THE EARLY LECTURES OF

Ralph Waldo Emerson

VOLUME I

1 8 3 3 - 1 8 3 6

THE EARLY LECTURES OF
Ralph Waldo Emerson

VOLUME I

1 8 3 3 - 1 8 3 6

Edited by

Stephen E. Whicher and Robert E. Spiller

HARVARD UNIVERSITY PRESS

Cambridge, Massachusetts

1 9 5 9

Typography by Burton Jones

Printed in the U.S.A. by Harvard University Printing Office

Bound by Stanhope Bindery, Inc., Boston, Massachusetts

Preface

Emerson's first fame was as a lecturer. All his books were first hammered out on the rostrum. His "low tones that decide," ostensibly disdaining tricks of oratory, are tones of the practiced rhetorician who wrote to be heard. Of his hundreds of lectures, only a relative few have been published from the many that still exist in manuscript. The later surviving lectures are in such a disorganized state that publication seems almost impossible. The purpose of this edition is to make available, in a readable and critical text, the surviving lectures of Emerson's earlier years (1833–1847).

The present volume contains the lectures from the apprentice period (1833–1836) when he was closest to the current Lyceum fashion and was working up subjects which were known to have popular appeal; they show him gradually working through to his proper subjects and lecture style. Manuscripts enough for two more similar volumes of lectures that reveal his rapidly growing independence and skill in the following decade are scheduled for later publication.

The editors are primarily indebted, as students of Emerson must always be, for essential information to the editorial work of James Elliot Cabot in his *A Memoir of Ralph Waldo Emerson* (2 vols., Boston: Houghton Mifflin Company, 1888), with its Appendix F (II, 710–803) containing the titles, dates, and many summaries of lectures and addresses known to him, and of Edward Waldo Emerson in the Centenary Edition of *The Complete Works of Ralph Waldo Emerson* (12 vols., Boston: Houghton Mifflin Company, 1903–04) and in the *Journals of Ralph Waldo Emerson*, edited with Waldo Emerson Forbes (10 vols., Boston: Houghton Mifflin Company, 1909–1914). Other sources of equal value are *The Letters of Ralph Waldo Emerson*, edited by Ralph L. Rusk (6 vols., New York: Columbia University Press, 1939), *The Life of*

Ralph Waldo Emerson, also by Ralph L. Rusk (New York: Charles Scribner's Sons, 1949), and two works by Kenneth L. Cameron, *Ralph Waldo Emerson's Reading* (Raleigh, N.C.: The Thistle Press, 1941), which contains notes on Emerson's withdrawals of books from the Boston Athenaeum and the Harvard College Library and Divinity School, and *Emerson the Essayist* (2 vols., Raleigh, N.C.: The Thistle Press, 1945), which contains much primary source material including similar notes on withdrawals from the Boston Library Society and a restudy of the lectures in this volume. Unless otherwise noted, most of the information upon which this edition of the early lectures depends is derived from one or another of these standard sources.

For permission to publish the texts of these lectures from manuscripts, which are now in the Houghton Library of Harvard University, and for unfailing cooperation and assistance in the editorial work, the editors are indebted to Mr. Edward W. Forbes and the Ralph Waldo Emerson Memorial Association as well as to the President and Fellows of Harvard College and to the Director of the Houghton Library, Mr. William A. Jackson, and his assistant, Miss Carolyn Jakeman. Professor Vivian C. Hopkins and Professor Carl F. Strauch have given us valuable information from their researches and Professor Kenneth W. Cameron has contributed generously from his unexampled knowledge of Emerson's sources.

Microfilms supplied by the Houghton Library were transcribed in typescript with exemplary accuracy by Mrs. Elizabeth C. Tompkins and these in turn were checked against the original manuscripts by the editors. Other valuable assistance was supplied by Miss Marianne Sommerfeld, Miss Jean Kirkpatrick, and Mrs. Elizabeth Whicher. H. Dan Piper, Verne H. Bovie, Philip L. Rizzo, and Robert A. McGill made studies of special aspects of Emerson's lectures in graduate seminars at the University of Pennsylvania.

Acknowledgment must also be made to the Modern Language Association for a grant to Mr. Whicher when he was planning a selective edition of passages from the lectures; to the Faculty Committee on the Advancement of Research of the University of

Pennsylvania for a grant to Mr. Spiller, and to the Faculty Research Grants Committee of Cornell University for a grant to Mr. Whicher, after publication of a more nearly complete text had been undertaken; and to the Ralph Waldo Emerson Memorial Association for a subsidy to assist in publication.

CONTENTS

CONTENTS

*Several manuscript pages are reproduced
following page 386*

x

INTRODUCTION

Introduction

FROM 1833, when he had just turned thirty, to the end of his active life almost a half century later, lecturing was Emerson's primary occupation, the profession which provided the main source of his earned income and the first form of public expression of his ideas.

Of his hundreds of lectures, only a few have been published from the many that still exist in whole or partial manuscript. A large proportion of these others were drawn upon by him, by his friend James Elliot Cabot, and by his son Edward Waldo Emerson for essays and books, and others contain passages which were taken almost verbatim from the journals and have since been published in that form. The remainder of the manuscripts, although carefully arranged in the collections of the Ralph Waldo Emerson Memorial Association in the Houghton Library of Harvard University, have presented an editorial problem which no one up to now has cared to face. The reaction of most scholars who have attempted to read these portfolios of manuscripts is reflected in a comment by Edward on a folder of 1866, when he was editing the Centenary Edition of his father's *Works* (1903–04):

> I have, preparatory to the editing of Vol. XII, looked through all these portfolios. Much has been printed and much has not; but they seem, for the most part, to be leaves seldom arranged by RWE or JEC: merely a miscellany of what was left on the subject named.

This is unquestionably a fair estimate of the state of a large proportion of these manuscripts, but the early folders — before the English lectures of 1847–48 — contain much fuller and more orderly manuscripts than do the later ones. These early lectures, prepared for specific occasions, were written out carefully in an easily legible hand on folded sheets of foolscap note paper, sewn or taped together to form booklets which generally survive intact. The handwriting is tighter and more regular than it became later, and most of the booklets have a title and a note on the date and place of first presentation.

Even at best, there are difficulties: all the early manuscripts contain cancellations; a few show evidences of revision for some later reading; many pages have been copied into other manuscripts, incorporated into essays and lectures of later date, or published in the *Journals*; pages, and occasionally an entire lecture in a series, are missing; of a few, only fragments remain. The earliest are in the best condition. Those of 1833–1839 offer no serious obstacle to publication; those of 1840–1847 are discouraging, but still offer some reward to the reader; only after 1847 does the restoration of a single text become almost impossible. There is justification, therefore, for a printed text of the early lectures, even though such an edition must stop at an arbitrary point at which rewards are no longer commensurate with editorial effort.

2.

It is fortunate that these early lectures are the ones which can be restored because they are the ones which students and readers of Emerson most need. They represent the bulk of his public expression during the period of his greatest intellectual and artistic growth, which can be definitely traced only with their help. When he stepped on the platform of the Masonic Temple in Boston on that November evening of 1833 to deliver his first lecture on Natural History, he was at last ready to become a spiritual leader in his own right, tempered in the fire of personal sorrow and failure, and prepared to devote his life to an open search for truth, goodness, and beauty in the modern American world of which he was so thoroughly a part. In the next few years he probably did more thinking than he had ever done before or was ever to do again. This was the turning point in his personal and professional life. Before it, he was a Unitarian clergyman with a clearly charted professional life in prospect; after it, he was a poet, a seeker, and a lay preacher of the self-reliance that he lived as well as taught. The early lectures, together with the book *Nature* (1836), reveal the probing and searching of mind and spirit which brought about this change into a new man with a new career; simultaneously, they exhibit the steady growth of the writer as he found his own form and voice.

When Emerson returned, on October 9, 1833, from a trip of almost a year in Europe, he faced the same uncertainties about his future that he had left behind him the previous December, but he was rested and more nearly ready to deal with them. During the remainder of that year and all of the next, he boarded with friends in Boston or visited his mother in her rooms in nearby Newton. His first wife, Ellen Tucker, had died early in 1831 after something more than a year of marriage, and he had resigned, in September 1832, the pastorate of the Second (Unitarian) Church of Boston. The two events were not directly connected except that both happened to him almost simultaneously, but together they marked the end of his youth. Two months later, he sailed for Italy.

After a cold and lonely month at sea, he welcomed the warm climate of the Mediterranean shores where, joining fellow Americans from time to time, he spent the winter and spring traveling and seeing the conventional tourist routes and shrines. Conscientiously he visited the art galleries and the churches, the notable places of natural beauty or historical association. He spent part of June in Switzerland, most of July in Paris, and August in England and Scotland. Another month at sea, and he was back in Boston as the leaves were turning.

The following winter was a busy but hardly less lonely one, though he saw much of his brothers, William, Edward, and Charles, of his long widowed mother, and of a few close friends. But the most important events of this period were the invitations to lecture to the Boston Natural History Society on November 5 and the several invitations to preach at Plymouth where he met and visited the physician-naturalist Charles Jackson and his two high-minded sisters. By September 1835, he had asked Lydia Jackson to change her name to "Lidian" Emerson, and to change her residence to Concord, where he had purchased the large

INTRODUCTION

framed Coolidge house on the Lexington Road. By this time he was well established as a public lecturer, having delivered during 1834 and early 1835 not only several more lectures on natural history, but also the series of six on "Biography" and the ten on "English Literature" before the Society for the Diffusion of Useful Knowledge at the Masonic Temple in Boston, as well as a "Historical Discourse" at Concord and several other addresses and sermons. With amazing rapidity he had rebuilt the structure of his personal and professional life. A legacy yielding some $1,200 a year from the Tucker estate supplemented his earnings from lecturing and occasional preaching as he settled into his new ways and slowly became a center of Concord's emerging cultural life. Even the deaths of his brothers Edward and Charles, as well as that of his infant son, in the next few years did not permanently disturb the impression of serenity and sense of direction that he maintained from this time until his break-down in 1870–1872. Even then, for more than a decade, the outward pattern of his life remained unchanged.

The inner meaning of this process of collapse and rebuilding of a life — apart from the events of death, love, and birth that studded these years — lay in his shifting of ground from a doctrinal to a personal base for religious experience. It was a New England version of Goethe's romantic experience of *Sturm und Drang*, echoed by Carlyle in *Sartor Resartus*, by Byron in *Childe Harold*, and by many another of that day. Against the background of a Puritan-bred conscience, however, both the experiences of depression and of subsequent elation were religious rather than narrowly personal. A seeker throughout his life, Emerson had been brought up in a Unitarian faith only slightly modified by the strong but eccentric Calvinism of his Aunt Mary Moody Emerson. As a boy, he had listened to the enlightened preaching of the elder William Ellery Channing, and at Harvard he had studied divinity under a strict Unitarian dispensation. Though itself a revolt against the stricter tenets of the Congregational Church, the new faith had its own doctrines and sacraments, now validated by reason rather than by dogma. Emerson's own sermons reveal a constant struggle of conscience against even this milder form of authority, and his resignation from his pastorate was immediately brought about by his request to be excused from administering the sacrament of the Last Supper. In the Divinity School Address of 1838, he made the grounds of his objection clear by distinguishing between historical and living Christianity. "Truth . . . cannot be received at second hand." But this was only after a long struggle. In the period 1832–1834, having decided to renounce the authority of both church and scripture, he craved, but as yet had not surely discovered, other categorical supports for the inner authority on which he would rebuild his religious life.

3.

It was more than coincidence that popular interest suggested the three alternatives to formal religion that he was most ready to explore: nature, the lives of great men, and literature.

Where could he better find grounds for his "First Philosophy" than in nature, already for over a century hailed as the Bible of the Deistic believer? And what faculty could be relied on for the finding with more confidence than the intuition of the individual man, made in the image of the Maker? In the doctrine of correspondence, the assumption of a parallelism between the moral and the natural laws, there was perhaps ground upon which religion and science could meet. If this doctrine would hold, the knowledge and the methods of the one could be applied to the questions of the other. Surely the seeker after truth must inform himself fully of the endlessly suggestive findings of science. Perhaps in the gradual unfolding of the natural law by the empirical methods so recently developed, a new confirmation of the moral law could be discovered. "Astronomy proves theism, but disproves dogmatic theology. . . . It operates steadily to establish the moral laws" (*J*, II, 491).

Here was the first formulation of the basic hypothesis of a reconstructed Christianity. But could the methods of science alone be trusted? Could the inner truth also be found by observation and experimentation? "The truth of truth consists in this, that it is self-evident, self-subsistent. It is light" (*J*, II, 516). Faith in Man's moral nature and in the validity of self-evident intuition could not be laid aside in favor of experiment and inductive logic. The moral law may be parallel to, but it is not identical with, the natural law. To distinguish differences is as important as to recognize similarities. In the romantic dichotomy between Reason and Understanding, Emerson found his answer to this problem. Reason is the faculty for perceiving spiritual truth beyond experience; Understanding, that for discovering the practical truths of this world. Derived chiefly from Coleridge by Emerson, this distinction was the common property of both German and English idealists of the day. "The *first* Philosophy," he writes in his Journal in 1833,

> that of the mind, is the science of what *is*, in distinction from what *appears*. . . . Reason, seeing in objects their remote effects, affirms the effect as the permanent character. The Understanding, listening to Reason, on the one side, which says, *It is*, and to the senses on the other side, which says, *It is not*, takes middle ground and declares, *It will be*. Heaven is the projection of the Ideas of Reason on the plane of the Understanding (*J*, III, 235–36).

In turning to science for truth, Emerson never thought of himself as a scientist, devoted to the search for truth through the Understanding. His was the voice of Reason always, to be trained like the Æolean harp to echo the music of the spheres. Even so, he could learn from science what to listen for, and he must know what science had to say. One must seek in nature the outward form of the inward truth. The book on Nature, which was to contain his new philosophy, was the finished expression of ideas first formulated in the lectures on science in 1833–34.

Perhaps it was Carlyle, perhaps it was Plutarch, who first suggested to Emerson that he might find a second test for truth in the lives of great men, but again the idea of hero worship was an integral part of the thinking of the day. Carlyle's *Heroes and Hero Worship* did not appear until 1841 and his own *Representative Men* in 1850 but, next to science, the experience of men who sought truth and fought for it most occupied his thought in 1831–1836. In each case, it was not so much the man's writing as the force of his personality that attracted him. "I would draw characters, not write lives. I would evoke the spirit of each, and their relics might rot. . . . I would walk among the dry bones, and wherever on the face of the earth I found a living man, I would say, here is life, and life is communicable" (*J*, II, 504). "When we look at the world of past men," he adds, "we say, what a host of heroes; but when we come to particularize, . . . none of them will bear examination, or furnish the type of a *Man*" (*J*, II, 505). His travels were marked with visits to Landor, Wordsworth, Coleridge, and Carlyle, and even then he contemplated the writing of a "modern Plutarch." The intention was partially realized in his first organized series of lectures on his return from Europe, that on Biography, and was repeated later, with a sharper definition of the central theme of *Man*, in the series on Representative Men.

The third source of inspiration — books and literature — was close to his nature and training as a man of letters. Yet he was not interested in the history of literature. He did not care whether an author was British or Persian as long as he said something of value; nor did he tie a man's thoughts closely to the facts of his life in a causal relationship. When he read books, he asked only that they give him ideas and that those ideas be well expressed. Even so, the lecture series on English literature, with its emphasis on Shakespeare, was a logical third topic for him to turn to in 1834–35 because of his interest in the symbolism of language. The three sources of inspiration for his ideal American scholar were now complete: nature (science), books (literature), and action (the lives of great men).

4.

There is no direct evidence that Emerson had thought seriously of the alternative career of public lecturer during the crisis in his career as a Unitarian clergyman. Rather he seems to have clung to an early dream of periodical publication, like Franklin, Dennie, Irving, and many others before him. Nevertheless, he was taking the first steps in preparation even before his trip to Europe. In a letter to his wife's cousin, Elizabeth Tucker, dated February 1, 1832 (*J*, II, 458–462), he suggests a "vacation scheme of study" which, after listing appropriate "Sunday books" such as the

Imitation of Christ and *Holy Dying,* turns to volumes in history and science which were currently being published by the American Society for the Diffusion of Useful Knowledge, the group before which two years later he was to present his first formal series of public lectures. References to scientific ideas, to scientists, and to popularizers of science fill the pages of his journal during the next few months — Brougham, Abernethy, Newton, Bacon, Aristotle, Galileo, and Galen — along with Milton, Shakespeare, Montaigne, Burke, and George Fox; and twice he speaks of possible lectures: one on the right use of the senses, after reading of Galileo's blindness (*J,* II, 466), and one on God's architecture on a winter's day (*J,* II, 532). It would seem that the current interest in the popularization of science, in literature, and in great men, which was being stimulated by the lyceum movement, was one means of turning Emerson's mind at this time to these subjects by providing him with readily available sources in lectures, magazine articles, and popular series like the London *Library of Useful Knowledge* and its American imitator which was just then being inaugurated.

When Emerson set out for Europe in 1832, the American lyceum movement was already beginning to gain momentum under the leadership of its founder, Josiah Holbrook. Holbrook, a popular lecturer on science himself, had published in 1826 a plan for a local, state, national, and even international lyceum bureau which was to sponsor lectures, foster libraries, develop natural history collections, and publish popularizations of knowledge. On November 28, 1828, an organization meeting was called in the Exchange Coffee House in Boston, with Daniel Webster in the chair, to discuss the founding of a local lyceum. Holbrook was appointed to a committee with Emerson's second cousin, George B. Emerson, and William Russell, the editor of the *American Journal of Education,* to form a Boston Society for the Diffusion of Useful Knowledge. Similar lyceums were founded during the next few years at Concord and Salem, and the movement spread rapidly to other New England towns and throughout the United States. By the time Emerson returned from Europe in 1833, there were highly organized systems of lectures and lecture series in almost every city or town he knew, with local committees of arrangement and membership audiences, ready to offer him a career at least supplementary to that of preaching and closely allied to it.

Under this system, it was not necessary to be an authority in order to present a subject. Louis Agassiz and George Catlin, to be sure, devoted much of their time to popular lectures on science, but so did the ex-schoolteacher John Griscom, whose subject was chemistry, and the Scotsman George Combe, whose subject was phrenology. Often a series was arranged on a single subject and different lecturers were assigned to the several lectures; on other occasions, entire series were offered by the same speaker. Clergymen and college professors were in demand, more because of their training in public discourse than for any special knowledge, and already, by 1833, there were many now-forgotten professional lecturers whose only gift was an ability to work up a subject quickly and to give an appealing performance on almost any level from the absurd to the profound.

Emerson's own turn from the pulpit to the platform was a gradual one, partly the result of a highly personal decision and partly a logical consequence of the circumstances of the time. His cousin, George Emerson, and his brother Charles made the arrangements for his first lecture, to be given less than a month after his debarkation on October 9, 1833. Emerson wrote to his brother William two days later, "I have engaged to deliver the introductory Lecture to the Natural History Society in November" (*L*, I, 397). Neither journals nor letters written during his European travels and his long sea voyage contain any hint that this was other than a surprise to him, and preparation, in spite of previous meditation on the topic, must have been hasty. Nevertheless, the understandable enthusiasm of Charles was probably warranted. "Last evening," he wrote to William on November 6, "Waldo lectured before the Natural History Society to a charm. The young and old opened their eyes and their ears — I was glad to have some of the stump lecturers see what was what and bow to the rising sun" (*L*, I, 397).

George Emerson seems to have had a major part also in arranging others of these early lectures, for he was an influential member of many of the groups from which Emerson received invitations to speak. Among these were the Franklin Lectures, a series arranged for people of modest means ("The Relation of Man to the Globe"), the Boston Mechanics Institution ("Water"), and the American Institute of Instruction ("A Correct Taste in English Literature"). The lectures on Italy were read before the New Bedford congregation, whose pulpit Emerson had been invited to fill in 1833, and lectures as well as sermons were read at Waltham and Plymouth as early as 1835. The next year he lectured or preached at Cambridge and Salem, and within the next few years at Waltham, Lowell, Roxbury, Framingham, Charlestown, Watertown, Portsmouth, East Lexington, and Concord. By 1843, his fame had extended and he was invited to lecture in Providence, Worcester, New York, Philadelphia, and Baltimore, but it was not until after his English tour of 1847–48 that he began his extended journeys to the West. By 1839, he had virtually given up preaching and could devote full time to his new career. In addition, he was invited to deliver occasional orations at the Concord sesquicentenial celebration (September 12, 1835), at the Green Street School in Providence (June 10, 1837), at the annual meeting of the Phi Beta Kappa Society at Harvard College (August 31, 1837), to students of the Harvard Divinity School (July 15, 1838), and at Dartmouth College (July 24, 1838), Waterville College, Maine (August 11, 1841), and Middlebury College, Vermont (July 22, 1845).

The lectures in the present volume are from Emerson's apprentice period and were obviously worked up for their occasions. Their sources are few and largely derivative and there is insufficient room among the facts to be presented for the larger ideas which the lecturer was already developing in his journals. In spite of the greater freedom of the platform, Emerson was at first almost as much bound to his audience by the lyceum system as he had been by the pulpit. The subjects upon which he was asked to speak were, at least in general terms, selected for him, and his times and places were arranged. Success depended in part on giving the audience what it expected, and a beginner could not depart too far from the formula which was already taking shape. There are many evidences that he chafed under these restrictions, and particularly the series on biography and on English literature show evidences of much the same kind of strain that is so obvious in some of the sermons, but now there was no organized authority to block his growing self-confidence. The subjects chosen for him were congenial and they offered him aid in seeking new foundations for his faith as well as means of supplementing his income. His rapid growth in depth and perspective is evident even in these partially assigned performances; by 1836 he was ready to declare his own terms.

The manuscripts of Emerson's lectures and sermons have been carefully preserved by him and by his heirs. As nearly as their history can be reconstructed, it would seem that it was his practice, at least during the early days of his lecturing, to use the standard letter paper of the day, a heavy double sheet in size suitable for folding to envelope shape and sealing. Taking several of these sheets, folded in two, he would fill both sides of each page in his legible and even hand; later the whole lecture was made into a kind of booklet by stitching or taping the folded edges. This practice gradually broke down as more and more single leaves were inserted until, between 1848 and 1870, his lecture manuscripts consisted of single sheets of various sizes and kinds without much logical arrangement. This change was largely the result of an increasing flexibility in his method of presenting his lectures; he used parts of old lectures to form new ones and repeated himself more and more as his itinerary became heavier.

When Emerson's health broke in 1870 and he found it increasingly difficult to concentrate, he called in his friend James Elliot Cabot to help him compile new books from old manuscripts. If he himself had not already started the practice, it was probably Cabot who placed the manuscript of each lecture in a large envelope and collected each series into folders tied with tape and carefully labelled. In this work he ultimately had some assistance from Emerson's daughter Ellen and possibly from his son Edward as well. At any rate it was Edward who, in 1900, took over the management of the papers and prepared both the Centenary Edition of the *Works* and the edition of the *Journals*, apparently respecting Cabot's arrangement and leaving the manuscripts much as he found them. Subsequent Emerson heirs have devoted their energies to preserving this store of material and keeping it open to modern scholars.

Cabot's list of the lecture manuscripts, with digests of their contents, appears as Appendix F of his *Memoir*. Most of the manuscripts so listed are still preserved, though Edward supplied about 160 single leaves, chiefly it would appear from the Concord "Historical Discourse" and perhaps other published texts, to Houghton Mifflin Company for their "Autograph Edition" of the *Works* and these are therefore now hopelessly scattered. A few pages from early lectures found their way into later folders, but only a few. Efforts to discover further manuscripts or parts of manuscripts in public and private collections have proved to be wholly futile. The lecture "Slavery" of 1837, quoted by Cabot (II, 425), is now missing. The lecture of that title, in a hand strikingly like Emerson's and dated 1835, now in the Houghton Library, has been identified as a lecture not by Ralph but by Charles Emerson, prepared by his brother for possible publication and then presented to Elizabeth Hoar and preserved in her family.

As Emerson never envisioned publication, the manuscript was prepared by him for only his immediate purposes as lecturer. It is therefore more than normally careless in orthography and repetitions, and full of alterations. Every effort has been made to restore the text itself to the form in which it was first heard by an audience. In so far as they have been identified, specific sources, both those indicated by Emerson and those subsequently discovered, are noted at the foot of the pages on which the references occur, together with indications of passages which have been substantially printed previously in the *Works* or the *Journals* and with such informational footnotes as the modern reader might need. Emerson's additions, corrections, and variant readings, as they appear in the manuscripts, or separately in the folders, have been noted in the textual notes at the end of the volume, with the exception of extensive working notes for the series on biography and on English literature. These have been described in the headnotes, but reproduced only in small part. A separate bibliography of sources, in the editions probably used by Emerson, has been supplied. Footnotes are numbered sequentially by lecture; textual notes are indicated by page and line of text.

Modern editorial practice is not fanatical with respect to alterations in punctuation, spelling, and capitalization. In preparing this text for printing, the editors have therefore:

(1) Expanded contractions and abbreviations.

(2) Regularized the use of quotation marks, except that Emerson's habit of using quotes around indirect speech has been retained where it occurs.

(3) Retained or supplied capitalization at the beginnings of sentences and for proper nouns, and retained it also, where it occurs, for certain emphatic abstractions ("Nature," "Spirit," etc.) or other words where such emphasis seems clearly intended; but we have eliminated possible capitalization where it seems merely an eccentricity of orthography. Emerson's practice is thoroughly inconsistent in this matter, in fact it is often impossible to determine from the manuscript whether he intends a capital or not.

(4) Supplied periods, question marks, exclamation points, commas, colons, and semicolons where they are unquestionably needed, as at the end of sentences or to separate items in a series or to introduce quotations.

(5) Added a minimum of further punctuation for clarity, all instances of this sort being recorded in the textual notes. No effort has been made to point the text in the style Emerson would have used if he had prepared it himself for publication. His own manuscript punctuation, even when eccentric, has rarely been altered, and the few such instances are all recorded in the textual notes.

(6) Regularized the forms of printing dates and numbers. With the former, we have been guided by Emerson's own practice when he edited the lecture "Michel Angelo" for publication, this representing presumably the way he was accustomed to read dates aloud before an audience. We have therefore replaced the usual manuscript form "15 March, 1572" with the form "the 15th

of March, 1572" in all cases. With numbers, we have followed modern press style.

(7) Corrected accidental misspellings. When in doubt we have followed the manuscript.

(8) Followed the manuscript for compound and hyphenated words but reserved the right to use common sense. Emerson's practice here is inconsistent and in a number of cases his intention is not clear.

(9) Used our judgment in paragraphing, since Emerson's manuscript practice is often not suited to the printed page.

With these minimum changes, the text follows Emerson's manuscript with no further attempt to eliminate his numerous inconsistencies and idiosyncrasies.

The following editorial marks have been used:

A. In the text:

(1) Square brackets [ ] indicate matter inserted by the editors. Matter in roman type within brackets forms part of Emerson's text; italics indicate editorial comments.

(2) Three dots indicate Emerson's omissions.

B. In the textual and other notes:

(1) Angle brackets ⟨ ⟩ indicate cancelled material; square brackets [ ], editorial comments; small braces { }, Emerson's brackets.

(2) Arrows ↑ ↓ indicate inserted material.

(3) A single slanted line / marks a page division in the manuscript.

(4) Three dots indicate editorial omissions.

(5) The symbol [E] in the footnotes means that all the preceding matter in the note is a marginal note or something similar transcribed from Emerson's manuscript.

This volume contains the lectures of Emerson from 1833 to 1836 inclusive listed by Cabot in Appendix F of his *Memoir* (Boston, 1888), pp. 710–724, with the exceptions of the two lectures on Italy, the "Historical Discourse at Concord," many times published, and the early lectures in the series on The Philosophy of History, which began on December 8, 1836, and ran into the following year. The text is that of the manuscripts, all but two of which (Nos. 1 and 4 in the Biography series) have been preserved in whole or in part, as they were arranged by Emerson and his literary executors, in the Collections of the Ralph Waldo Emerson Memorial Association in the Houghton Library of Harvard University.

The following abbreviations are used throughout the editorial notes:

W — *Works*, Centenary Edition (1903–04).

J — *Journals* (1909–1914).

L — *The Letters of Ralph Waldo Emerson*, ed. Ralph L. Rusk (1939).

Cabot — James Elliot Cabot, A *Memoir of Ralph Waldo Emerson* (1888).

Life — Ralph L. Rusk, *The Life of Ralph Waldo Emerson* (1949).

Cameron — Kenneth W. Cameron, *Emerson The Essayist* (1945).

Reading — Kenneth W. Cameron, *Ralph Waldo Emerson's Reading* (1941).

Cooke — G. W. Cooke, *Ralph Waldo Emerson* (1881).

I
SCIENCE

THE first four lectures of Emerson's new career were on natural philosophy, or science. He had already delivered three and was preparing for the other when he wrote to his brother William on January 18, 1834, "I seize the first vacation from this new drudgery of Lecturing to thank you for your kind letter. . . . Is it not a good symptom for society, this decided and growing taste for natural science which has appeared though yet in its first gropings? . . . I have been writing three lectures on Natural History and of course reading as much geology, chemistry, and physics as I could find." His reading, he explains, has been mainly in Playfair on the Huttonian Theory, Cuvier on the Revolutions of the Globe, and Mrs. Lee's Life of Cuvier. He has also looked into some of the 133 volumes of the Family Library, edited by the Rev. Dionysius Lardner (*L*, I, 404–405).

Emerson's interest in science was lifelong but his closest study of it is coincident with the intellectual crisis which led to his resignation as pastor of the Second Church (1832) and culminated in the publication of *Nature* (1836). It was perhaps the principal agent in his shift from a theological to a secular base for his moral philosophy. That this period exactly coincided with the rise of the lyceum movement with its strong emphasis on the popularization of science is merely historical fact, whether a result of coincidence or of a process of cause and effect.

A correlation of the journals in the early crisis months of 1832 with Kenneth W. Cameron's lists of his withdrawals of books from the Boston Athenaeum and the Harvard libraries suggests an upsurge of interest in science at that time. In 1831, only four of the books recorded were specifically on scientific subjects, but in 1832 there were some twelve, not counting the current issues of British magazines which may well have contained scientific articles of interest to him. Most of these books were borrowed between February and June. His journals of that same spring contain many references to science and scientists in what was obviously an effort to work out a system of natural symbols for moral truth. "Every form is a history of the thing" (*J*, II, 488). For example, the entries of May 3 and 11 refer to Charles's "dish of shells" as an illustration of how any collection of natural objects may be "an expression of the whole human mind"; then later in May he withdraws from the Athenaeum Leslie's *Elements of Natural Philosophy*, Mawe's *Linnean System of Conchology*, Drummond's *Letters to a Young Naturalist*, and from the Boston Library Society Haüy's *Elementary Treatise on Natural Philosophy*. At the same time he was reading in Mackintosh, Abernethy, Hartley, and Cousin, as well as in Carlyle, Milton, and Goethe, in an obvious quest for new grounds of moral certainty.

In Europe the following year, his disillusionment with literary men as a source of moral insight and his growing interest in works of art have been sufficiently noted; but his many references to science and scientists deserve more emphasis. In Florence, he visited Professor Amici and saw his optical instruments and he comments on the wax replicas of the human organs in the Museum of Natural History. In Padua, he heard Professor Caldania lecture on anatomy, and in Switzerland, he visited the watch factories as well as scenes which recalled Gibbon, Voltaire, and Calvin. George Emerson's brother Ralph greeted him in Paris and may have suggested auditing the lectures of Jouffroy, Thénard, and Gay-Lussac at the Sorbonne; he also visited the Collège Royale de France and the Jardin des Plantes. On July 13, 1833, he describes the collections in the Cabinet of Natural History in great detail and comments on the arrangements in Jussieu's system of plants outside in the garden. At the Mazarin Library, he attended a séance of the Class of Science in the Institute where he saw Biot, Arago, Gay-Lussac, Jouffroy, and others. In London, among other sights, he lists the Gallery of Practical Science, London University, and the Zoological Gardens. In his northern travels, he was impressed by his first ride on a railroad from Manchester to Liverpool with its hissing engine, its shower of sparks, and its cars which "dart by you like trout." Finally, in his summing up (*J*,III,185), it was the inventor of steam engines, Jacob Perkins, whom he met in the hotel at Liverpool and who illuminated him upon the science of heat, rather than Wordsworth, Coleridge, or even Carlyle, who is awarded the accolade of a man who knows his business and can speak of it with elevation. Such is the record of a clergyman on vacation.

The period of his intense interest in science did not long endure, but a curiosity to know the "secrets" of nature and the habit of regarding scientific facts as suggestive symbols of natural and moral laws never left him. He wrote only one more lecture specifically on science, "The Humanity of Science" (1836), after the four in this volume, and he never published any of the five. One of his closest friends of the period 1833–1836 was Dr. Charles T. Jackson, brother of his wife Lidian, whose chemical laboratory he visited frequently in those years, but otherwise he did not often seek out scientists as friends, and his indiscriminate reading of scientific publications diminished in later years, though general treatments of geology and astronomy, practical volumes on farming matters, and speculations on evolution continued to claim his interest. To a considerable extent, as *Nature* (1836) makes evident, his interest in science was absorbed into his interest in moral philosophy and by 1836 no longer served a special function in his thought.

The science which Emerson studied and professed was pre-Darwinian and concerned itself more with the classification than with the evolution of natural phenomena. Largely deductive in its theoretical base, it could serve as illustration of divine law and at the same time offer opportunities for observation and experimentation. Even current theories of evolution were in line with ideas of human progress and the progression of life from lower to higher forms could easily be considered new examples of the great chain of being. Biology was dominated by the theories and system of description and classification of Linnaeus as modified by the French naturalists who developed the Jardin des Plantes in Paris, Baron Georges Leopold Cuvier, Geoffroy Saint Hilaire, Antoine-Laurent de Jussieu, and Augustin Pyrame de Candolle.

Emerson could understand and respond to the larger concepts which motivated the work of such men without ever acquiring the technical competence to read their work intelligently in any but popularized versions.

The chief sources from which Emerson prepared these lectures, as far as the lectures reveal them, are listed in the Bibliography as well as cited in the footnotes to each lecture. Further evidence of Emerson's early reading in science, of course, is provided in the *Journals*, the *Letters*, and Cameron's lists, as well as in some of the manuscript journals. In addition, the lectures reflect his general reading in Plutarch and other classical authors, standard English authors such as Chaucer, Shakespeare, and Pope, and favorite "new lights" such as Goethe, Coleridge, Wordsworth, and the local Swedenborgians — above all, as always, Coleridge.

1

The Uses of Natural History

Although the manuscript dates this lecture November 4, 1833,[1] the announcement in the *Boston Daily Advertiser* places it one day later, which agrees with the letter dated November 6 of Charles to William, "Last evening Waldo lectured before the Natural History Society" (*L*, I, 397). Notes which E. W. Emerson conjectures were written in Liverpool while waiting for the boat are parallel in fact and idea to much in this and the following lectures, but may have been merely preparation for the book to which he refers while in passage (*J*, III, 192–93, 196). This lecture, as well as the others on science, were in turn used in preparation for the book which he actually did write on Nature. There is evidence in the text of the next lecture that both were read more than once. A journal entry of January 2, 1834 (*J*, III, 247) suggests that part of the concluding passage later used in *Nature* was added at a later date, though the manuscript does not support this view.

The only books specifically referred to by Emerson are Adam Smith's *Moral Sentiments* and Gilbert White's *Natural History and Antiquities of Selborne* (see textual notes); more important sources are listed in the Bibliography. Cabot has printed (I, 223, 227) and Cameron reprinted (I, 339–40) two short excerpts from this lecture.

IN accepting the invitation with which the Directors of this Society have honored me to introduce the course, I have followed my inclination rather than consulted my ability. My time has been so preoccupied as to prevent any particular course of reading or collection of novel illustrations of the subjects treated, which I should gladly have proposed to myself. I shall therefore say what I think on the subject of this lecture according to such imperfect general information as I already possessed.

[1] "Introductory Lecture read before the Natural History Society at the Masonic Temple November 4 1833" [E].

It seems to have been designed, if anything was, that men should be students of Natural History. Man is, by nature, a farmer, a hunter, a shepherd and a fisherman, who are all practical naturalists and by their observations the true founders of all societies for the pursuit of science. And even after society has made some progress, so that the division of labor removes men into cities, and gives rise to sedentary trades and professions, every man who is fortunate enough to be born in circumstances that require him to make any exertion to live, is compelled to pick up in his own experience, a considerable knowledge of natural philosophy, — as, an acquaintance with the properties of water, of wood, of stone, of light, of heat, and the natural history of many insects, birds and beasts.

And as if to secure this end in the constitution of all men, the eye is so fitted to the face of nature or the face of nature to the eye that the perception of beauty is continually awakened in all places and under the most ordinary circumstances. The beauty of the world is a perpetual invitation to the study of the world. Sunrise and sunset; fire; flowers; shells; the sea — in all its shades, from indigo to green and gray, by the light of day, and phosphorescent under the ship's keel at night; the airy inaccessible mountain; the sparry cavern; the glaring colours of the soil of the volcano; the forms of vegetables; and all the elegant and majestic figures of the creatures that fly, climb, or creep upon the earth — all, by their beauty, work upon our curiosity and court our attention. The earth is a museum, and the five senses a philosophical apparatus of such perfection, that the pleasure we obtain from the aids with which we arm them, is trifling, compared with their natural information.

It is frequently observed how much power, the influence of natural objects gives to the sentiment of love of country which is strongest in the most wild and picturesque regions. It deserves notice also as it is this which not [only] heightens but creates the charm which hunting has for many persons who would start at being thought to have any poetry in their constitution. If the running down a fox or hare were performed under cover, or in a street, it would soon lose its noble name, but great bodily exertion made along the mountain side, upon fields glittering with a million beads of dew, or in the shades of a wood — which always seem to say something, we cannot well make out what; — exhilarated by the fragrant scents, and cheered on by the trumpet of all the winds, — it is not strange that a man should learn to love these scenes, though he err in thinking he loves to kill his game.

Yielding ourselves to the same pleasant influences, let us inquire what are the advantages which may be expected to accrue from the greater cultivation of Natural Science.

They are in my judgment great and manifold, and probably more than can be now enumerated. I do not think we are yet masters of all the reasons that make this knowledge valuable to us. They will only disclose themselves by a more advanced state of science. I say this because we have all a presentiment of relations to external nature, which outruns the limits of actual science. I lately had an opportunity of visiting that celebrated repository of natural curiosities the Garden of Plants in Paris; and except perhaps to naturalists only I ought [not] to speak of the feelings it excited in me. There is the richest collection in the world of natural curiosities arranged for the most imposing effect. The mountain and morass and prairie and jungle, the ocean, and rivers, the mines and the atmosphere have been ransacked to furnish whatever was rich and rare; the types of each class of beings — Nature's proof impressions; — to render account of her three kingdoms to the keen insatiable eye of French science.

In spacious grounds skilfully laid out, and shaded with fine groves and shrubberies, you walk among the animals of every country, each in his own paddock with his mates, having his appropriate food before him, — his habits consulted in his accommodation. There towers the camelopard [2] nearly twenty feet high, whose promenade and breakfast attract as much attention as the king's; the lions from Algiers and Asia; the elephants from Siam — whose bath is occasionally performed with great applause from the boys; — our own countrymen, the buffalo and the bear from New Hampshire and Labrador. All sizes and all stripes of tygers, hyenas, leopards, and jackals; a herd of monkeys; not to mention

[2] Giraffe.

7

the great numbers of sheep, goats, llamas, and zebras, that sleep, browse, or ruminate in their several country fashions, (as much at ease as in their own wilds,) for the amusement of the whole world in the heart of the capital of France.

Moving along these pleasant walks, you come to the botanical cabinet, an inclosed garden plot, where grows a grammar of botany — where the plants rise, each in its class, its order, and its genus, (as nearly as their habits in reference to soils will permit,) arranged by the hand of Jussieu himself. If you have read Decandolle [3] with engravings, or with a *hortus siccus*,[4] conceive how much more exciting and intelligible is this natural alphabet, this green and yellow and crimson dictionary, on which the sun shines, and the winds blow.

The Cabinet of Natural History is contained in a large stone edifice in the centre of the grounds.

It is a prodigality to visit in one walk all the various halls in this great gallery of Nature. The ornithological chambers require an entire day: For who would mix and confound so fine and delicate sensations? This house of stuffed birds is a finer picture gallery than the Louvre. The whole air is flushed with the rich plumage and beautiful forms of the birds. The fancy coloured vests of those elegant beings make me as pensive as the hues and forms of a cabinet of shells have done before. They fill the mind with calm and genial thought. Some of the birds have a fabulous beauty that seems more appropriate to some sultan's garden in the Arabian Nights Entertainments than to a real tangible scientific collection. You see the favourites of nature, — creatures in whose form and coat seems to have been a design to charm the eye of cultivated taste. Observe that parrot of the parrot tribe called *Psittacus Erythropterus*. You need not write down his name for he is the beau of all birds and you will find him as you will find a Raffaelle in a gallery. Then the humming birds so little and so gay — from the least of all, the *Trochilus Niger* not so big as a beetle — to the *Trochilus Pella* with his irresistible neck of gold and silver and fire; and the *Trochilus Delalandi* from Brazil whom the French

[3] Augustin Pyrame de Candolle (1778–1841), author of a natural system of botanical classification.

[4] A "dry garden," or herbarium.

8

call the magnificent fly (La mouche magnifique) or glory in miniature. The birds of Paradise are singularly delicate and picturesque
in their plumage. The manucode or royal Paradisaea from New
Guinea, the red Paradisaea, and the Paradisaea Apoda, seem each
more beautiful than the last and each, if seen alone, would be
pronounced a peerless creature. I watched the different groups
of people who came in to the gallery, and noticed that they picked
out the same birds to point to the admiration of their companions.
They all noticed the Veuve à épaulettes — the widow with epau-
lettes — a grotesque black fowl called Emberiza Longicanda with
fine shoulder ornaments and a long mourning tail, and the Am-
pelis Cotinga. All admired the *Phasianus Argus*, a pheasant that
appeared to have made its toilette after the pattern of the peacock,
and the *Trogon pavoninus*, called also the Couroucon. But it were
vain to enumerate even the conspicuous individuals in the parti-
coloured assembly. There were black swans and white peacocks,
the famous venerable ibis come hither to Paris out of Egypt, —
both the sacred and the rosy; the flamingo with a neck like a
snake; the toucan, rightly denominated the rhinoceros; and a
vulture whom to meet in a wilderness would make the flesh creep,
so truculent and executioner-like he stood.

The cabinet of birds was a single and even small part of that
noble magazine of natural wonders. Not less complete, scarcely
less attractive is the collection of stuffed beasts, prepared with
the greatest skill to represent the forms and native attitudes of the
quadrupeds. Then follow the insects, the reptiles, the fishes, the
minerals. In neighboring apartments is contained the collection
of comparative anatomy, a perfect series from the skeleton of the
balaena [5] which reminds every one of the frame of a schooner, to
the upright form and highly developed skull of the Caucasian race
of man.

The eye is satisfied with seeing and strange thoughts are stirred
as you see more surprizing objects than were known to exist;
transparent lumps of amber with gnats and flies within; radiant
spars and marbles; huge blocks of quartz; native gold in all its
forms of crystallization and combination, gold in threads, in plates,

[5] Whale.

9

in crystals, in dust; and silver taken from the earth molten as from fire. You are impressed with the inexhaustible gigantic riches of nature. The limits of the possible are enlarged, and the real is stranger than the imaginary. The universe is a more amazing puzzle than ever, as you look along this bewildering series of animated forms, the hazy butterflies, the carved shells, the birds, beasts, insects, snakes, fish, and the upheaving principle of life every where incipient, in the very rock aping organized forms. Whilst I stand there I am impressed with a singular conviction that not a form so grotesque, so savage, or so beautiful, but is an expression of something in man the observer. We feel that there is an occult relation between the very worm, the crawling scorpions, and man. I am moved by strange sympathies. I say I will listen to this invitation. I will be a naturalist.[6]

Under the influence of such thoughts, I say that I suppose many inducements to the study of Natural History will disclose themselves as its secrets are penetrated. Besides that the general progress of the science has given it a higher and higher place in the public estimation is there not every now and then some inexplicable fact or new class of relations suggested which for the time seems not so much to invite as to defy scientific solution? For example, what known laws are to classify some of the astounding facts embodied in the Report of the Committee of the French Institute in 1830 upon the subject of Animal Magnetism[7] — a committee too, considering the persons and the circumstances, who might be regarded as a picked jury of the most competent scientific persons on earth? But not to venture upon this dangerous ground, the debateable land of the sublime and the ridiculous, let me confine my attention to the enumeration of certain specific advantages easily marked and understood which may serve as the commendation of the objects of this society.

1. It is the lowest and yet not a bad recommendation of the occupations of the Naturalist that they are serviceable to the

---

[6] "In spacious grounds . . . be a naturalist" (*J*, III, 161–64).

[7] The claims of Mesmer of ability to induce "magnetic" sleep were revived by the French physician Alexandre Bertrand and endorsed by the Paris Academy of Medicine in 1831. Their report is printed as an appendix to Colquhoun's Report on Animal Magnetism (see p. 332n).

health. The ancient Greeks had a fable of the giant Antaeus, that
when he wrestled with Hercules, he was suffocated in the gripe
of the hero, but every time he touched his mother earth, his
strength was renewed. The fable explains itself of the body and
the mind. Man is the broken giant, and in all his weakness he is
invigorated by touching his mother earth, that is, by habits of
conversation with nature.[8] It is good for the body exhausted by
the bad air, and artificial life of cities, to be sent out into the fresh
and fragrant fields, and there employed in exploring the laws of
the creation. The study of Botany deserves the attention of those
interested in Education, for this, if for no other cause. The wild
rose will reflect its hues upon the cheek of the lover of nature. It
is well known that the celebrated Wilson [9] was led to the study of
Ornithology for the benefit of his enfeebled health, and in his
enthusiastic rambles in the wilderness his constitution was established whilst he enlarged the domain of science.

The mountain minerals will pay their searcher with active
limbs and refreshed spirits. And he who wanders along the margin
of the sounding sea for shellfish or marine plants, will find strength
of limb and sharpness of sight and bounding blood in the same
places. Dig your garden, cross your cattle, graft your trees, feed
your silkworms, set your hives — in the field is the perfection of
the senses to be found, and quiet restoring Sleep, —

His poppy grows among the Corn.[10]

2. In the second place, the main advantage to be proposed
from the study of natural history is that which may seem to make
all further argument needless; to be itself the manifest ground on
which the study stands in the favor of mankind, I mean the direct
service which it renders to the cultivator and the world, the
amount of useful economical information which it communicates.
The proof of this assertion is the history of all discoveries, almost
the history of civilization itself. It is the earth itself and its natural
bodies that make the raw material out of which we construct our

[8] "The ancient Greeks . . . conversation with nature" ("History," W, II, 31).
[9] Alexander Wilson (1766–1813), author of *The American Ornithology*.
[10] Abraham Cowley, *Essays in Verse and Prose*, VI: "Of Greatness." Translation of Horace, Lib. III, Ode 1, stanza 4.

11

food, clothing, fuel, furniture, and arms. And it is the Naturalist who discovers the virtues of these bodies and the mode of converting them to use. In the most refined state of society, these are most accumulated; but these are now so numerous and the subdivision of labor has removed each process so far out of sight, that a man who by pulling a bell can command any luxury the world contains, is in danger of forgetting that iron came out of a mine, and perfume out of a cat.

You sit in your parlor surrounded by more proofs of the cultivation of natural science than books or cabinets contain. The water that you drink was pumped up from a well by an application of the air pump. The well ventilated chimney which every mason can build, derived its hint from Franklin and Rumford. The sugar in your dish was refined by the instruction given by a modern chemist on the adjustment of temperature for the crystallization of syrup; the brasses, the silver, the iron, the gold, which enter into the construction of so many indispensable articles, and indeed the glass, the cloth, the paints and dyes, have employed the philosopher as well as the mechanic; there is scarcely any manufacture whose processes are not assisted or directed by rules and principles derived from the observations of Naturalists. Apart from the consideration that all the foreign fabrics, drugs, fruits, and condiments, which are as familiar as salt, were transported hither across the sea by the aid of that map of the stars and the record of the predicted places of the sun and the earth, which the lovers of nature from the Chaldean shepherd [11] to Laplace and Bowditch have aided in bringing to perfection.

The history of modern times has repeatedly shown that a single man devoted to science may carry forward the mechanic arts and multiply the products of commerce more than the united population of a country can accomplish in ages wherein no particular devotion to scientific pursuits exists. This is forcibly illustrated by the historical fact of the influence produced in France by the appointment of the celebrated Duhamel to the professorship of the School of Mines. In 1822 it was stated to the Academy by its Secretary "that from the appointment of M. Duhamel to the time of

[11] The Chaldeans attempted to map the stars as early as 2000 B.C.

his death, the products of iron in France were quadrupled; the mines of this metal opened near the Loire in the region of coal, and in the midst of combustible matter, were about to yield iron at the same price as in England. Antimony, manganese, which we formerly imported, are now exported in considerable quantities. Chrome, discovered by one of our chemists, is also the useful product of one of our mines. Zinc and tin have already been extracted from the mines on the coast of Brittany. Alum and vitriol, formerly almost unknown in France, are collected in abundance. An immense mass of rock-salt has just been discovered in Lorraine, and all promises that these new creations will not stop here. Doubtless it is not to a single man, nor to the appointment of a single professorship that all this may be attributed but it is not the less true that this one man, this one professorship has been the primary cause of these advantages." [12]

But the advantages which science has presented to human life are in all probability the least part of her possessions. To the powers of science no limit can be assigned. All that has been is only an accumulated force to act upon the future. The prospective power, the armed hand, the learned eye are worth more than the riches they have acquired. It is a maxim in philosophy that a general truth is more valuable than all the particular facts which it has disclosed.

The natural history of water is not studied with less diligence or advantage at this moment than when Watt and Fulton made it a day laborer for mankind. It is but the other day that our countryman, Mr. Jacob Perkins, noticed the small bubbles that are formed on the sides and bottom of a vessel in which water is heated, and most rapidly on the hottest parts, and discovered that these bubbles operate as a screen between the fire and the body of water in the vessel, preventing the rise of the temperature within in any proportion to the increase of the temperature on the outside. He found especially that in the boilers of steam engines great inconvenience and danger frequently resulted from this cause because when the engineer quickened his fire it consumed the coats of the boiler more rapidly without making a proportionate ex-

[12] Lee, *Memoirs of Cuvier*, pp. 205–206.

pansion of the steam. This observation led to the thought that a
strong circulation in the water might be caused which should
continually rush against the sides of the vessel and break or remove these air bubbles. This thought he has recently executed
in the machine called the Circulators and which has already been
adopted in three of the locomotives on the Liverpool and Manchester Railroad with the best success and is about being introduced into all. And this may serve for a hundred examples of the
benefit resulting from these observations.[13]

3. But it is high time to enumerate a third reason for the
cultivation of natural history which is the *delight which springs
from the contemplation of this truth*, independent of all other
considerations. I should be ashamed to neglect this good, in too
particular a showing what profit was to accrue from the knowledge
of nature. The knowledge itself, is the highest benefit. He must
be very young or very sordid who wishes to know what good it will
do him to understand the sublime mechanism on which the stability of the solar system and the faithful return of the seasons
depend. What good will it do him? Why, the good of knowing
that fact. Is not that good enough? — Moreover is it not disgrace-
ful to be served by all the arts and sciences at our tables, and in
our chambers and never know who feeds us, nor understand the
cunning they employ? I cannot but think it becoming that every
gentleman should know why he puts on a white hat in summer,
and a woolen coat in winter; and why his shoes cannot be made
until the leather is tanned. Better sit still than be borne by steam,
and not know how; or guided by the needle and the quadrant
through thousands of miles of sea, without a mark in the horizon,
and brought to a little dent in the shore on the other half the
globe, as truly as if following a clew in the hand — and never ask
how that feat is accomplished.

Bias was asked what good, education would do for a boy; —
"When he goes there," pointing to the marble seats of the theatre,
he replied, "that he might not be a stone sitting upon a stone." [14]

---

[13] Cf. *J*, III, 184, 190–92.

[14] Bias of Priene (c. 550 B.C.), one of the "Seven Wise Men" treated in
Plutarch's *Morals*. This particular saying, however, has not been located.

Every fact that is disclosed to us in natural history removes one scale more from the eye; makes the face of nature around us so much more significant. How many men have seen it snow twenty or forty winters without a thought being suggested beyond the need of stout boots, the probability of good sleighing, and the country trade; until some kind philosopher has drawn our attention to the singular beauty of that phenomenon, the formation of snow; and shown us the texture of that self weaving blanket with which the parts of the globe exposed to cold, cover themselves in pile proportioned to their exposure, at the time when the animated creation on the same side of the earth whiten and thicken their fleeces. We cannot see again without new pleasure what the Latin poet calls the thick fleece of silent waters —

densum tacitarum vellus aquarum.[15]

You cannot go out when the snow is falling in a calm still air and catch the little hexagon upon the palm of your hand and measure the invariable angles of the radii of the star without a finer delight than ever sprang from the consideration of the convenience of the general railroad with which it covers the country for the woodcutter and the farmer. The snowstorm becomes to your eye a philosophical experiment performed in a larger laboratory and on a more magnificent scale than our chemists can command.[16]

To the naturalist belongs all that keen gratification which arises from the observation of the singular provision for human wants that in some instances requiring ages for its completion, was begun ages before the use of it was shown.

The science of Geology which treats of the structure of the earth has ascertained that before the period when God created man upon the earth very considerable changes have taken place in the planet. It is made probable that the various rocks that are now found broken upon it, as granite, slate, chalk, etc., covered it as so many concentric crusts or coats, like the coats of the onion,

[15] Martial, *Epigrams*, IV:3.
[16] The next five paragraphs have been lightly crossed out in the manuscript to indicate their use elsewhere. They are largely incorporated in the second lecture on science, which was read to a different audience (see pp. 29–30, 33–34).

one without the other. But the soils which now cover it are formed by the decomposition of these stones, so that in this position of them that mixture of them which is essential to the production of vegetable life could never have been affected. By internal volcanoes, or other means these several strata have been broken and raised and are now found lying as may be seen in mountain countries in oblique and perpendicular instead of horizontal layers so as to yield their various treasures to man and to the soil.

This is yet more striking in the case of Coal, so important to old countries, and recently to this, and has naturally attracted the particular attention of British naturalists.

It is well known how vastly the great development of the commerce of Great Britain and thence of the great civilization of that country is indebted to the boundless abundance of coal in its mines. In consequence of the abundance and accessibility of this mineral in that island, and its opportune association with beds of iron ore, and the invariable contiguity of limestone employed to flux the iron, the English have been enabled to surpass all other nations in the cheapness of machinery and thence in the extent of their manufactures.

But the discoveries of geologists have shown that the coal which is undoubtedly a vegetable formation is the relic of forests which existed at an unknown antiquity before the era of the creation of mankind, and by the overflowing of the sea and other changes of the surface had been buried below the surface at too great a depth to be reached by man. But before the creation of our race earthquakes or other convulsions of enormous force have lifted up these mineral beds into ledges so that they are found extending from 1000 feet above the level of the ocean, to unknown depths below it. And so it happens that these vast beds of fuel so essential to man's comfort and civilization, which would have been covered by the crust of the globe from his knowledge and use, are thus brought up within reach of his little hands; and a great work of Nature in an antiquity that hath no record — namely the deposit and crystallization of antediluvian forests, is made to contribute to our pleasure and prosperity at this hour.

Thus knowledge will make the face of the earth significant to

16

us: it will make the stones speak and clothe with grace the meanest weed. Indeed it is worth considering in all animated nature what different aspect the same object presents to the ignorant and the instructed eye. It only needs to have the eye informed, to make everything we see, every plant, every spider, every moss, every patch of mould upon the bark of a tree, give us the idea of fitness, as much as the order and accommodation of the most ingeniously packed dressing box. For, every form is a history of the thing. The comparative anatomist can tell at sight whether a skeleton belonged to a carnivorous or herbivorous animal — to a climber, a jumper, a runner, a digger, a builder. The conchologist can tell at sight whether his shell were a river or a sea shell, whether it dwelt in still or in running waters, whether it were an annual or a perennial covering, and many the like particulars. And this takes away the sense of deformity from all objects; for, every thing is a monster till we know what it is for. A ship, a telescope, a surgical instrument, a box of strange tools are puzzles and painful to the eye, until we have been shown successively the use of every part, and then the thing tells its story at sight, and is beautiful. A lobster is monstrous to the eye the first time it is seen, but when we have been shown the use of the case, the color, the tentacula, and the proportion of the claws, and have seen that he has not a scale nor a bristle, nor any part, but fits exactly to some habit and condition of the creature; he then seems as perfect and suitable to his sea-house, as a glove to a hand. A *man* in the rocks under the sea, would indeed be a monster; but a lobster is a most handy and happy fellow there.[17] So there is not an object in nature so mean or loathsome, not a weed, not a toad, not an earwig, but a knowledge of its habits would lessen our disgust, and convert it into an object of some worth; perhaps of admiration. Nothing is indifferent to the wise. If a man should study the economy of a spire of grass — how it sucks up sap, how it imbibes light, how it resists cold, how it repels excess of moisture, it would show him a design in the form, in the color, in the smell, in the very posture of the blade as it bends before the wind.

There is an excellent story in one of our children's books called

[17] "For, every form is a history . . . happy fellow there" (J, II, 488–89).

Eyes and No Eyes.[18] A dull dumb unprofitable world is this to many a man that has all his senses in health. But bring under the same arch of day, upon the same green sod, under the shadow of the same hills Linnaeus or Buffon or Cuvier or Humboldt and the sea and the land will break forth into singing, and all the trees of the field will clap their hands. The traveller casts his eye upon a broken mountainside, and sees nothing to detain his attention a moment. Let Cuvier regard the same thing; in the rough ledges, the different shades and superposition of the strata, his eye is reading as in a book the history of the globe, the changes that were effected by fire, by water, by pressure, by friction in ages long prior to the existence of man upon the planet, he is hearkening to infallible testimony of events whereof is no chronicle but in the memory of God, and taking down minutes of the same for the guidance and confirmation of future inquirers.

It has been felt by their contemporaries as a public calamity when such an observer who knew the value of his senses has been deprived of their use. One of the most touching incidents in biography is the affliction that befel Galileo, who, after announcing in rapid succession to the world his splendid discoveries, made by the aid of the telescope, namely, the uneven surface of the moon; the spots on the sun by which the revolution of that body was proved; that Venus was horned like the moon; the satellites, and the belt of Jupiter; the ring of Saturn; — was bereaved of sight. His friend Castelli wrote to one of his correspondents, "The noblest eye is darkened that nature ever made; an eye so priveleged, and gifted with such rare qualities, that it may with truth be said to have seen more than all of those which are gone, and to have opened the eyes of all which are to come." [19]

These men have used their senses to such good purpose, led on by the mere pleasure of observation, the high delight which they found in exploring the works of nature.

4. There is a fourth good purpose answered by the study of Natural History which deserves a distinct enumeration. I refer

---

[18] "Eyes and No Eyes; or, The Art of Seeing," John Aikin and Mrs. Anna Letitia Barbauld, *Evenings at Home*, 1792–96, Twentieth Evening.
[19] "Life of Galileo," *Lives of Em. Pers.*, p. 75. Cf. *J*, II, 466.

to its salutary effect upon the mind and character of those who cultivate it. It makes the intellect exact, quick to discriminate between the similar and the same, and greedy of truth.

Moreover I hope it will not be thought undue refinement to suppose that long habits of intimate acquaintance with nature's workmanship, which is always neat, simple, masterly, accustoms her scholars to think and work in her style. All our ideas of sublimity and beauty are got from that source. Our contrivances are good but will not bear comparison with hers.

An orrery is esteemed an ingenious and elegant machine to exhibit the relative motions of the bodies of the solar system, but compare it with nature's own orrery, as it would appear to the eye of an observer placed above the plane of the System. He should see the beautiful balls moving on self poised in empty space, no rods reaching from them to the sun — no wires fastening the moons to their planets, but all bound by firm but invisible cords, that never entangle, nor crack, nor wear, nor weigh, namely, those threads of attraction, that join every particle in creation to every other particle.

Or to take a much lower instance in an object at our feet of the simplicity of the means by which important ends are effected. Who are those that hoe and harrow the surface of the ground to keep it in a state of looseness fit for tillage, and to make the fallow land penetrable to the roots of the grasses and to the germination of forest trees? The Earthworms.

It has been observed by the entomologist [20] that worms promote vegetation by boring, perforating, and loosening the soil, and rendering it pervious to rains, and to the fibres of plants; by drawing straws and stalks of leaves and twigs into it, and most of all by throwing up such infinite numbers of lumps of earth called worm-casts which manure the grain and grass. Without the incessant aid of these little gardeners and farmers, the earth would soon become cold, and hardbound, and void of fermentation.

Thus Nature keeps the surface of the soil open; but how does she make the soil? Who are the strong and skilful architects that

[20] Gilbert White. The rest of the sentence is a quotation from *The Natural History of Selborne*, Letter XXXV.

build up the solid land from the bottom of the sea? A little insect, the coralline, the madrepore, almost too small for sight, possessing the power of extracting lime from the sea water, builds up the coral reefs from the bed of the ocean to the surface, and these make in the course of ages the broad floor, on which by the agency of the marine vegetation, and of the birds, and the accidents of drift timber, a coat of soil is gradually laid, and a new land opened for the accommodation of man.

There are numberless examples in the economy of bees, the celebrated discovery of Reaumur relative to the angles of the cells, the observations of Huber [21] upon the simplicity of the means by which the hive is ventilated, that are too long and too well known to be detailed.

Can the effect be other than most beneficent upon the faculties dedicated to such observations? — upon the man given

> To reverend watching of each still report
> That Nature utters from her rural shrine.[22]

Moreover the state of mind which nature makes indispensable to all such as inquire of her secrets is the best discipline. For she yields no answer to petulance, or dogmatism, or affectation; only to patient, docile observation. Whosoever would gain anything of her, must submit to the essential condition of all learning, must go in the spirit of a little child. The naturalist commands nature by obeying her.

And this benign influence passes from the intellect into the affections and makes not only the judgment sound but the manners simple and the whole character amiable and true.

Indeed I think that a superiority in this respect of truth and simplicity of character extends generally to people resident in the country whose manner of life so nearly resembles that of the professed naturalist. That flippancy which is apt to be so soon learned in cities is not often found in the country. Nor are men *there* all

[21] René A. F. de Réaumur (1683–1757), French naturalist; François Huber (1750–1831), Swiss naturalist.
[22] Wordsworth, "Written upon a Blank Leaf in 'The Complete Angler'," lines 5–6.

ground down to the same tame and timid mediocrity which results in cities from the fear of offending and the desire of display. But the peculiarities of original genius stand out more strongly which are the results of that framework which the hand of God has laid for each man and which it behoves every man to respect as it constitutes the only plan according to which his particular structure can ever rise to greatness. These peculiarities in the resident of the country are the effects no doubt of silence and solitude, and of constant familiarity with calm and great objects. Though this influence is often exaggerated, yet I believe none of us are quite insensible to it, as every man may prove who goes alone into a picturesque country. I apprehend that every man who goes by himself into the woods, not at the time occupied by any anxiety of mind, but free to surrender himself to the genius of the place, feels as a boy again without loss of wisdom. [23] In the presence of nature he is a child.

One thing more under this head of the effect of these studies upon the mind and character. It generates enthusiasm, the highest quality, say rather, the highest *state* of the character. It has been the effect of these pursuits and most conspicuously upon the first class of minds to absorb their attention. What was sought at first as a secondary object, to satisfy an occasional curiosity, or amuse a rainy day, gradually won upon their interest, excluding every former occupation, until it possessed itself of the whole man.

They have felt the interest in truth as truth which was revealed to their inquiries. The story of Archimedes running as a madman, around the streets of Syracuse, after discovering the mode of determining the specific gravity of bodies, crying out as he ran, "I have found it" is familiar to children. Scarce less notorious is that trait recorded of Newton, that, when after the new measurement of a degree of the earth's surface, he renewed his comparison of the earth's attraction of the moon, to the earth's attraction of a falling apple, — and saw, in the progress of the calculation, that he was approaching the result he had formerly anticipated, he was so much agitated by the grandeur of the fact about to be disclosed, that he was unable to go on, and was obliged to call in a friend

[23] Cf. *J*, III, 222.

to finish the computation.[24] As they say, the soldier who dies in hot blood never feels the wound, it is remarked of several physiologists, that they have continued their observations into the very doors of death. It is recorded of Haller, the celebrated Swiss physiologist, that he continued his observations in his last illness upon the progress of his disease with perfect calmness; taking note of the successive alterations in his system, and keeping his hand upon his own pulse, — until at last he exclaimed to his physician, "My friend, the artery ceases to beat," and expired.

And it is related of John Hunter that he retained the habit of critical observation to the last pulse, and said to a friend who sat beside him, "I wish I had power of speaking or writing that I might tell you how pleasant are the sensations of dying."

These are the heroes of science who have an instinctive preference of the value of truth, and who think that man has no nobler vocation than to watch and record the wonders that surround him.

Hence the high prophetic tone which they have sometimes assumed, speaking as with the voice of time and nature.

When Kepler had discovered the three harmonic laws that regulate the motion of the heavenly bodies, he exclaims, "At length, after the lapse of eighteen months, the first dawn of light has shone upon me; and on this remarkable day, I have perceived the pure irradiation of sublime truth. Nothing now represses me: I dare yield myself up to my holy ardor; I dare insult mankind by acknowledging, that, I have turned worldly science to advantage; that I have robbed the vessels of Egypt to erect a temple to the living God. If I am pardoned, I shall rejoice; if blamed, I shall endure it. The die is cast; I have written this book: — whether it be read by posterity or by my contemporaries, is of no consequence: it may well wait for a reader during one century since God himself during 6000 years has waited for an observer like myself."

The biography of chemists, botanists, physicians, geometers

---

[24] "Life of Newton," *Lives of Em. Pers.*, p. 17. The immediate sources of the following anecdotes have not been identified. See, however, *Encyclopaedia Americana* and "Kepler," *Lives of Em. Pers.*

abounds with the narrative of sleepless nights, laborious days and dangerous journeyings. There is no hazard the love of science has not prompted them to brave; no wilderness they have not penetrated; no experiment suggested, which they have not tried. And with all my honour for science, so much greater is my respect for the observer Man, than for any thing he observes, that I esteem this development of character — this high unconditional devotion to their cause, this trampling under foot of every thing pitiful and selfish in the zeal of their pursuit of nature, — to be worth all the stars they have found, all the bugs or crystals or zoophytes they have described, all the laws how sublime soever, which they have deduced and divulged to mankind.

It was my intention to have added the consideration of the effect of a diffusion of a general taste in these pursuits to counteract in the community the extreme and debasing influences of party spirit, and the excessive love of gain; as we would let in the west wind blowing from the wilderness into the polluted chambers of a hospital. But I am already trespassing on your time.

5. I have spoken of some of the advantages which may flow from the culture of natural science: health; useful knowledge; delight; and the improvement of the mind and character.[25] I should not do the subject the imperfect justice in my power if I did not add a fifth. It is in my judgment the greatest office of natural science (and one which as yet is only begun to be discharged) to explain man to himself. The knowledge of the laws of nature, — how many wild errors — political, philosophical, theological, has it not already corrected! The knowledge of all the facts of all the laws of nature will give man his true place in the system of being. But more than the correction of specific errors by the disclosure of particular facts, there yet remain questions of the highest interest which are unsolved and on which a far more profound knowledge of Nature will throw light.

The most difficult problems are those that lie nearest at hand. I suppose that every philosopher feels that the simple fact of his

[25] *Cf.* the list in *Nature* (1836): commodity, beauty, [language], discipline, [idealism]. He added "language" and "idealism" to the list in the lectures on English Literature.

own existence is the most astonishing of all facts. But I suggest the question, with great humility, to the reason of every one present, whether, the most mysterious and wonderful fact, (after our own existence) with which we are acquainted, be not, the power of *expression* which belongs to external nature; or, that correspondence of the outward world to the inward world of thoughts and emotions, by which it is suited to represent what we think.

There is more beauty in the morning cloud than the prism can render account of. There is something in it which reflects the aspects of mortal life, its epochs, and its fate.[26] Is the face of heaven and earth — this glorious scene always changing — yet always good — fading all around us into fair perspective, — overhung with the gay awning of the clouds, — floating themselves as scraps of down under the high stars, and the ever lasting vault of space, — is this nothing to us but so much oxygen, azote, and carbon of which what is visible is composed? Is there not a secret sympathy which connects man to all the animate and to all the inanimate beings around him? Where is it these fair creatures (in whom an order and series is so distinctly discernible,) find their link, their cement, their keystone, but in the Mind of Man? It is he who marries the visible to the Invisible by uniting thought to Animal Organization.

The strongest distinction of which we have an idea is that between thought and matter. The very existence of thought and speech supposes and is a new nature totally distinct from the material world; yet we find it impossible to speak of it and its laws in any other language than that borrowed from our experience in the material world. We not only speak in continual metaphors of the morn, the noon and the evening of life, of dark and bright thoughts, of sweet and bitter moments, of the healthy mind and the fading memory; but all our most literal and direct modes of speech — as right and wrong, form and substance, honest and dishonest etc., are, when hunted up to their original signification, found to be metaphors also. And this, because the whole of Nature is a metaphor or image of the human Mind. The laws of moral nature answer to those of matter as face to face in a glass. "The

---

[26] "There is more beauty . . . its fate" (*J*, III, 226).

visible world," it has been well said, "and the relations of its parts is the dial plate of the invisible one." [27] In the language of the poet,

> For all that meets the bodily sense I deem
> Symbolical, one mighty alphabet
> For infant minds.[28]

It is a most curious fact that the axioms of geometry and of mechanics only translate the laws of ethics. Thus, A straight line is the shortest distance between two points; The whole is greater than its part; The smallest weight may be made to lift the greatest, the difference of force being compensated by time; Reaction is equal to action; and a thousand the like propositions which have an ethical as well as a material sense. They are true not only in geometry but in life; they have a much more extensive and universal signification as applied to human nature than when confined to technical use. And every common proverb is only one of these facts in nature used as a picture or parable of a more extensive truth; as when we say, "A bird in the hand is worth two in the bush." "A rolling stone gathers no moss." "Tis hard to carry a full cup even." "Whilst the grass grows the steed starves." — In themselves these are insignificant facts but we repeat them because they are symbolical of moral truths.[29] These are only trivial instances designed to show the principle. But it will probably be found to hold of all the facts revealed by chemistry or astronomy that they have the same harmony with the human mind.

And this undersong, this perfect harmony does not become less with more intimate knowledge of nature's laws but the analogy is felt to be deeper and more universal for every law that Davy or Cuvier or Laplace has revealed. It almost seems as if according to the idea of Fontenelle, "We seem to recognize a truth the first time we hear it." [30]

[27] Quoted from Swedenborg's "apologist," Counsellor Samuel Sandels, in "Emanuel Swedenborg," *New Jerusalem Magazine* V (1831–32), 437. Cf. *J*, II, 500 and Cameron, I, 231–32.

[28] Coleridge, "The Destiny of Nations: a Vision," lines 18–20.

[29] "And this because the whole of Nature . . . moral truths" (*Nature*, W, I, 32–33 and "English Literature," Lecture 5, p. 290).

[30] "And this undersong . . . we hear it" (*J*, III, 226–27).

I look then to the progress of Natural Science as to that which is to develop new and great lessons of which good men shall understand the moral. Nature is a language and every new fact we learn is a new word; but it is not a language taken to pieces and dead in the dictionary, but the language put together into a most significant and universal sense. I wish to learn this language — not that I may know a new grammar but that I may read the great book which is written in that tongue.[31] A man should feel that the time is not lost and the efforts not misspent that are devoted to the elucidation of these laws; for herein is writ by the Creator his own history. If the opportunity is afforded him he may study the leaves of the lightest flower that opens upon the breast of summer, in the faith that there is a meaning therein before whose truth and beauty all external grace must vanish, as it may be, all this outward universe shall one day disappear, when its whole sense hath been comprehended and engraved forever in the eternal thoughts of the human mind.

[31] "Nature is a language . . . in that tongue" (*J*, III, 227).

2

On the Relation of Man to the Globe

The title page of this lecture has no place or date of delivery. Cabot has written on it: "This lecture must have been delivered in December 1833. See letter of R.W.E. to E.B.E. 1570 [*sic*]." The reference is to a letter of December 22, 1833 (*L*, I, 402) in which Emerson speaks of preparing a second lecture on natural history for "next Tuesday evening," December 24. Cameron, however, has discovered that the "Boston *Evening Transcript* for Monday evening, January 6, 1834, announced under 'Franklin Lectures' that the subject that evening would be 'The Relations of Man to the Globe' by the Rev. R. W. Emerson" (I, 340, n. 24). This later date sheds light on the comment by Charles Emerson on January 7: "Waldo is well and lectures well" (*L*, I, 402, n. 131). What lecture Emerson gave, if any, on December 24 is not known. The most plausible guess is that he referred to this one, which was given a trial reading somewhere on that date or, more probably, was for some reason postponed. The last sentence of the first paragraph, as the lecture now stands, and the cancellation of the words "this port" on p. 36 suggest that this lecture was read again somewhere together with "The Uses of Natural History" — possibly at Concord. Presumably at this time Emerson cancelled from the earlier lecture the passage on coal (see p. 15) which he had used again here.

The title and first paragraph are on the first and fourth pages respectively of the usual two-leaf sheet. On the third, Emerson jotted at some time the following pencilled outline:

1. preparation of the globe for man
2. proportion established between him and nature
3. adaptations of his system
4. necessities leading to commerce
5. fitness to the animals
6. command of inanimate nature
7. correspondence of Nature to the mind
8. high consequence of this to science
9. conclusion

Most of these headings were inserted also in the manuscript in pencil,

27

and the sections numbered accordingly. Each of these divisions is here indicated by a space in the printed text. The same careful formal organization can be observed in his other early scientific lectures and in *Nature*.

In this lecture Emerson draws on his reading in travel literature, such as Dampier and von Humboldt, as well as his own experiences and reflections on shipboard in 1833. Some notes in the journal of 1833 (*J*, III, 234) on hints taken by engineers and architects from nature, now printed in *Society and Solitude* (*W*, VII, 40–41), may well have been made with this lecture in mind. Cabot quotes two brief passages from this lecture (I, 223–24).

THERE are many facts which from their nature cannot suddenly be known and which can only be disclosed in long periods of time. The character of a climate cannot be known by one day nor safely judged by one year. The orbit of a planet cannot be determined until it has made a full revolution which may require several of our years. The precession of the equinoxes in our own planet, requires thousands of years for its cycle. There is a fact of this sort of much nearer interest to us but which only a series of ages could fully reveal, namely the fitness which the long residence of man upon this planet has discovered between his nature and his abode. I invite your attention to some considerations of the Relation of Man to the Globe. [As] the subject of the last was the uses so this will be found to involve the fruits of Natural Science.[1]

Since the middle of the last century, we have begun to study the history of organic nature by inference from certain marks left here and there about our abode; by putting together a most curious tissue of circumstantial evidence, of which Moses furnishes one fact; and the gypsum beds of Paris, another; and the mummies of Egypt, a third; and the rocks of Goat Island, a fourth; and the chance observation of some shipwrecked sailor, a fifth. We have come to look at the world in quite another light from any in which our fathers regarded it. It is not a mere farm out of which

---

[1] The last sentence is an insertion. Emerson did not originally read these two lectures before the same audience.

we can raise corn to eat; nor a battlefield on which the strongest arm can rob his neighbors of their property; nor a market where men set up each their various talents for sale; nor a mere abiding place which has no other interest than the action and suffering of which it is the scene; but it is found that it may serve the noblest purposes to the intellect; it is found that it is itself a monument on whose surface every age of perhaps numberless centuries has somewhere inscribed its history in gigantic letters — too deep to be obliterated — but so far apart, and without visible connexion, that only the most diligent observer — say rather — an uninterrupted succession of patient observers — can read them.

It was the opinion of a great man recently dead who long stood at the head of German literature and high in German science, "that Nature accidentally and as it were against her will became the telltale of her own secrets; that every thing was told — at least once; only not in the time and place at which we looked for or suspected it. We must collect it here and there, in all the nooks and corners in which she had let it drop. . . . That she was a book of the vastest, strangest contents from which however we might gather; that many of its leaves lay scattered around in Jupiter, Uranus and other planets." [2]

By the study of the globe in very recent times we have become acquainted with a fact the most surprising — I may say the most sublime, to wit, that Man who stands in the globe so proud and powerful is no upstart in the creation, but has been prophesied in nature for a thousand thousand ages before he appeared; that from times incalculably remote there has been a progressive preparation for him; an effort, (as physiologists say,) to produce him; the meaner creatures, the primeval sauri, containing the elements of his structure and pointing at it on every side, whilst the world was, at the same time, preparing to be habitable by him. He was not made sooner, because his house was not ready.

By digging into the earth anywhere it is found that the internal body of the planet is covered by successive concentric crusts lying one upon another like the coats of an onion. That envelope

[2] Austin, *Goethe*, I, 64.

which now forms the surface of the land, composed of mud, sand, clay, and broken stones, is formed by the decomposition and mixture of the several layers underneath it. Each of these several layers appears to have been at one time the external crust, until by a decomposition or mixture effected by fire or water, another was deposited over it. The lowest of all these crusts to which we have penetrated is granite, which seems to have been deposited in a state of fusion. When this formed the outer crust of the earth, there was no organic life, for no remains either of animal or vegetable fossils have ever been found in that hard rock; and how could life be supported on such a soil? By the fracture and crumbling of this stone, by a new distribution of the water or by other causes now unknown, new layers of gneiss, of slate, of clay, of limestone, were successively formed above it and then first faint traces of vegetable and animal life begin to appear, and in the lowest strata the most imperfect forms; — zoophytes,[3] shells, and crustaceous animals; then, fishes and reptiles. There is in nature a sort of boundary where the animate and inanimate seem to strive for mastery.

It appears that the most perfect animals were at that time formed which the earth in its then condition could sustain. Granite could not feed any creature and no vegetable is found thereon. Neither could gneiss; neither could slate. But when the vegetable race which is, you know, the laboratory or kitchen in which mineral substances — earths or stones — are decomposed and *cooked* for the nourishment of animal life — had existed, — then animal life could be sustained, and animals were created. But not all animals. The earth was not fit to support the more perfect species. In the first subsiding of the waters into the hollows which they occupy from covering the whole surface, there do not appear to have been any mountains. Mountains were later formations. The surface seems to have been nearly smooth. The shells and the gigantic grasses and reeds whose impression is found in coal, show that what was not sea was a vast marshy level, unfit for human habitation. It was the abode of enormous lizards, such as the iguanodon, whose remains indicate an animal seventy feet long,

[3] Plant-like animals, e.g. coral.

and of the bulk of an elephant; but there existed an atmosphere and a soil in which man could not subsist.

There was a time when the creatures of one sort had reached that number that it became necessary to check their multiplication; or, by their habits, had wrought such changes on the surface of the globe, as to make the earth habitable for a finer and more complex creation. Then a new formation — the remains of a new and higher order — begin to appear, more nearly resembling man, and giving earnest of his approach; and, as the new race waxes, the old race retires.

At certain epochs, convulsions occur to which the changes which we witness bear no comparison. Once, it would appear, the whole globe was in a state of vapor, (such at least was the opinion of Laplace and Mitscherlich and Cuvier); afterwards of fusion; afterwards solid; then broken up; and such action of waters and fire upon it as to crumble and mix the rocks to form soils; mountain chains were raised — blown up like a blister for several thousand miles together by fire underneath. In this hemisphere, there is one chain extending along the whole western side of the continent, about 8000 miles, from Cape Horn to Behring's Strait. There is another running east and west across the whole of the old world from Cape Finisterre in Spain through Europe and Asia to Behring's Strait.

Then there is a curious fact noticed by Lord Bacon, and though the inference might seem too daring, it is yet repeated by modern geologists, that the shape of the corresponding coasts of Africa and America would induce us to infer that the two continents of Africa and America were once united, the projecting or salient part of the former fitting exactly to the Gulf of Mexico, and the bulging part of South America about Paraiba and Pernambuco being about the size and shape of the Gulf of Guinea.

In fine, the conclusion at which in general geologists have arrived, is, that there had been repeated great convulsions of nature previous to the present order of things; that we now stand in the midst of the fourth succession of terrestrial animals; that after the age of reptiles, after that of palaeotheria,[4] after that of mam-

---

[4] A mammal of the Eocene era.

moths and mastodons, arrived the age in which the human species together with some domestic animals governs and fertilizes the earth peaceably; and that the present races are not more than five or six thousand years old.

Man is made; — the creature who seems a refinement on the form of all who went before him, and made perfect in the image of the Maker by the gift of moral nature; but his limbs are only a more exquisite organization, — say rather — the finish of the rudimental forms that have been already sweeping the sea and creeping in the mud; the brother of his hand is even now cleaving the Arctic Sea in the fin of the whale, and, innumerable ages since, was pawing the marsh in the flipper of the saurus.

Man is made; and really when you come to see the minuteness of the adaptation in him to the present earth, it suggests forcibly the familiar fact of a father setting up his children at housekeeping, building them a house, laying out the grounds, curing the chimneys, and stocking the cellar.

For, not to leave quite yet the external preparation of the house, modern chemistry has discovered some facts of striking fitness between the atmosphere and the creature who breathes it. Sir H[umphrey] Davy, it is well known, made experiments on many gases as to their power of supporting respiration; and placing animals in a given quantity of all those which can be breathed at all, he found that none would support life so long as the gas we breathe.

But another observation is much more singular. The common air, as you know, is made up of two gases named oxygen and azote; [5] and the mixture is found to contain four fifths of azote, one fifth of oxygen. Now these airs can be mixed in any proportion, just as salt may be mixed in any proportion with water. They have been mixed by experimenters in different proportions, and respired, and it is found that no other mixture will support respiration so well as four parts and one part. And what makes it more strange, nobody has found out what keeps this invariable proportion in their mixture, but, wherever you procure the air you analyze, whether from the tops of mountains, or the surface of the

[5] Nitrogen.

sea, or the bottom of mines, this uniform proportion of one of oxygen and four of azote is always found, this, namely, which is best suited to the health of man.

Then the texture and the magnitude of the earth are fitted to him. If it were stone, he could not till it. If it were slime, he could not build upon it, or stand upon it. And a strict relation is found to exist between the strength of the muscles and the gravity of the globe.

Finally, a hundred tribes of animals fit for food, and many thousand species of vegetables yielding wholesome and flavored fruits, grow upon and adorn the planet; a state of things for which slow and ancient preparation has been made. In one particular this is especially remarkable.

In the case of coal there is a most singular exhibition of the relation of a long forgotten past to the present hour.

It is well known how much the great development of the commerce of Great Britain and thence of the great civilization of that country is indebted to the boundless abundance of coal in its mines. In consequence of the abundance and accessibility of this mineral in that island, and its opportune association with beds of iron ore and the invariable contiguity of limestone employed to flux the iron, the English have been enabled to surpass all other nations in the cheapness of machinery and so in the extent of their manufactures.

But the coal which geologists have shown to be a vegetable formation, — the relic of forests which existed at an unknown antiquity before the era of the creation of mankind — had been by repeated overflowings of the sea and marine and fresh water deposits and other changes of the surface, buried below the surface at too great a depth to be reached by man.

But before the creation of our race, earthquakes or other convulsions of enormous force have lifted up these mineral beds into ledges, so that they are found extending from one thousand feet above the level of the ocean to unknown depths below it. And so it happens that these vast beds of fuel so essential to man's comfort and civilization, which would have been covered by the crust of the globe forever from his knowledge and use, are thus brought up within reach of his little hands; and a great work of Nature in an antiquity that hath no record — namely the deposit and crystallization of antediluvian forests, is made to contribute to our pleasure and prosperity at this hour.[6]

Well when the house was built and the lands were drained and the house was ventilated and the chimneys of the volcano opened as a safety valve and the cellar stocked — the creature man was formed and put into his habitation. He finds that he can breathe the air and drink the water, he finds too the temperature adjusted to his constitution. The temperature does not pass certain limits. The hottest place on earth by observation is La Guayra in Venezuela, the mean temperature being 82½°; yet at the time the observation was made, that town contained a population of eight thousand souls. The coldest temperature yet observed is about 54 degrees below zero. Yet it was found to be perfectly tolerable so long as the air was still and it is not the cold which has hindered men from reaching the pole, but the mechanical difficulties occasioned by the ice.

I have spoken of the preparation and adaptation of the abode to the inhabitant. I proceed now to the consideration of a fact not less remarkable and admitting no less variety of illustration, though — from whatever cause — it has been less frequently presented. It is this — that a proportion is faithfully kept, in all the arrangements of nature, between the powers of man and the forces with which he is to contend, for his subsistence.

This may be noticed in the animals which surround him. There are none so gigantic but man can tame or slay them. The enormous reptiles and beasts of the elder world have been destroyed before man was created. He is quite able, even in the savage state, to master all those that are alive. His traps or weapons follow every ceature into his element, and the whale is not large enough, nor the lion strong enough, nor the falcon swift enough to get away from man, a tender thin skinned creature, without tusks, or claws, or horns or scales. A man cannot swim like a whale, but a man in a boat, can. A man cannot rise into the air to overtake the eagle, but

[6] *Cf.* Lecture 1, p. 16.

a ball or an arrow can. And it is not only the New Bedford whale-
man in a ship of six hundred tons, with a forge and a furnace and
huge coppers on board and miles of hempen line and every equipment that American civilization can furnish, that can hunt the
behemoth of the waters wherever he swims round the globe, but
the poor Esquimaux also, with a harpoon pointed with bone, and
inflated sealskins tied to it, contrives to worry to death that enormous and formidable swimmer.[7]

In the first place, then, the animals on the earth are not an
overmatch for man. But the fact of the proportion kept between
the powers of man and the forces of nature may be observed in
many more respects than this one. And in all I think we shall be
struck with this fact, that man is made just strong enough to keep
his place in the world; that he is not any stronger than he need to
be; that the adjustment of his forces to the forces of nature from
which he would be in danger, is very nice, and if it had been a
little less, would have been insufficient.

And this is what I wish to illustrate.

More than three fifths of the earth's surface are covered by the
ocean. Of course, it behoved the creature who was to possess the
earth to find the means of crossing the sea. In Shakspeare's
comedy, the fairy Puck brags that he "can put a girdle round
about the earth in forty minutes." [8] We can scarce go so fast, but
the poet would not probably have thought of the thing, but that,
in his own time, Sir Francis Drake had done the feat of circum-
navigating the globe. It is the very language of his biographer that
"his fame will last as long as the world which he for the first time
surrounded." [9]

This capital art of navigation of the deep sea deserves much
attention, because it so often illustrates in the most forcible
manner the smallness of the odds (if I may say so) that exist in
favor of man, the nearness with which he comes to the edge of
destruction and yet has powers just sufficient to bring him off in
total safety. The man who has all his life been dwelling in the

[7] Cf. *J*, III, 261, for other whaling lore.
[8] *Mid. N. Dr.*, II, 1: 175–76.
[9] *Lives and Voyages*, p. 167.

interior, and who comes to the coast and embarks on the sea, and finds himself for the first time in a tempest, tossed upon a roaring ocean, cannot suppress his astonishment at the daring of this enterprize. It seems to him foolhardy — a rash encounter of a most unequal and tremendous risk. But it is not. These chances are all counted and weighed and measured, and a faithful experience has begotten this confidence in the proportioned strength of spars and rigging to the ordinary forces of wind and water. This confidence being habitual constitutes the essence of the sailor's fearlessness. The danger is incessant, and the safety of the ship requires incessant attention, but that not failing, the real risk is small. Every one who has been at sea remembers probably many moments of imminent danger. Every ship has all but struck — has been within an inch of destruction fifty times.[10] And yet how comparatively rare are fatal accidents.

A landsman at sea can scarce bring himself to rely on a reckoning scientifically kept. Much less, until he has learned the precision of a seaman's hand and eye, upon a longitude ascertained by so coarse and clumsy means as heaving the log once in two hours. But a skilful seaman seems to guess his way along with a success sometimes surprizing. About a year ago, I was a passenger on board a brig which sailed from Boston for the Mediterranean. Like most vessels of her class, she had no chronometer, and kept her reckoning by the log. At sunset, on the sixteenth day, we looked for St. Mary's, the southernmost of the Azores, but the weather was thick in the east, and we saw nothing. At nine o'clock in the evening, we descried that island, — a mere black hummock of land, — and the master's log-book being then produced, his reckoning was found to agree with our bearings within one mile.[11]

This result astonished himself. There was in it perhaps as much chance as skill. But the chronometer and quadrant make the traveller's way over the sea as plain as in a county road. It is told of an excellent seaman of our own, who made the shortest voyage that has yet been made across the Atlantic, — accomplishing the passage from Liverpool to Boston in fourteen days, — that he had

[10] *J*, III, 195.
[11] *J*, III, 196.

such confidence in the accuracy of his longitude, that on approaching the coast without seeing the land, he continued running in for Boston harbour though the weather was very thick. The passengers in a body intreated him to take in sail, and wait for clear weather, but in vain. Presently a man before cried "A sail!" "A sail, you simpleton," replied the Captain, "it is the lighthouse; starboard helm!" It was the lighthouse, and he ran round it, and presently came to anchor within the bay.

So narrow is the interval between perfect safety and total destruction. It is told of the same chivalrous sailor that in his voyages he rarely went below into the cabin, but slept on deck in the cable tier, for fear his mate should take in sail.[12]

I am tempted to add yet one more instance to show how slight a circumstance may turn the balance in human favor, so nicely adjusted are our dangers to our powers. This is a very odd but very simple expedient by which a ship was saved, which is related in the Voyages of Dampier, the excellent English navigator, in his account of a dreadful storm which he encountered off the Cape de Verd islands. "The ship was scudding before wind and sea, under bare poles, when, by the inadvertence of the master, she was broached to and lay in the trough of the sea; the waves at that time running tremendously high, and threatening to overwhelm her, so that if one had struck on the deck, she must have foundered. The person who had committed this nearly fatal mistake, was in a state of distraction, and roared for any one to cut away the mizenmast to give the ship a chance of righting. All was confusion and dismay, the Captain and the officer second in command objecting to this as [a] certainly hazardous and probably useless attempt to save themselves. The whole crew had given themselves up for lost, when a seaman called to Dampier to ascend the foreshrouds with him; this, the man alleged, might make the ship wear, as he had seen the plan succeed before now. As he spoke, he mounted, and Dampier followed him. They went half shrouds up, spread out the flaps of their coats, and in three minutes the ship wore, though such had been the violence of the tempest, that the mainsail having got loose, as many men as could

[12] J, III, 204.

lie on it, assisted by all on deck, and though the mainyard was nearly level with the deck, were not able to furl it." [13]

Now I say this is a striking example to show how nearly balanced are the chances of safety and destruction to man, when the ready recollection of one sailor, and so slight a circumstance as the purchase afforded to the wind by the skirts of the coats of two men, is sufficient to turn the odds in favor of man.

But these are solitary examples. Every one familiar with the sea and with histories of sea voyages will remember a multitude of similar escapes. By such simple expedients does the wit of man bring him off safe from hazards the most fearful. And so various and flexible has he contrived to make the form of his ship which in a few minutes the nimble sailors can change from the shape of a butterfly — all wing — to the shape of a log which the waves may toss and welcome; [14] and so they go on, through all that is sublime and terrible in nature, and lose entirely the feeling of the extraordinary; the thunder may roar, the "dirty southwester" may crack his cheeks; the ship's bulwarks may be swept clean off; but the cook in his caboose never fails one morning or evening of discharging his benevolent office, and, after an incessant peril of five or six months, brings back every old trunk and cracked plate safe across half the globe.

I think the history of navigation affords the most striking instances, but by no means the only ones, of the accurate adjustment of the powers to the wants of man. The same balance is everywhere kept. A man is always in danger, and never. It is said that in battle the eye is first conquered. "Primi in proeliis oculi vincuntur." [15] Let a man keep his presence of mind, and there is scarcely any danger so desperate from which he cannot deliver himself. For there is a very wide interval betwixt danger and destruction which men in peaceful pursuits seldom consider. A man in his parlor in this civil town, thinks that to meet a lion in the desert, or to stumble over an alligator in wading knee deep through a savannah, is certain destruction.[16] But the Fellatahs of Africa, or

[13] *Lives and Voyages*, p. 344n. Cf. *J*, III, 196.
[14] *J*, III, 204.
[15] Tacitus, *Germania*: 43.
[16] *J*, III, 195.

the Caribee Indians think no such thing. Their habitual acquaintance with these delicate circumstances, has taught them to see a wide distance betwixt danger and death, and in that discrimination their safety lies. Mungo Park rode slowly by a red lion, expecting every moment the fatal spring. Humboldt,[17] having left his boat on the river Orinoco, to examine some natural objects on the bank, suddenly found himself near a large jaguar, and "though extremely frightened, he retained sufficient self command to follow the advice which the Indians had so often given, and continued to walk without moving his arms, making a large circuit towards the edge of the water." The tiger did not move from the spot. An Indian girl at Urituco being seized by a crocodile — she immediately felt for his eyes and thrust her fingers into them and thus compelled the animal to let her go, though with the loss of an arm. And Dampier relates what befel one of his companions in Honduras — that wading in a meadow his knee was seized by an alligator; he quietly waited till the animal loosened its teeth to take a new and surer hold, and when it did, he snatched away his knee interposing the butt end of his gun in its stead, which the animal seized so firmly that it was snatched out of the man's hand, and carried off.[18]

Indeed I hardly know whether we need go so far to find the proofs of this adjustment between man and external nature. Perhaps an attentive consideration of the hazards that are daily met in the prosecution of many of the outdoor trades, and even in riding or swimming, or in many games, would furnish as conclusive evidence of the uniform existence of the fact. And when we have reckoned the numberless perils, to which a very superficial knowledge of the anatomy of man shows us we are exposed in every hour of the most peaceful and sheltered life, I cannot but think that the mere existence in full possession of all their organs of sense, of *old persons*, if it were not so familiar, would be a most surprizing phenomenon.

[17] Both the following stories are quoted in a review of Humboldt, Vol. IV, in the *Quarterly Review*, XXI (1819), 342, 344. Mungo Park (1771–1806) wrote *Travels in the Interior Districts of Africa*.
[18] *J*, III, 195–96. See *Lives and Voyages*, p. 301.

This leads me to another consideration upon which the balance we have been considering depends, namely, the manner in which man's supreme reason is seconded by the perfect constitution of his own frame. Behold the beautiful form of the skeleton, that elegant strong and flexible box in which is packed up his nervous and sentient organization; the delicate but durable health of the system; the exquisite sensibility of a skin so acutely alive to pain that, it has been well said, it makes a better guard to him from danger, than would the hide of a rhinoceros; his ear and lungs nicely adapted to the air; his eye to the light; his palate to the flavors of vegetables; and all his powers adapted to and concentrating their action upon his hand, that unrivalled machine.[19]

Nothing contributes more directly to human efficiency in the planet where we live, than the perfect inter-accommodation of all these senses. The eye is a miracle; the hand is another. A third is their mutual adjustment. Most of the gentlemen present, down to the very youngest, will remember the time when they studied the art of throwing a stone. I well remember my own vain endeavors to make the stone hit the mark, by all the nicety I could use in carrying the hand skilfully, until, by chance, I one day forgot to attend to the motion of my hand at all, and looking only at the mark, the stone struck it. There is a time when every boy learns this secret, that the eye and the hand are so wonderfully adjusted, that if the eye is fixed intently on the mark, the hand is sure to throw truly. I will not stop to draw the fine moral which speaks from this fact; but must not omit to mention the equal adjustment of the hand to the ear and voice in music, nay of the hand to the whole body. For you can put your hand upon any point of your body as well with your eyes shut as open.

In like manner are all the senses fitted to each other. Every one may observe the relation between the eye and the voice. It is a common rule given to young speakers, to fix the eye upon a person in the remote corner of the house, for, by so doing, the voice

[19] "This subject has lately attracted the attention it deserves in the beautiful treatise of Sir Charles Bell which cannot be read without delight" [E]. The reference is to a Bridgewater Treatise on *The Hand: its Mechanism and Vital Endowments as Evincing Design*, London, 1834. The lecture does not provide further evidence of Emerson's knowledge of this work.

naturally elevates itself to such a pitch that that person can hear.

I notice these adaptations in this connexion because this minuteness of finish in the human system is the essential element of his power. It has been said, "if the hand had not been divided into fingers, man would still be wild in the forest." This symmetry of parts is his equipment for the conquest of nature.

In pursuing these observations upon the reference that exists to Man in nature, another fact which commands our attention is the manner in which man is led on by his wants to the development of his powers and so to the possession of the globe. By the geographical distribution of animals, plants, and minerals, he is forced to be a traveller and a merchant as much as by hunger he is made a hunter or a shepherd. Nature has no capital city where she accumulates her splendid treasures. She has divided her goods among all the zones. It has been said, "Every degree of latitude has its own fruit." [20] Food is in one place, spice in another, medicine in a third, clothing in a fourth; arms in a fifth; beasts of burden in a sixth; ornaments in a seventh. And so she acquaints her children with each other, and contrives to impart whatever invention one man makes, to millions. On this great market of the world she gives opportunity to each, to ask after the family of the other, and what are the news.

May I add that there is a like equality in distributing even the decoration of the globe, as if that the shows of nature might attract so imaginative a creature from his native spot. In the south is hung the famous constellation of the Southern Cross and the Magellanic Clouds. But there is no rose in the southern hemisphere. That is one of the ornaments of the temperate zone. The equator is encumbered with magnificence of its vegetable and animal productions, and its atmospheric phenomena. But the gloom of the Pole is not without its glories, — its sublime twilights and unimaginable auroras. In the east is the baobab and the banian, and Himmaleh.[21] In the west, Niagara. In Sumatra is the

---

[20] The sources of this and the above statement have not been identified.
[21] The gourd of the monkey-bread tree of Africa; an East Indian tree which spreads underground; the Himalaya mountains.

largest flower, the Rafflesia, three feet in diameter. In the islands the cocoa, in the desert the date.

Another important fact which illustrates the relation between man's condition and his powers, is found in the servitude of the lower animals. Here is a new example of the accuracy with which he is adapted not to the elements only, but to the inhabitants of the earth, and of the pliancy of his own powers and habits which permit him to live in such strict relations to them. Ages ago it was settled that man should be master. But in some respects, these creatures are wiser than he is, as they have instincts, and he has none, or none that he does not outgrow. But he has eyes and reason, and contrives to avail himself of these instincts as he would of mechanical powers. And so he "learns from the dog the physic of the field." [22]

A species of cuckoo, called indicator, or honey-guide attracts the attention of the Hottentots by its shrill cry, and, as soon as he is observed, he flutters on to the hive of a wild bee, in hopes of sharing the honey. When the Buccaneers landed upon desert parts of South America or the West Indies, they were usually guided in their selection of unknown fruits by the birds, never eating any that were not pecked. [23]

We have long forgotten this humble origin of our most valuable knowledge, but the debt is probably very great. Why need I recur to the conspicuous fitness of the camel to the man of the desert, the reindeer to the man of the snow, the llama to the man of the cordilleras? I prefer the picture familiar to our own eyes. See how this wary lord of the world has gone into Persia and brought thence a beautiful species of pheasant and set him down in the farmyard to strut with his tidy family of hens around the barn door. He has brought home from Southern Africa the gloved cat, to be the sentinel of his pantry. He has tamed the jackal of Syria and by domestication and improvement of the race, has made the faithful dog. He has found in Tartary or Arabia a small wild lean ragged looking animal and by cultivation of the race has

[22] Pope, *Essay On Man*, III, 174.
[23] *J*, III, 196.

formed the domestic horse, the noblest of animals and the most important auxiliary of man, who flies over the ground at the rate of a mile in a minute. He has put the boar of Europe in a sty, and the sheep in a fold. On the sunny side of his house he puts a box of wood or straw for an insect family of little distillers who suck the honey from all the flowers within a mile of his dwelling, and bring it home to him. He has tamed the goose and the duck and the turkey and lives surrounded and beloved by his slaves.

One fact seems to mark a relation yet more intimate. He has learned from the chance experience of some dairy-maids to inoculate his flesh with a disease from the udder of a cow, and by that means to defend himself from a more dangerous disease to which his own race are subject.

Let us now proceed in our observation of man's aptitude to the surrounding objects from the animate to the inanimate creation. See what a skilful and beneficent hand he has laid upon the globe. Not finding the world in its original state sufficiently commodious, he has undertaken to alter and amend it. He may be said to keep the world in repair. A German naturalist [24] has shown that it is the tendency of every river in the course of time to elevate its bed. Two great rivers in the north of Italy, the Adige and the Po, are at this moment higher than all the land which lies between them. The territory is too valuable to be made a marsh. It is the garden of Lombardy and so the inhabitants build up their dikes above the tops of the houses of Ferrara. The whole province of Holland lies lower than the level of the sea, and a population of 820,000 souls see the waters of the Rhine and Meuse constantly suspended twenty or thirty feet above their heads. Wherever cities are built, the sea is kept out where it tends to encroach on the shore. The beds of rivers are cleared of obstructions and deepened by art to redeem the adjacent land from swamp. Bogs are drained and converted into firm land. Oaks are transplanted and a forest of fullgrown trees suddenly rises upon desolate heaths. The Swiss carries up the soil which is to form his garden, in baskets, and lays

[24] For what follows see Cuvier, *Discourse*, p. 97. The naturalist was French, a certain de Prony. A German is referred to shortly afterwards in Cuvier's text.

it down on the granite floor of the Alps. Downs formed by the blowing of the sand drifts from the seashore are confined by the beach grass, and the arable land saved from desolation. Climate is ameliorated by cultivation and not only the climate softened, but the air purified, and made healthful by the same cause.

> Yet nature is made better by no mean
> But nature makes that mean.[25]

By the study of nature he improves nature, and keeps the world in repair. For, if the human race should be totally destroyed, it would take no very long time for the sea and the sand and the rivers and the bogs to make most parts of the earth uninhabitable by men.

But perhaps the most striking effect of the accurate adaptation of man to the globe is found in his love of it. The love of nature — the accord between man and the external world, — what is it but the perception how truly all our senses, and, beyond the senses, the soul, are tuned to the order of things in which we live? The constant familiarity with the objects of nature, the use of water, of fire, of the air, and sunshine, are not more necessary than they are delightful. The exercise of all the senses is an intense pleasure, as any one will find, who recovers the use of one after being deprived of it. The effects of light and shade out of doors, the sight of an extended landscape, the wilderness of beautiful flowers by which the vegetable race is perpetuated, delight all men. Whoever has recovered from sickness, has remarked the picturesque appearance which the most common objects wore on his first ride or walk abroad. Perhaps he then found for the first time that the pigeon in the street was a handsome bird, that the trees grew in elegant forms, — and the outline of the mountains against the sky — he was never weary of gazing at.

Go into the country in the month of June or September, and stand upon a hillside in the morning, and listen to the sounds that rise from all the farms around; — the lowing of the cattle, the

[25] *Winter's Tale*, IV, 4:89–90.

sound of falling water, the various cries of the domestic fowls, the notes of wild birds, and the distant voice of man, — and judge if some adjustment has not been made to fit this concert to your ear. So the scents of flowers are fitted to the sense of smell.

So with the eye. In all the variations of nature the eye is still suited. I said go into the country in June — but go in December, go at midnight, go in the mist, in the rain, in hailstorms, with thunder and lightning, at blazing noon or at daybreak and you shall find there are states of feeling in your mind which correspond to all these phenomena.

This pleasure of a conversation with nature is conspicuously exhibited in the habits of savages who cannot be won by any luxuries from the wild enjoyments of the forest.

"It is no new thing," says an old traveller in Campeachy and Honduras, "for the Indians in these woody parts of America to fly away whole towns at once, and settle themselves in the unfrequented woods to enjoy their freedom; and, if they are accidentally discovered, they will remove again, which they can easily do, their household goods being little else but their hammocks and their calabashes. They build every man his own house, and tie up their hammocks between two trees, wherein they sleep till their houses are made. The woods afford them some subsistence, such as pecaree; but they that are thus strolling or *marooning*, as the Spaniards call it, have plantain walks that no man knows but themselves, and from thence they have their food till they have raised plantation provision near their new built town. They clear no more ground than what they actually employ for their subsistence. They make no paths, but when they go far from home they break now and then a bough letting it hang down which serves as a mark to guide them in their return." [26] Humboldt in his account of the Chayma Indians on the banks of the Colorado, attests the same fact. "Besides their cabin in the village, they usually have a smaller covered with palm or plantain leaves in some solitary place in the woods, to which they retire as often as they can; and so strong is the desire among them of enjoying the pleasures of savage life, that the children sometimes wander

[26] "Dampier" [E]. *Lives and Voyages*, p. 310.

entire days in the forests. In fact, the towns are often almost wholly deserted." [27]

Certainly the wild man exhibits his delight in God's world more steadily than we, but the walls of cities and their artificial modes of life have not yet tamed the savage in us. The festival of May Day finds such obstinate favor in our hearts, that even our cold winds cannot keep the young crowds at home. Every one has noticed, as well as Chaucer, that there is a season in the year when folk long to make journeys.

> Then longen folk to gon on pilgrimages,
> And palmers for to seeken strange strondes,
> To serve the holies known in sundry londes. [28]

And the greediness with which a rose, a dahlia, a bulbous root or an Aaron's rod or some green leaf is planted in every body's sitting room attests the universal presence of the same desires.

But the most interesting and valuable form which this inextinguishable propensity in us assumes is the love of the Natural Sciences. The same organization which creates in the Chayma Indian such thirst and hunger for his boundless woods, which makes a sunny meadow spotted with flowers and visited by birds such a paradise to a child, is the cause in cultivated men of that interest in natural objects and processes which expresses itself in the sciences of botany, of zoology, of chemistry, and astronomy. The pursuit of these sciences has gradually disclosed a new and noble view of man's relation to the globe.

With the progress of the cultivation of the species the globe itself both in the mass and in its minutest part, becomes to man a school of science. For, to begin with that which is the most perfect of the sciences, to what is owing that wonderful completeness of the records in which the complex revolutions of all the bodies in the immense spaces of the universe are computed and written down, as if this planet were a living eye sailing through space to watch them? Is it not because the earth is to the astronomer a *moveable observatory*, enabling him to change his place in the

---

[27] *Cf.* Humboldt, III, 237–38. Not Humboldt's words.
[28] Prologue to *The Canterbury Tales*, lines 12–14.

universe, and get a base of two hundred millions of miles, as a surveyor would take new stations in a field to form triangles? Whilst thus the astronomer makes the earth a platform to hold his telescope and vary his observations, the geologist finds the old ball to be a register of periods of time otherwise immeasureable. Shells and fossils are the coins from which he deciphers the history of forgotten ages. Some idea of the riches of the means which the earth affords to these investigations may be formed from the fact that the savans of France have detected more than eight hundred species of shells, almost all unknown in the existing seas, in the limestone of Paris; that Cuvier has determined and classed the remains of more than one hundred and fifty mammiferous and oviparous animals, ninety of which are wholly unknown at present among living species.

Professor Buckland [29] after having proved the identity of an antediluvian animal whose remains had been discovered, with the hyena now living in Africa, has confirmed the proof by an actual comparison of the relics of the last meal of the fossil animal — a mass of digested bone — with a similar mass that has traversed the organs of a living animal; and, it is said, an experienced eye does not readily discern the difference. And Cuvier has ascertained a disputed point — that the bird mummies which were found in the pyramids of Egypt, having a beak precisely similar to an ibis now found in the Nile not a serpent eater, *were serpent eaters*, by finding in the mummy the undigested remains of the skin and scales of serpents.[30]

Once upon this track of scientific research, every thing invites man, aids him and unexpected disclosures start up in every corner. It is already impossible to name an object large or small existing in nature which has not been the subject of searching inquiry. The habits of microscopic insects are examined as the habits of elephants. Classification has got down to them. In the Regne Animal, I find the genus of Monades thus defined: "A genus of insects of the order infusoria. The generic character is a worm invisible to the naked eye, simple, pellucid, and resembling a point.

[29] William Buckland (1784–1856), Anglican clergyman and geologist.
[30] Cuvier, *Discourse*, p. 243.

The genus includes five species."[31] Meantime the chemist decomposes bodies supposed to be simple, and almost anticipates the resolving all created things into a few gases, perhaps two, perhaps one. At the same time we seem to be approaching the elemental secrets of nature in finding the principle of Polarity in all the laws of matter, in light, heat, magnetism, and electricity. And how long before the laws of life will be laid open to the researches of the physiologist?

Now what is the conclusion from these hasty and to some it may appear miscellaneous sketches of the relations of man to the objects around him? I have spoken of the preparation made for man in the slow and secular changes and melioration of the surface of the planet. We have seen that as soon as he could live upon it, he was created; that the air was mixed to suit his lungs; that the temperature ranges between extremes tolerable to him; that the texture of the earth is fit; that the mineral treasures are conveniently bestowed for his use; then, that a most nicely adjusted proportion is established betwixt his powers and the forces with which he has to deal, — provided for in the excellent construction of his frame; then, that such an arrangement of the gifts of nature is made, as to invite man out to activity and commerce; then, that he forms mutually serviceable relations with his fellow creatures the brutes; then, that he improves the face of the planet itself; then, that not only a relation of use but a relation of beauty subsists between himself and nature, which leads him to Science; and, finally, that once embarked on that pursuit, all things stimulate and instruct him, — the dewdrop is a lecture, the rainbow a professor, the white Alps a specimen, the hurricane an experiment, the mine a book, and the planet in its orbit only a ship to transport the astronomer and his telescopes through the navigable heavens to more convenient stations of observation.

In the view of all these facts I conclude that other creatures reside in particular places as fishes in the sea, turtles in the mud, moles in the earth, camels in the desert, birds in the air, but the residence of man is the world. It was given him to possess it. I

---

[31] Cuvier, *Discourse,* p. 249, "Glossary." The *Regne Animal* was a larger work by Cuvier which we have no sure evidence that Emerson consulted.

conclude further, that the snail is not more accurately adjusted to his shell than man to the globe he inhabits; that not only a perfect symmetry is discoverable in his limbs and senses between the head and the foot, between the hand and the eye, the heart and the lungs, — but an equal symmetry and proportion is discoverable between him and the air, the mountains, the tides, the moon, and the sun. I am not impressed by solitary marks of designing wisdom; I am thrilled with delight by the choral harmony of the whole. Design! It is all design. It is all beauty. It is all astonishment.

Water

Emerson had long been interested in the symbolic possibilities of water. In a note written on a loose bit of paper and shut into the journal of March, 1831, he comments (*J*, II, 365):

A bubble of water, a grain of gunpowder.
A shell may teach more than a range of mountains.
Heat keeps the earth from assuming the shape of a small crystal.
Expansion of water by freezing.
Man comes in and turns the fishes out. Fishes and their senses fit for their element.
Atomic theory. Water the mirror, the solvent, the engineer, the presser, the scavenger.

Although dated 1833 on the title page, this lecture was delivered on January 17, 1834, before the Boston Mechanic's Institution at the Athenaeum (*L*, I, 402, 404; Cabot, II, 711; Cameron, I, 341). As in the case of the previous lecture, spaces in the text mark subdivisions to which Emerson as an afterthought attached labels and in a few cases numbers (see textual notes). For this most factual and least personal of his scientific talks Emerson rifled a wide variety of sources, notably Cuvier and Playfair.

"Water," said an ancient poet,[1] "is the best of things." Optima res, aqua. I have no such opinion, for I hold that every thing is good in its place. But there is so much foundation for the saying as this, that Water occupies a very large place among good things. Few people consider how large a place. No man yet knows how many offices this element fulfils. It needs much leisure and research and acuteness to find so many as are known. Perhaps as many remain to be found, for it hides itself very cunningly sometimes close by us, and sometimes becomes invisible, and some-

[1] Pindar, *Olympian Odes*, I: 1.

times works in places inaccessible to us that we can witness only its surface action, and can only by calculation approximate to a few of its numberless uses out of our sight.

The water in our pumps is so obedient, useful, and indispensable a household servant that we think we appreciate its merits pretty well and that no recommendation will increase our knowledge of its character. But a little research will show us that it is as serviceable in its universal mass as it is in petty quantities; that God makes as much use of it in the great order of nature, as man does in his washbowl or his cup; that we meet it oftener and owe it more than we imagine; that it is a friend who sends us favors unsuspected, that works when we sleep, circulates in our veins, is present in every function of life, grows in the vegetable, is a cement, and an engineer, and an architect, in inanimate nature.

The uses of Water make a large chapter in the encyclopedia of Nature. It ministers to our necessity, our comfort, and our delight. Even its least and incidental aids are of great importance. The food derived to man from the fisheries sustains a great population. And as it is the country of the ship and by means of the ship, as it is the bridge uniting all the countries on the planet, its influence on human civilization cannot be overestimated. But its most important services are general.

We think we have been very ingenious to set this strong laborer to work for us in so many ways; and contriving to take advantage of all his surprizing talents for industry, we have set him to cleanse our cities, to flood and fertilize our wastes, to carry our ship on the shoulders of his waves, to turn our mill wheel night and day, and if he must expand with such frightful force whenever he is hot, we have given him steam-pistons to lift of a few hundred tons with all his straining; and if he can pull so hard, and weigh so much as appears, we have thought he may as well press books, and spermaceti, and paper, as press himself with all his thousands of pounds.

And it cannot be denied, the element leads no idle life in most civilized countries. But his unseen services, over which we have no control, are greater than all these which we direct. For, he preserves the temperature of the globe in a fit condition for human life; he modifies the atmosphere; he washes away the filth of cities and continents; he plucks down the old Alps and Andes to make the habitable land of the plains; he makes new soil to repair the continual waste he occasions; he is present and active in every function of vegetable and animal structures; and he is the circulating medium having communication with every part of the earth through the rivers which ultimately pour their waters into the sea. And this action he performs under as many shapes as he has ways of working. It is surprizing to see how fast he can put on his masks, all new and all beautiful. Now he globes himself into a dewdrop. Now he reddens in the rainbow. Now he whitens into spray. Now he floats as a cloud. Now he shines as an icicle; now he crystallizes into the star of a snowflake; now he rolls as a wave, and then disappears from human eyes to make the transparency of the atmosphere.

It is the object of the present lecture to enumerate and describe in a general manner some of the properties of Water and the uses to which they are applied in Nature.

A drop of water is composed of two gases, oxygen and hydrogen. It is one of the most striking revelations of chemistry to inform us that all the most solid substances of the globe are made up by the mixture of elastic airs. At the polar regions ice hardens to so compact a texture that it can scarcely be broken by the hammer, yet is every block of that transparent stone composed of two gases, each of which is as invisible to the eye and as impalpable as the air we breathe. This is proved by putting eight parts of oxygen and one part of hydrogen [2] by weight in a glass receiver and passing the electric spark through the mixture; they burn, and water is immediately seen trickling down the sides of the vessel. This water being collected and accurately weighed is found exactly equal to the weight of the original gases.

The mass of this element upon the whole globe is immense. In all the changes it assumes no particle of water quits the earth, for it gravitates, and therefore there is as much now as at the

[2] Emerson is also familiar with Cavendish's ratio of one to two by volume (see textual notes).

creation. More than three fifths of the earth's surface are covered with it, and Laplace declares that to account for the observed phenomena of tides requires an average depth to the ocean of ten miles. It is elsewhere computed that if the waters covered the whole surface, instead of being collected in the hollows of the ocean, it would have a uniform depth of two miles. So vast a quantity of matter in a state of constant activity cannot but exert a very great agency both chemical and mechanical, not only through all the kingdoms of living nature, but also in the primary revolutions of the solid body of the planet itself.

And this is found to be true in our observation. It is never absent in the great agencies that have so changed the face of the earth. It is itself the laboratory of Nature in which new continents are manufactured to supply the waste of the old. As the chemist in his operations uses water as a receiver, a cover, a solvent, so does the great Chemist; and as our mechanicks have availed themselves of its immense force of pressure the same property is familiarly employed in the mechanism of the globe.

Let us then first inquire into its use in producing the great changes at the surface of the globe. Here its action is threefold, by its fluid level, by its solvency, and by pressure. Let us see the consequence of these properties.

Nineteen parts in twenty of the known solid matter of the globe are composed of five substances, Iron, Flint, Alumine, Lime, and Magnesia. These last, as well as iron, are metals disguised by oxygen, are crystallized into solid rocks. The soil on which we live and by which we are fed is nothing but a mixture of these rocks in a crumbled state together with remains of animal and vegetable matter to which the same soil had previously given birth. What broke them up? Water seeking its level. Something no doubt is to be ascribed to the incessant friction and to the chemical action of the air but more marked effects belong to the mechanical action of water.

Water everywhere "appears as the most active enemy of hard and solid bodies; and in every state, from transparent vapour to solid ice, from the smallest rill to the greatest river, it attacks whatever has emerged above the level of the sea, and labours incessantly to restore it to the deep. The parts loosened and disengaged by the chemical agents are carried down by the rains, and, in their descent, rub and grind the superficies of other bodies. Thus water, though incapable of acting on hard substances by direct attrition, is the cause of their being so acted on and when it descends in torrents carrying with it sand, gravel, and fragments of rock it may be truly said to turn the forces of the mineral kingdom against itself. No piece it breaks off is joined again, parts once detached can never be united save at the bottom of the ocean."

"On the shores the fragments of rock once detached become instruments of further destruction and make a part of the powerful artillery with which the ocean assails the land: they are impelled against the rocks from which they break off other fragments and the whole are thus ground against one another. Whatever be their hardness, they are reduced to gravel,"[3] whose smooth surface and round figure is the best proof of the irresistible force of this ceaseless friction.

Such is the provision that is made in nature first for forming and then for preserving the soil or the coat of vegetable mould spread out over the surface of the earth. Light and loose as this coat necessarily is, and subject to continual loss, being washed away by rains and continually carried down by the rivers into the sea, — yet such is the fidelity with which the balance of waste and repair is kept, that the soil remains the same in quantity, and has remained nearly the same, ever since the earth was inhabited by men. This continual repair, it is easily seen, can only be made by the activity of the waters in crumbling slowly but constantly the rocks. As much as the Hudson and the Mississippi carry away suspended in their stream is torn off and brought down by a thousand little brooks from the steep faces of the Alleganies, and the Rocky Mountains. And the permanence of the coat of vegetable mould on the surface of the earth is a demonstrative proof of the continual destruction of the rocks by water.

As the operations of Nature are restricted by no limits of time

[3] Playfair, I, 111–13.

the minute changes of every moment make vast revolutions in the course of ages so that the earth presents now no resemblance to its ancient appearance. And the immense effect of the incessant fall of waters for so many ages is apparent enough in the deep lines which they have cut into every part of the crust of the earth. Water has once flowed above the tops of the highest mountains. Regular strata deposited by the fresh or salt streams are found lying as they were formed in unbroken order 15,000 feet above the present level of the sea. Of course the ocean has subsided from them and they have been compared to pillars of earth which workmen leave behind them to afford a measure of the whole quantity of earth removed.

From every point of the surface does the rain glide into a lower bed and from thence into a lower until the countless streams after every variety of course combine to constitute the rivers which carry the collected waters to the sea. And by this the surface (on which they act) comes to exhibit a varied or undulated elevation of dry land with a beautiful arrangement of ramifying channels all sloping with a precision unattainable by art to the general mouth or receptacle.

Thus the mechanical action of the waters reduces continually the immense mountain chains of granite and porphyry and forms from their ruins a habitable region, and fruitful fields. But how is this continual loss and destruction repaired? The fruitful field is carried down little by little into the sea as well as the mountain brought down to the field. Every thing falls down and is decomposed. Nothing ascends. Avalanches fall but mountains do not grow as vegetables and animals. Iron rusts but new iron does not form along the ground. Diamond and granite decay under the wear and the chemical action of air and water but new diamond and new granite are not crystallized. How is all this waste repaired?

By the waters. The same power that destroys in different circumstances is made to reproduce. And few phenomena in nature are more full of interest than the series of changes by which new strata are formed and consolidated and mineralized to be again decomposed.

It dissolves and holds in solution a great number of substances and combining with some and floating all, it deposits them at last at the bottom of the sea. The sea by means of its rivers is in communication with every part of the earth. Its waters contain minute quantities of every substance in nature that is soluble in them, e.g. sal ammoniac; carb[onate] of lime; sulphur; magnesia; potash; iodine. Some rivers at a flood are so turbid that they are computed to carry one thirtieth of their bulk of solid matter down to the sea. All animal, all vegetable, all mineral particles one after the other are continually carried down from higher levels to lower levels and finally delivered into the sea. All this mass: the sand and gravel forming on the sea shore; all the shells and corals which in such enormous quantities are every day accumulated in the bosom of the sea; the drift wood and the multitude of vegetable and animal remains continually deposited in the ocean; from all these we cannot doubt that strata are now forming in those regions to which nature seems to have confined the powers of mineral reproduction; there, there is abundant reason to believe, they are acted upon by central heat and the vast mass of loose wreck and fragment of the continents melted and crystallized into new mineral, and then by further action of heat raised once more above the deep.

Various circumstances had made it probable that great accumulation of heat existed within the bowels of the globe; the observation that temperature increases as we descend; the hot springs; the phenomena of volcanoes; and the evident appearance in all rocks of having been once melted.

But it has been reserved for modern geologists by some singular but decisive experiments to show the true process by which this was accomplished and the very important part which water performs in the work of continual creation. It is found that water aids this consolidation of strata by pressure and by hindering the rapid cooling of the fused mass.

Dr. Hutton had advanced the opinion that beds of limestone were formed of the shells and exuviae of marine animals which had been melted by central fire and crystallized. But it was known that whenever fire is applied to these substances in the open air they are pulverized as soon as the fixed air is expelled by heat. To this objection it was replied that as the action of central heat on beds of marine shells took place under the ocean, the pressure of the water would prevent the escape of the fixed air and would probably render the calcareous earth more fusible. Sir James Hall at last determined to try the experiment and make a little quarry of marble himself.

Having calculated the resistance which a column of water of 1500 feet would present to the escape of fixed air, he inclosed a quantity of powdered chalk in a gun barrel and confined it in such a manner as to present an equal degree of resistance. He subjected the powdered chalk thus confined for some time to the action of a furnace; it was then drawn out and cooled and was found converted into crystalline limestone or marble: and in one instance where the chalk inclosed a shell, the shell had acquired a crystalline texture without losing its form.

All that extensive class of stones called trap rocks are fusible and most of them such as porphyry basalt form when melted a black glass. It was therefore supposed that they could never have been melted before or they would be found as glass at the surface. But Sir James Hall, reflecting that immense masses of melted rock under the pressure of the sea would cool so slowly as to assume a different appearance, made similar experiments on lava and basalt. He ascertained that if a small portion of liquid lava were suddenly cooled it formed a black glass, (as was well known to be the case with basalt), but, if the process of cooling were slow, both melted lava and basalt became stone. When the glass which had been formed by sudden cooling was melted again and suffered to cool very gradually it lost its vitreous character and was converted into a substance resembling basalt. One more experiment is still more striking. Every body knows of the famous basaltic columns that make the Giant's Causeway in the county of Antrim in Ireland and Fingal's Cave in Staffa which are composed of immense clusters of natural columns made of separate stones each fitting into the other like a ball and socket.[4] A son of the celebrated

[4] "The west banks of the Hudson for many miles above New York present this

SCIENCE

Mr. Watt made some experiments on the fusion and cooling of basalt in one of his father's furnaces. He fused seven hundred weight of the Dudley basalt called Rowley ragg and kept it in the furnace several days after the fire was reduced. It melted into a dark-coloured glass with less heat than was necessary to melt the same quantity of pig iron. In this glass small globules were formed which afterwards disappeared; and as the cooling proceeded, the mass was changed from a vitreous to a stony substance: other globes were again formed within the stony mass which continued to enlarge until their sides touched and pressed against each other, by which pressure the globes formed polygonal prisms. If part of the mass were cooled before the globular structure was destroyed these globes were harder than the surrounding stone and broke in concentric layers. What took place in the process easily showed when these globes were enlarged by a continuation of the same process they might press on each other and form prisms. The upper prisms pressing by their weight upon the lower might form concavities or sockets into which they would sink and remain jointed together or articulated.[5]

These experiments appear to disclose the mode in which nature operates in regions forever hid from human sight and to show the precise office performed by the pressure of great masses of water in the continual reproduction of continents.

Another very important use of water is its effect in keeping the equilibrium of temperature at the surface of the earth by its change of form. It was formerly thought that when a lump of ice was found at the temperature of 32°, that is, at the degree of freezing, it only needed a small addition of heat to melt it, and bring it to 33°. It is now well known that it needs a very great addition of heat, according to Black[6] 140°, to melt the ice to water over what it would have required to raise the ice, if it con-

rock in very well-pronounced columns which rise with more or less interruption to the height of 150 feet. Am. Encyc." [E]. Article "Trap-Rocks," *Encyclopaedia Americana*, XII, 323.

[5] See Playfair, para. 75; *Transactions of the Royal Society of Edinburgh*, V (1805) 43ff. and VI (1812) 71ff.; and *Philosophical Transactions of the Royal Society of London*, 1804, pp. 279ff.

[6] Joseph Black (1728–1799), Scottish chemist.

tinued ice, to 33°. In like manner it was formerly thought that when water was heated to 212°, that is, to the point where it is ready to become vapor, it needed only a small addition of heat to turn it to steam. It is now well known that in steam there are 940° of heat not indicated by the thermometer. On the other hand when steam is cooled and becomes water it gives out these 940°. And when water becomes ice it gives out 140° to become water [*sic*] at 32°.

This law that whenever solids are converted into fluids or fluids into gases there is always a great amount of heat absorbed and on the other hand whenever gases are converted into fluids or fluids into solids there is a great amount of heat set free — this law is of the utmost importance in the economy of nature. It was by observing the slowness with which ice and snow melted, that Dr. Black was led to this discovery of concealed or latent heat. If large quantities of heat were not necessary to enable ice and snow to melt, the moment the temperature rose in northern regions to 33°, a sudden and irresistible inundation would burst over the land with such fury as to sweep away men, animals, cities, and the very soil. Moreover the annual formation and destruction of ice within the Arctic Circle is a beautiful provision of Nature for mitigating the excessive inequality of temperature. Had only dry land been there opposed to the sun, it would have been absolutely scorched by his incessant beams in summer and pinched in the darkness of winter by the most intense and penetrating cold. None of the animal or vegetable tribes could have at all supported such extremes. But in the actual arrangement, the surplus heat of summer is spent in melting away the ice and its deficiency in winter is partly supplied by the heat given out by vapor forming into snow, and water into ice. (It always becomes warmer when it snows.) As long as ice remains to thaw, or water to freeze, the temperature of the atmosphere can never vary beyond certain limits. There and everywhere the formation of rain, hail, and snow tends to mitigate the severity of winter.

The next great office of water in the order of nature is its support of vegetable life. Without water all plants speedily wither and die. Its action upon this part of the creation is twofold. It is itself an important part of their food and it is the vehicle of all the rest.

A vegetable is unfurnished either with a mouth to masticate or a stomach to digest solid food; it can therefore only receive it when dissolved in water. The sap in roots is found to consist simply of water holding in solution a variety of crude ingredients such as lime, silex, magnesia, soda, and potash, and it is all sucked up by the spongioles or mouths of the roots by capillary attraction, just as water is absorbed by a lump of sugar dipped into it.

The water itself acts.

It gives the soft parts that degree of suppleness and succulency necessary for the performance of their functions; it exists in the form of water; and it conveys air into the plant.

There are some beautiful examples of the simplicity and perfection of natural contrivances in the manner in which plants are supplied with water. First the rain falls from the atmosphere in the form of small drops and therefore is thoroughly impregnated with air by the friction of its long fall and is warmed to the temperature of the atmosphere.

Its first good effect is to refresh the plant by washing off the dust, cleansing the evaporating pores clogged during a drought. But the simple rain cannot feed the plant. It must first go creeping about the earth in search of food and dissolving what it finds convey it to the mouths of the roots. It falls where it is wanted. It must be remembered that it is not at the bottom of the stem that the water is needed, but at some distance from the stem at the ends of the roots. And so the head of the tree by its green dome protects the stem from the rain like an umbrella. All around, the soil is exposed to the rain and the water penetrates the earth just where the extremities of the roots are situated to receive it. In addition to this, the greater part of the rain which has washed and refreshed the leaves trickles down from the ends of the branches and reaches the ground in the appropriate spot.

I shall have occasion presently to refer to another office water performs in the vegetable world in the form of dew.

The functions of this element are not less essential to animal life but its relations are there so complex, that I am forbidden to pursue the inquiry.

There is yet one other general use which the ocean and its rivers subserve in the world. It is itself one of the kingdoms of nature, maintaining its own vast proportion of vegetable and animal life. Vast tracts of the Atlantic Ocean are covered with meadows of floating seaweed which grows on submarine rocks from the equator to forty degrees of latitude on either side. The plants give food to minute marine insects and the insect tribes of the sea are inconceivable in their number and serve most important uses in the mechanism of the globe.

Even in the cold circles of the Pole amid eternal icebergs exists a swarming profusion of animal life such as is hardly found under the tropical sun. Here exists that incalculable swarm of animalcules called medusa or sea blubber which tinge the sea to their own olive green colour and exist to be the food of the crab and the shrimp and the herring who are the food of the whale. Here swims and blows the enormous whale with a respiration like the report of cannon. And hence issue out from beneath the solid vault of ice, the shoals of herring in close and countless columns which fill all the southern seas and supply food to nations.

In the dark recesses of this element a thousand species exist according to peculiar laws with systems adapted in every respect to the silent desarts through which they glide.

These creatures judged by our senses and powers in the upper air seem to be the creatures of privation. There is something almost pathetic in Cuvier's account of their adaptation to their element that I cannot deny myself the pleasure of reading the passage.

"Living in a liquid which is heavier and offers more resistance than air, their forces for motion have been disposed for progression and elevation. Hence arises that form of body which offers the least resistance, (the chief seat of muscular force being in the tail,) the shortness of their members, the smooth or scaly teguments, and the total absence of hairs or feathers. Breathing only through the medium of water, extorting, that is, the small quantity

61

of oxygen contained in the air which is mingled with water, their blood is necessarily cold and their vital energy less than in Mammalia and Birds. Their brain is much smaller and the external organs of their senses are not of a nature to admit powerful impressions. Fishes, in fact, are of all vertebrated animals, those which have the least apparent signs of sensibility. Having no elastic air at their disposal they have remained mute (or nearly so) and all those sentiments awakened or sustained by the voice have remained unknown to them. Their eyes almost immoveable, their bony and rigid countenance, their members deprived of inflexion, and every part moving at the same time, do not leave them any power of varying their physiognomy, or expressing their emotions. Their ear enclosed on every side by the bones of the skull, without external conch or internal labyrinth, and composed only of a few bags and membranous canals, scarcely allows them to distinguish the most striking sounds; and, in fact, an exquisite sense of hearing would be of very little use to those destined to live in the empire of silence, and around whom all are mute. Their sight in the depths of their abode would be little exercised, if the great number of the species had not by the size of their eyes been enabled to supply the deficiency of light, but even in these it cannot change its direction or accommodate itself to the distance of objects. Its iris neither dilates nor contracts and its pupil remains the same in every degree of light. No tear bathes this eye; no eyelid soothes or protects it; and in fishes it is but a feeble representation of that beautiful brilliant and animated organ of the higher classes of animals. Procuring food by swimming after a prey which also swims, having no means of seizing this prey but by swallowing it, a delicate sense of taste would have been useless. And their tongue, almost immoveable, often bony, and only receiving a few slender nerves, shows us how little sensible this organ is.

"Smell, even, cannot be as freely exercised by fishes as by animals which breathe air directly and whose nostrils are unceasingly traversed by odoriferous vapors. Lastly we come to the touch, which, from the surface of their body being covered by scales, and by the inflexibility of their members has been obliged to seek refuge at the end of their lips; and even these, in some species, are reduced to a dry and insensible hardness." [7]

Truly the ocean children seem to be in a destitute condition; but as men say one half the world does not know how the other half lives, much more is it true that one species have no organs for detecting the powers and satisfactions which exist in other species and are denied to itself.

Having run over these various general uses of the great mass of waters in the globe we cannot help returning with new interest to the beautiful phenomenon of its eternal circulation through nature. This makes the science of Meteorology. The action of the sun upon the surface of the sea is continually converting the water to invisible vapor. This vapor rising into the higher and of course colder parts of the atmosphere is condensed into clouds which attract each other and are attracted to the mountains which rise into the same region. Here they fall in mist or minute rain. These drops trickle down from every highland and are rapidly gathered into rivulets which run into rivers which, gathering into their beds all the rivulets through a valley of two or three thousand miles, pour out the whole into the ocean again, to be again evaporated and again returned. The circulation of the water in the globe is no less beautiful a law than the circulation of blood in the body.

The amount of the evaporation is very great. It is computed that from the surface of the globe 60,000 cubic miles of water are annually changed into vapor. Of course these suspended waters are present in the air when it is most dry and transparent and we have not only a visible ocean at our feet but we are thus always bathed in an invisible ocean overhead, and around us.

From hence comes the fine phenomenon of the deposit of dew. It is a consequence of the laws of heat. Hot [bodies] always emit their heat in right lines in all directions into space, some bodies faster, some slower according to the texture of their surface. All day the plants radiate heat which they receive from the sun and [which] would scorch them if accumulated; when the sun goes

[7] Lee, *Memoirs of Cuvier*, pp. 123–26.

down the plants continue [to] throw off this heat on all sides; but, as there is then no source from whence heat can be returned to them, they rapidly become colder than the superincumbent air. The adjacent air being thus cooled is no longer able to hold the vapour which while warm had floated invisible, and now deposits it in minute drops upon the cold surfaces of the plants. They are thus abundantly watered and most abundantly when they need it most, at midsummer, because then the air holds most water in solution. And they get all this wetting whilst stones and houses all around them are quite dry, and no vapor falls upon the sea from the simple circumstance that the plants are all good radiators of heat but stones, metals, air, and the surface of water are not.[8]

Another deposit of the invisible water is snow, a natural fleece which forms for the defence of the side of the earth exposed to cold in winter just as the wool thickens on the coat of animals at the same season in the same regions. The manner of its formation has been explained by observing the crystallization of ammoniac.

When the air is full of moisture and at a certain degree of cold a minute crystal forms and sinks as soon as it is formed. It descends slowly because its specific gravity is not much greater than that of the air which contains it. The first crystals produced at a great height in the atmosphere, determine, as they descend, the crystallization of other aqueous particles which without the disturbance of the air caused by their fall the surrounding air would have still retained in a state of solution, just [as] crystallization of sugar is aided by putting a thread or a stick [sic]. The result is the formation of stars of six rays when the air is calm and still and not so warm as to deform the crystals by melting off their angles, but when the wind blows and the snow falls from a great height the crystals clash together, unite in groups, and form irregular flakes.

Whilst the angles of the primitive crystal are invariable there is yet the greatest variety and beauty in the forms in which secondary crystals radiate from these. Mr. Scoresby in his Arctic Regions has delineated ninety varieties.[9]

The use of the snow is to protect the roots of plants which

[8] This passage owes a slight debt to Wells, pp. 10–11, 75–76.
[9] Scoresby, I, 426–432. Plates VIII–XI, Vol. II, illustrate ninety-six varieties.

it effectually does from the cold — Alpine plants die in winter in England for want of this protection — and to be the source by its gradual melting of fertilizing streams.

I cannot leave this part of my subject, the account namely of the different forms assumed by water, without taking notice of that most remarkable fact of its expansion by cold, — even at the risk of repeating a familiar fact.

It is well known that all bodies expand when they are hot and contract when they are cold. This is a general law of solids as iron, stone, and wood, but also of liquids. Mercury, oil, alcohol, brine, ether, sulphuric acid, and liquids in general expand in proportion to their heat. To this law water forms a remarkable exception. This expands a little when heated and contracts when it is cooled, but when you cool it to a certain point, say 40°, it then expands as if heat were applied, and enlarges to 32° the freezing point, when spicula of ice begin to shoot across its surface. This expansion is effected with prodigious force and we are all familiar with its effects. It not only breaks pitchers of glass or stone, if their shape do not allow of its expansion, but it rives granite blocks and splits trunks of trees and lifts up pavements of stone. A strong brass globe whose cavity was only one inch diameter was filled with water by the Florentine Academicians and frozen. The globe was burst although the force required was calculated to exceed 27,720 lbs.

The explanation of this fact is supposed to be that the particles when they crystallize and assume the solid state have a tendency to unite by certain sides in preference to others, arranging themselves so as to form right lines at determinate angles. This arrangement of the particles requiring more space and leaving numerous vacuities, the bulk of the whole must necessarily be enlarged.

But what has attracted in men of science so much attention to this property of water is the very important effects which result from it. If water followed the law of other liquids and contracted as it cooled until it arrived at the freezing point, ice would be heavier than water, and as fast as it formed, would subside to the bottom in successive flakes until the whole water however deep should become solid. The effects of such an arrangement can easily be conceived. A lake, a deep river, an arm of the sea, once frozen could never be thawed; — for what could a superficial heat effect upon such a base? Climates now the pleasant abodes of man and animals would be uninhabitable domains of frost. But in consequence of the irregularity in question, since water expands in freezing, ice is lighter than water, and floats upon its surface, and thus forms a thick coat to protect the water below from the influence of frost, so that a deep sea is never congealed.

Having thus spoken of the uses and appearances of this simple substance in the manifold architecture of nature I proceed to enumerate one or two of its virtues which man has learned to turn to good account in the arts. It is used as a mechanical power.[10]

From the law of the equal pressure of fluids two consequences follow; one is, that water though when unconfined it never can rise above its level at any point and never can move upwards, will yet by being confined in pipes or close channels of any kind rise to the height from which it came, i.e. as high as its source. And upon this principle depend all the useful contrivances for conveying water by pipes in a way far more easy, cheap, and effectual than those vast buildings called aqueducts by which the ancients carried their supplies of water in artificial rivers over arches for many miles.

The other conclusion is, that, the pressure of water upon any object against which it comes, any vessel which contains it, or any space upon which it rests, is not at all in proportion to the body or bulk of the water, but only to the size of the surface on, or against which it presses, and its own height above that surface.

In this way any quantity of water however small (a little scooped in the hollow of the hand, a drop of dew) may be so employed as to balance any quantity however great (as a reservoir, or the ocean).

Every thing depending upon the height and the surface and very little upon the bulk of the fluid, the greatest power may be exerted by a very small quantity of water if it is distributed so as

[10] Although the following section shows a slight debt to Lardner, which we know Emerson consulted, some of its facts come from elsewhere.

to stand high in however thin a column and to spread over a wide but confined and shallow space. Thus a very strong water cask being filled with water, screw tightly into its top a long small tube so narrow as not to hold more than an ounce of water. Pour water into this tube and the cask bursts with violence for it produces the pressure of a column of water of its own height upon every part of the cask.

This principle has been ingeniously applied in Mr. Bramah's Hydrostatic Press [11] by which a prodigious force is obtained with the greatest ease and within a very small compass; so that a man shall with a machine the size of a common teapot standing before him on the table cut through a thick bar of iron as easily as through a sheet of paper. A pressure of 41,472 tons might be produced by the agency of less than a pound of water, but we have no materials that can resist such pressure.

Another very pleasing application of Water as a mechanical power is by means of capillary attraction. Sir John Herschel relates that in some parts of France where millstones are made a mass of stone is first cut into a cylinder and it is then ready to be sliced into millstones. This is effected by chiselling little grooves quite round the cylinder at distances corresponding to the thickness intended to be given to the millstones, and into these grooves, wedges of dried wood are driven. These are then wetted or exposed to the night dew and next morning the different blocks of stone are found separated from each other by the irresistible expansion of the wood on its absorption of the water.[12]

But far the most powerful application of water to the mechanical arts remains to be noticed.

A drop of water in boiling expands into steam and occupies 1689 times the space it filled before. If it is made hotter, it expands more, and at 419° it exerts a force equivalent to nearly 15,000 lbs. upon every square inch of the vessel in which it is confined, a

---

[11] Joseph Bramah (1748–1814), English inventor of the hydraulic press. The manuscript reads 41.472 tons but that figure seems implausible. Why Emerson named this precise amount has not been discovered.

[12] Herschel, p. 48.

pressure so enormous that few vessels can be made strong enough to withstand it.

This property and the fact that it is capable of being immediately reduced in bulk by being cooled, make it fit for arming man with that prodigious strength which he now applies to every part of nature. There is no limit to its force except the limit of the cohesion of those natural bodies by means of which he prepares and concentrates its strength. It is convertible to the aid of every action of man precisely in the degree of his knowledge.

This great mainspring of natural power is too familiar to all to permit any repetition of its wonders. Every day is multiplying its applications to art and what was yesterday a ridiculous project is executed today. Its might and flexibleness seem to annihilate the obstinate properties of matter, to make the hard soft and the distant near.

Such virtue lies in a little water.

Such is an imperfect catalogue of the great general uses of Water in the economy of Nature. Superficial as this enumeration has been it is yet sufficient to show how mighty a benefactor is this most flexible and active of created things. It more than justifies the beautiful language of our own poet,

> See living vales by living waters blessed
> See ocean roll in glory dressed
> For all a treasure and round all a shield.[13]

It may serve to enlarge our perception of the boundless resources of the Creator, when we learn that in a bucket of water resides a latent force sufficient to counterbalance mountains, or to rend the planet, and when we trace the manifold offices which one atom of hydrogen and one of oxygen united in a particle of water may perform in the pulse, in the brain, in the eye, in a plant, in mist, in crystal, in a volcano, and it may exalt our highest sentiments to see the same particle in every step of this ceaseless revolution serving the life, the order, the happiness of the Universe.

[13] Charles Sprague, "Ode, Pronounced at the Centennial Celebration of the Settlement of Boston, September, 1830," Stanza XXIV.

4

The Naturalist

Unlike any other lecture in this volume, this one survives as a sheaf of half-sheets folded in half, as was often Emerson's practice when making notes. Though at some time most of them were sewn together, they are now loose and disarranged, appearing even to belong to different drafts. Consequently the lecture as printed here is a conjectural arrangement of fragments. A space in the text indicates a break in continuity. There is no evidence that Emerson's literary executors ever had any other text than this.

The lecture was prepared and read as an "Address to the Boston Natural History Society on their fourth Annual Meeting, 7 May, 1834," probably a more formal occasion than that of his first appearance before that Society. The usual title is found in the manuscripts only in a note jotted at the bottom of one of the sheets: " 'Naturalist' Read before the Nat. Hist. Soc. Boston." The first sheet is headed as above. We have accepted the more natural form of the title used by Cabot, sharing his apparent assumption that the manuscript form is an abbreviation. Since a passage entered in the Journals for May 16 (*J*, III, 298) appears in the section on Composition (pp. 73–74), Emerson may have revised and used the lecture elsewhere also; a lecture on Natural History was read at Concord on January 1, 1835.

The journals for a month before this address contain many reading notes and philosophical reflections on the topic in contrast to the simple facts and meanings of the previous lectures. He was checking his own observation of birds, shells, flowers, and other natural objects against their Latin names and classifications in Gray and other technical sources at the same time that he continued to read in such favorite philosophers of science as Coleridge and Goethe. "Well, my friend," he chides himself on May 6, "are you not yet convinced that you should study plants and animals?" (*J*, III, 296). Several passages in this lecture anticipate reflections in *Nature* and in "The American Scholar." Cabot prints four long paragraphs, with his usual silent cuts and elisions, from this lecture (I, 224–27).

The envelope also contains five full-sized leaves of rough notes headed "Naturalist." None of them is used in the address, except possibly the first, which quotes Sir Everard Home, *Philosophical Transactions of the Royal Society of London* for 1816. Others contain further botanical and chemical references.

Gentlemen,

The Curators have honored me with the task of preparing an Address to the Society agreeably to the custom of its annual meetings. I shall use the occasion to consider a question which though it have not equal interest for all has great interest for many of us: What is the place of Natural History in Education? It is but a small portion of this society who have time to devote themselves exclusively to Natural History. Perhaps it is better we should not.

But the question occurs to a man mainly engaged in far different pursuits whether it is wise to embark at all in a pursuit in which it is plain he must content himself with quite superficial knowledge; whether it is no waste of time to study a new and tedious classification. I shall treat this question not for the Natural Philosopher but for the Man, and offer you some thoughts upon the intellectual influences of Natural Science.

I shall say what in my opinion is to excuse such persons as myself who without any hope of becoming masters of any department of natural science so as to attain the rank of original observers, do yet find a gratification in coming here to school, and in reading the general results of Naturalists and learning so much of the classifications of the sciences as shall enable us to understand their discoveries.

That the study of Nature should occupy some place, that it will occupy some place in education, in spite of the worst perversion or total neglect, is certain. I knew a person who sailed from Boston to Charleston, S. C.[1] and never saw the water. But nature takes care generally that we shall see the water and the snow, the forest, the swamp, the mountain, the eclipse, the comet, the northern lights, and all her commanding phenomena.

The streets of towns cannot so completely hide the face of

[1] Emerson went by boat from Boston to Charleston, November 25, 1826, in quest of health.

heaven and the face of the earth but that every generous and penetrating genius is generally found to have an interest in the works of Creation. The imagery in discourse which delights all men is that which is drawn from observation of natural processes. It is this which gives that piquancy to the conversation of a strong-minded farmer or backwoodsman which all men relish.[2]

But it is said that Man is the only object of interest to Man. I fully believe it. I believe that the constitution of man is the centre from which all our speculations depart. But it is the wonderful charm of external nature that man stands in a central connexion with it all; not at the head, but in the midst: and not an individual in the kingdom of organized life but sends out a ray of relation to him.[3] So that all beings seem to serve such an use as that which is sought in comparative anatomy. We study our own structure magnified or simplified in each one.

In a generous education certainly the Earth, which is the bountiful mother and nurse, the abode, the stimulus, the medicine, and the tomb of us all, will not, nor will our fellow-creatures in it, fail of our attention. These objects are the most ancient and permanent whereof we have any knowledge. If our restless curiosity lead us to unearth the buried cities and dig up the mummy pits and spell out the abraded characters on Egyptian stones, shall we see a less venerable antiquity in the clouds and the grass? An everlasting Now reigns in Nature that produces on our bushes the selfsame Rose which charmed the Roman and the Chaldaean. The grain and the vine, the ant and the moth are as long-descended. The slender violet hath preserved in the face of the sun and moon the humility of his line and the oldest work of man is an upstart by the side of the shells of the sea.

But the antiquity of these objects is merely a claim upon the feelings. They have another claim upon the Understanding, which especially concerns us in this view of intellectual influences — they are perfect creatures. It is the result of all philosophy if it is

---

[2] "It is this . . . all men relish" (*Nature*, W, I, 29).
[3] Cf. *Nature*, W, I, 27.

not born with us — an assured optimism. When Lagrange and Laplace found out the periodicity of the errors of the heavenly bodies and thence the stability of the Solar System was the result unexpected by any mind? Whatever theology or philosophy we rest in, or labor after, the students of Nature have all agreed that in Nature nothing is false or unsuccessful. That which is aimed at is attained, and by means elegant and irresistible. The whole force of the Creation is concentrated upon every point. What agencies of electricity, gravity, light, affinity, combine to make every plant what it is, and in a manner so quiet that the presence of these tremendous powers is not ordinarily suspected. Woven in their loom every plant, every animal is finished and perfect as the world. A willow or an apple is a perfect being; so is a bee or a thrush. The best poem or statue or picture is not. This is the view which so much impressed the celebrated Goethe, whose life was a study of the Theory of Art, that he said "no man should be admitted into his Republic, who was not versed in Natural History."

There is deep reason for the love of nature that has characterized the highest minds. The soul and the body of things are harmonized; therefore the deeper is a man's insight into the spiritual laws the more intense will be his love of the works of nature.

"The smallest production of nature," says Goethe, "has the circle of its completeness within itself and I have only need of eyes to see with, in order to discover the relative proportions. I am perfectly sure that within this circle however narrow, an entirely genuine existence is enclosed. A work of art, on the other hand, has its completeness out of itself. The Best lies in the idea of the artist which he seldom or never reaches: all the rest lies in certain conventional rules which are indeed derived from the nature of art and of mechanical processes but still are not so easy to decipher as the laws of living nature. In works of art there is much that is traditional; the works of nature are ever a freshly uttered Word of God." [4] Perhaps it is the province of poetry rather than of prose to describe the effect upon the mind and heart of these nameless

[4] Austin, *Goethe*, II, 263–64.

influences. Certainly he that has formed his ideas of adaptation of beauty on these models can have nothing mean in his estimate and hence Fourier said of Laplace in his eulogy before the French Academy, "What Laplace called great, was great." [5]

It is fit that man should look upon Nature with the eye of the Artist, to learn from the great Artist whose blood beats in our veins, whose taste is upspringing in our own perception of beauty, the laws by which our hands should work that we may build St. Peter'ses or paint Transfigurations or sing Iliads in worthy continuation of the architecture of the Andes, [of] the colors of the sky and the poem of life. [6]

And as we have said in the first place these individual forms are perfect, let us speak now of the secret of their composition.

Nothing strikes me more in Nature than the effect of Composition, the contrast between the simplicity of the means and the gorgeousness of the result. Nature is particularly skilled in that rule of arithmetic called Permutation and Combination. Sometimes it is so amusing as to remind us of the French cook who could make forty dishes out of macaroni. A few elements has Nature converted into the countless variety of substances that fill the earth. Look at the grandeur of the prospect from a mountain top. It is composed of not many materials continually repeated in new unions.

Composition is more important than the elegance of individual forms. Every artist knows that beyond its own beauty the object has an additional grace from relation to surrounding objects. The most elegant shell in your cabinet does not produce such effect on the eye as the contrast and combination of a group of ordinary sea shells lying together wet upon the beach. I remember when I was a boy going upon the shore and being charmed with the colors and forms of the shells. I gathered up many and put them in my pocket. When I got home I could find nothing that I gathered, nothing but some dry, ugly mussels and snails. Thence I learned that Composition was more important than the beauty

[5] *Éloge. Mémoires de l'institut,* X, lxxxi (1831).
[6] *Cf.* "Art," W, II, 363.

of individual forms to effect. On the shore they lay wet and social by the sea and under the sky.[7] The smell of a field surpasses the scent of any flower and the selection of the prism is not comparable to the confusion of a sunset. A hillside expresses what has never been written down.

We are provoked by seeing how simple are the principles of her architecture. The tree is not, the botanist finds, a single structure but a vast assemblage of individuals. The difference between animal and vegetable textures is very slight at their commencement. Cellular tissue and animal fibre being similar and the vesicle and spiculum — hydrogen and oxygen deriving their original combination perhaps from their polarity — all grows up from plus and minus. How beautiful a shell is the Buccinum Harpa![8] but when we see that every one of these polished ridges that adorn its surface like harpstrings was in turn the outer lip the wonder is less. So many of the forms in conchology were originally determined perhaps by a mere projection. Give water in a cup a revolving motion, and it immediately assumes precisely the form most common in shells, that of the operculum[9] of the buccinums — or helix.

"I am persuaded," said Fontenelle, "that if the majority of mankind could be made to see the order of the Universe such as it is, as they would not remark in it any virtues attached to certain numbers, nor any properties inherent in certain planets, nor fatalities in certain times and revolutions of these, they would not be able to restrain themselves on the sight of this admirable regularity and beauty from crying out with astonishment, 'What! Is this all?' "[10]

There are specific advantages of such studies that deserve to be enumerated under the head of intellectual influences.

They restrain Imitation — Imitation, the vice of overcivilized communities. To take an example. Imitation is the vice eminently

[7] "I remember when I was a boy . . . under the sky" (*J*, III, 298). *Cf.* "English Literature," Lecture 6, p. 317.
[8] Cf. *J*, III, 287.
[9] The horny lid or cover of a shell.
[10] Quoted in Brown, I, 92.

of our times, of our literature, of our manners and social action. All American manners, language, and writing are derivative. We do not write from facts, but we wish to state facts after the English manner. It is at once our strength and weakness that there is an immense floating diction from which always we draw, to which by the ear we always seek to accommodate our expression.

It is the tax we pay for the splendid inheritance of the English literature. We are exonerated by the sea and the revolution from the national debt but we pay this which is rather the worst part. Time will certainly cure us, probably through the prevalence of a bad party ignorant of all literature and of all but selfish, gross pursuits. But a better cure would be in the study of Natural History. Imitation is a servile copying of what is capricious as if it were permanent forms of Nature. The study of things leads us back to Truth, to the great Network of organized beings made of our own flesh and blood with kindred functions and related organs and one Cause.

Another part of the intellectual discipline of Natural Science is that it sharpens the discrimination. It teaches the difficult art of distinguishing between the similar and the same. The whole study of Nature is perpetual division and subdivision and again new distinctions. And all these distinctions are real. There is no false logic in Nature. All its properties are permanent: the acids and metals never lie; their yea is yea; their nay, nay. They are newly discovered but not new. The Light yields to Dr. Brewster [11] its unequivocal answer when he puts the dilemma but it has published the same fact to the Universe every moment since the beginning undiscerned.

Natural objects are so sharply discriminated; an oak is so unlike an orange, wax and iron so different, and any mistake in practice is so promptly exposed that it is to be desired, that so many dull understandings who make no distinctions should be set to making chemical mixtures or classifying plants. What pity, instead of that equal and identical praise which enters into all biographies and spreads poppies over all, that writers of characters

---

[11] Sir David Brewster (1781–1868), Scottish physicist, inventor of the kaleidoscope (1816).

cannot be forced to describe men so that they shall be known apart even if it were copied from the sharp marks of Botany, such as *dry, solitary, sour, plausible, prosing,* which were worth a graveyard of obituaries.

These are specific advantages to be sought in Education from Science.

But as we have to do now with its true place and influences there are some important distinctions to be made. We are not only to have the aids of Science but we are to recur to Nature to guard us from the evils of Science.

We are the cossets of civilization, a refinement which consists very much in multiplying comforts and luxuries, which gives us pins and caoutchouc [12] and watches and almanacks and has the bad effect that crutches have of destroying the use of the limbs they are meant to aid.[13] The clock and compass do us harm by hindering us from astronomy. We have made civil months until the natural signs, the solstices and the equinoxes, most men do not know. Find me a savage who does not know them. Even the farmer is losing the power to tell the hour by the sun, or of finding the compass-points by the same means, or by the pole star; and even the botanist in his skill in names is ignorant of the properties of plants. We need study to repair just that loss. In cities we are in danger of forgetting our relation to the planet and the system. There are people in Venice it is said who never leave the quarter of the city where they are born. That is one of the uses the stars render us, looking down from their far and solemn heights into every narrow and deep lane, forcibly admonishing the eye that by chance catches their beam of higher relations than he ordinarily remembers.

I cannot but think that a ramble in the country with the set purpose of observation to most persons whose duties confine them much to the city will be a useful lesson. By such excursions the student will see a day perhaps in a light in which he never

[12] Rubber.
[13] *Cf.* "Self-Reliance," W, II, 85.

regarded it. We are so enslaved by art that we always know it is about half-past four or twenty minutes of five. But go out into the woods, break your hours, carry your biscuit in your pocket, and you shall see a day as an astronomical phenomenon. You shall forget your near and petty relations to Boston and Cambridge and see nothing but the noble earth on which you was born and the great star which enlightens and warms it. The contented clouds shall be to you an image of peace. The pines glittering with their innumerable green needles in the light every breath of air will make audible. "It is Day. It is Day." [14] That is all which Heaven saith. Then look about you and see the manifold works of which day is the occasion. At first all is solitary. You think nothing lives there. But wait a little. Hundreds of eyes and ears watched your approach. The rabbit bounded away as you entered the field. The snake glided off at the noise of your approach from the very rock on which you stand, the bee flew from the neighboring shrub, the titmouse has only taken the next pinetree, and listen a moment, and you shall hear the ground robin scratching the leaves at the side of the brook. The population of the fields is denser than that of the towns. More races here than families there.

Nature is the adroitest economist in her housekeeping and 'tis worth an especial visit to the fields to see how many creatures she contrives to tuck away in a single acre of ground without confusion or crowding. The schoolbooks say, to illustrate the porosity of matter: Fill a tub with cannon balls, then the interstices with bullets, then the interstices with shot, and the interstices with powder. But in nature every layer of the air and of the soil hath its population and every individual its parasite. She puts the ox in the field; the bird on the bough; the insect at the flower; the scaraboeus [15] in the rut; the turtle in the pool; woodpecker in rotten tree; the moth on the leaf; the squirrel; the hawk wheeling up to heaven; in the small interstices of the stones she hatches under a silver counterpane a spider's egg and every one of these creatures is ridden by some happy aphides and apply the microscope to the aphis and lo! the eater is eaten. Nor when you become

[14] "You shall forget your near and petty . . . 'It is Day'" (*J*, III, 271).
[15] Beetle.

acquainted with these centres of life will you despise them because their way of life is limited to a rood of ground. They have a life as large as yours. For their fine functions and senses stretch away into that other infinity of minute division which the microscope and the laws of polarization and chemistry have been opening to man, and there is as great an interval between a grain of sand and nothing as there is between the visible universe and the space in which it is swallowed as an atom.

As by aid of art we approach them, dust and mould quicken into races of beings, dots become genera, and, past the limit of unarmed vision, there is an infinite creation in intense activity between us and the negative Pole.

But having stated particular advantages I know that these may be met by statements of particular disadvantages and no study can be truly recommended but by showing in it an absolute Universal fitness that transcends all considerations of place, profession, age, and the like that induce us to prefer one or another liberal pursuit. Natural History seeks more directly that which all sciences, arts, and trades seek mediately — knowledge of the world we live in. Here it touches directly the highest question of philosophy, Why and How any thing is?

No reflecting man but asks these questions and however insolvable they appear would deem it brutish not to ask them of himself. We are possessed with a conviction that Nature means something, that the flower, the animals, the sea, the rock have some relation to us not understood which if known would make them more significant. As men have been fingering the characters that are carved on the Egyptian remains these thousand years, sure that they mean something if we could only find out the cipher, so for a much longer period men have been groping at the hieroglyphics of Nature to find out the cipher, assured that they mean something, assured that we shall understand ourselves better for what we shall read in the sea and the land and the sky. This their open secret is not translateable into words but is to make the face of the earth as much more to me than it is now as is a mountain chain to Humboldt than to his muleteer.

Natural History seeks directly to provide this key or dictionary by observing and recording the properties of every individual and determining its place in the Universe by its properties.

Men of extraordinary powers of a contemplative mind have in all ages pondered this secret: Pythagoras, Swedenborg, Goethe, not to mention the Brahmins. These have sought to give an explanation of Nature; of beasts, plants, minerals.

The Persian said that Oromasdes made good creatures, Ahriman the evil. Pythagoras said that the soul of man endured penance in the low forms of ferocious, gluttonous, obscene beasts. The pig was the purgatory of the glutton. A like faith had the Brahmin. Swedenborg taught that the soul creates evermore the body; that certain affections clothe themselves in certain forms as cunning in the fox, innocence in the lamb, cruelty in the laughing hyena. These opinions have failed to persuade men of their truth and yet are all valuable as the materials of truth, as proofs of an obstinate belief in the human mind that these creatures have a relation to itself.

This instinct is to be the guide, the god of inquiry or it will never come to anything. Natural History is making with knife and scales and alembic the Theory conform to the fact. It is for want of this marriage that both remain unfruitful. The poet loses himself in imaginations and for want of accuracy is a mere fabulist; his instincts unmake themselves and are tedious words. The savant on the other hand losing sight of the end of his inquiries in the perfection of his manipulations becomes an apothecary, a pedant.

I fully believe in both, in the poetry and in the dissection. I believe that we shall by and by know as The Arabian Nights tell us what the social birds say when they sit in the autumn in council chattering upon the tree, the caprices of the catbird, the affectation of the titmouse. I expect to know much of the biography of plants. Natural History is now little but a nomenclature. Nothing is known of the individuals yet who can doubt that in the history of the individuals lies all the charm as that of human history lies not in the races but in Luther, Napoleon and Webster. I should be glad to know what that delicate yellow Cistus does all the midsummer in those dry fields it inhabits. I should be glad to know what use the smilax subserves with its perennial greenness or whole wide fields of Empetrum and of brake.[16] I should be glad to know the biographies of the extraordinary individuals. It would be even pleasanter than it is now — to see a pumpkin in Hadley meadows or to shell corn in November in the cornbarn.

See that centipede: *c'est bien chaussée*.[17] Goethe said that Nature had cheated the snake of a body like the promise of his eyes and head and had sheathed him in a sack.[18] Among the insects few seem to be at home in their bodies, entire and content like a bird, but rather as efforts, foreshadowings. Here and there comes a very decided form like that odd Brentus Anchorago [19] which suggest[s] something very different from man, but in general man is the type by which we measure the insect.

I do not, whilst I lay stress on this point, undervalue the ordinary aids of science. The necessity of nomenclature, of minute physiological research, of the retort, the scalpel, and the scales, is incontestable. But there is no danger of its being underestimated. We only wish to insist upon their being considered as *Means*. We only wish to give equal and habitual prominence to the Love and Faith from which these should flow. This passion, the enthusiasm for nature, the love of the Whole, has burned in the breasts of the Fathers of Science. It was the ever present aim of Newton, of Linnaeus, of Davy, of Cuvier, to ascend from nomenclature to classification; from arbitrary to natural classes; from natural classes, to primary laws; from these, in an ever narrowing circle, to approach the elemental law, the *causa causans*, the supernatural force.

And the necessity of guarding this original taste, of keeping the mind of the student in a healthful state belongs especially to the consideration of the intellectual influences of science. When a reasoning man looks upon the Creation around him, he feels that

[16] Evergreen rockrose, greenbrier, crowberry, bramble.
[17] It is well shod.
[18] *Cf.* Austin, *Goethe*, I, 49.
[19] Elongated, long-snouted tropical beetle.

it is most fit as a part of the study of himself that he should inquire into the nature of these related beings. He sees that the same laws that govern their structure govern his own; that his very superiority is yet in strict harmony with their natures. He wishes to comprehend their nature, to have such knowledge as shall place him as it were at the heart of the Creation that he may see its tribes and races unfolding themselves in order (as the orbs of our system are seen from the sun) that he may have a Theory of animated nature, understand its Law, so that his eye may predict the functions and habits of the individual before yet they show themselves.

Now this is to be attained only by those who resolutely keep their reason in its seat, who guard themselves against their own habits, who persist in seeking the Idea in the particulars, the Type in the manifold forms. It seems the duty of the Naturalist to study in faith and in love, never to lose sight of the simplest questions, "Why?" and "Whence?" and "What of that?", to be a poet in his severest analysis; rather, I should say, to make the Naturalist subordinate to the Man. He only can derive all the advantage from intimate knowledge who forces the magnified objects back into their true perspective, who after he has searched the proximate atoms integrates them again as in nature they are integrated and keeps his mind open to their beauty and to the moral impressions which it is their highest office to convey. To him they suggest a feeling as grand as the knowledge is accurate.

To this end of furnishing us with hints, intimations of the inward Law of Nature, a cabinet is useful. It would seem as if there were better means of expressing these thoughts than words. 'Tis said that the idea which always haunted John Hunter, that Life was independent of organization, protecting and continually recreating the parts and wonderfully varying its means of action, he never succeeded in expressing but in his Museum.[20] So no intelligent person can come into a well arranged cabinet of natural productions without being excited to unusual reveries, without

[20] Cf. Coleridge, The Friend, III, 179–80, 213–15. John Hunter (1728–1793), Scottish physician, kept a collection of fish, bird, and animal specimens at his home in Brompton which was preserved after his death and which Emerson visited in 1833.

being conscious by instinctive perception of relations which he can only feel without being able to comprehend or define.

The later discoveries of naturalists seem to point more and more steadily at Method, at a Theory. The more superficial their observations the more unconnected and remote do the objects seem: the sticking of iron to the loadstone seems to have no connexion with the rainbow or the lightning or chemical changes but when the observation is more searching and profound the most remote objects are made to approach and seen to be various effects of one law: the spherules and spicula which the physiologist finds at the foundation both of vegetable and animal organization, these oxygenous, those hydrogenous; the little flower which makes lime and metals out [of] the elements of elements, and so promises to give us a course of chemical lessons worth knowing, and strip the little Proteus, Hydrogen, of his last coat, and the whole philosophy of their colours, the redundancy of oxygen in the red and yellow leaves in the autumn woods, the equilibrium of hydrogen and oxygen in the green leaf of midsummer; the application of polarized light as a chemical test; the new laws of crystalline architecture which the autophyllite in polarized light has suggested; Dr. Jenner's [21] derivation of the migration of birds and of fishes from a single organic change; Hatchett's analysis of the egg and its analogies in the intestinal secretions: [22] these seem to be most important steps and the most superficial reader cannot learn them without feeling himself in the precincts of that primary area whence the few great powers of Nature depart to produce by endless combinations their various and innumerable works.

I have great confidence, Gentlemen, that the spirit which has led you to such conspicuous efforts in the cause of Natural History, is founded in so true and deep a love of the laws of the Creation, in so simple a desire to explore and publish to others their precious secrets, as promises to our society the benefits without the pedantry of knowledge. The benefit to the community, amid the

---

[21] Edward Jenner (1749–1823), English physician, read a paper before the Royal Society in 1823 "On the Migration of Birds."
[22] *Cf.* Coleridge, *The Friend*, III, 180.

harsh and depraving strife of political parties, of these pure pursuits is inestimable.

We are born in an age which to its immense inheritance of natural knowledge has added great discoveries of its own. We should not be citizens of our own time, not faithful to our trust, if we neglected to avail ourselves of their light. The eternal beauty which led the early Greeks to call the globe κόσμος or Beauty pleads ever with us, shines from the stars, glows in the flower, moves in the animal, crystallizes in the stone. No truth can be more self evident than that the highest state of man, physical, intellectual, and moral, can only coexist with a perfect Theory of Animated Nature.[23]

[23] For other fragmentary passages from this lecture, see textual notes.

II

ITALY

SOMETIME during the "winter of 1834," Cabot tells us, Emerson gave two lectures on Italy, "in which he recounted the incidents of his tour very simply from his journal, for the benefit of his untravelled townsmen" (I, 227–28). In his appendix, these lectures are listed between January 17, 1834, the date of "Water," and May 7, the date of "The Naturalist," which would indicate that he believed them to have been delivered first during the later winter or early spring of 1833–34 (II, 712). The manuscripts, both of which survive complete, supply no dates, nor is there further conclusive evidence as to just when and where these lectures were first given or how often and where they were repeated. In his *Reminiscences of a Journalist* (quoted in Cooke, p. 36), Charles T. Congdon, who was a member of the congregation at New Bedford as a boy, recalls that, "He gave us afterwards two lectures based upon his travels abroad, and was at a great deal of trouble to hang up prints. There was a picture of the tribune in the Uffici Gallery in Florence, painted by one of our townsmen; and I recall Mr. Emerson's great anxiety that it should have a good light, and his lamentation when a good light was found to be impossible. The lectures themselves were so fine — so enchanting we found them — that I have hungered to see them in print, and have thought of the evenings on which they were delivered as 'true Arabian Nights.'" Rusk repeats this story and identifies the "townsman" as the artist William Wall (*Life*, 202). Cabot's phrase, "his untravelled townsmen" would apply as well to New Bedford as anywhere, because during 1833–34 he was constantly in that town while filling the pulpit of his kinsman, the Rev. Orville Dewey. Otherwise, he was variously boarding and visiting, chiefly with his mother or with Charles, in Boston, Newton, and Concord, but he did not settle in Concord until November, 1834. Rusk also suggests that the lectures might first have been read at Concord because of a letter from Dr. Edward Jarvis, dated November 17, 1843, inviting Emerson to appear there again and perhaps repeat the lectures on natural history and on Italy which he had once given, an invitation which Emerson declined because "the lectures you name are too old and musty for 1844" (*L*, III, 224). The record book of the Concord Lyceum lists lectures, without title, by Emerson on May 14 and November 26, 1834, either or both of which might have been on Italy, but probably not a first reading, as both dates would be later than any likely reading in New Bedford. Neither is Cameron's tentative suggestion likely that one of the lectures read in Boston in December, 1833, might have been on Italy (I, 340); and Edward Waldo Emerson gives no evidence for his statement, "Later in the winter [1833–34] he gave two lectures on Italy in Boston" (*J*, III, 246). If he is thinking of Cooke's similar conjecture (Cooke, p. 36), then the assertion has little authority. It is quite likely, therefore, that the lectures were prepared for and delivered first to the New Bedford congregation, probably about March, 1834, and that they were repeated later that year in Concord and possibly elsewhere, including Boston. Letters from him are dated from New Bedford on March 28 of that year, and letters from Charles to William indicate that he was there at least from March 22 to March 31. Earlier that month he had been in Plymouth and by April 12 he was back in Boston (*L*, I, 408). He moved with his mother to Newton in May.

Italy

Cabot is correct in his statement that these lectures are made up almost entirely from incidents recounted in the journal and, as the latter text has since been published (*J*, III, 62–147), and will soon be published more completely, the lectures are not reprinted from the manuscripts here; rather their approximate reconstruction is included in the textual notes to this volume. The only reading Emerson mentions is Byron's *Childe Harold*, which he recommends as a guide book. Cameron has pointed out that he withdrew John Bell, *Observations on Italy*, from the Athenaeum for two days on February 24, 1834 (Cameron, I, 342). The opening passages of the first lecture and the conclusion of the second are here given to provide a context.

1

I T is my present design to offer this audience a brief account of the most interesting objects of Italy as they present themselves to the notice of an American traveller. I wish to be understood as attempting nothing more. A just understanding of the Italian private society I have not. I wish I had. Into an account of their political relations I shall not venture. It may be found in the books and the newspapers. A learned criticism upon works of art is a very pertinent study for an Italian traveller, but I have no learning on the subject. But if any of my audience are curious to learn what impression the objects to which an unprivileged traveller can have access in that country have made upon one observer, I can promise them an independent and faithful testimony, though in many parts superficial.

When I recurred to such notes and memoranda as I had made in my recent visit to that country, it seemed to me the simplest method of presenting what I saw and felt, would be, not to attempt general observations upon Italy as one geographical region but to give an account of my own tour, and of the cities, the country, the people, and the works of art in [the] order in which I saw them. There is something to justify this method in the peculiar geographical shape of the peninsula and the situation of its chief towns. A long narrow district, its towns lie all upon the road and may all be visited in one journey beginning either at the south or at the north. . . .

2

. . . I have attempted to give a sketch of my own observations and sentiments as I passed through the chief cities of Italy. I am very sensible of the deficiencies of the picture. Every traveller must describe not what is, but what he sees. I have seen more than some and very much less than others. I was simply a spectator and had no ulterior objects. I collected nothing that could be touched or smelled or tasted, neither cameo nor painting nor medallion, but we come out there to see the utmost that social man can effect, and I valued much, as I went on, the growing picture which the ages had painted and which I reverently surveyed. And one is glad to find in how short a time we can learn what it has taken so many ages to teach. But no one can travel far without becoming aware that he is most profited by going abroad, who knows best how to spend his time at home. An eye that is not alive to the beauty of his own land, will find no excitement in the scenery of Italy. The mind that takes no interest in the history of the human race, that does not perceive the pathos and grandeur that belong to generations struggling with the ideas of freedom and greatness, will be unmoved amid the ruins of Rome. Moreover, it seems to me the best things we learn are only confirmation in unexpected quarters of our simplest sentiments at home. The stranger in a new costume and a foreign language only reminds you of some well known character and utters the old truths. And so perhaps the best result of all your experience is the conviction that names and places are of small importance, that the most diverse circumstances read the same lesson. A truly diligent and well regulated mind will attain to the same thoughts and feelings in Sicily, in Rome, in New England.

III

BIOGRAPHY

ON January 29, 1835, Emerson began his first planned series of public lectures, a series of six on Biography, before the Society for the Diffusion of Useful Knowledge at the Masonic Temple, Boston. He read one each Thursday evening. Judging by the journals of the latter part of 1834, his experience as a lecturer had not so far been altogether satisfactory. He was becoming dissatisfied both with the restraints imposed by the lyceum system and with the subject of science as there presented. "Natural history by itself has no value; it is like a single sex; but marry it to human history, and it is poetry" (*J*, III, 326–27). The lyceum system tended to emphasize the practical aspects of scientific inquiry by the collection of objects and apparatus rather than of moral ideas. Emerson was becoming less tolerant of the immediate concerns of the Understanding and was searching with increasing urgency for means of freeing Reason to its purer insights. "I would learn the law of the diffraction of a ray because, when I understand it, it will illustrate, perhaps suggest a new truth in ethics" (*J*, III, 343). Furthermore, he was not trained in science and each lecture required too much preparation, too much dependence on the work of others for ideas as well as information. "Henceforth," he vows on November 15, just after he had moved to Concord, "I design not to utter any speech, poem or book that is not entirely and peculiarly my work. I will say at public lectures, and the like, those things which I have meditated for their own sake, and not for the first time with a view to that occasion" (*J*, III, 361). "Remember," he cautions himself as he sets out to prepare the new series in December, "you are not to say, What must be said in a Lyceum? but, What discoveries or stimulating thoughts have I to impart to a thousand persons? not what they will expect to hear, but what is fit for me to say" (*J*, III, 409). At the same time, and in spite of his reminder to Charles that his "entire success, such as it is, is composed wholly of particular failures" (*J*, III, 334), he was gaining in confidence. "The high prize of eloquence may be mine, the joy of uttering what no other can utter, and what all must receive" (*J*, III, 345).

During these months his mind was turning from science to the examples of great men, a topic which was almost equally familiar to lyceum audiences, but his first approach to the topic was broadly philosophical. The idea of a "modern Plutarch" had been in his mind at least since 1832: "The British Plutarch and the modern Plutarch is yet to be written. They that have writ the lives of great men have not written them from love and from seeing the beauty that was to be desired in them" (*J*, II, 503). The general topic of biography may well have been assigned or at least suggested by the officials of the Society for the Diffusion of Useful Knowledge, but in the choice of individual men for biographical study, Emerson was faithful to his determination to lecture only on those things which he had meditated for their own sake, however heavily he drew upon his sources for his facts and illustrations. Milton had always been a favorite and it was to "Lycidas" that he turned for consolation on the long sea voyage after his own bereavement; Michelangelo had awakened him to the great movement and monuments of the Renaissance during his months in Europe; he was drawn to Luther as the man of will of the Protestant Reformation; and his Quaker friends in New Bedford had probably helped to recall his own feeling of kinship for George Fox. These four he had settled upon as early as October 29 (*J*, III, 351, 387; *L*, I, 428), but the fifth was more difficult. For whatever reasons, he had chosen Edmund Burke by December 27 for the concluding lecture (*J*, III, 414).

The pervasive influence of Plutarch is more apparent in these early lectures on Biography than it is in the later ones on Representative Men, when other influences such as Carlyle's had taken full effect. Emerson had known the *Lives* from childhood and the ideas of history as the lives of great men and of the great man as an example of good action were basic to his early thinking; and he turned from the *Lives* to the *Morals* as his own thought turned to a deepening concern for the principles of good conduct in themselves. All of the great men selected for the early course had in some way helped Emerson to resolve his own personal problems by furnishing examples of integrity and self-reliance. Others like Napoleon and Goethe, whose actions were morally ambiguous, he considered and rejected, returning to them and to the issue they presented in his later series on Representative Men. His uncertainty as to how to make individuals serve his larger ethical purposes is reflected in those passages of his Journals which deal with the problem of biography while he was preparing his own lectures. He is still strongly influenced by Plutarch's use of single incidents to illustrate general truths (*J*, II, 503–504; III, 386–87 and 439), but is seeking broader meanings. "The great value of Biography," he says, "consists in the perfect sympathy that exists between like minds. . . . We recognize with delight a strict likeness between their noblest impulses and our own. . . . We can find ourselves, our private thoughts, our preferences, our aversions, and our moral judgments perhaps more truly matched in an ancient Lombard, or Saxon, or Greek, than in our own family" (*J*, III, 440–42). This highly personal kind of parallelism leads him to the generalization, "I suppose the materials now exist for a Portraiture of Man which should be at once history and prophesy. Does it not seem as if a perfect parallelism existed between every great and fully developed man and every other?" (*J*, III, 362–63; see also II, 503–504; III, 249, 253, 267, 355, 362–63, 419, 430.)

To follow the course of Emerson's struggling thought from the particular to the general, from his personal use of specific great men, through the concepts of vocation and self-reliance which are expressed in the address on "The American Scholar" and other writings of the intervening years, to his final analysis of the great man as "an exponent of a vaster mind and will" in *Representative Men* (1849; *W*, IV, 34–35) would be to go beyond the editorial function. The early stages of the process are dramatically revealed in these lectures on biography. The larger aspects of the problem have engaged most serious students of Emerson's thought, especially and recently John O. McCormick, "Emerson's Theory of Human Greatness," *New England Quarterly*, XXVI (1953), 291–314; Henry N. Smith, "Emerson's Problem of Vocation," *NEQ* XII (1939), 52–67; Stephen E. Whicher, *Freedom and Fate*, pp. 50–71; and Sherman Paul, *Emerson's Angle of Vision*, pp. 132–169. Kenneth W. Cameron has provided evidences for the influences of Coleridge, Cousin, Reed, Swedenborg and others on Emerson's theory of great men (see Cameron, I, *passim*).

1

[*Introduction*]

The manuscript of this first lecture in the new series has disappeared, although a few notes, bound with similar notes for other lectures in the series and here printed with the textual notes at the end of this volume, give a rough idea of part of its content and organization. The lecture title "Tests of Great Men," used by Cabot and others following him (II, 712), is probably based on the caption for these notes, which is "Tests," but a reference by Emerson to this lecture in the later lecture on Fox (see textual notes to p. 165) suggests that tests were only one of several aspects of the problem of great men discussed in his introduction. This further content has not as yet been reconstructed, as the summaries of Cabot and Cameron do not go beyond these notes, and the introductory lecture in the series on Representative Men, delivered according to Cabot first on December 11, 1845, is written in the bolder, cursive script of that period and is not in key with the thinking of the earlier series. The Journals of 1834–35 are more likely to contain actual passages used in the lecture (for example, III, 249 and 440–42). This lecture was announced without title in the *Boston Daily Advertiser* for January 29, 1835 (*L*, I, 435n) and was entitled "The Study and Uses of Biography" in the record book of the Concord Lyceum when read on March 18 of that year.

Sources for this introductory lecture do not seem to be specific; Emerson was still reading in Coleridge, Goethe, de Staël and general works like de Gerando's *Histoire Comparée des Systèmes de Philosophie* and Stanley's *History of Philosophy*, withdrawn from the Athenaeum on October 18, 1834 (*Reading* p. 21), but as Victor Cousin's set of tests for greatness as listed in his *Cours de philosophie* (1829) differs from Emerson's, Cousin was probably only a general and not a specific source (Cameron, I, 343).

2

Michel Angelo Buonaroti

This lecture was read first on February 5, 1835, the second lecture in the series. Apparently it was not the second completed, for we find Emerson writing to Lydia Jackson on February 1, "If I succeed in preparing my lecture on Michel Angelo Buonaroti this week for Thursday, I will come to Plymouth on Friday. If I do not succeed — do not attain unto the Idea of that man — I shall read of Luther, Thursday" (*L*, I, 435). On the fifth, Charles Emerson wrote to William, "Waldo lectures tonight on Michel Angelo. A grand subject and he will do worthily by him I doubt not" (*L*, I, 435n). The *Boston Daily Advertiser* announces the same date.

The manuscript of this lecture is preserved, together with others in the series, in the Houghton Library and a somewhat revised text was printed in the *North American Review* for January, 1837, and again in the Centenary Edition of the *Works* (XII, 213–244). "In answer to your inquiry respecting the N. A. Review," Emerson wrote his English publisher a decade later, "I did write an article on Milton and one on Michel Angelo in that Journal. . . . I am not very eager to recall either of these papers to notice, — which I have never seen since they were printed, and which were printed only to oblige the editor. I had rather not have them printed with my name" (*L*, III, 359). Although he did not apparently consult the manuscript and not all his reasons are valid, Cameron's suggestion (I, 344–45) that the lecture was revised after its first delivery is probably correct, for two sheets defining Beauty were inserted in the manuscript after the lecture was sewed together (see p. 101). It was repeated at Concord on November 4, 1835.

Emerson's interest in Michelangelo dates back at least to April, 1833, when he saw — and coveted — the self-portrait in the Capitoline Museum and Gallery in Rome (*J*, III, 99). From then on, Italy was seen partly through the artist's eyes (*J*, III, 105–106, 109), and when he had returned to New England, he began to read about him (*J*, III, 252–53) almost immediately, attracted even more by his philosophy and poetry than by his painting and sculpture. When he set to planning his series on Biography, Michelangelo was one of the first names to be settled upon (*J*, III, 387, 394–403) although the actual preparation for the lecture seems to have been intensive and somewhat hurried. His principal sources are listed in the Bibliography. The envelope containing the notes for the introductory lecture also contains twenty-two pages of rough notes for this lecture, mainly items from his reading in these sources, together with translations of Sonnets 1, 3, 6, 21, 39, 51, and 56 as numbered by Biagioli. A few specimen passages are here given in the textual notes.

See also F. B. Newman, "Emerson and Buonarroti," *New England Quarterly*, XXV (1952), 524–535; J. P. Brawner, "Emerson's Debt to Italian Art," West Virginia University *Philological Papers*, VIII (1951), 49–58; and Vivian C. Hopkins, *Spires of Form*, Cambridge, Harvard University Press, 1951, pp. 95–96.

T HERE are few lives of eminent men that are harmonious: few that furnish in all the facts an image corresponding with their fame. But all things recorded of Michel Angelo Buonaroti [1] agree together. He lived one life: he pursued one career. He accomplished extraordinary works. He uttered extraordinary words and in this greatness was so little eccentricity: so true was he to the laws of the human mind that his character and his works like Isaac Newton's seem rather a part of Nature than arbitrary productions of the human Will. Especially welcome is his life as [one] which belongs to the highest class of genius inasmuch as it contains in it no injurious influence. Every line in his biography might be read to the human race with wholesome effect. The means, the materials of his activity were coarse enough to be appreciated, being addressed for the most part to the eye, the results sublime, and all innocent. A purity, severe and even terrible, goes out from the lofty productions of his pencil and his chisel and still more from the more perfect sculpture of his own life which heals and exalts. "He nothing common did or mean," [2] and dying at the end of near ninety years had not yet become old but was engaged in executing his sublime conceptions in the ineffaceable architecture of St. Peter's.

[1] The spelling is Emerson's. The Italian form of the name was Michelagnolo Buonarroti (1475–1564), but he was and is known also as Michelangelo. Emerson also refers to him as "Michael."

[2] Andrew Marvell, "Horatian Ode, on the Return of Cromwell."

Above all men whose history we know he presents us with the perfect image of the Artist. He is an eminent master in the four fine arts, Painting, Sculpture, Architecture, and Poetry. In three of the fine arts by visible means and in poetry by words he strove to express the Idea of Beauty. This was his nature and vocation. This Idea possessed his soul and determined all his activity. Beauty in the largest sense, Beauty inward and outward, comprehending grandeur as a part, and reaching to Goodness as its soul, — this to receive and this to express, was his genius.

It is not without pleasure that we see amid the depravity and griefs of the human race a soul at intervals sent into the world born to see and express only beauty. So shall not the indescribable charm of the natural world, the great spectacle of morn and evening that shut and open the most disastrous day, want observers. The ancient Greeks called the world κόσμος or *Beauty*; a name which in our present artificial state of society sounds fanciful and impertinent. Yet, in proportion as the mind of man rises above the servitude to wealth and a pursuit of mean pleasures he perceives that what is most real is most beautiful; and that by the contemplation of such objects, he is instructed and exalted. This truth, that perfect beauty and perfect goodness are One, was made known to Michael Angelo, and I shall endeavor by sketches from his life to show the direction and limitations of his search after this element.

When I say that I am to sketch the character of a man devoted to the love, the study, and the expression of Beauty, let not the laborer, the accountant, the manufacturer, the mechanic, the farmer turn away with ill-will or indifference as if this might be a very pretty subject for an idle hour but promised nothing of interest to them. It does concern them, if they take an interest in indefatigable laborers, in useful, noble, religious men. If they love that which ennobles their own nature, they must respect the means by which Michel Angelo pursued from first to last his singular vocation.[3]

In considering a life dedicated to the study of Beauty it is

[3] "M. A Buonaroti was born at Capresi in Italy in 1474 and early discovering a taste for the fine arts was educated under the patronage of the celebrated Lorenzo di Medici Duke of Tuscany" [E].

natural to inquire, What is Beauty? Is this charming element capable of being so abstracted by the human mind as to become a distinct and permanent object?

I answer: Beauty cannot be defined. Like Truth it is an ultimate aim of the human being. It does not lie within the limits of the Understanding. "The Nature of the Beautiful," says Moritz, a German critic, "consists herein, that because the Understanding in the presence of the Beautiful, cannot ask, 'Why is it Beautiful?' — for that reason, is it so. There is no standard whereby the Understanding can determine whether objects are beautiful or otherwise. What other standard of the Beautiful exists, than the entire circuit of all harmonious proportions of the great system of Nature?

"All particular beauties scattered up and down in nature, are only so far beautiful as they suggest more or less in themselves this entire circuit of harmonious proportions." [4] This great Whole the Understanding cannot embrace. Beauty may be felt. It may be produced; but it cannot be defined.

The Italian artists intimate this view of beauty by describing it as *il piu nell' uno*,[5] i.e. the many in one or Multitude in Unity, intimating what I doubt not we have all felt, that what is truly beautiful seems related to all nature. A beautiful person has a kind of universality and appears to have truer conformity to all pleasing objects in external nature than another. All persons feel related to a beautiful person. Every great work of art seems to take up into itself the excellences of all works and to present as it were a miniature of nature.

In relation to this element of Beauty the minds of men divide themselves into two classes. In the first place all men have an organization corresponding more or less to the entire system of nature and therefore a power of deriving pleasure from Beauty. This is Taste.

In the second place certain minds more closely harmonized with nature possess the power of abstracting Beauty from things and reproducing it in new forms on any objects to which accident may determine their activity, as stone, canvass, song, history. This

[4] Quoted from Goethe, *Werke*, XXIX, 311–13.
[5] A phrase picked up from Coleridge's *Table Talk*. *Cf.* Cameron, I, 323. With what follows, *cf. Nature, W*, I, 23.

is Art. The love of Beauty is Taste: the creation of Beauty is Art.

And because Beauty is thus an abstraction of the harmony and proportion that reigns in all nature it is therefore studied in nature and not in what does not exist. Hence the celebrated French maxim of Rhetoric, Rien de beau que le vrai; nothing is beautiful but what is true.[6] It has a much wider application than to Rhetoric; as wide, namely, as the terms of the proposition admit. In Art, Michel Angelo is himself but a document or verification of this maxim. He labored to express the Beautiful. This he did in the entire conviction that it was only to be attained unto by knowledge of the True. The common eye is satisfied with the surface on which it rests. The wise eye knows that it is surface, and if beautiful only the result of interior harmonies which to him who knows them, compose the image of higher beauty. Moreover he knew well that only by an understanding of the internal mechanism can the outside be faithfully delineated. The walls of houses are transparent to the architect. The symptoms disclose the constitution to the physician; and to the artist it belongs by a better knowledge of anatomy, and within anatomy, of life and thought, to acquire the power of true drawing.

Believing this Michel Angelo was very far from imagining that a life given to the love of beauty, could be a life given to ease. From his childhood to his death almost at the end of a century he was dedicated to toil. Few men have ever lived as industrious as this worshipper of beauty, none who proceeded more strictly step by step to the height of Art through the appointed means of study of nature. The first anecdote [7] recorded of him is proof of this habit of study and docility. Granacci, a painter's apprentice, having lent him a print of St. Antony beaten by devils, together with some colors and pencils, the boy went to the fish-market to observe the form and color of fins and of the eyes of fish. Cardinal Farnese one day found him when an old man walking alone in the Coliseum and expressed his surprise at finding him solitary amidst the ruins, to which he replied, "I go yet to school that I may continue to learn." And one of the last drawings in his portfolio is a sublime

[6] From Boileau, *L'art poetique* (1674). Cf. W, IX, 406.
[7] This and the following two anecdotes are from Duppa, pp. 5, 174, 175.

hint of his own feeling, for it is a sketch by him of an old man with a long beard in a go-cart and an hourglass before him and the motto "ancora inparo" [*sic*], I still learn.

"The manly form cannot be comprehended merely through seeing its superficies. It must be stripped of the muscles, its parts separated, its joints observed, its differences known, its action and counteraction learned, — the hidden, the reposing, the foundation of the apparent, must be searched, if one would really see and imitate what moves as a beautiful inseparable Whole in living waves before the eye." [8]

In this spirit he devoted himself to the study of anatomy for twelve years, — we ought to say, rather, as long as he lived. The depth of his knowledge in anatomy, I suppose has no parallel among the artists of modern times. Most of his designs, his contemporaries inform us, were made with pen, and in the style of an engraving on copper or wood. This manner is more expressive, but it admits not of correction. Other painters design with pencil instead of pen for want of sufficient acquaintance with anatomy. When Michel Angelo would delineate a figure, he began to make first on paper the *Skeleton,* then, upon another paper, the same figure clothed with muscles. The studies of the statue of Christ in the Church of Minerva at Rome are preserved made in this manner.[9]

To one who has never reflected on the subject, it may seem strange that there should be so much to study for the artist in a fabric of such limited parts and dimensions as the human body. But it is the effect of reflexion to disclose evermore a closer analogy between the finite form and the infinite inhabitant. Man is the highest and indeed but the only proper object of plastic art. There needs no better proof of our instinctive feeling of the immense expression of which the human figure is capable, than the uniform tendency which the religion of every country has betrayed towards anthropomorphism, or attributing to the Deity the human form. And behold the effect of this familiar object every day. No acquaintance with the secrets of its mechanism, no degrading views

[8] "Goethe" [E]. *Werke,* XXVIII, 264–65.
[9] *Cf.* Vasari, p. 137.

even of man, not the most swinish compost of mud and blood that was ever misnamed philosophy can avail to hinder us from doing involuntary reverence to any exhibition of majesty or of surpassing beauty in human clay.

Yet our knowledge of its highest expression we owe to the Fine Arts. It is probable no man living has acquired by himself such notions of the dignity or grace of the human frame as the student of art owes to the remains of Phidias, to the Apollo, the Jove, the paintings and statues of Michel Angelo, and the works of Canova.[10] There are now in Italy both on canvas and in marble forms and faces which the imagination is enriched by contemplating. The poet Goethe says that he is but half himself who has never seen the Juno in the Rondanini palace at Rome.[11] Seeing these works true to human nature and yet superhuman, "we feel that we are greater than we know." [12] Seeing these works we understand the taste which led Michel Angelo against the taste and against the admonition of his patrons to cover the walls of churches with unclothed figures, "improper," says his biographer, "for the place, but proper for the exhibition of all the pomp of his profound knowledge." [13]

The love of beauty that expires in gazing or that never passes beyond outline and color is too slight an object to occupy the powers of a great genius. There is a closer relation than is commonly thought between the fine arts and the useful arts, and it is an essential fact in the history of Michel Angelo that his love of beauty is made solid and perfect by his deep understanding of the mechanic arts. Architecture is the bond that unites the elegant and the economical arts and his skill in this is a pledge of his capacity in both kinds. His Titanic handwriting in marble and travertine is to be found in every part of Rome and Florence, and even at Venice, on defective evidence, he is said to have given the plan of the bridge of the Rialto.

[10] Antonio Canova (1757–1822), Italian sculptor whose romanticized studies of classic themes were highly popular at this time.
[11] Something like this is said of the Medusa at the Rondanini in *Italienische Reise*, Rome, July 29, 1787. *Werke*, XXIX, 40–41. *Cf.* January 6, 1787.
[12] Wordsworth, "The River Duddon," Sonnet XXXIV, last line.
[13] Vasari, p. 162. Cf. *J*, III, 394.

Nor was this a skill in the ornamental or in the outline and general designs of the art, but a thorough acquaintance with all its secrets, with all the details of economy and of strength.

When the Florentines united themselves with Venice and England and France to oppose the power of the Emperor Charles V, Michael Angelo was appointed military architect or engineer to superintend the erection of the necessary works.[14] He visited Bologna to inspect its celebrated fortifications and on his return proposed to his government to construct a fortification on the heights of San Miniato which command the city and environs of Florence.

On the 24th of October, 1529, the Prince of Orange, general of Charles V, encamped on the hills surrounding the city and his first operation was to throw up a rampart to storm the bastion of S[an] Miniato but his plan was frustrated by the providence of M[ichel] Angelo. He so annoyed the enemy that the Prince directed the artillery to demolish the tower. M[ichel] Angelo hung mattresses of wool on the side exposed to the attack and by means of a bold projecting cornice from which they were suspended, a considerable space was left between them and the wall. This simple expedient was sufficient, and the Prince was obliged to turn his siege into a blockade.

After an active and successful service to the city for six months M[ichel] Angelo was informed of a treachery that was ripening within the walls. He communicated it to the government with his advice upon it but was mortified by reproaches at his credulity and fear. He replied "that it was useless for him to take care of the walls, if they were determined not to take care of themselves," and he withdrew privately from the city to Ferrara, and thence to Venice. The news of his departure occasioned a general concern, and he was instantly followed with apologies and importunities to return. He did so, and resumed his office. [On the] 21st of March, 1530, the Prince of Orange assaulted the city by storm. Michel Angelo is represented as having so well ordered his means that the Prince was compelled to retire.

By the treachery however of the General of the Republic,

[14] The details in this and the next three paragraphs are from Duppa, pp. 87–100.

Malatesta Baglioni, all his skill was rendered unavailing, and the city capitulated [on the] 9th of August. The excellence of the works constructed by M[ichel] Angelo has been approved by Vauban who visited them and took a plan of them.

In Rome he was consulted by Pope Paul III in fortifying San Borgo and soon showed such errors in the plans of San Gallo as to cause the work he had commenced to be stopped. He built in Rome the stairs of Ara Celi leading to the Church once the Temple of Jupiter Capitolinus and then the Capitol itself with its porticos and staircase.[15]

In [1550] he was appointed to rebuild the bridge Pons Palatinus over the Tiber at Rome.[16] He prepared accordingly a large quantity of blocks of travertine and was proceeding on his own plan with the work when through the intervention of his rivals this work was taken from him and entrusted to Nanni di Baccio Bigio who plays but a pitiful part in Michael's history. Nanni sold the travertine and filled up the piers with gravel at a small expense. Michel Angelo made known his opinion that the bridge could not resist the current, and one day riding over it on horseback with his friend Vasari, he cried, "George, this bridge trembles under us, let us ride faster that it fall not, whilst we are upon it." It fell in five years in 1557, and is still called the Broken Bridge.

I delight in observing that beside the sublimity and even extravagance of his genius which all men admit, he possessed this unexpected dexterity in practical and even small contrivances. When the Sistine Chapel was prepared for him that he might paint the ceiling, he found the platform on which he was to work suspended by ropes which passed through the ceiling. Michel demanded of San Gallo how these holes were to be repaired in the picture. San Gallo replied,[17] That was for him to consider; for the platform could be constructed in no other way. M[ichel] Angelo had the whole removed and constructed a moveable platform to rest and roll upon the floor, which is understood to be the same simple contrivance that is used in Rome at this day to repair the

[15] *Cf.* Duppa, pp. 113, 123.
[16] Vasari, pp. 207–209.
[17] Duppa, p. 51; Vasari, pp. 94–95. San Gallo is in error for Bramante.

walls of churches. He gave this model to a carpenter who made it so profitable as to furnish a dowry for his two daughters.

He was so minutely faithful that he made with his own hand not only the wimbles, the files, and the steps but also the [rasps] and the chisels and all other irons and instruments which he needed in sculpture; and in painting he not only mixed but ground the colors himself trusting no one.[18]

And not only was this discoverer of Beauty and its Teacher among men rooted and grounded in those severe laws which are never intuitively known but must be learned by action and practice but he was tenacious in his industry as ardent in his love. His diligence was so great that it is marvellous how he endured its fatigues. The midnight battles, the forced marches, the winter campaigns of Julius Caesar or Charles XII do not indicate such strength of body and of mind.

He finished the gigantic painting of the ceiling of the Sistine Chapel in twenty months, a fact which enlarges, it was said, the known powers of man. Indeed he toiled so assiduously at this painful work that for a long time after he was unable to see any picture but by holding it over his head.

A little bread and wine was all his nourishment and he told [Vasari] that he often slept in his clothes both because he was too weary to undress and because he would rise in the night and go immediately to work.

"I have found," says his biographer, "some of his designs in Florence, where, whilst may be seen the greatness of his genius, may also be known that when he wished to take Minerva from the head of Jove there needed the hammer of Vulcan." He used to make to a single figure nine, ten, or twelve heads before he could satisfy himself, seeking that in the composition there should be a certain universal grace such as nature makes, saying that he needed to have his compasses in his eye and not in his hand because the hands work whilst the eye judges.[19]

He was accustomed to say, Those figures alone are good from which the labor is scraped off when the scaffolding is taken away,

[18] Vasari, p. 103.
[19] Vasari, p. 273. *Cf.* pp. 102, 286–87, 270.

i.e., wrought with such consummate art that they seemed natural objects. At near eighty years he began upon a block of marble a group of four figures for a dead Christ because, he said, to exercise himself with the mallet was good for his health.

And what did he accomplish?

Although it is no part of my design to give an account of his works of which something is known to every person present (and to many much more is known than I know) yet for the completeness of my sketch I will name the principal ones. *Sculpture*, he called *his Art*, and to it he regretted afterwards he had not singly given himself, and the style of his paintings is monumental and even his poetry partakes of that character.

In this art his greatest work is the statue of Moses in the Church of Pietro in Vincolo in Rome. It is a sitting statue of colossal size and seems designed to embody the Hebrew Law.[20] If the Laocoon is the most tragic, this is the most awful of statues.

In the Piazza del Gran Duca at Florence stands in the open air his David about to hurl the stone at Goliah. In the Church called the Minerva at Rome is his Christ. In St. Peter's is his Pieta or Dead Christ in the arms of his Mother. In the Mausoleum of the Medici at Florence are the tombs of Lorenzo and Cosimo with the noble statues of Night and Day and Aurora and Twilight. Many statues of less fame and bas reliefs are in Rome, Florence, and Paris.

His *Paintings* are in the Sistine Chapel of which he first covered the ceiling with the story of the Creation in successive compartments, with the great series of the Prophets and Sibyls in alternate tablets, and a series of greater and smaller fancy pieces in the lunettes; this is his capital work painted in fresco. Every one of these pieces, every single figure, every single hand and foot and finger is a study of anatomy and design. Disdaining the secondary arts of coloring and all the aids of graceful finish, he occupied himself exclusively as a stern Designer to express the magnificence and vigor of his conceptions. Upon the wall over the altar is painted the Last Judgment. Of his designs the most celebrated is that cartoon of the soldiers coming out of the bath and

[20] Cf. *J*, III, 99.

arming themselves; an incident in the War of Pisa. In the coarsest print and to an unpractised eye the wonderful merit of this sketch is evident.

Of his genius for *Architecture* it is sufficient to say he built St. Peter's, an ornament of the Earth. He said he would hang the Pantheon in the air, and he redeemed his pledge in suspending that vast cupola without offence to grace or to stability over the astonished beholder. He did not live to complete the work, but is there not something affecting in the spectacle of an old man on the verge of ninety years carrying steadily onward with the heat and determination of manhood his poetic conceptions into progressive execution, towering by the dignity of his purposes over all obstacles and all enmities and only deterred by the impossibility of equalling his designs? Very slowly came he after months and years to the Dome. At last he began to model it very small in wax. When it was finished he had it copied larger in wood and by this model it was built. Long after it was completed and often since to this day rumors are occasionally spread that it is giving way and it is said to have been injured by the unskilful attempts to repair it. Benedict XIV during one of these panics sent for the architect Marchese Polini to come to Rome and examine it. Polini put an end to all the various projects of repairs by the satisfying sentence, "The cupola does not start and if it should start nothing can be done but to pull it down."

The best commendation of his works is in their influence.[21] The impulse of his grand style was instan[taneous upon his contempories]. Every stroke of his pencil moved the pencil in Raphael's hand. Raphael said, "I bless God I live in the times of Michael Angelo." Sir Joshua Reynolds long after declared to the British Institution, "I feel a self congratulation in knowing myself capable of such sensations as he intended to excite."

It will be readily conceded that a man of such habits and such deeds made good his pretension to a clear perception and to accurate delineation of external beauty. But inimitable as his works are in all three arts his whole life confessed that his hand was all

---

[21] The next two paragraphs are based largely on "Michael Angelo Buonarotti," *Lives of Em. Pers.*, pp. 38–40.

inadequate to express his thought. "He alone," he said, "was an artist whose hands can execute perfectly what his mind has conceived." And such was his own mastery that they said "the marble was flexible in his hands." Yet contemplating ever with love the idea of absolute beauty he was still dissatisfied with his own work. The things proposed to him in imagination were such that for not being able with his own hands to express so grand and terrible conceptions he often abandoned his work. This is the reason why he so often only blocked his statue. A little before he died he burned a great number of designs, sketches, cartoons made by him in order that none should see the toils endured by him and the modes of trying his genius, that he should not appear unless perfect. Grace in living forms except in rarest instances, did not satisfy him. He never made but one portrait (a cartoon of Messer Tommaso di Cavalieri) because he abhorred to draw a likeness unless it were of infinite beauty.

Such was his devotion to Art, but let no man suppose that these images which his spirit worshipped were mere transcripts of external grace or that this profound soul was taken or holden in the chains of superficial beauty.

> As from the fire heat cannot be divided
> No more can beauty from the eternal.[22]

To him of all men it was transparent. Through it he beheld the eternal spiritual beauty which ever clothes itself with grand and graceful outlines as its appropriate form. He spoke of external grace as "the frail and weary weed in which God dresses the soul which he has called into Time." [23] He was conscious in his efforts of higher aims than to address the eye; he sought through the eye to reach the soul. Therefore as in the first place he sought to approach the Beautiful by the study of the True, so he failed not to make the next step of progress and to seek Beauty in its highest form, that of Goodness. The sublimity of his art is in his life. He did not only build a Divine Temple and paint and carve saints and

[22] Sonnet VI, *Rime,* p. 6.
[23] Sonnet LI, *Rime,* p. 118.

prophets. He lived out the same inspiration. There is no spot upon his fame. The fire and sanctity of his pencil breathes in his words. When he was informed that Paul IV desired he should paint again the side of the chapel where the Last Judgment was painted because of the indecorous nudity of the figures he replied, "Tell the Pope that this is easily done. Let him reform the world and he will find the pictures will reform themselves." [24] He saw clearly that if the corrupt and low eyes that could see nothing but indecorum in his terrific prophets and angels could be purified as his own were pure they would only find occasion for devotion in the same figures. As he refused to undo his own work Daniel de Volterra was employed to clothe the figures; hence ludicrously called Il Braghettone. When the Pope proposed to him that the chapel would be enriched if the figures were ornamented with gold, Michael replied, "In those days gold was not worn, and the characters I have painted were neither rich nor desirous of wealth, but holy men, with whom gold was on object of contempt." [25]

When he was in the seventy-third year of his age San Gallo, the architect of St. Peter's, died. The Pope Paul III first entreated then commanded the aged artist to assume the charge of this great work which though commenced forty years before was only commenced by Bramante and ill continued by San Gallo. Michael who believed in his own ability as a sculptor but distrusted his capacity as an architect at first refused and then reluctantly complied. His heroic stipulation with the Pope was worthy of the man and the work. He required that he should be permitted to accept this work without any fee or reward because he undertook it as a religious act; and furthermore that he should be absolute master of the whole design, free to depart from the plans of San Gallo and to alter what had been already done.

This disinterestedness and spirit, — no fee and no interference, — reminds one of the reward named by the ancient Persian when importuned to demand some compensation from the empire for the important services he had rendered it. He demanded that he and his should neither command nor obey but should be free.

---

[24] Vasari, p. 217.
[25] Duppa, p. 57; Vasari, pp. 101–102.

And does it not resemble the spirit of George Washington's acceptance of the command of the American armies? [26]

However as it was undertaken so was it performed. When the Pope, delighted with one of his chapels, sent him one hundred crowns of gold as one month's wages, Michael sent it back. The Pope was angry but the artist was immoveable. Embittered by the envious and pitiful machinations of the interested office holders and agents in the work whom he had displaced he steadily ripened and executed his vast ideas.

The combined desire to fulfil in everlasting stone the conceptions of his mind and to complete his worthy offering to Almighty God sustained him through numberless vexations with unbroken spirit. In answer to the importunate solicitations of the Duke of Tuscany that he would come to Florence he replies, that, to leave St. Peter's in the state in which it now was, would be to ruin the structure, and thereby be guilty of a great sin; that he hoped he should shortly see the execution of his plans brought to such a point that they could no longer be interfered with, and this was the capital object of his wishes, "if," he adds, "I do not commit a great crime by disappointing the cormorants who are daily hoping to get rid of me." [27]

Still further to illustrate the nobility of his character and sentiments I may adduce his admiration of Dante for whose works and whose character he had an ardent love.

> At whose coming did high heaven expand
> Her lofty gates to whom his native land
> Refused to open hers. Yet shalt thou know
> Ungrateful city, in thine own despite
> That thou hast fostered best thy Dante's fame
> For virtue when oppressed appears more bright.

He had a lofty sympathy with Dante: in common with him a "deep contempt of the vulgar, not of the simple inhabitants of lowly streets or humble cottages but of that abject and sordid crowd of

[26] Herodotus III. 83. Washington accepted only reimbursement of his expenses and took the command as an act of duty to his unanimous appointment.
[27] *Lives of Em. Pers.*, pp. 48–49. Other facts from Duppa and Vasari.

all classes and all places who obscure as much as in them lies every beam of beauty in the universe." [28]

In accordance with this sentiment he possessed an intense love of solitude. He lived alone and never or very rarely took his meals with any person. As might be supposed he had a passion for the country and in old age speaks with extreme pleasure of his residence with the hermits in the mountains of Spoleti, so much so, that he says, he is only half in Rome, since truly peace is only to be found in the woods.[29]

Traits of an almost savage independence mark all his history. Athough he was rich he lived like a poor man and never would receive a present from any person because it seemed to him that if a man gave him any thing he was always obligated to that individual. His friend Vasari relates one occasion on which his scruples were overcome. It seems that Michael was accustomed to work at night with a pasteboard cap or helmet on his head into which he stuck a candle that his work might be lighted and his hands at liberty. Vasari observed that he did not use wax candle[s] but a better sort made of the tallow of goats. He therefore sent him four bundles of them containing forty pounds. His servant brought them after nightfall, and presented them to him. Michel Angelo refused to receive them. "Look you, Messer Michel Angelo," replied the man, "these candles have well nigh broken my arm and I will not carry them back but just here before your door is a spot of soft mud and they will stand upright in it very well, and there I will light them all." "Put them down then," replied Michael, "since you shall not make a bonfire by my gate." [30]

Michel Angelo was of that class of men who are too superior to the multitude that surround them to command a full and perfect sympathy. They stand in the attitude rather of appeal from their contemporaries to their race. But he did not therefore fix his eye upon his own greatness and avert it from the good works of others. It has been the defect of some great men that they did not appreciate or did not confess the talents and virtues of others and so

[28] *Lives of Em. Pers.*, p. 59; Duppa, p. 166.
[29] Radici, pp. 256–57.
[30] Vasari, pp. 286–87.

lacked one of the richest sources of happiness and one of the best elements of humanity. This sometimes happens from preoccupied attention as from jealousy. Aristotle, Bacon, Napoleon hid their obligation to their fellow men and knew not the joy of frank admiration. It has been supposed that artists more than others were liable to this defect. But Michel Angelo's praise on many works is to this day the stamp of fame. Michel Angelo said of Masaccio's pictures that when they were first painted they must have been alive.

He said of his predecessor the architect Bramante that he laid the first stone of St. Peter's clear, insulated, luminous, with fit design for a vast structure. He expressed often his admiration of Cellini's bust of Bindo Altoviti. He expressed his admiration of Titian, of Donatelli, of Ghiberti, of Brunelleschi. And it is said that when he left Florence to go to Rome to build St. Peter's he turned his horse's head on the last hill from which the noble dome of the Cathedral is visible and said, "Like you I will not build; better than you I cannot." Come te non voglio meglio di te non posso.[31] Indeed the fame of many works of art now in Italy derives its best sanction from the tradition of Michel Angelo's praise. It is more commendation to say, This is Michel Angelo's favorite, than to say, This was carried to Paris by Napoleon. At the same time he had the philosophy to say, "Only an inventor can use the inventions of others."

Michael talking one day to his servant asked him, "What will become of you, Urbino, if I were to die?" He replied, "I must then serve another." "Poor fellow," said M[ichel] Angelo, "I will take care thou shalt not stand in need of another master," and immediately made him a present of two thousand crowns; an act only to be expected from Popes and Emperors. For this servant he had a sincere regard and during his last illness he himself waited upon him and sat up with him by night though he was then eighty-two years of age. His death after he had been in his service twenty-six years and had grown rich thereby was a great affliction to him.[32]

There is yet one more trait in Michel Angelo's history which

---

[31] *Lives of Em. Pers.*, pp. 49, 62.
[32] Duppa, pp. 171–72; Radici, p. 262; Vasari, p. 289.

humanizes his character without lessening its loftiness; this is his platonic love. He was deeply in love with the most accomplished lady of the time, Vittoria Colonna, the Widow of the Marquis di Pescara, who after the death of her husband devoted herself to letters and to the writing of religious poetry. She was also an admirer of his genius and came to Rome repeatedly to see him. To her his sonnets are addressed and they all breathe a chaste and divine regard which is not perhaps to be found in any works of literature but in Dante and Petrarch. They are founded on the thought that Beauty is the Virtue of the body as Virtue is the beauty of the soul; that a beautiful person is sent into the world as an image of the divine beauty, not to provoke but to purify sensual into an intellectual and divine love.[33] He therefore enthrones his mistress as a goddess or genius who is to refine and perfect his own character. Whether his views are truly or falsely conceived the poems themselves I am persuaded cannot be read without awakening sentiments of virtue. An eloquent vindication of their philosophy may be found in a paper by Signor Radici in the Retrospective Review and by the Italian scholar in the Lecture of Varchi upon the first sonnet of M[ichel] Angelo contained in the volume of his poems published by Biagioli from which in substance the views of Radici are taken. The testimony of Condivi, his friend, is this: "I have often heard Michel Angelo reason and discourse upon love but never heard him speak otherwise than upon platonic love. As for me I am ignorant what Plato has said on this subject; but this I know very well that in a long intimacy I never heard from his mouth a single word that was not perfectly decorous and had for its object to extinguish in youth every improper desire and that his own nature is a stranger to depravity." [34] As poems they are marked by truth of thought and sharpness of expression. Berni says of him, in rebuking the pompous poets of the time, "He utters things; ye utter words." [35]

Towards his end seems to have grown in him an invincible appetite of dying, for he knew that his spirit could only enjoy

---

[33] Radici, p. 253, *et al.*
[34] Duppa, p. 181.
[35] Biagioli, p. xxviii.

contentment after death. So vehement was this desire that he says his soul can no longer be appeased by the wonted seductions of painting and sculpture.[36] A fine melancholy not unrelieved by his habitual heroism pervades his thoughts on this subject. At the age of eighty-one years he wrote to Vasari sending him various spiritual sonnets he had been composing, and tells him he is at the end of his life, that he is careful where he bends his thoughts, that he sees it is already 24 o'clock, and no fancy arose in his mind but DEATH was sculptured on it.

Conversing on the subject of dying with one of his friends, that person remarked that Michael might well grieve that one who was incessant in his creative labors should have no restoration. "No," replied Michael, "it is nothing; for if Life pleases us Death being a work of the same Master ought not to displease us." [37]

But a nobler sentiment uttered by him is contained in his reply to a letter to his nephew Leonardo at Florence who had informed him of the rejoicings made there over the birth of another Buonaroti. Michael admonishes him "that a man ought not to smile when all those around him weep and that we ought not to show that joy when a child is born which should be reserved for the death of one who has lived well." [38]

Amid all these witnesses for his independence, his generosity, his purity, and his veneration am I not authorized to say that this man was penetrated with the love of the highest beauty, that is, goodness; that his was a soul so enamoured with grace that not possibly could it stoop to meanness or depravity; that Art was to him no means of livelihood nor road to fame but life itself, the organ by which he sought not to utter but to suggest the unutterable; that here was a man who lived to show his fellow men that to the human faculties on every hand worlds of grandeur and grace are opened which no profane eye and no indolent eye can behold but which to see and to enjoy demands a severest discipline of all the physical, intellectual, and moral faculties of the individual?

The city of Florence on the river Arno still treasures the fame

[36] Sonnet LVI, *Rime*, p. 123.
[37] Vasari, pp. 224, 290.
[38] Radici, p. 261.

of this man. There his picture hangs in every window; there the
tradition of his opinions meets the traveller in every spot. Do you
see that statue of St. George? Michel Angelo asked it why he did
not speak. Do you see this fine church of Santa Maria Novella?
It is that which Michel Angelo called his bride. Look at these
bronze gates of the Baptistery with their high reliefs cast by Ghiberti five hundred years ago. Michel Angelo said they were fit to
be the gates of Paradise. Here is [the] church, the palace, the
Laurentian Library, he built. Here is his own house. In the church
of Santa Croce are his mortal remains. Whilst he was yet alive he
asked that he might be buried in that church in such a spot that
the dome of the Cathedral might be visible from his tomb when
the doors of the church stood open.[39] And there is he laid. Almost
two years since I stood in that church which is to Florence what
Westminster Abbey is to England. I passed with consideration
the tomb of Nicholas Machiavelli the historian and philosopher.
I stopped before the tomb of Galileus Galileo the great hearted
astronomer; then of Alfieri the poet, and of Boccacio, but when I
came to the monument of Michel Angelo Buonaroti and saw his
venerable bust, I read the inscription with deep emotion of reverence.[40] Three significant garlands are sculptured on the tomb.
They should be four but that his countrymen feared their own
partiality. The forehead of the bust (esteemed a faithful likeness)
is furrowed with eight deep wrinkles one above another. As I
beheld that head I felt that I was not a stranger in the foreign
church for this man's great name sounded hospitably in my ear.
He was not a citizen of any country; he belonged to the human
race; he was a brother and a friend to all who acknowledge the
beauty that beams in universal nature and who seek by labor and
denial to approach its source in Perfect Goodness.

[39] *Lives of Em. Pers.*, pp. 12, 49.
[40] Cf. *J*, III, 106.

3

Martin Luther

This lecture, given on February 12, 1835, is the longest of the series and was the most industriously prepared. Emerson had early been attracted to Luther as, like Calvin, the originator of a personal theological system (*L*, I, 128) and, during his own battle of conscience, he saw in Luther's act of nailing his theses to the church door of Wittemberg a parallel to the action which he was himself meditating. While preparing his letter of resignation from the Second Church, he copied into his journal a statement by Luther which the anonymous Carlyle had incorporated in an article in *Frazer's Magazine*, "It is neither safe nor prudent to do aught against conscience. Here stand I, I cannot otherwise" (Rusk, *Life*, 151, 164–65). Yet the feeling of sympathy was and remained imperfect when pressed beyond the simple fact of man acting in complete freedom of conscience. The rebellious Milton, Fox, and Luther were inevitable first choices for biographical lectures, but the theory of learning how to shape one's own life by testing its parallels with those of great men was strained in the case of Luther. "I have not so near access to Luther's mind through his works as through my own mind when I meditate upon his historical position," he wrote when he had settled down to serious preparation for his lecture (*J*, III, 377), but he found that he could adjust Luther's "almanack" to his own meridian by translating a few of the leading phrases into their equivalent verities and he could accept his works while rejecting his creed (*J*, III, 382–83). His main purpose in these lectures required a successful engagement with the difficult Luther and he set to work.

Though the record indicates that he consulted a large number of sources, his main facts and some quotations come from two nineteenth century lives of Luther (see Bibliography); other "lustres" can be traced to Coleridge and Carlyle. In addition, he responded vigorously to Luther's vigorous *Table Talk* and quoted liberally from it. A passage in the later lecture on Bacon shows that Emerson used this one on Luther more than once. In the same envelope are some forty pages of working notes for this lecture: notes mainly on the biographies and the *Table Talk*, the first draft of some passages in the lecture, and other unpublished comments. At the bottom of one page we find, "Did he

118

reappear in George Fox?" and on another the comment, "Let it be his distinctive praise that he assumed and kept the erect position of a man above all men of his time." A notation on the first page of the manuscript, "Insert as footnote," would suggest that at one time Emerson started to prepare the lecture for publication.

IT sounds like a paradox but is a truth, that those talents and means which operate great results on society, are those which are common to all men. The greatest men are precisely those whose characters are easy to understand, and with whom we feel intimately acquainted. Whilst kings strive and armies are marshalled in vain; whilst great genius and incredible industry applied to bad ends produce no lasting consequence a simple honest man arises and accomplishes wonders without effort and fills the world with his fame. This salutary truth breathes from every page of the life of Luther.

Martin Luther the Reformer is one of the most extraordinary persons in history and has left a deeper impression of his presence in the modern world than any other except Columbus. Although copious materials exist for his biography it has never been worthily written.[1]

In this country his character has not, as far as I know, received much attention. In Germany his name is held in veneration, as in some sort the type of his nation, as the most German of the Germans. It is not my design to enumerate in detail the incidents of his life, but rather by extracts from his writings, and from the Records of his conversation, to form and exhibit a clear conception of the peculiar genius of the man.

The central fact in the history of Luther is the publication of his Thesis against Indulgences. This act is the crisis of his life, the cause out of which all his after actions flow. This involved him

---

[1] "Of these materials the book called his Table Talk, although of a somewhat obscure and questionable origin, yet receiving the sanction of great popularity among his friends soon after his death, and the formal sanction of the English Assembly of Divines and of the House of Commons February, 1646, is of great value, perhaps even more valuable to an insight into the man than his voluminous acknowledged writings" [E].

in the controversies, and nailed his attention to the ecclesiastical abuses which could not be seen by a sane eye without indignation. It happens that we can trace with some minuteness the genesis of this action. When Luther first took orders in the Augustinian Monastery at Erfurt, he suffered great torment from religious melancholy and what with his terrors and what with his habits of sedentary application he was seized with a sickness which threatened his life. A venerable monk of his order succeeded in impressing him with the conviction that "justification was of grace by faith." This doctrine which was to him not a theological formula but an expression for all his belief in God's Government, proved the seed of the Reformation. About the time when Tetzel, a worthless monk commissioned by Albert, Archbishop of Mentz, to sell Indulgences came to Wittemberg, where Luther was professor of theology in the college, Luther still absorbed in the examination of this doctrine had arrived at this solid conclusion: "A man is not made righteous by the performance of certain external actions, but he must first have righteous principles and then virtuous acts will follow of course." [2] The Church of Rome had taught him differently. It had taught him that certain forms being complied with, the mass, the sacraments, confession, penance, and alms, — eternal salvation was thereby secured, and that the religious profession of the monks and their mortifications were supererogatory merit and had a market value.

"When I celebrated that abominable idol the mass, then I presumptuously trusted and relied thereupon. But at that time I saw not the snare that thereunder lay hid. I did not put my confidence in God, but in my own Righteousness and good Works. I rendered no thanks for the Sacrament, but God must be glad to give me thanks, that I would sacrifice and offer up his son to him." [3]

Henceforward he held Works, by which he understood, a naked reliance on personal merits, in abomination. These sanc-

[2] Milner, pp. 281–82. The story of the "venerable monk" is in all accounts of Luther; for example, Bower, p. 16.

[3] *Table Talk*, p. 219. Some of the inaccuracies in Emerson's quotations from this text crept in as he transcribed his own notes. Here "snare" is "knave" in Luther and in the working notes.

timonious works, which he called "the White Devil," he declared "far more dangerous than the Black." [4]

This doctrine is henceforward his main theme: Works and Faith, or, what was to him synonymous, the Law and the Gospel. The Epistle of Paul to the Galatians did in terms magnify faith, and depreciate works; this epistle he made his study, and wrote a Commentary upon it, which was always his favorite work. For a similar reason he preferred the Epistle of John. "The letter of St. John is short but every word weigheth two tons." The Epistle of James on the contrary seemed to him to exalt works at the expense of faith, and therefore he contemptuously terms it an Epistle of Straw, *Epistola straminea.*[5]

Well now to his door, under his windows, comes an unprincipled hawker of Indulgences proclaiming to the people in the coarse language of the shops that Saint Dominic and St. Francis and St. Agnes having done all the works of the Law, and much more beside, that surplus is for sale in the Pope's hands; and that whatsoever crimes men have perpetrated, they may buy pardons for, at so much a crime; or, if they will purchase the deliverance of their deceased friends' souls from Purgatory, here is the article. "As soon as the money tinkles in the chest, your father's soul flies out of torment." [6] Luther listened with loathing and indignation. If the Catholic Fathers, — if the Apostle Paul taught that our best righteousness is filthy rags, and that to saint or martyr no hope can come, but through entire abandonment of self-righteousness and the act of total trust in God, what bottomless falsehood is this, that these mortal men had enough and to spare?

Then what ruin did not this leak threaten to let in upon private morals? What end would there be to fraud, lust, and assassination? On expressing his discontent to some [of] his friends Luther found himself fortified by the sympathy of some pious priests of his acquaintance and still more by the disgust which the indecent profanity of some of Tetzel's expressions had occasioned among the people. Samson (one of the coadjutors of Tetzel) entertained

[4] This distinction is made several times in *Commentary on Galatians.* Emerson found it in Chapter 1 : 4.

[5] Cf. *Table Talk*, p. 368.

[6] Scott, I, 23. *Cf.* Milner, p. 269.

121

the astonished audience with the sounds which the soul emits, when, its ransom being paid, it flies up out of purgatory. And on the 31st of October, 1517, Luther nailed his Ninety-five Propositions against Indulgences to the door of the College Church of Wittemberg.

This Thesis was a chain of propositions upon the nature of repentance, charity, and punishment showing the impossibility of sins being thus remitted by the sacrament of a priest and still more decidedly reprobating the pretension of delivering the souls of the dead. He invited all persons holding a different opinion to a public disputation, or to transmit their objections in writing.

No disputants appearing he printed and published his Thesis.

At this time Luther was a devout Catholic. He deferred with profound humility to the Pope to whom he appealed, for neither Pope or Council had by decree sanctioned this abuse. "If the Holy Father," he said, "knew the exactions of those mercenary preachers he would rather the palace of St. Peter's should be burned to ashes than built with the skin, flesh, and bones of his sheep." [7]

Many years afterward when he trenched on far more dangerous ground, he candidly republished his first Propositions with this remark.

"I have let these stand that it may be seen what a mad papist I then was. I was so drenched in the dogmas of the Pope, that I was quite ready to put to death persons who refused obedience to the Pope in any single article. Thus I was not ice in defending Papacy like Eckius [8] and his associates who appeared to me to act more from the belly than from conviction. I on the contrary was in thorough earnest, being dreadfully afraid of the day of judgment, and desirous from my inmost soul to be saved." [9]

This Thesis was everywhere circulated. Its boldness astonished men and because of Luther's piety and his known devotion to the Church, great numbers trusted him and espoused his cause. He refused to grant absolution to such as presented Tetzel's certificates. Tetzel caused a pile to be erected for the burning of heretics

[7] Bower, p. 48.
[8] Johann Maier von Eck (1486–1543), opponent of Luther at the Diet of Augsburg.
[9] Bower, pp. 30–31.

within sight of Luther's window, and burned his Theses. The students of the University took part with their professor, and burned Tetzel's propositions in answer. At first no notice was taken of his Thesis by persons of consequence; as Luther says, "the poor monk was despised." [10] But he was not idle. He addressed letters to various prelates; to the Elector, to the Pope, and to the Emperor. The clergy, the prelates, the Cardinal, the Emperor, and the Pope decided against him. At the public disputations he triumphed. This gave him new confidence, and of course every day new facts, new arguments flowed in to strengthen his position, and to impel him to take bolder ground. Every day he denied more. Every day the defenders of the Pope were more confounded, and the cause assumed more importance. Duke George at Leipsic hated him and broke up the dispute between Carolstadt [11] and Eck on the papal authority with the intelligent decision, "Be his right divine, or be it human, he is still Pope of Rome." [12] A legate was sent to Germany from Rome to coax or scare him back to his allegiance. But revolutions never go backward, and this monk and his ethical proposition was the revolution. Erasmus was consulted by Frederic the Wise, Elector of Saxony, Luther's native prince. Erasmus told the Elector, Luther was in the right; that the cause of all the uproar was that "Luther had touched the Pope on the crown, and the monks on the belly." [13] The Elector favored him. The University befriended him. He received offers of protection from noblemen in Suabia, Switzerland, Bohemia. But his help lay in himself; the thunder of his coarse unchosen words was the arsenal of his power which made men's ears to tingle, and stimulated their imaginations as the accents of a superior being. His words Richter called, "half battles," [14] and they well deserve the name. "Pomeranus," says Melanchthon, "is a grammarian, and explains the force of words; I profess logic and teach both the arrangement of the matter and the nature of argumentation; Justus Jonas is an orator, and discourses with copiousness and elegance; but Luther is *Omnia in*

[10] Bower, p. 55.
[11] Andreas Rudolf Bodenstein (Carlstadt) (1480–1541), Protestant reformer.
[12] Bower, p. 117.
[13] Scott, I, 104.
[14] Carlyle, "Richter Again," p. 42; *cf.* "Luther's Psalm," p. 743.

omnibus, complete in everything; a very miracle among men; whatever he writes, penetrates their minds, and leaves astonishing stings in their hearts." [15] With this account all agree. Never, it would seem, did the human Will clothe itself in more fit expression than in this man's words. It seemed as if in him dwelt a spirit of the most terrible determination that ever lived in a human breast.

He had appealed to the Pope. The Pope condemned his book. He appealed "from Leo X ill informed to the same most holy Leo X better informed." [16] A second bull appeared condemning as heretical and damnable forty-one opinions selected from his writings and denouncing the heretic himself. His books were burned at Cologne and Paris and Louvain. Luther caused a pile to be erected outside the walls of Wittemberg, and, in the presence of a vast assembly, burned the Bull.

In 1521, Luther was summoned to Worms by the Emperor Charles V, to give account of his opinions. The Elector had caused him to be made acquainted with the danger, and wished to know what he would do if cited. "If the Emperor would give him a safe conduct, he said, he should esteem it God's will that he should go; if violence should be done to him, it was not his business to determine whether more benefit would accrue to the Church from his life or his death. But he hoped otherwise, for the Emperor's sake. He had rather die by the Romanists, than have the reign of Charles commence with blood. But if I must die, God's will be done. You have here my resolution. Expect from me anything sooner than flight or retraction. I mean not to flee, much less to retract, so may the Lord Jesus strengthen me! I can do neither without scandalizing godliness, and hurting the souls of many." [17]

Still his friends admonished him of the terrible remembrance of Huss [18] who had been burned by the same Diet of the Empire in defiance of the Emperor's Safe Conduct.

But the same resolution appeared in all the answers of the

[15] Milner, p. 422; Scott, I, 40. Philipp Melanchthon (1497–1560), Johann Bugenhagen (Pomeranus) (1485–1558), Justus Jonas (1493–1555) were leaders of the Lutheran Reformation.

[16] Scott, I, 55.

[17] Scott, I, 121–22.

[18] John Huss (1369–1415), Bohemian follower of Wyclif, was condemned by the Council of Constance and burned as a heretic.

Reformer. The Emperor sent his safe conduct, requiring his appearance in twenty-one days, and forbid Luther to preach on his journey. But Luther preached to vast assemblies on the way, at Erfurt, and at Issenach. The population of the former town poured out to receive him. At Oppenheim again he found letters from his friends, even one from Spalatin [19] who had the Elector's confidence, urging him to stop. It was then that he made the declaration, "To Worms I will go, were there as many devils there, as there be tiles on the houses." [20] On the 16th of April, 1521, he arrived at Worms in his friar's cowl, seated in an open chariot, and preceded by the Emperor's herald on horseback, in his official dress. Several Saxon nobles came out to meet him, and before he reached his inn, he was attended by a procession of more than two thousand persons. Men surrounded his lodging in crowds, and seemed as if they could not be satisfied in beholding him. At four o'clock the next day, he was summoned before the Diet. The crowd was immense. The Official asked in Latin and in German two questions, 1. Whether Luther avowed himself the author of the books bearing his name? and 2. Whether he was disposed to retract or persist in their contents? Luther acknowledged the works. In answer to the second question, he spoke at some length. He said that his writings were very numerous; on many subjects; that he could not retract them all without retracting the most undoubted articles of faith. He urged on the assembled princes the peril of denying what had been forced on him by the study of the Scripture, and the corruption of the Church; and intreated any one present to point out any thing in his books inconsistent with the Scripture, and he would be the first to throw it in the fire.

The Official, as he was called, the agent of the Archbishop of Treves, declared that he had not spoken to the point, and demanded an explicit answer, Whether he recanted or not?

"Since," replied Luther, addressing the Diet, "a positive answer is required of me, be it known to you, that until such time as either by proofs from holy Scripture, or by fair reason and argument, I

[19] George Burkhardt (Spalatin) (1484–1545), secretary to the Elector Frederick III of Saxony and friend to Luther.
[20] Scott, I, 127.

have been confuted and convinced, I cannot and will not recant. It is neither safe nor prudent to do aught against conscience. Here stand I; I cannot otherwise. God assist me. Amen." [21]

Charles refused to violate his safe conduct, though it is said, importuned to do so. Luther was allowed to depart. But on his way home, was waylaid and carried prisoner to the Castle of Eisenach, by the friendly violence of his prince, who was apprized of the hostile intentions of the Catholics.

Thenceforward the whole life of Luther was given to the propagation in every manner, of the same opinions, by the translation and exposition of the Scriptures; by preaching; by counsel. The care of all the Churches rested on him. All men thirsted to see him. Fourteen thousand persons were collected at Zwickau to hear him preach. When the protestant martyrs were burned at Brussels Luther composed a hymn which was sung until recently in all the churches of Germany. A sharper trial than persecution followed, — that of bad friends. On hearing of the disorders at Wittemberg where the Protestants had thrown down the images in the Catholic Churches Luther to stop these outrages forsook his hiding place, disobeying the Elector his friend. He had broke with the Pope: he had broke with the Emperor: now he took the responsibility of offending his prince. He wrote a letter to the Elector in which he says he is persuaded that his manner of proceeding has not been sufficiently bold, and that his moderation tends to impede the march of the gospel. He will now no longer hide. "I write these things to your Highness that you may know that I return to Wittemberg under a protection far more powerful than that of an Elector. Your Highness's faith is weak, and I cannot think of relying on it for defence. You wish to know what you should do. I reply you have done too much. It is contrary to the will of God that your Highness or I should have recourse to arms in the defence of my cause." [22] The rapid progress of the Reform broke out into rebellion, and the "Peasants' War." Luther's behavior was irreproachable. He sharply reprobates the insurgents

---

[21] Carlyle, "Luther's Psalm," p. 743. Accounts of this famous scene were in all the biographies.
[22] Bower, pp. 187–88.

in his letters to them and denounces their leaders. On the other hand, he exhorts the Princes to moderation, affirming to them in language hitherto unheard, the rights of the people. When the friends of the new doctrines called themselves Lutherans, he writes to them, "Be not called after my name. Who am I? a lump of worms." [23]

One after another he assailed the practical corruptions of the Church, making good in every step his word by his act. At last having denounced the whole monastic institution, in 1524 he laid aside his cowl, and in 1525, he married Catharine of Born, a nun who had abjured the veil. The influence he attained was immense. He was the author or counsellor of every great act until 1529 when the Princes at the Diet of Spires signed the Protest which gave name to their Party, and in 1530 he drew up the Articles of the Confession of Augsburg.

Luther's singular position in history is that of a scholar or spiritual man leading a great revolution, and from first to last faithful to his position. He achieved a spiritual revolution by spiritual arms alone. Let it be his eternal praise, and let it stigmatize those who pretend the same cause with far different weapons, that Luther in the very spring and experiment of new Reformation, carrying with him the devotion of his countrymen, threatened though he was with prison and with fire by the papal power, and himself of that volcanic temper that his apologist Seckendorf says, "he will defend him against all charges but anger and jesting," [24] — that, Luther never appealed to force, and in every instance denounced those who did.

"I have never," he said, with literal truth, at the close of his life, "I have never caused the sword to be drawn from the scabbard." [25] He had such an unbounded confidence in the might of spiritual weapons that he would not degrade his cause by calling in the aid of flesh and blood. He believed a single truth was of strength to put to flight all the armies, all the kingdoms of the world. His ministry (to which he esteemed himself called by special impulses

[23] *Cf.* Scott, I, 168.
[24] Seckendorf, Book I, p. 22, column 1. Also cited in Milner, p. 285.
[25] Bower, p. 234.

127

from heaven) was to communicate the truths which he received and therewith to scatter the powers of darkness.

When Staupitz wrote him of the advantage that was taken of his first writings by dissolute persons he washes his hands of the consequences. "I am not master of events: my object has been by means of the written word to attack the system of impiety which now stands. The abominations, my father, the abominations of the Pope with his whole kingdom must be destroyed. And the Lord does this *Without Hand,* by the Word alone. The work exceeds all human comprehension and therefore we need not wonder that great commotions, scandals, and even prodigies should arise. Let not these things disturb you, my father. I cherish the best hopes. The counsel and the outstretched hand of God are plain in this matter." [26]

The magazine from which he drew his ammunition, the fleets and armies with which he hazarded his battle with an assurance like Prophecy of annihilating his enemies, was the Translating of the Scriptures and publishing them in the vulgar tongue. In his early youth he had discovered in a neglected corner of the convent library a copy of the Bible and with a presentiment of his Calling had given his days and nights to the study of it. The whole and every part of this book he esteemed omnipotent. He thought like Plato, "that the soul is unwillingly deprived of truth." [26a] He thought he saw the German nation — the European family — hungering after truth, and that it only needed to break down the barrier and let in the river of the Divine Word upon the impatient mind.

All his language and his actions are inspired with this thought. He scorned the use of outward force because it distrusted this divine force. He besought the Elector not to resist the Imperial Edicts but leave the Protestants to the care of Providence.

When he hears of the violences committed by Protestants, he writes: "Pull not by force any one person from the mass. Reflect on my conduct in the affair of the Indulgences. I had the whole body of the Papists to oppose. I preached, I wrote, I pressed on

[26] Scott, I, 58–59.
[26a] Cf. *Republic* II: 382.

men's consciences with the greatest earnestness the positive decla-
rations of the Word of God, but I used not a particle of force or
constraint. What has been the consequence? This same Word of
God has, while I was asleep in my bed, given such a blow to papal
despotism, as not one of the German Princes, not even the Emperor
himself could have done. It is not I, it is the Divine Word that
has done all." [27]

When he hears that Carolstadt had moved the people to throw
down the images in the churches, he admonishes them against this
course, but says he, Instruct the people and the Images will fall
of themselves. "My former sufferings," he writes to the Elector,
on hearing these violences, "were child's play to this alarm, which
goes to throw reproach on the Gospel itself." [28] And after the insurrection against the Papists at Cologne, Luther said, "I like not
such doings; I like not taking such forcible actions in hand; they
give therewith a great blow to the gospel. Popedom can by force
neither be destroyed nor preserved, for it is built upon lies, therefore such a kingdom must be turned upside down and destroyed
by the word of truth. I am an enemy to those that fall in by
force. Preach thou, and I will give thee strength." [29]

First by the Bible itself, then by his exposition of the Bible, did
he assure himself of victory. Thus the second of David's Psalms
seems to have drawn his attention in his controversy with the
Catholics. And he writes, "The second psalm is a proud Psalm
against those fellows. It begins mild and simply, but endeth stately and rattling. Fire will break out therefore, *Beati omnes qui con-
fidunt in eum*.[30] 'Tis a most excellent and a brave stately Psalm,
and I am much taken with it." And of this, and the Psalm CIV he
says, "If God would be pleased to give me a little time and space
that I might expound a couple of small psalms, I would bestir
myself so boldly that Samson-like I would take all the Papists away
with me." This verily is all his weapon, and he habitually esteems
it sharper than all the gross engines of War. Erasmus with too
much complaisance to the Pope had controverted his Doctrine of

[27] Scott, I, 167. Cf. *J*, III, 354.
[28] Bower, pp. 186–87.
[29] *Table Talk*, p. 489.
[30] Psalms 2:12: "Blessed are all they that put their trust in him."

Will. "So soon," he says in his sick bed, "as it shall please God to help me on my legs again, so will I write against him and cut his throat." [31]

His chief assault upon the power of the Pope, was, to translate and publish in the German tongue the Pontifical Mandates with marginal commentaries and these commentaries contain his incendiary jests upon the Ecclesiastical Dominion.

Thus upon the expression "The cure (of abuses) must proceed step by step," Luther writes, "You are to understand these words to mean that there must be an interval of some ages between each step." [32] When the Turks under Barbarossa became formidable to Europe before the battle of Lepanto, Luther surveyed the danger that menaced Christendom, and thought it sufficient to threaten that "to expose the Turk as he had done the Pope, he should one day publish a German version of the Koran." [33]

It is to be considered that this sublime reliance on the simple force of truth was favoured by the greatest auxiliary which the arts ever gave to the mind, to wit the Printing Press. The spring which this invention gave to Europe can only be understood now by considering what must take place in a civilized nation without books, if suddenly Books were introduced into it. The rarity and the cost of manuscripts had made all instruction oral, and now Books appear, and every body learns to read. Instead of that languid air with which we play with a book, in that age a book was seized with lively curiosity. There was no amusement, no prosing in its covers. It contained things which people wished to know, and it was read by people believing. What the fathers of the Reformation wrote, was read with fervency in all the towns of the Empire. Luther saw at once the value of this vehicle that carried his translations and his sermons to every cottage door. "Printing," he says, "is the chiefest and last gift through which God driveth on the cause of the gospel. It is the last flame before the extinguishing of the world." [34]

If there were time to pursue this comparison between the effect

[31] *Table Talk*, pp. 32, 59, 432.
[32] Scott, I, 181.
[33] Bower, p. 251.
[34] *Table Talk*, p. 535.

of a book then and now, it would be very easy to show that there was an equal difference in the nature of the books themselves. The truths that had been imprisoned a thousand years were then to be let out and to run their joyful race. Some notion of the care with which men wrote and of the solidity of their words may be derived from one of the letters of Luther to his friend Spalatin at Court, asking if it be possible that the Elector's collection of gems might be sent him at Wittemberg to assist him in translating the 21st Chapter of Revelations. They were sent, and, after a careful examination, returned.[35]

But we are born in an age when falsehood uses the press as freely as truth; when imitation is reckoned as good as nature; a book full of words is not discerned from a book full of things; and so literature degenerates, till it becomes the imitation of imitations, and losing all sterling value, loses presently all real hold of the hearts of men.

In order to obtain a better understanding of this reformer, and to comprehend how he was enabled to produce such extraordinary effects upon his own and the following ages, we shall attempt to reach a still more interior view of the man himself. He was not a philosopher; his speculations upon abstract questions are of no worth; Aristotle's logic had helped his dialectic, but not extended his views; he had no fitness to receive scientific truths, and he makes himself very merry with the recent astronomical discoveries, which he calls "starpeeping," [36] and confounds ignorantly with astrology. Nay his theology is Jewish: His reform is directed at the corruptions of the Roman Church, not at its ancient creed, and if he can attain the Christianity of the first ages, he is quite content.

His writings and his recorded conversation treat with the utmost gravity the most frivolous questions, such as the baptism of unborn infants, of signs in the air, witchcraft, angels, and devils. Even the ethical law which he saw so clearly, and which set him upon his attack on Indulgences, he did not state as a philosophical truth, but only as a Scripture doctrine on the article of Justification.

---

[35] Cf. *J*, III, 366: "vide Seckendorf, p. 204." The reference is to Book I.
[36] *Table Talk*, p. 505.

In his controversy with Zuinglius [37] he was wholly in the wrong.

He was not more a general scholar and not more a philosopher than was Isaiah or Ezekiel among the ancient Hebrews. He was like them the Prophet, the Poet of his times and country. Out of a religious enthusiasm he acted on the minds of his contemporaries. He believed deepest what all believed. Reared up in the solemn traditions of the Christian Church and becoming at a later period under agitating events accurately acquainted with the Scriptures, — of a pious temper and in a believing age, he was himself wholly immersed in the Bible. This book gave a determination to his force. Giving heed to a divine impulse upon his mind or, feeling as all men of the first class, a reverence for the Unseen Source of their thoughts, he saw the impulse and the God through the medium of the Bible alone. There never has been since Luther a great man of the first class who believed as he did, unless Cromwell be deemed a sort of continuation of him. All others, if religious men as Milton, Newton, Leibnitz, Bacon, Montesquieu, Fenelon, Pascal, Locke, Cuvier, Goethe have joined Nature to Revelation to form their religion or like Spinoza, Rousseau, Laplace have worshipped like the Indian, Nature alone. Luther's religion is exclusively and literally from the Scriptures.

Luther was a Poet but not in the literary sense. He wrote no poems, but he walked in a charmed world. Everything to his eye assumed a symbolical aspect. All occurrences, all institutions, all persons seemed to him only occasions for the activity of supernatural agents. God in a personal form, angels, Satan, and his devils, are never out of his mind's eye. All objects, all events are transparent. He sees through them the love or malignity which is working behind them. "I shall go to Worms: I am determined to meet Satan, and to strike him with terror." [38] The love and the hatred that are burning in his fervid mind, transform every object into similitudes and types of those things he loves and hates. His head is so full of Pope and friar and mass, that he sees nothing else look where he may, — at the walls, or the carpet, or the

[37] Huldreich Zwingli (1484–1531), Swiss humanistic Protestant reformer. Zwingli had argued, in opposition to Luther, that the Lord's Supper was commemorative and symbolical only.

[38] Bower, p. 163.

pictures in his apartment, or the herbs in the garden. "That yellow flower," he says, "which in the evening is like a bald friar," — "The Pope is turned to a Poppy, and to a frothy mushroom." He exhausts his vocabulary of figurative terms in finding names for the Pope: "Bear, Wolf, Huntsman, Ass, Sow, Ex-lex." "Popedom is a slaughterhouse of consciences." Luther took in his hand a young sparrow and said, "Thou barefoot friar with thy gray coat, thou art the most mischievous Bird." "I am a bitter enemy to flies, *quia sunt imago Diaboli et Hereticorum*, etc." [39] A pleasanter example of this poetic vision: "One evening Luther saw cattle going in the fields into a pasture and said, Behold there go our preachers, our milkbearers, butter-bearers, cheese and wool bearers, which do daily preach unto us faith toward God, that we should trust in our loving father who will nourish us." [40]

"I have been employed for two days in the sports of the field, and was willing myself to taste this bittersweet amusement of the great heroes. We have caught two hares and one brace of poor little partridges. An employment this which does not ill suit quiet leisurely folks; for even in the midst of the ferrets and dogs, I have had theological fancies. But as much pleasure as the general appearance of the scene and the mere looking-on occasioned me, even so much it pitied me to think of the mystery and emblem which lies beneath it. For what does this symbol signify, but that the Devil through his godless huntsman and dogs, the Bishops and Theologians, to wit, doth privily chase and catch the innocent poor little beasts. Ah! the simple and credulous souls came thereby far too plain before my eyes. Thereto comes a yet more frightful mystery; as at my earnest entreaty we had saved alive one poor little hare, and I had concealed it in the sleeve of my great coat and had strolled off a short distance from it, the dogs in the mean time found the poor hare. Such too is the fury of the Pope with Satan, that he destroys even the souls that had been saved and troubles himself little about my pains and entreaties. Of such hunting, then, I have had enough." [41]

It is true of him that his poetic vision mastered his own mind

[39] "Because they are the image of the devil and of heretics."
[40] *Table Talk*, pp. 300–301, 319, 416, 529, 43.
[41] Quoted in Coleridge, *The Friend*, I, 233–34.

and whilst other poets describe their imaginations, he believed and acted his. He held all his opinions poetically, not philosophically; with poetic force but with poetic narrowness also. In his religious faith, there is no approach to the conception of God as the Pure Reason, which is the faith dear to philosophic minds, but he adhered to the lowest form of the popular theology, — I had almost said, — mythology. His view of the Deity is so extraordinary that no understanding of his character can be obtained without it. The expressions that have come down to us from the Dark Ages, from the Saxon Chronicles, from Gothic ballads and sermons, touching Divine agency are such as Luther uses. An old chronicle quoted by Mr. Hallam speaking of the desolation of England under the civil wars in Stephen's time says, "Men said openly that Jesus and his saints were asleep." [42] It was a proverb in the height of the prosperity of the Swiss Canton of Berne that "God had been received a burgher of Berne."

This gross and heathen theism is almost precisely that of Luther. Under this God he regarded himself a chosen instrument, and felt his commission with so much more intensity from the distinctness of which this idea of God was capable.

God is in Luther's mind a Genius or local and partial tutelary Daemon, the lover of his Church, the hater of its enemy, the chief of which are the Pope and the Turk.

He addresses the Deity therefore much as a subject who is conscious that his great services to his king and his known devotion to his service entitle to use great liberties of speech.

"We tell our Lord God plainly, If he will have his Church, he must look how to maintain and defend it; for we can neither uphold nor protect it. And well for us that it is so. For in case we could or were able to defend it, we should become the proudest asses under heaven. Who is the Church's Protector that hath promised to be with her to the end, and the gates of Hell shall not prevail against her? Kings, Diets, Parliaments, Lawyers? Marry, no such Cattle." [43]

"Dr. Justus Jonas asked me if the cogitations and words of

[42] Hallam, II, 34n.

[43] Quoted from *Table Talk* in Coleridge, *Church and State,* as epigraph to the chapter, "Idea of the Christian Church."

Jeremy were Christian like where he curses the day of his birth? I answered him, We must now and then wake up our Lord God with such words. It was indeed a right murmuring in Jeremy."

Treating of the selfish ambition of the Papal hierarchy he says, "If I were as our Lord God and had committed the government to my son, as he hath done to his son and that these angry gentlemen were so disobedient as now they be, I would throw the world into a lump."

"God could be rich soon and easily if he would be more provident, and would deny us the use of his creatures. If he would but keep back the sun that it should not shine or lock up the air or hold up the rain or quench out the fire, Ah! then would we willingly give all our money and wealth to have the use of his creatures." [44]

There are many expressions so indecorously familiar that I should shock you by their repetition.

It is unavoidable that there should in every mind be some correspondence between its conception of good and its conception of evil agents. Luther's man-like God required the same outstanding distinctness in the form of the Devil. His fidelity to this idea is as unflinching as his faith in the Confession of Augsburg. "The Devil," he says, "is God's Ape." He seems to have seen that great Enemy in bodily figure reaching along the path of his life from the cradle to the grave. "We old people," he said, (at sixty-three years) "must live thus long, to the end we should see the tail of the Devil, to be witnesses that he is such a wicked Spirit." "The whole world is nothing else but a turned about Decalogue or the Ten Commandments backwards, a vizard and picture of the Devil."

"If I die through him (the Devil) he shall eat such a bit of me as will be his bane: he shall spew me out again and at the last Day I will in requital devour him." And in his chamber, he affirms, he was disturbed by sounds and alarums occasioned by devils until he scoffed and mocked at them; then they disappeared, for the Devil cannot bear contempt. Again: "We cannot vex the Devil

[44] *Table Talk,* pp. 233, 59, 37. Justus Jonas aided Luther to translate the Old Testament.

more than when we teach, sing, and speak of Jesus and his humanity. Therefore I like it well, when with loud voices, and fine, long, and deliberately, we sing in the church 'Et homo factus est; Et verbum caro factum est." [45] The devil cannot endure to hear these words, he flieth away." [46]

Brooding on such ideas, in the solitude of his convent or afterwards in his prison in the Castle of Warteburg, in hourly peril from the sword or the fagot, a man of tender conscience and seeing how far was the practice of the world, and (far worse) of the Church, from the plain letter of the Commandments, the movements of his heart took the form of visions, his thoughts became visible and audible, and he gave way to an irresistible conviction that he was summoned by God to set up a standard of Reform, and to do battle with the infernal hosts.

This persuasion betrays itself in all his writings and discourse. He esteemed himself a commissioned man, continuing the series of ancient prophets by whom the will of God was communicated to men. He called his prison, Patmos.[47] His Commentary on Galatians is evidently writ under the impression that there was a strict parallelism between the historical position of St. Paul and his own, and he uses the Epistle to defend and explain his own acts.

He deemed himself the conspicuous object of hatred to Satan and his kingdom, and to be sustained against their malice by special interpositions of God. This is the secret of his indomitable Will. No man in history ever assumed a more commanding attitude or expressed a more perfect self-reliance. His words are more than brave, they threaten and thunder. They indicate a Will on which a nation might lean, not liable to sudden sallies or swoons, but progressive as the motion of the earth.

Listen to his letter to Spalatin.

"I could wish that the Prince Frederic would be pleased to give a hint to his friend Cardinal St. George at Rome concerning this letter, etc., that my enemies may see that they will only make bad worse, by driving me from Wittemberg; for there are those

[45] "And He was made man; and the Word was made flesh."
[46] *Table Talk*, pp. 35, 70, 82, 378, 381, 108.
[47] An island near the coast of Asia Minor, scene of St. John's exile.

not in Bohemia, but in the middle of Germany, who both can and will protect me against all their ecclesiastical thunders. There most certainly I should expose the Roman errors and abuses with greater severity than I have thought it prudent to do at Wittemberg, where the authority of the Prince and the interests of the University are some restraint to my proceedings. As far as respects myself, the die is cast. Papal wrath and papal favor are equally despised by me. I no longer wish to communicate with the Romanists, or to be reconciled to them. Let them condemn me, and burn my books, and if, in return, I do not publicly condemn and burn the whole mass of pontifical law, it will be because I cannot find fire. They will not succeed in this contest. The Lord who knows me to be a most grievous sinner, will, I doubt not, finish his own work, either through me as his instrument, or through another."

When he hears of the persecutions at Leipsic, he says, "Should the city of Leipsic itself be in the same condition that Wittemberg is, I would not hesitate to go thither though I were assured that for nine days together the heavens would pour down Duke Georges every one of them many times more cruel than the present duke of that name." [48]

After quitting his asylum at Eisenach, his friends vainly importuned him to conceal himself. "Let Behemoth rage," he replied, "I will withdraw no more into a corner." [49]

Long afterwards he seems to have remembered his early daring with the belief that it was inspired.

"I thought, at first, that people had sinned ignorantly, and not out of set purpose to endeavor to suppress God's Word and ordinances. But it pleased God to lead me on in the mouth of the Cannon like a War-horse that hath his eyes blinded and seeth not who runneth upon him. Even so was I, as it were, tugged by my hair to the office of Preaching. But had I then known what now I know, ten horses should scarce have drawn me to it. Moses and Jeremy also complain that they were deceived." [50]

A short time before his death, he said at Eisleben, "Thus you

---

[48] Scott, I, 95, 162.
[49] Bower, p. 204.
[50] *Table Talk*, p. 11. "Bar-horse," the reading in Luther and the working notes, is deliberately altered in the manuscript.

perceive God can render a man undaunted; I know not now whether I should have courage to do so much." [51]

There is in Luther's character a very important element which qualified and ennobled this Enthusiasm. A man of his mighty heart and excessive Imagination is in danger of insanity, and, in such circumstances as he fell upon, of a Mohammedan fanaticism. How is it that he escapes all tinge of this madness and presents us the image of a simple erect Man great only because his head and heart are sound, a sort of Adam, one of that class of standard men in which the unsophisticated humanity seems ever and anon to be reproduced in its first simplicity, as model and leader of new generations? He is to us in the German age what Homer is in the Greek; Moses in the Hebrew; Alfred in the Saxon; Washington in the American epoch.

The healing principle, the balance-wheel that kept these dangerous powers from extravagant motions was his warm social affections. His heart was in the right place. His marriage with Catharine of Born, a nun who had abjured the veil, is an episode in his life which in Germany they are fond of representing in drama. All the incidental allusions to her in his letters or discourse, are full of interest. After he had been married many years, he writes of his favorite work, his Commentary on the Epistle to the Galatians: "My Epistle to the Galatians is that to which I am espoused; is my Catherine of Born. *Epistola ad Galatas est mea Epistola cui me despondi; est mea Catharina de Bora.*" [52] This single expression gives us a great insight into his character. So in his Table Talk, the conversation turning upon figures of speech Luther says, "The German tongue is full of metaphors; for instance: Catharine of Born is the Morning Star of Wittemberg." He sportively superscribes his letters to her, To the most wise, gracious, and most anxious Catharine.

There is an allusion to this lady something less complimentary on another occasion and yet not inconsistent with these. "I must have patience with the Pope. I must have patience with Heretics and Seducers. I must have patience with the roaring Courtiers.

[51] Bower, p. 163.
[52] Bower, p. 118.

I must have patience with my servants. I must have patience with Kate my wife; to conclude: the patiences are so many, that my whole life is nothing but Patience." [53]

Language like this is not to be mistaken. It is like a broad smile of good nature which cannot be counterfeited and inspires confidence. There is a vein of humor, sometimes playful, sometimes coarse, which is very obvious in his letters and in his sayings and which is strictly allied with this homely, affectionate temper. "Here is the Pope of Germany and Cardinal Pomeranus," [54] said he as he threw himself into the coach with his friend Dr. Pomer, to go and visit the Legate.

He writes to Spalatin when engaged in his Translation of Job, that, "Job seems a great deal more impatient of our translation than of the consolation of his friends; or he would certainly have sat forever on the dunghill." [55]

The following is a pleasing specimen of this childlike tenderness (bonhommie):

"Once towards Evening came flying into Luther's garden two birds and made a nest there but they were oftentimes scared away by those that passed by. Then said Luther, O ye loving pretty birds! fly not away. I am heartily contented with you if ye could but trust unto me. Even so it is with us: we can neither trust in God who notwithstanding showeth and wisheth us all goodness."

"I hear that the Prince Elector George begins to be covetous, which is a sign of his death very shortly. When I saw Doctor Goad begin to tell his puddings hanging in the chimney, I told him he would not live long, which fell out accordingly; and when I begin to trouble myself about brewing, malting, and cooking, then shall not I drive it long, but soon die." [56]

With the impression of good humor which these passages give, agrees the history of his life. And this fund of human kindness was a gift from heaven which made his other gifts available. We have a pledge of that man's sanity (especially the religious reformer so prone to fanaticism) who is good-natured, domestical, fond of

[53] *Table Talk*, pp. 481, 235.
[54] Bower, p. 262; *cf.* Scott, II, 75.
[55] Bower, p. 241.
[56] *Table Talk*, pp. 39, 87.

music in the house and who loves his joke. These traits show that the strength of his arm is not convulsive but natural, flowing from a sound heart. We are reminded of Epaminondas the greatest (some have thought) of the Greeks who said "that, the most agreeable incident in his life was the satisfaction his victory at Leuctra gave his old father and mother." [57] It reminds us of Agis whom the ambassador surprized riding on a stick with his children and who made the diplomatist wait till he had finished his ride.[58] There is more in this than our sympathy with the affection. It is a certificate of the man's cognizance of a whole new class of facts and feelings which a lawgiver, a teacher, ought to be acquainted with. The great philosophical poet of the present day in his sonnet addressed to Bonaparte laments his want of that discipline of the affections which is essential to Wisdom:

> 'Tis not in battles that from youth we train
> The governor who must be wise and good . . .
> Wisdom doth dwell with children round her knees,
> Books, leisure, perfect freedom, and the talk
> Man holds with weekday man in the hourly walk
> Of the mind's business; this is the stalk
> True sway doth grow on; these are the degrees
> True power doth mount by.[59]

In Luther it served to temper what would else have been a ferocious fanaticism to manly mildness. That it only tempered but did not tame his indignation is sufficiently manifest. That he found a certain delight in the exercise of his warlike genius he did not deny.

"I have no better work," he said among his friends, "than anger and jealousy; for, when I am angry I can indite well, I can pray and preach, as then my whole disposition is quickened, my understanding sharpened, and all unpleasant cogitations and vexations do depart."

"When I write against the Pope," he said elsewhere, "I am not

[57] Theban statesman of the 3rd century B.C. who twice defeated the Spartans. *Cf.* Plutarch, *Morals*, "Apothegms of Kings and Great Commanders"; *Lives*, I, 361.
[58] Something like this is told of Agesilaus in Plutarch, *Lives*, III, 69, and *Morals*, "Laconic Apothegms." *Cf. J*, II, 430.
[59] Wordsworth, Sonnet: "I grieved for Buonaparté," lines 5–14, considerably garbled.

melancholy for then I labor with the brains and the understanding; then I write with joy of heart; insomuch that not long since Dr. Reisenpusch said unto me, I much marvel that you can be so merry; if the case were mine it would go near to kill me. Whereupon I answered, Neither the Pope nor all his shaven retinue can make me sad, for, I know they be Christ's enemies, therefore I fight against them with joyful courage." [60]

Sometimes he reflected upon his own polemical bitterness. "I was born to fight with devils and factions. This is the reason why my books are so boisterous and stormy. It is my business to remove obstructions, to cut down thorns, to fill up quagmires, to open and make straight the paths. If I must necessarily have some great failing let me rather speak the truth with too great severity than once to act the hypocrite and conceal the truth." [61]

I have thought it necessary to expand these traits of his urbanity, because it combines so singularly with his overmastering enthusiasm. This is the key to his character. Here is an Enthusiast of a new order, a person of amiable and jocular habits, who had the will of Attila or Napoleon; a man of a courage so fierce that he held the brave Melancthon for a timid temporizer; and Erasmus, when he confessed he did not covet martyrdom, he treated with open scorn.

Out of this singular union came his prodigious efficiency. His violent impulses enable him to strike with effect and his simple good nature enables him to recover himself for a new blow. Other men have at critical moments launched the right word that fell like fire on the mine, and heaved society to and fro, but wanted a reserve of power to make good their enterprise. When the first force was spent, and men came back to the genius that had inspired them for aids to resist the reaction they had awakened, there was no force found in him to resist, much less, to furnish others for resistance. But Luther was a fountain of strength, and resembled the torpedo which from the inexhaustible electricity within it affords an unceasing artillery of new shocks, each more violent than the last. This is the everlasting advantage which the simple

[60] *Table Talk*, pp. 233, 388.
[61] "Luther," *Encyclopaedia Americana*, VIII, 152–53.

sincere man possesses over the defective or half man. For as each animal and plant contains within itself all means for its defence and continuance so much and more has God made the soul of man entire and selfsufficing when Vice has not mutilated and distorted it. It can stand and it can go. It is elastic enough to recover from a blow. It can in its most violent actions regain the erect position. But to this end is it indispensable that its motions should be natural. None of its acts should be self-divided. There must be no crack, no schism between the man's act and his conviction. Whereas if a man's bravery does not arise out of love to the thing he defends but is assumed for appearance and pride, no wonder it has a limit. The sincere man's bravery is his struggle for being: for he fights for no other cause than that which involves all. But a man's bravery in a bad cause, is mere sauciness, and can easily faint. As there was nothing artificial in Luther's first opposition to Rome, but a result he could not help, because he was really angry with the brazen impudence of the Indulgence-mongers, so he did not feel it necessary to keep up the appearance of a boiling resentment as vulgar antagonists do, but when his first passion subsided, he continued the attack in good humor, occasionally with loud laughter, then waxing grave again, then merry, and sometimes in a towering passion, but always just as he felt, on the emergences of the controversy.

Society has now become so imitative and artificial that he stands in glaring contrast. Very hardly now could the great man be true. Appearances are always to be kept up. Parties are to be drilled and encouraged by this and that manoeuvre. Statesmen are to be made to say this and that nothing for effect, and half that a man does, is for example. And presently our real existence will be bowed out of the world by its own shadow.

But that was an earnest age and Luther the most earnest man. He believed and therefore spake, hit or miss, please or sting whom it might. If you tickled him, he would laugh, — if you pricked him, he would bleed. He loved, he hated, he feared God, he dared the world and the devils, he prayed, he sang, he desponded, he married, he served his prince, he abhorred dependence and became free, he erred, and repented, he worked unceasingly, he advanced unceasingly.

MARTIN LUTHER

In the story of this singular person who was the instrument of the greatest of revolutions one moral appears, the superiority of immaterial to material power. His means being strictly spiritual called into life the deepest sentiments of men and the influence long outlived him who communicated it. A man mellowed by all the sweetness and tenderness of human nature, inspiring affection by the love in his own heart, astonishes and takes command of other men's minds by the energy of his own. Poor, loyal, abstemious, of irreproachable life, all men saw that it was not for earthly objects he contended, but taking his stand in the Invisible world as his basis, he operated on the sensible world. And so this enraged Poet, who did not write his visions in sonnets, but believed them, spoke them, and acted them, persuaded vast multitudes and many nations of their truth; and by the force of private thoughts, (with an impulse that is yet far from being exhausted), he shook to the centre, not only the Ecclesiastical empire, but, as all religious Revolutions must, the whole fabric of tyranny in the world.

4

John Milton

This lecture was announced in the *Boston Daily Advertiser* (L, I, 435) as to be given on February 20, 1835, but the Boston *Daily Evening Transcript* of February 19 refers to the lecture as of "this evening" (Cameron, I, 345n). As the other lectures in the series were all given on Thursday evenings, February 19 would seem to be the correct date. As the manuscript is missing, the present text is that of the *North American Review* (July, 1838), a text which, to judge by the lecture on Michelangelo, was probably revised from the lecture by incidental cuts and rephrasings which tightened but did not substantially alter the meaning. The lecture was included in *Natural History of Intellect* (1893), Vol. XII of the *Works*.

Emerson had been familiar with Milton's poetry from childhood and his enthusiasm for his character as a poet dates back at least to his college days when he wrote in his Journal, "What a grand man was Milton! so marked by nature for the great Epic Poet that was to bear up the name of these latter times" (*J*, I, 71). At his lowest point of distress in a storm at sea in late December, 1832, he tells us he "remembered up nearly the whole of *Lycidas*, clause by clause, here a verse and there a word" (*J*, III, 3). It was apparently more for his strength and his struggle of conscience than for his poetry that Milton was chosen among the first names for these lectures on great men (see *J*, II, 362, 364, 411, 504, and III, 205, 208, 328, 351, 362, 367, 372, 379, 414, 419, 440–41), but Emerson was not satisfied even at the time that he had succeeded in bringing the poet to life as an example of greatness. Three years later (March, 1838) he wrote to Hedge with reference to this lecture's publication that he had been "vamping up an old *dead* paper that more than a year since I had promised Dr. Palfrey and with all my chemistry and chirography I cannot make it alive" (L, II, 122).

In preparation for the lecture, Emerson reviewed the Prose Works and took notes on a recent biography by Joseph Ivimey. He was also familiar with the biography of Milton in Johnson's *Lives of the Poets*, but apparently used few other sources. The folder containing the notes on "Tests" also has some trial passages for the lecture (see textual notes) as well as sixteen pages of notes on Milton, many of them from Ivimey's life and from Symmons's introduction to the Prose Works which he had withdrawn from the Athenaeum (*Reading*, p. 21).

For discussions of Emerson and Milton, see R. C. Pettigrew, "Emerson and Milton," *American Literature*, III (1931), 45–59; J. D. Pollitt, "Ralph Waldo Emerson's Debt to John Milton," *Marshall Review*, III (1939), 13–21; G. R. Elliott, "Emerson's 'Grace' and 'Self-Reliance'," *Humanism and Imagination*, Chapel Hill: U. of N.C. Press, 1938, pp. 156–59; C. E. Jorgenson, "Emerson's Paradise Under the Shadow of Swords," *Philological Quarterly*, XI (1932), 289–292; and J. R. Roberts, "Emerson's Debt to the Seventeenth Century," *American Literature*, XXI (1949), 303–305.

THE discovery of the lost work of Milton, the treatise "Of the Christian Doctrine," in 1823, drew a sudden attention to his name. For a short time the literary journals were filled with disquisitions on his genius; new editions of his works, and new compilations of his life, were published. But the new-found book having, in itself, less attraction than any other work of Milton, the curiosity of the public as quickly subsided, and left the poet to the enjoyment of his permanent fame, or to such increase or abatement of it only, as is incidental to a sublime genius, quite independent of the momentary challenge of universal attention to his claims.

But, if the new and temporary renown of the poet is silent again, it is nevertheless true, that he has gained, in this age, some increase of permanent praise. The fame of a great man is not rigid and stony like his bust. It changes with time. It needs time to give it due perspective. It was very easy to remark an altered tone in the criticism when Milton re-appeared as an author, fifteen years ago, from any that had been bestowed on the same subject before. It implied merit indisputable and illustrious; yet so near to the modern mind as to be still alive and life-giving. The aspect of Milton, to this generation, will be part of the history of the nineteenth century. There is no name in literature between his age and ours, that rises into any approach to his own. And as a man's fame, of course, characterizes those who give it, as much as him who receives it, the new criticism indicated a change in the public taste, and a change which the poet himself might claim to have wrought.

The reputation of Milton had already undergone one or two revolutions long anterior to its recent aspects. In his lifetime, he was little, or not at all, known as a poet, but obtained great respect from his contemporaries as an accomplished scholar, and a formidable controvertist. His poem fell unregarded among his countrymen. His prose writings, especially the "Defence of the English People," seem to have been read with avidity. These tracts are remarkable compositions. They are earnest, spiritual, rich with allusion, sparkling with innumerable ornaments; but, as writings designed to gain a practical point, they fail. They are not effective, like similar productions of Swift and Burke; or, like what became, also, controversial tracts, several masterly speeches in the history of the American Congress. Milton seldom deigns a glance at the obstacles, that are to be overcome before that which he proposes can be done. There is no attempt to conciliate, — no mediate, no preparatory course suggested, — but, peremptory and impassioned, he demands, on the instant, an ideal justice. Therein they are discriminated from modern writings, in which a regard to the actual is all but universal.

Their rhetorical excellence must also suffer some deduction. They have no perfectness. These writings are wonderful for the truth, the learning, the subtilty and pomp of the language; but the whole is sacrificed to the particular. Eager to do fit justice to each thought, he does not subordinate it so as to project the main argument. He writes whilst he is heated; the piece shows all the rambles and resources of indignation; but he has never *integrated* the parts of the argument in his mind. The reader is fatigued with admiration, but is not yet master of the subject.

Two of his pieces may be excepted from this description, one for its faults, the other for its excellence. The "Defence of the People of England,"[1] on which his contemporary fame was

---

[1] A reply to a Latin defense of Charles I written, at the instance of the exiled royal family, by Salmasius, or Claude de Saumaise, a Dutch scholar, in 1649. It was controversially effective mainly for the reasons to which Emerson objects.

founded, is, when divested of its pure Latinity, the worst of his works. Only its general aim, and a few elevated passages, can save it. We could be well content, if the flames to which it was condemned at Paris, at Toulouse, and at London, had utterly consumed it. The lover of his genius will always regret, that he should not have taken counsel of his own lofty heart at this, as at other times, and have written from the deep convictions of love and right, which are the foundations of civil liberty. There is little poetry, or prophecy, in this mean and ribald scolding. To insult Salmasius, not to acquit England, is the main design. What under heaven had Madame de Saumaise, or the manner of living of Saumaise, or Salmasius, or his blunders of grammar, or his niceties of diction, to do with the solemn question, whether Charles Stuart had been rightly slain? Though it evinces learning and critical skill, yet, as an historical argument, it cannot be valued with similar disquisitions of Robertson and Hallam,[2] and even less celebrated scholars. But, when he comes to speak of the reason of the thing, then he always recovers himself. The voice of the mob is silent, and Milton speaks. And the peroration, in which he implores his countrymen to refute this adversary by their great deeds, is in a just spirit. The other piece, is his "Areopagitica," the discourse, addressed to the Parliament, in favor of removing the censorship of the press; the most splendid of his prose works. It is, as Luther said of one of Melancthon's writings, "alive, hath hands and feet, — and not like Erasmus's sentences, which were made, not grown."[3] The weight of the thought is equalled by the vivacity of the expression, and it cheers as well as teaches. This tract is far the best known, and the most read of all, and is still a magazine of reasons for the freedom of the press. It is valuable in history as an argument addressed to a government to produce a practical end, and plainly presupposes a very peculiar state of society.

But deeply as that peculiar state of society, in which and for which Milton wrote, has engraved itself in the remembrance of the

[2] William Robertson, author of *The History of Scotland* (1757); Henry Hallam, author of *Constitutional History of England* (1827).
[3] Something like this is in *Table Talk*, p. 510.

world, it shares the destiny which overtakes every thing local and personal in nature; and the accidental facts, on which a battle of principles was fought, have already passed, or are fast passing, into oblivion. We have lost all interest in Milton as the redoubted disputant of a sect; but by his own innate worth this man has steadily risen in the world's reverence, and occupies a more imposing place in the mind of men at this hour than ever before.

It is the aspect, which he presents to this generation, that alone concerns us. Milton, the controvertist, has lost his popularity long ago; and if we skip the pages of "Paradise Lost" where "God the Father argues like a school divine," [4] so did the next age to his own. But we are persuaded, he kindles a love and emulation in us, which he did not in foregoing generations. We think we have seen and heard criticism upon the poems, which the bard himself would have more valued than the recorded praise of Dryden, Addison, and Johnson, because it came nearer to the mark; was finer and closer appreciation; the praise of intimate knowledge and delight; and, of course, more welcome to the poet than the general and vague acknowledgment of his genius by those able, but unsympathizing critics. We think we have heard the recitation of his verses by genius, which found in them that which itself would say; recitation which told, in the diamond sharpness of every articulation, that now first was such perception and enjoyment possible; the perception and enjoyment of all his varied rhythm, and his perfect fusion of the classic and the English styles. This is a poet's right; for every masterpiece of art goes on for some ages reconciling the world unto itself, and despotically fashioning the public ear. The opposition to it, always greatest at first, continually decreases and at last ends; and a new race grows up in the taste and spirit of the work, with the utmost advantage for seeing intimately its power and beauty.

But it would be great injustice to Milton to consider him as enjoying merely a critical reputation. It is the prerogative of this great man to stand at this hour foremost of all men in literary history, and so (shall we not say?) of all men, in the power *to inspire*. Virtue goes out of him into others. Leaving out of view

[4] Pope, "The First Epistle of the Second Book of Horace," line 102.

the pretensions of our contemporaries (always an incalculable influence), we think no man can be named, whose mind still acts on the cultivated intellect of England and America with an energy comparable to that of Milton. As a poet, Shakspeare undoubtedly transcends, and far surpasses him in his popularity with foreign nations; but Shakspeare is a voice merely; who and what he was that sang, that sings, we know not. Milton stands erect, commanding, still visible as a man among men, and reads the laws of the moral sentiment to the newborn race. There is something pleasing in the affection with which we can regard a man who died a hundred and sixty years ago in the other hemisphere, who, in respect to personal relations, is to us as the wind, yet by an influence purely spiritual makes us jealous for his fame as for that of a near friend. He is identified in the mind with all select and holy images, with the supreme interests of the human race. If hereby we attain any more precision, we proceed to say, that we think no man in these later ages, and few men ever, possessed so great a conception of the manly character. Better than any other he has discharged the office of every great man, namely, to raise the idea of Man in the minds of his contemporaries and of posterity, — to draw after nature a life of man, exhibiting such a composition of grace, of strength, and of virtue, as poet had not described nor hero lived. Human nature in these ages is indebted to him for its best portrait. Many philosophers in England, France, and Germany, have formally dedicated their study to this problem; and we think it impossible to recall one in those countries, who communicates the same vibration of hope, of self-reverence, of piety, of delight in beauty, which the name of Milton awakens. Lord Bacon, who has written much and with prodigious ability on this science, shrinks and falters before the absolute and uncourtly Puritan. Bacon's Essays are the portrait of an ambitious and profound calculator, — a great man of the vulgar sort. Of the upper world of man's being they speak few and faint words. The man of Locke is virtuous without enthusiasm, and intelligent without poetry. Addison, Pope, Hume, and Johnson, students, with very unlike temper and success, of the same subject, cannot, taken together, make any pretension to the amount, or the quality, of

Milton's inspirations. The man of Lord Chesterfield is unworthy to touch his garment's hem. Franklin's man is a frugal, inoffensive, thrifty citizen, but savours of nothing heroic. The genius of France has not, even in her best days, yet culminated in any one head, — not in Rousseau, not in Pascal, not in Fenelon, — into such perception of all the attributes of humanity, as to entitle it to any rivalry in these lists. In Germany, the great writers are still too recent to institute a comparison; and yet we are tempted to say, that art and not life seems to be the end of their effort. But the idea of a purer existence than any he saw around him, to be realized in the life and conversation of men, inspired every act and every writing of John Milton. He defined the object of education to be, "to fit a man to perform justly, skilfully, and magnanimously all the offices, both private and public, of peace and war." He declared, that "he who would aspire to write well hereafter in laudable things, ought himself to be a true poem; that is, a composition and pattern of the best and honorablest things, not presuming to sing high praises of heroic men or famous cities, unless he have in himself the experience and the practice of all that which is praiseworthy." [5] Nor is there in literature a more noble outline of a wise external education, than that which he drew up, at the age of thirty-six, in his Letter to Samuel Hartlib. The muscles, the nerves, and the flesh, with which this skeleton is to be filled up and covered, exist in his works and must be sought there.

For the delineation of this heroic image of man, Milton enjoyed singular advantages. Perfections of body and of mind are attributed to him by his biographers, that, if the anecdotes had come down from a greater distance of time, or had not been in part furnished or corroborated by political enemies, would lead us to suspect the portraits were ideal, like the Cyrus of Xenophon, the Telemachus of Fenelon, or the popular traditions of Alfred the Great.

Handsome to a proverb, he was called the lady of his college. Aubrey says, "This harmonical and ingenuous soul dwelt in a

[5] "Of Education," Symmons, I, 277; "An Apology for Smectymnuus," Symmons, I, 224.

beautiful and well proportioned body." His manners and his carriage did him no injustice. Wood, his political opponent, relates, that "his deportment was affable, his gait erect and manly, bespeaking courage and undauntedness." Aubrey adds a sharp trait, that "he pronounced the letter R very hard, a certain sign of a satirical genius." He had the senses of a Greek. His eye was quick, and he was accounted an excellent master of his rapier. His ear for music was so acute, that he was not only enthusiastic in his love, but a skilful performer himself; and his voice, we are told, was delicately sweet and harmonious. He insists that music shall make a part of a generous education.[6]

With these keen perceptions, he naturally received a love of nature, and a rare susceptibility to impressions from external beauty. In the midst of London, he seems, like the creatures of the field and the forest, to have been tuned in concord with the order of the world; for, he believed, his poetic vein only flowed from the autumnal to the vernal equinox; and, in his essay on Education, he doubts whether, in the fine days of spring, any study can be accomplished by young men. "In those vernal seasons of the year, when the air is calm and pleasant, it were an injury and sullenness against nature, not to go out and see her riches and partake in her rejoicing with heaven and earth."[7] His sensibility to impressions from beauty needs no proof from his history; it shines through every page. The form and the voice of Leonora Baroni seem to have captivated him in Rome, and to her he addressed his Italian sonnets and Latin epigrams.

To these endowments it must be added, that his address and his conversation were worthy of his fame. His house was resorted to by men of wit, and foreigners came to England, we are told, "to see the Lord Protector and Mr. Milton."[8] In a letter to one of his foreign correspondents, Emeric Bigot, and in reply apparently to some compliment on his powers of conversation, he writes: "Many have been celebrated for their compositions, whose common conversation and intercourse have betrayed no marks of

[6] See Symmons, VII, 506–507 for this paragraph.
[7] Symmons, I, 284.
[8] Aubrey.

sublimity or genius. But, as far as possible, I aim to show myself equal in thought and speech to which I have written, if I have written any thing well." [9]

These endowments received the benefit of a careful and happy discipline. His father's care, seconded by his own endeavour, introduced him to a profound skill in all the treasures of the Latin, Greek, Hebrew, and Italian tongues; and, to enlarge and enliven his elegant learning, he was sent into Italy, where he beheld the remains of ancient art, and the rival works of Raphael, Michael Angelo, and Correggio; where, also, he received social and academical honors from the learned and the great. In Paris, he became acquainted with Grotius; [10] in Florence or Rome, with Galileo; and probably no traveller ever entered that country of history with better right to its hospitality, none upon whom its influences could have fallen more congenially.

Among the advantages of his foreign travel, Milton certainly did not count it the least, that it contributed to forge and polish that great weapon of which he acquired such extraordinary mastery, — his power of language. His lore of foreign tongues added daily to his consummate skill in the use of his own. No individual writer has been an equal benefactor of the English tongue by showing its capabilities. Very early in life he became conscious that he had more to say to his fellow-men than they had fit words to embody. At nineteen years, in a college exercise, he addresses his native language, saying to it, that it would be his choice to leave trifles for a grave argument, —

> Such as may make thee search thy coffers round,
> Before thou clothe my fancy in fit sound;
> Such where the deep transported mind may soar
> Above the wheeling poles, and at Heaven's door
> Look in, and see each blissful deity,
> How he before the thunderous throne doth lie.[11]

Michael Angelo calls "him alone an artist, whose hands can execute what his mind has conceived." The world, no doubt, contains

[9] Symmons, I, xxxi.
[10] Hugo Grotius, author of *De jure belli et pacis* (1625).
[11] "Anno Aetatis XIX. At a Vacation Exercise, etc." lines 31–36.

very many of that class of men whom Wordsworth denominates *"silent poets,"* [12] whose minds teem with images which they want words to clothe. But Milton's mind seems to have no thought or emotion which refused to be recorded. His mastery of his native tongue was more than to use it as well as any other; he cast it into new forms. He uttered in it things unheard before. Not imitating, but rivalling Shakspeare, he scattered, in tones of prolonged and delicate melody, his pastoral and romantic fancies; then, soaring into unattempted strains, he made it capable of an unknown majesty, and bent it to express every trait of beauty, every shade of thought; and searched the kennel and jakes as well as the palaces of sound for the harsh discords of his polemic wrath. We may even apply to his performance on the instrument of language, his own description of music:

> — notes, with many a winding bout
> Of linked sweetness long drawn out,
> With wanton heed and giddy cunning,
> The melting voice through mazes running,
> Untwisting all the chains that tie
> The hidden soul of harmony.[13]

But, whilst Milton was conscious of possessing this intellectual voice, penetrating through ages, and propelling its melodious undulations forward through the coming world, he knew also, that this mastery of language was a secondary power, and he respected the mysterious source whence it had its spring; namely, clear conceptions, and a devoted heart. "For me," he said, in his "Apology for Smectymnuus," "although I cannot say, that I am utterly untrained in those rules which best rhetoricians have given, or unacquainted with those examples which the prime authors of eloquence have written in any learned tongue, yet true eloquence I find to be none but the serious and hearty love of truth; and that whose mind soever is fully possessed with a fervent desire to know good things, and with the dearest charity to infuse the knowledge of them into others, when such a man would speak, his words, by what I can express, like so many nimble and airy servitors, trip

[12] "When, to the attractions of the busy world," line 80.
[13] "L'Allegro," lines 139–144.

about him at command, and in well-ordered files, as he would wish, fall aptly into their own places." [14]

But, as basis or fountain of his rare physical and intellectual accomplishments, the man Milton was just and devout. He is rightly dear to mankind, because in him, — among so many perverse and partial men of genius, — in him humanity rights itself; the old eternal goodness finds a home in his breast, and for once shows itself beautiful. His gifts are subordinated to his moral sentiments. And his virtues are so graceful, that they seem rather talents than labors. Among so many contrivances as the world has seen to make holiness ugly, in Milton, at least, it was so pure a flame, that the foremost impression his character makes, is that of elegance. The victories of the conscience in him are gained by the commanding charm, which all the severe and restrictive virtues have for him. His virtues remind us of what Plutarch said of Timoleon's victories, that they resembled Homer's verses, they ran so easy and natural.[15] His habits of living were austere. He was abstemious in diet, chaste, an early riser, and industrious. He tells us, in a Latin poem,[16] that the lyrist may indulge in wine and in a freer life; but that he, who would write an epic to the nations, must eat beans and drink water. Yet in his severity is no grimace or effort. He serves from love, not from fear. He is innocent and exact, because his taste was so pure and delicate. He acknowledges to his friend Diodati, at the age of twenty-one, that he is enamoured, if ever any was, of moral perfection. "For, whatever the Deity may have bestowed upon me in other respects, he has certainly inspired me, if any ever were inspired, with a passion for the good and fair. Nor did Ceres, according to the fable, ever seek her daughter Proserpine with such unceasing solicitude, as I have sought this τοῦ καλοῦ ἰδέαν, this perfect model of the beautiful in all forms and appearances of things." [17]

When he was charged with loose habits of living, he declares, that "a certain niceness of nature, an honest haughtiness and self-

---

[14] Symmons, I, 268.
[15] Plutarch, "Timoleon," *Lives*, II, 352.
[16] Elegia VI: "Ad Carolum Diodatum ruri commorantem."
[17] Symmons, I, ix. Cf. *J*, III, 205, 208.

esteem either of what I was or what I might be, and a modesty, kept me still above those low descents of mind, beneath which he must deject and plunge himself, that can agree" to such degradation.

"His mind gave him," he said, "that every free and gentle spirit, without that oath of chastity, ought to be born a knight; nor needed to expect the gilt spur, or the laying of a sword upon his shoulder, to stir him up, by his counsel and his arm, to secure and protect" attempted innocence.

He states these things, he says, "to show, that, though Christianity had been but slightly taught him, yet a certain reservedness of natural disposition and moral discipline, learned out of the noblest philosophy, was enough to keep him in disdain of far less incontinences than these," that had been charged on him. In like spirit, he replies to the suspicious calumny respecting his morning haunts. "Those morning haunts are where they should be, at home; not sleeping, or concocting the surfeits of an irregular feast, but up and stirring, in winter, often ere the sound of any bell awake men to labor or devotion; in summer, as oft with the bird that first rouses, or not much tardier, to read good authors, or cause them to be read, till the attention be weary, or memory have its perfect fraught; then with useful and generous labors preserving the body's health and hardiness, to render lightsome, clear, and not lumpish obedience to the mind, to the cause of religion, and our country's liberty, when it shall require firm hearts in sound bodies to stand and cover their stations. These are the morning practices." [18] This native honor never forsook him. It is the spirit of "Comus," the loftiest song in the praise of chastity, that is in any language. It always sparkles in his eyes. It breathed itself over his decent form. It refined his amusements, which consisted in gardening, in exercise with the sword, and in playing on the organ. It engaged his interest in chivalry, in courtesy, in whatsoever savoured of generosity and nobleness. This magnanimity shines in all his life. He accepts a high impulse at every risk, and deliberately undertakes the defence of the English people, when advised by his physicians that he does it at the cost of sight. There

[18] The preceding four quotations are from the "Apology," Symmons, I, 220–25.

is a forebearance even in his polemics. He opens the war and strikes the first blow. When he had cut down his opponents, he left the details of death and plunder to meaner partisans. He said, "he had learned the prudence of the Roman soldier, not to stand breaking of legs, when the breath was quite out of the body." [19]

To this antique heroism, Milton added the genius of the Christian sanctity. Few men could be cited who have so well understood what is peculiar in the Christian ethics, and the precise aid it has brought to men, in being an emphatic affirmation of the omnipotence of spiritual laws, and, by way of marking the contrast to vulgar opinions, laying its chief stress on humility. The indifferency of a wise mind to what is called high and low, and the fact that true greatness is a perfect humility, are revelations of Christianity which Milton well understood. They give an inexhaustible truth to all his compositions. His firm grasp of this truth is his weapon against the prelates. He celebrates in the martyrs, "the unresistible might of weakness." [20] He told the bishops, that, "instead of showing the reason of their lowly condition from divine example and command, they seek to prove their high preëminence from human consent and authority." He advises, that, in country places, rather than to trudge many miles to a church, public worship be maintained nearer home, as in a house or barn. "For, notwithstanding the gaudy superstition of some still devoted ignorantly to temples, we may be well assured, that he who disdained not to be born in a manger, disdains not to be preached in a barn." [21] And the following passage, in the "Reason of Church Government," indicates his own perception of the doctrine of humility. "Albeit, I must confess to be half in doubt whether I should bring it forth or no, it being so contrary to the eye of the world, that I shall endanger either not to be regarded, or not to be understood. For, who is there, almost, that measures wisdom by simplicity, strength by suffering, dignity by lowliness?" [22] Obeying this sentiment, Milton deserved the apostrophe of Wordsworth:

[19] "The Reason of Church Government," Symmons, I, 96–97.
[20] "Of Reformation," Symmons, I, 4.
[21] "The Reason of Church Government," *Selection*, I, 153; "The Likeliest Way to Remove Hirelings Out of the Church," *Selection*, II, 285.
[22] Symmons, I, 124, 126.

JOHN MILTON

Pure as the naked heavens, majestic, free,
So didst thou travel on life's common way
In cheerful godliness; and yet thy heart
The lowliest duties on itself did lay.[23]

He laid on himself the lowliest duties. Johnson petulantly taunts Milton with "great promise and small performance," in returning from Italy because his country was in danger, and then opening a private school. Milton, wiser, felt no absurdity in this conduct. He returned into his revolutionized country, and assumed an honest and useful task, by which he might serve the state daily, whilst he launched from time to time his formidable bolts against the enemies of liberty. He felt the heats of that "love" which "esteems no office mean." He compiled a logic for boys; he wrote a grammar; and devoted much of his time to the preparing of a Latin dictionary. But the religious sentiment warmed his writings and conduct with the highest affection of faith. The memorable covenant, which in his youth, in the second book of the "Reason of Church Government," he makes with God and his reader, expressed the faith of his old age. For the first time since many ages, the invocations of the Eternal Spirit in the commencement of his books, are not poetic forms, but are thoughts, and so are still read with delight. His views of choice of profession, and choice in marriage, equally expect a divine leading.

Thus chosen, by the felicity of his nature and of his breeding, for the clear perception of all that is graceful and all that is great in man, Milton was not less happy in his times. His birth fell upon the agitated years, when the discontents of the English Puritans were fast drawing to a head against the tyranny of the Stuarts. No period has surpassed that in the general activity of mind. It is said, that no opinion, no civil, religious, moral dogma can be produced, that was not broached in the fertile brain of that age. Questions that involve all social and personal rights were hasting to be decided by the sword, and were searched by eyes to which the love of freedom, civil and religious, lent new illumination. Milton, gentle, learned, delicately bred in all the elegancy of art and learning, was set down in England in the stern, almost fanatic,

[23] Sonnet: "London, 1802."

157

society of the Puritans. The part he took, the zeal of his fellow-ship, make us acquainted with the greatness of his spirit, as in tranquil times we could not have known it. Susceptible as Burke to the attractions of historical prescription, of royalty, of chivalry, of an ancient church illustrated by old martyrdoms and installed in cathedrals, — he threw himself, the flower of elegancy, on the side of the reeking conventicle, the side of humanity, but unlearned and unadorned. His muse was brave and humane, as well as sweet. He felt the dear love of native land and native language. The humanity, which warms his pages, begins as it should at home. He preferred his own English, so manlike he was, to the Latin, which contained all the treasures of his memory. "My mother bore me," he said, "a speaker of what God made mine own, and not a translator." He told the Parliament, that "the imprimaturs of Lambeth House had been writ in Latin; for that our English, the language of men ever famous and foremost in the achievements of liberty, will not easily find servile letters enow to spell such a dictatory presumption."[24] At one time, he meditated writing a poem on the settlement of Britain; and a history of England was one of the three main tasks which he proposed to himself. He proceeded in it no further than to the Conquest. He studied with care the character of his countrymen, and once in the "History," and once again in the "Reason of Church Government," he has recorded his judgment of the English genius.

Thus drawn into the great controversies of the times, in them he is never lost in a party. His private opinions and private conscience always distinguish him. That which drew him to the party was his love of liberty, ideal liberty; this therefore he could not sacrifice to any party. Toland tells us, "As he looked upon true and absolute freedom to be the greatest happiness of this life, whether to societies or single persons, so he thought constraint of any sort to be the utmost misery; for which reason he used to tell those about him the entire satisfaction of his mind, that he had constantly employed his strength and faculties in the defence of liberty, and in direct opposition to slavery."[25] Truly he was an

---

[24] "Areopagitica," Symmons, I, 295.
[25] John Toland, an early biographer, quoted in Ivimey, p. 250.

apostle of freedom; of freedom in the house, in the state, in the church; freedom of speech, freedom of the press, yet in his own mind discriminated from savage license, because that which he desired was the liberty of the wise man, containing itself in the limits of virtue. He pushed, as far as any in that democratic age, his ideas of *civil* liberty. He proposed to establish a republic, of which the federal power was weak and loosely defined, and the substantial power should remain with primary assemblies. He maintained, that a nation may try, judge, and slay their king, if he be a tyrant. He pushed as far his views of *ecclesiastical* liberty. He taught the doctrine of unlimited toleration. One of his tracts is writ to prove that no power on earth can compel in matters of religion. He maintained the doctrine of *literary* liberty, denouncing the censorship of the press, and insisting that a book shall come into the world as freely as a man, so only it bear the name of author or printer, and be responsible for itself like a man. He maintained the doctrine of *domestic* liberty, or the liberty of divorce, on the ground that unfit disposition of mind was a better reason for the act of divorce, than infirmity of body, which was good ground in law. The tracts he wrote on these topics are, for the most part, as fresh and pertinent to-day, as they were then. The events which produced them, the practical issues to which they tend, are mere occasions for this philanthropist to blow his trumpet for human rights. They are all varied applications of one principle, the liberty of the wise man. He sought absolute truth, not accommodating truth. His opinions on all subjects are formed for man as he ought to be, for a nation of Miltons. He would be divorced, when he finds in his consort unfit disposition; knowing that he should not abuse that liberty, because with his whole heart he abhors licentiousness and loves chastity. He defends the slaying of the king; because a king is a king no longer than he governs by the laws; it would be right to kill Philip of Spain making an inroad into England, and "what right the king of Spain hath to govern us at all, the same hath the king Charles to govern tyranically." [26] He would remove hirelings out of the church, and support preachers by voluntary contributions; requiring, that such only should preach, as have

[26] "The Tenure of Kings and Magistrates," Symmons, II, 285.

faith enough to accept so self-denying and precarious a mode of life, scorning to take thought for the aspects of prudence and expediency. The most devout man of his time, he frequented no church; probably from a disgust at the fierce spirit of the pulpits. And so, throughout all his actions and opinions, is he a consistent spiritualist, or believer in the omnipotence of spiritual laws. He wished that his writings should be communicated only to those who desired to see them. He thought nothing honest was low. He thought he could be famous only in proportion as he enjoyed the approbation of the good. He admonished his friend "not to admire military prowess, or things in which force is of most avail. For it would not be matter of rational wonder, if the wethers of our country should be born with horns, that could batter down cities and towns. Learn to estimate great characters, not by the amount of animal strength, but by the habitual justice and temperance of their conduct." [27]

Was there not a fitness in the undertaking of such a person, to write a poem on the subject of Adam, the first man? By his sympathy with all nature; by the proportion of his powers; by great knowledge, and by religion, he would reascend to the height from which our nature is supposed to have descended. From a just knowledge of what man should be, he described what he was. He beholds him as he walked in Eden:

> His fair large front and eye sublime declared
> Absolute rule; and hyacinthine locks
> Round from his parted forelock manly hung
> Clustering, but not beneath his shoulders broad.[28]

And the soul of this divine creature is excellent as his form. The tone of his thought and passion is as healthful, as even, and as vigorous, as befits the new and perfect model of a race of gods.

The perception we have attributed to Milton, of a purer ideal of humanity, modifies his poetic genius. The man is paramount to the poet. His fancy is never transcendant, extravagant; but, as Bacon's imagination was said to be "the noblest that ever con-

----

[27] Letter to Richard Jones, September 21, 1656. Varies from Symmons's version.
[28] *Paradise Lost*, IV, 300–303.

tented itself to minister to the understanding," [29] so Milton's ministers to character. Milton's sublimest song, bursting into heaven with its peal of melodious thunder, is the voice of Milton still. Indeed, throughout his poems, one may see under a thin veil, the opinions, the feelings, even the incidents of the poet's life, still reappearing. The sonnets are all occasional poems. "L'Allegro" and "Il Penseroso" are but a finer autobiography of his youthful fancies at Harefield. The "Comus" is but a transcript, in charming numbers, of that philosophy of chastity, which, in the "Apology for Smectymnuus," and in the "Reason of Church Government," he declares to be his defence and religion. The "Samson Agonistes" is too broad an expression of his private griefs, to be mistaken, and is a version of the "Doctrine and Discipline of Divorce." The most affecting passages in "Paradise Lost," are personal allusions; and, when we are fairly in Eden, Adam and Milton are often difficult to be separated. Again, in "Paradise Regained," we have the most distinct marks of the progress of the poet's mind, in the revision and enlargement of his religious opinions. This may be thought to abridge his praise as a poet. It is true of Homer and Shakspeare, that they do not appear in their poems; that those prodigious geniuses did cast themselves so totally in to their song, that their individuality vanishes, and the poet towers to the sky, whilst the man quite disappears. The fact is memorable. Shall we say, that, in our admiration and joy in these wonderful poems, we have even a feeling of regret, that the men knew not what they did; that they were too passive in their great service; were channels through which streams of thought flowed from a higher source, which they did not appropriate, did not blend with their own being? Like prophets, they seem but imperfectly aware of the import of their own utterances. We hesitate to say such things, and say them only to the unpleasing dualism, when the man and the poet show like a double consciousness. Perhaps we speak to no fact, but to mere fables of an idle mendicant, Homer; and of a Shakspeare, content with a mean and jocular way of life. Be it how it may, the genius and office of Milton were different, namely, to ascend by the aids of his learning and his religion, — by an equal perception, that is,

[29] Not located.

of the past and the future, — to a higher insight and more lively delineation of the heroic life of man. This was his poem; whereof all his indignant pamphlets, and all his soaring verses, are only single cantos or detached stanzas. It was plainly needful that his poetry should be a version of his own life, in order to give weight and solemnity to his thoughts; by which they might penetrate and possess the imagination and the will of mankind. The creations of Shakspeare are cast into the world of thought, to no farther end than to delight. Their intrinsic beauty is their excuse for being. Milton, fired "with dearest charity to infuse the knowledge of good things into others," [30] tasked his giant imagination, and exhausted the stores of his intellect, for an end beyond, namely, to teach. His own conviction it is, which gives such authority to his strain. Its reality is its force. If out of the heart it came, to the heart it must go. What schools and epochs of common rhymers would it need to make a counterbalance to the severe oracles of his muse.

> In them is plainest taught and easiest learnt,
> What makes a nation happy, and keeps it so.[31]

The lover of Milton reads one sense in his prose and in his metrical compositions; and sometimes the muse soars highest in the former, because the thought is more sincere. Of his prose in general, not the style alone, but the argument also, is poetic; according to Lord Bacon's definition of poetry, following that of Aristotle, "Poetry, not finding the actual world exactly conformed to its idea of good and fair, seeks to accommodate the shows of things to the desires of the mind, and to create an ideal world better than the world of experience." [32] Such certainly is the explanation of Milton's tracts. Such is the apology to be entered for the plea for freedom of divorce; an essay, which, from the first until now, has brought a degree of obloquy on his name. It was a sally of the extravagant spirit of the time, overjoyed, as in the French revolution, with the sudden victories it had gained, and eager to carry on the standard of truth to new heights. It is to be regarded as a poem on one of the griefs of man's condition, namely, unfit

[30] *Cf.* note 14.
[31] *Paradise Regained*, IV, 361–62.
[32] *The Advancement of Learning*, Book II; *Works*, I, 90.

marriage. And as many poems have been written upon unfit society, commending solitude, yet have not been proceeded against, though their end was hostile to the state; so should this receive that charity, which an angelic soul, suffering more keenly than others from the unavoidable evils of human life, is entitled to.

We have offered no apology for expanding to such length our commentary on the character of John Milton; who, in old age, in solitude, in neglect, and blind, wrote the Paradise Lost; a man whom labor or danger never deterred from whatever efforts a love of the supreme interests of man prompted. For are we not the better; are not all men fortified by the remembrance of the bravery, the purity, the temperance, the toil, the independence, and the angelic devotion of this man, who, in a revolutionary age, taking counsel only of himself, endeavoured, in his writings and in his life, to carry out the life of man to new heights of spiritual grace and dignity, without any abatement of its strength?

5

George Fox

The subject of this lecture, delivered first on February 26, 1835, was perhaps the closest to Emerson's heart of any in the series. Some notes written in July of 1832 (*J*, II, 497–500), when he was in the White Mountains meditating his resignation from his pulpit, show that he had with him William Sewel's history of the Quakers and probably Tuke's *Memoirs of the Life of Fox*. He is already linking Fox with Swedenborg for their ability to mix consistent mysticism with practical common sense. He sees Fox as "a natural growth, by reaction, of a formal church," and takes comfort in the simple directness of his rejection of all religious forms. In October of 1833, when he is starting to reshape his life, he again links Fox with Swedenborg as men to whom revelations "are made only in the woods or in the closet" (*J*, III, 222). On his visits to preach at New Bedford in 1834, he met and talked with the Quakers there, Deborah Brayton and Mary Rotch who attended the Unitarian Church after her dismissal from the Meeting, and Fox's name, with that of William Penn, begins to appear more frequently in the Journals. When he began to plan seriously for the lectures on Biography, Fox was his first choice as topic for one of them, and there are twenty pages of notes on him, mainly from Sewel and Fox's *Journal*, in the "Tests" folder. (They include also a reference to Thomas Hutchinson's *History of Massachusetts* and to *Sartor Resartus* on Hat Honor.) Though Emerson certainly knew other books on Quakerism, referring to some in the text, the lecture is based almost entirely on these two sources, chiefly Sewel. See the textual notes for a few excerpts from the working notes on Fox. On Emerson and the Quakers, see especially F. B. Tolles, "Emerson and Quakerism," *American Literature*, X (1938), 142–165 and M. C. Turpie, "A Quaker Source for Emerson's Sermon on the Lord's Supper," *New England Quarterly*, XVII (1944), 95–101.

IN the sketches taken in the preceding lectures we have contemplated men possessed of rare faculties and who had the advantage of rare cultivation. Each of them towers above his contemporaries and is not one man in a thousand men, but one man in a thousand years. But according to the true views of biography Man and not particular men are the subject of endless interest to man. We wish to hold these fellow minds as mirrors before ourselves to learn the deepest secret of our capacity. We wish not only to mark the extraordinary but to find the common and natural motions of the soul, what the cook, the peasant, and the soldier say. The nobility and splendor of conceptions never take us so much as when they appear in a vile form, neither borrowed from the palace nor from arts and sciences. There is both more delight to a wise mind and more profit in studying the symptoms of grandeur in the lowest of the populace, than in these brilliant anomalies who can be represented to be rather exceptions than examples of humanity. In passing by peculiar gifts and exhibiting the efficacy of universal principles the simplest discover their means and power. Portraits of common men who have accomplished much do human nature a kindness in showing it how much it can do of itself. "We are all of us richer than we think we are, but we are taught to borrow and to beg, and brought up more to make use of what is another's than of our own." [1]

There are such universal principles which seem to be the remedial force by which the decay and degeneracy of the human race is hindered, and which act continually to reproduce in the latest man or most formal age a novelty in the sentiments like that of the first man on the First Day. Such a principle is the passion of Love, and, of still greater efficacy, the sentiment of Religion.

George Fox was a man who possessed none of what are called the accidental social or personal advantages, but to whom the

[1] "Montaigne and sentence supra Vol 3 p. 421" [E]. The "sentence supra" reads: "He [Cato] has done humane nature a great kindness in shewing it how much it can do of it self." The essay is "Of Physiognomy."

latter principle, the Religious sentiment, was in the place of all, was father, mother, friends, house, and land. The great difficulty in estimating the religious principle and its effects philosophically is its extreme familiarity in lifeless and even absurd forms. At the name of Religion, our thoughts fly to a particular church and to modes of worship. We must aim to ascend to a more general view.

Upon this little globe of the Earth as it swings and spins in the deep of space, creep and run several pretty races of animals; among them one that speaks, and speaks of somewhat they call Reason, morals, God. Notwithstanding the very trifling and sordid works of many thousands and thousands of the members of this social tribe, certain among them affirm, that, in the hearts of them all shines a vital light which when observed by the mind it inhabits, not only fills the mind, but radiates outward upon all near and all remote objects (as there is no object in nature which intensity of material light will not make beautiful), until making visible, objects not before seen, adorning those that were seen and disclosing unexpected relations between the mind and those objects on which it falls, it pierces into infinite depths on every hand, and seems virtually to bring the Universe into the possession of the single soul. This pretension, in some views we are forced to take of man, might seem the very flourish of folly, did it not steadily reappear on frequent occasions in the remotest places and is never quite out of the head of some body wherever this species have any foothold. This alleged Light, or Conscience, or Spirit, takes different names in every new receiver, but its attributes are essentially the same.

Zoroaster in Persia, Confucius in China, Orpheus in Greece, Numa in Italy, Manco Capac in Peru [2] all asserted it. In terms and manner more remarkable Moses and Jesus in Palestine averred the same thing and an unbroken chain of witnesses ever since conspire in the same testimony.[3]

We think perhaps we understand how men of genius, kings,

[2] Numa Pompilius, second King of Rome, was reputed to have founded its religious institutions; Manco Capac, the first Inca of Peru and founder of its capital, Cuzco.

[3] "The Brahmins Mahomet" [E].

poets, great Captains should come to adopt this gay dream of eternizing their preeminence. But it happens that the most resist-less affirmations of this principle break out among what these would call the draff and refuse of the race. It is still originated in new breasts and wherever it makes its appearance, it supplies the place of poetry and philosophy and of learned discipline, and inspires by itself the same vastness of thinking.

The effect in this respect is striking enough of the Religious Sentiment. It communicates to the most narrow mortal a pro-digious elevation of thought. It uniformly persuades him that he is united in the most intimate manner to the Cause of all beings and so makes all the dominion of that Cause his own property. It gives him

> Eyes that the beam celestial view
> Which evermore makes all things new.[4]

Furthermore it is the most republican principle. "God is our Father and all we are brethren"[5] is its peremptory voice. It is above all the dogmas of the world the seed of Revolutions. Down topple before this enormous assertion of spiritual right, all the ty-rannies, all the hierarchies, all the artificial ranks of the earth. The stern question of Agesilaus when the Persian king was called the Great King, is the devout man's question concerning every man: "How is he greater than me if he is not more just?"[6] And hence wherever in history the religious element has appeared, it has exerted according to the confession of Hume an influence not to be computed, and does always threaten by its very existence the being of arbitrary government.

Meantime whilst there is a substantial identity of the religious sentiment in men under the widest disagreement in modes and terms, yet it happens that all attempts to confine and transmit the religious feeling of one man or sect to another age, by means of formulas the most accurate, or rites the most punctual, have hither-to proved abortive. You might as easily preserve light or electricity

---

[4] John Keble, *The Christian Year*, "Morning." Cf. *J*, II, 504.
[5] Not located.
[6] Agesilaus, King of Sparta. In Plutarch's *Morals* the anecdote is told twice, in "Apothegms of Kings and Great Commanders" and in "Laconic Apothegms."

in barrels. It must be lived. It cannot be writ. Therefore the newly stricken soul wanders among churches from sect to sect and never finds any that fits him, but in proportion to the depth of his convictions finds himself at first unlike all and alone, and afterwards to be in a degree of union with the good of each name.

These are the facts that make the simple life of George Fox interesting to the philosopher and philanthropist. He was one to whom the firm order of society promised nothing but bread for hard labor and no grace beyond. He was the son of a poor weaver and was apprenticed to a shoemaker in Drayton, Leicestershire, and by him employed part of the time to keep a few sheep in the pastures and part of the time to cobble shoes at his bench. But sitting in his stall amid tanned hides, pincers, rosin, swine's bristles, and nameless rubbish, this poor boy caught the glimpses of this Inward Light, and smit with its beauty amid the ugliness of his lot, he left all and followed it. It led him to that freedom and peace which he sought, and raised him out of the ashes of his fortune to that moral height which belongs to this principle. In the details of his history we shall find two facts to which we have alluded established: [1.] That religious enthusiasm opens the mind like liberal discipline of arts. It is better than an University and gives a far insight into its powers, so that in learning the religious thoughts of a strong though untaught mind you seem to have suggested in turn all the sects of the philosophers. 2. That the religionist is by necessity a reformer. He is at once an idealist seeking ever to accommodate the shows of things to the desires of the mind, and a realist putting ever a thing for a form.

George Fox was from a young child remarked for the gravity and thoughtfulness of his demeanor, and his habits of contemplation were favored by his employment as a grazier for part of the year in the service of his master. He was diligent in his business so that his master remarked his own success whilst G[eorge] was there. Impatient however of the routine of his trade, at the age of nineteen he forsook his craft, and gave himself up to a contemplative life. He wandered about in the country especially in the neighborhood of the Peak of Derbyshire with his Bible; he lived on berries and such food as the fields and woods could furnish him and sat and slept in hollow trees or a stack of hay and frequently in the night he walked mournfully about. He equipped himself for this singular life by making himself a leather suit of clothes both on account of cheapness and strength. At first he applied himself for a solution of his doubts and fancies to the clergy of the established Church, but fell among persons who treated his perplexities with levity. One related all George's confessions as soon as he was gone, to the milkmaids. One whom G[eorge] visited in his garden showed so much anger because G[eorge] trod upon a bed as disgusted him. One told him to "take tobacco and sing psalms." George told him "he did not love tobacco and was in no state to sing." Those who treated him with decency yet gave him no satisfaction either in private or public discourse. He listened anxiously but in vain in the churches. None of them, he complained, none of them spoke to his condition.

At last he fell to listening to himself only, for it was made known to him that the Lord Jesus Christ would speak to his condition.

A series of truths were impressed upon his mind some of more some of less importance and extent of bearing. He was moved to speak in any assemblies of people, and, when in churches, occasionally to interrupt the clergyman with interrogations or exhortations of his own. For this indecorum he was committed to jail and afterwards wherever he went often half famished from town to town the populace were easily excited against him and he was insulted, whipped, stoned, and many times almost bruised to death. These unmeasured severities had not the least effect upon his temper and conduct. More distinct and more happy thoughts of God and the soul opened upon him from time to time. He passed through many alternations of feeling and at one time fell into such a condition that he not only looked like a dead body but to many seemed really dead for fourteen days' time. In the first years his preaching consisted of some few but powerful and piercing words. He found as he said many "tender" persons who received his word gladly and ministered to his wants. In the course of months and years hundreds and thousands became his associates at the dear penalty of a furious persecution. But "the Lord had changed them," as two of their women replied in the prison of the Inquisition at Malta, "into that which changeth not."[7] Their constancy and meekness at length wearied out persecution and lived out calumny. Fox lived always the life of an itinerant, but was married [to] the widow of Judge Fell. In 1671 he came to America, to Barbadoes, to Maryland, and New England. He spent a year in A[merica]; afterwards in Holland. He frequently visited Oliver Cromwell at Hampton Court. In all companies, in all places, he bore his testimony for the truth, to judges, to churchmen, to merchants, to rulers, soldiers, jailers, convicts. He exhorted Charles II by letter. He had the best influence upon the whole society of the Quakers as long as he lived; and died in 1690 aged sixty-six years, and was followed to his grave by more than a thousand Friends.

But his true biography must be found in those revelations which in orchards, in lonesome places, and by the wayside, were made to him, and which are characterized by these two traits, 1. That they are of a liberal and philosophical tendency so as to agree well with the maxims of the schools of philosophy; 2. That they have a direct bearing on practical morals.

It was opened to him very early in life that he should keep God's word alway and not commit excess in eating and drinking. At Drayton it was opened to him that as the young went to vanity and the old to the earth, he should separate himself both from young and old and be as a stranger to all men. After this he was inwardly made sensible of Christ's sufferings; then, that not all called Christians were Christians; that to be bred at Oxford or Cambridge was not enough to make a minister of Christ; that believers needed no man to teach them but the anointing in man teacheth them; that the Scriptures cannot be understood but by the same spirit that gave them forth; that the Supreme Being dwelleth not in houses of brick and stone; that the natures of hurtful things that are without are also within the minds of evil persons, and that the natures of dogs, swine, vipers, etc., and those of Cain, Ishmael, Pharaoh were in the hearts of many people. As he walked one day by the steeple house in Mansfield, it was made known to

[7] Sewel, I, 525.

him, "That which people trample on, must be thy food." Then he perceived that they fed each other with words, but the true spiritula life of Christ, they trampled on.[8]

In a season of darkness it was impressed upon his mind, "All things come by Nature;" but presently, he sitting still, the cloud passed away, and it seemed to be affirmed to him, "No, there is a living God."

After this, he was made to see into the nature of creatures and proposed to practise physic, but it was taught him that he should betake himself to a spiritual cure. Then were opened to him the three great professions in the world, physic, law, and divinity, where he saw that the physicians wanting the wisdom of God by which the creatures were made, knew not their virtues; that the lawyers generally were void of equity and justice and so out of the law of God; and that the priests, for the most part, were out of the true faith which brings man to have access to God: so that these physicians, lawyers, and priests who pretended to cure the body, to establish the property of the people and to cure the soul, were all without the true knowledge they ought to possess.

There was to be a meeting of justices in a neighboring town for establishing some local regulation respecting the hiring of servants. Thither George felt constrained to go and exhorted them not to oppress servants; and many of the servants having come thither, he admonished them of their duties. He went and reproved a man of wild and vicious life.

Then it was made known to him that he should not give honor by lifting his hat or bowing his body before men. After this it was opened to him that men ought to say *Thou* to one, as *You* to more than one, that other things were of pride. Then that he should not swear at all; he should not take judicial oaths. Then that he should not fight with any carnal weapon but should seek peace with all men. He saw there was an ocean of darkness and death but withal an infinite ocean of light and love which flowed over that of darkness, in all which he perceived the immense love of God.

But that suggestion which contained and sanctioned all the

[8] Cf. *J*, II, 358, 498–99.

171

rest, which came first and remained with him to the end was the doctrine of the infallible guidance.

G[eorge] F[ox] believed in an infallible guidance which he called the Light: by which he understood nothing that was peculiar to himself but a leading that was tendered to every man who yielded himself to it. This doctrine was not new. The faith has always been in the world that every man was the care of a Genius who befriended him. Traces of this faith are in all story sacred or profane: in the story of Socrates' Daemon; in the poems of Homer; in the belief in fairies, and tutelar saints; in the doctrine of a special providence. All these are symbols or parables of the fact that an infallible Adviser dwells in every heart very silently, very peacefully, not obtruding his counsel, but to the ear sharpened by faith these intimations become words of fate, not one falls to the ground. What is made known to us by this Teacher is attended by a conviction which the opinions of all mankind could not shake and which the opinions of all mankind could not confirm.

These and such as these were the revelations made to the poor cobbler and grazier at his bench or amongst the hills. These were the thoughts whose influence upon his mind was so strong as to dwarf and dwindle all the considerations of thrift and decorum and safety.[9]

These were the thoughts which he communicated to men as poor and low as himself, — and to much meaner persons, — to the scullions and convicts and dragoons, with whom his persecutors drove him to associate, and which were received by such as they, with joy unfeigned, and followed by penitence and wisdom. They that heard him were for the most part ignorant men and women, many reprobate. Yet these lofty abstractions which Fox propounded to them on the sole authority of his own mind as the interpreter of the Scripture, they understood and adopted and extended. And when presently some of a gentler sort such as Robert Barclay, William Penn, Elwood and Pennington who had learning were added to their people, these men did at once perceive the perfect coincidence of this lowly village oratory with

[9] Primarily based on the early pages of Sewel. The ultimate source is, of course, Fox's *Journal.*

whatsoever doctrines of goodness and grandeur the poets and philosophers of the remotest ages and countries have conspired in teaching. It is, I think, the most remarkable fact in the history of the Quakers that the books and tracts written to announce and defend their faith are a string of citations from all the sages, such as one would expect to find in the lecture of Kant or Fichte on the Transcendental Philosophy.[10] This extends even to the more abstruse questions which are commonly thought to be out of the domain of exact science and left to theorists called visionary, to Schelling, Novalis, and Swedenborg: the nature of animals, of dreams, of names.

As a striking illustration of the degree to which this religious sentiment could exalt the thinking and purify the language even of uneducated men I am tempted to read the words of James Nayler who from the army where he had been eight years a common soldier had joined Fox. A few hours before his death he said to his friends:

"There is a spirit which I feel that delights to do no evil nor to revenge any wrong but delights to endure all things in hope to enjoy its own in the end. Its hope is to outlive all wrath and contention and to weary out all exaltation and cruelty or whatever is of a nature contrary to itself. It sees to the end of all temptations. As it bears no evil in itself so it conceives none in thought to any other: if it be betrayed it bears it: for its ground and spring is the mercies and forgiveness of God. Its crown is meekness, its life is everlasting love unfeigned, and takes its kingdom with entreaty, and keeps it by lowliness of mind. In God alone it can rejoice, though none else regard it or can own its life. It is conceived in sorrow and brought forth without any to pity it nor doth it murmur at grief and oppression. It never rejoiceth but through sufferings; for with the world's joy, it is murdered. I found it alone being forsaken. I have fellowship therein with them who lived in dens and desolate places of the earth who through death obtained this resurrection and eternal holy life." [11]

---

[10] "See Barclay's *Apology* and Penn's *Christian Quaker*" [E]. There is little further evidence in this lecture of Emerson's use of these books.
[11] Sewel, I, 289–90.

In the first place then his revelations agreed well with all philosophy. In the next place he commended himself to men by vitality of the doctrine and he demanded the same proof of faith from all.

He complained that the clergy were man made priests, that rails were built around the altar, that the wood, the lime, and the stone of a steeple-house were esteemed the Church and not the souls of men. "The visible," he said, "covereth the invisible sight in you." [12] He demanded radical reform of the church. This must every religious mind do that is born into an old church. The creed, the rites of one age can never fit the next. Let the Reformer define his creed never so accurately or establish what severe Rule of Discipline he will, in a short time he dies, and his friends who shared his spirit die, his own fire cannot be transmitted and soon their places are filled by a generation who read their prayers and observe their ceremonies with excessive punctuality, but the essence of religion, that is, its origin in the worshipper's soul, is wanting. But Nature never fails. Instantly the divine Light rekindles in some one or other obscure heart who denounces the deadness of the church and cries aloud for new and more appropriate practices. Thus every church, the purest, becomes speedily old and dead, and only a new church is alive. Thus the Protestants reformed the Catholic Church; the Presbyterians, the Protestant; the Independents, the Presbyterian; the Quakers, the Independent; but of the same new impulse arose still later the Methodist and now the Swedenborgian or New Jerusalem Church. Each is new only because the worshipper is in earnest; but all whilst they were new have taught the same things.

But a surer mark of the value of these meditations of Fox was their direct beneficial tendency. Not only was his life irreproachable, but every one of his impulses is a medicine to some one wound of human nature. All his actions and discourse breathe love to the race of man. His attitude from first to last is that of a consistent practical reformer. He exposes a falsehood but supplies a truth. He puts ever a thing for a hollow form. I have said he was

[12] Cf. *J*, II, 498–500 for quotations and ideas in the next few paragraphs. Like nearly all statements of fact in this lecture, they are based on Sewel.

an Idealist inasmuch as he would conform the outer to the inner world. And now he shows himself as all such consistent persons do, a Realist impatient of deception and pretence, eager for realities. I know it seems to many that a disorderly spirit is a very easy way to fame, and that to interrupt the religious services of churches was not the best mark of a true reform. This it is true the Quakers did and their Apology consists in the then state of the English Church. It must be admitted — it cannot be denied — that if an established church becomes utterly formal and dead the aggrieved pious man has a right to protest and denounce it. This is like the right of revolution in a tyranny which can never be denied. Now such had the English Church actually become at that time. Are there not some virtues higher than decorum? and in the bosom of a formal church may it not be pardoned to a fervid heart rejoicing in its new life to cry out, "Husks! Husks!" even in their solemn assembly? "Words! Words! Ye feed one another with words!" The sweetest psalms grated on his ear for he perceived that David's psalms were unsuitable to the states of the people.

All his prophetic rhapsodies are directed at some offence. His earliest inspiration at eleven years is that he should not commit excess in eating and drinking. They put him in jail. Forgetting immediately his private griefs he is pained by the mischiefs of the prison now first known to him. And he forthwith laid before the judges, what a hurtful thing it was, that prisoners should lie long in jail, because they learned wickedness one of another, talking of their bad deeds, and therefore that speedy justice ought to be done. Here too becoming sensible of the vices of the sanguinary criminal code of England he wrote to the judges concerning the evil of putting to death for stealing. In Derby jail among the felons was a conjuror who threatened to raise the devil and break down the house but George went to him and said, "Come, let us see what thou canst do, and do thy worst; the devil is raised in thee already but the power of God chains him down." At the calmness of this speech, the fellow slunk away. At Nottingham he testified against the licentiousness of the wakes and May games and the holidays of the Calendar; at the Market cross, against deceitful and covetous trading.

In [Derby] prison when his innocence and meekness had shamed the justices they bade the jailer leave the door of his cell unlocked but he would not take advantage of it. Then they gave him liberty to walk a mile. But he faithfully returned, and they were compelled honorably to discharge him. Afterwards, in the time of Charles II, by a premunire [13] he had become the King's prisoner, but he could not release him otherwise than by a pardon: and "I was not free to receive a pardon (writes George in his Journal) knowing I had not done evil. The king told J. Moore, that I need not scruple to receive a pardon, for many a man that was as innocent as a child, had had a pardon granted him; yet I could not consent to accept one; for I had rather have lain in prison all my days, than come out in any way dishonorable to truth." [14]

They offered him at [Derby] a bounty and a captain's commission if he would serve against Charles. But he declared that he did not fight with carnal weapon. Bowing to the creature he denied. "Wherein," said Judge Twisden, "do you show your respect to magistrates if you do not put off your hat to them?" "In coming when they call me," replied he. They brought him the Bible to administer the oath which they knew he would not take. "And thus," said he, "you would show your respect for the Bible, but the doers what the Bible says, you condemn." "Will you not," said the Judge, "take the oath of Allegiance?" "My allegiance," replied Fox, "does not consist in swearing, but in truth and faithfulness."

The usurpation implied in calling only the house of the episcopalians The Church, and the rails around the altar moved his indignation so much that on almost all occasions he preferred to preach out of doors, but when the church was offered and was manifestly the only convenient place he went in. He showed his good sense when, at Patrington, [at] the request of some one he lay down on a bed, to end the rumor that he never slept in a bed.

It is natural, especially for the student of Man, to ask what was the historical effect of a life so singular.

[13] Praemunire, an obsolete form of writ, originally used against Papists.
[14] Fox, *Journal*, II, 197.

We are told that there were at that time abundance of people in England who having searched all sects could nowhere find satisfaction. And these now understanding that God by his light was so near in their hearts, began to take heed thereunto. To men looking for better things and disgusted with venality and hollowness of the Church this doctrine of humility and simplicity seemed a welcome revelation. It was like the child returning to his father's house. It was as if the poor operative, begrimed, distorted in body, fleeing from his unhealthy forge and mill and hot and noisome lanes had escaped into a free horizon and the breath of the woods. Of all Revolutions a religious change is the greatest when not a nation is restored to its rights but one man made infinite, or with his principle more than a match for all nations without it. Like all revolutions this too promised in its dawn a better era.

> Of old things all are over old
> Of good things none are good enough
> We'll show that we can help to frame
> A world of other stuff.[15]

Peace, truth, unlimited prosperity and that on an immortal basis this sentiment promised, a promise which, could the sentiment be kept at the same pitch it now held, it surely would have made good. Peace, Temperance, Honesty, Love were the principles and practice of this undaunted man, and his companions caught from him the same spirit. That class, (as always there is a class,) whose minds were not deaf and dumb, heard themselves addressed with emotion. They were ready to say, The gods have come down to us in the likeness of men. Fox had great quickness and directness in speaking to the spiritual wants that presented themselves. Dr. Thomas Lower asking questions of [him] received such satisfactory answers from Fox that he said "his words were as a flash of lightning, they so ran through him, and that he never met with such wise men in his life." His father, who remained in the Old Church, saw with some grief the enthusiasm of his son and his extreme opinions but in 1654 he exclaimed, "Truly I feel, he that will but stand to the truth it will carry him out."

[15] Quoted in Coleridge, *Biographia Literaria*, p. 25.

As the sentiment was uttered so was it received with joy and hope, even at the peril and loss of goods, freedom, personal safety, and even life. The force that was in the Quakers made their senses so obtuse to danger, or so restored them by that power which the mind has over the body, that in reading the authentic narratives of these sayers of Yes and No, we seem to read the story of miracles. Women were whipped to blood and never startled at a blow, but sang. The wounded, nigh broken arm is instantly restored. The mastiffs that are set on them crouch and fawn upon them. The great stones that are thrown at them fell as nuts and beans. We are reminded of the adventurer favored by the fairies who found his pocket always replenished with money so long as he did not count it. The hay was not wasted in their barns nor the corn in their bins, though man and beast were lodged with unlimited hospitality at their meetings.

The solidity of these convictions was put to the test.[16]

The sufferings which George and his friends endured were indeed extreme. George was confined a year in Derby gaol, was barbarously used at Warnsworth, Doncaster, and Tichhill, was stoned at Lancaster, was denied a lodging from inn to inn, house, or barn at Patrington, and familiar with the prisons of almost every county. Pitiful insult and oppression was added to loss of freedom. After he had paid fifty shillings of his own money to repair his doleful prison room and keep out water, cold, and smoke the gaoler removed him into a worse.

No man was sentenced to die in England for this heresy, but no ridicule, no insult, no robbery which the law could connive at was spared. The magistrates hesitated not to break their canes over these wearers of hats. Their meetings were interrupted. A party of horse attempted to ride over an assembly of their people but the horses, more merciful than their riders, would not and turned aside. The Friends were imprisoned and put into holes not so large as some baker's ovens though higher. The turnkey nailed boards over the window to hide the light. Insults not to be repeated were added. They were fined and to pay the fine their

---

[16] The following passage, on loose sheets, was apparently intended for insertion here.

178

goods were confiscated. They took from a shop in Royston all but one skein of thread; they took beds from under the sick and when the child's pap stood in a pannikin they threw out the pap to take the pannikin away.

I grieve to say that in the Persecutions of the Quakers New England bore the fiercest part. On the arrival of two women of the Society at Boston in 1656 they were treated by the magistrates with great severity, imprisoned on their landing, and after five weeks sent away in a ship returning to England. This was done by the orders of Bellingham, Governor Endicot being out of town. The same treatment was shown to eight persons more who arrived later. But more arriving in 1658 the court sentenced three to lose their right ear by the hand of the hangman and passed a sharp edict of banishment on pain of death upon any members of the Society that should come into the province. In 1659 Robinson and Stevenson were hanged for remaining in the province contrary to this law. This horrible act entitles our town to the name of that bloody town of Boston which it bears in the history of this philanthropic sect. The effect of these severities in England was singular enough. There is in man an appetite for pain, a mysterious groping in certain states of enthusiasm to know the worst, "to tread the floors of hell." [17] And these poor Quaker men and women hearing the persecutions at Boston conceived an invincible appetite to come hither, and the masters of ships refusing to receive them, they sailed for Barbadoes, for Virginia, or any other port whence, by a circuitous route, through forests, bogs, and Indian camps, they might arrive hither to the prison, the whipping post, and the gallows.[18]

Is it asked, Did not the Quakers give cause for these severities? The great body of the Quakers did not. A few extravagances and indecencies were done under their name. As a sect in their early days no purer is to be found on the page of history. And I am persuaded that no lover of truth can now read the story of their sect, simple as it is, with the effort to place himself in their point of view, without feeling many chords struck in his own bosom,

[17] From Pindar by way of Plutarch, *Morals*, I, 303.
[18] See Hutchinson, I, 180–89.

and becoming sensible that the circumstances might present themselves, in which he should act the part of Fox and Howgill.[19] It is true that G[eorge] F[ox] and his friends did magnify some trifles, that they gave a ridiculous importance to their notions of plainness in speech, manners, dress. They cut their hair not in the best taste. They stripped all jewels and ornaments from their dress. They disused titles of honor. They said Thee and Thou, though they defended this practice with spirit. "The Pope," said George, "set up *you* to one, in his pride. Pride could not stomach the word *Thou*, which was before the Pope was, which was God's language and will stand when the Pope is ended." "Look now," said one of his friends, when he was bid uncover his head and say *You* to the magistrate, "they imprison me for speaking English and for not taking off my clothes." [20]

It is true that this plainness ran to a ludicrous excess. Beside plain speech, in Amsterdam they must have plain print, and books were published not having a capital letter from beginning to end. Isaac Furnier like another Diogenes used a split stick for tongs at his fire.[21]

But has it not been so with every combat for human right since the beginning, that the best cause is not at first defended on its merits, but the contention is ever hottest upon some minor and perhaps insignificant particulars? And this from necessity; for, the majority of society holding fast not to truths, not to things, but to usages, are keenly sensible when usages are invaded. They who have no care for religion or philosophy can see the least deviation from custom in manners or dress, and resent an omission of courtesy more than atheism. The Quakers being abused and tormented upon this ground, came unavoidably to exaggerate its importance. It came to be the badge of their tribe, and has been (as was far easier) preserved with exactness, when the spiritual distinctions have been obliterated.

But these slight things were not that whereon he and his friends laid stress but upon the doctrine of the infinitude of Man as seen

[19] Francis Howgill, a "Seeker" converted by Fox, who joined him in preaching.
[20] End of insert.
[21] This paragraph is based on Sewel, I, 252, which treats a "lunatic fringe" rejected by responsible Quakers.

in the conviction that his soul is a temple in which the Divine Being resides — that astounding paradox which is always lurking in the heart of every church and is at intervals announced anew with more or less clearness and fulness but whose limitations have never yet been written down in any book. All religious movements in history and perhaps all political revolutions founded on claims of Rights, are only new examples of the deep emotion that can agitate a community of unthinking men, when a truth familiar in words, that "God is within us," is made for the time a conviction. As an inference from this faith they claimed inspiration; but they observed the conditions within which that claim may be safely made, the act namely of total self renouncement. He who deals truly with himself and renouncing all wilfulness, acts after his clearest sight, can never repent his action, and has the assurance of the author of his constitution that it is for him the best action.

Preserving under the wholesome checks of persecution and controversy his simplicity of action Fox turned the divine light of this criterion upon one opinion and usage after another and justified or condemned them.

In some particulars his views have not spread beyond his sect.[22] That of silent meetings is peculiar. When he was reproached for them, he said, Better be silent than to tell lies.

There are two questions on which George Fox never ceased to exhort, on which his opinion is still confined to his own sect, that of a hired clergy, and that of the rites of Baptism, and the Lord's Supper.

The manner in which the ministers of religion shall be maintained, is still a question under constant debate, and it can scarce be said that society have acquiesced in any one mode. But to a true minister, the argument of Fox does not apply. The truth seems to be, that the true priest, as he does not preach because he is paid, so neither can he be overpaid. His pecuniary support is gladly contributed and is well earned, and is well spent. Nor can it be of much consequence in what manner his maintenance arises, whether from contribution or assessment. The false priest is too costly, if we only give the time to hear him. So that the only mate-

---

[22] This passage is on loose sheets also.

rial question, is, that which Fox puts to the minister himself, — "That which thou speakest, is it inwardly from God?"

On the rites of Baptism and the Lord's Supper, the Society held an opinion consistent with the general tenor of their doctrine. But whilst they rejected the use of the outward ceremony, they disclaimed the wish to judge those who found benefit in them. But setting aside these single opinions, let it be the praise of his truth and devoutness, that, in all important particulars, his decisions have been confirmed by the voice of the wise and good ever since.

He and his friends made a resolute stand in the English courts for the religious liberty of the subject. Calmly they disputed every oppression inch by inch. He and his friends originated the party in modern times which contends for the principles of Universal Peace. He and his friends first pointed the attention of men to the mischief of extrajudicial oaths, and to the ethical question of the expediency of an oath. He and they directed attention to the subject of Prison Discipline.

Following in these steps the Society of Friends have honorably led in the two philanthropic works of our age, the Abolition of Slavery and the Suppression of Intemperance. And slowly and silently their opinions sifted by time have passed into the public opinion of mankind, and whilst the Society founded by Fox remains a sect they now hold almost no peculiar opinion.[23]

Such are some of the facts recorded and words spoken by this single hearted peasant. One cannot look at the course of the great charities and best institutions of our age without following back their swollen stream until it begins in the little rill of this individual life at Drayton-in-the-Clay in Leicestershire. Nor can any one who deserves the name of man contemplate such a life as this, and see to what power this man attained and what were the sources of his power, without thinking better and hoping better of the race of Man.

[23] End of insert.

6

Edmund Burke

The choice of a subject for the last lecture, delivered first on March 5, 1835 (*L*, I, 439n), was difficult and the labor of preparation more irksome than for any other lecture in the series. Burke's name does not appear in the lists that Emerson drew up before the series started (*J*, III, 351, 387), but it had been high on his roll of the great for many years. As early as 1824, a journal entry makes a comparative study of Charles James Fox, William Pitt, and Edmund Burke as three kinds of statesmen and awards to Burke the role of "philosophical statesman" (*J*, I, 317–320). His eloquence also had an appeal, as did that of Everett and Webster, and later references (*J*, II, 122–23, 354) show a continuing concern for him as representative of "the gladiators on our political arena, here and in England." During the period of preparation of the lectures Burke's name is mentioned first on December 27, 1834, in connection with the idea that "every great man does in all his nature point at and imply the existence and well-being of all the institutions and orders of a state" (*J*, III, 414). Obviously the role of statesman had less personal appeal for Emerson than did those of poet, philosopher, and religious leader, but there was a logic in including one such name. It is perhaps worth noting that the Concord Lyceum Record Book records a debate on February 11, 1835, in which Emerson defended the French Revolution as having done more good than harm (*Life*, p. 203; *J*, III, 448–49), while his journals for this period contain many vigorous defenses of political conservatism, both in national politics and in general (see esp. *J*, III, 248, 250, 256–57).

On March 2, 1835, three days before the lecture was to be delivered, he writes from Concord to Lydia Jackson that, in addition to a heavy cold, "two biographies of Burke with eight volumes of his works to read, mark, and inwardly digest" (*L*, I, 439) had delayed his correspondence. One of these biographies was the *Memoir* by James Prior, which he followed closely in his lecture. If he read another, the lecture shows no evidence of it. In four pages of notes for this lecture surviving in the "Tests" folder, Emerson refers to Prior and to the "Boston edition of Burke's Works" (1826), which was in his own library together with other volumes of Burke's writings (*Cf.* Cameron, I, 346n). We have no

183

record of library withdrawals that relate to Burke at this time with the exception of Thomas Moore's *Memoirs of Sheridan* (*Reading*, p. 22), also mentioned by Emerson in his notes.

EDMUND Burke was born in Dublin, January 1, 1730, and was educated at Trinity College. He was a good scholar and was noticed to be fond of being alone. He preferred Plutarch to almost any other of the ancient writers. Demosthenes was his favorite orator. He preferred the Aeneid to the Iliad. He set the highest value upon Shakspear [1] and Bacon's Essays. He came to London to study law at the age of twenty. He soon gave up law for literature and politics. He supported himself in London by his pen and made acquaintance with many distinguished men, impressing all such persons at the first acquaintance with lively curiosity and respect for his genius. He became a candidate for the professorship of logic at Glasgow without success. He was married in 1756. In 1756 he published his Vindication of Natural Society and his Essay on the Sublime and Beautiful which attracted notice from all men of parts.

In 1765 he was recommended to [the] Marquis of Rockingham as private secretary and entered Parliament through his interest and spoke in the House of Commons, for the first time in 1766 at the age of thirty-six years.

He immediately took the lead of his party as a debater in the House and devoted himself for twenty-eight years to the interests of the Whig Party according to his construction of their interests, which was with a latitude worthy of the power of Great Britain.

He supported the Americans. He introduced and carried a plan of Economical Reform. He procured the Impeachment of Warren Hastings, Governor General of India. He opposed in every manner, at every step the French Revolution and predicted its course with surprizing sagacity. He was rejected by the majority of his party on his separation from Fox and Sheridan on this question. He published in [1790] the Reflexions on the French

---

[1] Emerson's variant spellings are retained here and elsewhere.

Revolution which for its effect on its day and its permanent value has no rival among political tracts. He received liberal abuse from the revolutionists and all tributes of respect from the sovereigns of Europe and from the intelligent and virtuous of all classes. After a parliamentary career of twenty-seven years in which he had taken an active part in every measure of public [*sic*], he resigned his seat in Parliament in 1794. The British Government conferred a pension on him in 1795. The death of his son of whom he was extravagantly fond, soon after this, almost broke his spirit. But he continued in retirement to take a strong interest in the French affairs, and to communicate his thoughts thereupon to the ministers from time to time until his death in 1797 at the age of sixty-seven years.

The great variety of this man's accomplishments, the superiority of his genius to all competitors at that time or before or since in the same walks, and the nearness of our position even at this hour to him and the events which he studied, make it difficult to speak of him with confidence as a man whose claims Time the judge has considered and decided. Certainly it is not in the formal biographies of him that his merits have been determined. I can almost call a biography the admirable satire in Goldsmith's Retaliation which with the allowance to be made for satire, embodies so much truth in every line and word, that, trite as it is, I shall be pardoned for repeating it.

> Here lies our good Edmund whose genius was such
> We scarcely can praise it or blame it too much
> Who born for the Universe narrowed his mind
> And to party gave up what was meant for mankind . . .
> Though equal to all things for all things unfit
> Too nice for a statesman, too proud for a wit,
> For a patriot too cool for a drudge disobedient
> And too fond of the right to pursue the expedient
> In short twas his fate unemployed or in place sir
> To eat mutton cold, and cut blocks with a razor.[2]

The great contemporaries of this man who cooperated with him and outran him in the race of power and personal consider-

[2] From Prior, pp. 155-56.

ation in society he has long already left behind. The once sun-bright names of Fox and Pitt and Sheridan have become pale and faint. Burke once interested the politician as a supporter or opposer of these men. They now derive all their interest from their relation to him. They now plead their rival pretensions before a very different tribunal from the people of London or the majority of the Parliament. There is no caprice and no chance in the final award upon human merit. A dim, venerable Public decides upon every work and upon every man. When a new book or a new man emerges into consequence a sort of perplexity, an uneasy waiting for judgment appears in the minds of the spectators and most in those who are the oracles of the day, but the new pretender presently takes his true place by a force which no furtherance can help and no opposition can hinder, namely, by the real importance of his doing and thinking to the constant mind of man.[3]

It may be that the very perceptible connexion between the events which Burke influenced and those amidst which we live, does not suffer us yet to escape from all optical illusion, exaggerating this or that part of characters related to the American and French Revolutions, yet we shall endeavor to ascend to that verdict which is formed or forming upon his life in the permanent public opinion.

It has rarely happened in history that a philosopher by genius should be called to take any important part in the administration of affairs. Not only a prejudice often envenomed is against them among vulgar minds, but for the most part their own incapacity for action and strong disinclination to business forbids. The emperor Marcus Aurelius is an eminent and almost solitary example within the period of certain history of a philosopher on a throne. But that excellent Stoic was not an intellectual but a moral speculator. His studies were directed not to the search of new truth but to a sublime yet simple theory of duties. His studies were rather in religion than in philosophy so that he did not find a distraction in business but endeavored to execute on the throne the pious conclusions of his closet.

[3] "A dim, venerable, Public . . . mind of man" (*J*, III, 300). Cf. *W*, II, 154 and p. 212.

Nicholas Machiavel, who in the beginning of the sixteenth century served the Florentine state with great ability in various employments for many years chiefly at foreign courts and gave on some occasions valuable advice at home, is another example of a philosopher engaged in politics. But the Florentine territory was so narrow and its foreign relations so unimportant that his influence is too small to be taken into the account of European history.

Lord Bacon is the first conspicuous example of modern times of the philosopher in action. He certainly possessed an eminent ability in both kinds. To him was given a sight like that of an archangel into the Present and the Future. He saw things before they were yet out of the doors of their causes, and has left the most remarkable generalizations of the history of literature, of science, and even of social man that are on record. He is in a long series of generations the great Secretary of philosophy. At the same time he was all too skilful in much meaner arts. He was by taste and by practice a cunning statesman, preferring on every occasion the expedient to the right and very adroit in the use of all means to petty ends.

I hesitate to censure his great name. No single mind since Plato has enriched his fellowmen with so many of those truths which by their dignity and extent of application we incline to call laws. He has so anticipated the progress of thought that his opinions and words are quoted often unconsciously in every professor's chair as the Scriptures in the pulpit. I gladly admit that his age which not so much legally as virtually was a despotism was singularly unfavorable to independence of character in persons possessing great accomplishments so that his very gifts, his eloquence, his address, his learning, proved snares for him, and that he might have leave to produce before the world such wonderful properties he was servile, shamefully servile. But Bacon, though the Prince of Philosophers, left his philosophy when he entered into politics. In his connexion with affairs there is nothing valuable and much that is very disagreeable to remember. The House of Commons of which he was a member for twenty years occupied a subordinate and mean place compared with their successors in

187

the eighteenth century, and though upon some practical abuses his dexterity abated mischiefs without offending either the Court or the Commons, yet the King always possessed an irresistible influence over him and he presently sunk into a courtier.

Edmund Burke, another philosopher who entered the House of Commons in 1765, has some points of resemblance to both these men. He had the piety of the Roman Emperor, a sentiment of reverence to virtue that was omnipresent with him and pervaded and exalted every thing he did or said. But by position and by genius he had an intellect infinitely more comprehensive and minutely informed. He saw all things from his own point of view but in a glance that shot so far and grasped so much that particular objects still seemed to occupy their proportionate place, and whilst he magnified them they did yet not break the harmony of nature. The concerns of the Roman Empire great as they were cannot vie in complexity or extent with those of the British Government at this period. Despotism is simple and as yet the people were governed as a mass and did not insist on being considered as individuals.

He can even be compared to Bacon in some of Bacon's excellences. As wonderful was his mastery of language; as minute his observation upon manners, trades, arts, ceremonies; as great his address in the dispatch of business; as perfect the dependence of his imagination upon his Understanding, so far as composition is concerned. Not so masculine a judgment as Bacon who never multiplies words. Burke is diffuse. He cannot deny himself the pleasure of fully expanding all the particulars. Bacon draws his grand designs. Every word is as essential as a figure in a date. Burke draws his design and finishes and decorates and gilds every head. (Bacon's Political Tracts are much inferior to Burke's.) With Bacon in literature, with Bacon as an observer and legislator for the human intellect, Burke can never compare. Then Bacon seems to be merely a mouth for the soul of the World. But in the House of Commons and in the part taken by them in public affairs, the advantage is forever with Burke, not only as it seems to me in the sincerity with which the latter acted, but in the enlargement of his view and the fitness and grace of his execution. Bacon treats particular affairs like a lawyer, devises expedients, and considers all the facts; Burke treats his business as a piece of the world, and quitting temporary expedients seeks to harmonize it with the whole constitution of Society.

Bacon's philosophy deserts him in business. His general remarks sound formal and pedantic. Burke actually applies his philosophy in good faith to the point in question. He was favored, as I have remarked, by the immensity of the province he had to govern. The government administered by leaders of opinion [of] the English House of Commons in the close of the eighteenth century was so vast, so complicated by the variety of gross interests and still more by the resistless importance of individuals, that it had really become of importance to a philosopher on its own account. In the other cases the philosopher might forsake his study to get the profit and rank of a part in government. Now, the public business had arisen to that dignity as to solicit the philosopher. It offered him a field for his study, a work worthy of his faculties, to introduce method into so great masses of facts and to second the natural efforts at organization of time and wealth by the direct application of principles.

This is the position which he occupies in the last age, the *philosophical politician*, not a man who, quoting Latin and German, Aristotle and Hume, acted with a total disregard to general principles, — but one who, drawing from the same fountain with these theorists, brought principles to bear upon the public business of England.

But this view is subject to some limitations. Mr. Burke was never a philosopher in the highest nor in the lowest use of that term. He was never of the French School or the recent English Schools of politics, neither agrarian nor Utopian. He did not propose to satisfy the wishes of the majority as they are, with one class, nor to legislate for human nature as it ought to be, with Plato and Rousseau. He did not establish his theory of government in his chambers and then go into Parliament with the design to make the experiment of it on the British nation. He did not begin at this end. But led by a strong delight which he took in watching public affairs he spent his days in the gallery of the House of Commons long before he was a member of that body and studying intensely, as was his habit, the course of business, and the characters of public men, he soon became a proficient and afterwards a master in the facts. But nothing could come out of his mind in the state in which it went in. His mental activity quickened and arranged without transforming every fact, every event. Things fell in his mind into associations of a new and natural kind. That which he saw disordered, assumed order in his own thought.

And all men were amazed to see how rapidly the most heterogeneous business took in his own mind a certain shape of proportion and yet without misrepresentation or neglect of any parts. I speak now not of particular instances, though there are several in point, but of the general character of his usefulness: That it is a characteristic of this man's wisdom, that he did not take his theory as a basis, and force the facts into a conformity thereto, but he took the facts as the base and reduced them by the illumination of his genius into the best order which they themselves admitted, and, as it always seemed when he announced it, a natural and perfect order.

The light therefore in which he appears to us is as the Conservative of modern times; but this in an exalted and quite peculiar sense, the teacher of order, peace, and elegance; the adorner of existing institutions, but, combining therewith a fire of affection, and a depth of virtuous sentiment that add heroism to his wisdom.

But almost the uniform tendency of men of thought coupled with ardent temper has been to the freest institutions; has been democratic rather than royalist. What made Burke who, even in opposition, is yet conservative, lean so strongly to establishments?

There are many elements which appear in the life of Burke, that serve to explain this determination of his character, and show why his love of liberty and his fondness for theory, did not produce their usual effect by making him a radical Reformer.

And first, his exquisite Taste. As a general observation I suppose it will hold, that men of fine taste are not fond of revolutions. As Fontenelle said, "I hate War, for it spoils conversation," [4] so, Taste is pacific; the objects on which it is conversant only collect

[4] From Stewart, *General View*, p. 153.

themselves in quiet and stable communities. Books, poems, the drama, learning, architecture, painting, sculpture, elegant society, fine manners, of all these was Edmund Burke very fond and in them all very skilful. Calm times and monarchy have always been observed to favor them, and he looked with affection to the historical names and renowned laws of his country, under whose shadow he had found them. The particular regard he gave to these objects, demonstrates his attachment. He wrote a Theory of Taste. He was the intimate friend of Sir Joshua Reynolds and of Barry.[5] He has been supposed to have given assistance to the former in his lectures; to the latter he gave advice which seems to show his eye for art to have been equal to his ear for eloquence.

Moreover not the least of his talents was his skill in conversation. He taxed the powers of Johnson, who declared that Burke was the only great man whose conversation was equal to his reputation, adding that "no man could talk with him under an archway during a shower, without finding him out." [6] And England has probably never contained more brilliant circles than at that moment.

Another trait in the character of Burke which would engage him to the support of the existing order is the strength of his attachments. Solitary thinkers who avoid others and are avoided may come to reckon their opinions at so high a rate, as to think that society had better be disturbed than these not adopted. But men who love their friends and meet no acquaintance without complacency, set a very great value upon all that tends to good will. Burke's heart was the seat of all beautiful affections. He was happy in his domestic relations and so entire was his affection to his wife that he drew her character under the title of "the Perfect Wife" and he repeatedly declared that under all the exhaustions, defeats and mortifications of his career every care vanished the moment he entered under his own roof. He dearly loved children; he called them his men in miniature; he spun top and tetotum [7] with them or trundled them in a baby coach. He was indeed a fine example of that trait so often remarked in men of genius that Mr.

[5] James Barry (1741–1806), Irish historical painter.
[6] Johnson, quoted in Prior, p. 69; see also Coleridge, *The Friend*, III, 134.
[7] A four-sided toy, spun like a top in a game of chance.

Coleridge calls it a distinction and moral accompaniment of genius, to carry "the feelings of freshness of childhood into the powers of manhood." [8]

It is said that he had on his estate among his cattle some favorite cows, and an affecting incident has been preserved that after the death of his son he gave orders that an old horse formerly much used by his son should be turned out to feed at will and should not be worked or molested. One day walking in his grounds this horse approached him and after looking at him a moment put its head on his breast. Mr. Burke was so much affected that he put his arms round the animal's neck and hugged and kissed it, with tears.

But these are affections that whilst their tendency may be easily observed to order, may yet admit of a coldness toward remoter relations. But this man's heart was the altar of love and every manly virtue. Every thing that is known of him attests the grandeur and the gentleness of his sentiments. His kindness to Barry was infinite. He found him poor, friendless, and unknown at Dublin. He sent him to London and kept him at his own house, introduced him to the artists and procured him employment. With the aid of William Bourke he sent him to Italy for his professional studies and maintained him there, and more than this, wrote him letters of advice which do his sense and taste and delicate courtesy equal credit. The infirm temper of Barry never wore out Burke's patient love. He introduced Hickey, an Irish sculptor, to notice. Only recently the affecting tale has been told of Burke's goodness to the poet Crabbe.[9]

In 1780 Crabbe having ventured to come to London in the hope of succeeding as a poet was nearly starved. The booksellers refused his manuscripts. He applied for employment in vain; he had no friends and his case became desperate. It came into his head to write to Mr. Burke. He told him that he had given his note for seven pounds to his landlord for lodgings and must go to prison if not paid in a week, that he had no claim upon him but

---

[8] Coleridge, *The Friend,* I, 183; cf. *Biographia Literaria,* p. 55.
[9] George Crabbe (1754–1832). See Crabbe, *Life,* I, 93. Emerson's language shows that he also saw the review of this book in the *Quarterly Review.*

as a good and great man and begged him to forgive if he could not relieve him. He enclosed some verses in the letter and left it at Mr. B[urke]'s house in Charles Street. He could not return home to sleep: he walked backwards and forwards on Westminster Bridge all night. In the morning he called for his answer, and was told Mr. Burke desired to converse with him. "He entered the apartment," says the son of Crabbe, "obscure, desponding, his last shilling gone, threatened with the jail; he came out of it, — his fortune virtually secured, his genius acknowledged by one whose verdict was unquestionable." Mr. Burke established him under his own roof, introduced him to Fox, Johnson, Reynolds. "The Village" and "The Library" were published from hence and Mr. C[rabbe] was through Mr. Burke's influence appointed Chaplain to the Duke of Rutland.

His own fortune was small and he needed a strict economy to live as his habits of society required. Yet always was his house open to the friendless and the poor. It is known that one night he was accosted by a wretched female in the streets of whom he inquired her history and upon her promises of penitence brought her to his housekeeper and retained her under her care until an opportunity occurred of providing for her permanent employment and the woman was saved. I delight, I delight in contemplating these facts in the obscure private history of a man who in broad daylight was the wonder and the light of Senates and the avenger of the wrongs of America and Asia and Europe. He whose heart feels and whose hand relieves secret distress has a right to shed tears and to cause others to shed tears in public for the griefs of millions.

The affectionate, childlike sweetness of this man's temper which endeared to him his friends, his neighbors, his countrymen, naturally inclined him to take favorable views of the laws and the historical institutions of the state. May I add the remark made to me by an ingenious friend upon Burke's strong partiality for Establishments: That as in every civilized country a man is exalted by the courtesy and respect he pays to woman, so Burke felt that the wise and influential citizen is exalted by the honor he pays to whatever venerable or elegant institutions exist in the land. It was a chivalrous feeling which led him freely to bestow a protection which he might have withheld.

Meantime it was the natural effect of the same elevation of his sentiments that he was no vulgar conservative. Believing that in the British Constitution rightly administered would be found within this boundary a remedy for every mischief he was found a steadfast friend of liberty, of humanity, the redresser of wrong. The British House of Commons whilst Burke was in it was an asylum of the earth. Every cause of humanity found in him its lover and defender. The terrors of the Constitution he turned against every cruelty and selfishness.

I cannot resist the temptation of reading a passage from the speech for repealing the marriage act which contains a just expression of his equitable position in the state:

"I am accused of being a man of aristocratic principles. If by aristocracy they mean the peers, I have no vulgar admiration nor any vulgar antipathy towards them; I hold their order in cold and decent respect. I hold them to be of an absolute necessity in the constitution but I think they are only good when kept within their proper bounds. I trust whenever there has been a dispute between these houses the part I have taken has not been equivocal. If by the aristocracy, which indeed comes nearer to the point, they mean an adherence to the rich and powerful against the poor and weak, this would indeed be a very extraordinary part. I have incurred the odium of gentlemen in this house by not paying sufficient regard to men of ample property. When indeed the smallest rights of the poorest people in the Kingdom are in question, I would set my face against any act of pride and power countenanced by the highest that are in it; and if it should come to the last extremity, and to a contest of blood, God forbid; God forbid, my part is taken — I would take my fate with the poor and low and feeble. But if these people came to turn their liberty into a cloak for maliciousness and to seek an exemption not from power but from the rules of morality and virtuous discipline, then I would join my hand to make them feel the force which a few united in a good cause have over a multitude of the profligate and ferocious." [10]

[10] "Bill for Repg the Marriage Act" [E]. *Works*, V, 392.

The oppression by the Crown of the Americans stimulated him to his great exertions in their behalf. He was member for Bristol. A proposition to revise some oppressive restrictions on the trade of Ireland, he advocated earnestly. Bristol which with other trading towns found its own advantage in this oppression, called upon him to maintain her views. Mr. Burke refused to comply, and in consequence lost his reelection. The East Indians had been cruelly oppressed by the Company. Burke never ceased to fill the House with his indignation and entreaty until at last the Governor [11] was impeached and the opportunity given him to open the whole enormous history of Indian tyranny. So was it with his voice of warning against the contagious spirit of the French Revolution until he had turned the tide of public sentiment.

On all these, on all his questions he squandered himself as if each were his own cause. Never labor hindered him, never fear, never pride. He was the Presiding Manager on the part of the Commons in W[arren] Hastings' Trial. He had in his mind reserved the plunder of the Rajah of Benares and the Begums of Oude for his own great effort. Sheridan had set his heart upon the same. Burke, finding this to be so, without hesitation, resigned it into his hands, "thus proving the sincerity of his zeal for the cause, by sacrificing even the vanity of talent to its success." [12] So always was he lofty, disinterested, ardent. Selfish views he had as little as any. He steadily refused to notice any calumny. He shoved by the gilded hand of corruption and declined those advantages that only his clear honor forbad him to use. Too ardent was he for his own peace. For the cause, for the cause he would resign connexion, ambition, even friends like Fox.[13]

Such were the traits [which] swayed his mind originally and habitually towards the side of the existing order and at the same time made him from first to last a wise reformer. He brought to the service of his country the lights of his philosophy, the almost novel ability of treating business according to higher laws than the rules of office or the interests of party, and the additional aid

[11] Warren Hastings (1732–1818).
[12] "Moore Life of Sheridan" [E]. I, 488–89.
[13] Charles James Fox (1749–1806).

of an industry as indefatigable. The effects were proportionate. By an insight into principles he foretold with eloquent boldness the course and issue of the measures he opposed. Nobody regarded the prediction until day after day and month after month still fulfilled them. This abstract metaphysician soon became the oracle of the House upon the whole subject of Commerce. Adam Smith declared that Mr. Burke was the only man who had arrived at his conclusions without previous communication. The House soon found that in the hands of this wonderful person who rivalled Shakspear in his fancy and a banker or tradesman in his acquaintance with details every business became a text of political and economical philosophy; the Ministers and the Opposition were alike instructed and did not fail to profit continually of the lesson, though they neglected their teacher. His influence over the great leaders of the Whig Party was unbounded especially over Mr. Fox. For his wisdom and his labor and his fervor gave him a habitual ascendency. He is the author of the measures which they often conducted to an end. Finally on the outbreak of the French Revolution he foresaw and foretold not only the whole course but almost the single incidents with such memorable accuracy that he seems ever to speak on secret information, and he sounded such an alarm through England and the World that he raised up everywhere a hostile party and did more than any except the atrocities of the French themselves to destroy the influence of revolutionary principles in England.[14]

But a philosopher and a partisan — how did Burke reconcile such incongruous characters? His answer was, "When bad men combine, good men must associate." Innocency, he says, is not sufficient to a man in a situation of public trust. "Public duty demands and requires that what is right should not only be made known but made prevalent. . . . When the public man omits to put himself in a situation of doing his duty with effect, it is an omission that frustrates the purposes of his trust almost as much as if he had formally betrayed it. He is to carry his plans into execution by the whole power and authority of the state. As this power is attached to certain situations it is their duty to contend for these situ-

[14] *Reflections on the Revolution In France*, London, 1790.

ations." [15] In the Thoughts on the Present Discontents may be found at length his Theory of Party from which I have drawn these few lines.

Long afterwards, he wrote to the Sheriffs of Bristol a similar apology for himself. "The only method which has ever been found effectual to preserve any man against the corruption of nature and example is an habit of life and communication of councils with the most virtuous and public spirited men of the age you live in. Such a society cannot be kept without advantage or deserted without shame. For this rule of conduct I may be called a party man. In the way which they call Party I worship the constitution of your fathers. And I shall never blush for my political company. All reverence to honor, all idea of what it is, will be lost out of the world before it can be imputed as a fault to any man that he has been closely connected with those incomparable persons living and dead with whom for eleven years I have thought and acted." [16]

And always let it be remembered what were the charges alleged against him: not that he was venal; not that he was negligent; not that any stain was on his life; not that he was ambitious; not that he was oppressive. "No!" said he to the Electors, "the charges [against me] are all of one kind, that I have pushed the principles of general justice and benevolence too far; further than a cautious policy would warrant; and further than the opinion of man[y would go along with me.] In every accident which may happen [through] life, in pain, in sorrow, in depression and distress — I will call to mind this [accusation; and be comforted]." [17]

It is necessary to speak of the great organ which made these gifts available, the eloquence of Mr. Burke. Some one asked Johnson whether Burke did not resemble Tullius Cicero. "No sir," he replied, "he resembles Edmund Burke." [18] That entitles him to his reputation that he is a new and original person, in manner, act, and word, that he derived his inspiration from the facts themselves to which he spoke and not from vanity or selfish ends. At college

[15] *Works*, I, 423.
[16] *Works*, II, 118–19.
[17] *Works*, II, 258. This paragraph is hastily jotted on an inserted scrap of paper with the indicated omissions.
[18] From Prior, p. 450.

it is remembered he loved Demosthenes and one may easily see why in his own character, for "the lamp of Demosthenes never went out," neither did his own. When Epicles twitted the Athenian orator with the assidvity of his preparation for his harangue, he answered as Burke might have done, "I should be ashamed to speak what comes uppermost to so great an assembly."

It is said of Demosthenes that when one day his voice failing him, the people hissed, he exclaimed, "Ye are to judge of players indeed by the clearness and tuneableness of their voice but of orators by the gravity and excellence of their sentences." Mr. Burke, whose voice was harsh, and whose action was not graceful but forcible, and who gave a half support never, but threw his whole soul into his cause, might have well put in the same plea against the occasional caprice and weariness of his audience. There is even a striking parallelism in the anecdotes related of the effect produced by these two. Philip of Macedon in a moment of enthusiasm on hearing the report of one of his speeches from an earwitness exclaimed, "Had I been there, I too should have declared war against myself." [19] And Warren Hastings attested by a similar confession the force of Burke's harrowing description of the crimes of the monster Debi Sing by whom he charged the Governor General with having been bribed. "For half an hour," said Mr. Hastings, "I looked up at the orator in a reverie of wonder, and during that space I actually felt myself the most culpable man on earth." And the existing report of that speech is singular in all recorded eloquence for the horror and indignation it awakens.[20]

I think that the evidence remaining on this subject warrants us in believing that there were moments in Mr. Burke's life when he did embody the idea of eloquence, when he did fill the ear and mind and heart of his hearers and produce the perfect triumph of the orator which consists in the oneness of his audience. And I must say that when such a man as he was, accomplished this end

[19] References concerning Demosthenes are from "The Lives of Ten Orators: Demosthenes," Plutarch's *Morals*, V, 41, 47.

[20] "See Boston Edit. of Burkes Works Vol VII p. 202–5–Fifth Day" [E]. The reference is to an account of the entire trial proceedings. Emerson's quotation is from Prior, p. 283.

by such means as he used, then was shown an art that soared above all the praise of Demosthenes or of any civil orator.

But I confess I see no strong resemblance between the Athenian and the Englishman. The points of difference admit of being more strongly marked. The obvious character of Demosthenes is his abstemiousness. King Philip said that his orations were soldiers. Mr. Burke's might be called, wise men. And as much more effective as is a soldier than a wise man in this world in coming directly to his end, that is the difference between the success of Burke and that of Demosthenes.

But it is known that Burke with all his inexhaustible riches of learning, of wit, of fancy, and of practical information was listened to with impatience, with weariness, and sometimes was coughed down and hindered from addressing the House. The fact whilst it reflects infinite discredit upon the assembly is yet one that could never befal a perfect orator. To persuade is his vocation as much as to conquer is a general's. Demosthenes wrote on his own shield as a motto, Good Fortune.

We may distinguish three kinds of eloquence. The first [is] what is commonly distinguished as Natural Eloquence and resides chiefly in certain felicities of voice and manner. There are in almost every man's knowledge two or three examples [of] speakers who impart their conviction as if by heart to their audience and not by the mind; whom every body delights to hear and by whom every body is instantaneously persuaded, but with this defect, that the heart has been addressed and not the mind; no arguments have been used, no ground of facts shown, and when the hearer returns home intoxicated with excitement and venting himself in superlatives, he cannot recal a reason, a statement, scarce a sentiment even for the curiosity of inquirers. We have had some eminent examples of this talent in our own community.

There is another sort of public speaking which for its importance and effect is often called eloquence, that of the man who takes what he calls the practical view, that treats it as a question of business and contemptuously setting aside all sentiment and all general considerations as remote, exhibits one prudential aspect of the affair and neither enlightening nor obscuring, awakens no emotion but extorts votes.

Neither of these classes describe Mr. Burke's oratory. There is still another sort grown up in modern times which aims to elevate the subject to its highest pitch; which takes of it a manly view such as the reason of nations might well consider; which strives to put the subject into harmony with all particular and all general views and which draws arguments and illustrations from all regions of nature and art as if to show that all nature and all society are in unison with the view that is presented, which seeks to concentrate attention upon the facts but to consider them in accordance with the immense expansion in modern times of all the powers of society.

Of this school of philosophic eloquence whose traces are very visible even now in the British and American Senates Mr. Burke is the founder and head. That his speeches monuments of genius as they are should have fallen without proportionate effect no intelligent reader of them will wonder. Men have more heart than mind. Their very excellence stands in their way. Their pomp of wisdom and wit and mass of information fatigues the faculties of ordinary men. The Present and the Future are always rivals. Fox and Pitt and Sheridan reaped laurels in the House, for they reap none elsewhere. Burke, who spoke to the world, the House of Commons felt at liberty to disregard.

If it were worthwhile to push this analysis any further I should be tempted to say that only rarely does Mr. Burke rise to Eloquence; that if the word Rhetoric had not by misuse acquired a hollow sound he might be called a consummate Rhetorician, being a sort of artist or painter with words and so fond himself of the exercise of this peculiar talent that he cannot deny himself the delight of adorning with his beautiful sketches every name and topic how flat and obscure soever that he touches.

Grace is natural to him like the genius of the Greeks. And as some countenances are so beautiful that no distortion of making mouths can make them otherwise, so is he incapable of an inelegance. Whatever he touched he adorned. Whatever he has said can never be repeated with equal happiness. His will be the accepted formula for that sentiment. His naming a man is fame, for always the image of that man reappears in the dress Burke bestowed.[21]

Whether or not Mr. Burke judged wisely in the part he took on the French Revolution is the question on which most persons according as they answer it fix their views of him. That he judged wisely for his own time and country will be by most conceded. No doubt he was unconsciously biased by his taste and imagination. When he espoused the cause of liberty in America, America was empty of all things that could dazzle his love of right, no establishments, no priveleges. But in Europe the same question was not simple but complicated with ruin to ancient institutions, laws, nobility, priesthood, and crown. And these [were] menaced and uprooted with such ferocity in France that I suppose the boldest lover of freedom if he love virtue also might well hesitate to decide between the continuance of tyranny and the outrageous abuses of freedom.

I have offered I am aware a very inadequate sketch of the character and influence of Burke, a man who drawing from the fountainheads of wisdom and goodness, endeavored to make a little light in the dark and corrupt mazes of politics. And his endeavors were crowned with success. His biographers lament loudly the opposition and defeats he encountered, the omission on the part of the government to raise him to the peerage, and almost regret that he did not use the opportunities which were repeatedly in his hands of enriching himself at the expense of the state. But a more lasting victory, a better nobility, a richer estate is his. He was so great that he was content to win the cause and give others the praise. He was content to strengthen the law and serve himself; he was content to instruct the present and the future ages with the devotion of a hero and the modesty of a child.

[21] "Howard Grenville Townshend Chatham Fox" [E].

IV

ENGLISH LITERATURE

IN November of 1835, Emerson began a new series of ten weekly lectures before the Society for the Diffusion of Useful Knowledge at the Masonic Temple in Boston. The previous June, he had written F. H. Hedge, "In the winter I must give eight or ten lectures before the Diffusion Society," and adds that he is contemplating a book of essays, "chiefly upon Natural Ethics" (*L*, I, 447). Cabot implies that the subject was suggested by the Society and quotes Emerson in his first lecture as referring merely to his plan to talk "on topics connected with English Literature" (I, 238). The *Boston Daily Advertiser* of November 3 printed an outline of the course and announced subsequently the individual lectures for November 5, 12, 26; December 10, 17, 24, 31; and January 7 and 14, 1836, without giving titles to any but that on Chaucer. In an unpublished journal of 1835, there are notes indicating Emerson's sources and outlining the course (Journal "L").

At first glance, the manuscripts of these lectures, all of which have survived, seem to show even less originality than the previous series on biography. For factual information Emerson relied heavily on a few general sources like Thomas Warton's *History of English Poetry* and Sharon Turner's *History of the Anglo-Saxons*. Even the copious quotations from English authors with which the manuscripts are filled are, as often as not, taken from one of these general works rather than from the original text. Preoccupied as he was during the summer by his move to Concord, his second marriage, and invitations to deliver frequent sermons as well as the "Historical Discourse" at Concord's Second Centennial Anniversary of its founding, he apparently had insufficient time for careful preparation. In August, he had to pull his ideas together for the lecture on Correct Taste for the annual meeting of the American Institute of Instruction; the course itself did not allow much time out for preparation between lectures.

The topic of English Literature nevertheless turned out to be the most congenial that the lecturer had undertaken up to this time because it allowed him a greater degree of freedom for the development of his ideas. The trend of his mind away from a view of scholarship as a process of gleaning illustrations from the past as guides to present conduct and toward the search for truth in natural ethics, from the study of books to the study of ideas, from (as Coleridge had taught him to say) Understanding toward Reason, was apparent as an unresolved struggle throughout the series on Biography; in the series on English Literature, the solution begins to appear more clearly. His very carelessness about factual knowledge and the use of sources is a symptom of a shift of emphasis; it was accompanied by a compensating care that his own ideas should be original and clear. In all of these lectures, but particularly in the first and last, as well as in the first of the two on Shakespeare, the poet and ethical philosopher launched out into abstract speculation more than he had dared to do in a lecture before, with results that encouraged him to greater boldness in the future. This was the last series to take an informational topic as springboard for the development of general ideas. The next three were to be on The Philosophy of History, Human Culture, and Human Life. By September, 1836, he was ready to publish *Nature*, the personal testament which he had been planning ever since his shipboard meditations of three years before. Much of the chapter "Language" in *Nature* evolved in these discussions, as well as a section or two of "Idealism" and one of "Beauty."

There is evidence also that the lecturer was gaining in platform confidence and elocutionary skill as he discovered that his audiences would respond to the ideas in which he was himself most involved and to his quiet, natural manner of presentation. In an unpublished letter of November 7, 1835, Charles remarked to William, "but you and I know how the pill is gilt and sugared" (*Life*, 238n) and Cabot reports that one of his hearers of that time told him that she still remembered and associated with Emerson's voice and manner some verses of Crabbe which she then heard for the first time (I, 240). No verses of Crabbe appear in our manuscript but we find many other indications that Emerson used these lectures partly as the occasion for "readings" from a well-stocked memory. Many of the quotations (which we give virtually unedited) are clearly set down from memory and others look like mere notations for recitation. For his hearers, if not for us, the series had not only the interest of his reflections but the charm of his abiding love of literature.

Other evidence of the success of these lectures is found in the manuscripts themselves. More than any of the previous lectures (but less than the subsequent ones), they have been cut and pasted together in new combinations for second and third readings. In the spring of 1836, Emerson gave in Salem a series of "six or more" (surely no more) lectures on English Biography and Literature; some or all of them were read in Lowell (*Life*, 239); a page or two were even borrowed for the series of readings on "English Poetry and Prose" which he gave in 1869. The problem of reconstructing the text of these early lectures as it was first presented to an audience begins to become complicated in this series. To judge from the manuscripts, he cut out the third, fourth, and sixth lectures, and probably the first as well, for a later reading. Parts of the third and fourth went into Lecture 2; 5 absorbed 6 and was also at some time enriched from 1. On another occasion, one conjectures, he borrowed from 1 and 2 for 9. There is also evidence that he once read the lectures on Bacon and Luther in one series. The result is that the lecture manuscripts as they now stand contain several duplicate passages, which are here repeated only when they are substantially revised.

At the time he undertook this series, Emerson was well read in English literature, many of the source books being in his own library. While in England, for example, he had bought Jonson, Wotton, Mackintosh, and doubtless others. The lectures and notes show that he supplemented these with some further reading, particularly in Warton and Turner. This was the period when he was most immediately under the spell of Coleridge's philosophy, and there are many evidences of a close reading of *The Friend* and other volumes but no memory of his personal disillusionment upon meeting Coleridge at Highgate in 1833. Mme. de Staël, Carlyle,

Goethe, and the Swedenborgians continue to provide sidelights. With the move to Concord, he found himself in the congenial circle which included Alcott, Thoreau, Elizabeth Hoar, Ellery Channing, the frequent visitor Margaret Fuller, and others who were to be main spiritual supports for his long and productive years. As soon as these lectures were over he turned to the composition of his first book, published that September. With the announcement of his first wholly original course of lectures on The Philosophy of History for the winter of 1836–37, his period of apprenticeship as public lecturer drew to a close.

On the Best Mode of Inspiring a Correct Taste in English Literature

The invitation to deliver an address at the sixth annual meeting of the American Institute of Instruction in August of 1835 caught Emerson at a crowded moment in his schedule. Again George B. Emerson, who had been elected a Vice President of the Institute in 1834, was Chairman of the Committee of Arrangements (Cameron, I, 346n; *L*, I, 449). Apparently the date, which had originally been announced as August 22, was changed on Emerson's request at the last minute to August 20, even though his friend William Henry Furness had addressed the Institute on the morning of that date (see the *Boston Daily Advertiser* for August 3, 12, 20, and 21, 1835). The title here used appears on the manuscript and is that announced; Emerson had early mentioned, in a letter to Hedge, that he was to "read a discourse to the Institute on the means of inspiring a taste for English Literature — or some kindred topic" (*L*, I, 447).

With the series on Biography concluded the previous March, Emerson was already preparing for the new series on English Literature, which was to begin in November. He was also deep in his preparation for his long "Historical Discourse" at Concord, which was scheduled for September 12. To crowd his thought further he was negotiating for the Coolidge house, which he bought on August 15, and was arranging to marry Lydia Jackson on September 14. No wonder he felt that a suitable emblem for the scholar might be the camel with his four stomachs (*J*, III, 537) and that he agreed with Charles that the summer "is a galloping consumption, and the hectic rises as the year approaches its end" (*J*, III, 533). While studying and taking notes on Warton's *History of English Poetry*, he was also still reading Plutarch, Montaigne, Lyell and other echoes of his interests in science and great men. His spirits were high.

The surviving manuscript of this lecture is in some disorder, with three rather long passages sewn, at points where they have no proper place, into what would seem to be too short a text to be that of the complete lecture as delivered. Brief passages from this lecture were used in later essays. Cabot quotes from a biographical note of the Rev. Dr. Hague (Cabot, I, 232–35) his memory that the address opened "with a brilliant paragraph containing a parenthetic affirmation of the uselessness of prayer," a passage which has not survived if it was ever more than an extemporaneous aside. Although it was the practice of the American Institute of Instruction to print lectures which were delivered before it in a volume of Annual Proceedings, Emerson's lecture is mentioned but not printed in the volume for 1835. The volume for 1841 states that Emerson delivered a second lecture on English Literature (announced only as "Introductory") in that year. No separate manuscript of this second lecture has survived; it may have been a rereading of the introductory lecture to the series, or it may have been made up of passages from several lectures on the subject.

I confess, Gentlemen, I have not much confidence in the application of any mechanical means to promote a spiritual end.[1] As all the physicians of the world cannot manufacture one drop of blood, neither can all the colleges make one scholar nor the best library a reader. If the genius of a country is wholly averse to learning and so warlike, or commercial, or dissolute, that they cannot hear the voice of their wise men I have no hope that any expedients will cure their deafness. Nor when a boy's mind is wholly given to horses or to trade or to sailing a ship should I attempt to convince him of the value of the Novum Organon or the Lives of English Poets nor reason with the Northwest Wind. I should acquiesce in the order of Providence which divides labor better than we and appoints sailors and soldiers as well as poets from the cradle and makes strong hands separate from strong heads. There are no doubt limits to these natural tastes and extraordinary conversions late in life which have brought the eminent in one class to eminence in the other, but the rod of this metamorphosis God holds in his own hand and does not make them so probable as to warrant our interference to forward changes of this sort. I see nothing to hinder us from accepting the general conviction of men that we cannot make scholars. They must be born.

Admitting this fact, which being expressed in other words is a canon of philosophy, that a truth or a book of truths can be re-

---

[1] The manuscript suggests several false starts before this one, including a long passage which is printed in the textual notes.

ceived only by the same spirit that gave it forth,[2] society divides itself into two classes in reference to any influences of learning:

1. The natural scholars, though now hindered by unfavorable circumstances from the knowledge of their powers and calling.

2. The much larger class in the community who bestow their leisure on those employments to which the custom of the day gives importance, those who if born in a military age would be soldiers in a trading community become speculators, and in a reading community become men of letters.

The main action of every lover of letters will of course be spent on the first of these classes. In bringing a scholar into acquaintance with himself and his proper objects we render all men such a service as he does to an army who nominates Washington or Napoleon to the Command in chief. Every suggestion that bears on this end has value.

Yet here again if we would not deceive ourselves we must content us with the stern simplicity of the means to which the Nature of the Mind confines us and believe that all concert or ingenious expedients or urgent appeals are quite insignificant — the one great means to be relied on is the bringing the man into acquaintance with the books. Life has few pleasures so pure and deep as that with which we sit down to read a new book of a favorite and venerated author. And I know few more agreeable offices in the opportunities of common life than to introduce a good mind to the writings of a kindred intelligence. It must be our main object to consummate this marriage between the mind of the scholar and the mind of the author. Literature resembles religion in many respects and their fortunes have been commonly related. It must be possessed by the man or it is naught. Sciolists are never nearer scholars than hypocrites are to saints.

If this is our only proper aim, to make ingenuous persons acquainted with the wealth of their mother tongue, it behoves all of us who by position or by profession have any supervision of education, to weigh the considerations which fall under this view.

The Instructor should consider that by being born to the in-

[2] Cf. p. 170 and Nature, W, I, 35. Attributed by Emerson to George Fox (J, II, 498; cf. 358; III, 225). He first heard it, perhaps, from Sampson Reed (Cameron, II, 26).

heritance of the English speech he receives from Nature the key to the noblest treasures of the world in the native and translated literature of Great Britain and America. I think the first step towards producing a revolution in our state of society would be to impress men's minds with a deep persuasion of the fact that the purest pleasures of life were at hand unknown to them; that whilst all manner of miserable books swarm like flies in the land, the fathers of counsel and of heroism lie neglected; care is not taken to bring them into the country. It cannot be doubted that they are little known. The farmer in winter kitchen, the maid in her chamber that love to read Milton and Thomson and Young without knowing they are literature are the true knowers, worth all study [?].

It will fortify him in his convictions and in his teaching the young, with whom always authority goes far, to observe the firm laws that determine literary reputation, to observe that there is no luck in literary reputation, but that a public not to be bribed and not to be entreated and not to be overawed, decides upon every man's fame. Only those books come down which deserve to last. Blackmore, Pollock, Bulwer may endure for a night but Homer and Moses last forever. There are not at any time in the world apparently more than a dozen persons who read and understand Plato; never enough to pay for an edition of his works; yet to every generation they come down, as if God brought them in his hand. And so with all sterling books, their permanence being fixed by no love or hatred but by their own specific gravity or the intrinsic importance of their thoughts to the constant mind of man.[3]

The teacher may well reflect that no man can teach more than he knows, or inspire a taste which he has not himself. Therefore let him acquaint himself with these treasures; let him mark, learn, eat, and digest these books as Scriptures approved by the voice of Human Nature in several ages. They shall be sweet in the mouth and sweet in the belly. These let him read to the exclusion of the crowd of mediocre writers. Multum non multa (Aphorism of Aquinas). The Persians read Hafiz, the Chinese Confucius, the Spaniards Cervantes. If the English should lose all but Shakspear,

---

[3] Cf. W, II, 154.

Milton, and Bacon the concentrated attention given to those writers might atone for all.

Let him consider that which belongs to literary discipline, an object of the first importance to every scholar. Dr. Johnson said, "Whilst you stand deliberating which book your son shall read first, another boy has read both. Read anything, five hours every day, and you will soon be knowing."[4] If you should read the same number of lines that you read in a day on the newspapers in Hooker's Ecclesiastical Polity or in Hume and Clarendon, Harrington[5] and Burke how few months would suffice to the examination of all the great British authors! Much of the difficulty that is supposed to hinder good learning is purely superstitious as for example the idle complaint of the number of good books.

Books are like the stars in the sky which seem innumerable but begin to count them and they diminish apace. There are scarce a dozen of the first magnitude. If you approach the study of European History it seems to be a library by itself. But the great facts are soon mastered. The feudal institution and the Saxon laws and customs by their union or opposition explain the earlier eras. And the life of Charles V and his contemporaries is the Eye of modern times. I have not the presumption to contemn the endless research of painful antiquaries. I only venture the opinion that study of these subjects is better than wide reading. So in English literature a very few names, Chaucer, Spenser, Shakspear, Bacon, Milton and Taylor, are a class by themselves that for mere number of volumes need never appal the readers of Southey and Scott. And to him who has read these books what remains to be read like them? For the second class of the same age, Ben Jonson, Herbert, Herrick, Marvell, Cowley, Cudworth, Dryden. And for the third, Pope, Addison, Swift, Hume, Butler, Johnson, Gibbon, Smith.

Let him read no mean books. The great and only true economy of time is not to do any thing unfit for you to do. Shun the newspaper, shun the spawn of the Press on the exciting topics of the

---

[4] See Boswell's *Life*, July 14, 1763. *Cf.* the essay on "Books" in *Society and Solitude* (*W*, VII, 194).

[5] Edward Hyde, Earl of Clarendon (1609–1674), author of *The True Historical Narrative of the Rebellion and Civil Wars in England*, 1704; Sir John Harington (1611–1677), political philosopher, author of *Oceana*, 1656.

day, for these things you shall learn in the street and in the stage-coach and save your time and your temper.[6]

And with these facts in his mind let him communicate to young men that which he has collected. Would you inspire in a young man a taste for Chaucer and Bacon? Quote them to him. Fear not to be like him who carried a tile as a sample of his palace; for the parallel does not hold unless the tile which the clown carried had been a diamond. It is a law of Wit that whoso can make a good sentence can make a good book. And to read a sentence of Hooker or Bacon is like offering a lump of gold as specimen of a mine or an apple to denote the quality of the tree; which would be right. Let the truths which we owe to Bacon and Taylor be communicated and let him judge of the writer not as a faultfinder but by the delight which is the proper attendant of great sentiments and profound observations.

No wise man thinks meanly of a book. These ships that sail in the sea of Time are the benefactors or the enemies of mankind. Nothing is more natural than the terror of the Southern planter at a Tract and nothing more vain than his resistance. They rend and they establish empires.

A good book is like the Ancient Mariner who can tell his tale only to a few men destined to hear it. It passes by thousands and thousands but when it finds a true reader it enters into him as a new soul. A good reader is rare. As we say translations are rare because to be a good translator needs all the talents of an original author so to be a good reader needs the high qualities of a good writer. Reading must not be passive. The pupil must conspire with the Teachers. It needs Shakspear, it needs a Bacon, to read Shakspear and Bacon in the best manner.[7]

When I have owed that pure feeling which we call the moral sublime to any writer I am not likely to forget his name or to doubt his genius. If the student could be accustomed to look in books for things then would he be competent to condemn the book in which he only found words. He should go to the book with the laws of the world in his mind and expecting to find the

---

[6] Cf. *W*, VII, 196.
[7] See textual notes.

page but a transcript of what he knows in nature. He expects there to find a refined nature or, in the words of Aristotle, *all of nature but the matter*.[8] Then an exact criticism is pertinent. When books are read in quest of the great laws of life and sentiment, then just judgments of them, of their style and method, will be formed. Let the power of his Author to impart instruction and raise happiness be the measure of his ability. Accustom the pupil to a solitude not of place but of thought. Entirely wean him from traditionary judgment. And will you not save him wholly that barren season of discipline which young men spend with the Aikins and Ketts and Drakes and Blairs [9] acquiring the false doctrine that there is something arbitrary or conventional in letters, something else in style than the transparent medium through which I should see new and good thoughts? Let him learn how false is the vulgar belief that in good writing anything else could be said than that which is said. I should aim to show him that the poem was a transcript of Nature as much as a mariner's chart is of the coast; that there was nothing arbitrary in the choice of words; that the pen of the true poet was guided by laws as rigorous as the pencil of the draughtsman.[10]

In presenting these considerations I have only in view the education of true scholars. They exist like ore in the mine wherever is society and we do the part of good citizens whenever we find one in the obscurity or when we train one more happily born.

Of inventions and contrivances to aid us, I have already stated I have no hope from them. The only mechanical means of importance which we have not, is cheap editions in good type but on cheapest paper of the best authors: Bacon, Milton, Shakspeare, Taylor. I should be glad to see cargoes of these books sailing up the Missouri and Red river and the bales unloaded by the half Indian hunter of the west prairie. Let them go out as magnets to find the atoms of steel that are in the mountains and prairies. For there are native poets and philosophers and I would give them a chance of being reached.

[8] See Cudworth, I, 336.

[9] Probably John Aikin (1747–1822), Nathan Drake (1766–1836), British critics; Henry Kett (1761–1825), minor Oxford wit; and Hugh Blair (1718–1800), author of *Lectures on Rhetoric and Belles Lettres*, 1783, an assigned text in Emerson's Harvard.

[10] Cf. *Biographia Literaria*, Chapter I, p. 11.

Another want that literature feels in this country is that of society. It is left altogether to the chance of private acquaintance and we have no effective literary associations. If something like union of like minded men were attempted, as formerly at Will's and Button's Coffee houses, where the wits of London assembled to hear the talk of Addison and Dryden, or in the back room of the bookseller's shop,[11] places where the scholar might come to utter himself to scholars without passing the piquet and guard posts of etiquette, it would add happy hours to the year. The want of fellowships in our colleges bereaves the University of that advantage of always affording a number of literary associates.

In these remarks I have confined myself to the single view of what should operate on scholars, for these make the lifeblood of the literary republic. I do not think it was designed that all should hold the pen any more than that all should hold the helm, or weave, or sing, or paint. Yet I think every man capable of some interest in literature; and I think it concerns the welfare of society that letters should occupy that subordinate place which if they do not fill arms or horses or huckster or riot will. For it is the most wholesome and honorable of all recreations. There is we know a contagion which affects communities and a whole generation and if the study even to idolatry of wise and learned men can be as it has been the object of this sympathy in lieu of War, Antimasonry,[12] or Commercial bubbles so much the better for the state.

There have been as we know periods of intense activity of the mind. The zeal which fired the nation's leaders was shared by all. A principle like a great wave bore up an entire generation upon its swell. And the tendency of exciting political events to send men to first principles, to pass out of all the nooks and continents of gain and expediency to the abstractions of reason, has made the names of Milton and Spenser popular in a Revolution.

[11] Many American publishers like John Wiley in New York, Matthew Carey in Philadelphia and James T. Fields in Boston encouraged authors to frequent the back rooms in their bookshops for literary discussions.

[12] The Anti-Masonic Party held its first and only convention in 1831.

1

English Literature: Introductory

The Boston series on English literature opened on November 5, 1835 with an introductory lecture, merely so announced, on the theory of literature in general. Cabot supplies the title "Introduction" and a generous summary of its contents (II, 716), which Cameron expands in detail and thoroughly annotates (I, 348–352), quoting also some notes headed "What is literature?" from Emerson's manuscript journal "L" (1835). The manuscript itself has no title, but the word "Introductory" appears in Emerson's hand on its cover.

The full text of the lecture as first given can probably not be accurately determined, as Emerson worked hard on this first statement of some of his basic ideas and subsequently used the result, not only for future lectures, but for *Nature* and other writings. In preparation he rewrote passages, used them again with amplification in a revision of a similar statement in his first lecture on Shakespeare (q.v.), then reworked the material for his chapter "Language" in *Nature*. A few sentences from the last paragraph were used much later in the Preface he supplied, with Cabot's help, for *The 100 Greatest Men* (Boston: Sampson, Low and Company, 1879). A version of this lecture may have been that read in 1841 before the annual meeting of the American Institute of Instruction and parts or all of it were doubtless included in the series read at Salem and elsewhere.

I am not so presumptuous as to undertake to present in this course of lectures a complete View of English Literature. There is no History of English Literature. Perhaps few men in this country are competent to such an enterprize. Our discipline in books is not extensive enough and is not exact and profound enough. But whoever is able, I am not. I have not read all the books that are popularly included under that name. Far less can I persuade myself that I understand the true place in history which each writer occupies, or know the master thought which is the key to his genius. At the request of the Society, I have attempted to prepare a course of lectures "on topics connected with English Literature." I shall endeavor in the present Discourse, by defining the nature and aim of Literature, and the interest which human nature has in it, to show how large a field of inquiry it opens, to show at once the attractions and the dangers of the road.

What is Literature? The name is derived from letters those cunning ciphers, the swarthy daughters of Cadmus,[1] by whose aid man gives perpetuity to his fleeting thoughts, by whose aid the delicate song with which an Eastern poet beguiled an hour thirty-five centuries ago, is preserved to us, line for line, and word for word, across so many perished empires, institutions, and generations. And the word Literature has an extent of meaning conformed to this etymology.

Literature, in its largest sense, is, the books that are written. It is the recorded thinking of man. It contains the utterance of man upon all knowables.

It has its deep foundations in the nature and condition of man. There is no accident or chance in its most fugitive line, but every form of composition, the epic, the novel, the history, and every song and chorus, and wild ejaculation, is holden and determined by firm laws. A man thinks. He not only thinks, but he lives on thoughts; he is the prisoner of thoughts; ideas, which in words he rejects, tyrannize over him, and dictate or modify every word of his mouth, every act of his hand. There are no walls like the invisible ones of an idea. Against these no purpose can prosper or so much as be formed. Rebellion against the thought which rules me is absurdity. For I cannot separate between me and it.[2]

Such are the ideas of God, order, freedom, justice, love, time, space, self, matter. It will be admitted that a man cannot take these in his hand and amuse himself with them as counters. He cannot exclude them from his mind. There they shine with their everlasting light upon him do what he will. He may wish them

[1] Founder of Thebes, who was said to have brought the Phoenician alphabet of sixteen letters to Greece.

[2] For "Emerson's Outline" in manuscript journal "L," see Cameron, I, 348.

away, he may make mouths at them. But their reality is never the less. They intrude into his dreams, and, compared with their fixity and stability, his being is a dream and a shade. Without going at present into the distinction between Ideas and notions,[3] it is sufficient to allude to these particular ideas of Freedom, Virtue, Love, that I may intimate the fact that certain invisible natures are to him the firmament itself of his being, are the powers whose divine despotism destroys all unbelief before it, and even man himself shrinks into a mere spectator, utterly insignificant in the presence of these magnificent laws.

The Ideas in every man's mind make him what he is. His whole action and endeavor in the world is to utter and give an external shape to those thoughts. He may deny them in words, and still he will serve them. He says there is no God; but every act and word proves his underconsciousness that he and all things are derived from a wisdom and firm law. He says he is not free; but every act proves his consciousness of freedom. Then his whole life is spent in efforts to create outside of him a state of things conformed to his inward thoughts. Observe how every belief and every error — each a thought in some man's mind — clothes itself with societies, houses, cities, language, ceremonies, newspapers. Observe the Ideas of the present day, — Orthodoxy; Skepticism; Missions; Popular Education; Temperance; Antimasonry; Antislavery. See how each of these abstractions has embodied itself in an imposing apparatus in the community; and how timber, brick, lime, and iron have flown into convenient shape, obedient to the master idea reigning in the minds of many persons.

Of the various ways in which man endeavors to utter the great invisible nature which gives him life, the most perfect vehicle of his meaning is Language. Let us consider how this is formed.

Everywhere we find man surrounded by the same company, that is, by what he calls Nature. He dwells with the multitude of his fellows; or alone in the misty fields; wet by the rains, pinched by the frost, cheered by the heat. Over him are the sun and moon; at his feet is the sea; around him are the mountains: the atmosphere embraces him in its soft arms. The stars shine on him with

[3] Emerson alludes here to a passage in Coleridge's *Stateman's Manual*, pp. 31–32.

pleasing light; beasts, fire, water, stones, and corn serve him. By continually dealing with these mute and brute natures he learns to make them more useful. Many of the great objects of nature, he is so weak he cannot use, nor explore. But in their friendly company, the little stranger finds himself, every day, more at home, and more skilful.

But the objects without him are more than commodities. Whilst they minister to the senses sensual gratification, they minister to the mind as vehicles and symbols of thought. All language is a naming of invisible and spiritual things from visible things. The use of natural history is to give us aid in supernatural history. The use of the outer creation is to give us language for the beings and changes of the inward creation. Every word which is used to express a moral or intellectual fact, if traced to its root, is found to be borrowed from some corporeal or animal fact. *Right* originally means *straight*; *wrong* means *twisted*. Spirit primarily means *wind*. Transgression, the *crossing a line*. Supercilious, the *raising of the eyebrow*. Light and heat in all languages are used as metaphors for wisdom and love. We say the heart to express emotion; the head to denote thought: and "thought" and "emotion" are in their turn mere words borrowed from sense, that have become appropriated to spiritual nature. Most of this process is now hidden from us in the remote time when our language was framed, but the same tendency we may observe now in children and in new words. Children and savages use only nouns or names of things, and continually convert them into verbs, and then apply them to some analogous mental act. Every truth we can learn concerning our Ideas, we find some symbol for, in outward nature, before we can express it in words. "And but for these emblems furnished by Nature herself, the moral and metaphysical world would have remained entirely buried in the eternal abyss." [4]

But this origin of all words that convey a spiritual meaning is only a small part of the fact. It is not words only that are emblematic: it is things which are emblematic. Every fact in outward nature answers to some state of the mind and that state of the mind can only be described by presenting that natural fact as a picture.

[4] "Oeggr" [*sic*] [E]. See Bibliography and Cameron, II, 87.

INTRODUCTORY

A fierce man is a lion; a brave man is a rock; a learned man is a torch. Light and Darkness are not in words but in fact our best expression for knowledge and ignorance. Who looks upon a river in a meditative hour, and is not reminded of the flux of all things? Throw a stone into the stream, and the circles that propagate themselves, are the beautiful type of all influence.

All the facts in Natural History taken by themselves have no value, but are barren and unfruitful like a single sex. But marry it to human history and it is full of life. Whole Floras, all Linnaeus' and Buffon's volumes are but dry catalogues of facts; but the most trivial natural property, the habit of a plant, the organs or work or noise of an insect applied to the illustration of a fact in intellectual philosophy or even associated to human nature affects us in the most lively and agreeable manner.[5]

It certainly will not be alleged that there is anything fanciful in this analogy between man and nature, when it is remembered that savages converse by these figures. In the writers in the morning of each nation such as Homer, Froissart, and Chaucer every word is a picture. As we go back in history, language becomes more picturesque, until its infancy, when it is all poetry; or, all spiritual facts are represented by natural symbols. The eldest remains of the ancient nations are poems and fables. And even now, in our artificial state of society, the moment our discourse rises above the ordinary tone of facts, and is inflamed with passion, or exalted by thought, it immediately clothes itself in images. Indeed if any man will watch himself in conversation, I believe he will find he has always a material image more or less luminous arising in his mind contemporaneous with every thought, [which] furnishes the garment of the thought.[6]

All poets, orators, and philosophers have been those who could most sharply see and most happily present emblems, parables, and figures. How much has a figure, an illustration, availed every sect, — as when the reabsorption of the soul into God was anciently figured by a phial of water broken in the sea. Jesus conversed in

[5] For this paragraph, see *J*, III, 326–27.
[6] "The use of natural history . . . garment of the thought" (*W*, I, 25–31). For the last sentence, cf. *J*, III, 227. A revision and expansion of this passage is in "English Literature," Lecture 5, p. 290.

221

parables. Plato, Luther, and Bacon scarcely less. All the memorable words of the world are these figurative expressions. "I see a chasm in the place of France," said Burke. Mirabeau remarked, "It is the chasm of a volcano." [7] Good writing and brilliant discourse are perpetual allegories. The imagery in discourse which delights all men is that which is drawn from observation of natural processes. It is this which gives that piquancy to the conversation of a strong natured farmer or backwoodsman which all men relish.[8] It is the salt of those semisavages, men of strong understanding, who bring out of the woods into the tameness of refined circles a native way of seeing things, and there speak in metaphors. "I showed him the back of my hand," said a backwoodsman, for *I broke friendship with him.* "We put finger in the eye," for childish complaint.

The strong humor of Jack Downing's letters has not contributed so much to their popularity as the just natural imagery in which all the thoughts are presented.[9]

Examples might be produced to any extent to show this habit of mind in the great writers. A few from the poets will suffice. Homer describes the terrible approach of Apollo to the Greeks: "He came like the Night." When his hero is down in the battle: "He fell as the great ash falls in the mountains and his arms crashed over him." Milton describes Proserpine gathering flowers in Enna, "Herself a fairer flower by gloomy Dis was gathered." [10]

> Within the infant rind of this small flower
> Poison hath residence and medicine power . . .
> Two such opposed foes encamp them still
> In man as well as herbs grace and rude will . . .

> Oh how much more doth beauty beauteous seem
> By that sweet ornament which truth doth give
> The rose looks fair but fairer we it deem
> For that sweet odour which in it doth live
> The cankerblooms have full as deep a die
> As the perfumed tincture of the roses

[7] Source unknown.
[8] For this sentence, see *W*, I, 29.
[9] Seba Smith, *Letters . . . . by Myself, Major Jack Downing*, 1833.
[10] *Paradise Lost*, IV, 270–71.

Hang on such thorns and play as wantonly . . .
But for their virtues only is their show
They live unwoo'd . . .

How like a younker and a prodigal
The scarfed bark puts from her native bay
Hugged and embraced by the strumpet wind
How like a prodigal doth she return
With overlabored ribs and weathered sides
Lean rent and beggared . . .[11]

Milton gives manly form to the abstraction of a state: "Methinks I see in my mind a noble and puissant nation rousing herself like a strong man after sleep and shaking her invincible locks (the laws): methinks I see her as an eagle muing her mighty youth and kindling her undazzled eyes at the full midday beam." [12] When Philip Van A[rtevelde] hears that Cassel has revolted, after the loss of Courtray, Thorout, and two other cities, he slights the new calamity:

> And for this forsooth
> What is it but that we are in the moult
> And here's a feather fallen.[13]

Hope and fear alternate swayed his breast
Like light and shade upon a waving field,
Coursing each other as the flying clouds
Now hide and now eclipse the sun.[14]

Not she: she tempts me not: tis I
Who, lying by the violet in the sun
Do as the carrion does, not as the flower
Corrupt with virtuous season.[15]

Mr. Burke happily compared the attempt of the British parliament to extort taxes from the hardhanded American farmers [to] an attempt to shear the wolf.[16]

---

[11] *Rom. and J.*, II, 3: 23–24, 27–28; Sonnet 54; *Merch. of V.*, II, 6: 14–19.
[12] "Areopagitica," Symmons, I, 324.
[13] Sir Henry Taylor, *Philip van Artevelde*, London, 1835, p. 191.
[14] "Douglas" [E].
[15] *Meas. for M.*, II, 2: 167–170.
[16] Cf. *J*, III, 510, 512, and *J*, IV, 24.

All reflexion goes to teach us the strictly emblematic character of the material world. Especially is it the office of the poet to perceive and use these analogies. He converts the solid globe, the land, the sea, the sun, the animals into symbols of thought: he makes the outward creation subordinate and merely a convenient alphabet to express thoughts and emotions. This act or vision of the mind is called Imagination. It is that active state of the mind in which it forces things to obey the laws of thought; takes up all present objects in a despotic manner into its own image and likeness and makes the thought which occupies it the center of the world. Lear thinks no evil can come to any man but through daughters. The intensity of thought gives the speaker the right to take hold of every high and vast thing as in common moods he uses familiar and trivial objects to explain his meaning. Lear, again feeling himself in his hoary hairs outraged, appeals to the heavens:

> O heavens if you do love old men if your sweet sway
> Allow obedience — if yourselves are old
> Make it your cause.[17]

And not less readily does it seize a resemblance in the small and obscure and dignify the object by uniting it to its emotion. The sublime author of the apocalypse in his great vision of the destruction of the world says, "The stars shall fall from heaven as the figtree casteth her untimely fruits." [18]

It is the standing problem which has exercised the wonder and the study of every fine genius since the world began, from the Egyptians and the Brahmins, through Pythagoras, to Plato, to Bacon, to Leibnitz and Swedenborg. There sits the Sphinx at the roadside and from age to age as each prophet comes by, he tries his fortune at reading her riddle.[19] It will no doubt be the effect of wiser and better times, if such earth shall ever see, to open the primitive sense of the permanent objects of nature, that so, all which the eye sees, may be a legible book in which every form, alone, or in composition, shall be significant.

Now, man standing on the point betwixt spirit and matter

[17] *Lear*, II, 4: 192–94.
[18] Revelation 6:13.
[19] "It is the standing . . . her riddle" (*W*, I, 34); cf. *J*, III, 525.

and native of both elements, only knows in general that one re-pre-sents the other; that the world is the mirror of the soul; and that it is his office to show this beautiful relation, to utter the oracles of the mind in appropriate images from nature. And this is Liter-ature. In a limited sense Literature, so far as it is pictures of thought, and excluding records of facts, is, the clothing of things of the mind in the things of matter.

I have said, *excluding records of facts*, that is, science and history. But Science goes to show what nature is and so read one side of the riddle. And for History, if I may be pardoned for fol-lowing out still one step farther the Theory of Literature, it should be added, that besides the instinctive belief we have of a strict analogy between the world and the mind, we have yet another in-stinctive belief, that there is a still higher harmony of *events with Nature*. Men have begun to study the philosophy of History, in the belief that Man acting under the control of Ideas, even the seemingly capricious workings of the Will may be found har-monious in long periods.

Every thing to be appreciated must be seen from the point where its rays converge to a focus. The most gorgeous landscape, the softest tinted clouds, what would they be, if I should put my eye to the ground? a few pebbles; or into the cloud? a fog. So of human history and of our own life. We cannot get far enough away from ourselves to integrate our scraps of thought and action, and to judge of our tendency and scope. We are in the battle and cannot judge how the day is going, much less of its picturesque effect.

Yet is there an inextinguishable conviction in the human mind that in the great Universe which bears us as its fruit and by which we are subdued and subordinated, the best is always done; the good of the whole is evolved, the discordant volitions of men are rounded in by a great and beautiful necessity so as to fetch about results accordant with the whole of nature, peaceful as the deep heaven which envelopes him, and cheerful as the green fields on which the sun finds him. Over men the purposes of Providence are thrown like enormous nets enclosing masses without restrain-ing individuals.

Here whilst acting and suffering the human mind endeavors evermore to compose its commentary upon events as the march of society proceeds, to record facts and thoughts, its joy and pain. So is the aim and effort of literature in the largest sense nothing less than to *give voice to the whole of spiritual nature* as events and ages unfold it, to record in words the whole life of the world.

Such is in general terms the nature and aim of Literature.

What interest have men in it? Is it made for a few? Is it made only for the Makers? Who are the Makers? and for whom do they work? What service is rendered us by the Thinker, or man of letters, and in what manner?

It is in the nature not of any particular man but of universal man *to think*; though the action of reflexion is very rare. The relation between thought and the world, of which I have spoken, is not fancied by some poet, but stands in the will of God, and so is free to be known by all men. It appears to men, or it does not appear.[20] But there it is. He who perceives it, and every man, whilst he perceives it, is a poet, is a philosopher. To perceive it, is to take one's stand in the absolute, and consider the passage of things and events purely as a spectacle and not as action in which we partake. This the poet, this the philosopher, this the historian does. The habit of men is to rest in the objects immediately around them, to go along with the tide, and take their impulse from external things. The Thinker takes them aside and makes them see what they did as *in dumb show*.

This is the familiar philosophy of us all. Custom is the defacer of beauty, and the concealer of truth. Custom presents every thing as immoveably fixed. But the first effort of thought is to lift things from their feet and make all objects of sense appear fluent. Even a small alteration in our position breaks the spell and removes the curtain of Custom. Thought is excited by seeing the shore from a ship, a balloon, or through the tints of unusual sky. The least change in our point of view gives the whole world a pictorial air. A man who seldom rides, has only to get into a coach and ride through his own town and what a ludicrous and pathetic picture

---

[20] "The relation between thought . . . not appear" (W, I, 33–34).

do the common streets present! The men, the women, talking, running, bartering, fighting, the earnest mechanic, the lounger, the beggar, the boys, the dogs, are unrealized at once, or at least [wholly detached from all relation to the observer, and seen as apparent, not substantial beings. What new thoughts are suggested by seeing a face of country quite familiar, in the rapid movement of the rail-road car! Nay, the most wonted objects, (make a very slight change in the point of vision,) please us most. In a camera obscura, the butcher's cart, and the figure of one of our own family amuse us. So a portrait of a well-known face gratifies us. Turn the eyes upside down, by looking at the landscape through your legs, and how agreeable is the picture, though you have seen it any time these twenty years!] [21]

In a German tale of Goethe, an effect like this is finely attributed to an improvisatore poet. "In a large hall, a wide circle of busy artists were engaged in sketching and moulding copies from a colossal group of sculpture standing in the centre of the apartment. Male and female forms of gigantic power, in violent postures, reminded one of that renowned battle between heroic youths and Amazons, wherein hatred and enmity ended in peace and alliance.

"The greatest silence reigned throughout the room; but the Superior raised his voice and cried, 'Is there any of you who in presence of this stationary work can with gifted words so awaken our imagination, that all we see here so massive, shall again become fluid without losing its character, and so convince us that what the artist has here laid hold of was indeed the best?' Called forth on all sides by name, a fair youth laid down his work; and as he stepped forward began a quiet speech seemingly intended merely to describe the present group of figures; but ere long he cast himself into the region of poetry, plunged into the middle of the action represented before them; by degrees his representation so swelled and mounted by lordly words and gestures, that the rigid group seemed actually to move about its axis, and the number of its figures to be doubled and trebled." [22]

[21] "Even a small alteration . . . these twenty years" (W, I, 50–51).
[22] Goethe, *Wilhelm Meisters Wanderjahre*, Book II, Chapter 8. A paraphrase of Carlyle's translation.

Something like this is always the effect of poetry and of eloquence. Mr. Hazlitt relates of his friend the late Mr. Coleridge, that he found him one day at Stowey holding forth to a large party of ladies and gentlemen upon his philosophical doctrines, and had already "made the whole material universe look like a transparency of fine words." [23]

To break the chains of custom, to see every thing as it absolutely exists, and so to clothe every thing ordinary and even sordid with beauty is the aim of the Thinker. All men are capable of this act. The very utterance of his thoughts to men, proves the poet's faith, that, all men can receive them; that all men are poets, though in a less degree. To succeed, he must be read in the same spirit in which he wrote.

But whilst the poetic vision seems to be not a partial gift to one man but a state of mind into which all occasionally pass, there yet subsist actually very great differences between men. The proud and cruel distinction of Machiavel divided men into three classes, "those who invent; those who understand; and those who neither invent nor understand." [24] The distribution, without satire, would be, the class which receives, the class which perceives, and the class which embodies truth. Most men are so much under the despotism of the senses that though they can see the truth or beauty that is pointed out they do not discover it themselves. A smaller class possess so much more of the same faculty that they not only receive but perceive. Still another and smaller class not only discern but can cast truths in living images. Men who can detain the busy and soothe the agitated mind with draughts of the everwondrous Spirit; chosen channels through which streamlets from the infinite abyss of thought pass into the knowledge and use of men; seers and prophets on whose minds first rise those truths which shine in the sky of the world, and never set; men who by the divine light of thought introduce order into groups of events, or groups of facts, and so create history and science; who give the most trivial facts importance by showing the principle: these are the men with whose endeavors literary history is conversant, and

[23] William Hazlitt, "My First Acquaintance With Poets."
[24] Coleridge, *The Friend*, I, 205–206; *Statesman's Manual*, p. 18.

such as these we think it wholesome to introduce to the notice even of those who have little leisure.

I know that the word Literature has in many ears a hollow sound. It does not sound practical. It is thought to be the harmless entertainment of a few fanciful persons and not at all to be the interest of the multitude. But the great Thinker thinks for all; and all have a property in his wisdom. These objections proceed on the very coarse supposition that nothing but what grinds corn and bakes bread is anything worth. But every attainment and discipline that increases a man's connexion with the invisible world raises his being. Every thing that gives him a new perception of beauty multiplies his pure enjoyments. Every object in nature rightly seen is related to the whole and partakes of the perfection of the whole; a leaf, a sunbeam, a moment of time, and no sane man can wish to lose his admiration. Shall not they who see its beauty say so? A river of thoughts is always running out of the invisible world into the mind of man. Shall not they who receive the largest streams spread abroad the waters? Shall not we fill our urns with precious drops? It was the symbolical custom of the ancient Mexican priests after the annual extinction of the household fires of their land, to procure in the temple fire from the sun, and thence distribute it as a sacred gift to every hearth in the nation. It is a faithful type of the service rendered to mankind by wise men. Aristotle, Homer, and Locke serve many more than have heard their names. The day laborer has the strongest interest in respecting the speechless solitude of Newton and Laplace. He has not less intimate interest that the poet or the moralist shall be yielded free to the impulses of his genius. There are those who prefer that Jesus should have wrought as a carpenter and St. Paul as a tentmaker.

A generous mind will own that they who have thrown into circulation thoughts that arm, cheer, or save us, have befriended the low and illiterate. Thought is the most volatile of things. It cannot be contained in any cup, though you shut the lid never so tight. But once brought into the world it runs over the vessel which received it, into all minds that love it. The very language we speak, thinks for us, by the subtle distinctions which already are marked

229

for us by its words, and every one of these is the contribution of the wit of one and another sagacious man, in all the centuries of time. Then, what a vast amount of wise sentences in the shape of fables, proverbs, or maxims, float in the discourse of the upper and middle circles of society and come to the unlettered in the caucus, or on the stage, or in the almanack, or newspaper. These humble tanks receive their water from aqueducts, which brought it from rivers, which flowed off the mountains, whose summits drew it from the heavens. And so are Chaucer, Bacon, Plato, Luther or some divine thinker, always the authors, through a remote paternity, of the truths and sentiments in common circulation among us.[25]

The influence of great minds is always salutary. The atmosphere they breathe exhilarates. Nature dilates, and the world of thought grows more profound as we talk with them. It befals us sometimes when the mind is inactive or has been dissipated by frivolous employments and frivolous company to believe that the cruse of truth is dry and will run no more oil; then we come to Shakspear and Bacon or to some living master and we believe again in her inexhaustible store.

Even of those numerous books of men of acknowledged genius which create an objection to the study of letters, books where no care has been used to guard the moral tendency of the invention or the dialogue, if there be vigor of thought, the general influence is safe. It has been finely said in defence of Schiller's drama The Robbers against the charge that the moral was bad, that his work has on the whole furnished nourishment to the more exalted powers of our nature; the sentiments and images which he has shaped and uttered tend in spite of their alloy to elevate the soul to a nobler pitch. And this is their sufficient defence.[26]

The English literature contains specimens in every kind of composition worthy to be compared for strength, for tendency, and for beauty with any works of man. We have confidence that even should we fail of our great end to analyze not its value to critics or to libraries but its worth to human nature, yet the study

[25] This passage was later prefixed to "English Literature," Lecture 9.
[26] Carlyle, *Life of Schiller*, p. 28. Cf. *J*, II, 526.

of works and particular thoughts will not be without its fruit.

But I must be permitted to say on the threshold, we must come to the examination of a great literature with meekness and self distrust. That man who thinks it is easily to be distributed into epochs by order of time, or into departments by the mere form of the composition, cannot much help us. There is no chance in its history. There is no insulated genius or book, but rather is it to be contemplated with patience and awe, as the striving for long periods, this way and that, of the great national mind, now under the opening and progressive force of one Idea, which, before it is spent, is opposed by or blended with another. Let us leave pedantry to pedants. If, as men, to any useful purpose you would study the literature of any cultivated nation, you must meet the majestic ideas of God, of Justice, of Freedom, of Necessity, of War, and of Intellectual Beauty, as the subject and spirit of volumes and eras.[27] The solemn powers of faith, of love, of fear, of custom, of conscience, which breathe into the books and men of any age the life [that] is in them, will yield no answer to petulance or haste or vanity. They are only to be seen and known by ascending to that height of calm reason whence as from a centre, the world is commanded.

Moreover a superficial inquiry is equally unworthy of the authors themselves. The great men who now make up the body of English literature, did not slide by any fortune into their high place. They have been selected for their place by the severest of all judges, Time. As the snow melts in April, so has this Mountain lost every age a new fragment; every year new particles have dropt into the flood as the average human mind found them wanting in permanent interest, until now of its elder ages the ephemeral reputations are all swept away and only the Titans remain. These august geniuses were men who had just views of their vocation as Teachers. They did not sing to the tune of the times; they were not decorous sayers of smooth things to lull the ear of society; they did not treat the great spiritual nature and aims which make man a man with silence or civil and distant respect, but they made themselves obedient to the spirit that was in them and preferred

[27] "If, as men, to any useful . . . and eras" (*J*, III, 551).

231

its whisper to the applause of their contemporaries. They had an instinctive belief that the office of a great genius was to guide the future, not follow the past; that these words which they launched were the bright thunderbolts of truth whose light flashes through ages without diminution. And it is fit that they should be read in honor and in a spirit which conspires with their own.

2

Permanent Traits of the English National Genius

The title of this second lecture, which followed the first by one week, on November 12, 1835, was supplied by Cabot from Emerson's announcement of his purpose in the second paragraph. The manuscript gives no title, but in his note in manuscript journal "L," he suggests the topic "British and Saxon Literature" for this lecture. Actually he discusses both topics, using the early English literature as a source for many of his generalizations about the national character. Although similar ideas appear in both, this lecture does not seem to have been used by Emerson in preparing his later book, *English Traits* (1856).

Unlike the first, this lecture depended largely on immediate preparation, his main source being Turner. In the envelope with this lecture are seven pages of notes on Warton, one containing quotes from the Saxon Ode on the Victory of Athelstan, the rest concerning Lydgate and Chaucer; also two pages of comments on the expressive power of language and the weakness of the superlative, headed "RHETORIC." They do not appear to have been used in connection with this lecture.

T HE inhabitants of the United States especially of the Northern portion are descended from the people of England and have inherited the traits of their national character. It has been thought by some observers acquainted with the character of both nations that the American character is only the English character exaggerated; that as some plants which grow in the temperate zone only one or two feet high, in the torrid zone are found to attain four or six feet, so the features of the English genius both good and bad, have, in the greater freedom of our institutions, become more prominent. Are they lovers of freedom? we more. Are they lovers of commerce? we more. Are they lovers of utility? we more.

Without undertaking to decide upon the justice of this view, I propose to offer you this evening some sketches of English history with a view to exhibit some of the permanent traits of the national genius.

That natural curiosity which the child must always feel in respect to the character of the parent, has given a perpetual interest, in this country, to innumerable works upon the history, the politics, the literature of Great Britain. Still, for the most part, History is not drawn from sufficiently deep sources. It ought to be written in a settled conviction that no event is casual or solitary, that all events proceed inevitably from peculiar qualities of the national character which are permanent or very slowly modified from age to age.

This remark is forced upon us by even a slight study of the unchangable features of national genius. The traits of national character are almost as permanent as the grander natural forms of a country, the mountains, rivers and plains. Amid all the multitude of causes that have operated for centuries to alter their laws, manners, customs, the English of the present day bear deeply engraven on their character the marks by which their ancestors are described by Caesar and Tacitus [1] 1800 years ago; "that they were blue eyed men, lovers of liberty, yielding more to authority than to command, and respecting the female sex." The Scots bear at this day a strong likeness to the portrait sketched of them by Servetus three centuries ago:

"The Scots are of rapid genius, quick at revenge and fierce. Brave in war, patient of the open air, watching, and frost; of comely person, but careless of dress; naturally envious and despisers of other men; very fond of showing their long descent, and, in the greatest poverty, tracing themselves to a royal line. They are moreover fond of dialectics, and acute at an argument." [2]

The historical virtues and vices of the French nation, at least as their enemies represent them, were sharply set down by Vopiscus and Salvian before the middle of the third century: "Francis familiare est ridendo fidem frangere: It is common with the Franks

---

[1] Referred to but not quoted in Turner, II, 4.

[2] Michael Servetus (1511–1553), theologian and comparative geographer. Quoted (in Latin) in Mackintosh, *General View*, p. 128.

to break their faith and laugh at it. The race of Franks is faithless. If a Frank perjure himself what wonder since they esteem perjury only a figure of speech and not a crime. The Franks are false but hospitable: Franci mendaces sed hospitales." [3] An union of laughter and crime, of deceit and politeness is the unfavorable picture of the French character as drawn by the English and Germans, and even by the French themselves.

The Island of Great Britain is the most pleasing spectacle which history shows. Its fair and ruddy population are known throughout the world as the paramount nation. Eight hundred years ago it was remarked in a Latin history, that England is the richest of all the northern nations. In the immense enlargement of the domestic wealth of the European nations to this day it has preserved its relative superiority. It has reached the highest point of civilization. It contains at this hour how vast an amount of human comfort and splendour. Nowhere is greater sincerity of benevolence. Nowhere greater ability of display. Its arts fill the farm, the sea, the cellar, the kitchen, the bedchamber, the drawing-room, with every utensil of wise economy. Its science is now one of the most potent agents in modern affairs. Its observatory at Greenwich is the calendar of the earth. England keeps the register of heat and cold; of the tides; of the magnetic variations annual and secular. By its charts, all ships are sailed; by its chronometers, time is measured; by its astronomical tables, the celestial phenomena are advertised. In concealed laboratories, its chemists are weighing airs and decompounding earths; splitting a ray of light and unloading a gas of all its mixtures; its inland country is a garden. Its dwellinghouses are models of comfort and its cottages of taste. The land is made venerable by the piles which were anciently constructed for defence or for religion or for learning. There stands Kenilworth and York Minster, and Oxford, and Westminster Abbey: and the modern arts and societies are as prolific in their edifices as the old.

Or if the traveller inquire for great men — it is peopled and transfigured with history and poetry; not a stone wall without its

---

[3] "Salvian" [E]. Turner, I, 51n. Flavius Vopiscus (Roman historian of fourth century A.D.); Salvianus (Christian writer of fifth century A.D.).

legend. And as they said of ancient Rome that there were more statues than men, so has England as many historical names as living citizens. And the living do not degenerate from the dead.

The moral weight of this singular nation is most worth. It is the country of established Law, where the principles of equity have been nicely analysed and applied with thorough system to all the parts of human business. It is a nation pervaded with a deep sense of moral obligation and where most of all nations a religious feeling has been most universally diffused.

Great and beautiful as is this spectacle he who sees the island of Great Britain sees its least part. Its domestic bear no proportion to its foreign relations. It is in the world a sort of ganglion or nervous centre. It radiates like a sun its light and heat. It holds the barbarous East in fee, as it has planted the barbarous West.[3a] England scatters by her speedy ships her power and her products over every sea and land. From point to point all round the globe are her military and naval stations, so that it is her proverb that the sun never sets on her flag and the four seasons are found at one moment within her far sundered domains. Where she has not power she has influence and where she is not loved, men buy her goods. This is more remarkable as England has very little natural wealth. The island when it was first explored was not found to yield anything but a little tin. But there Labor drudges in his iron apron all day, all night, year in, year out. There the pendulum, the wind, the water, the coal, the steam, the beast, even the insect are made to work. Its furnaces roar, its bellows blow, its Sheffields and Birminghams thunder and smoke to provide clothing, arms, furniture, and ornaments for mankind. All men eat of her meats, drink of her liquors, wear the garments of her loom, and are furthered by her inventions.

And what is greater, the political action of this people has been commensurate with this power. They have felt the dignity of their position and acted for the human race as became the leading nation. Its freedom and its moral sentiment have made it the Public of Europe. Its stormy and warlike press is the advocate of every unproved opinion and injured party in Europe as in the Islands. Its enterprises of science, of discovery, and its philanthropic policy

[3a] *Cf.* Wordsworth, "On the Extinction of the Venetian Republic."

have more than supplied the best legislation of the ancient Roman Empire.

If we inquire, as is natural, into the origin of this state, we learn that this wise and refined nation did not come of a very gentle stock.[4] They are descended with their ingenuity, their humanity, and their grandeur out of the loins of as abominable savages as any whom history describes.

That part of the ancestors of the English nation from whom the laws and language are derived, when history first mentions them, lived about the river Elbe, in the peninsula of Jutland, and in three small islands, — North Strandt, now nearly washed away; Busen, a perilous rock; and Heligoland or Holy Island opposite the mouth of the Elbe, forty miles distant in the German Ocean, a sea mark by day, a lighthouse at night, and peopled by pilots. Their territory on the main is partly a slimy marsh, partly a sterile sand, and partly forest.

The dwellers on these unpromising shores are described as men of huge frame with fierce blue eyes, and light or red hair, as more ferocious than any other enemy of the Romans. They enjoyed a disorderly freedom. They elected their chiefs by an equal suffrage, and held the female sex in great respect. Such was their passion for freedom, that one Roman historian relates that twenty-nine Saxons strangled themselves to avoid being brought into a theatre as gladiators. In battle was their delight. The horsemen were armed with an iron sledgehammer which they wielded without weariness and without pity.

But by sea they were more dangerous than by land. In boats framed of osiers and covered with skins sewed together the Saxons sported in the tempests of the German Ocean. For these skiffs no coast was too shallow, no river too small, and they carried them overland from stream to stream. They were pirates; and in the third century infested every accessible acre of coast of Belgium, Gaul, and Britain and seem at that period to have had the same hearty execration of all the sea-coasts of the Roman Empire in which we hold, at this day, the pirates of Cuba and the Spanish Keys.

[4] Facts about the Anglo-Saxons and Britons are based on Turner.

They arrived in England under Hengist and Horsa, A.D. 449, and were first employed there in small companies to aid the far descended Britons in their intestine wars.

The original tribe who gave [the] name of Britain to the country and to the rivers and mountains were probably Cimmerians [5] who came from Asia into Europe seven hundred years before Christ and faster or slower spread themselves along the western coast of Europe. They brought with them the oriental religion of the Druids and the oriental castes. The same immoveableness is seen in the institutions of the ancient Britons and the same man subduing superstition that has always been found in Eastern Asia. Their Druids monopolized learning and arts and really possessed great superiority of knowledge. They taught high doctrines of the transmigration of the soul and its imperishable nature; they taught many things concerning the stars and their motion; the size of the world and its countries; the nature of things and the force and power of the immortal Gods. They were educated by a strict discipline of twenty years.

The Asiatic Cimmerians dwelt underground; they ate the flesh and drank the milk of mares. They reverenced the oak and mistletoe. They were cruel and terrific in their fanaticism — much such people as are now found in the Pacific Islands: stained with woad, tattooed, with long hair, clothed in skins, and houses of reeds and mud.

Of these first settlers of Britain no architectural monuments remain but Stonehenge and a few similar circles. A few but very few words have descended from them into the English. The infusion of British words is very scanty. The word *Be* [6] is however of that high antiquity. The other inflections, *am, art, is,* etc. of this verb are perhaps not more than fourteen or fifteen hundred years old but this word Be, preserved alike in the Welsh, English, Germans, and Flemings, and in the Saxon, has come to us from Mt. Caucasus and may be one of the oldest monuments of man's Reason.

But indirect monuments of this maritime horde we have in

[5] Turner, I, 4–23, 108–109.
[6] *Cf.* Turner, II, 463.

the poetry of their descendants, the Irish, the Welsh, and the Scottish highlandmen. The very permanence of their national features leads us to believe the modern songs no unfair specimen of their ancient melodies. It appears that they had a distinct class of Bards. Aneurin and Llywarch Hen were princes; Taliessin the chief of the Bards was attached as minstrel to a prince. The earliest authentic poetry of these singers is about the period of Arthur, A.D. 530.

A poem of Taliessin called Gall from the Bards remains which gives us a pleasing insight into the poet's own views of the dignity of the poetic vocation, as it is a satire upon the wandering minstrels who descended from the dignity of their profession to amuse instead of instructing the people:

> The minstrels exercise themselves in false customs
> Their praise is not in the regular melody
> They sing the fame of foolish heroes
> They publish untruths
> The commandments of God they break.
> Married women, by their praise,
> With unwise thoughts they deceive;
> Beautiful virgins they corrupt;
> Let these beware how they trust them
> Or rank them with men of truth.
> Age and time they consume in vain;
> By night they carouse; by day they sleep;
> Idle, they eat without work;
> They hate the churches; they seek the liquor houses;
> The false thieves consent together
> For courts and feasts they inquire
> Each indiscreet discourse they repeat
> Each deadly sin they praise
> They wander over all the villages towns and lands
> They discourse on every filthy trifle;
> They despise the commandments of the Trinity
> They respect neither Sundays nor holidays
> They care not for the days of death;
> From every gluttony they refrain not;
> Tenths and family offerings they pay not;
> The men appointed they mock.
>   Birds fly; bees collect honey;
> Fishes swim; reptiles creep;

Every thing labors for its meat,
Except minstrels vagrants and thieves.
Blaspheme not among you, teaching, or the art of song!
For God gives anguish and melancholy
To those whose habit is false designs
In mocking the service of Jesus.
Be silent, ye Pos Bards! unhappy deceivers!
Ye know not to judge between truth and falsehood.
If ye be primary bards of faith,
Of the work of God the Artist,
Foretell to your King his misfortunes.
I am a diviner, and universal chief of the Bards;
I know every pillar in the caves of the west;
I released Elphin from the stone round tower.
Tell your king what will be his safety
If the Lord of the seacoast of Rhianedd come,
To avenge iniquity on Maelgwyn of Gwynedd.[7]

A poem of Llywarch Hen's is also preserved after the death of a chief and the desertion of his hold which breathes great dignity of sentiment:

The hall of Cynddylan is gloomy this night
Without fire without bed
I must weep awhile and then be silent

The hall of Cynddylan is gloomy this night
Without fire without candle
Except God doth, who will endure me with patience

The hall of C[ynddylan] gloomy seems its roof
Since the sweet smile of humanity is no more
Wo to him that saw it if he neglect to do good

The hall of Cynddylan is not easy this night
On the top of the rock of Hydwith
Without its Lord without company without circling feasts

The hall of Cynddylan is silent this night
After losing its master
The great the merciful God, what shall I do [8]

[7] Quoted, with some changes, from Turner, I, 115–16.
[8] Owen, pp. 77–79. Not consecutive stanzas.

Another begins

> Silent breathing gale long wilt thou be heard
> There is scarce another deserving praise
> Since Urien is no more.[9]

But these are very favorable specimens; for the most part the British poetry is so barren and bloody, a tiresome repetition of the same images, eagles, wolves, lions, and slaughter, that none can regret its loss.

A good deal of it is devoted to the exploits of Arthur, a prince of South Wales in the beginning of the sixth century who manfully resisted the Saxons and whose fortune it has been to enlist all the poetic sympathies of his countrymen, though Saxon themselves, ever since.[10] The old romance of Brut sums up his renown by saying, "In short God has not made since Adam was, the man more perfect than Arthur." He is described in [Joseph of Exeter's *Antiocheis* as] "praeteritis melior, majorque futuris: better than all past men, and greater than all men that shall come." [11] In all Britain it was believed that he was not dead but would return to expel the foreigners. And in the coasts of Brittany in France where the same race was settled and the same language spoken we are told in the twelfth century by Alanus, "Go into Brittany and mention in the streets or villages that Arthur is really dead like other men: you will not escape with impunity; you will be hooted with the curses of your hearers or stoned to death." [12]

But all the chivalry of Arthur and his native Britons was unable to defend that race against the strong savages who fleet after fleet arrived from the northern seas. Hengist and Ella and Cerdic brought, it has been computed, 300,000 men into Britain; gave it their name of England, or Land of the Angles; wrote their name on the districts and towns and rivers; and fixed their language, their laws and manners in the island. Presently after arrived the new tribes who are commonly known as Danes or Northmen, very little distinguish[ed] unless by even more beastly ferocity from the Anglo-Saxons. The Saxons had robbed by sea and by land; the

[9] "Elegy on Urien Reged," Owen, p. 39. Not the beginning.
[10] "Spenser" [E].
[11] Turner, I, 101n; Warton, I, clxvi.
[12] Turner, I, 113.

Northmen [13] were sea-kings or subsisted by piracy alone. These miscreants are represented as without a yard of land, without towns or any visible nation and making it their boast never to sleep under a smoky roof or drink the cup over a hearth. The king's eldest son remained ashore; all the rest mounted their ships which they called steeds of the ocean and sought their food by their sails and their swords. When the combat approached a class of fiends among them wrought themselves up to a voluntary madness, howled like wolves, foamed like mad dogs, bit their shields and tore off their clothing, and ran to the combat.

But even in the worst crimes of man the laws of nature force him to act with some regard to virtue.

Devil with devil damned firm concord hold.[14]

These barbarians at least preserved the stern Saxon principle of freedom. They kept the peace among themselves by studied equality. It was a law that the drinking vessel should pass round the whole crew as they sat, without distinction of persons.

We can hardly make this contrast between the refinement and virtue of the English and the ancient barbarism of their race without surprise. One is reminded of the remark of Alfieri upon his own countrymen: "The plant Man grows more vigorous in Italy than in any other country and even those atrocious crimes which are there perpetrated, are a proof of it." [15] The elements of human power seem to be *great activity of mind united with a strong will*. Where the intellect is torpid, as in the Asiatic races; or, where there is a defect of will, as perhaps exists in modern Germany, there is not much hope to be formed of political greatness. But this Northern horde had these qualities and combined them with a strong constitution of body. They were therefore not only capable but greedy of improvement, and, as the order of things in this world always bends man to virtue, they were led by necessity to make equal laws to protect the good and punish the bad, and their adoption of Christianity accelerated their moral discipline.

[13] Facts about Northmen from Turner, I, 205–212.
[14] *Paradise Lost*, II, 496.
[15] Vittorio Alfieri (1749–1803). Quoted (in Italian) in the letter to Hobhouse prefixed to Canto IV of Byron's *Childe Harold*.

I may add an observation which is one of the most pleasing conclusions of modern history, that in the course of nature, the moral sense is steadily reproduced; that the children of the convicts of Botany Bay are observed to have a healthful conscience, and to be, equally with the children of virtuous parents, under the operation of honor and shame.

But this was the rugged soil in which the splendid flowers of English wit and humanity should bloom. Out of the strong came forth sweetness.

As soon as the quiet possession of England was secured, the active mind of this race was rapidly turned from the arts of war to the arts of peace. Their maritime genius favored by their position out of the pirate created a merchant. A freeman not noble, was raised to the rank of thane by making three voyages at sea on his own account. Commercial and agricultural pursuits quickly mitigated their habits, whilst the love of freedom was never the less. The trial by jury and the representative council were instituted. The beneficent influence of literature was felt. The bards and gleemen forgot their sanguinary burden of wolf and raven and slaughter [and] showed themselves by a natural revolution the humanizers and civilizers of their countrymen. They succeeded in making infamous the odious insanity of the Berserkers, and then, the profession of piracy.

The earliest Saxon historical poem that has come down to us is an ode on the victory of Athelstan over Anlaff who with Hybernians and Scots entered the river Humber, A.D. 934:

> The earls of dead Edward fell
> For it was born within them
> Even from the loins of their kindred
> That they in battle oft
> Against every foe
> Should keep the land
> Hoard and homes
> The field swam
> With warriors' blood
> Since the sun rising
> On morning tide
> Mighty planet

Glided over the ground
bright candle of the Lord
till the noble creature
Sank to her seat . . .
Nor was there a greater slaughter
On this island
Ever yet
Of folk felled
Before this
by the sword's edges
of that they say in books
Old historians
Since eastward hither
Angles and Saxons
Up came
Over the broad seas
Britain sought
(When those) splendid warsmiths
Overcame the Welsh
And Earls exceeding bold
Obtained the earth.[16]

I read a few lines from Alfred's Translation of Boethius into Anglo-Saxon:

O in how gloomy
And how bottomless
A well laboreth
The darkened mind
When it the strong
Storms beat
Of the world's business
Then it contending
his own light
Again loseth
And with woe
forgets the
eternal joy.
Distressed with sorrows
Of this world
The Darkness then rushes on.

[16] Emerson's version differs from that of Turner (II, 289–290) and those of Warton (I, lxxxviii, and xl–xli).

O thou creator
Of the pure stars
of heaven and earth
Thou on high seat
Ever reignest.
And thou all the swift
Heaven turnest round
And through thy holy might
the stars compellest
that they obey thee . . .

O which on earth
of all creatures
obey thy commandments
As some
Do in heaven
With mind and power?
But man alone
he against thy will
Worketh oftenest

Oh thou eternal
And thou almighty
Of all creatures
Maker and governor
Pardon thy miserable
Offspring of earth
Mankind
Through the power of thy might.[17]

The wind is swiftest in the sky [18]
Thunder is loudest of noises
Great is the majesty of Christ
fortune is the strongest
Winter is the coldest
Spring has most hoarfrost
he is the longest cold
Summer sun is most beautiful
fierce harvest is the happiest
Truth is most deceiving

[17] Turner, II, 321–22.
[18] The following lines from Turner, II, 324–25, not part of Alfred's *Boethius*, are inserted in the manuscript without title.

treasures are most precious
And age is the wisest
Woe is a wonderful burthen
Clouds roam about

    The good man in his country
Will do justice
The gem in the ring
Will stand pendant and curved
The stream in the waves
Will make a great flood
The mast in the keel
Will groan with the sail yards

The woods will on the ground
Blow with fruit
The mountains in the earth
Will stand green

God will be in heaven
The judge of deeds
Fowl aloft
Will sport in the air
Salmon in the whirlpool
Will roll with the skate
The shower in the heavens
mingled with wind
Will come on the world
The thief will go out
In dark weather
The Thyrs will remain in the fen
In the dark weather

The salt ocean will rage
The clouds of the supreme Ruler
And the water floods
About every land
Will flow in wide streams
Good against evil
Youth against age
Life against death
Light against darkness
Army against army
Hate against hate

Shall every where contend
Sin will steal on

The Creator alone knows
Whether the soul
Shall afterwards roam
And all the spirits
That depart in God
After their death day
They will abide their judgment
In their father's bosom
Their future condition
Is hidden and secret
God alone knows it
The preserving father.

None again return
Hither to our houses
that any truth
May reveal to man
About the nature of the Creator
Or the people's habitations of glory
Which he himself inhabits.

Song on the Death of Edgar[19]

Ten nights before
from Britain departed
the bishop so good
in native mind
Cyneward was his name
Then was in Mercia
To my knowledge
Wide and everywhere
the praise of the supreme Governor
destroyed on the earth.
Many were disturbed
Of God's skilful servants
Then was much groaning
To those that in their breasts
Carried the burning love
Of their Creator in their mind.

[19] Turner, II, 292.

Then was the source of miracles
So much despised
the Governor of Victory
the Lawgiver of the Sky
When man broke his rights

And then was also driven
The beloved man
Oslac from the earth
Over the rolling of the waves
Over the bath of the sea fowl
Over the roaring of the waters
Over the country of the whales
the longhaired hero
wise and in words discreet
Of an home deprived. . . .

But besides these historical and lyric effusions the Saxons attempted something like romantic poetry. The feud of Beowulf, a metrical romance is the oldest epic of modern Europe. The poem on Judith in which the apocryphal story of the beheading of Holofernes is told, is another. Caedmon wrote a poem on the fall of the angels and the fall of man. All these poems though indicating simplicity of thought with some skill of invention are so stately and so encumbered with paraphrasis, or the repetition of the same sense in new words, as to be very fatiguing. This is the figure so familiar to us in the Hebrew poetry as in the Psalms of David where the second clause of the verse is usually an echo to the first. These historical poems indicate however the transition from that Asiatic form to the continuous narrative or sentence more agreeable to the European mind.

These poems are all written in Saxon; so are all the writings of Alfred, which consist chiefly of translations from the Latin. So is the Saxon Chronicle, a history of England from Hengist and Horsa to the reign of Stephen. This language is represented by those familiar with it as in the time of Alfred a very cultivated and even elegant speech. It interests us as it is the basis of our English. Saxon words make up four-fifths of the language we speak, and what is to our ears by far the most significant and strong part of it. Most of our monosyllables are Saxon and in general most words of necessity. Our written speech, or what children call *book-words*, are mostly Latin, which came to us by the Normans. In the Lord's Prayer of sixty-nine words only five are not Saxon.

It must be obvious to any student of history that this race and their descendants are distinguished by remarkable traits which continue and reappear with some modifications from age to age and in whatever country they are planted.

I will venture to enumerate a few of these traits:

1. A certain gravity in the constitution tending always to melancholy when not counterbalanced by the enterprise, which is also native to them. Whilst many barbarous tribes are of a joyous temper the Ancient Saxons were noticed to mark time by nights and winters. The modern Englishman is remarked in all countries for his taciturnity; for what a satirist has called "a silent fury."

2. Another trait is Humor, in a grave nature, a sense of the ludicrous.

3. The love of Home and an adherence in foreign lands to domestic habits so that the Englishman is said to carry his teakettle to the top of Mount Etna.

4. A certain economical taste or love of Utility which characterises all their arts, which is pleasantly expressed in the proverb that the French invented the ruffle and the English added the shirt.

5. Accuracy of perception and the strong love of truth. Add to this a passion for justice. The English from the highest to the lowest citizen — are lovers of fair play. This is so deepseated that it has given rise to the remark that the virtues of an Englishman never come out until he quarrels. Then you see that whilst there is in him a certain obstinacy of valor yet he is always just and will no more take himself than he will suffer another to take any unfair advantage.

6. A respect for birth.

7. A respect for women.[20]

---

[20] At some time after this lecture was first delivered, Emerson expanded it by adding a passage from Lecture 3 ("The popular origin of English letters . . . remembered in songs and ballads," pp. 263–65) and a passage from Lecture 4 ("In Chaucer are conspicuous . . . embellisher of manners," pp. 276–80). See the textual notes to this lecture for variants and additions.

Goethe has remarked that of all history he remembers nothing but a few anecdotes. It is indeed observable how small a part of all we read recurs with any vivacity to the memory in our involuntary thinking. The memorable events of the world are not the Assyrian Monarchy nor the Macedonian Era nor the fall of the Roman Empire or the conquest of Charlemagne but the story of Croesus and Solon, the sayings of Diogenes, the egg of Columbus, and here in England the story of Alfred and the herdsman's wife, Canute on the seashore.[21] These incidents, esteemed of trifling importance, when they occurred, are preserved by the moral quality that is in them which makes them always pertinent to human nature whilst laws, expeditions, books, and kingdoms are forgotten.[22] So it seems to me that in the literary history of the Saxons, we are more struck by a few oral expressions than by many elaborate compositions.

Edwin son of Ella besought asylum of Redwald king of East Anglia. Ethelfrith demanded the suppliant to be given up to him. But the queen of Redwald replied, "a King should not sell a distressed friend or violate his faith for gold. No ornament is so ennobling as good faith." [23]

Ina laid down his crown and dignity A. D. 721 after a successful reign of forty-seven years. His queen had long prayed him to do so but he would not. One day as they travelled in the country after a splendid feast Ethelburga the queen persuaded her husband to return to court. Ina consented but was amazed to find his banqueting hall filled with filth and rubbish and a swinish litter polluting his own couches. So had the relics of the feast been bestowed by order of the queen. Ina turned to the queen to know how this had happened. She cried out, "Where is the merriment, the splendor, the luxury, the flattery of yesterday? Are they not like vapors and as transient as the wind? As transitory are we who enjoy them. Are we not like the river hurrying to the dark ocean of illimitable time? Behold the foul spectacle of the dis-

[21] These stories are related in Turner, I, 256–57 and 437–38 but were surely already familiar to Emerson.

[22] Cf. *J*, III, 552–53.

[23] This and the following anecdotes are from Turner, I, 138–39; 159–60; II, 439; and I, 304n.

solving viands. In their miserable relics we may perceive what our pampered bodies will become. Let us then direct our pursuits to objects more suitable to the condition we approach." Ina resigned his crown, and travelled to Rome.

I seem to myself to find an analogy between the queen's words upon this singular and somewhat barbarous contrivance and the celebrated speech of the noble to Edwin when deliberating upon receiving the Christian missionaries. "The present life of man, O king, compared with that space of time beyond, of which we have no certainty, reminds me of one of your wintry feasts, where you sit with your generals and ministers.

"The hearth blazes in the middle, and a grateful heat is diffused around, while the storms of rain and snow are raging fierce without. Driven by the chilling tempest, a little sparrow enters at one door and flies delighted around us, till it departs through the other. Whilst it stays in our mansion, it feels not the winter's storm; but when this short interval of happiness has been enjoyed, it is forced again into the same dreary scene from which it had escaped, and we behold it no more. Such is the life of man, and we are as ignorant of the state which preceded our present existence, as of that which will follow it. Thus situated, I feel that, if this new faith can give us more certainty on this important subject, it merits our belief."

These words were spoken in the year 626 and it seems to me they mark already that contemplative and philosophical spirit which has been so largely unfolded in later ages by the countrymen of this Saxon Hume.

When Alfred knew that his end approached he gave his dying instructions to his son. "Without wisdom," quoth he, "wealth is worth little. Though a man had a hundred and seventy acres sown with gold, and all grew like corn, yet were all that wealth nothing worth, unless that of an enemy, one could make it become his friend."

We must read these anecdotes and we must read this poetry in the light of the national mind. As the clouds are bright on the side toward the sun so all this poetry faces the orbs of Chaucer, Shakspear, and Milton. Rude as these numbers are they have already an English cast of thought. There is a strong infusion of the religious sentiment. There is in them the melancholy that has cleaved to the Saxon race from the earliest period when they measured time by nights and by winters, until now, and what is still more indicative of their ingrained virtue is that each of these poems seems related to some work which we now acknowledge as a genuine English poem.

The identity of which I have spoken that adheres to the character of a nation for many hundred years is strikingly exhibited by the wonder and veneration which the English nation still cherish at this day for the name of the quiet Alfred, a prince who flourished a thousand years ago. Not the fabulous St. George, but this great man is the very Genius of the English nation already embodied. In the middle of the ninth century, he gave in his character and exploits, the pledge of all they are in the nineteenth. There is, indeed, a singular coincidence between the life of the king, and the history of England. His valor; his religion; the conscience and the discrimination which gave him in the early histories the surname of the *Truth Teller*; his literature; his economical inventions; his naval genius; his profuse patronage of learned men; his immense curiosity about distant countries which induced him to send Ohthere toward the North Pole, and an embassy to Jerusalem, and even to India, binding his fame to all the abodes of man, already indicate with curious fidelity the character and achievements of his race and foretell how far his posterity in both hemispheres should extend their influence, language, and laws.

3

The Age of Fable

This lecture was probably given at the regular weekly time and place, the Masonic Temple on November 19, 1835, although Rusk finds no notice of it in the *Boston Daily Advertiser* (*L*, I, 447n). For it Emerson depended mainly on Warton, whom he was reading and quoting in his Journal in the summer of 1835 (*J*, III, 494–95, 536–38, 544–45, 554).

The manuscript of this lecture supplies no title. Cabot's title is "The Age of Fable" (II, 717). Emerson's early note for this lecture (manuscript journal "L") proposed as its subject matter "Normans, Romance, Fable, Crusades." Apparently in later readings parts of it were merged with Lecture 2. The envelope contains a sheet in a later hand which concerns allegory in Greek and Northern myths.

T HE poems and histories of which some specimens were presented in my last lecture were translated for us out of the British and Saxon languages by the English antiquaries. We now arrive at the period when our native English tongue can speak for itself, when that rich composite dialect is forming and formed; and though at first it stammers and lisps with infirm utterance yet it already gives promise of the mellow and majestic tones in which it shall embody the wisdom and the will of a great nation. It marks the maturity and force of character that existed in the Saxons, the fact that the conquest of the island by the Normans in 1066 did not subvert the language. For two hundred years from that event, the court was wholly French. The laws were written in French for more than two centuries and a half. During this co-existence of two languages the common people holding steadily to the old Saxon adopted from the Normans, who spoke a corrupt Latin, all those words of chivalry, of romantic poetry, of science, and of learning, which they wanted, but conformed them by

Saxon terminations and inflections to their own ear. Whether it was that on the soil the natives had a right to give name to things of the soil, or that the strength of character was greater on the Saxon side, or from the disparity of numbers — from whatever cause the French tongue did not obtain a vernacular currency. The nobility yielded this proud privilege to the middle classes. At the beginning of the fourteenth century, the English language had undergone the whole change to which it was doomed by the irruption of Norman words. Edward III abolished the use of the Norman tongue in the public acts and in judicial proceedings, and even shortly after the reign of Edward I, the English language produced one of the earliest accounts of very remote regions, the Travels of Sir John Mandeville, who returned from his journeys in 1366.

We not only have the pleasure of hearing henceforward our own tongue, but we discern in its earliest compositions some distinctive traits of English genius. At first however by the channel of the Norman language England became acquainted with the metrical romances, the oral and written tales and poems of the troubadours and minstrels who made the only literature of the southern and western nations after the eighth century. The story of the War of Troy under the name of Dares Phrygius; a great prose romance on the same subject by Guido de Colonna (A.D. 1260); a profusion of Romances in prose or verse on the general subjects of Alexander the Great, on King Arthur and his Round Table, on Lancelot du Lac, who was but of the eighth degree from our Lord Jesus Christ, on Charlemagne and his Peers, and after the period of the Crusades on Richard Coeur de Lion made up the literary property of Europe. In this manner all the nations possessed common materials and a common taste, or shall I call it an equal degradation of intellect? In the use they made of them, in the progress of letters in the several states, very strong national peculiarities presently appeared.

The cause of this is to be looked for in the extraordinary political profusion of fable. If you look in the most general way at the history of the world from the fourth to the ninth centuries, you find it a period of universal war. It is singular that we can draw so firm lines of distinction between modern and ancient history. But it is easy to indicate a period during which the ancient systems of poetry, of philosophy, of social order were dissolved. If you consult the tables of chronology before the tenth century, you shall find no events but wars and their works. Come down a few centuries and you shall find the same table filled up with a quite different record: Invention of paper, of printing, of glass, of linen, the compass; discovery of the solar system; of America; manufacture of watches; the Post Office; the Bank; potato; coffee; tea; and silk.

But between these terms occurs a period of proper childhood. The barbarous age or age of War ruins not only the vanquished but the victors. So long as it lasts — however favorable it may be to hardihood and strength of will it destroys all that is good and valuable in society. Strong, boisterous, selfish persons rule: a nation is degraded into a camp: all cultivation is insolently set aside under pretence of want of time; even justice and humanity are turned out of doors on the same plea. The useful arts perish with the liberal. Without safety, the farmer will not plant his field. Without safety, the merchant will not load nor the sailor navigate a vessel. Nothing is so barren as a soldier's brain. War is one of those engrossing pursuits that like a passion for horses empties a man of all knowledge and all noble aims. War keeps every thing out of sight. In the terrific convulsions of the Middle Age the people were insignificant. Society being an army the organization is despotic. No soldier can have an opinion. To thought and freedom in individuals the whole system is hostile.

When these fires of war at last went out for want of fuel; when there was no longer any new Italy or France or Britain that promised an easy prey to Goth or Frank, the dismal effects of the disorder shewed themselves. The mind of Europe was reduced to a state of childishness. Men were ignorant and incapable. Their eyes were holden that they could not see. Of course the religion was superstitious and the government cruel in the same measure. The games, the grave enterprises, the civil institutions, even the learning of the times betray the incredible ignorance and folly. Then grew up in Europe that extravagant Romance literature which prevailed for some ages in all the south and western countries. The Poets sang as we do to children of war and witchcraft. The metrical and the prose romances left all nature and common sense far behind them: they set geography, chronology and chemistry at defiance: and piled wonder on wonder for the delight of credulous nations. The nobility undertook pilgrimages to countries that were never found in a map and amused themselves with challenging unknown antagonists to mortal combat for ladies whom they never saw.

The romances begin on some slender thread of history and spin to it an interminable string of gay or terrible or absurd adventures without order or reason. To that age we trace all the surprising fictions that still cheer the nursery: the giant, the dwarf, and the fairy.[1] Then arose the story of the seven sleepers who awoke in the reign of the emperor Theodosius after sleeping in a cave 187 years from [the] time of the persecution of Decius; the tale of the wandering Jew; then the renown of the giant Ritho killed by Arthur on Mt. Arabius who was drest in a robe woven of the beards of the kings whom he had slain; of monsters and monster killers at whose heroic voice a whole rookery flew from the giant's beard; the story of the giant's conveying the stones which compose Stonehenge (each of which was washed in herbs and has a medicinal virtue) out of the farthest coasts of Africa; of the terrible dragon who flew into England out of the west breathing fire and illuminating the whole country with the brightness of his eyes: "The fire was great, it made the island light";[2] of the wonderful horn by which Alexander the Great was wont to issue the word of command to his army, which was blown or sounded by sixty men at once and which might be heard sixty miles; of Mahomet's Angel whom he saw in heaven who was so large that it was seventy days' journey from one of his eyes to the other: in short of whatever is rare and amazing; of invisible powder to hide the hero and

---

[1] Most of these tales are found in Warton: Seven Sleepers (III, 12); the giant Ritho (I, xvi); giant building Stonehenge (I, xvii and 55); the terrible dragon (I, xix); Alexander's horn (I, 136); but Emerson's references contain material not in this source. On Mahomet's Angel, cf. *J*, III, 367.

[2] Something like this occurs in Geoffrey of Monmouth's *Historia Regum Britanniae*, X:2.

crystal mirrors that show his friend; of amulets that keep off disease and rings that telegraph an enemy; of swords that fight and shoes that walk of themselves; of faery mothers and inexhaustible purses.

Vast collections of tales of this character differing from the Arabian tales only in being joined with European manners and the Christian religion, exist in manuscript in the English public libraries of a date prior to the invention of printing and now make the first compositions in the English tongue. Many of them are the work of unknown authors which is the less important as they possess so little peculiarity of character. Many of them or parts of them have been printed by Ellis, Warton, Ritson, Southey but the most vogue they have at the present day is in the abridgments of Morte d'Arthur, Lancelot du Lac, and the Seven Champions of Christendom which have not yet lost all favor with the rising generation. I shall not quote any specimens of these as the language is for the most part too obsolete to be intelligible by the ear, containing many now forgotten Norman and Saxon words. But it seems necessary to make a few remarks in explanation of their nature and use.

Nobody can recal these without being struck with the immense difference between the Gothic fables and the fables of antiquity. In the beautiful creations of the Grecian muse every fable, though related as religious truth and believed by the multitude as history, is, at the same time a fine allegory conveying a wise and consistent sense. Those are properly creations of the Imagination; these merely of the Fancy. They beside superficial beauty have a deeper beauty to the wise. These only please us as long as they are new or only please the childish part of us. Compare the various incidents which we collect out of different poets respecting one of the Grecian Gods or demigods with the unchosen and miscellaneous prodigies which are related of Merlin and Arthur. Take for example the story of Prometheus.

The ancients relate that man was the work of Prometheus and formed of clay; only the artificer mixed in the mass particles taken from different animals. And being desirous to improve his workmanship and endow as well as create the human race he

257

stole up to heaven with a bundle of birch rods and kindling them at the chariot of the sun thence brought down fire to the earth for the service of men. Prometheus was repaid for this meritorious act by the ingratitude of mankind so that forming a conspiracy they accused both him and his invention to Jupiter. But the matter was otherwise received than they imagined for the accusation proved extremely grateful to Jupiter and the gods; insomuch that they not only indulged mankind with the use of fire, but moreover conferred on them a most acceptable and desireable present, viz. perpetual youth.

But men, foolishly overjoyed hereat, laid this present of the gods upon an ass, who in returning back with it being extremely thirsty and coming to a fountain, the serpent who was the guardian thereof would not suffer him to drink, but upon condition of receiving the burden he carried, whatever it should be. The silly ass complied; and thus the perpetual renewal of youth was, for a sup of water, transferred from men to the race of serpents.

Jupiter wishing to revenge himself on Prometheus but finding he could not punish him without afflicting the human race, commanded Vulcan to form a beautiful and graceful woman to whom every god presented a certain gift, when[ce] she was called Pandora, i.e. *all gift*. They put into her hands an elegant box containing all sorts of miseries and misfortunes; but hope was placed at the bottom of it. With this box, she first goes to Prometheus to try if she could prevail upon him to receive and open it; but he, being on his guard, warily refused the offer. Upon his refusal she comes to his brother Epimetheus, a man of a very different temper, who rashly and inconsiderately opens the box. When finding all kinds of miseries and misfortunes issued out of it, he, with great hurry and struggle, endeavoured to clap on the cover again: but with all his endeavor, could scarce keep in Hope which lay at the bottom.

Jupiter persisting in his wrath against Prometheus caused him to be carried to Mount Caucasus and there fastened to a pillar so firmly that he could not stir. A vulture stood by him which in the daytime gnawed his liver, but in the nighttime the wasted parts were supplied again, whence matter for his pain was never wanting.

This is one of those elegant fables invented by the Greeks which seem rather to have been gradually formed by the additions of successive poets than to have been devised by one for it was accepted by the people as a part of their sacred history. It seems to be a collection of pleasing allegories. Lord Bacon has drawn out of it a consistent sense explaining it of Providence.[3]

Such another is the fable of Orpheus, explained of natural and moral philosophy, of Atalanta and of Proteus, of Pan.

But see how unlike are these fables from those of our Romantic Literature. The meaning of the ancient apologues is so palpable and consistent, that we cannot persuade ourselves but they were made to convey it. Whereas in our Romance the whole object was amusement by the incidents of the story itself, and nothing was farther from the minstrel's intention than the discovery of a hidden sense.

Yet the obligations of our childhood to these excellent knights, fairies, and magicians, are too great to be hastily dismissed. The progress of refinement, Mr. Addison says, has not entirely plucked the old woman out of our hearts.[4] A skilful tale of superstition or faerie has its own claims on us. But beside the charm of gorgeous fiction for the fancy I believe a fairy tale draws some of its power over us from deep and legitimate sources. A fairy tale, a romance has often (I may say, always) a moral in spite of itself. He who constructs a beautiful fable only with the design of making it symmetrical and pleasing, will find that unconsciously he has been writing an allegory. He finds at the end of his task that he has only been holding the pen for a higher hand which has overseen and guided him. Poets, said Plato, utter great and wise things which they do not themselves understand.[5]

When Lucian, quite in the spirit of romance, relates that Pancrates a magician journeying from Memphis to Coptus and wanting a servant, took a door-bar and pronounced over it some magical words and it stood up and brought him water and turned a spit, and carried bundles, doing all the work of a slave.[6] Now we

---

[3] "Prometheus," *De Sapientia Veterum, Works,* X, 204–213.
[4] Not located.
[5] See *Apology* 22c. Cf. *Ion* and *Republic,* Book X. *Cf.* "History," W, II, 34.
[6] Lucian, *The Liar:* 35.

can in an instant make this idle tale an allegory of the progress of art, by reading for "Pancrates" Fulton or Watt, and for "magical word" read *steam*. For these magicians by this spell of steam have made an iron bar and half a dozen wheels do the work not of one but of one thousand skilful servants.

So with the similar fictions of our Arabian and English romance. Without the most remote intention of allegory on the part of the writer they still are such. Magic and all that is ascribed to it is manifestly nothing but a deep presentiment of the powers of science. The power of subduing the elements, of using the secret virtues of minerals, of understanding the voices of birds are only the obscure efforts of the mind in a right direction. Then the preternatural strength and success of the hero, the gift of perpetual youth and the like are only alike the endeavor of the human spirit to bend the shows of things to the desires of the mind. In endeavoring to make his hero agreeable the writer insensibly makes him virtuous. And being virtuous it is agreeable to our constitution to believe him powerful and successful. Many of these fictions are exceedingly beautiful. In Perceforest and Amadis de Gaul a garland and a rose bloom on the head of her who is faithful and fade on the brow of the inconstant.

In the story of the Boy and the Mantle even a mature reader may be surprized with a glow of virtuous pleasure at the triumph of the gentle Genelas.[7] Indeed there is quite a system of fairy ethics that an ingenious reader might collect; as: that the fairies do not like to be named; that their gifts are capricious and not to be trusted; that who seeks a treasure must not speak; and the like.

These remarks are capable of the most extensive application to romantic literature, even to its latest form the modern novel. I have before me Scott's fine novel *The Bride of Lammermoor*. It seems to me that the pleasure I derive from it arises chiefly from an unconscious extension of the meaning all the time as we read, making an allegory of it. Sir William Ashton is only a masked name for a vulgar temptation, Ravenswood Castle is a fine name for proud poverty, and the foreign mission of state only a Bunyan

[7] Warton, I, (60), for both references.

disguise for honest industry. We may all like the hero shoot a wild bull that would toss the good and beautiful by fighting down the unjust and sensual. Lucy Ashton is another name for fidelity which is always beautiful and always liable to great suffering in this world.[8]

Something like this is true of every fiction. Though composed for the mere pleasure of the picture quite undesignedly it becomes allegorical and expressive of some property of human nature. For example (though it is hardly safe to select one example when every verse of romance would serve equally well) what the fairies say in the ballad of Tamlane —

> Our shape and size we can convert
> To either large or small
> An old nutshell's the same to us
> As is the lofty hall —

is more true of the Intellectual power than it is of fairies. Or these verses, which caught my eye in a very different connexion, from the Little Garden of Roses:

> Little was king Laurin but from many a precious gem
> His wondrous strength and power and his bold courage came
> Tall at times his stature grew with shells of gramarye
> Then to the noblest princes fellow might he be.[9]

These lines describe the child of genius who borrows his culture from all objects and events and under the spell of a good cause is equal to the greatest favourites of fortune.[10]

It may be pardoned me in lectures on the history of English Literature to have pushed so far these speculations upon the nature of Fable. I return now to what belongs more strictly to our inquiry, the examination of its historical effect.

Whilst the predominance of the Romance betrays the puerility of the English taste and intellect and is in strict agreement with the shows and amusements and even the laws of that age, it is not to be concealed that it had indirect good effects that were more than a compensation.

[8] "Magic and all that is ascribed to it . . . in this world" (*W*, II, 34–35; *J*, II, 372).
[9] Warton, I, (51), for both references.
[10] Cf. *J*, III, 544–45.

It restored the poet to the people. The Latin literature had become formal and merely imitative. Nothing vigorous or useful any longer issued out of it. In the ignorance of the people it lost its hold on their reverence and could no longer cripple the natural efforts of the mind by its traditions. There was more hope for the poets and thinkers of the time in writing childish tales on the popular subjects than in imitating Virgil. For books only have life so long as they express the thoughts of living men, and as soon as speculation is divorced from human concerns and copies books instead of life it withers into pedantry. Literature is the oak which cannot grow in a figured porcelain flower pot, but needs for its sufficient support and nourishment the earth itself. The ear of the people was open to little else than war and magic. For war they knew and magic is the first and rudest form in which the human mind clothes its belief in its own power. But writing not after any accepted forms, but to stimulate and please men, they were led to avail themselves of all that familiar imagery which speaks to the common mind. Marvels are never so startling as when they begin in what is common and coarse. Presently, the Crusades, opening a world of new objects and traditions in the East, enlarged the domain of Poetry. Meantime war was mitigated and lessened by the antagonist principles of Christianity and Trade. The mind was exercised by new objects and juster principles. The people of England by their increasing share in political action grew wise. Then ensued the inevitable fall of the purely Romantic literature which of course must perish the moment the credulity of the multitude withdraws its aid. It fell into derision from its own excess for the more wild the wonders grew the sharper was the reprehension from the caustic sense and the moral indignation of shrewd and good persons who never fail in the end to exercise a sovereign influence on human affairs. And when it ceased to be believed it was no longer possible to create it. But in its flourishing state it had in England discovered new and permanent resources. It had already begun to be the vehicle of strong sense of satire and mainly of abundant images drawn from the ordinary face of nature and from common life. Nothing is more evident in every page of the old versifiers [than] that they

were men who used their eyes. And these traits it preserved when
the pure romance became obsolete or was softened into the mixed
poem and the novel.

The popular origin of English letters produced, or rather I
should say this popular origin favored, the unfolding of the peculiar genius of its poetry and elegant prose and which may be
already recognized in the earliest poems whose diction is completely intelligble to us.[11] I mean its homeliness, love of plain truth
and strong tendency to describe things as they are and without
rhetorical decoration. It imports into songs and ballads the smell
of the earth and the breath of cattle and like a Dutch painter seeks
the household charm of low and ordinary objects. It is the reverse
of the classic taste. I am tempted to quote as a specimen of this
tendency a little ditty which if Warton's reckoning is right is 635
years old:[12]

> Summer is icomen in
> Loud sing cuccu
> Groweth sed and bloweth med
> And springeth the wood nu
> Sing cuccu cuccu
> Ewe bleteth aftir lamb
> Loweth after calf cu
> Bullock sterteth buck verteth
> Merrie sing cuccu
> Well sings thou cuccu
> Ne swik thou never nu
> Sing cuccu nu
> Sing cuccu.[13]

The poems of Chaucer, Shakspear, Jonson, Herrick, Herbert,
Raleigh betray a continual instinctive endeavor to recover themselves from every sally of imagination by touching the earth and
earthly and common things. The English muse loves the field and
the farmyard. It holds fast by the highway, the market, and the
hearthstone. The English muse might adopt the expression of
Mme. de Stael about the people who would have her always say

[11] This and the following paragraphs were at some time inserted also in the
manuscript of "English Literature," Lecture 2 (p. 249).

[12] Warton, I, 28.

[13] Warton, I, 32, somewhat modernized.

fine things: "I tramp in the mire with wooden shoes when they would force me into the clouds." [14] The very burdens of English songs indicate this humor.

> The sun shines fair on Carlisle wall.
>
> The rain it raineth every day.[15]

I can explain my meaning by a few extreme instances. The winter song in *Love's Labors Lost*:

> When icicles hang by the wall
>   And Dick the shepherd blows his nail
> And Tom bears logs into the hall
>   And milk comes frozen home in pail
> When blood is nipped and ways be foul
> Then nightly sings the staring owl
>   To who
> Tu whit to-who a merry note
> While greasy Joan doth keel the pot.
>
> When all around the wind doth blow
> And coughing drowns the parsons saw
> And birds sit brooding in the snow . . .

Herrick's Ode to Ben Jonson:

> Ah Ben
> Say how or when
> Shall we thy guests
> Meet at those lyric feasts
> Made at the Sun
> The Dog the Triple Tunne
> Where we such clusters had
> As made us nobly wild not mad
> And yet each verse of thine
> Outdid the meat outdid the frolic wine.

All Sir Walter Raleigh's verse [is] so homely in [the] diction and allusion that it almost wears an air of defiance, as in the celebrated piece called The Soul's Errand:

[14] From a review in *Edinburgh Review*, XXXVI (1821–22), 61.
[15] These and the following four quotes are not from Warton or Turner but from Emerson's general stock of reading.

Go soul the body's guest

. . . .

Go tell the Court it glows
And shines like painted wood
Go tell the Church it shows
What's good, but does no good
    If Court and Church reply
    Give Court and Church the lie.

In Milton it is less conspicuous so deeply was he tincture[d] with the classic ideas but it is very marked in him. The whole imagery of the Allegro of Milton is of the same kind. And this is exclusively English poetry. It is neither French nor Italian nor Spanish nor Oriental. It is the poetry of a nation in which is much knowledge and much business so that their speculation and their fancy is filled with images from real nature and useful art. These are the verses of a people that require meat and not pap, to whom elegance is less native than truth, and who must even have their constitutional utility remembered in songs and ballads.

That I may give a few examples of the manner in which the best verses were written before the time of Chaucer, whilst yet the language had not settled down into polished metre, I will read a few lines written about five hundred years ago. Robert of Gloucester has left a long poem which is a history of England in verse from Brutus to the reign of Edward I. It was written about 1280. I quote a few lines from the description of the solemnities following Arthur's Coronation:

The king was to his palace tho the service was ydo
Ylad with his menie and the queen to hire also
Vor they hulde the old usages that men with men were
By themsulve and wummen by hemsulve also there
Tho they were eachone ysett as yt to her state becom
Kay king of Anjou a thousand knights nome
Of noble men yclothed in ermine each one
Of one suit and served at this noble feast anon
Bedwer the butler king of Normandy
Nom also in his hall a fair company
For to tell all the nobley that there was ydo
Tho my tongue were of steel me should nough dure thereto.[16]

[16] Warton, I, 52–53.

Robert Langlande wrote the poem called the Vision of Pierce Plowman about 1362. It is a satire upon the vices of the day but especially upon the clergy. The characters are Kynde, that is Nature, Do wel, Do evel, Do bet and Do best, Thought, Wit, and Charity.

There is a rough sublimity in the following passage which one may easily see suggested a well known passage in Paradise Lost. It describes Kinde (that is, Nature) sending forth diseases from the planets at the command of Conscience and of his attendants age and death.

> Kynde Conscience then heard and came out of the planets
> And sent forth his forreous Feveris and Fluxes
> Coughs and Cardyacles Cramps and toothaches
> Reumes and Redegounds and roynous Skalles
> Boils and botches and burning agues
> Frenesies and foul evils foragers of Kind
> There was Harrow and Helpe here cometh Kynde
> With Death that is dreadful to undon us all
> The lord that lived after lust then loud cried
> Age the hoar he was in the vawward
> And bare the banner before death by right he it claimed
> Kynde came after with many keen soris
> Pock pits and Pestilence and much people shent
> So kynde thro Corruptions killed full many
> Death came dryving after and all to dust pashed
> Kings and knights kaisors and popis
> Many a lovely lady and lemans of knightis
> Swowed and sweltid for sorrow of Deths dents
> Conscience of his courtesy to Kynde he besought
> To cease and suffer and see whether they would
> Leave pride prively and be parfyt Christene
> And Kynde ceased then to see the people amend.[17]

There remains an elegy on the death of Edward I who died in 1307. I quote it more willingly to show how early the most pleasing metres now in use were brought to perfection.

> All that be of huert trewe
> Astoundé hearken to my song

[17] Warton, II, 119–120, where is also found the comparison to Milton, *Paradise Lost*, II, 475–494.

Of duel that Deth hath diht us new,
 That maketh me sigh and sorrow among.
Of a knight that was so strong,
 Of whom God hath done his will
Methinketh that Deth has done us wrong
 That he so soon shall ligge still.

Before that our king was ded
 He spake as man that was in care
Clerkès, knights, barons, he said
 I charge you by your sware
That ye to Engelonde be true,
 I die, I ne may live na more
Help my son and crown him new
 For he is nest to ben ycore

The messenger to the pope come
 And said that our king was dead
In his own hand the letter he nom
 I wis his harté was ful great
The pope himself the letter read
 And spake a word of great honour
Alas he said is Edward dead
Of Cristendom he ber the flower

The pope of Peter's stood at his mass
 With full great solempnete
There me began the soulé blesse
 King Edward honoured thou be
God leve thy son come after thee
 Bring to end that thou hast begun,
The holy cross ymade of tree
 So fain thou wouldest it have won

Jerusalem thou hast ilore
 The flower of all chivalerie
Now King Edward liveth na more
 Alas that he yet should die
  He would have reared up full high
Our banners that he brought to ground
 Wel longe we may clepe and cry
Ere we such a king have found.[18]

---

[18] Warton, I, 106–109, somewhat modernized.

We shall have occasion to see that many of the most musical metres of Scott and Campbell and Moore are among the oldest in England.

The writers of whom I have spoken this evening have little importance in themselves. They only deserve attention from the historical position they occupy. Of such we shall not again have occasion to speak. The genuine English muse of Chaucer will introduce us to a style of thought and expression more consonant with our own.

4

Chaucer

The lecture was first read at the Masonic Temple on Thursday, November 26, 1835. Emerson had planned from the start to devote his fourth lecture to Chaucer (manuscript journal "L"), and there is no other title. He withdrew the first volume of Godwin's *Life of Chaucer* from the Boston Library Society as early as 1816 and he returned to his interest repeatedly in later life; an edition of *The Canterbury Tales* was in his own library. For background information he relied largely on Warton. B. J. Whiting has pointed out (*American Literature*, XVII [1945], 75–78) that the (mis)information on Chaucer which Emerson included in his essay on Shakespeare in *Representative Men* (W, IV, 197–98) derived from Warton. The immediate source, it is now clear, was this lecture, additional errors creeping in as Emerson revised his own earlier statement.

When Emerson refers to Chaucer as in the unanimous opinion of scholars "the earliest classical English writer," he is obviously thinking of "classical" as synonymous with "great" or "major" and is not referring either to the ancient classics or to critical distinctions between the "classic" and "romantic" modes in art. In fact, the main emphasis of this lecture is on the English tradition in literature and Chaucer's place in it. His first three lectures had dealt with a general theory of literature and with the English national character in its origins as providing the setting for the great writer. Chaucer is the first to merit full-length treatment.

Geoffrey Chaucer was born in London in 1328. He studied at Oxford and spent several years in France after leaving the University. At the age of thirty he became connected with the English Court and received many honorable and lucrative offices from Edward III. John of Gaunt, Duke of Lancaster, the patron of Wicliffe, was Chaucer's patron and friend. This nobleman in 1396 married Lady Catherine Swinford, sister of Chaucer's wife. This connexion aided the interests of the poet. In a contention between the city of London and the Court, 1384, respecting the election of Mayor the Duke and Chaucer espoused the party of the City and of Wicliffe. In consequence of this opposition Chaucer was obliged to escape into the Low Countries, and, on his return to England, his offices were taken from him and he was imprisoned in the tower. He did not recover his liberty and employments without some discreditable confession and impeachment of his old associates. He died at the age of seventy-two.

The most remarkable circumstance in his biography is that being sent by the king on a mission to Genoa in 1370 he met with Petrarch at the wedding of Violante, daughter of Galeazzo, Duke of Milan, with the Duke of Clarence. Froissart, the French Historian, was present; and it is not improbable that Boccacio was of the party.

Of himself and his habits of study he has related thus much in the House of Fame:

> And also beau sire of other things
> That is thou haste no tidings
> Of loves folke if they be glad
> Ne of nothing else that God made
> And not only fro ferre countre
> That no tidings commen to thee
> Not of thy very neighbors
> That dwellen almost at thy dores
> Thou hearest neither that ne this
> For when thy labor all done is
> And hast made all thy reckenings
> Instead of rest and of new things
> Thou goest home to thine house anon
> And also dombe as a stone
> Thou sittest at another book
> Till fully dazed is thy look
> And livest thus as an hermite.[1]

Geoffrey Chaucer in the unanimous opinion of scholars is the earliest classical English writer. He first gave vogue to many Provençal words by using them in his elegant and popular poems,

[1] Lines 643–659. The line references are to F. N. Robinson's edition, Cambridge, 1933.

and by far the greater part of his vocabulary is with little alteration in use at this day. He introduced several metres which from
his time have been popular forms of poetic composition until ours.
Moreover he either is the author or the translator of many images
and fables and thoughts which have been the common property
of poets ever since; and more or less exist in the common speech
of men so that the reader of Chaucer finds little in his page that
is wholly new. He is struck everywhere with likeness to familiar
verses or tales; for, he is in the armoury of English literature. 'Tis
as if he were carried back into the generation before the last, and
should see the likeness of all his friends in their grandfathers.

The single fact that he continues to be read by his countrymen
now for near five hundred years, might well draw our attention
to him. It is more remarkable in the present case as our poet set
out with competitors whom his own age did not think of inferior
merit. In the first hundred years of his fame, it was common to
speak of Lydgate, Gower, and Chaucer as the English poetical
triumvirate. By and by Lydgate was dropt; but the stern verdict
of Time has now sentenced Gower also to silence and the name
of Chaucer remains alone. In literature, one is ever struck with
the fact that the good once is good always, the excellent is brand
new forever. The average physical strength is so fixed, that among
thirty jumpers the longest jump will be likely to be the longest of
three hundred; and a very long jump will remain a very long jump
a century afterward. Not less stable are intellectual measures.
Richard Hooker wrote good prose in 1580. Here it is good prose in
1835. There have not been forty persons of his nation from that
time to this who could write better.[2] Often the superiority of the
bard whose writings go down to posterity over the bard who is
forgotten, is not very great. What Shakspear says of Coriolanus,

> I think he'll be to Rome
> As is the osprey to the fish, who takes it
> By sovereignty of nature,[3]

is a good account of the successful poet in whom sometimes a
skilful analyst could hardly show the immediate causes of his

[2] "In literature, one is ever struck . . . write better" (*J*, III, 508–509).
[3] *Coriolanus*, IV, 7: 33–35.

popularity and first decided claim of preference to his rivals. But having once secured that preference, having had the good fortune to survive from his age, he now receives a hundredfold additional honor as the representative of the entire humanity of that period. Like the Chickasaw chosen on slight grounds to act for his tribe at Washington, he there is the object of attention from distinguished men of all nations not at all proportioned to his personal merits but he monopolizes the curiosity which his tribe excite.

But the poems of Chaucer have great merits of their own. They are the compositions of a man of the world who has much knowledge both of books and of men. They exhibit strong sense, humor, pathos, and a dear love of nature. He is a man of strong and kindly genius possessing all his faculties in that balance and symmetry neither too little nor too much which constitute an individual a sort of Universal Man and fit him to take up into himself without egotism all the wit and character of his age and to stand for his age before posterity. He possesses many of the highest gifts of genius and those too whose value is most intelligible to all men. The milk of human kindness flows always in his veins. The hilarity of good sense joined with the best health and temper never forsakes him. He possesses that clear insight into life which ever and anon perceives under the play of the thousand interests and follies and caprices of man the adamantine framework of Nature on which all the decoration and activity of life is hung.

He possesses the most authentic property of genius, that of sympathy with his subjects so that he describes every object with a delight in the thing itself. It has been observed that it does not argue genius that a man can write well on himself, or on topics connected with his personal relations. It is the capital deduction from Lord Byron that his poems have but one subject: himself. It is the burden of society, that very few men have sufficient strength of mind to speak of any truth or sentiment and hardly even of facts and persons clean of any reference to themselves and their personal history. But the wise man and much more the true Poet quits himself and throws his spirit into whatever he contemplates and enjoys the making it speak that it would say. This power belonged to Chaucer.

With these endowments he writes though often playfully yet always as a sincere man who has an earnest meaning to express and nowise (at least in those poems on which his fame is founded) as an idle and irresponsible rhymer. He acknowledges in House of Fame that he prefers "sentence," that is, sense, to skill of numbers. He would make

> the rime agreeable
> Tho some verse fail in a syllable
> And though I do no diligence
> To show crafte but sentence.[4]

But he felt and maintained the dignity of the laurel and restored it in England to its honor.

No modern reader can fail to be struck with the manner in which the ancients, as Plato, Plutarch, and Cicero, quote the poets. It is very much in the manner of our quoting Scripture. A single clause, often a single word is adduced with great emphasis from Pindar, Hesiod, or Euripides, as precluding all argument, because thus they said, these writers evidently proceeding on the supposition that there was something divine, something of strict inspiration in the language of a genuine bard; that he was the teacher of mankind and spoke not his own words, but the words of some God. This exceeding respect stands in broad contrast with the levity and indifference with which the Americans and English at this hour regard the writings of any poet as merely ornamental but as nowise profitable to life and action. In my last lecture I remarked the downfal of the stately Latin literature in the Middle Age as a happy event; for its strength was exhausted, and an imitation of it in our English would have been exceedingly unfavorable to the prospects of the new age. With it however fell also the remains of this reverence for the Poet. The English poets of the middle and modern age were forced to quit the raised platform from which elder bards had talked down to the multitude and win their attention by the study of the taste and genius of the people. To get any audience at all they were forced to amuse the people

[4] Lines 1097–1100.

and so they told the monstrous and endless fables of war and magic which characterised that period. They were forced instead of studying books to recur to the primitive and permanent sources from which the human mind draws excitement and delight, namely to natural objects and the common incidents of human business and adventure, and thus laid the foundations of a new literature in nature and truth. As good sense and increased knowledge resumed their rights, and happier poets arose who could draw their chief strength from these legitimate sources the poet began by instinct to reclaim for himself that reverence, to retake that attitude of a prophet and priest and to acquire a professional conscience and set a value upon his own words.

This is very observable in the old English poets. The distinction was broader then between "the learned," and "the lewed";[5] and a high responsibility of this sort is conspicuous in the graver pieces of Chaucer, Gower, Spenser, Shakspear, Ben Jonson, and throughout Milton. It is a pleasing trait, as it is the instinctive claim of the seer of truth to the ear and heart of his species. Even God himself, said Luther, cannot do without wise men.[6] It is a consciousness that truth is the property of no individual but is the equal treasure of all men. And in proportion as any writer has ascended to just and pure prospect of man's nature and condition he has adopted this tone as Dante, Shakspear, Spenser, and Milton among the moderns have preeminently done. But when the French school came into English ground, when Dryden, Pope, and Swift and Gay, Darwin and many men of less genius were the popular writers with a frivolous style of thought, down went again the respect of the poet as a priest or divine man, and Scott, Byron, and Moore have done nothing to recal the right state of things.

No one can read Chaucer in his grave compositions without being struck with his consciousness of his poetic duties. He never writes with timidity. He speaks like one who knows the law, and has a right to be heard. He is a philanthropist, a moralist, a reformer. He lashes the vices of the clergy. He wrote a poem of

[5] "The uncultivated."
[6] Not located.

274

stern counsel to King Richard. He exposes the foibles and tricks of all pretenders in science [and] the professions, and his prophetic wisdom is found on the side of good sense and humanity.

I do not feel that I have closed the enumeration of the gifts of Chaucer until it is added as a cause of his permanent fame in spite of the obsoleteness of his style (now 500 years old) that his virtues and genius are singularly agreeable to the English mind; that in him they find their prominent tastes and prejudices. He has the English sincerity and homeliness and humor, and his Canterbury tales are invaluable as a picture of the domestic manners of the fourteenth century. Shakspear and Milton are not more intrinsically national poets than is Chaucer. He has therefore contributed not a little to deepen and fix in the character of his countrymen those habits and sentiments which inspired his early song.

The humor with which the English race is so deeply tinged, which constitutes the genius of so many of their writers, as, of the author of Hudibras, Smollett, Fielding, Swift, and Sterne, and which the English maintain to be inseparable from genius, effervesces in every page of Chaucer. The prologue to the Canterbury Tales is full of it. A pleasing specimen of it is the alarm in the farmyard in the Fable of the Cock and the Fox.

> The sely widow and her daughters two
> Herden these hennes crien and make wo
> And out at the dores they sterten anon
> And saw the fox toward the wood is gon
> And bare upon his back the cock away
> They crieden out Harow and Wala way!
> A ha the fox! and after him they ran
> And eke with staves many another man
> Ran Col our dog and Talbot and Girland
> And Malkin with the distaff in her hand
> Ran cow and calf and eke the very hogs
> So fered were for barking of the dogs
> And shouting of the men and women eke
> They ronnen so them thought their hearts would break
> The duckes crieden as men would them quell
> The geese for fear flewen over the trees
> Out of the hive came the swarm of bees

Of bras they broten beemes and of box
A horn and bone in which they blew and pooped
And therewithal they shrieked and they whooped
It seemed as if the very Heaven would fall.[7]

In Chaucer are conspicuous some of those ideas which re-appear continually in the Saxon race.[8] One of these is that of Gentilesse, or the doctrine of gentle behaviour founded upon Honor, which adheres in all times and fortunes to the English mind. Mr. Coleridge has remarked that "Chaucer represents a very high and romantic style of society among the gentry." [9] But beyond his delineation of actual manners he is possessed with the idea of the gentleman in no less strength and clearness than it existed in the minds of Spenser, Sidney, Milton, Clarendon and Addison and Burke. It may be worth while to dwell a moment on the historical development of this idea from its first narrow condition to its present liberal and just acceptation. It is remarked by the historian of the Anglo-Saxons[10] that that semibarbarous people paid a great regard to birth, and in all their laws and customs yielded a ready deference to a noble stock. And the natural faith that noble moral qualities of the sire will reappear in the son, is both the first form in which this virtuous respect is shown and is the cause of gentle behavior as it constitutes a claim beforehand on the son of a generous man. Sir James Mackintosh in his account of the reign of Edward I very happily describes the extension of this natural aristocracy.

"The principle of birth continued to lie at the foundation of the body of gentry and lent to every newly received candidate some portion of a feeling which is so much mingled with the moralities of education, with the means of generosity and with lasting exemption from grievous and disreputable toil that except where it is counteracted by jealousy, it never can fail, with or without the aid of legal privilege, to be an agreeable object of contemplation, whether in our own possession, or in that of others.

[7] Lines 3375–3401. Partly quoted in Warton, II, 254.
[8] This and the following paragraphs appear also in Lecture 2 of this series, probably moved there for a later reading (see p. 249).
[9] Coleridge, *Table Talk*, II, 101.
[10] Turner, II, 90.

But in the course of ages, the body gradually opened their arms to receive among them all men of liberal education and condition. It became a species of voluntary aristocracy, which, after some silent trial adopted every man who appeared to be distinguished from the multitude. It was bestowed neither by kings nor laws: and it was only to be withdrawn silently on strong appearances that the delicacies and refinements of honor which were imposed when the rank was granted, had been disregarded by some of its possessors. One of its last and most modern results was an unbroken chain of connection extending from the steps of the throne to the lowest limit of liberal education." [11]

Whilst thus in England the possession of the rank of a gentleman was at first ingrafted on the hereditary aristocracy and afterwards extended to persons of liberal education, the increasing ambition and activity of modern society, especially here in America has given a new enlargement to this species of rank. The disuse of wearing arms, badges, or any peculiar dress has opened the doors of this aristocracy to every man who can place himself within it. It is now on its true foundation. Neither birth, nor law, nor wealth, nor academick education can confer it. It is now to be obtained only by gentle behaviour. It is now thrown wholly as it ought to be on its moral distinctions. It is not the less a stable idea in the English and American mind with all the lapse of time and of institutions that were supposed its essential guards. Mr. Landor has finely said, "all titulars else must be created by others, a knight by a knight, a peer by a king while a gentleman is self existent." [12] It wears no badge but it is not the less inimitable by pretenders. Its distinctions are moral, but you need wait but a little and they shall give infallible proof of their presence. The most obvious of these marks of the gentleman, it has been said, is a certain generosity in trifles.[13] The deeper characteristic[s] stand in ludicrous contrast to the vulgar attributes. Lord Byron thinks the hand is the mark of a gentleman, another judge a fine voice. Three things,

[11] "Hist of Eng. Vol 1 p 269" [E]. Actually p. 226.
[12] "William Penn and Lord Peterborough," *Imaginary Conversations*, Second Series, London, 1829, Vol. II, 267. Most of the following quotations are transcribed from the page "Gentleman" in Emerson's manuscript journal "Encyclopaedia."
[13] Coleridge, *The Friend*, III, 323.

ENGLISH LITERATURE

says a lawgiver of Almacks,[14] constitute the gentleman, the hat, the boots, and the collar. I am happy to oppose to these an American witness. The late Mr. Randolph in a letter that does his memory great credit, remarks that "Truth is the distinction of a gentleman," that if his condition in the world is easy its greatest benefit is, that it releases him from the temptations that interest offers to speak falsely.[15]

In a similar spirit Mr. Wordsworth has defined the term Honor in one of his poems:

> O what is Honor? 'tis the finest sense
> Of Justice which the human mind can frame
> Intent each lurking frailty to disclaim
> And guard the way of life from all offense
> Suffered or done.[16]

An element of the gentlemanly character [is] a certain mildness and sweetness — which I think is oftener exhibited in England than in this country — a certain affectionateness and domesticity of deportment which carries with it an irresistible conviction that the party has no doubtful pretensions to defend, but a real desire to create cheerfulness and comfort around him. Hence a mark of a gentleman is a countenance in cheerful repose, intimating that he feels himself at home.

Chaucer is a teacher of this doctrine expressly and by implication throughout his works. In the Wife of Bath's tale he has given us excellent advice which embodies the most liberal and republican creed:

> But for ye speken of such gentillesse
> As is descended out of old richesse
> That therefore shullen ye be gentilmen
> Such arrogancè n'is not worth an hen.
>
> Loke who that is most vertuous alway,
> Prive and apert, and most entendeth ay
> To do the gentil dedes that he can,

[14] A famous London club. Saying ascribed to "W.W." in "Encyclopaedia." Mr. Worldly Wiseman?
[15] *Letters of John Randolph to a Young Relative*, Philadelphia, 1834, p. 15.
[16] Wordsworth, Sonnet: "Say, what is honour . . .", lines 1–5.

278

And take him for the gretest gentilman.
Crist wol we claim of him our gentillesse,
Not of our elders for their old richesse
For though they gave us all their heritage
For which we claim to be of high parage
Yet may they not bequethen for no thing
To none of us their virtuous living
That made them gentilmen called to be
And bade us folwen him in such degree

      Take fire and bere it into the darkest house
Betwixt this and the Mount of Caucasus
And let men shctte thc doorés and go thenne
Yet wol the fire as faire be and brenne
As twenty thousand men might it behold
His office naturel ay wol it hold
Up peril of my lif till that it die.

      Here may we see wel how that genterie
Is not annexed to possession
Sith folk ne don their operation
Alway as doth the fire ló in its kind
For God it wot men monn ful often find
A lordés son do shame and vilanie
And he that wol han pris of his genterie
For he was boren of a gentil house
And had his elders noble and vertous
And nill himselven do no gentle dedes
Nor follow his gentil ancestore that ded is
He n' is not gentle be he duke or erl
For villains sinful dedes make him a churl
For gentilesse is but the renomée
Of thin ancèstors for their high bountee
Which a strangè thing to thy person;
Thy gentilesse cometh from God alone.
Then cometh our veray gentilesse of grace,
It was nothing bequethed with our place.

The speaker refers to Valerius, to Seneca, and to Boethius as
authority.

      There shall ye seen expresse that it no drede is
That he is gentil that doth gentil dedis.[17]

[17] Wife of Bath's Tale, lines 1109-24, 1138-64, 1169-70.

This is the highest doctrine of gentle behaviour and one is glad it has been printed and read for five centuries.

I cannot forbear to remark how well it falls in with a saying of Mr. Coleridge: "Religion is in its essence the most gentlemanly thing in the world. It will alone gentilize if unmixed with cant, and I know nothing else that will alone. Certainly not the army which is thought to be the grand embellisher of manners." [18]

Chaucer exhibits in all his sustained pieces such carriage in his knights as comports with this opinion and carries it as Clarendon and other chivalrous spirits have done to extravagance, as when in the Frankelein's tale Dorigen has been entrapped by her own innocent words, having declared that she would receive the unlawful love of Aurelius when all the rocks of Brittany were taken away. A magician in the service of Aurelius raises the tides over all the rocks, and Aurelius renews his suit and relates her dilemma to her husband, Arviragus. He declares that Truth is the highest thing that man may keep and bids her tell Aurelius she will keep her word, and the magnanimity of Arviragus produces its just effect upon Aurelius who restores to her her rash word.

I have represented as a historical feature in the English race the respect for women, for want of which trait the ancient Greeks and Romans as well as the Oriental nations in all ages have never attained the highest point of Civilization. A severe morality is essential to high civilization and to the moral education of man it needs that the relation between the sexes should be established on a purely virtuous footing. It is the consequence of the unnatural condition of woman in the East that even life to a woman is reckoned a calamity. "When a daughter is born," says the Chinese Sheking, "she creeps on the ground: she is clothed with a wrapper: she plays with a tile: she is incapable of evil or of good." [19] Our venerable English bard fully shared this generous attribute of his nation. I suppose nothing will more forcibly strike the reader of Chaucer than his thorough acquaintance with the

[18] Coleridge, *Table Talk*, I, 91.

[19] Sheking, or Shih Ching, a collection of poems said to be compiled by Confucius. This is from Part II, Book IV, Ode 5.

female character. He does indeed know its weakness and its vice and has not shunned to show them. I am sorry for it. Well he had observed all those traits that in rarely endowed women command a veneration scarcely to be distinguished from worship. The whole mystery of humility, of love, of purity, and of faith, in woman, and how they make a woman unearthly and divine, he well knew, and has painted better than any other in Griselda and Blanche. The story of Griselda in the Canterbury Tales, is, I suppose the most pathetic poem in the language. And the Book of the Duchess, though the introduction be long and tedious, seems to me a beautiful portraiture of true love. All the sentiment is manly, honorable, and tender. I admire the description of Blanche who knew so well how to live

> That dulness was of her adrad
> She n'as too sober nor too glad
> In all thinges more measure
> Had never I trowe creature:

And though she drew all eyes, she knew it not,

> But good folke over all other
> She loved as man may his brother
> I have not wit that can suffice
> To comprehend her beaute
> But thus much I dare sain that she
> Was white ruddy fresh and lifely hewed
> And every day her beauty newed
> And nigh her face was alderbest
> For certes Nature had soch lest
> To make that faire, that truly she
> Was her cheif patron of beaute,
> And cheif ensample of al her werke
> And monster; for be it never so darke
> Methinketh I see her evermo
> And yet, moreover, though all tho
> That ever lived were now alive,
> They would not have found to descrive
> In all her face a wicked sign
> For it was sad, simple, and benign.[20]

[20] Lines 879–882, 891–92, 902–918.

To counterbalance his sarcasms in the Knight's Tale of Palamon and Arcite where he informs us that

> Women, as to speken in commune,
> They folwen all the favor of fortune,

and the cry of the attendants around the corpse of Palamon,

> Why woldest thou be dead? these women cry,
> That haddest gold enough and Emelie,[21]

he draws, in the Doctor's tale, the charming picture of Virginia. I must at least read the commencement. She was fair

> For Nature hath with soverain diligence
> Yformed her in so great excellence
> As though she wolde sayn Lo! I, Nature,
> Thus can I form and paint a creature,
> When that me list; who can me counterfeit?
> Pigmalion? Not though he aye forge and bete
> Or grave or paint, for I dare wel sain
> Apelles, Zeuxis shoulden werke in vain.
> For he that is the former principal
> Hath maked me his vicar general
> To form and painten earthly creatures
> My Lord and I ben ful of one accord
> I made hir to the worship of my Lord.[22]

The devotion of woman to passion is a frequent theme and is presented with exquisite pathos in the story of Theseus and Ariadne.

He shows his skill in man in the Alchemist's apprentice when he says,

> And yet for all my smert and all my grief
> For all my sorwe labor and mischefe
> I coulde never leve it in no wise;[23]

in the jangling and hard thoughts of the multitude concerning the hors of bras:

[21] Lines 2681–82, 2835–36.
[22] Lines 8–26.
[23] Canon's Yeoman's Prologue, lines 714–17.

As lewed peple demen comunly
Of thinges that ben made more subtilly
Than they can in their lewdness comprehend
They demen gladly to the badder end;[24]

in the caution which mine host gives to the clerk of Oxenford when he is to tell his story:

Speketh so plain at this time I you pray
That we may understonden what ye say; [25]

his remark upon the sergeant of the Law:

Nowhere so busy a man as he there n'as
And yet he seemed busier than he was.[26]

The Destinee ministre general
That executeth in the world over al
The purveiance that God hath sen beforne
So strong it is that though the world had sworne
The contrary of a thing by yea and nay
Yet sometime it shall fallen on a day
That falleth not efte in a thousand yere
For certainly our appetites here
Be it of war of pees or hate or love
All this is ruled by the sight above.[27]

The pious tenderness of the prioress' tale is known to all in the modern version of Mr. Wordsworth. And the Man of Law's tale is of equal beauty. Milton seems to have preferred the Squier's tale of Cambuscan bold.

The influence of Chaucer I have remarked already is very conspicuous on all our early literature. Not only Pope, Dryden, and Milton have been indebted to him but a large unacknowledged debt is easily traced. From Chaucer succeeding writers have borrowed the English versions of the celebrated classic mythology. Phebus, Diana and Mars, Priam, Hector, Troilus, Dido, Theseus, Ariadne reign as much in his poems as in those of the ancients, though in quite new costume of manners and speech. Chaucer

[24] Squire's Tale, lines 221–24.
[25] Clerk's Prologue, lines 19–20.
[26] General Prologue, lines 321–22.
[27] Knight's Tale, lines 1663–72.

however did not invent this modern dress for the old gods and heroes. In the year 1260 Guido de Colonna, a native of Messina in Sicily, published a grand prose romance in Latin in fifteen books, called Historia de Bello Trojano. This was founded on the apocryphal Greek history of Dares Phrygius and enriched by all paraphrases from Ovid and Statius. This is Chaucer's chief magazine. This is the book which was turned into English poetry by Lydgate at the command of Henry V and translated into English prose by Caxton the printer in 1471. Chaucer's other sources are Petrarch, Boccacio, Lollius, and the Provençal poets. The Romaunt of the Rose is translated from William of Lorris and John of Meun. Troilus and Creseide from Lollius of Urbino. The House of Fame is from the French or Italian. The Cock and the Fox is from the Lais of Marie a French poetess.[28] And the extent of Chaucer's obligations to his foreign contemporaries and predecessors is so great as to induce the inquiry whether he can claim the praise of an original writer.

The truth is all works of literature are Janus faced and look to the future and to the past. Shakspear, Pope, and Dryden borrow from Chaucer and shine by his borrowed light. Chaucer reflects Boccacio and Colonna and the Troubadours; Boccacio and Colonna elder Greek and Roman authors, and these in their turn others if only history would enable us to trace them. There never was an original writer. Each is a link in an endless chain. To receive and to impart are the talents of the poet and he ought to possess both in equal degrees. He is merely the marble mouth of a fountain into which the waters ascend and out of which they flow. This is but the nature of man, universal receiving to the end of universal giving. The great theory of the Solar System published by Copernicus in the sixteenth century is but the revival of a very ancient system of astronomy known to Archimedes, and in his writings attributed to Aristarchus of Samos. The sublime prayer which Jesus taught his disciples, Grotius has shown to be a compilation of existing Jewish petitions,[29] and learned

[28] "The influence of Chaucer I have remarked . . . French poetess" (*W*, IV, 197–98). Based on Warton, I, 128–131. *Cf.* Warton, II, 179–180, 292–304.

[29] Hugo Grotius (1583–1645), author of *De Veritate Religionis Christianae*, 1627.

oriental scholars find the leading thought of many of his precepts in Hebrew proverbs current in his time. Where is the doctrine of the newest sect of religion or philosophy that we cannot match with its counterpart from some primeval verse or proverb? Jefferson is not less the author of the Declaration of Independence because every clause of it had been suggested by some Memorial or Remonstrance of the period.

And the nobler is the truth or sentiment concerned the less important becomes the question of authorship. It never troubles the simple lover of truth, said Mendelsohn,[30] from whom he derived such or such a sentiment. Whoever expresses to me a noble thought makes ridiculous the pains of the critic who should tell him where such a thing had been said before. For truth is always in the world: "It is no more according to Plato than according to me." Truth is always present; it only needs to lift the iron lids of the mind's eye to read its oracles. But the fact is it is as difficult to appropriate the thoughts of others as it is to invent.

Every great man, as Homer, Milton, Bacon, and Aristotle, necessarily takes up into himself all the wisdom that is current in his time. It is only an inventor [can use the inventions of others].

There is a recorded conversation of Goethe with Dumont, the nephew of the celebrated Dumont who had been the secretary of Mirabeau, upon the disclosures which that writer had made of Mirabeau's obligations to the men of talent who surrounded him. "The French want that Mirabeau should be their Hercules. And they are right: — but a Hercules must be abundantly supplied with food. They forget, good people, that this colossus is composed of parts; — that this demigod is a collective being. The greatest genius will never be worth much if he pretends to draw exclusively from his own resources. What is genius but the faculty of seizing and turning to account everything that strikes us, of coordinating and breathing life into all the materials that present themselves; of taking here marble, there brass, and building a durable monument with them. If I were not assured that Mirabeau possessed in the highest possible degree the art of appropriating the knowledge and the thoughts of those around him, I

[30] Moses Mendelsohn (1729–1786), author of *Phädon*.

should not believe the stories told of his influence. The most original young painter who thinks he owes everything to his invention cannot, if he really has genius, come into the room in which we are now sitting and look round at the drawings with which it is hung without going out a different man from what he came in and with a new supply of ideas. What should I be — what would remain to me if this art of appropriation were considered as derogatory to genius? What have I done? I have collected and turned to account all that I have seen, heard, observed. I have put in requisition the works of nature and of man. Every one of my writings has been furnished to me by a thousand different persons, a thousand different things: the learned and the ignorant, the wise and the foolish, infancy and age have come in turn — generally without having the least suspicion of it — to bring me the offering of their thoughts, their faculties, their experience. Often they have sowed the harvest I have reaped. My work is that of an aggregation of beings taken from the whole of nature. It bears the name of Goethe." [31]

The literary man who feels his position and duties should be solicitous to supply men with intellectual light, which he can often do better by direct importation from foreign sources than by the composition of new works, as when Alfred translated Boethius and books of travels for his countrymen or Wicliffe and Luther the Bible. Morality is concerned only with the spirit in which it is done; if the writer appropriates the praise and conceals the debt he is a plagiarist. If he generously feel that the thought most strictly his own is not his own and recognizes with awe the perpetual suggestion of God he then makes even the oldest thoughts new and fresh when he speaks them. Chaucer is never anxious to hide his obligations; he frankly acknowledges in every page or whenever he wants a rhyme that his author or the old book says so; and thus is to us in the remote past a luminous mind collecting and imparting to us the religion, the wit, and humanity of a whole age.

[31] Austin, *Goethe*, III, 75–77.

Shakspear [first lecture]

After an interval of a week, Emerson again took up his series with two lectures, on December 10 and 17, 1835, on Shakespeare. He had originally planned only one, with a lecture on Spenser for the fifth of the series, but on reconsideration, Spenser was dropped out altogether and Shakespeare given a unique position of importance (manuscript journal "L"). There is evidence both in the text itself and in the working notes that these lectures were read more than once, both in an expanded form and compressed into one. The entire passage on language and the nature of the imagination in the early pages is a revision, presumably for a later reading, with insertions from Lecture 1 of this series and from "The Uses of Natural History." Most of this material in turn went into *Nature*, chiefly the chapter "Language," which thus has a complicated manuscript history, now partly lost. There is no textual correspondence between these lectures and the later lecture on Shakespeare included in the series on Representative Men (1845), nor is it likely that they were repeated in the course of readings at Chickering's Hall, Boston, in 1869.

Emerson's familiarity with Shakespeare's works was lifelong. An eight-volume set was among the books in his father's library sold at auction in 1811 when he was only eight years old (Cameron, II, 137), and his own library contained at least three editions that he could have used at the time he was preparing these early lectures. Actually, to judge from the sixty-three pages of working notes now in the envelope for Lecture 6, he depended chiefly on Malone's edition of which he withdrew the first three volumes, or "Prolegomena," from the Athenaeum and Harvard during this year (*Reading*, 104). The same notes quote opinions from Herder, Goethe, Heine, Hazlitt, and Mme. de Staël, but some of these notes were clearly made after the date of the lecture. Coleridge's opinions in "Letters, Conversations, etc." and in "Quart. Rev. no. 105" are cited; and there is a reference to "Langbaine Account of the Eng. Dram. Poets Article *Shakespeare*," but the bulk of these notes are quotations from the plays and comments on them. Virtually every quotation in these lectures appears in these notes, often in similar context. The notes on *Henry VIII* attempt to identify

Shakespeare's contributions to that play. Some passages are transcribed from the journals for 1832–35, in which there are many references to Shakespeare (see especially *J*, II, 422–23, 481–82; III, 260, 287, 290, 307, 327, 329, 408, 414, 451, 499, 573).

Emerson's somewhat contradictory expressions of opinion about Shakespeare have been the subject of some scholarly concern. Actually, as Robert P. Falk has pointed out ("Emerson and Shakespeare," *PMLA*, LVI [June, 1941], 523–543), all of it is favorable except for the "one derogatory criticism" in *Representative Men*. The full text of the early lectures confirms this opinion, providing further evidences of his view of Shakespeare as the Ideal for the poet and of his pleasure in reading aloud from the poems and plays, which he obviously did well. In fact, these two lectures, even more than others in the series, are as much public readings as critical essays. Later, when the poet was asked to represent the more rigorous demands of the "moral sentiment," Shakespeare — and all but the most ethical of poetry — suffered temporary eclipse; here, and more consistently throughout his life, Emerson justifies by theory and example the most unstinting recognition of Shakespeare's "universal mind." Some comments from the notes which are not in either Journals or Lectures are quoted in the textual notes.

It is impossible in the brief limits of the few lectures I am engaged to read to the Society to treat of all the great names of English literature. I am compelled to omit all notice of Mandeville, of Wicliffe, of Sir Thomas More, of Latimer. I am compelled, though with great reluctance, to pass by in silence the great name of Spenser, in order to present notices of those writers whom chiefly I wish to examine. The subject of the present lecture is the genius of Shakspear.

The life of Shakspear makes an extraordinary part of modern history. His immense and evergrowing influence over the human mind places him alone among poets. The silence and steadiness with which this kingdom of the intellect has been reared, a stone cut out from the mountain without hands to form the most great and durable of edifices, add to the interest of the event, and stimulate our inquiry into the sources of his power. It is not without cause, this irresistible dominion. It proceeds from a structure of mind as remarkable. To analyze the powers of such an individual is to analyze the powers of the human mind. In the very humble endeavor I shall make to separate the elements of his genius, I must ask the pardon of my audience if I tax their patience with something of metaphysical inquiry. He possessed above all men the essential gift of the Poet, namely, the Imaginative Power, and as this is a power which all men possess in greater or less degree and yet is not I think rightly defined in our popular criticism I shall endeavor to show its foundation in one of the most interesting facts with which we are acquainted.

The power of the Poet depends on the fact that the material world is a symbol or expression of the human mind and part for part. Every natural fact is a symbol of some spiritual fact. Light and darkness are our familiar expression for knowledge and ignorance and heat for love. Who looks upon a river in a meditative hour and is not reminded of the flux of all things? Throw a stone into the stream and the circles that propagate themselves are the beautiful type of all influence. All the facts in natural history taken by themselves have no value but are barren like a single sex but marry it to human history and it is full of life. Whole Floras, all Linnaeus' and Buffon's volumes are but dry catalogues of facts but the most trivial of these facts, the habit of a plant, the organs, the work, or noise of an insect applied to the illustration of a fact in intellectual philosophy or in any way associated to human nature affects us in the most lively and agreeable manner. The seed of a plant; — to what affecting analogies in the nature of man is that little fruit made use of through all conversation up to the voice of Paul who calls the human corpse a seed. "It is sown a natural body; it is raised a spiritual body." [1] The motion of the earth round its axis and round the sun makes the day and the year. These are certain amounts of brute light and heat. But is there no intent of an analogy between man's life and the seasons? and do the seasons gain no grandeur or pathos from that analogy? The instincts of the ant are very unimportant considered as the ant's but the moment a ray of relation is seen to extend from it to man, and the mite is seen to be a monitor, a little body with a

[1] I Corinthians 15:44.

289

mighty heart, then all its habits even that recently observed that it never sleeps become sublime.[2]

This omnipresent analogy of the visible to the invisible world itself opens so wide a field of inquiry that I can at present only indicate its borders. But the laws of moral nature answer to those of matter as face to face in a glass. The axioms of physics translate the laws of ethics: the whole is greater than a part; reaction is equal to action; the smallest weight may be made to lift the greatest, the difference of weight being compensated by time; and the like, which have an ethical as well as physical sense. Observe too these propositions have a much more extensive and universal sense when applied to human life than when confined to technical use. In like manner the memorable words of history and the proverbs of nations consist usually of a natural fact selected as a picture or parable of moral truth. Thus, "A rolling stone gathers no moss;" "A bird in the hand is worth two in the bush;" "A cripple in the right way will beat a racer in the wrong;" " 'Tis hard to carry a full cup even;" "Vinegar is the son of wine;" "The last ounce broke the camel's back;" "Long lived trees make roots first;" and the like. In their primary sense these are trivial facts but we repeat them for the value of their analogical import.

The more attention is bestowed on this subject the more clearly it is seen that there is nothing lucky or capricious in these analogies but that they are constant and pervade nature. This relation between thought and the world is not fancied by some poet but stands in the will of God. It appears to men or it does not appear but there it is. All men sometimes perceive it. The moment our discourse rises above the region of familiar facts and is inflamed with passion or exalted by thought, it clothes itself in images. A man conversing in earnest, if he watch his intellectual process will find that always a material image more or less luminous arises in his mind cotemporaneous with every thought which furnishes the garment of the thought. Hence good writing and brilliant discourse are perpetual allegories.[3]

[2] "Every natural fact . . . becomes sublime" (*W*, I, 26–29; *J*, III, 326–27); *cf.* "English Literature," Lecture 1, p. 221.

[3] "This omnipresent analogy . . . perpetual allegories" (*W*, I, 32–34, 30–31); *cf.* "The Uses of Natural History," pp. 24–25; cf. *J*, III, 510, 227.

Now the office of the Poet is to perceive and use these analogies. He converts the solid globe, the land, the sea, the air, the sun, the animals into symbols of thought. He makes the outward creation subordinate and merely a convenient alphabet to express thoughts and emotions. And this act or vision of the mind is called Imagination. It is the use which the Reason makes of the material world, for purposes of expression. It is not therefore a separate part or member but is the act of the total mind. It is that active state of the mind in which it forces things to obey the laws of thought, takes up all present objects in a despotic manner into its own image and likeness, and makes the thought which occupies it the centre of the world. Lear thinks no evil can come to any man but through daughters. The difference between an imaginative and an unimaginative mind is this, that one conforms things to its thoughts and the other conforms its thoughts to things. The one views all nature as fluid and impresses its own character thereon, the other views nature as rooted and fast. In Holinshed's Chronicle [4] all events are narrated as they fell out in such or such a year, in such or such a county. In the play of Richard III the same events are made to flow from the will and character of Richard, and from the laws of human nature.

As soon as a man is inflamed with passion he immediately finds picturesque language, as soon as his intellectual faculties are active he does the same. He magnifies the small. He micrifies the large. He makes the refractory world ductile and flexible in his hands and treats nature as merely apparent and thought as the only reality.

The intensity of thought gives the speaker the right to take hold of every high and vast thing as in common moods he uses familiar and trivial objects to explain his meaning. Thus Lear feeling himself in his hoary hairs outraged appeals to the heavens:

> O heavens!
> If you do love old men, if your sweet sway
> Allow obedience if yourselves are old
> Make it your cause.

[4] Raphael Holinshed, *The Chronicles of England, Scotland, and Ireland* (2nd ed. 1587), a principal source for Shakespeare's historical plays.

And not less readily does it seize a resemblance in the small and obscure and dignify the object by uniting it to its emotion. The sublime author of the Apocalypse in his great vision of the destruction of the world, says, "The stars shall fall from heaven as the figtree casteth her untimely fruits."

Shakspear possesses the power of subordinating nature for the purposes of expression beyond all poets. His imperial muse tosses the creation like a bauble from hand to hand to embody any capricious shade of thought that is uppermost in his mind. Open any page grave or gay and you shall still find this despotism of the imagination summoning the elements at will to illustrate his momentary thought:

> How like a younker and a prodigal
> The scarfed bark puts from her native bay
> Hugged and embraced by the strumpet wind
> How like a prodigal doth she return
> With overlabored ribs and weathered sides
> Lean rent and beggared by the strumpet wind.

In Measure for Measure Lord Angelo's exculpation of Isabel:

> Not she she tempts me not, but tis I
> Who lying by the violet in the sun
> Do as the carrion does not as the flower
> Corrupt with virtuous season.

What can exceed the hyperbole in the gay song

> Take those lips away
> Which so sweetly were forsworn;
> And those eyes the break of day
> Lights that do mislead the morn.

The power to make any object great or little at pleasure as suits his purpose may be shown from two or three passages from The Tempest. Prospero says,

> The strong based promontory
> Have I made shake, and by the spurs plucked up
> The pine and cedar.

He soothes the frenzy of Alonzo and his companions with music and says,

The charm dissolves apace,
And as the morning steals upon the night
Melting the darkness so their rising senses
Begin to chase the ignorant fumes that mantle
Their clearer reason. . . .
Their understanding
Begins to swell and the approaching tide
Will shortly fill the reasonable shores
That now lie foul and muddy.

Sometimes the picture is conveyed in a single word as where Hamlet says of the king his uncle,

If his occulted guilt
Do not itself unkennel in one speech,[5]

which immediately compares his evil thoughts to dogs and unclean beasts.[6]

Though this imaginative power pervades all his dramas yet it was never so purely manifested as in his sonnets, a little volume of poems whose wonderful merit has been thrown into the shade by the splendor of his plays; yet I know not where in English or in foreign poetry more remarkable examples can be found of the tyranny of the imagination or the perfect control assumed of all nature by the poet.

These poems are written at the same time with such closeness of thought and such even drowsy sweetness of rhythm that they are not to be dispatched in a hasty paragraph but deserve to be studied in the critical manner in which the Italians explain the verses of Dante and Petrarch. One opens them as a little volume of love songs as indeed many of them are and finds them the production of a mind exalted to that pitch that he treats time, space, the world, works of art, the sea, the generations of men, the whole series of thought — with a sovereignty as if they existed to him alone and to be subordinated to the subject that for the moment now occupies his mind.

[5] *Lear*, II, 4: 192–94; Revelation 6:13; *Merch. of V.*, II, 6: 14–19; *Meas. for M.*, II, 2: 167–170; IV, 1: 1–4; *Tempest*, V, 1: 46–48, 64–68, 79–82; *Hamlet*, III, 2: 85–86.

[6] *Cf.*, for the above four paragraphs, W, I, 51–54 and "English Literature," Lecture 1, pp. 223–24.

I will read a few lines from some of them to show how different they are from common amatory poetry and with what solemn and costly materials he rears his temples:

If my dear love were but the child of state
It might for fortune's bastard be unfathered
As subject to time's love or to time's hate
Weeds among weeds or flowers with flowers gathered
No it was builded far from accident
It suffers not in smiling pomp nor falls
Under the blow of thralling discontent . . .
It fears not policy that heretic
Which works on leases of short numbered hours
But all alone stands hugely politic
That it nor grows with heat nor drowns with showers . . .

Great princes' favorites their fair leaves spread
But as the marigold at the sun's eye
And in themselves their pride lies buried
For at a frown they in their glory die
The painful warrior famoused for worth
After a thousand victories once foiled
Is from the book of honor razed quite
And all the rest forgot for which he toiled
   Then happy I that love and am beloved
   Where I may not remove or be removed.

Full many a glorious morning have I seen
Flatter the mountain tops with sovereign eye
Kissing with golden face the meadows green
Gilding pale streams with heavenly alchemy
Anon permit the basest clouds to ride
With ugly rack on his celestial face . . .

That thou are blamed shall not be thy defect
For slander's mark was ever yet the fair
The ornament of beauty is suspect
A crow that flies in heaven's sweetest air . . .

Did not the heavenly rhetoric of thine eye
Gainst which the world could not hold argument
Persuade my heart to that false perjury . . .

Not mine own fears nor the prophetic soul
Of the wide world dreaming on things to come . . .

294

He uses time or duration as the casket in which his beloved is inclosed:

> So am I as the rich whose blessed key
> Can bring him to his sweet uplocked treasure,
> The which he will not every hour survey
> For blunting the fine point of seldom pleasure.
> Therefore are feasts so solemn and so rare
> Since seldom coming, in the long year set,
> Like stones of worth they thinly placed are,
> Or captain jewels in the carcanet.
> So is the time that keeps you, as my chest
> Or as the wardrobe which the robe doth hide
> To make some special instant special blest
> By new unfolding his imprisoned pride.
> Blessed are you whose worthiness gives scope
> Being had to triumph being lacked to hope.

Many of them are written on a singular topic, to persuade a beautiful young man to leave his single life and enter the married state. This topic gives him occasion for all the most beautiful allusions to the passage of time:

> Ah yet doth beauty as the dial hand
> Steal from its figure and no pace perceived . . .

> Thou by the dial's stealthy pace mayst know
> Time's peevish progress to eternity . . .

> When I consider every thing that grows
> Holds in perfection but a little moment
> That this huge stage presenteth nought but shows
> Whereon the stars in secret influence comment
> When I perceive that men as plants increase
> Cheered and checked even by the selfsame sky
> Vaunt in your youthful sap, at height decrease
> And wear their brave state out of memory etc.[7]

They deserve on many accounts the most accurate criticism. But I refer to these poems as informed throughout with the presence of an overmastering imagination or the power of subduing all

[7] Sonnets 124, 25, 33, 70; *Love's L.L.*, IV, 3: 60–62 (also lines 29–31 of "The Passionate Pilgrim"); Sonnets 107, 52, 104, 77, and 15.

nature and compelling it to be the organ of the poet's mind. They form perhaps as striking an example of this intellectual function as any book in the history of literature.

It is very much to be regretted that there are commonly printed in the same volume some mean and base poems, whether Shakspear's or not, which have no title to their place.

But it is plain that however gorgeous and elevated is this power of creation or of subjecting nature to the thought of man yet it has this vice that it leaves us without any measure or standard for comparing thought with thought. Each passing thought or emotion filling the whole sky of the poet's mind and bringing a new world of images to embody and adorn it, he is no way differenced from the man of diseased mind. Of this fact Shakspear has expressed his own sense in the well known lines:

> The lunatic the lover and the poet
> Are of imagination all compact
> One sees more devils than vast hell can hold
> That is the madman the lover all as frantic
> Sees Helen's beauty in a brow of Egypt
> The poet's eye in a fine frenzy rolling
> Glances from Heaven to earth from earth [*sic*]
> And as imagination bodies forth
> The forms of things unknown, the poet's pen
> Turns them to shapes and gives to airy nothing
> A local habitation and a name.[8]

This cannot be denied. Such an imagination alone, untempered by other elements, would be a disease. In many men of fine powers the imagination has been morbid from its own excess. Even Luther with all his coarseness was not able always to distinguish thoughts from events, the symbol his imagination availed itself of from the thing.[9] The antidote provided in nature against the influence of any part is in the influence of the whole. There is a state of repose, an integrity to the mind, in which all objects are thrown back to stand in their due proportion. This vision of all being we call Reason. We speak of it generally as the mind's Eye.

[8] *Mid. N. Dr.*, V, 1: 7–17.
[9] *Cf.* the discussion of Luther in Coleridge, *The Friend*, First Landing Place, Essay II.

It is the Reason which affirms the laws of moral nature and thereby raises us to a region above the intellect.

The healthful mind keeps itself studiously open to all influences and like the earth receives a ray from every star in the concave sphere in which it hangs. If its bold speculation carries one thought to extravagance presently in its return it carries another opposite truth to its extreme limitations. Moreover the special check to the excess of imagination is the appetite which leads man to introvert his eye, to explore the grounds of his own being, to compare his own faculties. This is philosophy when applied to man, criticism when applied to his works, and of all faculties esteemed the most fatal to the triumphs of the poetic art, because it seems necessary that the poet should believe his own fable and be the first convert to his own inspiration.

Shakspeare added to this towering Imagination this self-recovering, self collecting force. Universality is the trait that all men remark in him. It is exceedingly difficult to extract an autobiography from his works, so impartial and devoid of all favorite moods and topics are his works. And he recognizes in certain thrilling strains the spiritual truths which are the basis and fountain of our being. Moreover he joined to it a habit of the most subtile and searching speculation into the cause and foundation of man's being and faculties.

His reflective powers are very active. The questions are ever starting up in his mind as in that of one of the most resolute skeptics concerning life and death and man and nature. What is this conscious being? Has the world any real existence, or do we dwell only in a picture gallery which the sovereign Mind paints on Space and Time? The solid globe melts away and leaves not a rack behind. He doubts if any thing is, he doubts if he doubt. Hamlet subscribes himself, "Thine evermore, O dear lady, whilst this machine is to him." He arrives at the conclusion that there's nothing either good or bad but thinking makes it so. This brave o'erhanging firmament, this majestical roof fretted with golden fire appears no other thing to him than a foul and pestilent congregation of vapors.

297

> And we fools of nature
> So horridly to shake our disposition
> With thoughts above the reaches of our souls [10]

> Man proud man
> Drest in a little brief authority
> Most ignorant of what he's most assured
> His glassy essence

> We are such stuff
> As dreams are made on and our life
> Is rounded with a sleep

> Since I suppose we are made to be no stronger
> Than faults may shake our frames.

> Ham. Poor Ophelia
> Divided from herself and her fair judgment
> Without the which we are pictures and mere beasts

> Imog. I thought I was a cavekeeper
> And cook to honest creatures but 'tis not so
> 'Twas but a bolt of nothing shot at nothing
> Which the brain makes of fumes.

> Life's but a walking shadow; a poor player
> That struts and frets his hour upon the stage
> And then is heard no more; it is a tale
> Told by an idiot full of sound and fury
> Signifying nothing.[11]

How strong a spirit of morbid speculation is acknowledged when Prince Hal says to Poins, "Indeed these humble considerations make me out of love with greatness. What a disgrace is it to me to take note how many pair of silk stockings thou hast, namely, these and those that were the peach-coloured ones, or to bear the inventory of thy shirts; as one for superfluity and one other for use." [12]

[10] *Hamlet*, II, 2: 123–24, 310–15; I, 4: 54–56.
[11] *Meas. for M.*, II, 2: 117–120, 4: 132–33; *Tempest*, IV, 1: 156–58; *Hamlet*, IV, 5: 84–86; *Cymb.*, IV, 2: 298–301; *Macb.*, V, 5: 23–27.
[12] *Henry IV, Pt. II*, II, 2: 14–20.

In general Shakspeare accepts and uses the popular religion of his day but ever and anon he puts all afloat:

> How his audit stands who knows but heaven
> But in our circumstance and course of thought
> 'Tis heavy with him.

I forbear to enlarge upon this topic by adducing the well known soliloquies of Hamlet and Macbeth upon the secret of nature. But it would be easy to show from the sonnets this obstinate self scrutiny which dictated the saying in Hamlet,

> All that live must die
> Passing through Nature to Eternity.[13]

I discover in many passages in the sonnets the cunning dreams of oriental contemplation. He believes that he has preexisted and all the shows of Time are recent and new beside his soul.

> No Time thou shalt not boast that I do change
> Thy pyramids built up with newer might
> To me are nothing novel nothing strange
> They are but dressings of a former sight
> Our dates are brief and therefore we admire
> What thou dost foist upon us that is old
> And rather make them born to our desire
> Than think that we before have heard them told.[14]

Thus singularly did he unite the faculties of the Poet and the Philosopher. But had Shakspear possessed only these faculties he might have still been thrust by the derision of the world into the class of mere contemplators and visionaries with Pyrrho, Plato, Plotinus, Kant, with students and philosophers, whom however they may be reverenced after they are dead, when alive the world bows aside as amiable enthusiasts whose speculations tend to no human purpose. These however deal in the real world of truths, of thoughts and slight the apparent world and are slighted by it.

Porphyry relates that his master Plotinus was all his lifetime affected with shame because he had a body [15] and Diogenes in

---

[13] *Hamlet*, III, 3: 82–84; I, 2: 72–73.
[14] Sonnet 123.
[15] Porphyry, *Life of Plotinus*, opening sentence.

the many indecencies and impertinences related of him is evidently impelled by a similar philosophic shame. The philosopher converses only with thoughts or with truths abstracted from all personal relations. He considers man as an object of study and not at all as an object of affection. But in the actual world nature as we say is too strong for us and we are compelled to love and to hate, to go with the tide of men's opinions and see things coloured by our partialities; we hug our little local prejudices, we exaggerate trifles and become slaves of our love of comfort and use.

But the vast majority of men though by nature all related to and having access to this world of thought, yet live and act mainly in quite another region, that is, in the apparent world of the senses, acting with simple reference to their actual relations, that is, as mortals, as fathers, as tradesmen, as householders. They go in and out providing for the body and taking council of their eyes and ears quite unembarrassed by any skeptical fancies. This material world is the natural discipline which God has fastened upon the human spirit. Some men perceive more clearly than others the relations of the outward or apparent world and act agreeably to them. The name we give to this perception is Common Sense. And we are wont to think a conformity of the spirit to this condition of its being so important, as to express it by the word *humanity*, which we contrast with the divine aspirations of the soul.

Shakspear possessed this quality of clear perception of the relations of the actual world in at least as remarkable a manner as he had the perception of truth. Shakspear delights in the earth and earthly things. He soars indeed to [a] heaven of thought and there poises himself as if it were his natural element but he returns instantly to the ground and walks and plays and rolls himself in hearty frolic with his humble mates. All the little that we know of his personal history falls in perfectly with this impression. He was so much like other men that his genius was not suspected in his own time. He impressed men as a prudent, pleasant man in the management of his theatre, whilst Beaumont and Jonson were evidently thought the true poets. Ben Jonson unquestionably esteemed himself the better writer. Even the fables and traditions about him are coloured with an earthly not a romantic hue. 'Tis said he was obliged to flee to London for stealing deer. 'Tis said he held horses at the theatre door. 'Tis known that he married early, was a thrifty, pleasant man, easy, fond of good fellows, making epigrams and biting jokes upon Jonson and others but mentioned by his contemporaries as upright in his dealings: and the papers that are extant show that he was a lender of money, that he built a new House, that he left a good estate accumulated by himself in his will to his children. "He was," says Aubrey, "a handsome well shaped man, very good company, and of a very ready pleasant and smooth wit." Fuller in his Worthies of England informs us, "Many were the wit combats between Shakspear and Ben Jonson. I behold them like a Spanish great galleon and an English Man of War. Master Jonson like the former was built far higher in learning, solid but slow in his performances. Shakspear like the latter lesser in bulk but lighter in sailing could turn with all tides, tack about and take advantage of all winds by the quickness of his wit and invention."

Aubrey tells us that "he went up and down gathering humors wherever he came and that the Constable in Much Ado About Nothing he happened to take at Grendon in Bucks (I think it was Midsummer Night that he happened to be there,) on the road from London to Stratford and there was living that Constable about 1642 when I first came to Oxford."

The epitaph he wrote for himself is a work of the same sort. The same sympathy of a quiet householder who in dying is chiefly desirous that his bones shall lie undisturbed.

> Good friend for Jesus sake forbear
> To dig the dust enclosed here
> Blest be the man that spares these stones
> And cursed he that moves my bones.[16]

It was this overpowering instinct of Nature, this fitness for and pleasure in the common social world in business and society and amusement that drew Shakspear to the drama. In his earlier poems Venus and Adonis, Tarquin and Lucrece, and the Sonnets he had displayed prodigious imaginative and reflective power.

---

[16] The above biographical facts and quotes come from Malone, Vol. II.

But for all that, — wonderful as they are — they are not attractive poems. I cannot otherwise account for the neglect in which they have lain. They are like a monotonous tune of delicate music which inclines us to sleep. They are like a philosophical theory which we leave in our study and which is never remembered in the street. He himself laughs at them when he describes

> the lover
> Sighing like furnace with a doleful ballad
> Made to his mistress' eyebrow.[17]

The action of ordinary life in every sort, the heroic, the wretched, the humorous, yielded him the aliment he longed for. See him unbutton himself in unrestrained glee in the jokes and faults of Falstaff. He is the very impersonation of fun and animal comfort taking his ease in his inn. The man is portrayed with such unmixed delight that we feel that he must be painting himself. In the unfeigned joy with which he brings in his varied platoon of clowns, scoundrels, and braggarts; in the love of money and of revenge of his Jew; in the country manners of his shepherds and lasses; in the delicate and beseeching affection of the lover for the maid; of the wife for the husband; in the outraged affection of Othello and Lear; in the pride of Coriolanus; in the fierce ambition and love of War which glitters and bristles in King John and Henry V and Henry VI we behold the overflowing love of life, the hearty sympathy of this great man with every pulse and sensation of flesh and blood, with the sweet and bitter lot of mortal man.

Such then I take to be the grand elements of his genius that, whilst the author of the book of Job, whilst Ossian, whilst Bunyan has been made eminent by possessing the imaginative power in a high degree and so was a poet; and whilst Aristotle, or David Hume, or Im[manuel] Kant has possessed the reflective faculty in as extraordinary a degree and so was a philosopher; and very many persons have possessed the accurate perception of things as they stand in the world around us and so have been practical men: Shakspear united in himself all these faculties as no man had joined them, he was a poet, a philosopher, and a man.

[17] *As You Like It*, II, 7: 147–49.

It will be easy to draw the best examples from the writings of Shakspear of each of the three great intellectual faculties of man, the Imaginative, the Reflective, and the Practical. They can be drawn thence as they cannot from the writings of any single author beside. Milton however exalted above him by the purity and religious elevation of his life may compete with Shakspear in the first of these great attributes but cannot in the two last.

I have distinguished these faculties and endeavored to exhibit proofs of the separate action of each of them. But the secret of his transcendant superiority as a writer lies in the joint activity and never ceasing presence of them all. What he writes is the dictate of the truest reason thrown into the fittest image and warmed with life.[18]

His wisdom draws men to him. We do not go to him to have our ear tickled with the tune of his verse nor our fancy amused with flowers and rainbows. But we go to him because whilst he yields us these gratifications, this wondrous Sage takes possession of our heart and mind and instructs and elevates us. He gives us truth, clear, wholesome, and practical. He knows what is great and noble in man and also what is ludicrous and what is base and in every line he communicates his knowledge. His verse never halts from weakness and repeats the same thing but advances unceasingly and gives us things and not words.

I should gladly add to these already extended remarks a notice of his rhythm, his language, his characters, his maxims but when would the subject of Shakspear be exhausted? I hasten to recapitulate the view of the Lecture.

Why is it that this great man is his own silent eulogy to all thoughtful men and almost to all men? Why is it that our power to apprehend and love him has become a sort of gauge of our degree of culture and his mind a measure of the human mind? It is because this soul reaches through the three kingdoms of man's life, the moral, the intellectual, and the physical being; because taking his stand in that empyrean centre out of which the Divinity speaks, he possessed the organ of embodying the oracles of that

---

[18] Emerson later inserted here a passage from the next lecture ("These wise sentences . . . in the cold wind"), pp. 313–15. For variants, see textual notes.

divine nature in selectest words, of sharply defining the subtle boundaries of truth and thence darting his glance through the whole sphere of man's life to its outmost circumference, representing the terrific, the true, the beautiful, and the comic with equal ease and with unrivalled grace; that every man finds in him what delights and what instructs him and the most enlarged mind learns that the dominion of human nature is broader than it knew whilst a spirit of beauty and of joy broods over it from side to side.

It needs then in order to any just understanding of this shining genius that we dismiss from the mind at once all the tavern stories that circulate, as if he were an untutored boy who without books or discipline or reflection wrote he knew not what, and see in him what he was, a Catholic or Universal mind of very great cultivation and one who by books, by discourse, and by thought formed his own opinions, who wrote with intention and who knew that his record was true and in every line he penned has left his silent appeal to the most cultivated mind.[19]

[19] Cf. *J*, III, 452,450.

6

Shakspear [second lecture]

IN my last lecture I attempted to distinguish the leading elements of Shakspear's Genius. It was shown chiefly from his earlier poems that he possessed in prodigious degree the Imaginative power, the primary talent of a poet.

It was then shown that the dangers incident to the mind from the preponderance of this faculty were averted from him both by the natural check of a clear Reason, or the state of the mind when its faculties are in equipoise and admit all impressions with equal freedom, and also by the extraordinary activity of his reflective powers, which had they been alone, would have made him the extremest of Skeptics.

It was then shown that to this double faculty of Imagination and of Philosophy was added a third in quite equal energy, that of Common Sense, a clear perception of and a strong interest in the ongoings of the actual world. So that he was by these three rarely united gifts, the imaginative, the spiritual, and the practical faculties, at once a poet, a philosopher, and a man.

I proposed to add to the view then given, a few remarks, necessarily somewhat miscellaneous, upon his Rhythm; his Language; upon his characters; and upon his sentences and maxims.

The most extraordinary fact in literary history is, without doubt, the neglect of Shakspear by his contemporaries. It is strange that a sensible man could read a scene, even a sentence of his poorest play without being made aware of his transcendant superiority. He writes for the most refined of a refined age. All our education only makes us better readers of Coriolanus and Hamlet. Yet he lived among a cloud of intelligent witnesses unpraised, unmentioned. It is with difficulty that we glean a very few passages from the writings of the day, in which his name is noticed, and B[en] Jonson sums up his praise of his friend with the frugal encomium that there was ever in him more to be praised than to be pardoned. Sir Philip Sidney, who probably sat for the portrait of Hamlet in Ophelia's lament for his madness, writes a Defence of Poesy and treats of the English Drama and does not mention Shakspear. Spenser in a long list of English poets of the day has left four bare lines concerning one *Aetion*, which, it has been conjectured, might refer to Shakspear. Herrick has written a list of the poets in an ode to Ben Jonson in which Beaumont, Fletcher, Marlow, are all named, and Shakspear not. Lord Bacon, the English Plato, who from his clear understanding surveyed the whole horizon of human wit and made catalogue of all its stars in all the volumes of his works, has not once alluded to the existence of his mighty contemporary.[1] We should say that the excess of wit at that remarkable era hid the merit of individuals, had not some of the lights of that constellation been favorably distinguished.

We must leave this singular fact quite without comment. It is pleasant to observe that from the first a very small number of sensible persons have selected Shakspear with very significant commendation, viz. Jasper Mayne, the author of some fine lines prefixed to the first edition of his Plays; Southampton; and Essex; the Ever Memorable John Hales; Lord Falkland; Selden;[2] Milton; Dryden; Addison, since whose time he became the wonder of the world.

The commendation which was withholden at first has been given in the present age without stint, and often without wisdom, until it seems useless to add to his eulogy: but it may be pleaded there is reason for our panegyrics on Shakspear because it is just now that his preeminent merit is breaking into light. He is of that merit that needs a long perspective to show it truly and the judgments of men could not be trusted which had assigned a con-

---

[1] Cf. *W*, IV, 202. These statements are based on Malone.

[2] Jasper Mayne (1604–1672), dramatist; Henry Wriothesley, 3rd Earl of Southampton (1573–1624); Robert Devereux, second Earl of Essex (1566–1601); John Hales (1584–1656), Canon of Windsor; Lucius Cary, second Viscount Falkland (c. 1610–1643); John Selden (1584–1654).

temporary the superlative praise we have awarded him. We indulge our admiration at first timidly, until we see that a man who has been dead in England two hundred and twenty years is no longer aided by any accidental advantages at all adequate to the [witchcraft] which he exercises over our minds. And that influence reaches not over one faculty, but over all. We are first taken by the magic of the story. No art is omitted to carry to its height the interest of the tale and our imaginations are carried captive by the distress or adventure of his kings and queens, his lovers and knights. Then we are delighted by the truth and life of the individual persons of the drama; by the wit and eloquence of the dialogue; by the splendor of the poetry; by the delicacy of the expression; and lastly by the weight and profoundness of the sentences.

Hence he takes, in the common mind of the English race, the place which no other writer ever took. A very large number of his expressions have passed into the stock of vernacular speech: "milk of human kindness," "chewing the food of sweet and bitter fancy," "Nothing extenuate nor set down aught in malice," "Time was the brains were out the man would die." Next to the English Bible he contributes most of all books to the authority and permanence of the language.

As it is said of Milton's "Paradise Lost" that the theological dogmas there taught are continually confounded with the teachings of Scripture; so it is affirmed, and I doubt not truly, that Englishmen know more of English history from Shakspear than from Hume.

Add also this praise that the fancy creations of this obscure poet have come to be esteemed Ideas, and speculated upon and analyzed on the belief that nothing accidental or capricious went to their composition. Whether Hamlet was truly insane, what was the real character of Othello, and the fate of Ophelia are questions which wise men have not thought it unworthy to debate as if Hamlet and Othello were historical personages; such is our confidence that a truly great genius will never write capriciously but is always obeying with fidelity the law of thought.

Of the minor excellences of Shakspear not the least remarkable

307

is his rhythm, or the music of his verse. There is a curious remark of Madame de Stael which might show us how unfit is the most exalted genius to speak of matters of this sort in a foreign language. She says that the English do not admit much imagination into their prose because such is the facility of the structure of their blank verse that every one reserves for poetry all exalted thoughts.[3] Now the fact is, as we well know, that of all our metrical structures the blank verse is the most difficult to use with success, and of all the English only five or six writers have ever succeeded in it, namely, Shakspear, Milton, Young, Thomson, Cowper, and Wordsworth. The newspapers and albums are filled with essays on all subjects written in blank verse. It is mere metrical prose. We feel as we read, that these thoughts were conceived in prose, and after turned laboriously by cutting off syllables and substituting worse words, into verse. But in Shakspear we are sensible instantly that the thought first took body in this melodious form, that the sentence was born Poetry, according to Milton's fine definition of Poetry, "Thoughts that voluntary move harmonious numbers."[4] Shakspear indeed has no rival but Milton in the sweetness of his numbers. His verse has this perfection, — that the sense of the verse determines its tune; and this makes him of all writers the least of a mannerist and so the hardest to imitate. For in every sentence the new sentiment gives a new cadence. Read the verse so as best to express its sense, and you will most truly bring out the music of the line.

> Your mind is tossing on the ocean
> There where your argosies with portly sail,
> Like signiors and rich burghers of the flood,
> Do overpeer the petty traffickers
> That curtsey to them, do them reverence
> As they fly by them with their woven wings.
>
> I saw young Harry with his beaver on,
> His cuisses on his thighs, gallantly armed,
> Rise from the ground, like feathered Mercury,
> And vaulted with such ease into his seat

[3] de Staël, II, 8–9. Cf. *J*, III, 554.
[4] *Paradise Lost*, III, 37.

SHAKSPEAR [SECOND LECTURE]

As if an angel dropped down from the clouds
To turn and wind a fiery Pegasus
And witch the world with noble horsemanship.[5]

The sweetness of this verse will be felt by comparing it with that of the blank verse of Beaumont and Fletcher or Massinger or Otway or Dr. Johnson's Irene which is all poetry of the manufactory and not of the muse. This distinction which I am now re-marking will be felt by comparing it with one play of Shakspear or at least universally ascribed to him, Henry VIII, which is distinguished from the other dramas by a very remarkable structure of verse in which there is an overpowering tune whilst a large proportion of the lines have also a double ending, that is, the verse has eleven syllables instead of ten.

Buck. It has done upon the premises but justice
But those that sought it I could wish more Christians
Be what they will I heartily forgive them
Yet let them look they glory not their mischief
Nor build their evils on the graves of great men . . .

Yet I am richer than my base accusers
Who never knew what truth meant I now seal it . . .

Cromwell I charge thee fling away ambition,[6]

a sort of amble in the verse quite unlike the nimble, erect, variable stanza of Shakspear.

The fair Ophelia; Nymph in thy orisons
Be all my sins remembered.

Ill met by moonlight proud Titania.

Not poppy nor mandragora
Nor all the drowsy syrups of the world
Shall ever medicine thee to that sweet sleep
Which thou owdst yesterday.[7]

Indeed Shakspear is so perfect in his melody as if it had been a principal aim with him. In the many passages which have been

[5] *Merch. of V.*, I, 1: 8–14; *Henry IV, Pt. I*, IV, 1: 104–110.
[6] *Henry VIII*, II, 1: 63–67, 104–105; III, 2: 440.
[7] *Hamlet*, III, 1: 88–89; *Mid. N. Dr.*, II, 1: 60; *Othello*, III, 3: 330–33.

adduced as the originals from which he borrowed a thought or expression it will always be found that he has mended the harmony of the phrase. His contemporaries observed this fact. Jonson compliments him on his "true torned and well filed lines" and Meres [8] thinks the soul of Ovid has revived in this melodist. But it is ever so. The telescope and the microscope arrive at perfection together. The great masters of wisdom and the heart are the masters of words. We speak as if literature in more recent days had descended to finery and word-catching but the cunning of Moore or Pope or Addison is but coarse prentice-work compared to enchantments of Shakspear in that sort.

In connexion with his Rhythm it is necessary to say a few words of his Language.

One page of Shakspear does not repeat the words of the last page. His rich vocabulary searches all the provinces of language, the court, the camp, the farms, the sea, the market, for every phrase and term of strength or delicacy. His pedlar gabbles, his statesman mystifies, his hero thunders, his fool puns, his maiden pleads, each perfect in their dialect, and new supernatural beings are introduced, like Caliban, for whom he has devised a new language.

Whilst the words minister so much delight to the ear that they seem to be chosen for their beauty only, they are so exactly proper that it would be difficult to express the sense in a simpler or shorter form. Coleridge remarks that it would be as easy to push a stone out of the pyramid with the bare hand as to alter a word of Shakspear for the better in any of his more elevated passages.[9] It must be remarked that it may be characterized as an immortal style. It is not now at all obsolete. The speeches of passion in Lear and Othello are as fresh and modern now in 1835 as they were in 1600:

> I tax not you, you elements, with unkindness
> I never gave you kingdoms called you children
> You owe me no subscription why then let fall

[8] Francis Meres (1565–1647), *Palladia Tamia, Wits Treasury*, 1598, contains a list of Shakespeare's plays and a comment on him.

[9] *Biographia Literaria*, p. 20. Cf. *Table Talk*, II, 109, quoted in *Quarterly Review*, LII (1834), p. 7.

Your horrible pleasure; here I stand, your slave,
A poor, infirm, weak, and despised old man.
But yet I call you servile ministers,
That have with two pernicious daughters joined
Your high engendered battles gainst a head
So old and white as this.

Put out the light and then put out the light
If I quench thee thou flaming minister
I can again thy former light restore
If I repent me but once put out thine
Thou cunningest pattern of excelling nature
I know not where is that Promethean heat,
That can thy light relume.[10]

The perfection of the writing is such as centuries of collation and revision could not mend, so that one is almost tempted to believe in a Philonic inspiration [11] which guided the pen of the poet and held the hands of the players, scriveners, and editors that none should tamper with the precious text. How else should so marvellous lines, pages, and books have come safe through such shiftless and casual channels as the prompters' books and players' editing, his plays being first published [in] 1624 by the players seven years after the death of Shakspear.

Of the persons of his Drama it is not easy to say a little. They are so sharply drawn as if always he was painting from real life, and yet all are idealized or made more true to the laws of thought than heroes in actual life are ever found. Brutus in Julius Caesar is finished with as delicate yet firm discrimination as Othello or Falstaff. Antony in that play and in Antony and Cleopatra is a very noble figure in whom all manly accomplishments are neutralized by the love of pleasure. Cleopatra, a female Sardanapalus,[12] [whom] the poet offers as a lass unparalleled wholly given up to voluptuous passion but distinguished abundantly from the common voluptuary by the self-abandonment that postpones life and crown even to her devotion to her lover, is a new image in poetry

[10] *Lear*, III, 2: 16–24; *Othello*, V, 2: 7–13. Cf. *J*, III, 327–28.
[11] The Jew and Neo-Platonist, Philo Judaeus (c. 20 B.C. — c. 50 A.D.), taught that through the Logos man could receive revelations from God.
[12] Luxurious Assyrian king, the subject of a tragedy by Byron (1821).

and for the first time makes even luxury sublime. How noble the sentiments of the lovely suicide, after the death of Antony:

> Then is it sin
> To rush into the secret house of death
> Ere death dare come to us . . .
> We'll bury him and then what's brave what's noble
> Let's do it after the high Roman fashion
> And make death proud to take us.
>
> My desolation does begin to make
> A better life. 'Tis paltry to be Caesar
> Not being fortune he's but fortune's knave
> A minister of her will. And it is great
> To do that deed that ends all other deeds
> That shackles accidents and bolts up change
> Which sleeps and never palates more the drug
> The beggar's nurse and Caesar's.[13]

In Macbeth he has fairly earned the title which Mme de Stael gives him, that Shaksp[ear] like Death is the King of Terrors.[14] Every thing in that piece is so skilfully combined to affright and yet the terror so modulated and kept from extacy by the intermingling of the most natural and even pleasing parts, such as Duncan's remark upon the pleasantness of the air indicated by the temple haunting martlet which resorts ever where the air is delicate; the dagger in the air, the imaginary voices, the sleepwalking of Lady Macbeth, and the ghost at the banquet are so just and various pictures of fear, the progress of the story is so natural, and the event so just that it is too high to praise.

In the historical plays I think we are much affected by the romantic state of society described and our imagination awed by the magnificent figure of the feudal barons, Gloster, Warwick, Northumberland, Salisbury, these rich and wilful gentlemen who take their honor into their own keeping and defy the world, so confident are they of their personal courage and strength. In dangerous times these pretensions are presently tried; therefore their very name becomes a flourish of trumpets. It is the blazon

[13] IV, 15: 80–82, 86–88; V, 2: 1–8.
[14] de Staël, I, 293–94.

of an approved reality. They are the stuff of which that age and world is made.

The plays let us into the ancient creed of loyalty and the barbarous ethics and religion of the age. Richard II, Henry V, Henry VI all speak in earnest faith of their duties as kings, though their religion is singular enough. We praise Scott for taking kings and nobles off their stilts and giving them simple dignity but Scott's grandees are turgid compared with the princeliness of Hamlet or Prince Hal.[15]

In Dryden's time they were wont to commend Shakspear for his men and to suppose he did not draw women:

> But stronger Shakspear felt for man alone.[16]

It seems to show that he was little read, or they would have found the truth of Imogen, Isabel (purity), Juliet, Cato's daughter Portia (heroism), Desdemona, Cordelia (piety), Cleopatra (luxury), Lady Macbeth (ambition), Beatrice (satire). And lastly the supernatural agents that are introduced satisfy the imagination, which is the highest praise: Ariel, Caliban, the Witches, the Ghosts, Titania and her fairies.

It is impossible to leave the details without a particular mention of a class of passages which bear to be separated from their connexion as single gems do from a crown and choicely kept for their intrinsic worth. The occasions of his story are continually suggesting to the mind of Shakspear the most subtle and profound reflexions on life and manners which he drops in a style often as simple as the stage directions but which fix themselves in the reader's memory and become oracles which all the events of our lifetime are interpreting and verifying. These wise sentences make in fact a large part of that treasury of proverbial wisdom which floats in the daily speech of all who use the English tongue being long ago so familiar that they who use them do not know their author. Such sentences are the observation of Brutus,

> There is a tide in the affairs of men
> Which taken at the flood leads on to fortune

[15] J, III, 327. Cf. W, III, 148.
[16] Not from Dryden's poetry. *Cf.* Preface to "Troilus and Cressida," 1679.

Omitted all the voyage of their life
Is bound in shallows and in miseries,

the conviction of Macbeth,

Even handed Justice
Commends the ingredients of our poisoned chalice
To our own lips,

the saying of [Edgar] in Lear,

Our pleasant vices
Are made the whips to plague us,

the remark of Hamlet,

Our indiscretion sometimes serves us well
When our deep plots do pall and that should show us
There's a divinity that shapes our ends
Rough hew them how we will,

the melancholy sentiment of Enobarbus on the diminution of his captain's (Antony's) brain,

I see men's judgments are
A parcel of their fortunes and things outward
Do draw the inward quality after them
To suffer all alike,

the words of Antony,

But when we in our viciousness grow hard . . .
the wise gods seel our eyes
In our own filth drop our clear judgments make us
Adore our errors laugh at us while we strut
To our confusion.

In a different humor, what satire was ever uttered upon false religion, upon the grossness with which the popular mind holds the sweet and awful verities of faith, to surpass Dame Quickly's naif account of the death of Falstaff?

How now? Sir John, quoth I; what, man! be of good cheer. So he cried out, 'God, God, God!' three or four times. Now I, to comfort him bid him he should not think of God; I hoped there was no need to trouble himself with any such thoughts yet.

What portrait breathes more knowledge of the world in which we all live than that of the knave Parolles in "All's Well That Ends Well"?

> Yet these fixed evils sit so fit in him
> That they take place when Virtue's steely bones
> Look bleak in the cold wind.[17]

Of this character is the whole dialogue of Ulysses with Achilles in Troilus and Cressida; the advice of Polonius to his son in Hamlet; and an abundance of other passages among which each of us has his favorites. They are speculations that being stript of all local and accidental features have an equal interest to all men.

With all the deductions that can be made by the most thorough research into his materials enough remains to astonish us. It is the part of a just criticism to separate what is admirable from what is merely fortunate in the history of this genius, not by any means to depreciate Shakspear, whom we wish neither to raise nor to sink, but that we may better judge of what man has done and may do. Yet the immense body of annotation that has been accumulated on Shakspeare has brought to light only two general facts of much moment.

It is to be considered then that he lived in the age of Queen Elizabeth, a fortunate era prolific in men of great parts and great action, in the time when Sir Francis Drake had, for the first time, sailed round the world: when Sir Walter Raleigh kept the expectations of men erect by his irregular greatness: when Sir Philip Sidney stimulated the imagination of men not less by that wit which was the measure of congruity, than by the courtesy and adventure by which he went before all gentlemen: when the ambition of Essex and Leicester decorated and defended England: when the Court was served not only by Burleigh and Cecil but by the transcendant abilities of Bacon: when Spenser was already publishing the Faery Queen, and Chapman, and Marlowe, and Herbert, Herrick, poets of exquisite delicacy of genius, were writing

[17] *J. Caesar*, IV, 3: 218–221; *Macb.*, I, 7: 10–12; *Lear*, V, 3: 170–71; *Hamlet*, V, 2: 8–11; *Ant. and Cl.*, III, 13: 31–34, 111–15; *Henry V*, II, 3: 17–22; *All's W.*, I, 1: 113–15.

their classical or pious poetry: when Ford, Massinger, Beaumont, Fletcher, and Ben Jonson, all were writing for the stage and when the stage was greedily attended by all classes of men. Lord Bacon, in speaking of that period, commends it in Elizabeth that "Some ages are so barbarous and ignorant, that men may as easily be governed as sheep, but this princess lived in a learned and polite age when it was impossible to be eminent without great parts and a singular habit of virtue." [18] At such periods there is a contagion of wit which keeps the powers of men tense and active by emulation and the genial impulse of noble minds. Now the conversation, the religion, the spirit of the Court of that age our poet represents to us. It was impossible that such an observer as Shakspear could walk in the same city from year to year with this renowned group without gathering some fruit from their accomplishments and learning. It must be reckoned fortunate that the dramatist, the painter of manners and society, should live at a period of great activity and on a conspicuous scene. We must not think Shakspear less indebted to it, that his contemporary dramatists were too unskilful to make a good use of the same knowledge.

In the next place it is true his fables were furnished to his hands. The Criticism of two hundred years has labored to make a Catalogue of Shakspear's library. It is found that the works of Homer, Plutarch, of Ovid, of Seneca, of Terence, of Herodotus had all been translated into English. It is found that a great number of the French and Italian Romances were open to him in English versions; that Holinshed's and Harrison's Chronicles were at hand; that many old plays on the same subjects as his own had already possession of the stage. Of all these materials, Shakspear frankly and unscrupulously availed himself. Many plays he merely altered and embellished. In Coriolanus he borrowed whole paragraphs from Plutarch. In Henry VIII from Holinshed. Undoubtedly we should find his debts very large had not time destroyed these materials. Nor will it be denied he shows the greater and more excellent to us, because the scaffolding and rubbish is removed, by the help of which his structure was built.

[18] "In felicem memoriae Elizabethae," *Works*, X, 280. "Burleigh and Cecil" (above) refers to William Cecil, Lord Burghley (1520–1598), and his son, Robert Cecil, Earl of Salisbury (1563?–1612), both ministers to Queen Elizabeth.

But is not this the ordinary course of humanity that one man is made to take up into his genius whatsoever is excellent and worth preserving in his age? He becomes the Secretary for that Century or Nation. The happy conception of extraordinary events is more the product of tradition than of poets.

It is the inevitable effect of meditating upon these wonderful productions to see that they are no rhapsodies cast forth at a heat but like all other truly great productions are the union of many parts each of which came solitary and slowly into the mind and did not at first attain its full expansion. This indeed is a law that lies at the foundation of literature and is well expressed by the word Composition, i.e. putting together. It is the most powerful secret of Nature's workmanship. In Nature a most gorgeous result is continually produced by the mere union of common elements. Fontenelle said if the secret of Nature were out, if men saw of how simple elements the universe was made up they would cry with mortification, Is this all! What grandeur in the prospect from a mountain summit! It is made up of many similar and in themselves, not striking objects.[19] In like manner, in all art, Composition is more important than the elegance of individual forms. Every artist knows that beyond its own beauty the object has additional beauty from relation to surrounding objects. The most elegant shell in a cabinet does not please the eye like the contrast and combination of a group of the most ordinary sea shells lying together wet upon the beach. The boy walks upon the shore and charmed with the colors and forms of the shells he gathers them up and carries them home. When he comes home he can find nothing in his pocket but dry ugly mussels and snails. They have lost all the beauty which they had when they lay wet and social on the shore touched by the sea and under the sky.[20] Now, an advantage precisely analogous, do our thoughts obtain when put together by their natural affinities. It is the second aphorism of the Novum Organon, "The naked and unassisted hand however strong and true is adapted only to the performance of few and easy works but when assisted by instruments becomes

[19] Cf. *J*, III, 287–88. *Cf.* "The Naturalist," note 10.
[20] "The boy walks upon the shore . . . under the sky" (*J*, III, 298); *cf.* "The Naturalist," p. 74.

able to perform much more and of much greater difficulty: and the case is exactly the same with the mind." [21] Composition or methodical union is this instrument. The orator who astonishes the senate is nowise equal to the sudden creation upon a new subject of the brilliant chain of sentiments, facts, and illustrations whereby he now fires himself and you. Every link in this living chain he found separate: one ten years ago; one last week; some in his father's house or at his first school; some of them by his losses; some in his sick bed; some through his crimes. [He] probably admires his own speech as much as the hungriest hearer in the assembly and knows himself to be nowise equal, unarmed that is, without this instrument of Synthesis, to the splendid effect which he is yet well pleased should be attributed to him.

This makes the difference between the rhapsody of the Pythoness [22] or the chant of the improvisatore [23] (if it were possible there should be any strictly extempore poetry) and the elaborate written poem. No human wit unaided is equal to the production at one time of such a result as the Hamlet or Lear, but by a multitude of trials and a thousand rejections and the using and perusing of what was already written one of those tragedies is at last completed — a poem made that shall thrill the world by the mere juxtaposition and interaction of lines and sentences that singly would have been of little worth and short date. The poet derived the greatest advantage from the first part of his work to complete the remainder, just as the part of St. Peter's that is already built elevated the conception of the following architects and instructed them to build the rest. So do the collated thoughts beget more and the artificially combined individuals have in addition to their own a quite new collective power. The main is made up of many islands, the state of many men, the poem of many thoughts each of which in its turn filled the whole sky of the poet, was day and happiness to him.[24]

[21] Bacon, *Works*, VIII, p. 1, free translation.

[22] Priestess of the Delphic Oracle.

[23] A poet who composes verse extempore, such as were found in Italy from the sixteenth to the eighteenth century.

[24] "It is the second aphorism . . . day and happiness to him" (*J*, III, 477–79, revised).

The plays of Shakspear are works of art altogether of too great and grave a cast to be supposed to have been thrown off at a heat or as little men wish to think in the fumes of wines and youth. There is no juggle of this sort in Nature, least of all in her costliest productions. The laws of the mind are never eluded. It takes an ounce to balance an ounce, and deep thought and the most keen insight into all parts of society and all the acts of life cannot be evinced by a profligate and buffoon.

The gifts exhibited in the dramas of Shakspear indispensably demand habits of wisdom and goodness, a mind beyond experience candid and open to all impressions with the utmost tenacity in hoarding its observation, the most daring flights of imagination, the most gentle and magnanimous spirit, and the more profound the study of him will excite the most wonder.

7

Lord Bacon

For the seventh lecture in the Literature series, delivered on December 24, 1835, Emerson did not have to do much preparation, as Bacon's writings had been a constant accompaniment to his thoughts since college days. "I have been reading the *Novum Organum*," he wrote in his Journal on August 8, 1820. "Lord Bacon is indeed a wonderful writer; he condenses an unrivaled degree of matter in one paragraph" (*J*, I, 26–27). Yet the paradox of Bacon the writer vs. Bacon the man was still unresolved when he commented in 1854, "The whole is told in saying Bacon had genius *and* talent. Genius always looks one way, always is ideal, or, as we say, Platonist, and Bacon had genius. But (a common case, too) he had talents and the common ambition to sell them. Hence his perfidies and sycophancy" (*J*, VIII, 492–93). In the year of this lecture, he thought of Bacon's "universal mind" as he endeavored to work out his own "first philosophy" (*J*, III, 489), and Emerson here uses him to exhibit, somewhat unwittingly, most of the unresolved personal and philosophical issues with which he was struggling; the "censure of Bacon" which he had wished to include in his British Plutarch (*J*, II, 504) turns out to contain its share of praise.

The lecture is based mainly on the London, 1824, edition of Bacon's *Works* which Emerson owned, but he is also indebted to Coleridge's discussion of Bacon in *The Friend* (Cameron, I, 353–54n) and he refers to Francis Osborn's *Advice to a Son*. An alternate paragraph for the introduction to the lecture (see textual notes) shows that at some time it was read in series with that on Luther. Among the Journal references to Bacon at the time of this lecture are: III, 226, 363, 386, 475, 477, 554. An excellent recent article is Vivian C. Hopkins, "Emerson and Bacon," *American Literature*, XXIX (1958), 408–430.

Great men of the first class do us many good offices. They exhilarate the spirit by the scope they give to admiration and hope. In hours of depression when annoyed by trifles and by littleness and degraded by crimes, man seems a sort of vermin. But these persons by taking hold on the bright durable objects of the intellect and at the same time, making us feel a community of nature with them, encourage us again. It is a fatal blow to the mind to remove from it all objects of veneration. These restore them. We make before these divinities that heartfelt, childlike obeisance which honors them and us. Then they are antidotes to each other's excessive influence. By remaining long in the neighborhood we are drawn into the mighty orb of Plato or Dante or Milton and we should presently from the habit of submitting our understanding and finding our teacher always wise lose the power of recovering the erect position: but then comes by another luminary, of different light and course, and with equal claims on our wonder, and affords us at once the power of self recovery, and that of comparing system with system, influence with influence, and, at last, man with man.

We have just now considered Shakspear the poet, whose mind was coextensive with nature.

Bacon is another universal mind, one who to quite different ends exercised powers scarcely inferior, possessed an imagination as despotic as Shakespear's, which he yet employed rigorously as an instrument merely to illustrate and adorn the objects presented under the agency of the Understanding.[1]

Bacon was born in 1561 and educated in the Court of Queen Elizabeth. His genius was early ripe for he entered the University of Cambridge in his twelfth year, and at nineteen he wrote a sketch of the state of Europe which both in style and matter indicates a mature mind. The Queen was a coquette in her policy as well as in her love, and kept Bacon a suitor for place as long as she lived. He was a member of the House of Commons for twenty years. In 1597 he published the Essays. After the accession of James, in 1607 he was made solicitor general. In 1617 he was made Lord Keeper and in 1619 Lord Chancellor of England. In 1620 he published the Novum Organon. In 1621 on the presentment of certain charges of corruption he was impeached before the House of Peers, and declining to defend himself he was found guilty and

---

[1] See textual notes for an alternate introduction.

condemned to a fine of £40,000 and to imprisonment in the Tower during the King's pleasure. The King restored him to liberty and forgave him the fine. In 1622 he published his history of Henry VII. In 1626 he died.[2]

He was by nature and by discipline a most accomplished man. Of his rare eloquence and of his singular weight of personal character we possess the most decisive testimonies from his contemporaries. The reverence of genius always followed him and while yet alive he was called Venerable Bacon.

Francis Osborn gives us some additional particulars:

"Lord Bacon in all companies did appear a good proficient if not a master in those arts entertained for the subject of every one's discourse treating with every man in his respective profession and what he was most versed in. I have heard him entertain a country Lord in the proper terms relating to hawks and dogs and at another time outcant a London Chirurgeon. His most casual talk deserveth to be written. Nor did an easy falling into arguments appear less than an ornament in him. The ears of his hearers receiving more gratification than trouble and no less sorry when he came to conclude than displeased with any that did interrupt him. Now this general knowledge he had in all things, husbanded by his wit, and dignified by so majestical a carriage strook such an awful reverence in those he questioned, that they durst not conceal the most intrinsic part of their mysteries from him. All which rendered him no less necessary than admirable at the Council Table, where, in reference to Impositions, Monopolies, etc. the meanest manufactures were an usual argument; and, as I have heard, he did in this baffle the Earl of Middlesex that was born and bred a citizen." Osborn says, "A censure for innovation fell upon Venerable Bacon till over balanced by a great weight of glory from strangers."[3]

The testimony of Ben Jonson is very explicit and discriminating.

---

[2] This paragraph suggests that Emerson had checked through the article on Bacon in the *Encyclopaedia Americana*, I, 513–14.

[3] "Francis Osborn, *Advice to a Son*" [E], in *Works*, Eighth Edition, London, 1682, First Part, p. 151.

"Yet there happened in my time one noble speaker who was full of gravity in his speaking. No man ever spake more neatly, more pressly, more weightily, or suffered less emptiness, less idleness in what he uttered. No member of his speech but consisted of his own graces. His hearers could not cough or look aside from him without loss. He commanded where he spoke, and had his Judges angry and pleased at his devotion. No man had their affections more in his power. The fear of every man that heard him was lest he should make an end." [4]

Sir Walter Raleigh said that the Earl of Salisbury was an excellent speaker but no good penman; that Lord H[enry] Howard was an excellent penman but no good speaker: Sir Francis Bacon was alike excellent in both.

James Howel calls him "a man of recondite science born for the salvation of learning and I think the eloquentest that was born in this isle." [5]

But this shining picture has a sad reverse. He was a servile courtier, a low intriguer; he was an ungrateful friend. It is well known that he was tried on the charge of Bribery and found guilty. This however is not a very grave charge against him. It was proved that in conformity with a dangerous custom he permitted his servants to receive presents from parties suing at his court. But he was not himself corrupt. And no sentence of his was ever reversed. His ruin was permitted by King James to save Buckingham on whom the national vengeance was ready to fall. James thrust in the Chancellor as a victim and forbade him to defend himself, promising to annul the sentence. The grave charge against him is the servility of which his letters are too many proofs, the suing to the King, to the favorite, and to the favorite's favorite. Please recommend me. Your kind word for me with the king. Speak of me to him when Burleigh is by, that he may commend me also, and the suppleness of such an one as Bacon to such an one as Buckingham — who can remember without pain?

He was the rival and enemy of Sir Edward Coke [6] and certain-

[4] Emerson could have found this in Stewart, p. 244.

[5] William Rawley, *The Life of . . . Bacon*, London, 1670, p. 7. James Howel, *Epistolae Ho-Elianae*, Book I, section 4, Letter to Dr. Pritchard.

[6] Sir Edward Coke (1552–1634), Chief Justice of the King's Bench (1613).

ly descended to some low shifts to hinder the prosperity of his rival.

But the worst fact in his history is his servile obedience to Elizabeth who thrust Bacon forward in the prosecution of the Earl of Essex for treason. Essex, one of the most generous of men, loved and cherished Bacon and had employed him in his affairs and was wont to come to this young sage for advice. To recompense him he used all his interest with the Queen and her Council to secure him the vacant place of Solicitor. His letters which still remain plead with heat and importunity for his friend. The Queen refused him. Essex went to Bacon and told him of the refusal and forced him to accept a piece of land of him which was worth more than £1800.

When presently the imprudences of the Earl had brought him into the guilt of treason, Elizabeth commanded Bacon to act in the prosecution of Essex. Bacon sought to excuse himself but the Queen insisted and Bacon complied. Essex was executed. Then Bacon was called upon to publish a Narrative of his Treasons. Even to this most ungracious office of laying open to the world all the errors of his friend and benefactor did Bacon's love of preferment and fear of disgrace bend his sense of honor and friendship.

"After the Queen had denied me the Solicitor's place for which his Lordship had been a long and an earnest suitor in my behalf it pleased him to come from Richmond to Twickenham Park and brake with me and said 'Mr. Bacon the Queen hath denied me the place for you and hath placed another; I know you are the least part of your own matter but you fare ill because you have chosen me for your mean and dependance. You have spent your time and thoughts in my matters. I die (these were his very words,) if I do not somewhat towards your fortune; you shall not deny to accept a piece of land which I will bestow upon you.'" [7]

It is with pain I recur to these deformities in the moral character of this highly endowed person; with pain; for I believe no man reads the works of Bacon without imbibing an affectionate

[7] "Letter to Earl of Devonshire" [E]. *Works*, III, 214.

veneration for their author. We owe to him sentiments so exalted; we see the deep thirst he had for all noble thoughts; we
follow with toil the bold excursions of his masculine understanding, that we come to regard him as an Archangel to whom the
high office was committed of opening the doors and palaces of
knowledge to many generations. But his works are coloured also
with infusions of this alien spirit of courts and contemptible selfishness. We are reminded of those cases of Double Consciousness
in which an individual is afflicted with intervals of insanity during
which a totally different character is exhibited from his own. The
word King seems to be the fatal word that brings back his madness
for then the great Teacher makes an Asiatic prostration, fawns
and eats dust. His spirit of compliment is nauseous.

Much palliation no doubt is to be found in his education and
in the depraved politics of his times and in the hard necessity
which threw such a prophet at the whim of so foolish and contemptible persons as Buckingham and King James. Yet there are
also favorable parts of his moral character which evidently made
a deep impression on his contemporaries since Aubrey informs
us, that "all who were great or good loved and honoured him."

And Ben Jonson writes thus of him:

"My conceit of his person was never increased toward him by
his place or his honors, but I have and do reverence him for the
greatness that was only proper to himself, in that he seemed to
me ever by his work one of the greatest men and most worthy of
admiration that had been in many ages. In his adversity I ever
prayed that God would give him strength, for greatness he could
not want. Neither could I condole in a word or syllable for him
as knowing no accident could do harm to Virtue but rather help
to make it manifest." [8]

His own letters and other works contain incidental expressions
of regret that ever he was enticed from those intellectual labors
in which his strength and prosperity lay.

Let us hasten then to the blameless and exalted side of his
character, and contemplate him as the Lawgiver of science
and the profound and vigorous thinker who has enlarged our

[8] Emerson could have found these in Stewart, p. 245.

knowledge in the powers of man, and so our confidence in them.

The most obvious trait in the genius of Bacon, is, the extent combined with the distinctness of his vision. Not less than Shakspear, though in a different way, he may claim the praise of Universality. He had a right to pass the censure upon others which he is fond of quoting from Heraclitus, that, "Men rather explore their own little worlds, than the great world which God made," [9] for he is free from that fault himself. His expansive Eye opened to receive the whole system, the whole inheritance of Man. He did not appreciate only this or only that faculty, but all the divine energy that resides in him, and sought to make it all productive. None ever hoped more highly of what man could do.

It is inferior men who think meanly of human nature. Great men think greatly of it. In our age Goethe has summed up in an admirable sentence the powers of man: "From the first animal tendency to handicraft attempts, up to the highest practising of intellectual art; from the inarticulate tones and crowings of the happy infant, up to the polished utterance of the orator and singer; from the first bickerings of boys, up to the vast equipments by which countries are conquered and retained; from the slightest kindliness and the most transitory love, up to the fiercest passion and the most earnest covenant; from the merest perception of sensible Presence up to the faintest presentiments and hopes of the remotest spiritual future: all this and much more also lies in man, and must be cultivated, yet not in one but in many." [10] This sphere of life and power Bacon beheld. He saw what all saw and also what few see and what none understand.

All these powers he looked upon as productive. Truth was not barren. The perfect man was, to use his expression, "the interpreter of Nature and the priest of the world" [11] and so he went over nature to make an inventory of man's kingdom. There in the great magazine of beings his genius finds room and verge enough.

He has not like others any favorite views into which as into

[9] Emerson's translation of Bacon's Latin version in Aphorism 42 of *Novum Organum, Works*, VIII, 8.

[10] *Wilhelm Meisters Lehrjahre*, Book VIII, Chapter 5, Carlyle's translation.

[11] Aphorism 1 of *Novum Organum, Works*, VIII, 1, freely translated. *Cf.* Cameron, I, 351, 333.

a mould he is ever forcing all objects. He is content to view them where they lie and for what they are. He does not magnify the facts that make for his view and conceal or neglect all others. The system grinder hates the truth. Every object had some interest for him as a fact for he was wise enough to know that every object had value could he find its place. He as readily cites what is sordid as what is great. This he has nobly declared in his works:

"But for impolite or even sordid particulars which as Pliny observes require even an apology for being mentioned even these ought to be received into a natural history no less than the most rich and delicate; for natural history is not defiled by them any more than the sun by shining alike upon the palace and the privy. And we do not endeavor to build a capital or erect a pyramid to the glory of mankind; but to found a temple in imitation of the world and consecrate it to the human understanding so that we must frame our model accordingly. For whatever is worthy of existence is worthy of knowledge, which is the image of existence. Nay as some excrementitious matters, for example, musk, civet, etc. sometimes produce excellent odours so sordid instances sometimes afford great light and information." [12]

Thence he is omnivorous and his keen eye pierces all nature and society and art for facts. He is greedy of truth and of fancies and of falsehoods.

He conceived more highly than perhaps did any other of the office of the Literary Man. Believing that every object in nature had its correlative in some truth in the mind he conceived it possible by a research into all nature to make the mind a second Nature, a second Universe. The perfect law of Inquiry after truth, he said, was, that nothing should be in the globe of matter, which should not be likewise in the globe of crystal; [13] i.e. nothing take place *as event*, in the world, which did not exist *as truth*, in the mind.

Nothing was so great, nothing so small, nothing so vile but he would know its law. The literary man should know the whole theory of all that was done in the world whether by nature or by

[12] "Nov. Org. 120" [E]. *Works*, VIII, 64.
[13] *Works*, VII, 406.

men and this in no general and vague way but with sufficient particularity to make him if need be master of the practice also. He would have the literary man master of the whole theory of business, of courts, of trades, of arts, of armies, of navigation, of luxury, and also of cunning, of dissimulation, of fraud, of poison. He seems to have taken to heart the taunts which are thrown out against speculative men as unfit for business, sharpened no doubt by his remembrance that Cecil had objected this to Bacon's qualification for office in the ear of the Queen, and aimed in his own Scheme of an Education to make the Scholar not only equal to useful oversight and direction of business, but to outshoot the drudge in his own bow, and even to prove his practical talent by his ability for mischief also.

"To teach men how to raise and make their fortune is an unwonted argument," he says, "but the handling thereof concerneth learning greatly both in honor and in substance: in honor because pragmatical men may not go away with an opinion that learning is like a lark that can mount and sing and please herself and nothing else; but may know that she holdeth as well of the hawk that can soar aloft and can also descend and strike upon the prey. In substance, because there should not be anything in being and action which should not be drawn and collected into contemplation and doctrine." [14]

This last sentence contains the theory of his life and labors as a philosopher: "There should not be anything in being and action which should not be drawn and collected into contemplation and doctrine." It is not an occasional expression but his settled creed. This happy constitution of mind, this Universal Curiosity determined undoubtedly his election of his literary task. He would not dedicate his faculties to the elucidation of the principles of law, though his law tracts are highly commended. He would not found a sect in moral, or intellectual philosophy, though familiar with these inquiries; nor in natural nor in political science; but he would put his Atlantean hands to heave the whole globe of the Sciences from their rest, expose all the gulfs and continents of error, and with creative hand remodel and reform the whole. In

[14] "Advancement of L." [E]. *Works*, I, 200.

the execution of his plan there is almost no subject of human knowledge, especially none of human action, whereto he has not directed some attention and some experiment in the manner of one who was in earnest by acting to learn the facts.

Lord Bacon is surely not an author who can be rashly disposed of, in a superficial sketch. His massive sentences and treatises slowly collected and consolidated from year to year must be studied with a humble mind from year to year if we would apprehend the scope of his philosophy. Without attempting any minute analysis I shall content myself with an enumeration of his works, to intimate the ambition of his genius.

His great literary labor considered collectively is called the Instauration of the Sciences and consists of several parts.

The Advancement of Learning is one of the principal books in the English language, one on which the credit of the nation for wisdom mainly depends. The treatise itself is a survey of the literature of the world, the Recorded Thinking of Man, to report its sufficiency and its defects, but it is the survey as of a superior being so commanding, so prescient. As if the great chart of the Intel[lectual] world lay open before him, he explores every region of human wit, the waste and the cultivated tracts, and predicts departments of literature that did not then exist. It is made up of passages each of sufficient merit to have made the fame of inferior writers. Its style is an imperial mantle, stiff with gold and jewels. It is full of allusion to all learning and history. The meaning is everywhere embodied or pictured to the eye by the most vivid image. No man has done with this book who has read it but once. The sentences are so dense with meaning that the attention is withdrawn from the general views to particular passages.

Though the book is one stream of sense and splendor so that a passage selection cannot without injustice be made yet I am tempted to read the concluding sentences of the first book:

"Lastly leaving the vulgar arguments that by learning man excelleth man in that wherein man excelleth beasts; that by learning man ascendeth to the heavens and their motions, where in body he cannot come, and the like; let us conclude with the dignity and excellency of knowledge and learning in that whereunto man's nature doth most aspire which is immortality or continuance; for to this tendeth generation and raising of houses and families; to this tend buildings, foundations, and monuments; to this tendeth the desire of memory, fame, celebration and in effect the strength of all other human desires. We see then how far the monuments of wit and learning are more durable than the monuments of power or the hands. For have not the verses of Homer continued 2500 years or more without the loss of a syllable or letter; during which time infinite palaces, temples, castles, cities have been decayed and demolished? It is not possible to have the true pictures or statues of Cyrus, Alexander, Caesar: no nor of the Kings and great personages of much later years, for the originals cannot last and the copies cannot but lose of the life and truth. But the images of men's wits and knowledges remain in books exempted from the wrong of time and capable of perpetual renovation. Neither are they fitly to be called images because they generate still and cast their seed in the minds of others provoking and causing infinite actions and opinions in succeeding ages. So that if the invention of a ship was thought so noble which carrieth riches and commodities from place to place, and consociateth the most remote regions in participation of their fruits, how much more are letters to be magnified which, as ships, pass through the vast seas of time, and make ages so distant to participate of the wisdom, illuminations, and inventions, the one of the other."

The second part of the Instauration was designed to invigorate the powers of the mind by a juster application of its reasoning faculty to the works of nature.

Bacon was forcibly impressed with the vagueness and uncertainty of all the physical speculations then existing, and the entire want of connexion between the sciences and the arts.

Knowledge he said, was barren. From a few facts they rush to general propositions which are of no use to the arts, but very fruitful of debate. He proposed a new method, Novum Organon, namely a slow Induction which should begin by accumulating observations and experiments and should deduce a rule from many observations, that we should like children learn of nature and not dictate to her. His favorite maxim was "Command Nature by obeying her." [15]

And before laying down the rules to be observed he enumerates the Causes of Error under the name of Idols, intimating that the mind of man is an edifice not built with human hands which needs only to be purged of its idols and idolatrous services to become the Temple of the true and livng light. These are

1. The Idols of the Tribe, or the causes of error founded on human nature in general or on principles common to all mankind, as the Spirit of System.

2. Idols of the Den, those that spring from the character of the Individual. Each individual has his own dark cavern or den into which the light is imperfectly admitted and to some error there lurking truth is sacrificed.

3. Idols of the Forum, those that arise from commerce or intercourse of society and especially from language.

4. Idols of the Theatre, those which arise from the dogmas of different systems of philosophy.

Having exposed the causes of error he proceeds to expound the method in which a true History of Nature should be formed and to show how by a rigorous exhaustive method an answer might be extorted from nature to every inquiry of man.

This book was a new logic not to supply arguments for dispute but arts for the use of mankind, not to silence an academical antagonist but to subdue nature by experiment and inquiry.

To test his logic he began to show himself its use by making collections of facts in Natural History, and instituted thousands of experiments so costly and so minute as to be fit for the laboratory of the alchemist. And to these he added observations on all parts of nature. Some of these observations are of greatest value. He anticipated by happy conjecture some great astronomical discoveries. Some of them are of no value and have exposed him to the derision of very inferior men, especially those investigations which were favorite speculations in his age.

[15] This maxim is repeated three times in the *Novum Organum*: in the "Distributio Operis," and in Aphorisms 3 and 129 (*Works*, VII, 44, and VIII, 1 and 73). *Cf.* p. 20 and Cameron, I, 333.

His curiosity was attracted by all parts of nature, those which are occult not less than those which are manifest. The whole mass of facts that stand on the confines of the spiritual and material world and which for want of name are sometimes called Natural Magic he studied with equal calmness though I think with no success, the influence of the Eye in love, in envy; the supposed virtues of amulets.

This obscure class of facts, coincidences, auguries, dreams, animal magnetism, omens, sacred lots, etc. have great interest for some minds. They run eagerly into this twilight and cry to the unwilling beholder, there's more than is dreamed of in your philosophy. Certainly these facts are interesting and are not explained. They deserve to be considered. A theory of them is greatly to be desired. But they are entitled only to a share of our attention and that not a large share. Let their value as exclusive subjects of attention be judged by the infallible test of the state of mind in which much notice of them leaves us. They savour of nothing great or noble. Read a page of Cudworth or Milton and we are exhilarated and armed to manly duties. Read Cornelius Agrippa or Scott's Demonology or Colquhon's Report on Animal Magnetism [16] and you are only bewildered and perhaps a little besmirched. We grope and stumble. They who love them say they shall reveal to us a world of unknown and unsuspected truths. No doubt; all nature is rich but these are her least valuable and productive parts. If a diligent collection and study of these occult facts were made they could never do much for us. They are merely physiological, pointing at the structure of man, opening to our curiosity how we live but throwing no light and no aid on the superior problem why we live and what we do.[17] It is wholly a false view to couple them in any manner with the religious nature and sentiments and a most dangerous superstition to raise them to the lofty place of motives and sanctions. This is to prefer haloes and rainbows to the sun and moon.[18]

[16] Henry Cornelius Agrippa von Nettesheim (1486–1535), *De Occulta Philosophia*, 1531; Sir Walter Scott, *Letters on Demonology and Witchcraft*, 1830; J. C. Colquhoun, *Isis Revelata; an Inquiry into . . . Animal Magnetism*, Edinburgh, 1833.

[17] "This obscure class . . . and what we do" (*J*, III, 484; *W*, X, 23–24).

[18] "It is wholly . . . sun and moon" (*W*, X, 26).

Lord Bacon's speculations [and] proposed experiments on this class of facts have no scientific value whatever; they are only material as they show his all-seeing curiosity.

Newton, Davy, and Laplace have put in execution the plan of Bacon. The whole history of Science since the time of Bacon is a commentary and exposition of his views.

The book of Lord Bacon that gets out of libraries into parlors and chambers and travelling carriages and into camps, is his Essays. Few books ever written contain so much wisdom and will bear to be read so many times. Each reader is struck with the truth of the observations on that subject with which he happens to be most familiar. Yet almost all the topics are such as interest all men. They are clothed meantime in a style of so much splendor that imaginative persons find sufficient delight in the beauty of expression.

They delight us by the dignity of the sentiments whenever he surrenders himself to his genius, as when he writes in the first Essay, "Certainly it is heaven upon earth to have a man's mind move in charity, rest in Providence and turn upon the poles of truth." [19] How profound the observation in this passage! "This same truth is a naked and open daylight that doth not show the masks and mummeries and triumphs of the world half so stately and daintily as candle lights. Truth may perhaps come to the price of a pearl that showeth best by day, but it will not rise to the price of a diamond or carbuncle that showeth best in varied lights. A mixture of a lie doth ever add pleasure. Doth any man doubt that if there were taken out of men's minds vain opinions, flattering hopes, false valuations, imaginations as one would and the like, but it would leave the minds of a number of men poor shrunken things, full of melancholy and indisposition and unpleasing to themselves?" [20] And let us believe that the following sentence contains his own apology to himself for submitting to the mortifications of ambition. "Power to do good is the true and lawful end of aspiring; for good thoughts though God accept them yet towards men are no better than good dreams except they be put

[19] "On Truth" [E], *Works,* II, 254.
[20] "On Truth" [E], *Works,* II, 253–54.

in act, and that cannot be, without power and place, as the vantage and commanding ground." [21]

How noble is the view which he takes of personal deformity as being more a spur to virtue than a cause of malevolence: "Because there is in man an election touching the frame of his mind and a necessity in the frame of his body, the stars of natural inclination are sometimes obscured by the sun of discipline and virtue; therefore it is good to consider of deformity not as a sign which is most deceivable but as a cause which seldom faileth of the effect." [22]

The uses of Friendship are nobly set forth: "Certain it is that whosoever hath his mind fraught with many thoughts, his wits and understanding do clarify and break up in the communicating and discoursing with another; he tosseth his thoughts more easily; he marshalleth them more orderly; he seeth how they look when they are turned into words; finally he waxeth wiser than himself and that more by an hour's discourse than by a day's meditation." [23]

The defects of this book stand in glaring contrast to its merits. Out breaks at intervals a mean cunning like the hiss of a snake amid the discourse of angels. But these passages need no index and no brand. The finger of a child can point them out.

What wisdom is shown in the essay on Travel and in that of Studies! What criticism on manners in that on Ceremonies and Respects! What nicety and curiosity of taste in those on Gardens and Masks and Buildings!

If I may adventure a criticism upon Lord Bacon's writings, it would be to remark a fault not easily separable from so colossal undertakings. His works have not that highest perfection of literary works, an intrinsic Unity, a method derived from the Mind. If a comparison were to be instituted between the Instauration and the Epic of Milton or the Hamlet of Shakspear I think the preference must remain with these last as the production of higher faculties. They are the mind's own Creation and are perfect

---

[21] "On Great Place" [E], *Works*, II, 276.
[22] "Of Deformity," *Works*, II, 358.
[23] "Of Friendship," *Works*, II, 318.

according to certain inward canons which the mind must always acknowledge. But Bacon's method is not within in the work itself, but without. This might be expected in his Natural History but not in his elaborated compositions. Yet in his Essays it is the same. All his work lies along the ground, a vast unfinished city. He did not arrange but unceasingly collect facts. His own Intellect often acts little on what he collects. Very much stands as he found it — mere lists of facts material or spiritual. All his work is therefore somewhat fragmentary. The fire has hardly passed over it and given it fusion and a new order from his own mind. It is sand without lime. It is a vast collection of proverbs, all wise but the order is much of it quite mechanical, things on one subject being thrown together; the order of a shop and not that of a tree or an animal where perfect assimilation has taken place and all the parts have a perfect unity. The Novum Organon has taken this form of separate propositions and the Essays would bear to be printed in the form of Solomon's proverbs, that is, in total disconnection.

So loose a method had this advantage, that it allowed of perpetual amendment and addition. And every one of his works was a gradual growth. Three times he published the Essays with large additions. Twelve times he wrote over the Novum Organon, that is once every year from 1607. Many fragments remain to us among his works, by which we may see the manner in which all his works were written. Works of this sort which consist of detached observations and to which the mind has not imparted a system of its own, are never ended. Each of Shakspear's dramas is perfect, hath an immortal integrity. To make Bacon's works complete, he must live to the end of the world.

Two reflections are forced upon the mind by this hasty retrospect of Bacon's achievement.

1. A new courage and confidence in the powers of man at the sight of so great works done under such great disadvantages by one scholar. This he has himself suggested in a passage in the Novum Organon:

"If any one should despair, let him consider a man of as much employment in civil affairs as any other of his age; a man of no great share of health, who must therefore have lost much time, and yet in this undertaking he is the first that leads the way, unassisted by any mortal, and steadfastly entering the true path that was absolutely untrod before, and submitting his mind to *things*, may have thus somewhat advanced the design." [24]

2. The other moral of his history, is, the insufficiency we feel in his mighty faculties to varnish the errors of his life. We are made sensible, in his example, of the impossibility of welding together vice and genius. The first will stand out like a loathsome excrescence in its old deformity, nor wit, nor eloquence, nor learning will whiten ingratitude, or dignify meanness. There in the stream of Time he rears his immortal front nor seems "less than Archangel ruined, and the excess of glory obscured," [25] dividing our sentiments as we pass from point to point of his character, between the highest admiration and the highest pity.

[24] "Nov. Org." [E]. Aphorism 113, *Works*, VIII, 59.
[25] *Paradise Lost*, I, 593–94.

8

Ben Jonson, Herrick, Herbert, Wotton

Emerson's choice of four relatively minor seventeenth century writers for his eighth lecture, delivered on December 31, 1835, after having bypassed both Spenser and Milton, would seem to provide evidence for the influence of the English "metaphysical" poetry of that century, which has been pointed out by N. A. Brittin in "Emerson and the Metaphysical Poets," *American Literature*, VIII (1936), 1–21; J. R. Roberts in "Emerson's Debt to the Seventeenth Century," *American Literature*, XXI (1949), 305–308; and other critics from Bronson Alcott to F. O. Matthiessen. Doubtless he depended largely on volumes in his own library, as Warton discusses none of these writers and there is no record of his having withdrawn library copies at this time. His notes in manuscript journal "L" indicate that he first thought of choosing Herbert and Jonson for his seventh lecture and including Bacon and Chapman in his eighth; Bacon then changed places with Herbert and Jonson, and Wotton was substituted for Chapman. As to topic, the two lectures were obviously one in his mind.

Apart from the problem of reconciling the writer and his works, ethical principles and literary enjoyment, which underlies all of these lectures, that of the function of language as symbol was most persistent in Emerson's thinking at this time and may have motivated his choices of writers. He was reading Jonson and Barrow as early as 1820 "merely because they are authors where vigorous phrases and quaint, . . . may be sought and found" (*J*, I, 24), and in 1831, he comments on Herbert that "his thought has that heat as actually to fuse the words, so that language is wholly flexible in his hands and his rhyme never stops the progress of the sense" (*J*, II, 415). He was similarly attracted to Herrick by "the simplicity and manliness of his utterance, . . . a perfect plain-style from which he can at any time soar to a fine lyric delicacy, or descend to the coarsest sarcasms without losing his firm footing" (*J*, III, 483). Almost his only journal reference to Wotton is the quotation of his remark about Sidney that "his wit was the measure of congruity" (*J*, III, 488). "For language of nature," he sums up, ". . . in the 17th century, it appeared in every book" (*J*, III, 529). Most of these scattered remarks, with much other appropriate comment, went into the lecture, but there they are not tied up into any generalizations which might be useful for his own book. "Do not expect," he reminds himself, "to find the books of a country written, as an encyclopaedia by a society of *savants*, on system, to supply certain wants and fill up a circle of subjects. . . . In the world of living genius all at first seems disorder, and incapable of methodical arrangement. Yet there is a higher harmony whereby 't is set" (*J*, III, 555–56).

I proceed this evening to give account of some of the minor poets of between the age of Elizabeth and Charles.

Ben Jonson is a person of much importance in English literature, not only on account of his own merits but because of his relation to the remarkable circle of men of wit who flourished in England in the beginning of the 17th century. Of humble birth, in his early life a soldier of fortune, and carving his own way to honor by his industry and resolution, his learning, wit, and manly character made him a favorite in the court and among the poets; so that no literary man has come down to us with so many honorable notices from his contemporaries. We are accustomed to regard him as the President of that brilliant society of men of letters which illuminated England in Elizabeth and James's reign, consisting of Spenser, Shakspear, Marlow, Camden, Chapman, Beaumont, Herbert, Bacon, Herrick, Donne, Hooker, Sidney, Selden. Most of these writers have in some manner connected their names with his. The Latin historian Camden was his teacher. Shakspear is said to have introduced him to the stage. For Lord Bacon he is said to have translated the Novum Organon into Latin. Herrick, Chapman, Donne, and Beaumont, have written panegyrics of him and he has written eulogies of Sidney, Selden, Shakspear, Spenser, and Donne.

Ben Jonson is the author of several regular dramas, both tragedies and comedies. He was in his age a sort of master of revels to King James. He supplied the Court with dramatic poems which were spoken and acted on holidays, on nuptial occasions, and on the occasion of Royal Visits to great houses.

It is I think the general vigor of his genius, the unquestionable proof occasionally given by him of poetic power, and not the dramatic merit of his pieces that has preserved the credit of his name to this day. He who takes up the volumes of Ben Jonson at this day with the fame of his great name in his mind and with any expectation of a rivalry or even a resemblance to Shakspear must incur a heavy disappointment. His plays must be read with great indulgence. They are very dull yet with no vulgar dulness. The diction is pure. The sentences are perfect and strong. There is abundance of allusion to Greek and Roman writers. In his Comedies the characters are usually made to represent some extravagant folly of that day, some sickness of the manners, or choice piece of nonsense in fashionable life, as the Euphuism which Scott has represented in Sir P[iercie] Shafton in [The] Monastery, but oftener the styles of dress and the old and heavy pleasantries of coxcombs at the awkwardness of a novice on his entrance into high life. The whole dialogue and incident is prosaic and formal in the last degree unrelieved by one sally of wit or sparkle of mirth. The names, the plot, the costume are those of comedy yet all creeps so heavily forward that one would think them parodies of some popular piece, or written with some latent design of excessive ridicule; but this supposition is forbidden by the prefaces accompanying many of them, in which our author appears very angry and scornful, because his play with all its unspeakable merits had been rejected. Dulness so rich and pedantic as Jonson's makes us feel the full sense of the proverb, There's no fool like your learned fool. His tragedies are not better. Catiline and Sejanus are translated much from his Latin reading but he never comes over us with one stroke of pity or terror; and they seem to have been very properly hissed from the stage.

What is it then that has given such honor to the name of Rare Ben Jonson? I think it cannot be contested that dull and pedantic as he is he has claims to the reputation he wears. What made him the favorite of the most discerning men that were ever in England? I think it is because his writings presuppose a great intellectual activity in the audience, suppose an Elizabethan age and even their dulness is the dulness of learned and of fanciful people. All savors of the kingdom of wit. I suppose in his times he made his pedantry very agreeable to the crowd. We should never allow of such pedantry now. Why? Because we have not the learning of which it is the abuse. Then his vocabulary [is] ample and his language scrupulously correct. There is always good sense. He is on all general topics a correct and vigorous thinker. His moral sense is very clear and is always present. That highest office of the bard, namely, that of being priests and divine teachers and in melodious numbers enjoining the practice of virtue Ben Jonson discharged in his age.

In his preface to the Fox addressed to the two Universities he gives utterance to his sentiments:

"If men will impartially and not asquint look towards the offices and functions of a poet they will easily conclude to themselves the impossibility of any man's being the good poet without first being a good man. He that is said to be able to inform young men to all good disciplines, inflame grown men to all great virtues, keep old men in their best and supreme state or as they decline to childhood recover them to their first strength; that comes forth the interpreter and arbiter of Nature, a Teacher of things divine no less than human, a master in manners; and can alone (or with a few) effect the business of Mankind: this I take him is no subject for pride and ignorance to exercise their railing rhetoric upon." After alluding to the gross licentiousness of the stage, he adds, "For my particular I can and from a most clear conscience affirm that I have ever trembled to think toward the least profaneness; have loathed the use of such foul and unwashed bawdry as is now made the food of the scene. . . .

"Let me not then lack the continuance of your favor to the maturing of some worthier fruits wherein if my Muses be true to me, I shall raise the despised head of Poetry again, and stripping her out of those rotten and base rags wherewith the times have adulterated her form, restore her to her primitive habit, feature, and Majesty, and render her worthy to be embraced and kissed by all the great and master spirits of our world. I have laboured to reduce not only the ancient forms but manners of the scene, and last, the *doctrine*, which is the principal end of Poesy, to inform men in the best Reason of living." [1]

This is his confession of faith. And he is always a moral poet. Amidst the frivolity and fantastic buffoonery which he displays with a coarse lumbering pencil, out shine flashes of Roman virtue. He delights in uttering wise moral sentences.

Ben Jonson and Donne and Chapman and Marlow in their better writings have given proof of a sort of conventional reverence for first thoughts, those moral decisions of the Reason which are said to proceed from the Divinity. They felt that in receiving and reporting these they might safely cast behind them the study to please and all remembrance of the Town. And this they did with their eyes open, — knowing that whatever is done to gain the approbation of the few, ensures a sacrifice of the favor of the many. They wait long for a reader but he comes at last. They paint for eternity. "A writer," says Mme de Stael, "who searches only into the immutable nature of Man, — into those thoughts and sentiments which must enlighten the mind in every age, is independent of events. They can never change the order of those truths which such a writer unfolds." [2]

But Jonson had no skill to blend by just degrees his jest and earnest. Voltaire said wittily that the use of sense was to learn to live well with those who had none. [3] So that his very wisdom seems impertinence like a sermon in a beargarden.

In the New Inn, otherwise a tedious and foolish piece, is introduced a young philosopher who in grave earnest teaches the doctrine of love and of valor in the style and with the eloquence of Plato. In Cynthia's Revels among clouds of fops and coquettes quite run mad, walks Arete, the Goddess of Virtue and Crites her votary uttering the sense of Seneca or Fenelon. If this shows the virtue of the Poet I cannot but think that this is miserable drama. 'Tis a mad world with one sane man but he the victim of all the rest.

[1] "Works. Vol 2, p 112" [E]. This edition (see Bibliography) Emerson bought in London in 1833. The last sentence is from earlier in the Preface.

[2] de Staël, II, 76–77.

[3] Voltaire, *Socrate*, I, vii. Cf. *L*, I, 182; *J*, II, 125; *W*, VI, 243.

In a manner quite analogous for its clumsiness and infelicity in The Poetaster he introduces Virgil and Horace oppressed by the dunces in the Court of Augustus and then produces by main force a triumph for them and makes them utter the language of Aristotle amid the vanities of braggarts and knaves.

This scene where Horace, Tibullus, and Gallus are commanded by Caesar to express their opinion of Virgil contains undoubtedly the author's deliberate judgment and rises at once far above the flat of the rest of the piece to the dignity of thought and feeling. I will read the passage.

Caesar says to Gallus and Tibullus:

> You both have Virtues shining through your shapes
> To show your titles are not writ on posts
> Or hollow statues which the best men are
> Without Promethean stuffings reached from heaven
> Sweet Poesy's sacred garlands crown your gentry
> Which is of all the faculties on earth
> The most abstract and perfect; if she be
> True born and nursed with all the sciences
> She can so mould Rome and her monuments
> Within the liquid marble of her lines
> That they shall stand fresh and miraculous
> Even when they mix with innovating Dust
> In her sweet streams shall our brave Roman spirits
> Chase and swim after death, with their choice deeds
> Shining on their white shoulders; and therein
> Shall Tyber and our famous rivers fall
> With such attraction that th'ambitious line
> Of the round World shall to her centre shrink
> To hear their music.

Virgil being announced Caesar turns to Horace:

Caes.   Say then lov'd Horace thy true thought of Virgil.

Hor.   I judge him of a rectified spirit
        By many revolutions of Discourse
        In his bright Reason's influence, refined
        From all the tartarous moods of common men;
        Bearing the Nature and similitude
        Of a right heavenly Body; most severe

In fashion and collection of himself
And then as clear and confident as Jove.

Gallus. And yet so chaste and tender is his ear
In suffering any syllable to pass
That he thinks may become the honoured name
Of issue to his so examined self
That all the lasting fruits of his full merit,
In his own poems, he doth still distaste;
As if his mind's piece which he strove to paint
Could not with fleshly pencils have her right.

Tibullus. But to approve his works of sovereign worth
This observation methinks more than serves
And is not vulgar. That which he hath writ
Is with such judgment labored and distilled
Through all the needful uses of our lives
That could a man remember but his lines
He should not touch at any serious point
But he might breathe his spirit out of him.

Caes. You mean, he might repeat part of his works,
As fit for any conference he can use.

Tib. True, Royal Caesar.

Caes. Worthily observed
And a most worthy virtue in his works
What thinks material Horace of his learning?

Hor. His learning savors not the school like gloss
That most consists in echoing words and terms
And soonest wins a man an empty name:
Nor any long or far fetched circumstance
Wrapped in the curious generalities of arts
But a direct and analytic sum
Of all the worth and first effects of Arts
And for his Poesy 'tis so ramm'd with life
That it shall gather strength of life with being
And live hereafter more admired than now.[4]

These are lines which obviously will not help the dramatic effect of a Comedy but which can proceed only from a wise and

[4] *The Poetaster* (1601), Act. V, Sc. 1, lines 88–139. *Works,* I, 481–85.

disciplined intellect. The same merit of clear insight of the heroi-
cal character by the clearness of his perception of right and wrong
and of true and false shines to more advantage in his minor poems.

I am unable to see the merit of his dramas. I think him the
worst dramatist of any reputation in English. There is not a scene
nor situation nor single speech in all of great dramatic power.

We must measure modern plays by Shakspear and there is not
a scene in all Ben Jonson of equal interest to the worst scene in
Shakspear.

But as a poet he has great merits. He has the poetic eye and
the poetic ear. Heavy and prosaic as his drama is, he has written
some of the most delicate verses in the language with a melody
and sweetness equal to the cunning of Milton himself. Let me
read from one of his masques called the Vision of Delight the
Invocation of Phantasy by Night:

> Song of Night in a Masque
> Break Phantasy from thy cave of cloud
>   And spread thy purple wings
> Now all thy figures are allowed
>   And various shapes of things
> Create of airy forms a steam
> It must have blood and nought of phlegm
> And though it be a waking dream
>   Yet let it like an odour rise
>   To all the senses here
>   And fall like sleep upon their eyes
>   Or music in their ear.

In another masque are the songs of Daedalus to the Dancers
which have the same sweetness. He sends the youth to choose
partners among the maids:

> Go choose among — but with a mind
> As gentle as the stroaking wind
> Runs o'er the gentler flowers
> And so let all your actions smile
> As if they meant not to beguile
>   The ladies but the hours
> Grace laughter and Discourse may meet
> And yet the Beauty not go less

344

For what is noble should be sweet
But not dissolved in wantonness.

Will you that I give the law
    To all your sport and sum it
It should be such should envy draw
    And overcome it.

These masques abound in beautiful poetry; and he is fond of endulging his fancy in the grotesque, of which this incantation is an example:

The faery beam upon you
The stars to glister on you
A moon of light
In the noon of night
Till the fire drake hath o'ergone you

The wheel of fortune guide you
The boy with the bow beside you
Run aye in the way
Till the bird of day
And the luckier lot betide you.

I will quote one more of his pieces, an Ode to himself which expresses the dignity of his sentiments:

Where dost thou careless lie
Buried in ease and sloth
Knowledge that sleeps doth die
And this security
It is the common moth
That eats on wits and arts and quite destroys them both

Are all the Aonian springs
Dried up Lies Thespia waste
Doth Clarius' Harp want strings
Or droop they as disgraced
To see their seats and bowers by chattering pies defaced

If hence thy silence be
As 'tis too just a cause
Let this thought quicken thee

345

> Minds that are great and free
> Should not on fortune pause
> 'Tis crown enough to Virtue still her own applause.[5]

The prose productions of Jonson are an English Grammar and a book of miscellaneous aphorisms called Discoveries. It is thrown together wholly without method and even many sentences are imperfect. But it contains some valuable opinions upon life and upon books.

A contemporary and friend of Ben Jonson was Robert Herrick (born 1591) the author of the Hesperides and Noble Numbers, a genuine English Poet. His verse is exclusively lyric, composed [of] short fugitive compositions upon all topics grave and gay, dainty and coarse, upon the objects of common life. I cannot better enumerate his subjects than by giving the argument of his book:

> I sing of brooks of blossoms birds and bowers
> Of April May of June and July flowers
> I sing of maypoles hock carts wassails wakes
> Of bridegroom's brides and of their bridal cakes
> I write of youth of love and have access
> By these to sing of cleanly wantonness
> I sing of dews of rains and piece by piece
> Of balm of oil of spice and ambergrease
> I sing of times transshifting; and I write
> How roses first came red and lilies white
> I write of groves of twilights and I sing
> The court of Mab and of the fairy king
> I write of Hell; I sing and ever shall
> Of Heaven and hope to have it after all.

All these objects and still homelier ones which he has not here specified have their poetic side, and may properly become the subject of affecting verse. The man of poetic temperament never feels his privelege more proudly than among common and mean objects. The drudge is exalted by the sight of a volcano, an eclipse, or a conflagration but the poet's eye gilds the dullest common or street, his kitchen or hen coop with light and grace. He delights in this victory of genius over custom. He delights to show the muse

---

[5] *Works*, V, 330, 346, 382–83, 175.

is not nice or squeamish, but can tread with firm and elastic step in sordid places and take no more pollution than the sun-beam which shines alike on the carrion and the violet. Herrick by the choice often of base and even disgusting themes, has pushed this privelege too far, rather I think out of the very wantonness of poetic power, than as has been said by his biographers, to make his book sell, by feeding the grosser palates of his public.

His talent lies in his mastery of all the strength and lighter graces of the language so that his verse is all music, and, what he writes in the indulgence of the most exquisite fancy is at the same time expressed with as perfect simplicity as the language of conversation. No better example of this felicity need be cited than the well known ode to Blossoms:

> Fair pledges of a fruitful tree
>> Why do ye fall so fast
>> Your date is not so past
> But you may stay yet here awhile
>> To blush and gently smile
>> And go at last
>
> What were ye born to be
>> An hour or half's delight
>> And so to bid good night
> 'Twas pity Nature brought ye forth
>> Merely to show your worth
>> And lose you quite
>
> But you are lovely leaves where we
> May read how soon things have
> Their end though ne'er so brave
> And after they have shown their pride
>> Like you awhile they glide
>> Into the grave.

Star Song

> Tell us thou clear heavenly tongue
> Where is the babe but lately sprung
> Lies he the lily banks among
>
> Or say if this new birth of ours
> Sleeps laid within some ark of flowers

Spangled with dew light thou canst clear
All doubts and manifest the where

Declare to us bright star if we shall seek
Him in the morning's blushing cheek
Or search the beds of spices through
To find him out

No this ye need not do
But only come and see him rest
A princely babe in's mother's breast.

A beautiful example of the delicacy of his poetic vision is in the little stanza "To Silvia":

I am holy while I stand
Circumcrost by thy pure hand
But when that is gone again
I like others am profane.

Many of his poems are mere couplets or stanzas of four lines like his "Clothes for Continuance,"

The garments lasting evermore
Are works of mercy to the poor
And neither tettar time or moth
Shall fray that silk or fret this cloth,

or his definition of Beauty,

Beauty no other thing is than a beam
Flashed out between the middle and extreme,[6]

which may serve as a counterpart to Winkelmann's fine criticism upon the antique: "Beauty with the ancients was the tongue on the balance of expression."[7] There is an air of magnanimity in the confidence with which the poet gives us on many grave topics his sense in so little compass as a stanza of two, four, or six lines. It evinces his belief in what I take to be an admitted fact in Criticism, that there may be as unquestionable evidence of wit in a sentence as in a treatise, or that whosoever has written one

[6] Herrick, I, 5, 247; II, 243, 38, 282; I, 44.
[7] See Johann Joachim Winckelmann, *Geschichte der Kunst des Alterthums*, Book IV, Chapter 3, para. 5.

good sentence has given proof of his ability to write a book. For a good sentence is not merely a proposition grammatically stated but one which contains in itself its own apology, or the reason why it was said. A proposition set down in words is not therefore affirmed. It must affirm itself or no propriety and no vehemence of language will give it evidence.

Herrick's merit is the elegance and manliness of his utterance and only rarely the weight of his sentences. He has and knows he has a noble idiomatic use of English, a perfect plain style from which he can at any time soar to a fine lyric delicacy or descend to the coarsest sarcasms without losing his firm footing. But this power of speech was accompanied by an assurance of fame.[8] One of the most agreeable among his smaller pieces is one entitled "Not every day fit for verse":

> Tis not every day that I
> Fitted am to prophesy
> No, but when the spirit fills
> The fantastic pannicles
> Full of fire then I write
> As the Godhead doth indite
> Thus enraged my lines are hurl'd
> Like the Sibyl's through the world
> Look how then the holy fire
> Either slakes or doth retire
> So the fancy cools, till when
> That brave spirit comes again.

Another poet in that age was George Herbert, the author of the Temple, a little book of Divine songs and poems which ought to be on the shelf of every lover of religion and poetry. It is a book which is apt to repel the reader on his first acquaintance. It is written in the quaint epigrammatic style which was for a short time in vogue in England, a style chiefly marked by the elaborate decomposition to which every object is subjected. The writer is not content with the obvious properties of natural objects but delights in discovering abstruser relations between them and the subject of his thought. This both by Cowley and Donne is pushed to affectation. By Herbert it is used with greater temperance and

[8] "Herrick's merit is the elegance . . . assurance of fame" (J, III, 483).

to such excellent ends that it is easily forgiven if indeed it do not come to be loved.

It has been justly said of Herbert that if his thought is often recondite and far fetched yet the language is always simple and chaste.[9] I should cite Herbert as a striking example of the power of exalted thought to melt and bend language to its fit expression. Language is an organ on which men play with unequal skill and each man with different skill at different hours. The man who stammers when he is afraid or when he is indifferent, will be fluent when he is angry, and eloquent when his intellect is active. Some writers are of that frigid temperament that their sentences always seem to be made with grammar and dictionary. To such the easy structure of prose is laborious, and metre and rhyme, and especially any difficult metre is an insurmountable bar to the expression of their meaning. Of these Byron says,

> Prose poets like blank verse
> Good workmen never quarrel with their tools.[10]

Those on the contrary who were born to write, have a self-enkindling power of thought which never knows this obstruction but find words so rapidly that they seem coeval with the thought. And in general according to the elevation of the soul will be the power over language and lively thoughts will break out into spritely verse. No metre so difficult but will be tractable so that you only raise the temperature of the thought.

"For my part," says Montaigne, "I hold and Socrates is positive in it, that whoever has in his mind a lively and clear imagination, he will express it well enough in one kind or another and though he were dumb by signs." [11]

Every reader is struck in George Herbert with the inimitable felicity of the diction. The thought has so much heat as actually to fuse the words, so that language is wholly flexible in his hands, and his rhyme never stops the progress of the sense.[12]

---

[9] Coleridge, *Biographia Literaria*, p. 20.
[10] *Don Juan*, I, 201.
[11] "Of the Education of Children," Montaigne, I, 261.
[12] "And in general according to the elevation . . . progress of the sense" (J, II, 415–16).

The little piece called Virtue beginning,

> Sweet day so cool so calm so bright
> The bridal of the earth and sky,

is well known. I will quote a few lines from "The Confession":

> No screw no piercer can
> Into a piece of timber work and wind
> As God's afflictions into man
> When he a torture hath designed
> They are too subtle for the subtlest hearts
> And fall like rheums upon the tenderest parts
>
> We are the earth and they
> Like moles within us heave and cast about
> And till they foot and clutch their prey
> They never cool much less give out
> No smith can make such locks but they have keys
> Closets are halls to them and hearts highways
>
> Only an open breast
> Doth shut them out, so that they cannot enter;
> Or, if they enter, cannot rest,
> But quickly seek some new adventure
> Smooth open hearts no fastening have; but fiction
> Doth give a hold and handle to affliction.

There is a little piece called the Elixir of which a mutilated copy has crept into some of our hymn books:

> Teach me my God my king
> In all things thee to see
> And what I do in any thing
> To do it as for thee
>
> Not rudely as a beast
> To run into an action
> But still to make thee prepossessed
> And give it its perfection
>
> A man that looks on glass
> On it may stay his eye
> Or if he pleases through it pass
> And the heaven espy

All may of thee partake
Nothing can be so mean
Which with this tincture *for thy sake*
Will not grow bright and clean

A servant with this clause
Makes drudgery divine
Who sweeps a room as for thy laws
Makes that and the action fine

This is the famous stone
That turneth all to gold
For that which God doth touch and own
Cannot for less be told.

How finely dost thou times and seasons spin
And make a twist chequered with night and day
Which as it lengthens winds and winds us in
As bowls go on but turning all the way

The sea which seems to stop the traveller
Is by a ship a speedier passage made
The winds who think they rule the mariner
Are ruled by him and taught to serve his trade

Sometimes thou dost divide thy gifts to man
Sometimes unite The Indian nut alone
Is clothing meat and trencher drink and can
Boat cable sail and needle all in one.[13]

What Herbert most excels in is in exciting that feeling which
we call the moral sublime. The highest affections are touched by
his muse. I know nothing finer than the turn with which his poem
on affliction concludes. After complaining to his maker as if too
much suffering had been put upon him he threatens that he will
quit God's service for the world's:

Well, I will change the service and go seek
    Some other master out
Ah, my dear God, though I be clean forgot
Let me not love thee if I love thee not.[14]

[13] Three stanzas from "Providence."
[14] Cf. *J*, III, 248. Last four lines of "Affliction." Quoted in Walton.

Herbert's Poems are the breathings of a devout soul reading the riddle of the world with a poet's eye but with a saint's affections. Here poetry is turned to its noblest use. The sentiments are so exalted, the thought so wise, the piety so sincere that we cannot read this book without joy that our nature is capable of such emotions and criticism is silent in the exercise of higher faculties.

It is pleasant to reflect that a book that seemed formed for the devotion of angels, attained, immediately on its publication, great popularity. Isaac Walton informs us that 20,000 copies had been sold before 1670, within forty years.[15] After being neglected for a long period several new editions of it have appeared in England and one recently in America.

There is a name which deserves some attention among this remarkable company more for his fortune than his merit, I mean Sir Henry Wotton inasmuch as it would be hard to find in history another man who had stood in relations of personal acquaintance with so great a number of extraordinary men. Sir Henry Wotton was born in 1568 and was a kinsman and correspondent of Lord Bacon. Pursuing his studies at Oxford he became the friend of Albericus Gentilis, then Professor of Civil Law, and of his fellow student Dr. Donne. In his travels into Switzerland and Italy he became acquainted with Arminius, at Leyden, Theodore Beza, and at Geneva he lodged with Isaac Casaubon. At Venice he lived on terms of intimacy with Father Paul the historian of the Council of Trent. He visited Kepler at Lintz, and gave him Lord Bacon's Novum Organon, and Vieta at Venice and Robert Bellarmine at Rome. The Earl of Essex, Bacon's benefactor and Shakspear's friend, made Wotton his secretary and W[otton] accompanied him in a voyage to [the] Spanish main. He was the friend of the ever memorable John Hales, and Cowley, of Sir Walter Raleigh, and Sir Philip Sidney. He was in habits of intercourse with John Pym the patriot, and Sir Henry Vane. Isaac Walton the Angler was his friend and biographer, and Milton had a short acquaintance with him, presented him his Comus, and received from him a letter of advice on setting forth on his travels. He was employed

[15] Isaac Walton, "Life of Mr. George Herbert," *Lives.*

by Elizabeth and by King James abroad and finally made Provost of Eton College at home. Beside this wonderful circle of friends, each [or] any one of whom would make the fame of a common man, his acquaintance with Spenser, with Shakspear, and Ben Jonson may be fairly presumed, though we have no record of the fact; and thus he appears to us though a man of uncommon merit yet in his individual ability quite insignificant, compared with the relation he sustained to so many illustrious men as a hoop of gold to hold them staunch by mutual love and good offices.[16]

Wotton is the author of the epigrammatic hymn now in use in our churches called the "Happy Life." He has left a few essays and some of his correspondence with his gifted contemporaries.[17] But he is better known by a few wise maxims which he pleased himself with venting from time to time. Thus, he desired it might be writ in Latin on his tombstone not his name but that here lay the author of the maxim, "The itch of disputation will prove the scab of the Church." A better specimen of his wit is his satire upon Criticism, saying that "Critics were brushers of nobler men's clothes." He wrote in an Album at Augusta in Germany that "An Ambassador was an honest man sent abroad to lie for his country." Another maxim which he wrote in an album was this, that in much travel he had learned that "Souls grow wiser by resting." When he was at Eton one of his friends who had received diplomatic employment abroad came to him for advice, to whom he gave this for an infallible aphorism, "That to be in safety himself and serviceable to his country he should always and upon all occasions speak the truth. For," says Sir H[enry] W[otton], "You shall never be believed, and by this means your truth will secure yourself if you shall ever be called to account and 'twill also put your adversaries who will still hunt counter, to a loss in all their disquisitions and undertakings." Another: "Sir Philip Sidney's wit was the measure of congruity." His advice to Milton is well-known: il viso sciolto i pensieri stretti. "Thoughts close the countenance loose" will go through the world.[18]

---

[16] Cf. *J*, III, 211.

[17] In Wotton's *Remains* (see note 19).

[18] The facts on Wotton, and some of his sayings, derive from Walton's "Life of Sir Henry Wotton." Other sayings are cited in the Journals (*J*, II, 284; III, 488).

Sir Henry Wotton projected a life of Luther and afterwards a history of England but died without writing either. The little volume called his remains [19] compiled by his friend the Angler, Isaac Walton, is chiefly valuable as illustrating the history of English literature by anecdotes and correspondence of the baronet and his friends.

There are many other writers of this period whose works deserve notice: Hooker, usually called "the judicious," author of the Eccles[iastical] Polity; Roger Ascham, a tedious writer; Donne, Marlowe, Chapman, Crashaw; Raleigh (Hist[ory] of the World), and Philip Sidney, the author of Arcadia and of the Defence of Poesy — writers into whose works as we have no space to enter fully we will not dishonor by a slight notice.

I close the lecture with one general remark. By far the most copious department of English literature in the age of Elizabeth and James is the Drama. I cannot help thinking that there yet remain several false reputations on which justice is yet to be done of which the chief [is] Massinger. I cannot help thinking that there is a good deal of tradition and custom in their praise. Anyhow there are many books of which a wise man would wish to remain ignorant and a very little reading in their volumes will I think satisfy him that these are of the number. The curious reader who opens much the volumes of old English plays cannot fail to be struck with the barbarity of manners and the depravation of morals, and if these scenes of profanity and indecency really exhibit the existing tone of fashionable society we may safely thank God that he has permitted the English race in both hemispheres to make a prodigious advancement in purity of conversation and honesty of life.

We find two of them jotted on the last page of a manuscript journal of 1828–29 (Houghton H 21). The last appears in Johnson's "Life of Milton" (cf. *J*, III, 435).

[19] Emerson bought Wotton's *Reliquiae Wottonianae*, London, 1685, when he was in England.

9

Ethical Writers

For his ninth lecture, on January 7, 1836, Emerson abandoned his first plan to discuss a group of seventeenth and eighteenth century writers — Milton, Dryden, Clarendon, Locke, Addison, Johnson — on what would apparently be merely eclectic principles and substituted the ethical formula which was implicit in many of the previous discussions. Dryden was crossed off the list in manuscript journal "L." Milton received scant attention (perhaps because of his presence as a feature topic in the earlier series on Biography, delivered to the same Society). Addison was also slighted, and Cudworth (in a footnote) added, with Samuel Johnson receiving major if not too sympathetic a treatment. As Cameron (I, 57–68) and Vivian C. Hopkins (*American Literature*, XXIII [1951], 80–98) have pointed out, Cudworth's influence dates back to early years, but his inclusion here was an afterthought — probably because of the shift from an emphasis on literature to one on ethics.

The problem of establishing the text of the first reading is complicated by the presence in the same folder of an alternate introduction and at least two other passages, from Lecture 2, which were added later, indicating that the lecture was read on one occasion apart from the series. There is no internal evidence to suggest that Emerson used sources other than those on his own shelves.

A COURSE of criticism on English authors arranged chronologically may be convenient for the memory but has no intrinsic propriety. We cannot class them in epochs and schools for nothing is so saltatory and unaccountable as the appearance of the Bards. Wit is not a torch reached from one to the other, but a meteor observing no laws of ours. After Wicliff the Church is more corrupt, the doctrine more superstitious. After Chaucer, Lydgate, and Gower, the poetry is more mean, prosaic, and voluminous, and nothing indicates an improved language. By and by come Spenser and his cohort.

But they come as stars, now single now in constellations, and the laws of their grouping we have not found. It were better, where such an order is attainable to link the writers by their natural affinities. That I may have an opportunity to name a few writers whom by following the course of time I should not reach, I shall speak this evening of a Class.[1]

There is very great difference in the order of thoughts and emotions to which different literary works are addressed. Many of the English writers of most reputation in their day have been prodigious scholars, readers of all unchosen learning, and have claimed and received fame from the number of the books they have read. Such is the praise of Bentley, Selden, Porson, Pocock, Parr, Walton, Bryant, a merit which only scholars can understand and very subordinate when unaccompanied by other accomplishments. These are the clerks and librarians of the Muses. It is a merit that excites a species of admiration among superficial readers, because their own impatience of a book raises their reverence for a thorough scholar.

But it is not a merit which a philosopher will highly prize. To value a thing because it is old or because it is rare is the part of a virtuoso[2] not of a wise man. To prize a name or an unimportant date in the Assyrian Dynasty or the fixing the use of an accent or force of a particle recovered with infinite pains and proved after a learned controversy may rank in consequence with a Byzantine coin dug up or a new autograph of Tasso, or the finding of a hybrid insect but will never enlarge the limits of valuable knowledge [nor] cheer the solitude of sickness and despondency.

The poets who write elegant trifles whose aim and success is only to say better than any other what has often been said before — Suckling, Prior, Gay, Waller, Garth, Warton — or those whose aim is some momentary occasion as the panegyrics of the laureate poets — Chaucer, Jonson, Dryden, Tate, Southey — have no permanent interest.

[1] The first two paragraphs are bracketed by Emerson to indicate the substitution of the alternate introduction (see textual notes).

[2] Collector of curios.

357

All works of science which are merely empirical and experimental of course lose their value as science improves, as the Century of Inventions of the Marquis of Worcester,[3] or Bacon's Centuries of Natural History, or Gilbert, or Boyle. In like manner, books upon the subjects of religion and philosophy, when written in accordance with the mere opinions of the time, have as brief a date as most of the partisans among the divines on each of the successive questions that have agitated the Church. In the view of all these, the man of the world feels a species of contempt which he imagines is directed against Literature. The philosopher also perceives that these have no inherent vitality.

But there is a class of writers who carry an antidote against oblivion in the very direction of their thought, who address certain feelings and faculties in us which are alike in all men and which no progress of arts and no variety of institutions can alter; those writers, namely, who have to do not with opinions but with Principles; those who write not upon local institutions or particular men and to particular ends but to the general nature of man.

There is a class of writers who do not please but who help us by addressing not our taste but our human wants, who treat of the permanent nature of man, who treat of duties and aim with Socrates to make fair and perfect souls and whose writings keep sweet through all ages. These yield not beauty to the Imagination but Bread on which the mind can feed and grow. The permanence of writings of this kind may be judged by endeavoring to ascertain the date of the common maxims that are in daily use among us, that are repeated not only from the pulpit, the bench and senate, but in the market and the sitting room, which make the mottoes of newspapers and seals and signposts. They come from an antiquity to which the memory of man goeth not back. The proverbs or maxims attributed to the seven wise Masters of Greece,[4] Bias, Chilo, Solon, Pittacus, Cleobulus, Periander, Thales, have lost none of their freshness. Of all the writings of the ancients what is now most effective, least mortal, and that which in the burning

---

[3] Edward Somerset, Marquess of Worcester (1601–1667), *Century of the Names and Scantlings of such Inventions as at present I can call to mind to have tried and perfected*, 1663.

[4] See "Banquet of the Seven Wise Men," Plutarch's *Morals*.

of libraries and kingdoms the smell of the fire hath not passed upon? It is the Golden Sayings of Pythagoras, of the Banquets of Xenophon, of Plato, and of Plutarch, all reciting the fine moral precepts of the sages in connexion with the manners and pleasures of common society, the simple aphorisms of Diogenes, of Zeno, of Socrates, and the books professedly ethical as Epictetus, Marcus Antoninus, Tully's Offices, and Seneca's Morals, and the ethical passages in the poems of Homer, Juvenal, Lucretius, Horace, Euripides, Sophocles.[5]

It is a base thing to think meanly of man and he does us a disservice who depreciates and defames the human soul. On the contrary a remark dropt by any writer expressing the depth of man's nature and powers raises our opinion of his genius and our love and courage in human beings. It is related of Heraclitus that one day sitting alone in a smoky cabin, and seeing an acquaintance pass by he cried to him, "Come in, for the Gods are here also." [6] It was a saying of Seneca that "the good man differs from God in nothing but duration." [7] Sentiments of this sort stimulate and enliven for they speak to faculties in us the most deep and sublime. The various faculties of man have been happily represented as bearing to each other the relation of several concave spheres one within another. It seems as if many of our habits of thought and action were quite superficial and temporary and did scarcely call into exercise the central faculties. There is a state of mind [to which it seems as if] all evil and error were superficial. The noble aphorism "Man is good but men are bad" [8] indicates, that, under the vicious peculiarities of each individual, is a common nature which is pure and divine. In proportion to the inwardness of the thought or feeling a writer addresses, in that proportion are his compositions durable. The gossip of our street or neighborhood is unintelligible in the next street or town. A piece of political or scientific information will interest men further off. But an utterance out of the heart's conviction of a social right or of a

[5] The paragraph from "English Literature," Lecture 2, "Goethe has remarked . . . and kingdoms are forgotten" (p. 250) was inserted here at some later date. For variants see textual notes.

[6] This story Emerson found in Cudworth, II, 243.

[7] *De Providentia*, cap. I. *Cf.* Cameron, I, 183, 382.

[8] Ascribed by Emerson to Rousseau.

moral sentiment will be equally pertinent in the ears of all men and to the remotest times. Moral science is that Muse who alone hath immortality.

This is that sibyl whereof the ancient Plutarch speaks who expressed not herself in the fine measures of Sappho, to tickle the ear and fancy of her hearers, but who plain and harsh, "uttering sentences altogether thoughtful and serious, neither fucused nor perfumed, reaches with her voice to a thousand years, by the favor of the Deity that speaks within her."[9] This is the perpetual miracle that brings down to us unhurt the prophecies and histories of the ancient Hebrews and insures their equal efficacy over the human mind for the ages that are to come.

In the English mind this capacity for Ethical truth, the decided taste for it, is very conspicuous from the earliest dawn of Anglo-Saxon history until now and contrasts with the less decided love of the French, the Italian, or the Scandinavian race.[10] From the same ethical genius flows the excellence of English laws, the precision and energy with which at every period the Courts have drawn and defined the theory of rights. Hence the zeal with which the cause of the Reformation was so early espoused in England by Wicliff, Lord Cobham, Tindal. Hence the fact that the island seems never to have been without its sect of puritans or separatists. Hence the early versions of the Scriptures. The liturgy was written in Henry and Elizabeth's time and pervaded as every one may see with the deepest sentiment of piety. Again in James's reign the Bible was anew translated and in a manner not to be surpassed. All men may discern by the weight with which its verses sink into our memories and have given a bias to the forms of our speech that it was translated with the spirit in which a new work is written, that into the lines of Shakspear or Dryden not more vivacity enters, than into the verses of our Bible, though of course a very slow interrupted work, done with manuscripts, lexicons, and grammars. Hence the fragrant piety of so great a number of English devotional writers giving to that nation a

[9] "Wherefore the Pythian Priestess," etc., *Morals*, III, 104.

[10] The passage from "English Literature," Lecture 2, "Ina laid down . . . become his friend" (pp. 250–51) was inserted here at some later date. For variants see textual notes.

character of religion without superstition that has no resemblance but in the Hebrew race.

The effect in the history of the nation is manifest.

And as the English mind was thirsty for this truth so has England produced a large number of writers who could gratify this taste. Such among the writers of Elizabeth's time are Bacon, Spenser, Sidney, Hooker. In the following reigns appeared a still larger company: John Smith, Henry More, who were philosophical writers; Jeremy Taylor, the great light of the English Church; Archbishop Leighton; Harrington and Algernon Sidney, the political philosophers; Milton; Donne; Sir Thomas Browne, author of Religio Medici; John Bunyan, who in Bedford jail where he was confined twelve years wrote the Pilgrim's Progress; Lord Clarendon the historian. All these were men of a philosophical mind who had an insight into the moral laws of man's nature and who either expressed or implied the existence of these laws in everything they wrote, and therefore have written passages and books from which the thoughtful and serious draw comfort and courage at this hour. They were moreover persons of a more methodical and laborious education than is now in use in public or private seminaries, and as Plato is the most conspicuous of the ancient ethical writers and breathes the most universal spirit of all others they were for the most part versed in his works and called Platonists.

Partly the cause, partly the effect of writers of this class was the moral revolution which, commencing in the reign of Henry VIII, if indeed it were not older, by the agitation of the questions of the Reformation imported from Germany, Switzerland, and France but imported into a soil where like fruit had long been growing, proceeded in private during the reigns of Elizabeth and James, and in that of Charles I, broke out in civil war and changed the constitution. Certain it is, that the public mind of that day was exercised by much deeper thought than the public of any other period known in history. Witness the character of the massive volumes printed at that period in which "almost every possible question that could interest or instruct a reader whose whole heart was in his religion were discussed with a command

361

of intellect that seems to exhaust all the learning and logic, all the historical and moral relations of each several subject." "Jeremy Taylor and Dr. Donne," we are told, "were the most popular preachers of their times and were heard with enthusiasm by crowded and promiscuous audiences, and the effect produced by their eloquence was held in reverential and affectionate remembrance by many attendants on their ministry, who were not like themselves men of learning and education." "The very length of the discourses with which these rich souls of wit and knowledge fixed the eyes, ears, and hearts of their crowded congregations are now a source of wonder." In that memorable period "all the possible forms of truth and error bubbled up on the surface of the public mind as in the ferment of a chaos. It would be difficult to conceive a notion or a fancy in politics, ethics, theology or even in physics and physiology which had not been broached in the fertile brain of that age." [11]

About the same period seem to have been added to the fund of vernacular wisdom a great number of translations from the Latin and Greek classics and also from the French, when anything of value appeared in that tongue, as the philosophy of Malebranche; and the Essays of Montaigne which were admirably translated by Cotton.

Among the writers already noticed we have had occasion to observe the richness of their minds in this property. I proceed to single out a few more of later date.

Among these writers we distinguish the name of Milton as one by whose genius human nature itself is consoled and exalted. The Fall of Man was the subject of his Muse only as a means whereby he might help to raise man again to the height of his divine nature and proportion. We cannot name Milton without feeling some infusion of virtue, some scorn of self indulgence. With his name are associated all the riches of learning, all the vigor of independence, and all the virtues of an austere republican who out of the elegancy of his nature trampled upon errors and vices.

The Comus of Milton is a shield against the temptations of

[11] Coleridge, *Statesman's Manual*, pp. 183–85; *The Friend*, III, 69.

youth and has been and will be an eloquent argument to fortify the generous resolutions of the noble minded. He it was who sung,

> Virtue could see to do what Virtue would
> By her own radiant light though sun and moon
> Were in the flat sea sunk
> He that has light within his own clear breast
> May sit in the centre and enjoy bright day.

The second Book of his Tract called Reason of Church Government urged against Prelaty is a provocative to a manly and pure ambition such as was never addressed to scholars and the piece called Apology for Smectymnuus is a better plea for Chastity and Temperance than the spurs and scarfs of chivalry and the Comus contains the same sentiment in charming numbers:

> So dear to Heaven is saintly Chastity
> That when a soul is found sincerely so
> A thousand liveried angels lackey her
> Driving far off each thing of sin and guilt
> And in clear dream and solemn vision
> Tell her of things that no gross ear can hear
> Till oft converse with heavenly habitants
> Begin to cast a beam on the outward shape
> The unpolluted temple of the mind
> And turn it by degrees to the soul's essence
> Till all be made immortal.[12]

He commended not less by precept and by practice the virtue of Temperance. He thought he who would write good poems ought to make his own life a heroic poem. And his whole life and doctrine is a prevailing argument for every virtue and has enlarged our conception of the offices of the citizen and the man.

Another ethical teacher who is less known is Lord Clarendon,[13] author of the History of the Rebellion. His fault is, that he is a partisan, as the very name of his book betrays. Loyalty was indeed with him a passion, which he carried to an extravagance which those who remember his personal history will easily believe was never exceeded. And this colours all his narrative, and re-

[12] Lines 378–382, 453–463.
[13] Edward Hyde, 1st Earl of Clarendon (1609–1674).

quires that the reader should be on his guard against this bias. I call him an ethical writer. His book is indeed a civil history. But if a book is to be judged by the impression it leaves upon the reader, no writer better deserves the name of a philosopher than Clarendon. His characters stimulate our moral sentiments and provoke us to noble actions. He is a wonderful painter and as his own heart was made of honor so he understood how to delineate every quality and grace that belong to the perfect character of a gentleman. It is not easy to read his sketches of the virtues and talents of the leading men in England without unconsciously forming to ourselves a nobler outline of the manly character and better resolutions for our particular life.

Let me read a few lines from his character of Hampden whom he regarded as a public enemy, and therefore praises sparingly:

"He was very temperate in diet and a supreme governor over all his passions and affections and had thereby a great power over other men's. He was of an industry and vigilance not to be tired out or wearied by the most laborious; and of parts not to be imposed upon by the most subtle or sharp; and of a personal courage equal to his best parts, so that he was an enemy not to be wished, wherever he might have been made a friend, and as much to be apprehended where he was so, as any man could deserve to be."

The character of Lord Falkland is so noble a portrait that it deserves to be read by all entire, yet I must borrow from it a few sentences:

"In this time, his house being within little more than ten miles from Oxford, he contracted familiarity and friendship with the most polite and accurate men of that University; who found such an immenseness of wit, and such a solidity of judgement in him, so infinite a fancy, bound in by a most logical ratiocination; such a vast knowledge that he was not ignorant in any thing, yet such excessive humility as if he had known nothing; that they frequently resorted and dwelt with him, as in a college situated in a purer air; so that his house was a university in a less volume: whither they came, not so much for repose as study, and to examine and refine those grosser propositions which laziness and consent made current in vulgar conversation.

"He submitted to the King's command and became his secretary: yet two things he could never bring himself to, whilst he continued in that office, that was, to his death. . . . The one, employing of spies, or giving any countenance or entertainment to them. . . . The other, the liberty of opening letters upon suspicion they might contain matter of dangerous consequence.

"For the first he would say, 'that no single preservation could be worth so general a wound and corruption of human society as the cherishing such persons would carry with it.' The last he thought 'such a violation of the law of nature that no qualification by office could justify him in the trespass.' . . . When his friends passionately reprehended him for exposing his person unnecessarily to danger, he would say that his office could not take away the privelege of his age, and that a secretary of war might be present at the greatest secret of danger."

It is of Falkland that he elsewhere tells us that "he was so severe an adorer of truth that he could as easily have given himself leave to steal as to dissemble."

He tells us of Sir Thomas Coventry that "he had a strange power of making himself believed, the only justifiable design of eloquence." [14]

His characters of Selden, of Cromwell, of Buckingham, of Vane are all in like manner the sketches of an erect and heroic mind.

In the next reign Locke appeared as a metaphysical and ethical writer. The name of Locke will be always respectable, but, as has been well said, "the mind of Locke will not always be the measure of the Human Understanding." [15] His epoch marks the decline and not the rise of a just philosophy. With him disappeared the class of laborious philosophers (More, Smith, Cudworth,[16] Norris) who had studied Man with Plato in the belief that man existed in connexion with the Divine Mind, and his reputation

---

[14] Clarendon, IV, 94, 242–256; II, 95; I, 83.

[15] Probably a paraphrase of a passage in Sampson Reed's "Oration on Genius" (Cameron, II, 11).

[16] "Cudworth was excited by the evil tendency of the writings of Hobbes to compose the Immutable Morality and the Intellectual System a vast storehouse of wisdom. He has little original matter but reminds us of a Corinthian brass composed by the melting down of ancient temples of steel and silver and gold" [E]. Cf. *J*, III, 489.

and example gave leave to a crowd of Essayists who referred the unfathomable mysteries of human knowledge, thought, and action, the impression of heaven and continual creation upon our plastic clay, to the low sources of sensation. Locke was a virtuous and able man but we scarcely owe to him a profound observation. His merit, if it be one, seems to be that he made philosophy popular, and drew the attention of good society to these studies.

In the reign of Anne appeared Addison and performed much in that revolution of modern times which has brought books into every house. Twenty thousand copies of the Spectator were duly scattered three days in the week in and about London; and elegant speculations upon manners, morals, and books were cast into every coffee house and upon every tea table. Addison's heart was in the right place and his influence has been undoubtedly benefi-cent. His own mind was not very original, but he was a reader of all the lively Essayists among the ancients and moderns, and has transplanted into English what had lain forgotten in Plu-tarch, Lucan, Xenophon, Rabelais, and Montaigne.

The pride of ethical writers in later times was Dr. Samuel Johnson, who more than any other of the English authors im-presses us by the peculiarities of his personal character. A man whom it is always a refreshment to remember because with what-ever faults and whatever mountainous prejudices encumbered he was a man of principle and therefore had the inexhaustible resources of principle and the power which always attends it to inspire respect into men of every degree and every character. He is always accompanied by something of the majesty proper to virtue. His intellect is not very subtle nor do his observations indicate very profound philosophy yet always is his sense so vigorous and his sympathy with virtue so perfect, and moreover so deeply does he stamp every sentence with his own mode of thought that the faults of his learning and the limits of his own speculation have not diminished his fame or influence. He is most fortunate certainly in having been painted in the best biography that is in any language.

Johnson's obstinate prejudices color every one of his per-formances and therefore the lovers of Milton have never forgiven him the petulance with which he depreciates the private and public merits of the republican poet. Nevertheless he has written by far the best life of Milton. Though he hated a Whig, he loved and embraced a great Man; and it is easy to see the deep respect with which Milton fills him and which breaks out ever and anon in heartfelt eulogies which are the more effective from the taunts and sarcasms that went before:

"Before the greatness displayed in Paradise Lost, all other greatness shrinks away." And at last he confesses, "Milton's great works were performed under discountenance and blindness; but difficulties vanished at his touch; he was born for whatever is arduous and his work is not the greatest of heroic poems only because it is not the first." [17]

There is in the genius of Johnson a shade of majestic pathos that seems to me more sublime than the passages that are usually so called in books of rhetoric. It appears in a somewhat juvenile form in the letter to Lord Chesterfield, in many of his Essays, but nowhere better than in the conclusion of his Preface to his Dictionary:

"It may gratify curiosity to inform it that the English Dictionary was written with little assistance of the learned, and without any patronage of the great; not in the soft obscurities of retirement, or under the shelter of academic bowers, but amid inconvenience and distraction, in sickness and in sorrow. It may repress the triumph of malignant criticism to observe that if our language is not here fully displayed I have only failed in an attempt which no human powers have hitherto completed. If the lexicons of ancient tongues now immutably fixed and comprized in a few volumes be yet after the toil of successive ages inadequate and delusive; if the aggregated knowledge and cooperating diligence of the Italian academicians did not secure them from the censure of Beni; if the embodied critics of France when fifty years had been spent upon the work were obliged to change its economy and give their second Edition another form; I may surely be contented without the praise of perfection, which if I could obtain

---

[17] "Life of Milton," in *Lives of the Poets*. Emerson's edition of Johnson is listed in the Bibliography. The text makes the sources of the remaining quotations plain.

367

in this gloom of solitude what would it avail me? I have protracted my work till most of those whom I wished to please have sunk into the grave, and success and miscarriage are empty sounds. I therefore dismiss it with frigid tranquillity having little to fear or hope from censure or from praise."

The Rambler I suppose most persons find a tedious book. Yet it contains many of those passages which we are stronger and happier for having read. He himself declared in its conclusion, of its ethical essays "that it would be found exactly conformable to the precepts of Christianity without any accommodation to the licentiousness and levity of the present age. I therefore look back on this part of my work with pleasure which no blame or no praise of man shall diminish or augment. I shall never envy the honors which wit and learning obtain in any other cause, if I can be numbered among the writers who have given ardor to virtue and confidence to truth."

Let me read the sublime sentence on the capacity of endurance which occurs in the 32d Number, on the Necessity of Patience: "I think there is some reason for questioning whether the body and the mind are not so proportioned that the one can bear all that can be inflicted on the other, whether virtue cannot stand as long as life and whether a soul well principled will not be separated sooner than subdued.

"Yet lest we should think ourselves too soon entitled to the mournful privileges of irresistible misery it is proper to reflect that the utmost anguish which human wit can contrive or human malice can inflict has been borne with constancy and that if the pains of disease be as I believe they are sometimes greater than those of artificial torture they are therefore in their nature shorter: the vital frame is quickly broken, or the union between soul and body is for a time suspended by insensibility; and we soon cease to feel our maladies when they once become too violent to be borne."

The whole of the 68th Number of the Rambler under the humble title of "The Opinion of Servants Not to be Despised," contains a beautiful moral lesson, which imparts a sympathetic activity to our torpid powers. Of similar influence is the fine Essay on Perseverance in the 43d Number:

"All the performances of human art at which we look with praise or wonder are instances of the resistless force of perseverance. It is by this that the quarry becomes a pyramid and the distant countries are united with canals. If a man was to compare the effect of a single stroke of the pickaxe, or of one impression of the spade, with the general design and last result, he would be overwhelmed with a sense of their disproportion; yet those petty operations incessantly continued in time surmount the greatest obstacles, and mountains are levelled and oceans bounded by the slender force of human beings.

"It is therefore of the utmost importance that those who have any intention of deviating from the beaten roads of life, and acquiring a reputation superior to names hourly swept away by time among the refuse of fame, should add to their reason and their spirit, the power of persisting in their purposes; acquire the art of sapping what they cannot conquer and vanquishing obstinate resistance by obstinate attacks."

From the writings of Burke the contemporary and friend of Johnson many sentences of equal weight and beauty could be extracted. His reflections on the French Revolution, on the Regicide Peace, and many of his speeches beside their surpassing rhetorical merits are the philosophy of English politics and are full of ethical wisdom.

The whole body of English sermons is also a very valuable collection of ethics containing the great names of Butler, Tillotson, Barrow.

I am persuaded that a selection might be made of moral sentences from English literature from the works of Bacon, Shakspear, Milton, Taylor, from Sir T[homas] Browne, Barrow, South, Johnson, and Burke that should vie with that which any language has to offer, quicken the pulse of a virtuous ambition and inspire [in] men the feeling of perpetual youth; for as these truths concerned are immutable, so our apprehension of them is the certificate of man's immortality.

The law which Ethics treats is that we mean by the nature of things; the law of all action which cannot yet be stated, it is so simple; of which every man has glimpses in a lifetime and values that he knows of it more than all knowledge; which whether it be called Necessity or Spirit or Power is the law whereof all history is but illustration; is the law that sits as pilot at the helm and guides the path of revolutions, of wars, of emigrations, of trades, of legislation, and yet is fully exemplified in all its height and depth in the private life of every man.

10

Modern Aspects of Letters

The full title of Emerson's last lecture in the literature series, which he read on January 14, 1836, appears on the manuscript as, "Byron, Scott, Stewart, Mackintosh, Coleridge; Modern aspects of letters." He had originally thought of writing a lecture on Gibbon for this occasion (manuscript journal "L"), but at some point dropped Gibbon out of the series entirely. The vogue of Byron and Scott was high in Boston at this time, and he was himself indebted to Coleridge for much of his basic thinking in the series as a whole. Dugald Stewart had been, as Sir James Mackintosh currently was, one of his chief sources of "useful knowledge," and his journals of this period are spotted with references to all five authors (Cameron, I, 355–56n). He probably would also have expanded his references to Wordsworth and Carlyle had it not been for his decision to speak only of those whom "death has removed beyond the circles of prejudice or change." He seems to have drawn upon his own knowledge and ready-formed opinions for this lecture; no special preparation was necessary. A large part of his peroration found its way into the chapter "Beauty" in the book *Nature* for which in so many ways these lectures had been the preparation and to which he now turned his full attention. It was advertised in Boston on September 9, 1836.

In his paper, "Thoughts on Modern Literature," in the *Dial* for October, 1840 (based on a lecture of the previous winter), Emerson returned to Byron without any noticeable change of attitude (*W*, XII, 318–19) but the only direct quotation from this lecture is in Edward Emerson's note (*W*, XII, 471). He also returned to Scott in a memorial note read before the Massachusetts Historical Society on August 15, 1871 (*W*, XI, 463–67). See, J. T. Flanagan, "Emerson as a Critic of Fiction," *Philological Quarterly*, XV (1936), 30–45 and F. T. Thompson, "Emerson's Indebtedness to Coleridge," *Studies in Philology*, XXIII (1926), 55–76, as well as Cameron, *passim*.

ALTHOUGH Time has little to do with the interest of genuine literary works, yet obvious circumstances knit so close ties of relationship between every reader and those writers who belong to his own age, that I willingly yield to the attraction of the eminent names of the nineteenth century which death has removed beyond the circles of prejudice or change. I pass again by some masters to speak of a few whom the fortune of birth has placed nearer to us, and to suggest a few remarks upon the literary complexion of the times.

Lord Byron's genius attracted so much attention a few years since, that the ear is almost weary of the topic, and the more so that men begin to feel that his claims to a permanent popularity are more than dubious.

He owed his strong popularity to something. Certainly his knowledge is very little; his truth of sentiment very little; his taste was just; his power of language and that peculiar gift of making it flexible to all the compass and variety of his emotion without ever marring the purity of his diction, is as remarkable in him as in any English writer since Dryden. No structure of verse seemed laborious to him. How perfect is the flow in the difficult stanza of Childe Harold. He could not speak more simply in prose:

> I twine
> My hopes of being remembered in my line
> With my land's language if too fond and far
> These aspirations in their scope incline
> If my fame should be as my fortunes are
> Of hasty growth and blight and dull oblivion bar
>
> My name from out the temple where the dead
> Are honored by the nations let it be
> And light the laurels on a loftier head
> And be the Spartan's epitaph on me
> Sparta hath many a worthier son than he.[1]

This power of language is a very compound faculty and involving as it does a certain facility of association is one of the rarest and best gifts of the poet. But in Byron, as if merely from moral

---

[1] *Childe Harold*, IV, 9–10.

faults, from the pride and selfishness which made him an incurious observer, it was hindered of its use, it lacked food. Instead of marrying his Muse to Nature after the ordination of God, he sought to make words and emotions suffice alone, until our interest dies of a famine of meaning. We must try his pretensions by the old and stern interrogatories of higher literature.

What faculties does he excite? What feelings does he awaken? What impressions does he leave? The malevolent feelings certainly have their interest and their place in poetry but only for a short time or in company with and under the counteraction of others. Volumes upon volumes of morbid emotion disgust.

Cursing will soon be sufficient in the most skilful variety of diction. Yet several of his [poems are] little else. I know no more signal example of failure from this cause than in the celebrated imprecation in the Fourth Canto of Childe Harold which begun and continued with great magniloquence ends in utter nonsense, not from the fault of the writer who is certainly a great genius but from the poverty of thought. When a man knows nothing let him say nothing. Occasionally, he utters a true and natural sentiment; as in that burst of bitter remembrance in which the spirit of beauty and youth seem to return upon us:

No more no more oh never more on me
The freshness of the heart can fall like dew
Which out of all the lovely things we see
Extracts emotions beautiful and new
Hived in our bosoms like the bag o' the bee
Think'st thou the honey with those objects grew
Alas 'twas not in them but in thy power
To double even the sweetness of a flower

No more no more oh never more my heart
Canst thou be my sole world my universe
Once all in all but now a thing apart
Thou canst not be my blessing or my curse
The illusion's gone forever.[2]

The fourth Canto of Childe Harold surpasses his earlier productions and he had made some improvement in his knowledge by his travels so that he had at last another subject than himself, and

[2] *Don Juan*, I, 214–215.

that Canto is the best guidebook to the traveller who visits Venice, Florence, and Rome.[3]

I think the Island one of the most pleasing of his poems; but how painful is it to feel on looking back at the writings of one who should have been a clear and beneficent genius to guide and cheer human nature the emotions which a gang of pirates and convicts suggest.

One of the most pleasing names in modern English literature is Dugald Stewart, the Scottish philosopher. Though in form an ethical and metaphysical philosopher I believe he has laid down no one valuable principle and established no valuable distinction in either science. His true merit is that of an excellent Scholar and a lively and elegant Essayist. His works delight us by the satisfaction of our taste and the aliment his own purity and elevation furnish to our moral sentiments, and especially by his acquaintance with all elegant literature. Every page is enriched with quotations or allusions to his reading. They form a picture gallery in which we find originals or copies of all choice works of ancient and modern art. As his book on Metaphysics [4] has been the textbook for many years in this country most scholars will remember the brilliant promise of the Introduction to his Philosophy of the effects to follow from the new analysis of the human mind; what visions floated before the imagination of the student, and how heavily they are disappointed. One is reminded of Dr. Clarke's well known description of the entrance of Moscow which at a distance showed a splendid collection of domes and minarets and filled the traveller with a tumult [of] pleasing expectations, but when once he had passed the gates and entered the city he found nothing but narrow streets and plain tenements.[5] As we enter he tells us what he will do, as he goes on, he tells us what he has done.

The chapters on the Being of God and that on the immortality of the soul in the Essay on the moral powers of man are interesting reviews of the history of literature on those subjects. His Disserta-

[3] *Cf.* Introduction to "Italy"; also *J*, III, 98–99.
[4] *Elements of the Philosophy of the Human Mind*, 1792.
[5] *Cf. J*, II, 308. Edward D. Clarke, *Travels in Various Countries.* . . , New York, 1813, Part I, Section 1, pp. 29–30.

tions on the Progress of Eth[ical] and Metaphysical Philosophy are the most agreeable of his works and breathe the spirit of the gentleman and the scholar.

The debt of all the civilized world to Sir Walter Scott, [the] entertainment he has given to solitude, the relief to headache and heartache which he has furnished, make it ungrateful to speak of him but with cheerful respect. Though a very careless and incorrect writer he is always simple and unaffected. Strong sense never leaves him; his good nature is infinite; he has humor; he has fancy; and unsleeping observation. In the high and strict sense of Imagination he can scarcely be said to exercise that faculty. The Lear and Hamlet and Richard are sublime from themselves; Ravenswood and Meg Merrilies, Norna, only from situation and costume.[6] Jeanie Deans, Di Vernon, Burley, certainly have a degree of interest from character also, but it is not very deep and we do not remember anything they say. That in which he is unrivalled, is, the skill of combining dramatic situations of painful interest.

The dialogue, though far superior in natural grace and dignity to the tone of vulgar romances, is often quite artificial and pedantic. He rarely makes us shed a tear; but sometimes he does. The fate of Fergus, the devotion of Evan Maccombich, the trial of Effie Deans, I think must be admitted to be passages of genuine pathos.

If Scott is advanced from the crowd of his contemporaries and compared with the standard English authors, I apprehend, it will be found that he has done little for permanent literature. He has been content to amuse us. He has not aimed to teach. Let it not be said that this is not to be expected from the novelist. Truth will come from every writer, let the form be what it may, who writes in earnest. "Fictions have often been the vehicle of sublimest verities." What Scott has to contribute is not brought from deep places of the mind and of course cannot reach thither. Always we ought to hear sounding in our ears that first canon of criticism: "What comes from the heart that alone goes to the

[6] Cf. *J*, III, 327.

heart: what proceeds from a divine impulse that the Godlike alone can awaken." [7] The vice of his literary effort is that the whole structure was artificial. Scott is no lover or carer for absolute truth. The conventions of society are sufficient for him and he never pondered with the higher order of minds, Milton, Jonson, Wordsworth, De Stael, Rousseau, the enterprise of presenting a purer and truer system of social life. He was content instead to have an idol. His taste and humor happened to be taken with the ringing of old ballads and the shape and glitter and rust of old armor, and the turrets of old castles frowning among Scottish hills and he said, I will make these tricks of my fancy so great and so gay that for a time they shall take the attention of men like truths and things. By the force of talent he accomplished his purpose but the design was not natural and true and daily loses its interest as swarms of new writers appear.

A writer of elevated views and many accomplishments was Sir James Mackintosh, who had almost equal reputation as a scholar, a jurist, a statesman, a historian. He has been long favorably known in this country as the author of some very valuable critical articles in the Edinburgh Review upon Madame de Stael's Germany; upon Partitions; and two upon Stewart's Introduction to the Encyclopedia. They contain his literary opinions upon many important questions.

His first important original work was his Dissertation upon the history of Ethical Philosophy, of which an edition was published a few years since in Boston, a book in which he followed up the hint which he had dropped many years before in the Edinburgh Review that the whole of Ethical Science perhaps now lay in fragments in various books if the hand could only be found to gather them up. It is what it professes to be, a history of the science; and as such is valuable for the luminous finger with which he discriminates the aim and effect of each philosopher. It contains also several definitions of much worth, as of Taste; of the Will; [the] Emotive part of nature; and of the Moral sentiments. It touches or opens many speculations of great interest though I have no belief that Sir James will bring all readers to his opinions: but

[7] Coleridge, *The Friend*, III, 265.

it will be found full of suggestion and written with great urbanity and elegance.

At the time of his death he was occupied with the History of England, three volumes of which have appeared in Lardner's Cabinet Cyclopaedia, and the History of the Revolution of 1688 by itself.

His English History is rather a Dissertation upon history than a complete narrative. But it is chiefly valuable, as it shows how history ought to be written; [it] allowed scope for the introduction of his opinions on all the incidental topics and instead of being the narrative of the royal family and a few persons in attendance on it, it treats generously of all the topics that interest humanity in a great nation: Arts, Literature, Language, Customs, the genius of institutions, and the philosophy of history. Furthermore over the whole series of events and persons the unerring moral judgment of the historian presides as a god among men.

Mackintosh is not a writer of that elevation and power of thought to justify a belief that his works shall never be superseded; yet he had but one contemporary philosophical writer whose studies may expect a longer date.

The grave has only recently received the body of Samuel Taylor Coleridge, a man whose memory may comfort the philanthropist as he showed genius and depth of thought to be still possible which but for this solitary scholar we might think not genial and native to our age.

It is very certain that Coleridge was not popular in his lifetime. That fact certainly warrants the charge we make upon the times, of superficialness or deficiency of interest in profound inquiries, though it does not at all affect him. He was a person of great reading and a passion for learning that made him a profound scholar in books of a philosophical character, though his learning certainly was not of that robust and universal character as that of the famous scholars of England such as Bentley and Gibbon. It was a lake that had some flats, and some fathomless places, and not one whose waters were everywhere overhead. His interest in all sciences was equal. He was of that class of philosophers called Platonists, that is, of the most Universal school; of that class that take the most enlarged and reverent views of man's nature. His eye was fixed upon Man's Reason as the faculty in which the very Godhead manifested itself or the Word was anew made flesh. His reverence for the Divine Reason was truly philosophical and made him regard every man as the most sacred object in the Universe, the Temple of Deity. An aristocrat in his politics, this most republican of all principles secured his unaffected interest in lowly and despised men the moment a religious sentiment or a philosophical principle appeared. Witness his reverential remembrance of George Fox; Behme; De Thoyras; of his poor miner; his private soldier of the Parliament, from whom he drew the sublime passage in the Friend; and of so many of his poetic persons.[8]

His true merit undoubtedly is not that of a philosopher or of a poet but a critic. I think the biography of Coleridge is written in that sentence of Plato, "He shall be as a god to me who shall rightly define and divide." [9] He possessed extreme subtlety of discrimination; and of language he was a living dictionary, surpassing all men in the fineness of distinctions he could indicate, touching his mark with a needle's point.

And that is the most valuable work he has done for his contemporaries and for all who hereafter shall read the English tongue, that he has taken a survey of the moral, intellectual, and social world as it interests us at this day, and has selected a great number of conspicuous points therein and has set himself to fix their true position and bearings.

He has made admirable definitions, and drawn indelible lines of distinction between things heretofore confounded. He thought and thought truly that all confusion of thought tended to confusion in action; and said that he had never observed an abuse of terms obtain currency without being followed by some practical error. He has enriched the English language and the English mind with an explanation of the object of Philosophy; of the all-important distinction between Reason and Understanding; the distinction of an Idea and a Conception; between Genius and

[8] *Biographia Literaria*, pp. 86–89; *The Friend*, III, 81–83, 70–77.
[9] Cf. *J*, III, 529. See *Phaedrus*: 266.

Talent; between Fancy and Imagination; of the nature and end of Poetry; of the Idea of a State.[10]

But what definitions and distinctions are these to the reader of his fervent page? How unlike the defining of school logic and formal metaphysicians! Out of every one of his distinctions comes life and heat. They light the road of common duty: they arm the working hand with skill. They fill the mind with emotions of awe and delight at the perception of its own depth. Take the single example of the distinction so scientifically drawn by him between Reason and Understanding. We do not read the popular writers of our own day, those I mean of the best class in this country, without seeing what confusion of thought the study of this one subject would have saved them, and that with his theory of Reason he could not fail to impart to them his own sublime confidence in Man.

In like manner, his singular book called Biographia Literaria, or his own literary life and opinions, is undoubtedly the best body of criticism in the English language. Nay for the importance and variety of the questions treated; for the clearness with which the truth is pointed and the beauty that adorns the whole road,

> Pitching her tents before us as we walk
> An hourly neighbor,[11]

I do not know a book on criticism in any language to which a modern scholar can be so much indebted. His works are of very unequal interest; the Aids to Reflexion, though a useful book I suppose, is the least valuable. In his own judgment, half the Biography and the third volume of the Friend from the beginning of the Essay on Method to the end with a few of his poems were all that he would preserve of his works. In this judgment, if you add the invaluable little book called Church and State which was written afterwards, I suppose all good judges would concur.

The unpopularity of Coleridge during his lifetime is un-

[10] The two items before the last refer to *Biographia Literaria*, the rest mainly to *The Friend*, though the last alludes also to *Church and State*. Reason and Understanding are much discussed in *Aids to Reflection*, but this volume, though Emerson certainly knew it, figures curiously little in these lectures.

[11] Wordsworth, "The Recluse"; quoted in the Preface to "The Excursion," lines 46–47.

doubtedly to be attributed very much to the abstruseness of the speculations in which he delighted and which tasked the intellect too sorely to be the favorite reading of the loungers in reading rooms. Undoubtedly his genius is disfigured by some faults which his critics were glad to lay hold on as reasons for dislike and contempt. He indulges much in expressions of censure and contempt at the low state of philosophical and ethical studies in England; and at the impatience of the public of any writings exacting severe thought; and especially at the arrogance and unscrupulousness of the periodical critical journals. As he had himself some private griefs to complain of, his lovers will always regret that he should have allowed the supercilious remarks upon his writings in the Reviews or the very limited circulation of his own books to affect his serenity. We feel that a man of his discernment should know that by the eternal law of Providence the Present and the Future are always rivals; he who writes for the wise alone writes for few at any one time and writing for eternity he does not write for the mixed throng that make up a nation today. Another fault with which he is taxed in this country is his excessive bigotry to the Constitution of the Church of England. This is so apparent and so separate from the general tendency and texture of his philosophy that it will never disturb the student who is accustomed to watch his moods of thought and will skip the unnecessary pages. But [the] disinterestedness with which he put behind him all the baits of lucre and pleasure, the heartiness of his patriotism, the manliness of his sympathy with all great and generous thoughts and actions, the piercing sight which made the world transparent to him, and the kindling eloquence with which both in speech and in writing this old man eloquent[ly] masters our minds and hearts promises him an enduring dominion.

But death hath now set his seal upon him, and already his true character and greatness begin to be felt. Already he quits the throng of his contemporaries and takes his lofty station in that circle of sages whom he loved: Heraclitus, Hermes, Plato, Giordano Bruno, St. Augustine.

We must here close our brief notices of English authors. There remain at least two now alive [12] (and may they live long!) who deserve particular attention as men of genius who obey their genius: who write what they know and feel, and who therefore know that their Record is true. In general, we cannot but feel that with the exceeding multitude of English books reason and virtue do not gain in proportion. It must be felt that a torpidity has crept over the greater faculties which the Masters were wont to touch which is ill supplied by incessant appeals to the passion, to the love of literary gossip, and to superficial tastes.

Moreover another grief cannot fail to touch us in view of this illustrious company of great men. A degree of humiliation must be felt by the American scholar when he reviews the constellation of great geniuses from Chaucer down who in England have enlarged the limits of wisdom and then returns to this country where Humanity has been unbound and has enjoyed the culture of Science in the freedom of the Wild and reckons how little has been here added to the stock of truth for mankind. Where are the bards [who] have sung? Where are the scholars who have collected? Where are the philosophers' digested maxims that not only run through all the corners of America, but go current in Germany, Italy, and Spain?

It seems very important that just notions of what literature is and can do, should prevail in this country, that we may neither make nor encourage others to make counterfeit books and reputations. There certainly is visible among us a great deal of false taste, a want of intellectual principles, an uncertainty in criticism and the perpetual mistake of notoriety for reputation.

There is in every civilized community a disposition to put the forms for things, the plausible for the good, the appearance for the reality. It were much to be desired that the laws of the human soul should be studied and published unweariedly in the ears of all men. The men who at public meetings of whatever kind; the writers who in books or papers of whatever kind, put manner for matter, should learn that they have lost their time. The writer who takes his subject from his ear and not from his heart, should

[12] Wordsworth and Carlyle.

know he has lost as much as he seems to have gained, and when the empty book has gathered all its praise, and half the people say what poetry! what genius! it still takes an ounce to balance an ounce. Nature cannot be cheated. That only profits which is profitable. Life alone can impart life. And though we burst we can only be valued as we make ourselves valuable.

There are two ends to one or both of which all works of literature are or should be composed: Truth and Beauty. A work must be written to one of these ends or it is naught. Truth is not the same thing as truism. If a book of general speculation only contain propositions that cannot be denied, it may not yet carry on its face the reason why it is written. Every man besides his access to universal truth, has a law of *his* being. And in Composition he must respect that law, or he cannot write well: he must write such a book as he was born to write; he must accept the high advice of Sir Philip Sidney, "Look in thy heart, and write"; he must write to himself, and he writes to an eternal public. Let every book, of whose merit we would judge, be tried by this test. Is this written to communicate one new truth? Does it contain things which had a necessity that they should be uttered?

The other principle to which the mind lives, is Beauty, which includes goodness, as the highest beauty. The rhythm of verse, the splendor of imagery, the sallies of wit, lyrics, tragedy, romance, devotional writings aim purely to express and gratify the love of beauty that haunts the human mind. This, like the other, is felt to be a spiritual and eternal principle, and a sufficient reason for the existence and publication of any word or work in which it inheres.

It is further to be observed that Truth and Beauty always face each other and each tends to become the other.

These I take it are the accepted principles of criticism, yet these tests are not very severely applied to the bales of books which every year produces, but a book full of words is thought every whit as good as a book full of things and literature becomes the imitation of imitations.

A suspension of the creative spirit of literature in England and America shall not convince me that it shall not resume its work. I am very far from believing that the age of original poetry or philosophy is past or that the cruse of truth shall run no more oil.

Nothing is infinite but truth, and the first lessons and degrees which we take in it teach us that nothing which has been done forecloses any of its avenues. It is that sphere out of which we cannot go, whose centre is everywhere, and whose circumference is nowhere. It is not made poorer by so much as a thought for all the wit and science that has been in the world, but replenishes itself forevermore and makes itself entire to every mind. It was the sublime ejaculation of St. Austin to Truth: "And yet, as rich as thy furniture is, O city of God! thy gates stand always open, free to all comers. For thy immoveable Wealth needs no guard, the Exchequer of Light and Truth is secure against all thievish attempts, and the treasures of Wisdom, though common to all, can yet be rifled and carried away by none." [13]

The unreflecting person who goes into great libraries and runs over the subjects of books and sees the infinite divisions and subdivisions of literary and scientific research is wont to think that every acre and rood and square inch of Truth's field has been digged and ransacked and no more treasures can be brought thence. The wise man ever finds himself conscious of knowing nothing but being just ready to begin to know. He is as if just born and ready to ask the first questions. Truth is new and perfect to every mind and to every moment. And herein is the ground of encouragement we have for all the future. The foundations of Literature, Truth and Beauty, are as strong and deep for us as for any.

Every man — by the gift of intellectual powers is made and prepared to be a literary man. He has intellectual capacities and duties. He has a nature far greater than he knows and resources on which he has never drawn. Let him know that the great questions affecting our spiritual nature are not one of them decided. They are all open to discussion and every candid and inquiring mind is a candidate for truth. Liberty, immortality, theism, rights, taste, the laws of beauty, the laws of love, education, physiology, the laws of thought, the system of Compensations in moral and material nature, and a hundred other questions of

[13] Not located. Probably not *The City of God.*

primary concernment to the state of man, are all open to discussion, nor has Aristotle closed the canons of criticism, nor Luther nor Swedenborg those of religious faith, nor Newton those of nature, nor Scott those of romance. A man by his intellectual nature may derive a similar evidence of his immortality to that which comes from the moral sense. A contemplation of the nature of scientific truth, a study of the principles of beauty leads the man at once into an enduring region. No man is yet fully a man or has had half the consciousness of being until his intellect has been so stimulated that he has awaked from the sleep of custom, and beheld himself and all nature from the ground of the Absolute. When that is done the whole character and complexion of events is changed to his eye. What was painful is pleasing, what was foul is fair. And the same difference is produced as when a common landscape is reflected in still water and every leaf and stake and stone loses its vulgarity and becomes an object of delight.

The present moment against all time. Wherever is Man there as from its embryo point the Universe of light and love unfolds itself anew as it had never been. I believe in the riches of the Reason and not of Plato or Paul. "He that has been born has been a First Man." [14] The stars and the celestial shell that overarch *our* spot of ground, are as brave and deep as those which Pindar or Petrarch saw, or those that shone on the faces of Ben Jonson and Shakspear, of Dryden and Milton, of Addison and Pope. Every rational creature has all nature for his dowry and estate. All nature, nothing less, is totally given to each new being.

It is his potentially. He may divest himself of it, he may creep into a corner and abdicate his kingdom as most men do but he is entitled to the world by the constitution. He is entitled to it; only he must come and take it. "The winds and waves," said Gibbon, "are always on the side of the ablest navigators." [15] What is not? I pray. When a noble act is done, — perchance in a scene of great natural beauty, — when Leonidas and his three hundred martyrs consume one day in dying and the sun and moon come each and look at them, once, in the steep defile of Thermopylae; when

[14] Not located.
[15] Gibbon, *Decline and Fall*, Chapter 68.

Arnold Winkelreid [16] in the high Alps amid the glittering terrors of the glaciers gathers in his side a sheaf of Austrian spears and so breaks the line for his comrades; are not these heroes entitled to add the beauty of the scene to the beauty of the deed? When the bark of Columbus nears the shore of America; before it the beach lined with savages fleeing out of all their huts of cane, the sea behind and the purple mountains of the Indian archipelago around, can we separate the man from the magnificent picture? Does it not come and clothe him as fit drapery? And when and where does not natural beauty steal in like air, and envelope great actions? In the most obscure places, even in sordid objects, an act of truth, of heroism seems at once to draw to itself the sky as its temple, the sun as its candle.

Nature stretcheth out her arms to embrace man, only let his thoughts be of equal grandeur. Willingly does she bend her lines of grandeur and grace to the decoration of her darling child. Only let his thoughts be of equal scope and the frame will suit the picture. A virtuous man is in keeping with the works of Nature and makes the central figure in the visible sphere.[17] It is we who by error and crime thrust ourselves aside and make ourselves impertinent lodgers, not citizens of the world. The fruitful source of all crime, the chief source of all the misery in the world is in-consideration, the want of habits of severe reflexion; men open the eye of the sense, but the iron lids of the Reason are slow to unclose.

[16] Arnold von Winkelreid, semi-legendary Swiss hero, who by his act is said to have won the victory of Sempach over the Austrians in 1386.

[17] "Every rational creature has all Nature . . . in the visible sphere" (*W*, I, 20–22); cf. *J*, III, 570.

The Uses of Natural History.

Introductory Lecture read before the Natural
History Society at the Masonic Temple
November 4 1833

In accepting the Invitation with which
the Directors of this Society have honored me
to introduce the Course, I have followed
my inclination rather than Consulted my a-
bility. My time has been so pre occupied as to
prevent any particular Course of reading or
Collection of novel illustrations of the subjects
treated, which I should gladly have proposed to
myself. I shall therefore say what I think on the
subject of this Lecture according to such imperfect general information as I already posses-
ed.

From "The Uses of Natural History." See p. 5.

nature of art & of mechanical

processes but still are not so easy

to decipher as the laws of

living nature. In works of art

there is much that is traditional

the works of nature are ever a

freshly uttered Word of God."

Perhaps it is the province of poetry rather than of prose
to describe the effect upon the mind & heart of these nameless influences. informing
that of mind & heart

He that has formed his ideas of ~~this source~~ adaptation

~~of order~~ *certainly* of beauty on these models

Can have nothing mean in his estimate

and hence in his eulogy before yᵗ Academy

Fourier said of Laplace "What La

Place called great, was great. "

Insert X

It is a moral influence of

such studies that alone might be

the recommendation of them

in the view, we are now

of intellectual influence

From "The Naturalist." See pp. 72–73.

X   It is fit that man should

Let us ~~Continue~~ to look upon
Nature with the eye of the Artist.
to learn from the great Artist whose
blood beats in our veins, whose
taste is upspringing in our own
perception of beauty, the laws by
which our hands should work
that we may build St Peterses or paint
Transfigurations or sing Iliads
in worthy ^Continuation of^ relation to the Architecture
of the Andes to the Colors of the
Sky & the poem of life.

And ~~as~~ we have said in the first
place these ^individual^ forms are perfect let us
speak now of the secret of their com
position.

From "The Naturalist." See p. 73.

"Water.

" "Water," said an ancient poet, is the best of things." Optima res, aqua. I have no such opinion, for I hold that every thing is good in its place. But there is so much foundation for the saying as this, that Water occupies a very large place among good things. Few people consider how large a place. No man yet knows how many offices this element fulfils. It needs much leisure & research & acuteness to find so many as are known. Perhaps as many remain to be found for it hides itself very cunningly sometimes close by us, & sometimes becomes invisible

From "Water." See p. 50.
See p. 50.

The use of Natural history is to give us aid in supernatural history. The use of the outer creation is to give us language for the changes & objects of the inward creation. Every word which is used to express a moral or intellectual fact, if traced to its root, is found to be borrowed from some corporeal or animal fact. Right originally means straight; wrong means twisted. Spirit primarily means wind. transgression, the crossing a line. Supercilious the raising of the eyebrow. Light & heat in all languages are used as metaphors for wisdom & love. The heart is used for feeling the head for thought: And but for these emblems furnished by nature herself the moral & metaphysical world would have remained entirely buried in the eternal abyss. And "thought" & "emotion" are in their turn mere words borrowed from sense, that have become appropriated to spiritual nature. Most of this process is now hidden from us in the remote time when our language was framed, but the same tendency

From "English Literature 1." See p. 220.

a cripple in the right way will beat
a racer in the wrong.
Tis hard to carry a full cup even
Vinegar is the son of wine
The last ounce broke the camels back
Long lived trees make roots first
                        and the like.

In their primary sense these are
trivial facts but we repeat them
for the value of their analogical
import

From "English Literature 5." See p. 290.

~~Lord Bacon who was born 1561~~

The writings of Lord Bacon ~~make~~ so material a portion of English literature that ~~it is almost~~ some notice is due to ~~impossible~~ to speak of them ~~without a slight~~ ~~notice of the~~ remarkable man who wrote ~~them~~. Bacon was born in 1561 & educated in the Court of Queen Elizabeth. His genius was early ripe for he entered the University of Cambridge ~~at 13 years~~ in his 12th, & at 19 he wrote a Sketch of the State of Europe which both in style & matter indicates a mature mind. The Queen was a coquette in her policy as well as in her love, & kept Bacon a suitor for place as long as she lived. He was a member of the House of Commons for 20 years.

In 1597 he published the Essays. After the accession of James
In 1607 he was made Solicitor general.
In 1617 he was made Lord ~~Chancellor~~ keeper and
In 1619 ~~he was made~~ Lord Chancellor of England.
In 1620 he published ye Novum Organum
~~In 1621 he fell~~
In 1622 he published his history of Henry 7.
In 1626 he died.

From "English Literature 7." See pp. 321–322.

but he never comes over us with one stroke,
of pity or terror; and they seem
to have been very properly hissed from
the stage.

What is it then that has given such honor to the name of
Rare Ben Jonson. I think it cannot be contested that
dull & pedantic as he is he has claims to the reputation
he wears. That made him the favorite of the most discerning men
that were ever in England. I think it is because his writings presuppose a
great intellectual activity in the audience suppose an Elizabethan age
and every their dulness is ye English & learned that fanciful & of
all that is it then that makes the merit of Ben
all savors of the kingdom of wit
Jonson. I suppose in his times his to be made
his pedantry very agreeable to ye crowd; because
We shd. never allow of such pedantry now! Why? because
we have not the learning of which it is the abuse.
Then his vocabulary ample & his language

scrupulously correct. There is always
good sense. He is on all general topics a
correct & vigorous thinker. (But his especial
merit is that) his moral sense is very
clear & is always present. That highest
office of the bard (which in the earliest
times they fulfilled), namely, that of being
priests & divine teachers & in melodious
numbers enjoining the practice of virtue
Ben Jonson worthily discharged in his age

From "English Literature 8." See pp. 339–340.

Bibliography
Textual Notes
Index

Bibliography of Principal Sources

I. GENERAL

Austin, Sarah (Trans.), *Characteristics of Goethe; from the German of Johann Daniel Falk and Others*, London, 1833.

Brown, Thomas, *Lectures on the Philosophy of the Human Mind*, Philadelphia, 1824.

Carlyle, Thomas, *Life of Schiller*, London, 1825.

Coleridge, Samuel Taylor, *Biographia Literaria*, New York and Boston, 1834.

Coleridge, Samuel Taylor, *On the Constitution of the Church and State*, London, 1830.

Coleridge, Samuel Taylor, *The Friend*, London, 1818.

Coleridge, Samuel Taylor, *Specimens of Table Talk*, London, 1835.

Coleridge, Samuel Taylor, *The Statesman's Manual*, Burlington, 1832.

Encyclopaedia Americana, Philadelphia, 1829.

Goethe, Johann Wolfgang von, *Werke*, Stuttgart und Tübingen, 1828–33.

Goethe, Johann Wolfgang von, *Wilhelm Meister*, tr. Thomas Carlyle, Boston, 1828.

Hallam, Henry, *View of the State of Europe during the Middle Ages*, Philadelphia, 1824.

Lives of Eminent Persons, London: Society for the Diffusion of Useful Knowledge, 1833.

Montaigne, Michael, Seigneur de, *Essays*, tr. Charles Cotton, London. Vols. I, III, 1693; Vol. II, 1700.

Oegger, G., *The True Messiah* . . . Pub. by E. P. Peabody, Boston, 1842. (Available to Emerson in manuscript).

Plutarch, *Lives*, tr. John Langhorne and William Langhorne, New Edition, Philadelphia, 1822.

Plutarch, *Morals*, tr. "several hands," London, 1718. (Volumes II and IV are missing from Emerson's copy.)

Staël-Holstein, Anne Louise Germaine, baronne de ("Mme. de Staël"), *The Influence of Literature upon Society*. (The edition Emerson used is unidentified. Our references are to the Second Edition, London, 1812.)

Stewart, Dugald, *A General View of the Progress of Metaphysical, Ethical, and Political Philosophy*, Boston, 1822.

[Swedenborg], "Emanuel Swedenborg," *New Jerusalem Magazine* V (1831–32).

II. SCIENCE

Cuvier, Baron G., *A Discourse on the Revolutions of the Surface of the Globe*. . . , Philadelphia, 1831.

Herschel, John, *On the Study of Natural Philosophy*, London, 1830.
Humboldt, Alexander von, *Personal Narrative of Travels in Equinoctial Regions of the New Continent*, London, 1814.
Lardner, Dionysius, *Treatise on Hydrostatics and Pneumatics*, Cabinet Cyclopaedia, London, 1831.
Lee, R. [Mrs. Sarah], *Memoirs of Baron Cuvier*, London, 1833.
Lives and Voyages of Drake, Cavendish and Dampier, Early English Navigators, Edinburgh Cabinet Library, Edinburgh, 1831.
Playfair, John, "Illustrations of the Huttonian Theory of the Earth," *Works*, Edinburgh, 1822, Vol. I.
Scoresby, William, *An Account of the Arctic Regions* . . . , Edinburgh, 1820.
Wells, William C., *An Essay on Dew* . . . , Second Edition, London, 1815.
White, Gilbert, *The Natural History and Antiquities of Selborne*, London, 1825.

III. BIOGRAPHY

Michelangelo

Biagioli, Giambattista, ed., *Rime de Michelangelo Buonarroti il vecchio* . . . , Parigi, 1831.
Duppa, Richard, *The Life of Michel Angelo Buonarrote* . . . , Second Edition, London, 1807.
[Radici], Review of the *Rime*, *Retrospective Review* (London) XIII (1826) 248–265.
Vasari, Giorgio, *Vite de' Piu Excellenti Pittori, Scultori, e Architetti*, Milano, 1807–11, Vol. 14.

Luther

Bower, Alexander, *The Life of Luther* . . . , London, 1813.
Carlyle, Thomas, "Luther's Psalm," *Fraser's Magazine* II (January 1831) 743–44; "Jean Paul Friedrich Richter Again," *Foreign Review* V (1830) 1–52.
Luther, Martin, *A Commentary upon the Epistle to the Galatians*, London, 1635?
Luther, Martin, *Divine Discourses* . . . *Table Talk*, tr. out of High German by H. Bell, London, 1652.
Milner, Joseph and Isaac, *The History of the Church of Christ*, Boston, 1809, Vol. IV, Part 1.
Scott, John, *Luther and the Lutheran Reformation*, New York, 1833.
Seckendorf, Veit Ludwig von, *Commentarius Historicus et Apologeticus de Lutheranismo* . . . , Francofurti et Lipsiae, 1692.

Milton

Aubrey, John, *Letters* . . . *and Lives of Eminent Men*, London, 1813.
Ivimey, Joseph, *John Milton: His Life and Times* . . . , New York, 1833.
Johnson, Samuel, "Life of Milton." See "Johnson" in Section IV.
A Selection from the English Prose Works of John Milton, Boston, 1826.
Symmons, Charles, ed., *The Prose Works of John Milton; with a Life of the Author* . . . , London, 1806.

BIBLIOGRAPHY

Fox

Fox, George, *A Journal* . . . , Fourth Edition, New York, 1800.

Hutchinson, Thomas, *The History of Massachusetts*, Boston, 1795–1828.

Sewel, William, *The History of the Rise, Increase, and Progress of the Christian People called Quakers*, Philadelphia, 1823.

Burke

Burke, Edmund, *Works*, Boston, 1826.

Crabbe, George, *Life of the Rev. George Crabbe, By his Son*, London, 1834.

Moore, Thomas, *Memoirs of the Life of the Right Honourable Richard Brinsley Sheridan*, London, 1827.

Prior, James, *The Life and Character of Edmund Burke*, Philadelphia, 1825.

IV. ENGLISH LITERATURE

Bacon, Francis, *Works*, London, 1824.

Byron, George Gordon, Lord, *Works*, Philadelphia, 1829.

Clarendon, Edward, Earl of, *The History of the Rebellion and Civil Wars in England*, Oxford, 1827.

Cudworth, Ralph, *The True Intellectual System of the Universe*, London, 1820.

Herrick, Robert, *Poetical Works*, London, 1825.

Johnson, Samuel, *Works*, London, 1806.

Jonson, Ben, *Works*, London, 1716.

Mackintosh, Sir James, *A General View of the Progress of Ethical Philosophy*, Philadelphia, 1832.

Mackintosh, Sir James, *History of England*, Cabinet Cyclopaedia, Philadelphia, 1830.

Owen, William, *The Heroic Elegies and Other Pieces of Llywarç-Hen* . . . , London, 1792.

Malone, Edmond, ed., *The Plays and Poems of William Shakespeare*, London, 1821.

Turner, Sharon, *The History of the Anglo-Saxons*, Second Edition, London, 1807.

Walton, Isaac, *Lives*, Library of Old English Prose Writers, Boston, 1832.

Warton, Thomas, *The History of English Poetry*, ed. Richard Price, London, 1824.

Textual Notes and Variant Passages

These notes, keyed to the text by page and line, are intended to record all of Emerson's manuscript cancellations and insertions, as well as any editorial changes not covered by the general editorial principles set forth on pages xxiv–xxvii of the introduction. A number of changes that are so covered are included also, as well as some variant passages and some supplementary material from Emerson's working notes. The text printed here is a literal transcription of the manuscript and thus differs in some respects from the edited version above. Minor eccentricities and slips of the pen, a few doodlings and other ephemera, and merely mechanical material (such as "Insert A," pointing hands, etc.) are usually omitted.

The symbols used in these notes are explained on page xxvi. The symbol [E] here applies to what immediately precedes it, when that might otherwise be mistaken for an editorial insertion. When matter in these notes immediately follows a cancellation, without a space, as in "The⟨se⟩y," "⟨was⟩proved," etc., it is partly or wholly written over the cancellation in the manuscript; a space is left when the new matter follows the cancellation in the text. A small superior number represents a number inserted by Emerson, usually subscript, to indicate a reversal in the order of words or longer units.

I. SCIENCE

1. THE USES OF NATURAL HISTORY

Lines   *Page 6*

4–5   Societies for the ⟨diffusion of useful knowledge⟩ pursuit of science.

11   acquaintance with the ⟨history⟩ properties

30–33   ↑It is frequently . . . which not↓ ⟨And I saw the other day in a little book which had no other good remark an observation upon the power of natural objects not only to⟩ heighten ↑s↓ but ⟨to⟩ create ↑s↓

30   how much ⟨the⟩ power, ↑the↓ influence

32   picturesque ⟨countries⟩ ↑regions↓

34–35   persons who would ⟨be ashamed to be⟩ ↑start at being↓

37   noble name, but ⟨what is done⟩ ↑great bodily exertion made↓

Page 7

2   dew, or in the ⟨shady⟩ shades

3–4   make out what, exhilarated by the fragrant ⟨air⟩ ↑scents↓

4–5   of all the winds, — ⟨I do not wonder⟩ ↑it is not strange↓

393

Lines
5   love the↑se↓ ⟨life⟩ ↑scenes↓
6   though he ⟨miscalls it the love of hunting⟩ err
8   advantages which ⟨will⟩ ↑may be expected to↓ accrue ⟨to
           individuals & to the community⟩
17   Repository of Natural Curiosities
18   except ↑perhaps↓ to Naturalists ⟨I might hesitate to⟩ ↑only
           I ought to↓
19–20   excited in me. ⟨It may not be known to all though it is well
           known to most of this audience that⟩ there is the richest col-
           lection in the world of ⟨all⟩ natural ⟨objects⟩ ↑curiosities↓
           ⟨classified scientifically &⟩ arranged ⟨in such a manner as
           to produce⟩ ↑for↓ the most imposing effect. ⟨upon the eye⟩.
21–22   ⟨Not only⟩ the mountain and morass & prairie & jungle, ⟨but⟩
           the ocean, ↑&↓ ⟨the⟩ rivers,
22–23   ransacked ⟨to furnish⟩ ↑⟨for⟩ to furnish↓
29   his habits ⟨of⟩ consulted
30–31   Cameleopard nearly 20 feet high, ⟨browsing on the trees⟩ whose
           promenade & breakfast attract⟨s⟩
34   our own countrym⟨a⟩en, the buffalo

Page 8

2–3   country fashions, ⟨⟨apparently⟩ as much . . . own wilds⟩ for
4   Capital of France.
5–6   pleasant walks ⟨as fast as your curiosity will permit⟩, you . . .
           Cabinet,
6   where grows a ⟨botani⟩ grammar
9–10   Jussieu himself. ⟨Any body who has ever studied the classes
           of plants by⟩ ↑If you have read Decandolle with↓ engrav-
           ings, or ⟨by⟩ with a *hortus siccus*, ⟨may easily⟩
12   crimson dictionary, ⟨whereon⟩ ↑on which↓
14   ⟨Not stopping long at the aviary, you come to⟩ the Cabinet
           of Natural History, ⟨which⟩ is contained
16–20   It is a prodigality . . . rich plumage [substituted for] ⟨I
           have no hope of being able at this distance of time to com-
           municate⟩ / the pleasure I derived from this Great Gallery of
           Nature, ⟨n⟩or the emotions I felt. As I wander⟨ed through the
           various halls, I was more surprized & gratified at every step.
           It was too much to be seen at one time. When I entered the
           Ornithological Chambers, I wished that I had come there
           only, to receive the full effect of the agreeable impressions
           which there awaited me. It was as fine a picture gallery as
           the Louvre. The whole air of the place is flushed with⟩ the
           rich plumage
18–19   delicate sensations.
23   The↑y↓ ⟨spectacle⟩ fill⟨s⟩ the mind
25   appropriate to some ⟨seraglio⟩ ↑sultan's↓
28–29   cultivated taste. ⟨I refer to such birds as one parrot of a
           fellow⟩ ↑Observe that parrot of the parrot tribe↓

394

Lines

30   You need not ⟨put it in your memorandum book⟩ ↑write down his name↓

34   *Trochilus Pella* ⟨who hath such a⟩ ↑with his↓

Page 9

1   magnificent fly ↑La mouche magnifique↓

1–2   glory in miniature. / ⟨chilus niger not so big as a beetle, to the Trochilus pella who hath such an irresistible neck of gold & silver & fire, & the Trochilus Delalandi from Brazil whom the French call the magnificent fly ↑or glory in minia-ture↓ is a glorious little tot. There too is⟩ The birds of Paradise ⟨also⟩ are singularly ⟨handsome⟩ delicate

5   than the last & ↑each↓

6   peerless ⟨bird⟩ ↑creature↓ ⟨Th⟩ I watched

8   same birds to ⟨show⟩ ↑point to the admiration of↓

10   black fowl ↑called Emberiza longicanda↓

11   ornaments & a ⟨lugubrious⟩ ↑long mourning↓ tail.

12–13   Phasianus Argus a pheasant that appeared to have ⟨dressed itself⟩ ↑made its toilette↓

14   Coucouron ⟨pavonin⟩

14–16   ↑But it were vain . . . assembly↓

16   There ⟨I saw⟩ ↑were↓ black swans

17   come hither ↑to Paris↓ out of Egypt

18   the rosy; ⟨There was⟩

19   Toucan rightly ⟨called⟩ ↑denominated↓

20   & a vulture ⟨that would make the flesh creep⟩ ↑whom↓ to meet in a wilderness ↑wd. make the flesh creep↓ so

22   ⟨But⟩ the cabinet of birds was ⟨but⟩ a single

23   Magazine of natur⟨es⟩al ⟨productions.⟩ ↑wonders.↓ ⟨Scarcely less attr⟩ Not less complete scarcely

24   collection of ↑stuffed↓ beasts

25–26   attitudes of ⟨All⟩ ↑the quadrapeds↓.

26   Then ↑follow↓ the insects

27   In ⟨a⟩ neighboring

28   anatomy ↑a perfect series from↓

30   upright form & ⟨large⟩ highly developed

33–35   as you see ↑more surprizing . . . lumps of↓ amber with ⟨musquitoes⟩ ↑gnats & flies↓ within; ↑radiant spars & marbles↓ huge blocks

36–(10)1   combination ↑gold in↓ threads, ↑in↓ plates, ↑in↓ crystals, ↑in↓ dust

Page 10

3   enlarged ⟨to your eye⟩

8–10   organized forms. ⟨If⟩ ↑Whilst I stand there↓ I am impressed with ↑a singular↓ conviction ⟨of the⟩ that

15   such thoughts, ↑I say that↓ I suppose ⟨there may be⟩ many

Lines
18   Science has given it a ⟨very⟩ higher
21   defy scientific solution.
24–27   Institute ↑in 1830↓ . . . Animal Magnetism a committee
            . . . persons on earth.
28–29   ridiculous let me

Page 11

29–30   I mean the ↑direct↓ service
32–33   all discoveries almost . . . civilization itself. ⟨Who is not
            indebted for the comforts & accommodations of every day to
            the investigations which have been carried into every kingdom
            of nature.⟩
34   out of which we ⟨are fed & clothed & warmed & armed⟩ con-
            struct

Page 12

3–4   these are most ⟨debt is greater⟩ ↑accumulated↓
5–6   process so far ⟨from our⟩ ↑out of↓ sight, that ⟨it⟩ a man ⟨stands
            in danger of forgetting that iron came out of the mine & per-
            fume from the cat⟩ who by ⟨ringing⟩ ↑pulling↓ a bell
18   the cloth, the ⟨dyestuffs⟩ paints
18–19   philosopher ↑as well as the ⟨ch⟩ mechanic;↓
20   processes are not ↑assisted or↓ directed
21   derived from ⟨scientific men⟩ the observations
24–25   Record of the predicted
33–34   produced in France by the ⟨celebrated⟩ appointment

Page 13

2–3   region of coal, ⟨in⟩ and in
6   one of our chemists is
16   But ⟨it is not alone⟩ the advantages
17–18   possessions. To ⟨these to⟩ the powers
18   assigned. ⟨The power⟩ All that
19   future. The ⟨power⟩ prospective
24   The natural history of water is not studied [written under-
            neath in pencil:] Perkins steam engine
25   advantage ⟨today⟩ ↑at this moment↓ than when
26–27   the other day ⟨since⟩ ↑that↓ our countryman
29–30   these bubbles ⟨acted⟩ ↑operate↓

Page 14

4   air bubbles — this thought he has recently ⟨put in practice⟩
            ↑executed↓
5   machine called his ↑the↓ Circulators

THE USES OF NATURAL HISTORY

Lines

7–8	best success ↑& is about being introduced into all.↓
13–14	too particular a a showing
17–18	stability of the Solar System
23	cunning they employ.
32	education ⟨had done⟩ ↑would do↓
33–34	When he goes ⟨to the theatre⟩ ↑there, pointing to the marble seats of the theatre↓ he replied,

Page 15

3–4	significant. ⟨We⟩ ↑How many men ⟨livi[?]⟩↓ have seen it snow ⟨all the⟩ ↑20 or 40↓ winters
4–5	beyond the ↑need of stout boots, the probability of↓ good
8	and shown us ⟨how⟩ the texture
10–11	animated creation ⟨in⟩ on
12	We cannot see again ↑without new pleasure↓ what the latin
15–16	still air & ⟨see⟩ ↑catch↓
16–17	↑& measure . . . the star↓
19–20	covers the country for the farmer [2] & the woodcutter.[1]
21–22	laboratory & ↑on↓ a more
22–(16)36	can command.
	Coal To the naturalist . . . provision for human wants ⟨that is made sometimes ages before it is needed⟩ that in some instances ⟨was begun ages before⟩ requiring . . . the use of it was shown. / [written in pencil; cancelled by two pencilled lines]
	The science of Geology . . . prosperity at this hour. / [these four paragraphs lightly cancelled by one pencilled line]
29–30	structure of the Earth
33	upon it as granite

Page 16

6	now found as may be seen lying as may be seen
7	perpendicular ⟨la⟩
12–13	development of the Commerce
17–18	iron ore, ⟨the English have⟩ ↑and the invariable . . . flux the iron, the English have↓
21–22	the Coal which is undoubtedly
31	essential to ⟨human⟩ ↑man's↓
35	crystallization of Antediluvian
37	↑Thus↓ Knowledge will make

Page 17

1	clothe with ⟨new life⟩ ↑grace↓
16	it is for. a ship, a telescope,
21	the use of the ⟨color⟩ case, the color
27–28	in nature so mean ⟨n⟩or ⟨so⟩ loathsome, ⟨neither⟩ not a weed, not a / not a toad

Page 18

Lines

1   Eyes and no Eyes.

2   senses in health. ⟨Eyes have they, but they see⟨n⟩ not; ears
        have they, but they hear not; and noses, but they smell not.⟩

4–5   same hills⟨ides⟩ ↑Linnaeus or Buffon or↓ Cuvier or Hum-
        boldt or ↑⟨Linnaeus, Buffon, Huber⟩↓ ⟨Kirby or Spence or even
        some accomplished countryman of ours, and will⟩ & the sea

6   clap their hands. ⟨Let a person of inattentive mind⟩ ↑The
        traveller↓ cast↑s↓

7   mountain side, ⟨he⟩ sees

8–10   Let Cuvier ⟨or Humboldt⟩ regard the same thing ⟨& mark the
        difference⟩ . . . the globe the changes [no punctuation]

11   effected ⟨in ages⟩ by fire

12–13   planet, he is ⟨conversing by⟩ ↑hearkening to↓

15   future inquirers. [Here follows a much corrected paragraph
        about Galileo, all afterwards cancelled heavily in ink:] ⟨Gali-
        leo⟩ ⟨Who has not mourned over the⟩ ⟨calamity⟩ ⟨public⟩ ↑⟨It
        was felt by their contemporaries as a public⟩↓ calamity, when
        such an observer who knew ⟨how to use his eyes⟩ ↑the value of
        his senses,↓ has been deprived of their use. ⟨I refer the cele-
        brated instance of⟩ ↑One of the most touching incidents in
        ⟨history⟩ biography is the affliction befel↓ Galileo who after
        ⟨his⟩ announcing in rapid succession to the world his splendid
        discoveries namely ↑uneven surface of the moon↓ ↑the spots
        on the sun by wh. the revolution was proved.↓ ⟨the⟩ that
        Venus ⟨had phases⟩ ↑was horned↓ like the moon, the satellites
        ↑and the belt↓ of Jupiter, the ring of Saturn — was ⟨afflicted
        with the loss of⟩ ↑bereaved of↓ sight. His friend wrote to
        [blank] The noblest eye is darkened that nature ever made
        etc. / "⟨The noblest eye is darkened (said Castelli) which
        nature ever made: an eye so priveleged and gifted with such
        rare qualities, that it may with truth be said to have seen
        more than all of those who are gone, & to have opened the
        eyes of all who are to come."⟩
        ⟨Galileo himself writes — "Alas, your dear friend & servant
        Galileo has become totally & irreparably blind; so that this
        heaven, this earth, this universe, which with wonderful ob-
        servations I had enlarged a hundred & a thousand times be-
        yond the belief of bygone ages, henceforward for me is shrunk
        into the narrow space which I myself fill in it.⟨"⟩ So it pleases
        God: it shall therefore please me also."⟩
            And every ones memory will serve him with numerous in-
        stances in the biography of naturalists of the ⟨strong⟩ keen
        delight they found in the prosecution of their inquiries. / [All
        the above sheet is heavily crossed out in ink.]

Page 19

Lines

8–9 contrivances are good ⟨until they are compared with hers⟩ ↑but will not bear comparison↓ with hers.

11–12 Solar System but . . . nature's own orrery, as ⟨the system⟩ ↑it↓ would appear ⟨if seen⟩ to the eye

14–15 self poised in empty space no rods

24–25 grasses, and ↑to↓ the germination of forest trees. The Earth-worms. —

26 observed by ⟨a keen eyewitness of the habits of insects {White of Selborne}⟩ ↑the entomologist↓

31–32 grain & grass. ↑Without the ⟨aid of these⟩ incessant aid of these little↓ Gardeners & farmers, ⟨may complain of worms, but they would find, that, without them,⟩ the earth

34 Thus ⟨then, by these tiny workmen⟩, Nature keeps

34–35 how does she ⟨rear⟩ ↑make↓

Page 20

1 build ↑up↓ the solid

1–2 little insect, the coral ⟨-insect⟩ ↑line↓,

4–5 surface, & th⟨i⟩↑e↓s↑e↓ make⟨s⟩ ↑in the course of ages↓ the ↑broad↓ floor

6–7 accidents of drift ⟨wood⟩ timber

9 numberless ⟨ins⟩ examples

14–15 beneficent upon the ⟨mind given⟩ ↑faculties dedicated↓ to such observations? — ↑upon the man↓ given

27 whole character ⟨true and⟩ amiable and true. ⟨Stewart's remark upon the difference of the character of poets & men of science is familiar to all.⟩ [Here is crossed out a hand pointing to two sentences inserted on the following (otherwise blank) page:]
{Fontenelle who wrote the lives of the members of the French Academy of Sciences, a society of natural philosophers & mathematicians takes notice of the amiable simplicity of their manners which rather seemed common to that class of men of letters than peculiar to any individual. D'Alembert who wrote the lives of the Members of the Academy — a society of poets & fine writers nowhere pretends to represent this amiable quality as characteristical of this class of men of letters.}
(See Adam Smith — Mor. Sent.) [Philadelphia, 1817, p. 203]

28 I think that ⟨every one's experience⟩ a superiority

Page 21

1–2 mediocrity ↑which results in cities from↓ the fear

2 display. ⟨being the ruling passions.⟩

Lines
5–6 each man & which ↑⟨which⟩ it behoves every man to respect as it↓ constitutes

7–8 These ↑peculiarities in the resident of the country↓ are the effects

12 I apprehend that ⟨no⟩ every

22–23 amuse a ↑rainy↓ leisure day

24 the whole man.

⟨The biography of chemists of botanists of physicians & the whole race of naturalists abounds with narratives of sleepless nights & laborious days of painful watchings & dangerous journeyings There is no hazard the love of science has not prompted them to brave, no wilderness they have not penetrated, no experiment suggested which they have not tried. Hence the high prophetic tone which they have often assumed speaking as with the voice of nature herself.⟩

28–29 "I have found it" is ⟨almost a nursery tale⟩ ↑⟨as wel⟩ familiar to children↓

Page 22

1 computation. ⟨It is⟩ As they say

2 remarked ⟨that⟩ of several

4–5 Haller ⟨& Hunter⟩ the celebrated ↑Swiss↓ physiologist

5–6 observations ⟨upon his own disease⟩ ↑in his last illness upon the progress of his disease↓

6 calmness; ⟨observing⟩ ↑taking note of↓

7 system, ⟨and until⟩ ⟨at last⟩ ↑and↓

8 exclaimed ↑to his physician↓

12–13 had power ⟨to⟩ ↑of speaking or writing that I might↓ tell

15 value of truth ⟨to the comfort of the observer⟩, & who

29 time & nature. ⟨Kepler⟩

31–32 one century ⟨when⟩ ↑since↓ God

Page 23

1–2 laborious days & ⟨painfu⟩ dangerous

8 to their cause, this ⟨loss of all⟩ trampling

15–16 party spirit, & the ↑excessive↓

20 natural science health;

24–25 discharged) ⟨is⟩ to explain

27 already corrected.

27 all the facts ⟨will give ma⟩ of all

28–32 system of being. ⟨and then it will answer the highest questions The whole of Nature, no man can doubt, will be found agreeing to the whole of mind⟩ ↑but more than . . . unsolved and ↑on↓ which . . . throw light.↓ /

⟨The deepest problems ⟨in⟩ [?] are those that lie nearest at hand. Is not the most mysterious and wonderful fact, after

Lines

our own existence, with which we are acquainted, ↑be not,↓ the power of expression that belongs to external nature? Or that Correspondence of the outward world to the inward world of thoughts and emotions by which it is suited to be typical of what we think. [The rest of this page is heavily scored through.] Is the face of heaven & earth this glorious ⟨combination⟩ scene always changing yet always pleasant fading all around us into ↑fine↓ ⟨near⟩ perspective overhung with the ever varying awning of the clouds ⟨sailing⟩ floating themselves as ↑scraps of↓ down under ↑the high stars &↓ the everlasting vault of space — is this nothing to us but the oxygen & the azote & the carbon of which what is visible is composed? Is there not more beauty in the morning cloud than the prism can render account of. Is there not something in it that resembles the aspects of mortal life its epochs & its fate?⟩ / ⟨The most difficult problems are those that lie nearest at hand. I suppose every philosopher feels that the simple fact of his own existence is the most astonishing of all facts. But I suggest the question with great humility to the reason of every one present whether the most mysterious & wonderful fact (after our own existence)⟩

Page 24

4	existence) ⟨be not⟩ with which
7	suited to ⟨be typical of⟩ ↑represent↓ what we think.
20	Mind of Man
30	thots of sweet & bitter moments of
35–36	The laws of ⟨external⟩ ↑moral↓ nature

Page 25

7–25	{Thus, a straight . . . points The . . . part The . . . greatest the . . . time Reaction . . . action; in life they have a much . . . technical use And harmony with the human mind.}
20	but we ⟨respect⟩ ↑repeat↓ them
26	this undersong this perfect

2. ON THE RELATION OF MAN TO THE GLOBE

Page 28

1–14	↑There are many facts . . . fruits of Natural Science↓ / [in pencil: added for a later reading?]
2	suddenly be known ⟨There are many facts⟩ & which

Lines

2–3   periods of time. ⟨From their nature they cannot suddenly be known. One of these⟩
     The character

4   by one year. The ⟨laws that determine⟩ orbit

6   our years. ⟨The irregularities of these orbits as⟩ the precession

8–9   interest to us ⟨but which could not be known to Adam as it is known to us⟩ ↑only a series of ages could fully reveal↓ namely

11   nature & his ⟨residence⟩ abode.

12–14   The subject of ye last was [?] ye Uses so ⟨I hop⟩ . . . Natural Science

Page 29

10–11   say rather — . . . patient observers can

22   1. ↑The preparation of the Globe for Man↓
     By the study

22–23   we have ⟨learned⟩ ↑become acquainted with↓

24   sublime, ↑to wit,↓ that

32   house was not ready. ⟨for him⟩

Page 30

2   broken stones is

25   earths or stones are

Page 31

12   Once it would appear,

19   along the ↑whole↓ western side

Page 32

28–29   four fifths of ⟨oxygen⟩ ↑azote↓, one fifth of ⟨azote⟩ ↑oxygen↓

Page 33

4   then the ⟨weight⟩ texture

9–10   many thousand ⟨veg⟩ species of vegetables

24–25   their manufactures.
     Playfairs fossil   But the coal

28–29   fresh water deposites

Page 34

19   ↑2.↓   I have spoken of the preparation

22   been ↑less↓ frequently

29   He is quite ⟨equal⟩ ↑able↓,

THE RELATION OF MAN TO THE GLOBE

Page 35

Page 36

Page 37

Page 38

Page 40

Page 41

Page 42

Page 43

Lines	
14	↑6.↓ ↑Relation to inanimate creation↓ Let us now proceed ⟨from⟩ in our
27–28	constantly ↑suspended↓ twenty

Page 44

2–3	confined by the ⟨bind weeds⟩ ↑beach grass↓,
9	totally destroyed it
13	↑7↓ ↑Correspondence of Nature to the soul↓ But perhaps the most striking
17	things in which we live.

Page 45

34	to which they ret⟨urn⟩ire as often

Page 46

3	exhibits ↑his↓ delight
18	which ⟨gives⟩ ↑creates in↓ the Chayma
22	which ⟨has built up⟩ ↑expresses itself in↓
24–25	new & noble ⟨relation⟩ view

Page 47

7–8	Some idea of the ⟨diligence with which⟩ ↑riches of the means which the earth affords to↓ these investigations ⟨have been pursued⟩ may be
10	shells almost
23	Egypt having
24	the Nile ↑not a serpent eater↓,

Page 48

4–8	⟨In the theo⟩ ↑At the same time we seem . . . researches of the physiologist.↓ [no punctuation]
27	instruct him, — ⟨T⟩the dewdrop
29–30	orbit only a ⟨bark⟩ship to transport

3. WATER

Page 51

6	pretty well & ↑that↓ no recommendation
12	unsuspected that works

Lines

17–18	are of ⟨the first⟩ ↑great↓ importance. The ⟨sustenance⟩ ↑food↓
18	fisheries ⟨is⟩ sustains
19–20	of the ship ⟨its influen⟩ & by means of / of the ship
24	ways; & ↑⟨to⟩↓ contriv⟨ing⟩⟨e⟩ing
25	talents for ⟨work⟩ ↑industry↓,
27–28	mill wheel night & day, / [upside down at bottom of sheet:] ⟨of changes by which new strata are formed & consolidated & mineralized to be again raised decomposed. The water dissolves & holds in solution⟩
33	thousands of ⟨tons⟩ pounds.
36	all these. ↑wh. we direct↓ For,

Page 52

1–6	human life; ↑he modifies the atmosphere↓ he washes . . . make ⟨new⟩ the habitable . . . plains, he . . . occasions, he . . . & animal ⟨life⟩ ↑structures↓ ↑structures [pencil]↓ and he is . . . medium having
10	masks all new
10–13	Now he globes . . . dew drop. Now . . . rainbow Now . . . spray Now . . . cloud Now . . . icicle now . . . snow-flake now
19	↑{Composition of Water}↓

Water	by weight	by volume
Oxygen	8	1
Hydrogen	1	2

↑A drop of↓ Water is composed of two gases oxygen

21	all the ⟨iron & granite⟩ ↑the most solid substances↓ of the globe ⟨is⟩ are
22	elastic airs. ⟨In⟩ At the polar regions ⟨water⟩ ice hardens to ⟨a⟩ ↑so↓ compact ↑a↓ texture ⟨which⟩ ↑that it↓ can
24–26	yet is ⟨it⟩ ↑every block of that transparent stone↓ composed of two ⟨substances⟩ ↑gases↓ each of which is ↑as↓ invisible to the eye & ↑as↓ impalpable ⟨gas⟩ ↑as the air we breathe↓.
27–28	glass ⟨vessel⟩ ↑receiver↓ & passing
32	↑{Mass of Water on the Globe}↓

Page 53

2	that The mass ↑to account for the observed↓ ⟨the⟩
7–8	but exert ⟨the greatest⟩ a very great
8–9	mechanical ↑not only↓ through
9	kingdoms of ↑living↓ nature
14–19	As the chemist . . . mechanism of the globe. [no punctuation] ⟨The first use then in dignity.⟩ Let us then first inquire into its use in ⟨the changing the⟩ producing
20–21	threefold by its

Lines
21–34

Let us ↑see↓ trace ⟨this action of Water seeking its level.⟩ ↑the consequence of these properties↓ Nineteen parts in twenty . . . These last as well as iron are . . . oxygen are . . . into solid rocks / What broke them up? . . . mechanical action of Water. ⟨The incessant action of the rains & the rivers which they form, on every point of the vast surface of the dry land with the force of gravitation always aiding them⟩ /
↑{Fluid Level}↓
⟨Let us trace this action of water seeking its level.⟩

Nineteen parts in twenty of the known solid matter of the globe are composed of five substances Flint, alumine, lime, magnesia, (& iron.) These which are all metals disguised by oxygen are crystallized into solid rocks. The soil on which we live & by which we are fed is nothing but a mixture of these ⟨crumbled⟩ rocks in a crumbled state together with remains of animal & vegetable matter to which ⟨had previously subsisted on⟩ the same soil had previously given birth. Now what broke up these solid rocks on which no blade of grass could grow into small powders which by their mixture with each other & with air & water could feed vegetable life & in that new form support animal life? ⟨The continual action of⟩ ↑Water seeking its level↓ ⟨air & water⟩ ⟨the incessant wear of the wind & of the rain ↑on every point of the vast surface of ye dry land↓ with the force of gravitation always aiding them, affects a great deal in long periods of time, but withal there / is a continual chemical action also by the same elements.

But the mechanical forces of destruction are more easily marked than the chemical.⟩ "⟨And⟩ Water everywhere appears   [It is possible that when Emerson abridged this passage on the previous leaf (i.e. "What broke . . . aiding them)" above) he intended to supersede all the above. The arrangement of the text on the pages concerned suggests, however, that he intended a composite text such as has been adopted.]

Page 54

9
20–21
27
31–32

against itself. ⟨Every separ⟩ ↑No↓
made in nature ↑first for forming & then↓
has remained ⟨the s⟩ nearly
in their ⟨waters⟩ ↑stream↓ is ⟨taken down⟩ torn off & brot down ↑by a thousand little brooks↓

Page 55

3

ancient appearance. ⟨The geologist accounts the great chains of mountains⟩   And the

3–4   of the ⟨everlasting⟩ ↑incessant↓ fall

7   deposited by the ⟨sea⟩ ↑fresh or salt streams↓

9–10   from them & ⟨it has been said they are left⟩ they

16   & by this ⟨change⟩ the surface

36–(56)1   to be again decomposed./

↑⟨111⟩↓ ↑{Solvency}↓ ⟨I have spoken of the effect of water in Nature by pressure & by its tendency to seek a level I proceed to a third property of greatest use in Nature its solvency.⟩ It dissolves & holds

Page 56

5–7   soluble in them ↑e.g. sal . . . iodine;↓.

9–14   All animal . . . in the / the bosom of the sea; [no commas, colon, semicolon]

18   reproduction; There,

24   heat existed ⟨at the centre⟩ within

25–26   the hot springs the . . . volcanoes and

33–34   cooling of the fused mass. /

⟨4⟩ /

↑{Pressure}↓ Dr Hutton ∧ had advanced

Page 57

7   & make ⟨a bed of limestone himself⟩ a little

18   All ↑that extensive class of stones called↓

19   ↑such as porphyry basalt↓

22   Hall ⟨that⟩ reflecting

24   appearance, ⟨He therefore⟩ made ↑similar↓ experiments

25   basalt. ⟨&⟩ ↑He↓ ascertained

36n   {The west banks . . . Am. Encyc.}

Page 58

14–15   concentric layers. ⟨In this manner the balls of basalt & porphyry which fall out of decomposing rocks were probably formed; they derived their superior hardness from the crystalline arrangement of the particles when in a melted state⟩ ↑What took place in the process easily showed↓ When these

19   jointed ↑together↓ ⟨&⟩ or articulated."

21–22   & to show ⟨how⟩ the precise

22   ↑the pressure of great masses of↓

23   of continents.

↑Equalizes temperature↓

25   temperature ⟨in the⟩ at the surface

26   of form. ⟨It is now⟩ It was

28–29   heat to tur melt it & ⟨to⟩ bring

30   ↑according to Black 140°↓

Page 59

Lines	
2	water was at ⟨21⟩ heated
5	940° degrees of heat
6	when steam ⟨becomes⟩ is cooled
10–11	a great ⟨loss of heat⟩ amount of heat ⟨set free⟩ ↑absorbed↓ & on
12	amount of heat ⟨absorbed⟩ ↑set free↓ —
18	a sudden ⟨inundation⟩ & irresistible
19–20	men animals cities & the very soil ⟨Moreo⟩ /
31–32	water to freeze the temperature
33–34	↑There & every where the formation of rain hail & . . . severity of winter.↓
	↑Supports Vegetation↓
36	vegetable (& animal) life.
36–(60)1	wither & die. It act⟨s⟩ion upon

Page 60

2	itself ⟨their⟩ ↑an important part of their↓
5	solid food it
6–10	The sap in roots . . . dipped into it. / [no punctuation]
11	⟨Water a⟩ The water itself acts
17	First the ⟨water⟩ ↑rain↓ falls
23	But the ↑simple↓ rain
24–26	and dissolving what it finds convey it to the mouths of the roots. ↑It falls where it is wanted.↓ ⟨& it is observed⟩ ↑It must be remembered↓ that it is not
28–29	tree in ⟨the form of a⟩ ↑by its green↓ dome protects the the
30	to the rain ⟨& the ends of the branches shed it off⟩ & the water
35	refer to ↑another↓ the office

Page 61

1	↑In Animal life↓ ⟨I shall not⟩ The functions
2	but ⟨the⟩ its relations
4	↑A kingdom of life↓ 6. ⟨In the⟩ There is yet one
5	It is itself ⟨a kingdom⟩ one of the
15–18	↑Here exists that . . . food of the whale.↓
20	issue out ⟨of the⟩ from
23	⟨Here⟩ In the dark & recesses
27–28	↑There is something almost pathetic in↓
28–29	their element. ⟨is almost pathetic⟩ that I cannot
30	heavier ⟨tha⟩ & offers

Page 62

3	smaller & the⟨ir⟩ external
15	of a few ⟨membranous⟩ bags

Lines	
28	also swims, ⟨with greater or less rapidity⟩,
29	useless ⟨to fishes. had nature bestowed it on them.⟩
30	often bony, ⟨or armed with dentated plates⟩
31–32	sensible ⟨is⟩ this organ is.

Page 63

2	insensible hardness."
	Cuvier
3	Truly the⟨y⟩ ↑ocean children↓
8	⟨H⟩ ↑{Meteorology}↓ ↑7↓ Having run over
11	↑This makes the science of Meteorology.↓
12	upon ⟨all⟩ the surface
15–16	which rise ⟨as high as their⟩ ↑into the same↓
16	fall in ⟨minute⟩ mist
18	rivers which ⟨return the waters⟩ gathering
19–20	3000 miles ⟨length⟩ pour
23–24	computed that ⟨om⟩ from
29	↑Dew↓ ↑8↓ ↑⟨invisible ocean⟩↓ ⟨Another⟩ ↑From hence comes the fine↓ phenomenon ⟨in the economy of meteorology is⟩ ↑of↓ the deposit⟨ion⟩ of dew.
30–32	laws of heat. ⟨All bodies⟩ ↑hot↓ ⟨The earth itself & all bodies containing heat⟩ always ⟨radiate⟩ ↑emit↓ their heat in right lines ↑in all directions↓ into space. Some bodies ⟨more⟩ ↑faster↓, some ⟨less⟩ ↑slower↓ ⟨in⟩ according
32–(64)1	⟨As soon as⟩ ↑All day the plants radiate ⟨this⟩ heat which they receive from ye sun & would scorch them if accumulated; ⟨but⟩ when↓ the sun goes down the plants ⟨therefore⟩ ↑continue↓ throw off this heat ⟨which they have received⟩ ⟨i⟩on all ⟨directions⟩ ↑sides↓;

Page 64

5–6	invisible, ⟨but is⟩ ↑and↓ now deposit⟨ed⟩s ↑it↓ in
7–8	and most ↑abundantly↓ when ⟨most needed in the hot season⟩ ↑they need it most, at midsummer↓, because
9	And ⟨all this happens⟩ ↑they get all this wetting↓
9–10	houses ↑all around them↓
11	simple ⟨fact⟩ ↑circumstance↓ that
12	heat but stones . . . are not. / [no commas]
13	Another ⟨beautiful meteor⟩ ↑deposit of the invisible water↓ is snow a natural ⟨blanket⟩ ↑fleece↓
17	by ↑observing↓ the crystallization
21	of the ⟨liquid⟩ ↑air↓
25–26	solution ↑just crystallization of sugar is aided by putting a thread or a stick↓.
27–28	calm & still & ⟨the⟩ not ⟨to⟩ so warm

Lines

28–30   angles. but when . . . irregular flakes. [no commas]
31   angles of the ⟨cr⟩ primitive

Page 65

1–2   from the cold ↑Alpine plants . . . protection↓ & to be
9–10   This is ⟨true of liquids & of solids⟩ ↑a general law . . . also
         of liquids.↓ [no commas]
10–11   Mercury . . . sulphuric acid ↑& liquids in general↓ [no com-
         mas]
21   brass globe ⟨the⟩ whose
22–23   Academicians & ⟨was⟩ frozen.
27   others arranging
31–32   to this ⟨fact⟩ ↑property of water↓
37   become ⟨one⟩ solid.

Page 66

11   virtues ⟨of⟩ which
12   account ↑in the arts↓.
13   ↑Hydrostatics↓   ⟨In consequence⟩ ↑From th⟨is⟩e law↓
14   follow; one
26–27   on, or, against which
33–34   fluid the greatest ⟨mischief⟩ ↑power↓ may be ⟨done⟩ ↑exerted↓
34   water if it ⟨happens to be⟩ ↑is↓ distributed

Page 67

2–3   water cask ⟨bursts with violence⟩ ↑being↓
3–4   small tube ⟨that will⟩ so narrow
13–14   41.472 ↑tons↓ ⟨is⟩ might . . . pound of water. but
18   where mill stones are made
25–26   by the ↑irresistible↓ expansion
29   ↑Steam↓   A drop of water ⟨at 212°⟩ ↑in boiling↓
30   1689 times the ⟨bulk it had⟩ ↑⟨occupied⟩↓ ↑⟨filled⟩↓ ↑space it
         filled↓ before.
31   exerts a ⟨pressure⟩ force equivalent to ⟨14,700⟩ ↑nearly 15 000↓
         lbs

Page 68

4   make it ⟨susceptible of⟩ ↑fit for↓ arming
5   strength ⟨with⟩ which he
8–9   its strength. ⟨There is more force in a pail of water than
         mountains can counterbalance &⟩ it is convertible to ↑the aid
         of↓ every action
14   matter to make
16   Such ⟨are the⟩ virtue⟨s⟩ lies

4. THE NATURALIST

Page 69

Page 70

Page 71

Page 72

Page 73

Lines

1–2   ideas of ⟨contrivance of order⟩ ↑adaptation↓ of beauty

3–4   ↑and hence↓ Fourrier said of Laplace ↑in his eulogy before ye F. Academy↓

5–13   ↑It is fit that man should . . . secret of their Composition.↓

5   ⟨Let us continue⟩ ↑⟨learn⟩↓ ⟨to⟩ ↑It is fit that man should↓ look upon

9–10   worthy ↑continuation of↓ relation to the Architecture of the Andes, to the colors

12   these ↑individual↓ forms

13   perfect let us

13   secret of their composition.
         ⟨It is a moral influence of such studies that alone might be the recommendation of them in the view ↑of intellectual influence↓ we are now⟩ /

14   ↑Composition↓ Nothing strikes

16   the result. ⟨A few elements⟩ Nature

17–19   Combination ⟨A few elements she has⟩ ↑Sometimes it is so amusing as to remind us of↓ The French cook ↑who↓ . . . maccaroni.

33   gathered . . . mussels & snails. ⟨shells⟩. [no commas]

Page 74

6–7   principles of ⟨the⟩ her architecture. ⟨The radical⟩

7–8   a single ⟨work⟩ structure

8   assemblage of ⟨vegetable⟩ individuals

12   polarity all

13–14   Buccinum Harpa but when we see that that every one of these ⟨ele⟩ polished

17   projection Give

21   Hence "I am persuaded

30–32   intellectual influences.
         1. They restrain imitation. /
         III ⟨considering, namely, that they⟩ restrain Imitation — Imition ⟨is⟩ the vice of overcivilized Communities. ↑To take an example. Imitation↓ ⟨& it is⟩ ↑is↓ the vice

Page 75

2   writing ⟨is⟩ ↑are↓ derivative

4   ↑It is at once our strength & weakness that↓ ⟨T⟩there

7   It is the ⟨consequence of having a literature⟩ tax we pay

11   bad party ⟨forgetful⟩ ignorant of ⟨English⟩ ↑all↓ literature

13–14   ↑as if it were permanent forms of Nature.↓

15   back to ⟨Nature⟩ ↑Truth↓

17   & one ⟨Maker⟩ ↑Cause↓.

18   Another ⟨obvious effect of the⟩ ↑part of the intellectual↓

Lines

23 All prop-↑its↓erties are permanent:

25 The Light ⟨answers⟩ ↑yields↓

29 ⟨The distinctions of⟩ natural objects are . . . discriminated. An

30 orange ↑wax & iron so different↓ and

32 many dull ⟨per[?]⟩ understandings

33–34 plants. ⟨For example⟩ what pity instead of

Page 76

2 from the ⟨terse⟩ ↑sharp↓ marks

2–4 Botany — such . . . graveyard of obituaries. / [no commas or italics. Vertically under the last six lines:] Dear Charles,

3 sour ⟨philopropagenitive⟩ plausible

10–11 evils of Science. [bottom of page:]
   "Naturalist"
Read before the Nat. Hist. Soc. Boston. /
IV ⟨But perhaps I ought to take for granted the general fact that a knowledge of Nature is desireable for it sounds like arguing a truism to set out to prove that Nature is perfect No that I will leave But it is my business to show that the time is not lost by the student which is given to its laws.⟩

 ↑There is a general influence needed from recurrence to Nature to save us from evils owing to Science.↓

 ⟨And here let me urge an advantage it promises much needed in our times.⟩ We are the cossets of civilization. a

13 pins & ⟨knives & forks⟩ ↑caoutchouc↓

14 bad effect of / that crutches

15–16 meant to aid. ⟨We depend so much on our clocks that we have lost the knowledge of the time by the sun.⟩ ↑⟨In this way⟩ ⟨t⟩The clock . . . from astronomy↓

17 Natural ⟨marks⟩ ↑signs↓

19–22 farmer is ⟨getting⟩ losing . . . by the sun. or of finding the compass-↑points↓ . . . pole star. ↑& even the botanist . . . of plants.↓ We need ↑study↓ to repair just that ⟨amt we should otherwise have attained by study⟩ ↑loss↓ In ⟨the walls of⟩ cities

23 system ⟨It seems to me that is one of the use⟩

25–29 That is one . . . ordinarily remembers. [lightly cancelled: used elsewhere?]

26–27 render us ⟨solemnly⟩ looking . . . deep lane forcibly

30–31 ↑with the set purpose of Observation↓

32–33 will be ⟨of high moral influences⟩, ↑a useful lesson.↓ By ⟨so doing he⟩ ↑such excursions the student↓

Page 77

1 regarded it. ⟨before.⟩

3 Carry your biscuit in your ⟨hand⟩ ↑pocket↓

Lines
8   shall ⟨reflect their⟩ be to you an image of peace.
           The pines /
           V   The pines glittering
9–10   needles in the ⟨wind⟩ light ⟨speak with⟩ every breath of air
           ↑will make audible↓.
10–11   It is Day. It is Day   That is all which ⟨trees & birds & waters
           & insects declare⟩ ↑Heaven saith↓
11–12   see the ⟨book which opens⟩ ↑manifold . . . occasion↓.
13–15   ↑wait a little. . . . entered the field.↓ ⟨Are you sure of that.⟩
           The snake glided ⟨away⟩ ↑off↓
16–17   the bee ↑flew↓ from the ⟨flower you pluck⟩ ↑neighboring
           shrub↓ the
24–25   crowding. ⟨It reminds us of the image given in⟩ the School-
           books ↑say↓ to illustrate . . . matter   Fill
30–31   the turtle ↑in the pool↓ woodpecker ⟨climbing⟩ ↑in rotten
           tree↓; the moth ↑on the leaf;↓
33   counterpane ⟨the⟩ ↑a ⟨moth's[?]⟩↓ egg ⟨of an insect⟩ ↑spider's↓
34–35   microscope ↑to the aphis↓

Page 78

7   sand & nothing ⟨as there is between the farthest century of
           which we have record & the eternity which encircles it; or⟩
           as there is between the ⟨whole⟩ visible
9   As by ⟨enlarged powers⟩ ↑aid of art↓
11–12   activity ⟨on this side nothing.⟩ ↑between us & the negative
           Pole.↓ ⟨Darting, feeding, building, procreating; hating to be
           nothing as much as we & as far on this side nothing as we
           in a privacy of littleness these elephantules & egglets exist &
           prosper the yelk & ingredient of nature eggs of bigger⟩ /
24–25   Nature means something that
29–30   ↑if we could only find out the cipher↓ so
31–32   of ⟨the world⟩ Nature ↑to find out the cipher↓ assured that
           they mean something assured

Page 79

1   provide this Dictionary[2] or key[1]
5   this secret. Pythagoras
7–9   minerals.
           ⟨Pythagoras said that⟩
           The Persian . . . creatures Ahriman
14–15   cruelty in the ⟨hyena⟩ laughing hyena
16   yet are ↑all↓ valuable . . . of truth as proofs
18–19   relation to itself.
           These
           This instinct . . . the guide the god
20   anything. ⟨Science⟩ Natural History

Lines	
23–24	accuracy ↑is a mere fabulist↓ his
24–25	tedious words. ⟨For want of⟩ The savant
25	sight of the ⟨object⟩ end
28	believe in both in
30–31	autumn ↑in council↓ chattering

Page 80

7	centipede. *c'est*
9–11	Among the insects . . . foreshadowings. [no punctuation]
13	different from man. but
15	The a
	I do not whilst I
	A {⟨⟨Let me not be supposed by the⟩ lay stress ⟨laid upon a ↑this↓ single⟩ ↑on this↓ point, ⟨in these remarks, to⟩ undervalue
16	The ⟨absolute⟩ necessity
17	the scales ⟨to which we are so much indebted⟩,
19	wish ↑to↓ insist upon
23	Fathers of ⟨the⟩ Science.
27	causa causans [no italics]
32	looks ⟨around him⟩ upon the Creation

Page 81

2–3	sees that the same / ⟨VIII⟩ laws that
6–7	he may see ⟨their⟩ ↑its↓ tribes
10–11	they show themselves.
	⟨This has been the ever present aim of all the great men who have devoted themselves to science ↑of Newton, of Linnaeus, of Davy,↓ to ascend from nomenclature to classification from arbitrary to natural classes from natural Classes to primary laws from these in an ever narrowing circle to approach the elemental law, the causa causans ↑the supernatural force.↓⟩
15–17	Naturalist ⟨rather⟩ to study . . . "Why" & "Whence" & "What of that?" to be
21	perspective. who ⟨inte⟩ after he
23–24	↑& keeps his mind . . . office to convey.↓
25	knowledge is accurate.
	⟨It is not a mass of facts so much as tendencies which we seek in nature & it is indispensable that the observing eye be kept in a healthful state.
28–30	Words. ↑Tis said yt↓ The idea ↑always↓ which haunted John Hunter, ⟨it is said⟩ . . . organization protecting
31–32	parts & ↑wonderfully↓ varying its means of action / he never
32–33	So no⟨body can⟩ intelligent
34–(82)1	reveries without being ⟨haunted⟩ ↑conscious↓ by

415

Page 82

Lines

2   or define ⟨Nothing seems of equal importance to the naturalist as keeping his eye for natural Characters⟩

10   one law. the spherules & ⟨vesicles⟩ ↑spicula↓

11–12   organization; ⟨the chemistry of⟩ ↑these oxygenous those hydro-
genous↓ the

14–15   worth knowing, & ⟨explain the tricks of⟩ ↑strip ⟨the Pro⟩↓
th⟨at⟩e th⟨at⟩e little

15–16   ↑of his last coat, and . . . colours the

17   the ↑red & yellow↓ leaves in the ⟨crimson fall⟩ ↑⟨yellow⟩↓
↑autumn woods↓,

18–19   ↑the application . . . chemical test;↓

19–20   laws of ↑crystalline↓ architecture which the ⟨apo⟩ ↑auto↓phyl-
lite ⟨has suggested⟩ in

22–23   change the ↑Hatchetts↓ analysis . . . secretions these

26   whence the ↑few↓ great

26–27   depart ↑to produce by endless combinations↓ ⟨to⟩ their

30–31   the creation, ⟨as⟩ in so simple

32   secrets, as ⟨shall secure th⟩ ⟨shall secure⟩ promises

Page 83

1   parties of

2–6   inestimable. It /
⟨With regard to the common objection, the want of time, it
will affect those only whose curiosity is not very keen. If we
wish to know any thing there is time to ask it. The best books
are always few, For each new one supersedes some other &
the progress of science ever is to reduce all foregoing facts
into one formula. ↑And in the case of Natural history the
students of the present day may command ⟨the⟩ excellent
compends↓

Another objection is
Is a man less a man for not knowing the polarization of light
& the internal architecture of a crystal. Is it not true that the
primary Powers & emotions appear in every situation & find
their appropriate occasions or excitements in every one; that
Washington was no less that he never heard of the optical
powers of a tourmaline or of the electricity ⟨powers⟩ of a
magnet. ⟨the practical answer is⟩ Very probably; but you,
Gentlemen, have heard of the ⟨optical⟩ tourmaline, & of elec-
tromagnetism. They are before you they are your Trenton &
your Jerseys. ⟨They⟩ The field of the Delaware is won but
the discoveries of ↑Newton↓ Herschel Cuvier Arago Brewster
Fresnel have ⟨altered⟩ modified our intellectual place & relations as much as the voyage of the pilgrims to Plymouth or
the sword of the Revolution have ⟨affected our⟩ determined

our social relations. We must see by the lights we have⟩ We
are born in an age . . . discoveries of its own.
   We should not be citizens of our own time not faithful
to our ⟨calling⟩ ↑trust↓ if

6   of their light. ⟨It would be a rejection of all spiritual & all
sensible philosophy⟩ The eternal

8–9   in the flower ⟨breathes⟩ moves

9–12   No truth . . . Animated Nature. [no punctuation]

[The following three sheets appear to belong to an earlier draft:]

{⟨Although undoubtedly specific reasons exist & may be assigned why natural
history ought to be cultivated yet it is still a matter which is more sure
to be felt than it is easy to be defined. I should prefer to press it as
a piece of natural religion, so confident am I that it has all our instincts in
its favor than to argue its cause
   I would say to the most ardent & active in view of the calamities to
which all are exposed. We cannot give ourselves too many advantages.
Study Natural History to provide you a resource when business friends &
your country fail you that you may never lose your courage nor be without
soothing & uplifting occupation.
   In solitude, in old age, & I think even in madness it will yet cheer you
that the mellow voice of the robin is not a stranger to you that the flowers &
the forest trees are reflections to you of ⟨earlier⟩ happier & thoughtful
hours⟩} [cf. *J*, III, 297]
   There are two ⟨evils⟩ faults to one or the other of which the lover of
nature is prone. The savans are apt to be unpoetic. the poets to be unscien-
tific. Yet are the facts & the feeling both indispensable to the ⟨true⟩ wise
Naturalist.
   ⟨But ↑as↓ it was my design in these Remarks not simply to commend the
Study but to speak of its true place & influences it is necessary to take some
distinctions⟩
   ↑2↓ The end which science proposes to itself needs to be strongly
⟨B⟩ marked out. Books, it is said, can never teach the use of books. Neither
does science, when it becomes technical, keep its own place in the mind.
Men are so prone to mistake the means for the end, that even Natural History has its Pedants who mistake Classification for Science. It is of the
utmost importance that he who seeks the Natural Sciences, ⟨in⟩ as a part
of a just education, should understand & keep steadily in view the nature
of Classification. that all Classification is arbitrary or only approximate to
natural divisions; that all Classification is only introductory, — only temporary, — convenient for collection of facts, & awaiting the discovery of
the Theory which is to supersede it. [cf. *J*, III, 293] Let us state this fact a
little more particularly. An individual led by the universal passion for Natural
Objects, commences the study of ⟨conchology⟩ shells or of plants.

⟨It is fit that every man who seeks to educate to understand himself should
inquire into the nature of his fellow-creatures on the planet should de-

sire to place himself at the heart of the Creation to see their tribes & races unfolding themselves in order as the orbs of our system are seen from the sun that is to have a theory of animated Nature to understand its Law, so that the observer may predict all the functions & habits of the individual⟩ to understand that wonderful law of life independent of organization which yet protects & ↑continually↓ recreates every part & wonderfully varies the means of its action

⟨This it is obvious is the ever present aim⟩ ↑⟨He wishes this because he sees that their law is his own. that in his very superiority is in strict harmony with them⟩↓ He wishes to know what ⟨laws⟩ facts the students ↑of Nat Hist.↓ have collected & the masters have arranged that he may have insight into its tendencies He does not want facts but tendencies

⟨This it is obvious has been the ever present aim of all geniuses that have entered that field to ascend from nomenclature to classification; from arbitrary to Natural Classification from Natural Classification to primary laws from these in an ever narrowing circle to approach the elemental law the causa causans, the vis formativa⟩

It is neither desireable to look at things merely for show & quite superficially — the show of color & form, as poets, nor for sensual profit as the farmer & lumber merchant but by means of the intimate knowledge of the properties of things possessed by the last to exalt & embody the vision of the first. The inside of the tree is ⟨no⟩ as curious as its outside & determines the shape & color of its outside. & to a person thoroughly acquainted with timber the ⟨outwa⟩ bark & leaves would ⟨give⟩ be signs not to be mistaken of internal qualities. A thorough knowledge of all the habits & uses of a plant would give new meaning to all the signs & motions of the plant in the different seasons & ⟨under⟩ ↑affected by↓ different accidents Would not that be to understand its language

To know a robin or a titmouse intimately, would make us acquainted with its cries of affection, fear, complaint, hunger, would show us the different coats of different months the manners ⟨of the bird⟩ ⟨⟨⟩ & (as we say) the morals of the bird. Would it not greatly inhance the expression of these natural signs We should understand the meaning of signs in the wood that now convey quite no meaning to us. Well then here poetry & fact meet The Arabian Nights said they understood what the birds said.

A thorough knowledge of the mineral & the plant would continually disclose its relation to man ⟨so that every⟩ & explain some corresponding secret in man so that every plant in its little year would be prophet physician astronomer moralist to us.

Accuracy then that we may really know something. But under the guidance of this pious sentiment of curiosity to understand ourselves & the Whole. Studying with this sentiment every acquisition will be indeed gratifying. Studying with this sentiment every effort will be natural & not cog-wheelwise. we shall receive knowledge as into a vessel opened under water & not drop by drop.

ITALY

[With the exception of an occasional passage of simple description for his untravelled audience, the 133 manuscript pages of Emerson's two lectures on Italy are based on passages from the Journals expanded, cut, or re-arranged, but not essentially different in import. The text is here described, page by page, with an occasional verbatim transcript of a selected passage. Textual notes for the two passages printed in our text are included. All editorial comment and references to the printed Journals and other sources are given in the usual square brackets.]

[Two half sheets of what appear to be working notes precede the first sewed gathering of manuscript sheets. On the last page is an early variant of the concluding paragraph of Lecture II, as quoted on p. 90. Cf. *J*, III, 131–32, Cabot, II, 712, and Cameron, I, 342.]

LECTURE I

[*pp. 1–2*: Opening paragraph as quoted on pp. 89–90 above. Textual notes:]

Page 89

Lines
1–2	audience a ⟨sketch of the present appearance of the chief cities⟩ ↑brief account of the most interesting objects↓
5	⟨An⟩ ↑Into an↓ account
6	It ⟨is to⟩ ↑may↓ be found
8	pertinent ⟨task⟩ ↑study↓
12	faithful ⟨if a superficial⟩ testimony
17–18	Italy as one ⟨country⟩ ↑geographical region↓ but to ⟨describe⟩ ↑give an account of↓
18–(90)1	the country, ⟨the works of art⟩ the people & the works of art in / order

Page 90

2	⟨It may⟩ There is something
5–6	or at the North, ⟨just as a traveller in this country twenty years ago before the days of Cincinnati & New Orleans by taking the direct road from Portsmouth to Washington would pass thro Boston New York Philadelphia Baltimore would & have seen all the noted towns except Charleston⟩

[*p. 3*: Statistical facts on Italy for "the younger members of my audience."]
[*pp. 4, 5, 6, 8, 10, 12, 15, 18*: Blank]
[*pp. 7–11*: Naples, revision of *J*, III, 62, "And what . . . at home."]
[*pp. 13–19*: Naples. Size; activity; Villa Reale; lazzaroni; high spirits]
[*pp. 20–21*:] But there is a dark side to this picture   These circumstances

419

that dispose the people to indolence & pleasure lead them to crime & to miserable poverty   The woes of this city are scarcely less conspicuous than its enchantments [*J*, III, 71 "Goethe says . . . every mouthful,"] & waits til you come out if indeed he does not come in. When you ride, the blind & the deformed run screaming ⟨after⟩ at the side of the coach, Carita ⟨signore⟩ ↑Eccelenza↓ per amore di Dio / ⟨Every⟩ ↑Many a↓ hand ⟨almost⟩ in the street is outstretched for alms; the boys beg piteously pointing ⟨at⟩ with their fingers at their open mouths, "Ho molto fame, mio caro signore." Indeed they speculate on their infirmities ⟨&⟩ farm them out, & go snacks in misery. One old woman (in Syracuse) in my street having begged several times in her own right, beset⟨s⟩ me ⟨now⟩ ↑afterwards↓ with an old blind wretch whom she le⟨ads⟩d up, pointing at her eyeballs which she rolled dreadfully — "Ella e cieca signore, — vedova miserabile."

[*p. 22*: Cancelled sentence]

[*pp. 23–24*: Description of churches. *J*, III, 70, "The Cathedral . . . nave of the Cathedral"; 70–71, "They were well attended . . . then on that."] ↑nor putting a bust of a saint upon the heads of the votaries to keep them from headache for a year, a ceremony I watched in F.↓ [i.e., Florence. Cf. *J*, III, 122–23]

[*pp. 25–26*: The Academy of Sciences. *J*, III, 66, "I have been . . . your youth," expanded]

[*pp. 27–28*: Blank]

[*pp. 29–32*: Walk to Pozzuoli, etc. Revision of *J*, III, 66–69, "This morn . . . *con amore.*" Much personal comment cut. Page 32:] Still every thing is a lesson & these manifold chagrins give us valuable instruction as a volcano or the ruin of a city.

[*pp. 33–36*: Blank]

[*pp. 37–38*: Trip to Baiae. *J*, III, 72–73, "And today . . . Judges of Hell." Bracketed for omission]

[*p. 39*: Blank]

[*p. 40*: One penciled sentence]

[*pp. 41–43*: Ascent of Vesuvius, based on a passage in the manuscript "Pocket Note-book." On p. 43 is a penciled passage, added presumably for a later reading, the last sentence of which is copied from p. 47:] I pass by my visit to Pompeii as ⟨you have⟩ an account of ⟨th⟩ its remains has already made one Lecture of the Course. But there especially the eye reverts to the form of the solemn mountain, author of all this ruin, without one blade of grass upon its black cone & a little smoke stealing out of the summit as if to say   The fire that again & again has ravaged this fair ⟨region⟩ ↑garden↓ is not quenched.

[*p. 44*: Blank]

[*pp. 45–48*: Herculaneum and Pompeii. Based on a passage in the "Pocket Note-book" of which the beginning only is given in *J*, III 74]

[*p. 49*: Trip to Rome. *J*, III, 75, "But we rode . . . Gate of St. John."]

[*p. 50*: First impression of Rome:] ⟨My first vis⟩ It is difficult to describe the experiences of a traveller in Rome for so much of the interest of the place consists in that which cannot be spoken in ⟨what⟩ something that can neither be numbered nor measured nor painted — in the genius of the place, — in the sentiment which is continually suggested by the sound of every name, & by slight but certain marks in so many buildings that you stand in the centre of history. It is good & pleasant & instructive to be here. We grow wiser here by the day & by the hour   Here are the manifest footprints of the nations & the ages   Here is the town of Centuries the Capital of the ancient & ↑of the↓ modern world. All is large magnificent secular and the treasury of the arts is evidently the Contribution of the whole Civilized world.

[*pp. 51–53*: St. Peter's, incorporating *J*, III, 87, "When night . . . and walking," and *J*, III, 89–90, "I love . . . of the beautiful." Page 53:] There is no fact that interests me more in relation to the church than Michel Angelo's connexion with it as the architect.

[*p. 54*: Blank]

[*pp. 55–56*: Views from St. Peter's; incorporating *J*, III, 91–92, "I went up to the top . . . marble wilderness below."]

[*pp. 57–61*: Vatican Museum; incorporating *J*, III, 77–79, "I went to . . . did not expect," and *J*, III, 93, "Few pictures . . . look at him," the latter cancelled in pencil. Page 61:] One more reflexion is forced upon you in the view of a picture which is so intelligible in its excellence as the Transfiguration whilst you hear the manifold criticisms which the throng of ⟨young artists⟩ ↑⟨[?]⟩↓ ↑connoisseurs↓ affect to make up on it, that if they cannot admire, it was not meant for them but it was meant for you; that the painter painted for you; — for those who had eyes capable of being pleased with simplicity & ⟨soul⟩ ↑lofty emotions↓. And every person of quiet tastes is glad to feel a sort of union across three hundred years between the mind of Raphael & his own. [cf. W, II, 362]

[*p. 62*: The Arch of Titus, for insertion in what follows]

[*pp. 63–64*: Forum, Coliseum, Pantheon]

[*pp. 65–67*: Vatican Museum continued, including *J*, III, 78, "In one apartment . . . it is magnificent," and *J*, III, 91, "How have . . . living man," revised]

[*p. 68*: Blank]

[*pp. 69–72, 75*: Religious ceremonies, including adaptations of *J*, III, 81–83, "I have been . . . pictures and music," *J*, III, 85–86, "The famous *Miserere* . . . forms and faces," and *J*, III, 88–89, "This morning . . . went his way."]

[*pp. 73–74*: One leaf; recto, jottings on Roman remains that once followed immediately after p. 64; verso, cancelled passage in pencil on washing of pilgrims' feet (cf. *J*, III, 86)]

[*p. 76*: Art and artists. Cf. *J*, III, 92, "Rome fashions . . . louis d'or."]

[*p. 77*: Conclusion, with adaptation of *J*, III, 102–103, "In Rome . . . other's is your own."]

●

LECTURE II

[*pp. 1–3*: Journey from Rome to Florence. *J*, III, 106–108, "The journey occupied . . . lake of Thrasimene," and *J*, III, 104, "Passed a peaceful

. . . fair Florence." Two short quotes on Velino and Thrasimene (imperfect, probably from memory) from Byron's *Childe Harold*, Canto IV, Stanzas LXXI and LXIII]

[*p. 4*: Blank]

[*p. 5*: Florence; paraphrase of *J*, III, 104–105, "And how do you like . . . its wondrous Campanile."]

[*p. 6*: The Cathedral. Two anecdotes of Michel Angelo's opinion of the Cathedral (see pp. 114 and 117)]

[*p. 7*: The Campanile and anecdote of Dante, based on *J*, III, 115]

[*p. 8*: The Baptistry. Interior of the Cathedral]

[*pp. 9–10*: The Uffizi Gallery, the Venus, etc.; incorporating *J*, III, 105, "I saw . . . Laocoon are," and *J*, III, 108, "I reserve . . . genius of the artist."]

[*p. 11*: Pitti Palace; including sentence from *J*, III, 105, "I think . . . come hither."]

[*p. 12*: Blank]

[*p. 13*: Santa Croce. *J*, III, 105–106, "I have been . . . over his dust." Cf. *J*, III, 118]

[*p. 14*: Blank]

[*pp. 15–16*: Piazza of Santa Croce. *J*, III, 118–19, "When I walk . . . *senza più*," and *J*, III, 123, "Is not . . . candle-light."]

[*pp. 17–18*: Comment on Florence. *J*, III, 120–21, "Six or seven . . . Carrara."]

[*pp. 19–24*: Florence and environs: the vineyards, the villas, the historical associations, the palaces, the houses, the statues. Page 22: The Michelozzi villa. *J*, III, 121–22, "I passed . . . foreign artists." Page 23: Santa Maria Novella; Michel Angelo. *J*, III, 124–25, "I have been . . . sculptor's puzzle." Page 24: Reference to Lord Byron. *J*, III, 108. Added as a footnote:] I ought to say that Italy is Lord Byron's debtor [cf. *J*, III, 99] especially the cities of Venice Florence & Rome   The fourth Canto of Childe Harold was my best guide book in those places & a comparison of his descriptions with the objects only demonstrates the justness of his thoughts & their superiority [adaptation of passage on Professor Amici, *J*, III, 111–12, and reference to Landor.]

[*p. 25*: Gaiety of the Florentines. *J*, III, 111]

[*pp. 26–28*: The Order of Misericordia. *J*, III, 114–15]

[*p. 29*: Blank]

[*p. 30*: Notes on Bologna and Ferrara]

[*pp. 31–33*: General description of Venice]

[*p. 34*: Blank]

[*pp. 35–36*: General description of the Piazza of St. Mark's, with some debt to *J*, III, 130 and 136]

[*p. 37*:] {No one can fail to be excited to much emotion by the ⟨wh⟩ sight of this superb square in the centre of an ⟨ancient city⟩ old city of such importance in the history of Commerce & whose very soil is won by art & industry from the waves and all its greatness earned — every trophy & town — by victor⟨y⟩ies of energy & wisdom. Every thing around you reminds you of its ⟨his⟩ contests with Germany with Pisa & Genoa. ⟨Its long contest with Genoa.⟩ In the symbols of grandeur going to decay you remember ⟨its former⟩ the day of its former peril, when Doria of Genoa ⟨returned the famous answer⟩ & Carrara of Padua ↑in 1379↓ thundered at its suburbs. You cannot see the horses over the portico without recalling the proud answer of the Genoese.

[*p.* 38: Blank]
[*p.* 39: Answer of the Genoese quoted]
[*p.* 40: Blank]
[*pp.* 41–42: The Ducal Palace; the Bridge of Sighs; the Campanile. Based on *J*, III, 134–35, "Thence we . . . Faliero," and "After seeing . . . its shape & extent."]
[*pp.* 43–44: The Arsenal; cf. *J*, III, 135. General opinion of Venice; debt to *J*, III, 136–37]
[*pp.* 44–45: History of Venice] Perhaps it may not be unwelcome to the younger part of my audience . . .
[*p.* 46: Blank]
[*p.* 47: Journey to Milan via Padua, Verona, Vicenza, etc.; based in part on *J*, III, 141]
[*pp.* 48–50: Blank]
[*pp.* 51–53: Milan Cathedral, including *J*, III, 142–43, "This morn . . . separate picture," *J*, III, 143, "Underneath . . . I *Promessi Sposi*," and *J*, III, 144, "Then we visited the Triumphal Arch . . . to Milan."]
[*pp.* 54–55: General comments on Milan; based on *J*, III, 145–46, "Milan is a well-built town . . . and fresco painting."]
[*p.* 56: Blank]
[*p.* 57: Fertility of Italy. *J*, III, 125]
[*p.* 58: Cancelled note]
[*pp.* 59–60: Italian towns and peasants; based on *J*, III, 140, "All the Italian towns . . . red umbrellas."]
[*p.* 61: Blank]
[*p.* 62: Insert for final paragraph]
[*pp.* 63–65: Concluding paragraph, quoted on p. 90 above. Based on *J*, III, 131–32. Textual notes:]

Page 90

Lines	
8–9	⟨Nobody can be more alive to⟩ ↑I am very sensible↓ of
9	picture. ⟨than myself.⟩
10	more than ⟨a younger or a less observant eye⟩ ↑some↓
11–18	↑I was simply . . . ages to teach.↓
13	tasted. neither
13–14	but we ⟨go⟩ come out
18	But ⟨nob⟩ ↑no↓ one
20	beauty ⟨at⟩ ⟨in⟩ of
21–22	The ⟨memory⟩ mind that takes
28	& a ⟨different⟩ foreign language only ⟨repeats to you⟩ ↑reminds you of↓
30–32	↑names & places . . . same lesson↓ a truly

III. BIOGRAPHY

1. [INTRODUCTION]

[The following notes, presumably used in the preparation of this lecture, are found among the working notes for this lecture series:]

Tests

Bonaparte undoubtedly was a great kill-cow, the very bully of the common & knocked down ↑most↓ indubitably his antagonists; he was as heavy as any six of them. But if you would consider the worth not the size of the parties you will have a different result & Napoleon will skulk out of sight, kick the beam. In order to this take the tests of Character

1 Test.   My first question concerning a man is, Has he any aim which with all his soul he pursues? My second question is, Is that aim good or bad?
    {Well Napoleon had an Aim & a Bad one

2 Test.   Is a man in earnest believing in his ends or does he work for show
    Luther, Washington, Lafayette, ↑Laplace,↓ believed in their ends Napoleon was no more a believer than a grocer who disposes his shop-window invitingly, quite French. ↑Je devrois mourir à Waterloo was his ⟨Roscian⟩ greenroom remark.↓

3 Test.   The health of the mind is to work in Sport   In good humor I shd prefer. Napoleon worked gloomily alone. Luther Lafayette Alfred Shakspear in broad daylight with smiles & red cheeks. Julius Caesar was a great man; goodhumored ambition. N. Bonaparte pitiful jealous /

4 Test.   A great man must not only be able to control the storms of his mind ⟨but⟩ ↑and↓ must be able to turn to good account the worst accidents of his fortune but he must have that intellect which sets in motion the intellect of others. / [E] Is Lafayette in Olmutz or Napoleon in Helena great? As to Intellectual action on others in any generous sense, it is out of the question, cannot be predicated of this iron Hand. Mirabeau
    Bonaparte's greatness seems to be a quite numerical thing. It is a pun on the word *great* to apply it to him. He is great by armies, by kings, by physical power but by one generous sentiment never. But I will not sacrifice the truth one iota of his merit to an antithesis or even B. mt rise & condemn me but think of him in connexion with ↑Mme↓ De Stael   Of Napoleon the strength consisted of his renunciation of all Conscience. The devil helps him. /

5 Test.   I cannot conceive of a great man who does not believe in Superhuman influence   Without it all is low flat & beastly
Alaric (or Attila) esteeming himself Scourge of God opens thus into himself Supernal influence   So does Mahomet Cromwell Burley   So does Washington Alexander the Great Cicero Luther Milton Newton Angelo   But I am not sure that Bonaparte does
Nothing seems less than an insulated man   an ant an acorn is each united to the World by a stream of relation which flows thro them.

424

6 It must be a distinctive mark whet [sic] that the aim has no reference to Self   So had not Washington's Luther's Archimedes' Shakspears' & genius in general wh. works *with love*   Luther took his life in his hand   Socrates Epictetus Geo Fox Lafayette Burns Henri IV Washington's ass [cf. *J*, III, 333] Jesus /

7 I ask if it be not another characteristic of truly great minds that they appreciate objects justly and are therefore absolved from the prejudices of their age & treat trifles as trifles. {Baron Swedenborg treats the Romish Church with the exaggeration of his age, not as a philosopher.} Julius Caesar did. The hobgoblins of the Bank Antimasonry the Catholics seem to show a peculiar aptitude in our people to be duped

↑the various hobgoblins social polit relig with which our community is amused & abused seem to betray a deficiency in our organ of measure.↓

[written vertically at the bottom of the page:]
Is he in earnest
Is he not selfish
Is he goodhumored
Is he an intellect-mover
Is he a believer in the Super human?
Is he able to appreciate things justly

2. MICHEL ANGELO BUONAROTI

Page 99

Lines	
2	that furnish ⟨a⟩ in
3	But ⟨every⟩ ↑all↓ thing↑s↓ ⟨that is⟩ recorded
6	so little excentricity
8–9	arbitrary ⟨fruits⟩ ↑productions↓
9–10	as ⟨one⟩ ⟨of that⟩ ↑which belong⟨ing⟩s to the↓ highest
10–11	genius ↑inasmuch as it↓ contain⟨ing⟩s
13–14	appreciated ↑being addressed for the most part to the eye↓
15	purity, ⟨a⟩ severe and even terrible ⟨⟨like that of Milton's Comus⟩⟩ goes out
19–20	was ⟨busily⟩ engaged in executing

Page 100

2–3	↑He is an eminent . . . & Poetry↓ In
5–6	Vocation This Idea possessed his soul ⟨& moulded his purposes⟩
9	↑this to receive and↓ this to express, ⟨of⟩ ↑⟨in⟩↓ ⟨this to⟩ ⟨be⟩ ↑⟨live⟩↓, was
12–14	⟨Yet⟩ ↑So shall not↓ the indescribable ↑⟨so shall⟩ ⟨charm of the natural world⟩↓ ↑⟨the great⟩↓ ⟨spectacle of⟩ ⟨sunset & sunrise⟩ ↑⟨morn & evening⟩↓ ⟨that shut & open every day⟩ ↑charm of the natural world, the great . . . shut & open↓ the most

Lines

15–16	a name ⟨& an idea⟩ which in our
17–18	the ⟨desire of⟩ ↑servitude to↓ wealth
18–19	of mean ⟨objects⟩ ↑pleasures↓ he perceives that ⟨the beautiful⟩
20–21	This truth, ⟨was⟩ that
25	this element. /

⟨When Beauty ⟨becomes⟩ ↑is esteemed↓ a science, & is to be ↑methodically↓ studied it begins in Accuracy.⟩

　　When I say that I am to sketch
[written in pencil under the above:] ⟨I shall seek in this Lecture to show the direction & the limitations of his search after this element & how he sought by just degrees to rise to that love which moves the sun & all the stars⟩

26	Beauty ⟨I hope⟩ let not
29	subject ↑for an idle hour↓ but promised
30	It does ⟨interest⟩ ↑concern↓ them,
30–31	interest in ⟨men⟩indefatigable
34	singular vocation.* [E]

When Beauty is esteemed a science & is to be methodically studied it begins in Accuracy

34n	{M. A. Buonaroti
34n	↑early discovering a taste for the fine arts↓
34n	Lorenzo ⟨Cosimo⟩ di Medici Duke of Tuscany /
35–⟨102⟩6	↑In considering . . . but what is true.↓ / [on sheet inserted after the lecture was sewed]

Page 101

4	I answer; Beauty
4	↑Like Truth↓ It is
8	Beautiful⟨;⟩?" —
9	There is no standard ⟨of the beautiful⟩
12	the great ⟨All⟩ ↑system↓ of Nature? ⟨which no understanding can embrace.⟩ /
18	beauty by ⟨their expression for⟩ describing
19	*nell' uno* i.e. the

Page 102

2–6	And because . . . Rhetoric ⟨Rien . . . vrai⟩　　Nothing . . . what is true. / ↑Nothing is beautiful but what is true.↓ 'Rien de beau que le vrai' is a celebrated maxim of Rhetoric.
6–7	application ↑than to Rhetoric↓;
7	In ⟨the⟩ Art,
9	⟨I have said⟩ he labored to express
12	rests　　The ⟨master⟩ ↑wise eye↓ knows
13–14	knows them, ⟨give⟩ ↑compose↓ the image
14–15	that only by an ⟨Uno⟩ understanding
17	⟨To the physician⟩ ⟨t⟩The symptoms disclose

Lines
17–18   ↑to the physician;↓
21   ⟨In common with all minds of the first class⟩ ↑Believing this↓ Michel Angelo
24–27   ↑Few men have ever lived . . . beauty. none . . . step by step ⟨in⟩to the ⟨appointed[?]⟩ height . . . study of nature↓
28–29   ↑habit of study & docility↓. Granacci a painter's apprentice having
30   ↑t↓he ↑boy↓ went
31–35   fish ↑Cardinal Farnese . . . ruins to which . . . continue to learn."↓
35   one of the last ⟨sketches⟩ ↑drawings↓ in his portfolio ⟨when grown old⟩ ↑⟨in his last year⟩↓ is a

Page 103

1   for ⟨there remains yet⟩ ↑it is↓ a sketch
1–2   an ⟨old⟩ ↑old↓ man with a long beard ⟨bent with age⟩
2   ↑and an hourglass before him↓
3   inparo" I
6–7   & counteraction ⟨known⟩ learned, —
11   ↑in th⟨e⟩is spirit ⟨of this faith⟩↓
13   knowledge in ⟨this matter⟩ ↑anatomy↓,
13–14   parallel ⟨in⟩ ↑among the artists of↓
14–15   designs ⟨says one of⟩ his contemporaries ↑inform us [over same in pencil] were↓ ⟨are⟩
16–17   expressive, ⟨as⟩ ↑but↓
17–18   design ⟨not⟩ with ⟨pen but⟩ pencil ↑instead of pen↓
21   studies of the ↑statue of↓ Christ
25   to study ⟨in⟩ for the Artist ↑in↓
28–29   ↑Man is the highest . . . plastic Art↓   There
31   human ⟨form⟩ ↑figure↓
33   Anthropomorphism. or ⟨giving⟩ ↑attributing to↓
34   this familiar ⟨sight⟩ ↑object↓ every day

Page 104

5   Yet ⟨this seems to be a lesson which⟩ ↑our knowledge of its highest expression↓
6   acquired ↑by himself↓
10–20   ↑There are now in Italy . . . Rondanini palace at Rome↓ Seeing these works true . . . superhuman "we . . . know" seeing . . . figures 'improper . . . proper ⟨to⟩ for . . . his profound knowledge.' /
   ⟨So dearly did he delight in the contemplation & delineation of beauty that he abhorred to take a portrait unless it were one of surpassing loveliness & actually never took any but that of the Cavalier Tomasso⟩

Lines
21   ⟨Beauty⟩ The love
30   Florence. and

Page 105

1–2   or in the ⟨extensive aims⟩ ↑outline & general designs↓
12–13   On the 24 October 1529 the Prince of Orange general of Charles V encamped
31   followed with importunities [2] & apologies [1]
32–33   21 March 1530, — the Prince

Page 106

2   capitulated, 9 August
7–10   ↑He built in Rome ye stairs . . . porticoes & stair⟨s⟩case↓
11   In [blank] he was appointed
19   resist the ↑force [pencil]↓ current
20–21   trembles under us let us
26–27   prepared for him ↑that he might↓ to paint the ceiling he
27–28   suspended ⟨fr⟩by ropes
31–32   M. Angelo ⟨had⟩ the
33   floor which

Page 107

1   gave this ↑model↓ to a carpenter who ⟨wu⟩made
3   ⟨In his painting⟩ he was so minutely
4   the steps but also the cacagnuoli [calcagnuoli]
8   His incredible industry
            And not only was this discoverer of Beauty & its ⟨priest⟩ Teacher
18   In ⟨fact⟩ ↑deed↓ he toiled
21–22   nourishment & he told ⟨Vasari⟩ that
29–30   make to ⟨one of his⟩ ↑a single↓ figure⟨s⟩ 9, 10 or 12 heads, ↑before he cd. satisfy himself↓
31   certain ⟨concord of⟩ ↑universal↓ grace ⟨in all⟩ such
33   eye judges: ⟨that this was true also in Architecture.⟩
35–(108)1   taken away i.e. wro't

Page 108

1–2   seemed natural objects.
            ⟨At 75 year⟩
            At near 80 years
9–10   ⟨In⟩ *Sculpture*, ⟨which⟩ he called *his Art*, & to ⟨which⟩ ↑it↓
11   himself. & ⟨his⟩the style
13–14   ↑In this art↓ his greatest . . . in Rome   It
18–19   In the Church ⟨at⟩ called . . . Christ   In

Lines
21   Florence ⟨is⟩ are
25   *Paintings* ↑are in↓ The Sistine
33   exclusively ⟨in the⟩ ↑as a↓ stern Designer
35–(*109*)1   Last Judgment
                    Of the
                    Of ↑his designs↓ the most . . . themselves. an

Page 109

4   Architecture
5   St. Peters an ornament
9–14   something ⟨sublime⟩ ↑affecting↓ . . . execution towering . . . designs.
15–16   in wax   When
24–25   pull it down."
                       ↑The historians↓
                    The best ⟨result⟩ ↑commendation↓ of
26   ↑The impulse of his grand style was instan↓
27–29   Every ⟨im⟩stroke of ⟨the⟩ his . . . hand   Raphael . . . Angelo   Sir
32–(*110*)23   ↑It will be readily conceded . . . beauty from the eternal.↓
                    [on sheet inserted after lecture was sewed]
35   are in ⟨sculpture⟩ all three arts

Page 110

1   his thought. ⟨His practick skill panted after his Idea⟩
4   in his hands"   Yet
5–6   he was ⟨ever⟩ ↑still↓ dissatisfied with his own work   The
6   to him in ⟨idea⟩ ↑imagination↓ were
8   abandoned his work. / ⟨nay spoiled many.⟩
9   blocked his ⟨marbles⟩ statue.
10–13   made by him . . . unless perfect. [lightly run through in pencil]
12   trying his genius that
13   ↑Grace in↓ Living ↑forms↓ ⟨beauty⟩ except
17   devotion to ⟨images of beauty⟩ ↑Art↓ but
17–18   suppose that ⟨this profound soul was taken or holden⟩ these images ↑which his spirit worshipped↓
21–23   As from . . . eternal. / [lightly jotted in pencil]
                    ⟨It will readily be conceded that a man of such habits & such deeds was thoroughly versed in the perception & ⟨imitation⟩ delineation of external beauty.⟩ But let no man suppose that his profound soul was taken or holden in the chains of superficial beauty. To him of all men
25–26   He ⟨called⟩ ↑spoke of↓ external grace ↑as↓
26   which God ⟨imprisons⟩ ↑dresses↓ the soul

28–29   the eye   He sought through the eye to ⟨address⟩ ↑reach↓ the soul.

31   progress & / & to seek

31–32   highest form that of Goodness.

Page 111

8   corrupt & low ⟨men[?]⟩ eyes

9   prophets ↑& angels↓ could

11   ⟨The⟩ As he refused to undo

14–15   with gold, ⟨but⟩ Michael

18–19   San Gallo the . . . St. Peters died.

21   before was in ⟨a⟩ only

23   in his ↑own↓ ability

24   ↑at first refused & then↓

27   reward ⟨as⟩ ↑because↓

29   free to ⟨change⟩ depart

32   reward ⟨dem⟩ named

34   rendered it, He

34–35   that ↑he &↓ his ⟨family⟩ should ⟨be⟩ neither

Page 112

2   American armies.

4–5   Pope delighted . . . sent it back. [no punctuation]

6   ↑was angry but the artist was immovable.↓

10   fulfill in ⟨an⟩ everlasting

13   ⟨He⟩ In answer to

19–20   wishes. 'if,' he . . . cormorants who ⟨were⟩ ↑are↓

32   with Dante in common

Page 113

4   ⟨Vasari asserts that he⟩ ↑He lived alone &↓

5   ⟨But⟩ ↑As ⟨was⟩ might be supposed↓

14   Vasari relates one ⟨incident⟩ occasion

19   goats   He

21   after ⟨dark⟩ ↑nightfall↓,

31   to their race ⟨from their time to all time⟩.

32   greatness and ⟨shut⟩ avert

Page 114

2–3   ↑This sometimes . . . from jealousy↓ Aristotle

6–7   ↑But Michel Angelo's . . . stamp of fame↓ [?] Michel

10   Bramante. that

11   luminous ↑with↓ fit

14   Brunelleschi   And

Lines
15   Florence ⟨he turned his⟩ to go
17–18   will not build better
20–22   It is ⟨as much⟩ ↑more↓ commendation to say ↑This is↓ Michel
           Angelo's ⟨studio⟩ ↑favorite↓ than to say this ⟨picture or statue⟩
           was carried
29   2000 crowns. an act
30   from ⟨kings⟩ ↑popes↓ & Emperors. ⟨D⟩For this servant
31   he ↑himself↓ waited

Page 115

3–4   time ↑Vittoria Colonna↓ the . . . Pescara who
11   soul that a beautiful
12–13   divine beauty, ⟨&⟩ not . . . divine love   He
15   Whether his ↑views↓ thoughts
17   An ↑eloquent↓ vindication
18   found in ⟨an eloquent article⟩ ↑a paper↓ by Signor
19   Italian Scholar
22–24   {The testimony of Condivi his friend is this. . . . depravity /
           as poems
31   Berni says of him in
32   "He ⟨speaks⟩ ↑utters↓ things ye
34   dying for

Page 116

1   contentment ⟨beyond the grave.⟩
4   this subject   At
10–11   friends that person remarked ⟨It was fit⟩ that Michael ⟨should⟩
           ↑might well↓ grieve ⟨forasmuch as he⟩ ↑that one↓
13   it is nothing for
22   his independence his his generosity,
25   goodness that his was a soul so ⟨thoroughly⟩ enamoured
27–29   the ⟨simplest means⟩ ↑organ↓ by which he sought ↑not↓ to utter
           ↑but to suggest↓ the unutterable. ⟨or rather to suggest that
           which cannot be attained⟩ that

Page 117

1–9   ↑There his picture hangs in every window there ⟨his⟩ the
           tradition . . . Here is his own house.↓
4–7   speak   Do . . . Novella   It . . . 500 years ago   Michel
8   Here is ⟨his ho the⟩ church, the palace,
10   are his ⟨bones⟩ mortal remains
11–12   spot that the ⟨glorious⟩ dome
13–14   stood open. ↑And there↓ And so is he laid. ⟨It is not yet⟩
           ↑Almost two↓
16–17   philosopher   I stopped ⟨long⟩ before

Lines

19–20   Buonaroti & ⟨saw its three significant garlands which should be four⟩ saw & his ↑venerable↓ bust,

20–22   reverence ⟨the more perhaps that Italy is so full of his⟩ fame. ⟨The forehead of the bust (esteemed a faithful likeness) is furrowed with eight deep wrinkles one above the other.⟩ Three significant . . . tomb   They

23–24   bust esteemed a faithful likeness is . . . another   As

25–26   I felt that ⟨this ma⟩ I was . . . church for

27–28   He was not . . . country. he . . . human race he was

29   beams in ⟨all⟩ ↑universal↓ nature

[The following entries, not in either lecture or journal, appear among the working notes for this lecture:]

Helps he not me? ⟨wh⟩ The moral of M. Angelo. While he is moulding the cornices & carving the rosettes of his ⟨sculp⟩ entablature to express impatiently the beauty that intoxicates him can I not polish my expressions sweeten my temper impart a moments delight to those next me & thus express the divinity that haunts me.

The question of draped or naked figures in the Last Judgment is in painting the reappearance of the everlasting dualism which makes in Temperance ye question of *Pledges*; the Absolute opposed to the Relative. . . .

Vasari records with care the popes & princes (Soliman) who caressed M. Angelo & yt Cosimo of Florence held ⟨in⟩ his ⟨hat⟩ cap in his hand while he talked with him. As soon as the popular element comes in as in a religious war the prince holds back & does not see Luther. Aforetime the prince representing mankind honors the genius.

3. MARTIN LUTHER

Page 119

1   ⟨It is a⟩ It sounds like a paradox

1–2   that those ⟨powers of men⟩ ↑talents and means↓ which produce ⟨vast effects⟩ ↑operate great results↓ on society

5–6   Whilst ↑kings strive and armies are marshalled in vain; whilst↓ great

15n   {⟨Of these . . . acknowledged writings.⟩} [marginal note:] Insert as footnote.

15n   Of these ↑materials↓ the book

15n   is of great ⟨,perhaps of chief⟩ value

15n   more valuable ↑to an insight into the man↓ than his ⟨acknow⟩ voluminous

16   character has not ⟨that⟩ ↑as far as↓ I know

Lines

19   {⟨In conformity with the plan of these Lectures⟩} it is not my design

20–21   and from the ⟨r⟩ Records of his conversations

23–24   is the ↑publication ⟨hi⟩ of his↓ Thesis

24–25   This act is ⟨his guiding Star⟩ ↑the crisis of his life↓, the cause

Page 120

1–2   attention to the ↑ecclesiastical↓ abuses

3   ⟨It fell out that when Tetzel a worthless monk came to Wittemburg where Luther was professor of [blank] in the College⟩ It happens that we can trace

7   seized with a ⟨dangerous⟩ sickness

8   monk of his order ⟨brought consolation to his mind by⟩ ↑succeeded in↓

10–11   not a theological ⟨phrase⟩ ↑formula↓ but an expression (⟨as we shall presently see⟩) for ↑all↓ his belief

11–12   Government, ⟨was⟩ proved

12   ⟨Devoting himself to the works of St Bernard and St Augustine he arrived⟩ About the time when Tetzel

14   Indulgences ⟨arriv⟩ came

15   in the college, ⟨his mind⟩ ↑Luther↓ still

16   doctrine ⟨was⟩ had arrived at this ↑solid↓ conclusion; "A man

20   differently. ⟨The Chu⟩ It had taught

21   confession, ⟨and⟩ penance,

22–23   and that the ⟨mon[?]⟩ religious profession

32–33   understood, a ↑naked↓ reliance ⟨up⟩on ⟨bare⟩ personal

33–(*121*)1   sanctimonious works ↑which↓ he called

Page 121

3   henceforward his ⟨fav⟩ ⟨perennial⟩ ↑main↓ theme. Works

5   Galatians did ↑in terms↓ magnify

6   works; ⟨and therefore he seized on⟩ this epistle ↑he made his study,↓

7–9   ⟨a⟩ his favorite work. ↑For a similar reason he preferred the Epistle of John. ⟨"St John he said wrote little but every⟩ ↑"The letter of St John is short but every↓ word weigheth two tons."↓

13   "Well now

13–14   comes an ⟨coarse⟩ ↑unprincipled↓ hawker

14–15   in the ⟨style of an auctioneer⟩ ↑coarse language of the shops↓

16–17   Law, and ⟨so⟩ much more

18   crimes ⟨they⟩ ↑men↓ have

19   so much ⟨per⟩ ↑a↓ crime; or, ⟨that⟩ if

22   out of torment."

27   that these ↑mortal↓ men had enough ⟨enough⟩ and to spare.

33–(*122*)3   among the people ↑Samson . . . Purgatory.↓ And on the 31 October 15 17.

Page 122

Lines

4	door of the ↑College↓ Church
10–11	all persons ↑holding a different opinion↓ to a public
16	knew ⟨of⟩ the exactions
19	⟨Long⟩ ↑Many years↓ afterward
27	conviction ⟨Even x x x x⟩ I on the contrary
30	circulated. ⟨and read.⟩
34	Tetzell caused

Page 123

2	took part ⟨of⟩ ↑with↓
3–4	At first ↑no notice . . . consequence.↓ as Luther says
5	not idle. ⟨a moment⟩.
5–6	letters to ⟨the⟩ ↑various↓ prelates
6–7	Emperor. ⟨The Elector of Saxony Frederic surnamed the Wise favored him⟩ The clergy the prelates
9	confidence, ⟨in his cause,⟩
12	confounded, ⟨Every day⟩ ↑and↓ the cause
13–14	Leipsic ⟨decided⟩ hated him and ⟨closed⟩ broke up
14–15	Eck ↑on the papal authority↓ with the ⟨famous⟩ ↑intelligent↓
16	A legate ⟨Cardinal Caietan⟩
18	But ⟨R⟩↑r↓evolutions ⟨⟨it is said⟩⟩ never
18–19	this monk⟨s⟩ and ↑his↓ ethical proposition was the ⟨R⟩↑r↓evolution
23	belly." ⟨He had appealed to the Pope The pope⟩
24–25	protection from ↑noblemen in↓ Suabia
25	But ↑this help lay in himself;↓
26	the ⟨artillery⟩ ↑arsenal↓ of his ⟨might⟩ ↑power↓
28–29	as the ⟨manifestation⟩ ↑accents↓ of a superior being. ↑His words ⟨were⟩ ↑Richter↓ called, 'half battles,' and they well deserve the name. ⟨Never⟩ "Pomeranus,"
31–32	matter and the ⟨force⟩ nature

Page 124

2	and leaves ⟨the most⟩ astonishing
6	human breast. ⟨It was a Will on which a nation might lean⟩
7	⟨I cannot pretend to trace with any detail the incidents of his life. The Pope condemned his⟩ He has appealed to the Pope
9	⟨The⟩ A second bull
11	the heretic ⟨it⟩ ↑him↓self ⟨The⟩ His books
15	⟨It needs to give a more particular account of the Diet of Worms i⟩ In 1521, ⟨when⟩ Luther was summoned ↑to Worms↓
16–18	his opinions. ⟨His friends admonished him of the danger he incurred in vain.⟩ ↑The Elector ↑had↓ caused . . . acquainted with ↑the↓ danger, . . . cited.↓

Lines
19–20 should go; ↑if violence shd. be done to him, it↓ ⟨It⟩ was
22–23 his death. ↑But he hoped otherwise, for the Emperor's sake.↓
30 burned by the ↑same↓ Diet
31 of the ↑Emperor's↓ Safe Conduct. ⟨of th⟩
32 But the same ⟨fire⟩ ↑resolution↓

Page 125

1 Reformer ⟨He was determined to strike Satan with terror⟩.
1–2 safe-conduct, ↑requiring his appearance in 21 days, and↓ ⟨but⟩
3 preached ↑to vast assemblies on the way,↓
5 Oppenheim again ⟨his friends yet a lect[?]⟩
6 Spalatin ⟨the⟩
7 stop. ↑It was↓ ⟨T⟩then ↑that↓ he made ⟨his⟩ the
8–9 there, as ↑there be↓ tiles
9 On 16 April ⟨On 16 April⟩ 1521,
14–15 men . . . beholding him. [written over the same in pencil]
15–16 At ⟨4⟩ ↑four↓ o'clock
17 ⟨Luther⟩ The Official ⟨demanded⟩ asked
19 ⟨& wh⟩ and 2. whether
20 persist in ⟨aft⟩ their
20–21 In answer ⟨In answer⟩
22–23 he could not ⟨deny⟩ retract
23–24 retracting ⟨every⟩ ↑the most undoubted↓ articles
30 not ⟨answered⟩ ↑spoken↓
30–31 demanded a ⟨categorical⟩ ↑an explicit↓

Page 126

4 violate ⟨the⟩ ↑his↓ safe conduct, tho⟨'⟩ugh
6 waylaid and ⟨taken⟩ ↑carried↓
7–8 who . . . Catholics. [written over the same in pencil]
13 Zwick⟨au⟩↑au↓
17–32 ↑On hearing of . . . defence of my cause. . . . ⟨I, at least, believe them."⟩↓ [on inserted sheet, on the back of which, upside down, in pencil, is:] . . . Germans. It is not . . . [torn] . . . the incidents of his life but rather by extracts from his writings & from the Records of his conversation to ⟨give⟩ ↑exhibit↓ some idea ↑form a clear conception↓ of the ↑peculiar↓ Genius of the man
The materials exist of obtain [?] are his own voluminous writings & the Colloquia Mensalia not published in Germany until 1626 & ⟨approved⟩ Eng Translation approved by a committee of Eng Parliament in Nov 1646
17 On hearing ↑of↓ the disorders
19 Churches ⟨he⟩ ↑Luther to stop these outrages↓
20 hiding place ⟨though conse[?]⟩ disobeying the Elector ⟨his patron and⟩ friend.

Lines
21   with the Pope: He
32   defence of my cause. ⟨If you put belief in these things you
              will be saved; if not, I, at least, believe them."⟩

Page 127

9–10   in 1524 . . . in 1525, he [written over the following in pen-
              cil:] 11,000 persons were collected at Zwickau to hear
10   Catharine ⟨de Bore⟩ ↑of Born↓
11   The influence he attained ⟨The influence he attained⟩
14–15   and in 1530 . . . Augsburg. [written over the following in
              pencil:] On hearing the disorders at Wittemburg he forsook
              his hiding place risking the displeasure of the Elector   He had
              broke with the Pope he had broke with the Emperor   Now
              he took upon himself the responsibility of offending ⟨the⟩ his
              Prince
16   ⟨Let us now contemplate⟩ Luther's
16   history ⟨,⟩ ↑is↓
18   He ⟨led⟩ ↑achieved↓
26   Luther never ⟨on any occasion⟩ appealed
27–28   those who did. /
                  ⟨Let us now contemplate Luther's singular position in
              history a scholar or spiritual man leading a great revolution
              and ⟨without interval⟩ ↑from first to last↓ faithful to his posi-
              tion. He led a spiritual revolution by spiritual arms alone.⟩
              "I have never,"

Page 128

9   The ⟨subject⟩ ⟨matter⟩ ↑work↓
15   The ⟨magazine⟩ ⟨arsenal⟩ from which . . . ammunition the
              fleets
23–24   He thought ⟨the⟩ he saw
24–25   the ⟨human race⟩ ↑European family↓ [over same in pencil]
              hungering ⟨and thirsting⟩
25   it only ⟨to this end was he born⟩ ↑needed↓
26   Word ⟨to⟩ ↑upon↓ the impatient
29   He ↑scorned↓ hated ⟨he abominated⟩
32–33   he writes; "Pull
35   Papists ⟨against me⟩ to oppose

Page 129

3   consequence   This same
8   Carolostadt
9   churches, he ⟨is filled with regret and⟩
13–14   And after the insurrection ⟨And after the insurrection⟩
16   blow to the gospel ⟨⟨they give offence to many people; they

436

Lines

fish before the net   The Prophet Isaiah and St Paul do say
'I will grind them to powder with the breath of my mouth'
'I will slay him with the spirit of my lips.' With such weapons
we must beat the Pope.}⟩

18–19   destroyed by the / ⟨I a⟩
22   second ⟨Psalm⟩ of David's
28   and the ↑Psalm CIV↓ ⟨104 Ps⟩
32   This ⟨indeed⟩ ↑verily↓ is all
33–(*130*)1   ↑Erasmus ⟨had been required to write against⟩ with too much
        complaisance to the Pope had controverted his Doctrine of
        Will,↓

Page 130

1   he says ⟨as it shall⟩ in his sick⟨ness⟩ ↑bed↓
1–2   God to ⟨set⟩ ↑help↓
2–3   write against ⟨Erasmus⟩ ↑him↓ and cut his throat."
        ⟨After Henry VIII had written his book ⟨against him⟩ ↑for
        which he received the title Defender of Faith↓ he says to a
        friend "I must answer the grim Lion that passes himself off
        for king of England."⟩
9   step by step;" Luther
11   When ⟨When⟩ the Turks
11–12   to Europe ⟨in⟩ before
12–13   danger that ⟨threatened⟩ ↑menaced↓ Christendom, ⟨with calm-
        ness declaring⟩ ↑and thought it sufficient to threaten↓
16   this ⟨absolute reliance⟩ sublime
19   this ⟨I⟩↑i↓nvention
20   place in a ↑civilized↓ nation
23   ⟨Of course i⟩Instead
24–25   with which we ⟨take up⟩ ↑play with↓ a book, ⟨it⟩ ↑in that age
        a book↓ was seized with ⟨intense⟩ ↑lively↓ curiosity.
26   It ⟨was written⟩ contained
29   Luther saw ⟨well⟩ ↑at once↓ the ⟨immense importance⟩ ↑value↓

Page 131

3–4   were then to be ⟨freshly uttered⟩ ↑let out↓.
4–5   care with which ⟨they⟩ ↑men↓ wrote
6   derived from ⟨the⟩ one of
7   that the ↑Elector's↓ Collection
8   sent him ↑at Wittemburg↓
9   They were sent ⟨to Wittemburg⟩, and, after
10   returned
        ⟨But⟩
11   But ⟨now comes the⟩ ↑we are born in an↓ age
12–13   nature; ⟨words⟩ a book
14–15   imitations, and ⟨so⟩ losing

Lines

17   a ⟨nearer⟩ ↑better↓ understanding of this ⟨extraordinary char-
            acter⟩ ↑reformer↓
19–20   ages, ⟨it is necessary to get⟩ ↑we shall attempt to reach↓
20–23   ⟨If we examine his writings or the records of his conversation
            we shall find that he⟩ ↑He↓ was not a philosopher; ⟨that⟩ . . .
            worth; ⟨that⟩ Aristotle's . . . views; ⟨that⟩ he had
23–24   truths, and ↑he↓ makes himself very merry with ⟨familiar[?]⟩
            ↑the recent↓ astronomical
26   Nay ⟨that⟩ his
26–27   ⟨his is merely a⟩ ↑His↓ reform ↑is↓ directed at the ⟨abuses⟩
            corruptions
27–28   Church ↑, not at its ancient creed↓
30   ⟨So little did he value the genius of the Stagirite that he de-
            clared in 1516 to John Langus "If I did not know that Aristotle
            was a Man I should not be ashamed to say that he was the
            Devil."⟩ His writings and his
33   Even ⟨the⟩ ethical ⟨Even the⟩ ethical law
34   upon his ⟨opposition⟩ attack

Page 132

1   ↑In his controversy . . . wrong.↓
2   He was not more ↑a general scholar and not more↓ a
4–5   ↑Out of a religious enthusiasm he↓ ⟨He⟩ acted ⟨with prodigious
            energy⟩ on ↑the minds of his contemporaries↓ ⟨his age⟩ ⟨out of
            the abundance of his religious enthusiasm.⟩
10   This ⟨venerable⟩ book
10–11   to his ⟨enthusiasm⟩ ↑force↓. ⟨He felt⟩ ↑Giving heed to↓
11   his mind ⟨he felt⟩ ↑or, feeling↓
12   first class, ⟨have⟩
13   thoughts, ⟨but⟩
16–18   All others, ↑if religious men as↓ Milton, Newton ↑Leibnitz↓
            Bacon ↑Montesquieu↓ Fenelon Pascal Locke ↑Cuvier Goethe↓
19–21   their religion. ⟨Luthers Religion is from the Scriptures alone⟩
            ↑I have already intimated↓ [pencil]   ⟨He very naturally
            therefore came to consider⟩ ↑⟨another class from Nature
            alone.⟩↓ /[inserted on previous page:] ↑or like Spinoza . . .
            from the Scriptures.↓ / ⟨himself as a commissioned man, con-
            tinuing the series of ancient prophets by whom the Will of
            God communicated to men. ↑The Com. Epist ad Gal.↓ ↑and
            Moses↓ ↑He called his prison Patmos↓ He esteemed himself
            as the peculiar object of hatred to Satan and his kingdom of
            evil angels, and as ⟨en⟩countering him in every especial
            occasion.
                It is ⟨vi[?]⟩ material to a just view of his character that
            we observe ⟨what⟩ the marked Jewish character of his idea
            of God   It has all the anthropomorphism of the Jewish
            thought. God is with him a Genius or local and partial tutelary

Lines

Spirit the lover of his Church the hater of the Turk as much as David's God. I could not without offending ⟨the serious⟩ devout persons repeat many of ⟨his⟩ ↑the↓ expressions of this man the most religious of his age, touching the Deity⟩

22–23 ⟨In calling him a Poet, I do not speak figuratively⟩ Luther was a Poet ⟨without writing Poems. He⟩ ↑but not in the literary sense. He wrote no poems, but he↓

25 only ⟨the⟩ occasions

25–26 of ⟨Spiritual⟩ ↑supernatural↓ agents.

27 are ⟨everpresent to⟩ ↑never out of↓

27 ⟨He⟩ All objects,

30 ⟨In his fervid⟩ The love

Page 133

1 in his ⟨room⟩ apartment,

5–9 ⟨The cuckoo⟩ ↑Popedom is a slaughterhouse . . . *et Hereti-corum*, etc."↓

10 poetic vision; ⟨which he possessed is the following⟩

12–13 butter-bearers, cheese- [end of line] and wool bearers

27 Thereto comes ↑a↓ yet more frightful

35 It is true of him ⟨that he did not write but acted poems⟩

Page 134

2 opinions ⟨with⟩ poetically

10 from ⟨the⟩ Gothic

13 Stephen's time says. "⟨You might travel all day and not find an inhabited village.⟩

15 Berne ⟨to⟩ that

17 Th⟨ese⟩is gross &, ⟨as it were⟩, heathen ⟨idea of God⟩ ↑theism↓ is ⟨that⟩ almost

21 ⟨It is material to an understanding of his history that we observe the marked Judaism of his idea of God. It has all the anthropomorphism of the Jewish thought.⟩ God is in Luther's

22–23 enemy, ⟨whether Pope ⟨or⟩ and Turk⟩. ↑the chief of which are the Pope and the Turk.↓

24 therefore ⟨continually⟩ much

25 known ⟨entire⟩ devotion

28 for we ↑can↓ neither

Page 135

3 murmuring in Jeremy. ⟨Our Saviour Christ spake in that sort (Luke 9) Moses also in such manner set God the stool before the door, as we say, when he said Have I begotten this multitude of people I am not their father.' It is not possible but a man must grieve very much when from his heart he meaneth good and yet is not regarded. I can never be rid

of these cogitations in wishing I had never begun this business with the Pope. Likewise I wish myself rather dead than to hear God's word and his servants contemned   This is our nature's frailty.(") Those that contemn such passions are Theologi in arte Speculativa who play with thoughts and ⟨deal with speculations⟩ ↑love to theorize↓; but when they come themselves into that case, then they will well find it and be sensible thereof. Such Histories are very great and we ought not to dispute of them with cogitations and speculations.")

7   disobedient as now they ⟨are⟩ be

8   into a lump."

⟨Commenting upon the Second Psalm he says "I have now angered the Pope about his images of idolatry and how the Sow raiseth her bristles! I have a great advantage of him for the Lord saith *Ego suscitabo vos in novissimo die* and then will he call and say, Ho Martin Luther, Philip Melancthon, Justus Jonas, John Calvin Arise!   come up! Well ↑on,↓ let us be of good comfort.")

12   fire Ah! then

18   between ⟨the idea⟩ its ⟨idea⟩ ↑conception↓ of good and its ⟨idea⟩ ↑conception↓

19   God ⟨gives⟩ ↑required↓ the same

20   distinctness ⟨to⟩ ↑in↓

23   bodily ⟨form⟩ figure

32   devour him."

⟨And in his chamber he affirms he was disturbed by ⟨noises⟩ ↑sounds↓ and commotions occasioned by devils until he scoffed and mocked at them   Then they disappeared for the Devil cannot bear contempt⟩ [written under the same, in pencil]

35   Again; "We cannot vex
       ⟨"We cannot vex⟩ the Devil

Page 136

1   teach ⟨preach⟩ sing

6   [upside down at the bottom of the page:] To the Atlan /
       Brooding ↑on such ideas↓

7   peril ⟨of the⟩ from

14   infernal hosts. ⟨This persuasion is continually expressed in his writings and discourse. This is the secret of his indomitable will   No man in history ever assumed a more commanding attitude or expressed a more perfect self reliance. His words have been called "half-battles.")

15–29 ↑This persuasion . . . motion of the earth↓

15   This persuasion ⟨is abundantly obvious⟩ ↑betrays itself↓ in ↑all↓ his

Lines	
18–19	to men. ↑He called his prison, ⟨Patmos⟩ Patmos.↓ His Commentary on ⟨the⟩ Galatians
20	position of ↑St↓ Paul
21	Epistle ⟨therefore⟩ to defend
21	own acts.
	⟨He called his prison Patmos⟩
23	and ⟨as⟩ ↑to be↓ sustained
23–24	by ⟨the outstretched arm⟩ ↑special interpositions↓
26–29	His words ⟨have been called half battles⟩ [pencil:] ⟨They well deserve the name. They indicate a Will on which a nation mt lean not liable to sudden sallies or⟩ [written under:] are more than brave, . . . motion of the earth.

Page 137

15	persecutions ⟨of⟩ ↑at↓ Leipsic
15	Were the ↑Should↓
16	itself ↑be↓ in the same
23	I will ⟨retire⟩ ↑withdraw↓ no more
24	seems to ↑have↓ remembered
25	inspired.
	⟨"Had I known when I first began to write what I now see that people had been such enemies of God's Word and so fiercely had bended themselves against the same truly I had held my peace for I never should have been so courageous as to have fallen upon the Pope and to have angered him and almost the whole Christian World.⟩
29	like a W⟨B⟩War ↑War-↓

Page 138

4–5	⟨With⟩ ↑A man of↓ his ⟨stormy⟩ ↑mighty↓ heart and restless ↑excessive↓
8–9	and heart are sound, a sort of ↑He is one of that class of men that give us the impression stabil↓ Adam, ↑one of that class of Standard men↓
11–12	in its ⟨primitive⟩ ↑first↓ simplicity . . . generations.
16	was his ⟨kind[?]⟩ ↑warm↓ social
18	Catharine ⟨de Bore⟩ ↑of Born↓
23–26	Galatians; "My Epistle to the Galatians is ↑that to which I am espoused; is↓ my Catharine ⟨de⟩ ↑of↓ Bor⟨e⟩n." ↑This single . . . character↓
27–29	Table Talk, ⟨he says⟩ ↑the conversation . . . Luther says↓ . . . for instance; Catharine

Page 139

5–6	confidence. ⟨wherever it is seen.⟩
6–8	There is a vein . . . temper. [no commas]

Lines
16 ⟨I hear he s⟩ The following
21–22 fly not away I . . . with us we can
31 fund of ⟨kindliness⟩ human kindness

Page 140

1 Th⟨i⟩ese traits ⟨confirm our confidence in him⟩ show⟨ing⟩
11–22 ↑The great philosophical . . . doth mount by.↓
16 wise and good
⟨And temper with the sternness of the brain
Thoughts motherly and meek as womanhood⟩
24 fanaticism to ⟨the⟩ manly
25 manifest. ⟨It seems⟩ ↑That↓
26 his ⟨controversial powers⟩ ↑warlike genius↓

Page 141

3–4 said unto me I . . . merry if the
8 own ↑polemical↓ bitterness. ⟨in controv⟩
30 had ⟨occasioned⟩ ↑awakened↓
33–34 within it⟨self supplies⟩ affords

Page 142

3–4 man ⟨*totus in seipso teres et rotundus*⟩ [Horace, *Satires* 2.7.86]
↑entire and self-sufficing↓
5 stand and ↑it can↓ go
20 good humor, ⟨&⟩ occasionally
21 merry, and ⟨now and then⟩ ↑sometimes↓
22 controversy. ⟨He surrendered himself to his natural emotions.⟩
25 Appearances are ⟨he⟩ always

Page 143

5–6 all the
⟨A man mellowed by all the⟩ sweetness and

[overleaf from the final paragraph, in pencil:]
Lauterbach
Aurifaber
Order of the house of Commons sanctioning Henry Bell's translation is dated Feb. 1646   It states that it had been already approved by the Assembly of Divines

4. JOHN MILTON

[Since this volume went to press, manuscripts of the Milton and the Michel Angelo lectures have been discovered in the Houghton Library among the papers now on deposit there of John Gorham Palfrey, editor of the *North*

American Review between 1835 and 1843. Although the manuscripts are evidently printer's copies with the printer's marks on them, both contain a number of alterations by Emerson. Collation with the surviving manuscript of the Michel Angelo lecture shows that in that case Emerson transcribed the text of the lecture and then revised this to produce the text of the article published by Palfrey. There is every reason to believe that he followed the same procedure with the Milton lecture. We have prepared, therefore, a complete set of textual notes from the Palfrey manuscript, from which something like the text of the original lecture as delivered may be reconstructed. The first draft material presented in our textual notes to other lectures is of course still not available for this one, having disappeared with the original manuscript.

Our thanks are due to Dean John Gorham Palfrey of Columbia College for making this material available to us. The textual notes have been prepared by Mr. Wallace E. Williams.]

Page 145

Lines

2	1823, ⟨attracted a new⟩ ↑drew a sudden↓
3	time the ⟨periodical⟩ literary
12–13	↑new &↓ temporary ⟨eclat⟩ ↑renown↓ of the poet ⟨has faded⟩ ↑is silent↓ again, it is n⟨o⟩evertheless true
14	not ⟨f⟩ rigid
16–18	It was ⟨very⟩ [light cancellation] easy to remark a↑n↓ ⟨very⟩ altered tone in the criticism ⟨to which we have alluded⟩ ↑when he reappeared as an author fifteen years ago↓ from ⟨th⟩ any
19	merit ⟨long put beyond all question⟩ ↑indisputable & illustrious↓
21–22	history of the ⟨time⟩ ↑nineteenth century↓
23	↑And as↓ A man's

Page 146

1	receives it, ⟨It therefore⟩ ↑the new criticism↓
3–4	wrought.
	⟨A very great change had long since befallen the reputation of Milton⟩ The reputation of Milton⟨'s reputation⟩ had
5	its ⟨pre⟩ recent
6	not ↑at↓ all
7–8	formidable controversialist. His
12	ornaments ⟨yet⟩ ↑but↓
14	what ⟨are⟩ ↑become↓
15–16	↑the history of the↓ American ⟨Debate⟩ ↑Congress↓. Milton⟨'s tracts never⟩ seldom ↑deigns a↓
17	are ⟨first⟩ to be overcome ⟨to⟩ before
18–19	but ⟨haughty⟩ ↑peremptory↓ & impassioned he demands ⟨at once⟩ ↑on the instant↓

Lines

19–20	discriminated from ⟨the⟩ modern
21	is ↑all but↓
29	integrated [not underlined]
30	mind⟨; and t⟩The reader
32–33	one for its ⟨defect⟩ ↑faults↓

Page 147

1	divested of ⟨his⟩ its
4	Paris, at Tholouse, & at London, had ⟨quite⟩ ↑utterly↓
5	genius ⟨must heartily deplore⟩ ↑will always regret↓
6	taken cou⟨s⟩nsel of
8–9	liberty. ⟨Far different would have been then its prophetic tone from⟩ ↑There is ⟨no⟩ ↑little↓ poetry or prophecy in↓
14	slain? ⟨The topics of the mob the teacher the poet might have scorned & instead of winding about to follow the argument of Salmasius he should as at all other times have lent his erect ear to the oracle within & thence drawn the theory of English rights⟩ Though
15	as a historical
15–16	valued with ⟨the⟩ ↑similar↓
18	thing, then always he recovers
19	speaks, and the ⟨conclusion⟩ peroration
23	press, ⟨in our judgment⟩, the
29	magazine of ⟨thoughts & arguements on the subject of⟩ ↑reasons for↓
31–32	peculiar ⟨people & crisis for⟩ ↑state of society↓
34–(*148*)1	wrote, ⟨have⟩ ↑has↓ engraved ⟨themselves⟩ ↑itself↓ in the remembrance of the world, ⟨they⟩ ↑it↓ share↑s↓

Page 148

4	oblivion. ⟨Our⟩ ↑We have lost all↓
4–5	redoubted ⟨debater⟩ ↑disputant↓ ⟨& orthodox champion⟩ of a sect. ⟨Creed, sermon, pamphlet, & divine ↑of the purest party↓ find little favor ⟨in our eyes⟩ ↑beyond three generations↓⟩, but
7	mind of ⟨every wise lover of his race⟩ ↑men↓
8–10	It is ⟨his fa[?]⟩ the aspect which he presents to th⟨e⟩is ⟨present⟩ generation which alone concerns us. ⟨Not only has⟩ Milton the controversialist ↑↑has lost his↓ ⟨has no longer any⟩ popularity ↑long ago,↓↓ ⟨lost all interest for us⟩ and ↑if↓ we
10	Paradise ⟨l⟩Lost
11–12	divine," ⟨but⟩ so did the next age to his own. ⟨b⟩But
12–13	kindles ⟨some admiration⟩ ↑a↓ love & emulation in us which he ⟨[?]d⟩ ↑did↓ not ⟨f[?]⟩ ↑in↓
22–24	articulation that ⟨now first was the⟩ ↑now first was such↓

perception & enjoyment ↑possible; — the perception & enjoy-
ment↓ of all ⟨that⟩ his ⟨perfect⟩ ↑varied↓ rhythm, & ⟨the⟩ ↑his
perfect↓

25   style↑s↓. ⟨was now for the first time possible.⟩ This ⟨must
always be;⟩ ↑is a poets right;↓

32–33   ↑But it would be . . . critical reputation↓
⟨But whilst Milton is no longer a polemic and whilst he
stands at a greater height on the mount of song neither is
his reputation with this age merely critical. But i)It is

35   & so, shall we not say of all men,

Page 149

1–2   our cotemporaries ⟨always an in-⟨estimable⟩ ↑calculable↓ influence,⟩

2–3   acts ⟨with great energy on the⟩ ↑on the↓

4–5   Shakspear undoubtedly transcends, ⟨but⟩ & far

6   but Shakspear

7   not. ⟨But⟩ Milton

13–14   fame as that of a near ⟨relative⟩ ↑friend↓. ⟨He is loved by us
as nature is, whose laws he loved & celebrated.⟩ He is

16–17   we think that no man

18   character. ⟨as did John Milton⟩. Better

21   such ⟨harmonious union⟩ ↑a composition↓

24   philosophers ⟨since Milton have formally dedicated⟩ in England

26–27   impossible ⟨to name one⟩ ↑⟨pronounce a⟩↓ ↑recal one↓ in
those countries ⟨which awakens⟩ ↑who communicates↓

28   Milton ⟨inspires⟩ awakens.

30   shrinks & palters

31   Bacon's ⟨e⟩Essays

35   poetry, very uninteresting & daily growing more so. ⟨Pope⟩
Addison

Page 150

1   man that Lord Chesterfield has described, is ⟨not⟩ unworthy

3–4   heroic. ⟨It were unjust to the Nor has t⟩The genius of France
↑has not↓

27   advantages. ⟨Such p⟩Perfections

29   been ⟨corroborated⟩ in part

30–32   political ene⟨ne⟩mies, ⟨we might doubt his biographers were
drawing ideal portraits as of Xenophon⟩ ↑would lead us
to suspect the portraits were ideal like the↓ Cyrus ⟨or Tele-
machus⟩ ↑of Xenophon, the Telemachus of↓ Fenelon ⟨in his
Telemachus⟩ or ⟨in⟩ the popular

445

Page 151

Lines

1   beautiful & ⟨pro⟩ well proportioned

4–6   ↑Aubrey adds a sharp trait, . . . sign of a ⟨[?] &⟩ satirical genius."↓

8   was so ⟨delicate⟩ ↑acute↓

9–10   ↑and his voice, . . . sweet & harmonious.↓

11–12   education. ⟨His⟩
           With these

14   midst of ⟨l⟩London

16   order of ⟨nature⟩ ↑the world↓

24   Baroni seem ⟨wholly⟩ to

28   wit & fore↑i↓gners came

29–30   one of ⟨these⟩ his

Page 152

5   his own e⟨[?]⟩ndeavor

6–7   treasures of the Latin, Greek, ⟨&⟩ Hebrew

9–10   Michel Angelo, & Correggio: where ↑also↓

12   ↑or Rome↓

20–21   consummate ⟨s mastery⟩ skill in the use of his own. No individual writer has been an equal benefactor of the English tongue

25–26   his choice to
           (leave trifles /
           ⟨There is such a wide difference between the powers of t⟨[?]⟩wo m communication Between two men of equal quickness of apprehension there appears such a wide difference in the power of expressing thought as to justify the separate consideration of the power of language. In Milton the skill in foreign tongues & a matchless skill in his own are of that so conspicuous traits as to fasten attention. There is no individual writer to whom the English tongue is so much indebted as to him. His power of language amazes those who study it most. Very early in life he became conscious that he had more to say to his fellow men than they had fit words to embody At nineteen years in ⟨c⟩a college exercise he addresses his native language, saying to it that it would be his choice to⟩ / leave trifles

29   Such where the ⟨[?]⟩deep

33   Michel Angelo

Page 153

7   Shakspear, he ⟨swelled its⟩ ↑⟨vied with him in the⟩↓ ↑scattered in↓

8   ↑his pastoral & romantic fancies;↓

Lines	
9	strains he ⟨showed⟩ ↑made ⟨it⟩↓ it
10–11	majesty, and ⟨the[?]⟩ bent it to express every ⟨shifting emotion, every subtle distinction, yes⟩ ↑trait of beauty, every shade of thought,↓
13	apply to his ⟨own⟩ performance
21	conscious of ⟨this⟩ possessing this ⟨penetrating⟩ ↑intellectual↓
22–23	ages & ⟨multiplying⟩ ↑propelling↓ its melodious undulations ↑⟨o[?]⟩↓ ↑forward↓ through ⟨out⟩ the
26–27	said in his ⟨a⟩Apo⟨[?]⟩logy for Smectymnuus

Page 154

4	devout. ⟨In him⟩ He
7	↑the old↓ eternal ⟨virtue⟩ ↑goodness↓
11–12	holiness ⟨[?]⟩ ↑ugly↓, in Milton, at least, it ⟨dwelt⟩ ↑was↓ so pure⟨ly⟩ ↑a flame↓
16	resemble Homer's
17	were ⟨severely ascetic⟩ ↑austere↓
19	the lyri⟨c⟩st ⟨poet⟩ may
22–23	love, ⟨&⟩not from fear. He is innocent & exact because ⟨so⟩ his taste was so pure & delicate. ⟨out of his adoration of beauty⟩. He
24	twenty ⟨one, "⟩ ↑one↓ that

Page 155

13	keep ⟨me⟩ ↑him↓
31	↑in gardening↓
32–33	whatsoever ⟨breathed a⟩savored of ⟨anything⟩ genero⟨us⟩sity & noble↑ness↓
35	English ⟨p⟩People

Page 156

1	forbearance in his polemics even.
6–7	added ⟨[?] still higher g[?]ce⟩ ↑the genius of↓ the Christian ⟨holiness⟩ ↑sanctity↓
8	in the Christian ⟨doctrine⟩ ↑ethics↓
17–18	weakness." He ⟨taxed⟩ ↑told↓ the bishops ⟨with this⟩ "that instead
27	own ⟨deep sense⟩ ↑perception↓
32	lowliness?" ⟨And by⟩ ↑Obeying↓
33	deserved the ⟨pr⟩ apostrophe

Page 157

15–16	sentiment ⟨inspired⟩ ↑warmed↓ his writing & ⟨action⟩ ↑conduct↓ with the highest ⟨c[?], that⟩ ↑affection↓

Lines
17   which ⟨he made⟩ in
19   his ↑old↓ age
19–20   ages, the ⟨devout⟩ invocations
22–23   choice in ⟨matrimony⟩ ↑marriage↓
24   Thus ⟨singular in⟩ ↑chosen by↓
25   & all that is ⟨just⟩ ↑great↓
33   love of ↑freedom↓

Page 158

1   Puritans. ⟨Susceptible as Burke to all the attractions of his-
        torical prescription, of royalty, of chivalry of an ancient
        church illustrated by old martyrdoms, & enshrined in cathe-
        drals, he threw himself the flower of elegancy on the side
        of the reeking conventicle, the side of the unlearned & un-
        adorned.⟩ The part he took ⟨the side he chose⟩ the zeal
3–4   Burke to ⟨all⟩ the
24   times: ⟨but⟩ in them
31   thought ⟨a⟩ constra↑i↓nt of

Page 159

13–17   He maintained the doctrine of {*literary* liberty, . . . He
        maintained the doctrine of} *domestic* liberty
14   press ⟨& [?]⟩ & insisting
18   mind was better
23–24   human ⟨liberty⟩ ↑rights↓. They are all ⟨new⟩ ↑varied↓
36   requiring ↑that↓

Page 160

6–7   He ⟨desired⟩ ↑wished↓
18–19   nature; by the ⟨perfect⟩ proportion of his ⟨own⟩ powers;
        ⟨raised⟩ by great knowledge & ⟨animated⟩ by ⟨goodness⟩ ↑re-
        ligion↓
25   Round from his ⟨manly⟩ ↑parted↓ forelock ⟨parted⟩ ↑manly↓
        hung
30–31   Milton of a ⟨loftier humanity⟩ purer ideal of humanity, ⟨than
        poet had yet described⟩ modifies
33–(161)2 said ↑to be "the noblest that ever contented itself↓ "to minis-
        ter to ⟨his⟩ ↑the↓ ⟨u⟩Understanding," so Milton's ministers to
        character

Page 161

5   life ↑still↓
8   The Comus is but a transcript
23   Shall we ⟨own⟩ say

JOHN MILTON

Page 162

Lines	
4	single cantoes
10	Milton ⟨inspired⟩ ↑fired↓ "with ⟨f[?]⟩ [erased] dearest [over erasure]
11–12	imagination, & ⟨the⟩ exhausted
15–16	↑common↓ rhymers would it need to ⟨present⟩ ↑make↓
19	prose ⟨as⟩ ↑and↓
21	more ⟨real &⟩ sincere
24	Aristotle; 'Poe⟨try⟩sy not
28–29	apology to be ⟨pleaded⟩ ↑entered↓ for his plea

Page 163

2	yet have ⟨they⟩ not
6	We have ⟨n⟩offered no
9	labor ⟨never⟩ or
9–10	love of the ⟨most⟩ supreme
14	endeavored ⟨to⟩ [erased] in [over erasure]

[The following entries, not for the most part in either lecture or journal, appear among the working notes for this lecture:]

Milton a realist. Poetry is now unreality. Once it was Reality by Emphasis. The theogonys iliads hymns Odes expressed not the fancy but the faith of men. ⟨Milt⟩ Now poetry is a mere carcass   The deep reverence it once acquired & the instinct now in men that they are related to something better than beef & stone keep its dead life along. imitative. But it is not any longer as it was once the voice of society as direct & natural an utterance as is the cry of a child that is in pain   Once in an age awakes out of the multitude a man who becomes the voice of a certain real emotion or thought who sings because he cannot help it and such a man is as much distinguished from the poets of the time as he is from other writers. Burns was such a man & with great deductions Beranger among the French. The Cowleys Grays Popes & ⟨Campbells⟩ ↑Crabbes↓ write from elegancy & merely write verse from the want of a more proper vehicle   That is the one in use   But Spenser, Shakspear, Milton & Burns write verses because the⟨y⟩ thoughts are musical & cannot otherwise find fit expression. And such persons create their verse. Shakspears is new & peculiar & ⟨Miltons would never remi⟩ it is not the least praise of Paradise Lost to say that ⟨it⟩ written in the same stanza as Lear & Hamlet it is so essentially different in its structure as never to remind the ear of Shakspear
This is the characteristic of Milton. He does not write verse by stealth & blush if you find it, as men do now. It is grave earnest with him. And he means every thing he says.

In them is plainest taught & easiest learnt
What makes a nation happy & keeps it so. [cf. p. 162]

This reality is his force   ↑If↓ out of the heart it came ⟨&⟩ to the heart it must go. [cf. pp. 375–76]
Now his Paradise Lost is not all Real. His Comus is. Th⟨is⟩e defects of Paradise Lost are the fictitious part. The Reason of Ch. Gov & Areopagitica, are. better poems than whole books of P.L.

The tragic part is his knowledge that he was alone. Like Jeremiah he says Wo is me my mother that thou hast borne me a man of strife. ⟨the⟩ he feels the sad condition of Vision. that unhappy handful of men whose misfortune it is to have understanding.
    {the two classes of men the theorist always at the ↑extreme↓ end of human judgment ⟨belie⟩ affirming the perfectibility legislating for men as for wise & amiable angels; & the practical man managing wheedling complying bargaining for safety & plenty anyhow only anxious that the world shd last his day — these two classes ⟨from⟩ on whose endless struggle the peace of society is built}
one the men of principle
other   men of fact
See J. 1834 p 91 [i.e., *J*, III, 349 (c. Oct. 27). Not this passage]

5. GEORGE FOX

Page 165

Lines

1–5   In the sketches . . . a thousand years. [An alternative opening appears in pencil on the (otherwise blank) previous page:] In the heads ⟨usually⟩ selected for biographical sketches men have an eye in ordinary to persons of rare faculties and to such as had the advantage of rare cultivation   Luther Shakspear Columbus Washington each tower above his contemporaries.

1   ↑George Fox born, 1624; died, 1690↓
         In the sketches

4   & is not ⟨so much⟩ one man in a thousand men, ⟨as⟩ ↑but↓ one man

5–6   to the ↑true↓ views of biography {stated in my first lecture} Man & not

6–7   are ⟨our⟩ ↑the↓ subject ↑of endless interest to man↓.

8–9   We wish ↑not only to make the extraordinary but↓

10–11   what the ⟨women⟩ ↑cook↓ the peasant and the soldier say. ⟨Better is⟩ The

11–12   conceptions ↑never take us so much as↓ when

12–13   from ↑the↓ palace⟨s⟩ nor from ⟨the⟩ Arts

16   represented ⟨rather as⟩ to be

17   ↑⟨Men of exalted genius are marked because they are rare⟩ In passing by peculiar gifts &↓ & ⟨In⟩ exhibiting

Lines
19–20   means & power. ⟨We see the power of them that retire & creep. These⟩ ↑Portraits of common men who have accomplished much↓ do human
25   the ↑decay &↓ degeneracy ⟨& decay⟩
27   formal age ⟨the⟩ a novelty
27–28   sentiments ⟨a freshness of action⟩ like that
28   First Day. ⟨The sentiment of Religion &⟩ ↑Such a principle is↓
30–31   Religion. /
         In passing by peculiar gifts /
         George Fox was a man ⟨to⟩ who

Page 166

1   principle the Religious sentiment was
2   was ⟨now⟩ father, mother,
5–6   and to ⟨forms⟩ ↑modes↓ of worship. ⟨Let us⟩ ↑We must↓
12   works of ↑many↓ thousands
13   social ⟨race⟩ ↑tribe↓, certain
14   shines a ↑vital↓ light ⟨wonderful vital⟩
16–17   remote objects ↑as there is no . . . make beautiful↓ [marginal note; no mark of insertion]
24   reappear on ⟨all⟩ ↑frequent↓ occasions in the ⟨widest spaces⟩ ↑remotest places↓
27   new receiver but
29–30   Zoroaster ↑in Persia↓, Confucius ↑in China↓, Orpheus ↑in Greece↓, Numa ↑in Italy↓, Manco Capac ↑in Peru↓
31   Jesus ↑in Palestine↓
33   testimony   the Brahmins   Mahomet

Page 167

2–3   the most ⟨staggering⟩ ↑resistless↓ affirmations
5–6   it ⟨supersedes⟩ ↑supplies the place of↓ Poetry & philosophy & ⟨inspires education⟩ ↑of learned discipline↓,
8   respect ⟨of this singular sentiment⟩ ↑is striking enough↓
9   the most ⟨obscure⟩ ↑narrow↓ mortal
10–11   uniformly ⟨instructs⟩ ↑persuades↓ him that he ⟨sustains the closest relations⟩ ↑is united in the most intimate manner↓
12   the ⟨property⟩ ↑dominion↓ of that Cause
16   ⟨Then⟩ ↑Furthermore↓ it is the most
16–17   ↑"God is our . . . peremptory voice↓ [written in ink over "God is . . . brethren" in pencil]
20   of the earth. ⟨"God is our . . . peremptory voice.⟩
22–23   every man "How
25   ↑according to the confession of Hume↓
28   substantial ⟨agreement⟩ ↑identity↓ ⟨between⟩ ↑of↓ the
28–29   religious sentiment(s) ⟨of⟩ ↑in↓
33   You might as ⟨well⟩ easily

Page 168

Lines	
1	barrels. ⟨It is infinitely more volatile than either.⟩ It must be lived.

5–6	good of each name.
	        In this
	        These are the facts

7	philanthropist. ⟨Both⟩ He
10–11	Drayton Leicestershire and
14	this poor ⟨cobbler⟩ ↑boy↓ caught
15	beauty amid ⟨all⟩ the ugliness
17–18	↑out of the ashes of his fortune↓ to that ⟨height of⟩ moral ⟨elevation⟩ ↑height↓ which belongs to this principle. ⟨,out of the ashes of his fortune.⟩
19–20	we shall ↑find↓ two facts . . . established, that
20–21	↑liberal discipline of arts It is better than↓
23	tho' un⟨informed⟩ ↑taught↓ mind
23–24	suggested ⟨all⟩ in turn
25	reformer. ⟨an⟩ ↑He is at once an↓ ⟨true⟩ idealist
27	thing for a form. ⟨as George Fox ever complained that none spoke to his condition.⟩
31–33	↑He was diligent . . . George was there.↓
33–35	the ↑routine↓ interruptions of his trade, ↑at the age of 19↓ he forsook his ⟨business He⟩ ↑craft and gave himself up to a contemplative life.↓
36–37	Derbyshire ↑with his Bible↓; he lived on ↑berries &↓
37–(*169*)2	furnish him & ↑at &↓ slept in hollow trees. ↑or a stack . . . mournfully about↓

Page 169

4	↑both on account of ⟨as being⟩ cheapness & strength↓.
5–6	clergy of the ⟨church⟩ established
7–10	with levity. ↑⟨none of ym spoke to his condition⟩↓ ↑One related . . . as disgusted him.↓
13	public discourse. ↑None of them spoke to his condition.↓
14–15	None of them he complained none
22	clergymen with ⟨contradiction⟩ ↑interrogations↓
24	afterwards ⟨from⟩ wherever he went ↑often half famished↓
25–26	and he was ↑insulted,↓ whipped
29–33	↑He passed through . . . for 14 days time↓ [added in margin; no insert mark in text] ↑In the first years . . . piercing words.↓ [added above the line]
36–37	hundreds and thousands ⟨listened⟩ became ⟨hearers and doers of his word⟩ ↑his associates↓ at the dear penalty ↑of↓ a furious persecution. ⟨until by⟩ But "the Lord

Page 170

Lines	
1	as two ↑of their↓ women ↑replied↓
2–3	Their ⟨inflexible⟩ constancy and meekness
4–5	itinerant. ↑but was ⟨G F⟩ married the widow of Judge Fell↓ [no mark of insertion]
5–6	came to America to Barbadoes
6–7	↑He spent a year in A. afterwards in Holland.↓
8–10	Hampton Court ↑⟨According to the company⟩ In all companies . . . jailers convicts↓ [no punctuation]
17	made to him. And
19–20	That they ⟨all⟩ have a direct
20	practical morals.
	⟨But his true biography must be found in those revelations that in orchards, in lonesome places, & by the wayside were made ⟨known⟩ to him⟩
23	(Drayton)
26–35	Christs sufferings Then, . . . hearts of many people. [semicolons in text replace periods in ms.]
28–29	minister of Christ
	⟨That⟩
	That believers
30–32	↑That the Scriptures . . . that gave them forth.↓ That ⟨God⟩ ↑the Supreme Being↓ dwelleth not in ⟨temples made with hands⟩ ↑houses↓ ↑of brick & stone↓ /
	{There is one even Jesus Christ that can speak to thy condition}
33–35	persons. ↑and that the natures of ⟨the seethings which were hurtful⟩ dog swine vipers . . . hearts of many people.↓

Page 171

2	with words, but ⟨trampled on⟩ the true
5	presently, ⟨the⟩ he sitting still,
8	he was made to ⟨perceive⟩ see
11–16	professions of the world physic, . . . virtues that . . . God and . . . God. so that
19–22	ought to possess. ⟨He was then constrained to go to⟩ ↑There was to be↓ a meeting of justices ⟨met[?]⟩ in a neighboring town for ⟨deliberating on⟩ ↑establishing some local regulation respecting↓ the hiring of servants; ↑Thither George felt constrained to go↓
27	bowing ⟨himself⟩ his body
28–29	*You* to more than one that
34	darkness in all
36–(172)17	↑But that suggestion . . . mankind could not confirm.↓ [added on separate sheet]

Page 172

Lines

1   which came first & ⟨lasted longest⟩ remained

9–10   profane in the . . . Daemon: in . . . Homer: in . . . fairies; in tutelar saints: in

12–15   silently very peacefully not . . . counsel but to the ear sharpened by faith ⟨he utters⟩ ↑these intimations become↓ words of fate. not one falls to the ground. ⟨The⟩ What

17   mankind could not confirm. ⟨The philosopher expresses the same supreme power of the Soul by the word Reason when used in its highest sense in opposition to the Understanding⟩

18   These ↑ & such as these↓

18–19   poor cobler

20   was so strong & ⟨stormy[?]⟩ as to

21   considerations of ⟨prudence⟩ ↑thrift↓

23–24   communicated ⟨as a gospel⟩ to men as poor

25   scullions & ⟨gaol birds⟩ ↑convicts↓ & dragoons,

31   Scripture they understood ⟨& when⟩ & adopted

33–34   William Penn, Pennington [2] & Elwood [1] ↑who had learning↓ were added to their people, ⟨who had learning⟩, ⟨&⟩ these men

Page 173

3   most remarkable ⟨circumstance⟩ ↑fact↓

4   Quakers that the ⟨tracts &⟩ books & tracts

9–10   called visionary to ⟨Swedenborg⟩ Schelling Novalis & Swedenborg the

10–11   of dreams, of names.

                 ⟨And I am persuaded that no lover of truth can read the history of the Quakers simple as it is with the effort to place himself in their point of view without feeling many chords struck in his own mind, & becoming sensible that the circumstances might present themselves in which he should act the part of Fox or Howgill.⟩

13   sentiment could ⟨purify⟩ ↑exalt↓ the thinking & purify the ⟨expression⟩ ↑language↓

14   tempted to read the ⟨language⟩ words

20   enjoy its own ⟨at⟩ in

Page 174

1–2   ↑In the first place . . . with all philosophy↓

2–3   himself to men by ⟨his rigid morality⟩ ↑vitality of the ⟨puren⟩ doctrine↓. ⟨His own life was irreproach⟩able & he demanded

8–9   ↑"The visible . . . sight in you"↓

9   radical reform ⟨regeneration⟩ of the church

Lines

12–13 establish ⟨his⟩ what severe Rule of Discipline ⟨he will⟩ ↑the will↓, in a short time ⟨his own⟩ he dies,

14–15 spirit ↑die↓, ⟨&⟩ his own fire cannot be transmitted & ⟨in a short time⟩ ↑soon↓ their places

20–21 more appropriate ⟨forms⟩ ↑practices↓. Thus every church the purest becomes

22–23 Thus ⟨Luther⟩ ↑the Protestants↓ reformed the Catholic

25–26 Methodist & [?] now the Swedenborgian

27 earnest; but ⟨teaches⟩ all whilst

32 human nature. ⟨His whole preaching & life⟩ ↑All his actions & discourse↓ breathe⟨s⟩

33 race of man. ⟨Hence⟩ ⟨h⟩His attitude

35 ever a thing ⟨for a word⟩ for

Page 175

4–13 ↑I know it seems to many . . . actually becomes at that time.↓ [added on the previous (otherwise blank) page; written over the same passage in pencil, with variants as follows:] I know it seems to many ⟨a re⟩ that disorderly spirit is a very easy way to fame, and that to interrupt the religious services of churches was not the best mark of a true reform. This it is true the Quakers did and their apology consists in the ⟨then⟩ state of the English Church. ⟨It had then become a dead & merely formal church & the ⟨only⟩ ↑right↓ to denounce it emphatically like the right of Revolution in a tyranny can never be denied⟩ It must be admitted — it cannot be denied that if an established church becomes utterly ⟨dead⟩ formal and dead the aggrieved pious man has a right . . . become at that time.

7 in the ⟨st⟩ then state

8–9 denied that if an

13–17 decorum . . . with words. [no punctuation]

13–14 ↑in the bosom of a formal Church↓

17–18 ↑The sweetest psalms . . . states of the people.↓

19–20 His ⟨first⟩ earliest inspiration

27 becoming sensible of of the vices

31–32 Come . . . the devil [no punctuation]

36 Calendar
At the Market cross against

Page 176

1 In [blank] prison

5–14 ↑Afterwards, in ye time of Charles II . . . accept one; For, . . . in any way dishonorable to truth."↓ [on a separate slip]

15 They offered him at [blank] a bounty

27 The ⟨pretence⟩ usurpation implied

Lines

29	that on ↑almost↓ all occasions
31–32	place he, went in. He showed his ⟨practical⟩ good sense when at ↑Patrington↓ the request

Page 177

2–3	satisfaction ⟨for their hungry souls⟩. And these
4–6	thereunto To ⟨such⟩ ↑men looking . . . hollowness of the Church↓
7–8	returning to ⟨its⟩ ↑his↓ fathers house.
8–9	operative begrimed distorted in body ⟨had escaped⟩ ↑fleeing↓ from
9–10	↑& hot & noisome lanes↓
19	prosperity ⟨this promised to⟩ and that on
20	sentiment promised, ↑a promise which↓ ⟨as⟩ could
25	whose ⟨opinions⟩ ↑minds↓ were not
27–29	in the likeness of man. ↑Fox had great . . . presented themselves↓ [added on next ⟨otherwise blank⟩ page]
28	directness in ⟨satisfying⟩ speaking to the spiritual ⟨cases⟩ ↑wants↓
29	⟨Many attested the power of G. F.⟩ Dr Thomas Lower asking questions of / received
30–32	"his words were . . . wise men in his life." [no punctuation. Marginal note:] G. F.'s father
32–35	↑His father who . . . Old Church saw . . . it will carry him out↓ ⟨They said that when his friend I Coate "spoke to the ungodly world his face had an awful gravity & his words were like a hammer & a sharp sword."⟩

Page 178

3	that was in ⟨them⟩ ↑the Quakers↓ made
11–13	↑We are reminded . . . replenished with money ⟨until one day ⟨he⟩ it came into his head to count it after which it diminished daily.⟩ ↑so long as he did not count it↓↓ [this sentence written after the following one, but marked for insertion here]
14	bins though
15	at their meetings.

⟨It is true that George Fox and his friends did magnify some trifles. It is true that they gave a ridiculous importance to their notions of plainness in speech manners and dress. They cut their hair not in the best taste. They stripped all jewels and ornaments from their dress. They disused titles of honor. They said Thee and Thou though they defended their practice with spirit "The Pope," said George, "set up *you* to one, in his pride. Pride could not stomach the word *Thou,* which was before ⟨the father⟩ the Pope was, which was God's

Lines

language, and will stand when the Pope is ended." "Look now," ⟨he⟩ said ↑one↓ when ↑he was↓ bid ⟨him⟩ uncover his head, and say *You*; — "They imprison me for speaking English, and for not taking off my clothes."⟩ /

18–22	extreme. ⟨They were⟩ George was confined . . . every county. [no punctuation]
21	familiar with the ⟨doleful⟩ prisons
23–24	repair ⟨the⟩ ↑his doleful prison↓ room
24–25	cold & smoke the⟨y⟩ ↑gaoler↓ removed
26–32	↑No man was sentenced . . . & turned aside.↓ [added on previous (otherwise blank) page]
28–29	canes over these ⟨offending⟩ wearers of hats.
31	horses more . . . riders would not
32	⟨No man was sentenced to die in England for this heresy but⟩ the friends were ↑imprisoned &↓
35	↑They were fined & to pay the fine↓ Their

Page 179

2	thread they
3	pap stood in ⟨the⟩ ↑a↓ pannikin
7	they were treated ↑by↓ the magistrates
13–14	sharp edict ⟨to⟩ of banishment
22–23	hearing the ⟨horrid⟩ persecutions at Boston
29	Is it asked Did . . . severities.
31	their name. ⟨In⟩ As a sect
33–34	can ↑now↓ read the story of their sect

Page 180

8–9	set up you to one in his pride.
9–10	the word Thou which
15	plainness ran to a ⟨ridiculous⟩ ↑ludicrous↓
16	plain print, ⟨also⟩ & books
17	capital letter ⟨in the whole book⟩ ↑from beginning to end↓
21	beginning that the best cause is not ↑at first↓ defended
23	insignificant ↑particulars↓ circumstances. ↑And this from necessity↓ For
24–25	holding fast not to ⟨tho[?]⟩ truths, but to ⟨forms⟩ ↑usages↓, are keenly sensible when ⟨forms⟩ ↑usages↓ are ⟨assailed⟩ ↑invaded↓.
26	philosophy can see ⟨if⟩ the
29–30	its importance. ⟨a⟩ It came
30	tribe. & has been

Page 181

1	his soul is ⟨but⟩ a temple
2	resides. That astounding

457

Lines

3   of every church & is ⟨every⟩ at intervals announced ⟨a⟩ anew
6–7   Claims of ⟨Liberty⟩ ↑Rights↓,
9   is made ↑for the time↓ a conviction.
10   ⟨On this conviction⟩ ↑As an inference from this faith↓
12–13   He who deals ⟨faithfully⟩ ↑truly↓ with
18   criterion upon ⟨the⟩ one opinion
19   condemned them.

⟨↑In some particulars his views have not spread beyond his sect. That of silent meetings is peculiar. When he was reproached for them he said "Better be silent than to tell lies."↓ [inserted after the next sentence, but marked for insertion here; a second insert indicated, but missing]   Let it be the praise of his truth and devoutness that in all important particulars his decisions have been confirmed by the voice of the wise and good ever since.

He and his friends made a resolute stand in the English courts for the religious liberty of the subject. Calmly they disputed every oppression inch by inch.

He and his friends originated the party in modern times that contends for the principle of Universal Peace.

He and his friends first pointed the attention of men to the mischief of extrajudicial oaths and to the ethical question of the expediency of an oath / [leaf torn out]

He and they directed attention to the subject of Prison Discipline

Following in these steps the society of Friends have honorably led in the two philanthropic works of the age the Abolition of Slavery and the ⟨Abstinence from the use of Ardent Spirits.⟩ ↑Suppression of Intemperance↓ And slowly and silently their opinions sifted by time have passed into the public opinion of mankind and whilst the Society ↑founded by Fox↓ remains a sect they now hold almost no peculiar opinion.⟩

Page 182

19   works of our age the Abolition
22   of mankind & whilst
27   until it ⟨ends in⟩ begins in
28   ↑at Drayton-in the-Clay in Leicestershire↓.

[The following pencilled entries, written over in ink with other material, appear among the working notes for this lecture:]

I say natural but who shall tell me the limits of the natural? spiritual helps are natural they are part of the nature with which every man is endowed and the life of all his nature.

It seems to me as if we ought solemnly to congratulate one another that we exist, that we live embosomed in the love of God, that out of all ⟨the⟩ ↑our↓ vexations & wants ⟨of our⟩ we ⟨can⟩ withdraw into a shelter of peaceful & divine thoughts, that we may there set up our everlasting rest   that whilst our feet walk in the material world & our hands work there & our lungs breathe ⟨the⟩ material air each one of us does at the same time inherit an entire spiritual world of thought & affection   that to that world no change no decay no decrepitude approaches   That creation is ↑this moment↓ as fresh as it was in its morning prime & shall be as fresh when they have fallen out of heaven for the soul of man can retire to the very presence & communion of God & devoting itself to him become a part of Him & take hold on his eternity.

[The working notes also include this passage:]
The philosophy of the common human heart is Religion. This warfare with Nature this wrestling with Nature & demanding of it Infinite Gratifications for the very lowest of human kind interests us in George Fox & the scullions & gaolbirds with whom he dealt   upon these Metaphysics what said Cousin?
   "Abundance of people in Eng^d who having searched all sects cd. no where find satisfaction for yr hungry souls. And these now understanding yt God by his light was so near in their hearts began to take heed thereunto" &c p. 147   [Sewel]
   A deep consideration this subject deserves to see how the Reason of the philosopher is the Religion of the people & how deep an emotion can agitate a whole community of unthinking men when the ⟨familiar words⟩ truth familiar in words that God is within us is made a conviction. Then is the greatest of all Revolutions not a nation restored to its rights but one man made Infinite. See p. 193 vol 1   [Sewel]

6. EDMUND BURKE

Page 184

Lines	
1	Dublin 1 Jan. 1730 and
2	Trinity College. ⟨Dublin⟩
3	fond of being alone. ⟨His ⟨preference of⟩ ↑taste in↓ books is characteristic.⟩
4–5	his ↑favorite↓ orator.
12	logic at Glasgow ⟨&⟩ without success. ⟨In⟩He was married in 1757(?).
13	Natura Society
21	devoted himself ↑for 28 years↓
23	Power of Great Britain. ⟨for 28 years in the House.⟩
24	He introduced ⟨a⟩&
26	Hastings Governor
27	manner at every step
30	He published in [blank] the

Page 185

Lines	
1–2	Revolution which for ⟨a political tract is perhaps the most powerful ever written⟩ ↑its effect . . . political tracts.↓
2	He received ⟨every kind of⟩ ↑liberal↓
3–7	revolutionists & ⟨the⟩ all tributes of respect from the ⟨moderate⟩ ↑sovereigns . . . every measure of public↓ He resigned
7–8	↑The British . . . in 1795↓
10	to take a⟨n i⟩strong interest
15	genius to ⟨any of⟩ all competitors at th⟨is⟩at
16–17	the same walks and . . . the events ⟨on⟩ which he studied make
20–21	determined. ⟨The only good biography that has yet been written of him is⟩ ↑I can almost call a biography↓ the admirable ⟨passage⟩ ↑satire↓
22	↑with the allowance to be made for satire,↓
28	meant for mankind [in margin:]
	Too deep for his
	tho fraught

Page 186

1–2	The ⟨bri⟩ once sunbright
2–5	pale & faint. ⟨Fox⟩ ↑Burke once interested . . . their relation to him.↓
6	tribunal from the ⟨majority⟩ people
7–8	↑There is no caprice . . . human merit.↓
10–12	perplexity an uneasy . . . oracles of the day but
13	takes his true place by ⟨no effort friendly or hostile⟩ ↑a force↓
26	among ⟨the⟩ vulgar minds, but ⟨C⟩ for the
30–31	moral speculator. ⟨&⟩
32	sublime ⟨but⟩ ↑yet↓ simple theory of duties. ⟨And the throne⟩
35	the ↑pious↓ conclusions

Page 187

1–2	Machiavel ⟨is another example of a philosopher engaged in political affairs⟩ ↑who in the beginning of the 16 Century↓ ⟨He⟩
3	↑chiefly at foreign courts↓
4–7	advice ⟨to the⟩ at home ↑is another . . . in politics.↓ ⟨But the extent of⟩ ↑But↓ the Florentine territory was so ⟨small⟩ ↑narrow↓ & its foreign relations so ⟨feeble⟩ ↑unimportant↓ that his influence is ⟨of no account whatever⟩
9	first ↑conspicuous↓ example
15–16	He is in a ⟨great⟩ ↑long↓ series
18	cunning statesman preferring
25	quoted ⟨almost⟩ ↑often↓ unconsciously

Lines	
27	not so much ⟨by law⟩ ↑legally↓ as virtually
32–34	servile shamefully servile. ⟨Then B⟩ ↑But Bacon though . . . Philosophers left . . . into politics↓ In his connexion
37–(*188*)1	subordinate & ⟨little⟩ ↑mean↓ place . . . century and though upon ⟨questions requiring dexterous⟩ some practical

Page 188

3	yet the ⟨Court⟩ ↑King↓ always
5	Edmund Burke ↑another philosopher↓
6	1765 ⟨may be⟩ has some points
7	Emperor a sentiment
12–13	that ⟨they⟩ particular objects
13–14	& ⟨not⟩ whilst he magnified them ↑they did↓
15–16	cannot ⟨compare⟩ ↑vie↓ in complexity
21	as ⟨perfect the dependence of his⟩ minute his
22–23	↑as great his address in the despatch of business↓ as
24	Understanding, ⟨as⟩ ↑so↓ far as
25	Not so ⟨healthful⟩ ↑masculine↓ a judgment
29–30	⟨Bacon's Political Tracts are ⟨not to be compared with⟩ ↑much inferior↓ to Burkes.⟩ ⟨All Bacons⟩
36	enlargement & of his view

Page 189

2	Burke treats ⟨a particular affair⟩ ↑his business↓
9	The government administered ↑leaders of opinion↓ by [inserted words above the line, no insertion mark]
11	was so vast ⟨the⟩ so
12	still more by ⟨command⟩ ↑the↓ resistless
14	philosopher ↑might↓ for⟨sook⟩sake
17–18	to introduce ⟨the⟩ method
19	efforts ↑at organization↓
21–22	age the ⟨political philosopher⟩ *philosophical politician*, ⟨the⟩ ↑not a↓ man who ⟨not⟩ quoting
24–26	one who drawing . . . theorists ⟨attempted to ⟨con-⟩reduce⟩ ↑brought principles to bear upon↓ the public business of England. ⟨to a natural & principled regularity⟩
27	But this view is ⟨to be regarded⟩ ⟨held wit[?]⟩
30	politics ⟨no⟩ ↑neither↓ agrarian nor ⟨fanatic⟩ ↑Utopian↓
31–32	with one class nor
33	He ⟨never proposed to⟩ did not establish
37	gallery of the H. of Commons

Page 190

1	that body & ⟨with⟩ studying
5–6	quickened & ⟨in some measure⟩ ↑arranged without↓ transform⟨ed⟩ing

Lines
10   business ↑took↓ in his own mind ⟨took⟩
11   & yet ⟨remained still the⟩ without misrepresentation
13   usefulness. That
15   & ⟨en⟩force the facts into a conformity ↑thereto↓,
25–28   ↑But almost the uniform tendency of ↑men of thot coupled with↓ ardent temper . . . lean so strongly to establishments?↓

Page 191

1–2   Books poems, ⟨music⟩ ↑the drama↓,
6   renowned ⟨chival⟩ ⟨orders⟩ laws of his country,
13   Moreover ⟨his⟩ not the least
16   no man could ⟨meet him⟩ ↑talk with him↓
18–19   never contained ↑more brilliant circles↓ better society than at that moment. / [one leaf missing, probably blank]
20–21   which would ⟨bind⟩ ↑engage↓ him
21–22   attachments. ⟨His heart was⟩ Solitary thinkers
22–23   avoided may ⟨easily⟩ come to reckon their ⟨U⟩
26   complacency, ⟨esteem the⟩ set
27–34   affections. ↑He was happy in his domestic relations↓ ² {He dearly loved children he . . . miniature he . . . a baby coach} ¹ {and so entire . . . under his own roof.}

Page 192

1–2   genius to carry
7   turned out ⟨in⟩ to feed
10–11   he ⟨hugged⟩ put his arms round
19–20   own house introduced
20–21   With ↑the aid of↓ William Bourke
21–22   Italy ↑for his professional studies↓ &
23   letters ↑of advice↓ which
25   Hickey an Irish sculptor to
30–31   in vain he had
34   in a week that

Page 193

6–10   converse with him. ⟨Mr. Burke after an interview established him under his own roof introduced him to Fox Johnson & Reynolds   His Village & Library were published from hence & he was thro' Mr. B.'s means appointed Chaplain to the Duke of Rutland⟩. He entered the apartment, says . . . unquestionable." [written over the same in pencil]
11   own roof introduced
17   open to the ⟨friend. It is known that one night⟩
21   opportunity ⟨for⟩ occurred
22   I delight I delight

Lines
26   relieves ↑secret↓ distress
30–31   countrymen, ↑naturally↓ ⟨&⟩ inclined
32–33   the remark ↑made to me by↓ ⟨of⟩ an
33–34   Establishments. That
35   woman so Burke

Page 194

2–4   might have withheld.
    ⟨But I quote these facts with a double purpose first to show the
    affectionate childlike sweetness of this man's temper which
    ⟨inclined him to take pleasant views⟩ which endeared to him
    his friends, his neighbors, his countrymen, & ⟨bent⟩ ↑inclined↓
    him to ↑take↓ favorable views of ⟨all surrounding⟩ home, of the
    laws & the country ⟨and further in showing the elevation⟩ ↑and
    then to show further↓ invariable⟩ ↑Meantime it was the natural
    effect of the same↓ elevation of his sentiments ⟨to show⟩
4   conservative. ⟨but⟩ ⟨b⟩Believing
6   ↑within this boundary↓
7–8   redresser of wrong /
    ⟨His own fortune was small & he needed a strict economy to
    live as his habits of society required   Yet always was his
    house open to the friendless & poor. It is known that one night
    he was accosted by a wretched female in the streets ⟨with⟩
    ↑of↓ whom he inquired her history & upon her promises of
    penitence he brought her to his house keeper & retained her
    under his care until an opportunity occurred of providing for
    her permanent employment, & this woman was saved. I de-
    light I delight in contemplating these facts in the ↑obscure
    private↓ history of a man who in broad daylight was the won-
    der & the light of senates & the avenger of the wrongs of
    America & Asia & Europe. He whose heart feels & whose hand
    relieves secret distress has a right to shed tears & cause others
    to shed tears in public for the griefs of millions⟩ The British
    House of Commons
12–36   ↑I cannot resist the temptation . . . of the profligate & fero-
    cious."
      Bill for Repg ye Marriage Act↓   [on separate sheet]
12–14   ↑I cannot resist . . . position in ye state↓ [inserted in pen-
    cil]
30   God forbid. God f. my part
35   which a few ⟨joined⟩ ↑united↓ in a good cause

Page 195

2   his great ⟨& successful⟩ exertions
3   ⟨On a⟩ A proposition
5   found ⟨an⟩ its own

Lines

6   maintain her ⟨opinion⟩ views

8   never ceased to ⟨ring⟩ fill

14   all these on all

14–15   as if ⟨it⟩ each

17   He had ⟨in⟩ in

27   For the cause for

29–30   Such were the traits ⟨in his mind which determined⟩ swayed his mind ↑originally & habitually↓

32   his philosophy the almost

Page 196

4   prediction ⟨but⟩ ↑until↓ day

5   fulfilled them. ⟨This classic scholar⟩ this ↑abstract↓ metaphysician

5–6   oracle of the house upon ⟨all⟩ the

11   every ⟨question⟩ business became a ⟨topic⟩ ↑text↓

14   lesson though

21   secret information and

23   hostile party & ↑did↓ more

24   French themselves ⟨he⟩ to destroy

26   partisan. How

Page 197

13   to honor all idea of what it is will be

17–26   ↑And always let it be remembered . . . I will call to mind this↓/ [jotted hastily on a smaller leaf and loosely inserted here, with lacunae as noted in the text; no punctuation except the "!"]

27–28   ↑It is necessary to speak of↓ The great . . . available the eloquence

28–29   Some one ⟨said to⟩ ↑asked↓ Johnson

32–33   facts themselves ↑to which he spoke↓

33   At ⟨sch⟩ college

Page 198

9   tuneableness of their voice⟨s⟩

11   Burke whose voice

12   but forcible, & who ⟨threw⟩ gave

14   the ↑occasional↓ caprice

17   one of his ⟨prodigious⟩ speeches

19–20   And ⟨the Marquis of⟩ ↑Warren↓ Hastings attest⟨s⟩ed ↑by a [?] similar confession↓ the ⟨prodigious⟩ force of Burkes

21   Debi Sing ↑by↓ whom

22   having been bribed ⟨to appoint in⟩

26   horror & ⟨abomination⟩ ↑indignation↓

Lines
27   ⟨And⟩ I ⟨suppose⟩ think that the evidence
28–31   when he did ⟨fill up⟩ ⟨fulfil⟩ ↑embody↓ the idea of eloquence
        when he did fill the ear & heart ² & mind ¹ of his ↑hearers↓
        audience

Page 199

1   as he used, ⟨it was⟩ ↑then was shown↓
2   Demosthenes or of any ⟨speaker⟩ ↑civil orator↓
3   But I ⟨have no⟩ confess I see
19–20   ⟨There are⟩ ↑We may distinguish↓ three kinds of eloquence.
        ⟨one is⟩ ↑The first↓ what
21   chiefly in a certain felicities of voice & manner. ⟨&⟩ ⟨t⟩There
24–25   every body is ⟨at once⟩ instantaneously
26–27   mind no ⟨grounds of⟩ arguments have . . . facts shown and
28–29   excitement ⟨he can only⟩ ↑and↓ vent↑ing↓ himself in superla-
        tives, ⟨but⟩ ↑he↓
33–36   often called eloquence that ⟨effective⟩ ⟨exclusive⟩ ⟨business
        speaking which leaving everything but the narrowest view of
        the matter in debate⟩ ↑that of the man who takes what ⟨is
        called⟩ ↑he calls↓ the practical view that . . . considerations
        as remote↓ exhibits

Page 200

3–5   oratory. ⟨He⟩There ↑is still another ⟨class⟩sort . . . aims to↓
        elevate⟨d⟩ ⟨his⟩ the
5   pitch; ⟨He took⟩ ↑which takes↓ of it a ⟨grand⟩ manly
6–7   strives to put the ⟨questions⟩ subject
10   presented which
11–12   in accordance{⟨with⟩ the improvements of science & with} the
        immense
14–15   eloquence ↑whose traces . . . American Senates↓
17   without ⟨effect⟩ proportionate effect
18–19   ↑Men have more heart than mind↓
19   excellence ↑stands ⟨is⟩ in their way.↓
22   reaped ⟨the⟩ laurels
27   word ⟨r⟩Rhetoric
28   called a ⟨finished⟩ ↑consummate↓ Rhetorician being
29   painter ⟨in⟩ with words ⟨of consummate skill⟩
33   ⟨It⟩ ↑Grace is↓ natural to him ⟨is grace⟩ ⟨that he is incapable
        of an inelegance⟩ like the
33–34   and as ⟨a⟩ ↑some↓ countenances ↑are↓ so
34–35   distortion ⟨not even making faces⟩ ↑of making mouths↓

Page 201

3,3n   Burke bestowed. Howard . . . Fox
7–8   country will be ⟨for⟩ by most conceded. ⟨I confess⟩ ⟨I believe⟩
        ↑No doubt↓ he was

Lines

9–10	America ⟨the⟩ America was empty
10–11	right no establishments
14	uprooted ⟨in such a manner⟩ ↑with such ferocity in France↓
20	goodness endeavored
27–28	He was content so great

[On blank page at the end of the lecture:] Burkes voice was a sort of lofty cry

IV. ENGLISH LITERATURE

1(A). ON THE BEST MODE OF INSPIRING A CORRECT TASTE IN ENGLISH LITERATURE

[The following is on a half-size sheet folded in two and sewn in with the lecture to precede page 1:]

⟨Whilst the order of God is yt one man shall be a scholar & one a farmer it is also true that⟩ ↑So much delight arises from the intellectual powers & of so pure a nature↓ ⟨e⟩Every man is in a ↑has some tendencies to literature & some cultivation↓ degree a literary man, inasmuch as he is a man or possesses the intellectual powers. He is in the practice of ⟨these⟩ compositions purely intellectual when ever his conversation departs from the straight line of business into the region of wit or fancy or history or sentiment & is so far a competitor with the poet & the man of letters. Whenever he pursues truth as an end wh. is ye object of some conversation I hope every where & even now he is pursuing the end of these writers

And the Newspaper with its poetry in its northwest corner and its notices of new books and its [sic] is a certain proof of the existence of such tastes in the crowd if every album & circulating library & popular literary magazine did not show the same thing

I say then that every man as far as he is a man is capable of being addressed as an intellectual being is to some extent a scholar. The sailor has his song & his Robinson Crusoe & bible and every house in this city a closet or a shelf of books or a book upon the shelf.

At the same time it is no less evident that in most men this taste is secondary or exists in the lowest degree ⟨being almost⟩ the ⟨[?]⟩ active powers of the man being ⟨monopolized by⟩ usurped by quite other tastes & desires. Whilst a few persons are born with eminent fitness for study & unfitness for all else

I believe these distinctions are drawn by nature & therefore are not to be erased. Nature who works in infinite time can alone bring either the scholar or the ⟨h⟩Craftsman into the perfect communication of gifts   That shall be in a purer state of sensation & existence./

466

Page 210

Lines	
1–2	confidence in the ⟨accumulating⟩ ↑⟨efficiency⟩↓ ↑application↓
3	Physicians of the world cannot ⟨make⟩ ↑manufacture↓
4–5	↑nor the best library a reader↓.
6	& so ⟨martial⟩ ↑warlike↓
7	voice of th⟨e[?]⟩eir ⟨Muses⟩ ↑wise men↓
7–8	any ⟨tricks⟩ ↑expedients↓
8–9	Nor when ⟨individuals show a turn of mind wholly⟩ a boy↑s mind↓ is wholly ⟨absorbed⟩ ↑given↓ ⟨in⟩ to ⟨a⟩ horses or ⟨in⟩ to trade or ⟨in⟩ to sailing
11	Eng. Poets nor ⟨talk⟩ ↑reason↓ with the North West Wind.
17–18	class to ⟨be⟩ eminent in the other but the ⟨spell⟩ ↑⟨wand⟩↓ ⟨that works⟩ ↑rod of↓ th⟨is⟩ese enchantment↑s↓ ↑metamorphosis↓
19	our ⟨action⟩ interefence [sic]
23–24	⟨Admitting this Canon also⟩ ↑⟨also⟩↓ ↑Admitting this fact which . . . canon of philosophy↓ that a ⟨s⟩ truth

Page 211

1–3	forth ⟨there remain only⟩ ↑society divides itself into↓ two classes ⟨on which we can ⟨aim⟩ ↑expect↓ to work with any hope of fruit⟩ ↑in reference to any influences of learning↓
	1. on the ⟨potential⟩ ↑natural↓ scholars ⟨in other words those who are scholars by nature⟩ tho' now
5	2. on the much larger
7	importance those who
9	men of letters
	1 On the life of the scholar & ⟨say rather⟩ 2 On the leisure of the whole community.
11	classes. ⟨Eve⟩ In bringing
16–17	content ⟨ourselves⟩ ↑us↓
19–20	the ⟨only⟩ one great means
20–21	bringing the ⟨person⟩ ↑man↓ into acquaintance with the ⟨authors⟩ ↑books↓.
23–24	offices ↑in the opportunities of common life↓ ⟨we can show⟩
24–25	to the ⟨work⟩ ↑writings↓
25–26	⟨But⟩ ↑It must be ⟨this is⟩ our main object to consummate↓
27	author. ⟨must be consummated⟩ ⟨There is no alternative⟩ Literature resembles
31–32	our ↑only↓ proper aim to . . . Mother tongue
33	who by ⟨education⟩ ↑position↓
35	The Instructor shd. consider
	1. That by being

Page 212

3	I ⟨wish⟩ think the first
4–5	would be ⟨p[?]⟩to impress

Lines
6   unknown to them that
7   books ⟨lik[?]⟩ swarm like ⟨flights of musquitoes⟩ ↑flies↓
9–13   ↑It cannot be doubted that they are little known   What sig-
nifies [?]   The farmer in winter kitchen the maid in her
chamber that . . . literature are ye . . . worth all study
[?]↓ /
⟨2 Meantime no man teach more than he knows or inspire a
taste he has not himself⟩
⟨⟨It will fortify him in his tastes & in his teaching to the young
with whom authority always goes far to meditate on the fact
that there is no luck in literary reputation that only the great
minds of a nation survive their century⟩⟩ /
14–27   It will fortify . . . constant mind of man. [on a separate leaf
sewn into the lecture between the sheet ending "library by
itself. But the" and the sheet beginning "great facts are soon
mastered" (see below, p. 213). Its intended position is conjectural, but see the cancelled passage above]
14   ↑A↓ {It will fortify him
16   reputation. to observe
20–21   ↑Blackmore Pollok Bulwer may endure for a night but Homer
& ⟨Milton [?]⟩ ↑Moses↓ last forever.↓
23–24   yet ⟨always⟩ ↑to every generation↓
25   sterling books their
26–27   or the ⟨actual⟩ intrinsic importance
27   constant mind of man.}
28   ⟨3 Let him then⟩ ↑The Teacher may well↓ reflect
30–32   treasures these let him ⟨lear⟩ mark learn . . . voice of Human Nature
32–33   sweet in ⟨his⟩ ↑the↓ mouth and sweet in ⟨his⟩ ↑the↓
34–35   the ⟨great⟩ crowd of mediocre writers. ↑Multum non multa
Aphorism of Aquinas↓

Page 213

3–4   4. Let him consider . . . discipline an object
4–6   Dr Johnson said "⟨Do not consider too carefully what ⟨your⟩
book your boy shall read first.⟩ Whilst ⟨he⟩ ↑you↓ stand⟨s⟩
deliberating ↑which . . . first↓
6   Read anything, ⟨no matter what⟩,
9   Hookers Ecclesiastical ⟨History⟩ ↑Polity↓
10   how ↑few↓ many months
11   great ↑British↓ authors.
17–18   library ↑by↓ itself. But the / [inserted leaf; see above under
p. 212, line 14]
18–21   mastered. ⟨The life of Charles V & his contemporaries is the
Eye of⟩ The feudal . . . Eye of modern times.
22   I only ⟨say in general⟩ ↑venture the opinion↓
23   better than ⟨much⟩ ↑wide↓ reading.

Lines
24–25   few names Chaucer . . . Taylor are a class
32–(*214*)1   Newspaper shun . . . of the day for

Page 214

4   ⟨I asked a good scholar how he w⟩Would ↑you↓ inspire
5–7   ⟨He replied "I would q⟩Quote them to him." Fear not to ↑to
               be like him who↓ carr⟨y⟩ied a ⟨brick to show the⟩ ↑tile as a
               sample of his↓ palace; for the ⟨analogy⟩ ↑parallel↓ does not
               hold unless the tile which ⟨Scholasticus had⟩ ↑the clown↓
               carried
10   like ⟨carrying⟩ ↑offering↓ a lump
13   not as a ↑faultfinder↓ critic
16–29   No wise man thinks meanly . . . & Bacon in the best man-
               ner. [on a separate leaf sewn into the lecture between the
               sheet ending "Let the power of his author to impart instruc-
               tion" and the sheet beginning "and raise happiness be the
               measure of his ability" (see below, p. 215). Its intended posi-
               tion is conjectural]
16   ⟨None but⟩ No wise man
17   Time are the ⟨best[?]⟩ benefactors or the ⟨most formidable
               foes⟩ ↑enemies of mankind↓.
19–21   They rend ⟨empires⟩ & they establish empires. /// [E] ⟨It
               passes by thousands & thousands & finds⟩ ⟨It⟩ ↑A good book↓
24   ⟨As⟩ ⟨Therefore is⟩ a good reader ↑is↓ rare.
28   Shakspear it needs a Bacon to

Page 215

4–5   then ⟨an⟩ just judgments of them of their style & method will
5–7   ⟨All the⟩ ⟨Accustom the pupil to love or slight his Author as
               these conditions of instruction⟩ ↑Let the power of his Author
               to↓ impart⟨ing⟩ instruction / [inserted leaf; see above under
               p. 214, line 16] & raising happiness ⟨are complied with or
               not.⟩ ↑be the measure of his ability↓
12–14   conventional in letters something . . . good thoughts.
17–18   coast. that . . . words that
22–23   find ⟨a true⟩ one in the obscurity
24   us, ⟨as⟩ I have already stated
26   is ⟨the want of⟩ cheap editions
27   best authors. Bacon

Page 216

3   & [blotted] ⟨that⟩ we have no effective
4–9   attempted as . . . of etiquette. [no commas] It would ⟨make⟩
               add happy
10   colleges ⟨takes⟩ bereaves

469

Lines

11   literary associates. / [The cancelled draft of a letter appears upside down at the bottom of this page:]

         Concord, Mass. 11 Aug. 1835.

My dear sir,

     ⟨I have the pleasure of introducing to your acquaintance two of my friends David L Child Esq of Boston & his lady.⟩

12   to the ⟨case of⟩ single view of

21–22   & if the ⟨cultivation⟩ study even

25–26   ⟨A⟩ ↑There have been as we know↓ periods of intense activity of the ⟨leading⟩ mind⟨s⟩ The

26–27   all. The causes which A ⟨great⟩ principle

[Upside down on the verso of the last (otherwise blank) leaf appears this cancelled draft of a letter:]

         ⟨Concord Mass 11 August 1835⟩

⟨My dear Sir,

     This letter will be presented you by my friend Mrs Child of Boston⟩

1. INTRODUCTORY

Page 217

1–2   undertake ⟨a⟩ to present ⟨a⟩ ↑in this↓ course

3   ↑There is no Hist. of Eng Lit.↓ ↑Perhaps↓ Few men

4   such an ⟨undertaking⟩ ↑enterprize↓

5   discipline ↑in books↓

6   I am not. ⟨I have⟩ ⟨At the request of the Society I have endeavored to prepare a Course of lectures on topics connected with Eng.⟩ I have not ⟨even⟩

8   understand the ⟨place⟩ true place

Page 218

1   or ⟨the⟩ know the ⟨idea⟩ ↑master thought↓

2–3   I have ⟨promised⟩ ↑attempted↓

5–6   interest which ⟨all⟩ human nature

9–10   derived from ↑letters↓ . . . ciphers the . . . Cadmus by

12   delicate ⟨verses⟩ song ⟨of⟩ ↑with which↓ an ⟨Hebrew⟩

12–13   an hour thirty- ↑5↓ centuries

15   word ↑Literature↓ has

17   written. ⟨it is the public depository of the thoughts of the human race⟩

21–23   line, but ⟨it⟩ ↑every form of composition the . . . ejaculation↓ is holden

24–25   laws. A man ⟨is capable of thought⟩ ↑thinks↓. ⟨This is the largest admission of the superficial.⟩ ↑⟨The most superficial admit this fact⟩↓ ⟨But they who deal strictly with the facts

Lines	
	of his nature, see that he is) ↑⟨But⟩ he↓ not only ⟨so⟩ ↑thinks,↓ but ⟨that⟩ he lives on thoughts; ⟨that⟩ he is
25	thoughts; ⟨that⟩ ideas,
26	rejects, ⟨do⟩ tyrannize
28–29	these ⟨the fiercest purpose struggles in vain⟩ ↑no purpose can prosper or so much as be formed.↓ ⟨All r⟩Rebellion
31	ideas of God, ↑Order↓ freedom.
32	matter. ⟨I suppose⟩ it will

Page 219

2	into his ⟨very⟩ dreams,
3–5	& a shade. (⟨I may have occasion by & by to define accurately an Idea, & show the distinction between Ideas & Notions, but⟩ ↑Without going . . . Ideas & notions↓ it is sufficient ⟨for my present purpose⟩ to allude
5–6	Love, ⟨to establish the positi⟩ ↑that I may intimate ye fact↓ that certain
7	his being, are the ⟨law⟩ ↑⟨forces⟩↓ ↑powers↓ whose
11	⟨I say that⟩ the Ideas in every man's mind ⟨are that⟩ ↑⟨they⟩↓ ⟨which⟩ make⟨s⟩ him what
17	whole life is ⟨the⟩ spent
18	create ⟨a⟩outside
19–20	& every ⟨prejudice⟩ ↑error↓ — each a thought
20	societies, ⟨citie⟩ houses,
21–22	language, ⟨events⟩ ceremonies ↑newspapers↓. ⟨You⟩ Observe the Ideas of the ⟨time⟩ ↑present day↓, —
27	many persons. {Insert X} [This insert is lost or copied into the later text.]
28	⟨Whilst thus in⟩ ↑Of the↓ various ways ↑in wh.↓ man
29	invisible ⟨spiritual⟩ nature
29	perfect ⟨of all expressio⟩ vehicle⟨s⟩

Page 220

6	& more skilful. / ⟨Everywhere we find man surrounded by the same company, that is, by what he calls Nature; ↑He dwells with the multitude of his fellows, or alone in the misty fields over him are↓ the sun & moon; ↑at his feet↓ the sea; ↑around him are↓ the mountains. the atmosphere embraces him in its soft arms; the stars shine on him with harmless light; beasts, fire, water, stones & corn serve him. ⟨With his fellows he builds towns, &⟩ by continually dealing with these mute & brute natures, he learns to make them ↑⟨ma⟩↓ more useful. ⟨In this friendly company the little stranger finds himself every day more at home & skilful⟩ Many of the great objects of nature he ⟨cannot for weakness⟩ ↑is so weak he cannot↓ use, ⟨& cannot⟩

Lines

↑nor↓ explore. But in their friendly company the little stranger finds himself every day more at home, & skilful.〉

9   mind as 〈keys〉 ↑vehicles↓ & symbols

12–13   language for the ↑beings &↓ changes 〈& objects〉 of

18   *eyebrow.* [marginal note:] consider   ponder   conceive

19–20   wisdom & love. ↑We say↓ The heart 〈is used for feeling〉 ↑to express emotion;↓ the head 〈is used for〉 ↑to denote↓ thought: 〈"And but for these emblems furnished by Nature herself the moral & metaphysical world would have remained entirely buried in the eternal abyss."〉 And "thought" & 〈feeling〉 ↓"emotion"↓ are in

27   mental act.
amalgam
bench
calumet
unkennel
〈A〉 Every truth

32   words 〈expressing〉 ↑that convey↓

Page 221

1–2   learned man is a 〈light〉 torch.

12   applied to the 〈interpreta〉tion ↑illustration↓

13–14   nature 〈is beauty is poetry is truth.〉 ↑affects us . . . agreeable manner↓

17–19   converse by these 〈symbols.〉 ↑〈pictures〉↓ ↑figures. In the writers . . . such as ↑Homer↓ Froissart . . . picture.↓

21   symbols. The 〈first〉 eldest

22–23   now, in 〈the〉 our

25   in images. 〈It is remarkable that all poets orators & philosophers〉 Indeed

27–29   luminous ↑arising↓ in his mind 〈for〉 ↑with↓ ↑contemporaneous with↓ every thought, 〈which〉 furnishes

30   〈It is remarkable that〉 all poets

32–33   figure an illustration availed every sect. As

34   in the sea. 〈Plato, Luther, & Bacon〉

Page 222

2–4   ↑I see a chasm . . . of a volcano.↓

8–9   all men relish. It is the 〈salt〉 of those

9–10   understanding who

11   way ↑of↓ seeing things,

16–17   imagery ↑in↓ which

17   are presented.
〈Fisher Ames happily said — contrasting our form of govt with those of Europe — that a Monarchy was a good ship & sailed well but it was liable to strike a rock & be wrecked.

Lines

A republic, on the other hand, was a raft: it could not go to the bottom, but then your feet were always in water.) [written over the same in pencil:] Fisher Ames said that [etc.]

18–(*223*)31 Examples might be . . . shear the wolf. [All this was crowded onto one ms. page as Emerson thought of additional examples. Quotations added last are indicated below. Except for omission marks and final stops, and the colon in the Milton, the pointing (or lack of it) in these quotations is Emerson's.]

18–19 produced to any ⟨amount⟩ ↑⟨number⟩↓ ↑extent↓ to show this ⟨ima[?]⟩ habit of mind in ⟨Homer in Shakspear in Milton &⟩ the great

19–20 will suffice Homer

22–23 his arms ⟨resounded⟩ ↑crashed↓ over him.

28 grace & rude will
⟨And where ye worser is predominant
Full soon ye canker death eats up ye plant⟩

Page 223

4–9 ↑How like a younker . . . rent & beggared↓

10 ↑Milton gives . . . of a state↓

12–13 (the laws) methinks

21–24 ↑Hope & fear alternate . . . eclipse ye sun.
Douglas↓

25–28 ↑Not she: ⟨it is [?]⟩ she tempts me not: ⟨but⟩ ↑tis↓ I
Who lying ⟨like⟩ by ye . . . virtuous season↓

29 ⟨When⟩ Mr Burke

Page 224

2–24 ↑Especially is it the office . . . casteth her untimely fruits↓

15 outraged appeals

26–27 from ↑the Egyptians &↓

30 fortune ⟨to⟩ at

31 if ↑such↓ the earth shall ↑ever↓ see, ⟨such,⟩

Page 225

5 In a ⟨high⟩ ↑limited↓ sense   Literature so far

7 things of matter. /
⟨All reflexion goes to teach us the strictly emblematic character of the material world   It will be the united effect of the progress of science & the progress of virtue to open the primitive sense of the permanent objects of nature that so all which the eye sees may be to the mind that legible book in which every form, alone or in composition, shall be significant.
Man stands on the point betwixt spirit & matter, the

Lines

native of both elements. The true thinker sees that one represents the other, that the world is the mirror of the soul
& it is his office to show this beautiful relation, to utter the
oracles of the mind in appropriate images from nature. Literature celebrates the marriage of Nature & the Mind. Thereby
is Man as Bacon said the priest of the earth & the Interpreter
of Nature.⟩

8–10   ↑I have said . . . And for History,↓ ⟨But⟩ if

15–18   History. ↑in the belief . . . the seemingly ⟨arbitrary⟩ capricious . . . in long periods.↓

29   the great ⟨theatre of Nature on which we now play visibly so
transient a part⟩ ↑Universe ⟨All⟩ which ⟨has borne⟩ ↑⟨yields⟩↓
↑bears↓ us as its fruit↓

32   rounded in [in margin:] p. 73

32–33   so as to ⟨produce⟩ fetch about . . . whole of nature peaceful

35–36   Over men the ⟨[?] of earth⟩ ↑purposes of Providence↓ are
thrown ⟨only as immense[?]⟩ ↑like enormous↓ nets

Page 226

1–2   human mind ⟨utters⟩ endeavors evermore to ⟨utter⟩ ↑compose↓
its⟨elf⟩ ↑commentary upon events↓

3   to record ⟨events⟩ ↑facts↓ &

6   unfold it. to . . . of the world. / [two pages missing in the
ms.; probably blank]

7   ⟨We ha⟩ Such is ⟨the⟩ in . . . the Nature

7–8   Literature.
⟨Let us now consider ⟨in what manner⟩ what service is rendered us by the Thinker or man of letters & in what manner.
Important questions arise concerning the⟩ ↑What↓ interest
⟨that all men⟩ have ↑men↓ in it?

10–11   work? ⟨Let us consider⟩ what service . . . what manner.

17   appear. ↑But there it is.↓

18–19   philosopher. ⟨It⟩ ↑To perceive it,↓ is to

24   Thinker ⟨awakens their attention⟩ takes

26–27   defacer of ⟨all⟩ beauty . . . of ⟨all⟩ truth

29–30   sense appear ⟨visionary⟩ ↑⟨fluxional⟩ fluent↓.
⟨There are very familiar illustrations of this fact in every man's
experience.⟩ Even a small

31–32   curtain ↑of Custom. Thought . . . unusual sky.↓

Page 227

1–2   talking ⟨earnestly⟩ ↑running,↓ bartering,

3   at once, or at least / [The next leaf is missing. The paragraph
is completed as it was printed in *Nature* (*W*, I, 50–51).]

23   Superior rais⟨ing⟩ed

32   before them; ⟨⟨and ruled this element like a master;⟩⟩

Page 228

Lines	
2	his friend ↑the late↓ Mr Coleridge,
3	↑one day at Stowey↓
4	↑upon his philosophical doctrines,↓
7–8	every thing ⟨from an⟩ ↑as it↓ absolutely
12–13	same spirit in which he wrote. / ⟨The poet writes in the faith that all men are poets, though in a less degree. To please, he must be read in the same spirit in which he wrote.⟩
15	one man but ⟨share⟩ a state
16–17	The cruel ² & proud ¹ distinction
19	invent ⟨or⟩ ↑nor↓ understand." ⟨A truer⟩ The
21	class which ⟨not only perceives but⟩ embodies
22	senses that ⟨they do⟩ though
26	but can ⟨body forth⟩ ↑cast↓ truths
28	ever wondrous Spirit [new line] Chosen
28–30	↑streamlets from↓ the infinite ⟨truth⟩ ↑abyss of thought↓ . . . use of men! Seers
30–31	truths which ⟨then⟩ shine . . . & never set. Men
33–(229)2	who ⟨turn⟩ ↑give↓ the most . . . principle; ↑These are the men with whose ⟨ef⟩ endeavors . . . have little leisure↓

Page 229

3	↑the word↓ Literature
4–5	practical It is thought to be the ⟨interest⟩ harmless
6–7	↑But the great . . . his wisdom.↓ ⟨But⟩ these
8	nothing but ⟨that which⟩ ↑what↓ grinds
13–14	seen is ⟨beautiful⟩ ↑related to the . . . of the whole.↓
18–19	the waters. Shall . . . drops. It
22	as a ⟨solemn⟩ ↑sacred↓ gift
24–25	↑Aristotle . . . heard their names↓
25	day laborer ⟨th⟩ has
31	A ⟨more⟩ generous mind
35	tight. But ⟨it runs⟩ once bro't

Page 230

2	wit of ↑one & another↓ sagacious m⟨e⟩an
4	proverbs, or ⟨verses⟩ maxims,
5	unlettered ⟨in the Church or⟩ in the Caucus,
6	in the ↑Almanack, or↓ newspaper.
11–12	circulation among us. / [at the bottom of this page, the end of a sheet, upside down:] Concord 1835
13	⟨Always⟩ the influence of great minds is ↑always↓
14	Nature ⟨around us⟩ dilates
17–18	that the cru⟨i⟩se of truth
18	oil; then ⟨comes by⟩ ↑we come to↓

Lines
21   Even ↑of↓ those numerous
24   dialogue, ⟨the general influence⟩, if there
25–26   Drama the Robbers . . . moral was bad. that
30   pitch. ↑& this is their sufficient defence↓ /
            ⟨In the confidence ⟨that⟩ of the correctness of these views
            we presume to ask the attention of the Society to some con-
            tinuous examination of the great English writers. ⟨In the
            belief that thought is the highest interest of man⟩⟩ The English
34–35   end to ⟨represent⟩ ↑analyze↓ not its ⟨verbal or conventional⟩
            ↑value to critics or to libraries↓

Page 231

1   of ↑works↓ books &
1   its fruit. ⟨We must aim at much to⟩ be sure of some.
2   ↑But I must . . . threshold↓
6   help us ⟨We must⟩ There
12–13   you would ⟨know⟩ ↑study↓
16   The⟨se⟩ solemn powers
18   yield no ⟨solution⟩ ↑answer↓
19–20   known by ⟨calm⟩ ascending
22   Moreover ⟨it⟩ ↑a superficial inquiry↓
27   lost every ⟨da⟩ age
27   particles have ⟨been⟩ dropt
29   ↑of its elder ages↓

Page 232

2   belief ⟨that these words were the bright thunderbolts of truth⟩
            that the office
2–3   the future not follow the past that these words ↑wh they
            launched↓
4   of truth ⟨which the true scholar launches & which⟩ whose
            light
6   honor & ⟨love⟩ in a spirit

2. PERMANENT TRAITS OF THE ENGLISH NATIONAL GENIUS

Page 233

6   grow in ⟨our⟩ the temperate
7   two feet high in the torrid
8   genius ⟨have⟩ both good
9   have, in ⟨this countr⟩ ⟨the freedom of this country⟩ ↑the greater
            freedom of our institutions↓
10   freedom⟨,⟩? we more;

Page 234

Lines

2–4   traits of the National genius /
↑Sketches of English history with a view to exhibit some of the permanent traits of the national Genius.↓
⟨The subject of this Lecture is the Genius of the English nation.⟩ That natural curiosity

8   part History is not ⟨written⟩ ↑drawn↓ from sufficiently deep ⟨foundations⟩ ↑sources↓.

9   in a ⟨deep⟩ ↑settled↓ conviction

13–15   ⟨It is very remarkable how⟩ ↑This remark is forced upon us by even a slight study of the↓ unchangable ⟨are the⟩ features of National genius. ⟨almost as much so⟩ ↑The traits of national character are almost as permanent↓

20   Tacitus ↑1800 years ago;↓

25   genius quick

30   acute at an argument." / ⟨I spoke in my last lecture of the value of Literature as it is ⟨the history of thought⟩ the record of the rise power prevalence & ⟨disappearance⟩ ↑succession↓ of Ideas. ⟨We ought to of⟩ History is read carelessly as a Chronicle of unconnected events. If ⟨we will⟩ instead of reading passively, ↑if we↓ read actively, ↑&↓ conspire with our teacher, we may find its pages full of cheerful wisdom. Thus it is very remarkable how permanent are ⟨nationa⟩ the features of national character. The English ⟨& Germans⟩ of the present day bear deeply engraven on their character the marks ↑by↓ which ⟨T the ancient Romans described in⟩ their ancestors are described by Caesar & Tacitus ↑yt they were blue eyed men lovers of liberty yielding more to authority yn to ⟨force⟩ command, & respecting ye female sex↓. The Scots bear at this day a strong likeness to the portrait sketched of them by ⟨Scaliger (?)⟩ Servetus 3 centuries ago {Insert A} ["A" missing] that they were fervid, ↑fond of dialectics↓ acute at a metaphysical argument, and that every one believed himself descended from a royal or noble family.⟩

31–32   French nation at least as ⟨the English⟩ ↑their enemies↓

34–(235)4   frangere. ↑It is common . . . laugh at it.↓ ⟨Gens Francorum infidelis est. Si perjuret Francus quid novi faciet qui perjurium ipsum sermonis genus putat, non esse criminis.⟩ ↑The race of Franks . . . not a crime↓ (Salvian) ↑The Franks . . . hospitable↓

Page 235

5   crime of deceit

6–7   & Germans. ↑and even by the French themselves.↓
⟨In like⟩
⟨In like manner the Ancient Cimmerians from whom the Irish

Lines

descend were distinguished by superstition by the immoveable establishment of castes & their ⟨ar⟩ by the singular custom of subterranean architecture. Who sees the different mode in which an English & an Irish peasant at this day go to work in building a house will be ⟨reminded of the⟩ find some hint of the Cimmerian architecture in the manner in which the Irishman will construct his shanty⟩ / [upside down at bottom of sheet:] Concord

11 ago it ⟨is⟩ ↑was↓ remarked ⟨by⟩ ↑in↓

12–14 ²{It has preserved its relative superiority ¹{in the immense enlargement of the domestic ⟨resources⟩ ↑wealth↓ of the European nations to this day. ⟨It has worked hard ever since & like other capitalists growing old has grown rich.⟩ It has ⟨attained⟩ ↑reached↓

15 It ⟨has⟩ contains

18–23 drawingroom, with ⟨whatever⟩ ↑every utensil↓ of wise economy ⟨they have⟩. ↑Its science is now . . . of the tides of ye . . . annual & secular.↓ ⟨Its sciences; behold its watchtower at Greenwich is the Calendar of the world.⟩

24 time is measured by

26 weighing ⟨earths⟩ ↑airs↓ & decompounding ⟨gases⟩ ↑earths↓;

27–28 gas of all ↑its↓ mixtures its inland country is ⟨not less beautiful than its shops are useful.⟩ ↑a garden↓ Its dwellinghouses are ⟨proverbs⟩ ↑models↓

29 piles which ⟨ancient piety or chivalry⟩

30 defence or for ⟨piety⟩ ↑religion,↓

34 inquire for ⟨the⟩ ↑great↓ men.

35–(236)1 poetry not . . . without its ⟨tradition⟩ ↑legend.↓

Page 236

2–3 men, so ⟨is⟩ ↑has↓ England ⟨more⟩ ↑as many↓ historical names ↑as↓ than living citizens.

5 Law where

6 analysed ⟨& weighed⟩ & applied ⟨to⟩

7 It is a ⟨free⟩ nation

9–10 universally diffused ⟨It is ⟨thus⟩ from this cause the Public of Europe. Its stormy ↑& warlike↓ Press is the advocate of every ⟨downtrodden⟩ ↑unproved↓ opinion & ↑injured↓ party in Europe as in the islands⟩ ⟨Its speedy ships⟩ Great & beautiful

11–12 least part. ↑Its domestic ⟨relations⟩ bear no proportion to its foreign relations.↓

14 West. ⟨⟨By the sea as by a ring the nations are married.⟩⟩

16 sea & land. ⟨Two thirds of the longitude of the globe⟩ From point to

17–18 her ↑military & naval↓ stations, so that it is ⟨well known⟩ ↑her proverb↓ that ⟨her f⟩ the sun

478

Lines
20–21   men buy ⟨of⟩ her ⟨wares⟩ ↑goods↓. ↑This is more remarkable
         as↓ England ⟨mighty as it is⟩ has
22   wealth. ⟨but is what it is by cultivation⟩ The island
23–24   Labor ⟨is sits on⟩ ↑drudges in↓ his iron ⟨throne⟩ ↑apron↓
26–28   Its furnaces . . . for mankind. [no punctuation]
29   liquors, ⟨&⟩ wear
31   greater the ⟨legislation⟩ ↑political action↓
33–34   leading nation. ⟨Their enterprizes of science, of discovery, &
         their philanthropic policy have more than supplied the best
         legislation of the ancient Roman empire.⟩ Its freedom

Page 237

3–4   ↑If we inquire . . . we learn that↓
5   descended with ⟨wisdom⟩ ↑their↓
6   loins of ⟨th⟩ as ⟨truculent⟩ ↑abominable↓
8   ↑That part of↓ The
8–9   ↑from whom the laws & language are derived↓ when History
10–11   and ↑in↓ three small
15   Their ⟨continental⟩ territory
18–19   & ↑light or↓ red hair, as more ⟨untameable &⟩ ferocious
24   In battle ⟨they were terrific⟩ ↑was their delight↓.
25–26   sledgehammer. ↑which they . . . without pity↓
30   shallow no river too small and
33–34   had the ⟨e⟩ ↑same↓ hearty
34–35   Empire ⟨that we⟩ in which

Page 238

3–5   intestine wars. /
         ⟨And who are these wonderful people & whence did they
         spring. Though mainly of one family they are in part of a
         fourfold stock that is of British Saxon Northman & Norman
         lines. They are descended with their gentleness & craft &
         science out of the loins of the most truculent savages that
         have disgraced history.⟩
         The original ⟨Britons⟩ ↑tribe who↓ who gave name ↑of Bri-
         tain↓ to the country ↑& to the rivers & mountains↓
12–13   Druids ⟨accordingly⟩ ⟨had great superiority of knowledge as
         they⟩ monopolized learning & arts. ↑& really possessed great
         superiority of knowledge↓
14–18   ↑& its imperishable . . . of twenty years↓
19   They ↑Asiatic Cimmerians↓ dwelt
20   reverenced the ⟨mistletoe⟩ oak
21–23   fanaticism much . . . islands stained . . . skins and houses
26   few similar ⟨simple structures⟩ ↑circles↓ ⟨The⟩ A few
31–32   Be preserved . . . ↑English Germans & Flemings↓

Lines

33–34   mans Reason.
⟨The Druids were educated by a strict discipline of 20 years. Their lessons were conveyed in verses.⟩

Page 239

1   descendants the Irish
5   princes Taliessin
7   singers is ⟨the⟩ about
11   vocation as it
22–23   trust them
⟨And⟩ ↑Or↓ rank them

Page 240

9   primary bards of ⟨truth⟩ faith,
15   will be his ⟨security⟩ ↑safety↓
17   Maelgwyn of Gwynedd./ [upside down at the bottom:] Concord 86
18   preserved ⟨which⟩ after
19   desertion of his ⟨castle⟩ hold
21–22   The hall of Cyndyllan is gloomy this night
Without fire without bed

Page 241

5–7   specimens for . . . images eagles . . . slaughter that
9–13   Arthur a . . . countrymen though Saxon themselves ever since. Spenser   The old romance of Brut ⟨says⟩ sums up
12–13   Saxon themselves ever
15–17   He is described in [blank] (praeteritis . . . futuris) better . . . shall come.
17–19   ↑In all Britain . . . the foreigners↓
26   that race ⟨before the strong arms⟩ against
27–28   Cerdic ⟨established⟩ bro't it . . . computed 300,000 men into Britain ⟨established th⟩ gave it
29–30   Angles wrote their name on the ⟨counties⟩ ↑districts↓ & towns & rivers; & ⟨established⟩ ↑fixed↓
32   commonly ⟨distinguished⟩ ↑known↓ as Danes or Northmen very

Page 242

Lines

1–2   piracy alone. ⟨They are represented⟩ These . . . land without
5   remained ashore all
5–6   ↑which they called steeds of the Ocean↓
14   These ⟨madmen⟩ barbarians
15   They ⟨were⟩ kept the peace

Lines

21	countrymen. "The plant
22	country and ⟨th⟩ even
23–24	human ⟨greatness⟩ ↑power↓ seem to be
24–25	Where the ⟨mind⟩ ↑intellect↓
26–27	there is not ⟨the sam⟩ ⟨great⟩ ↑much↓ hope
28	horde ⟨combined⟩ ↑had↓ these qualities, ↑& combined them↓
29	capable but ⟨inquisitive⟩ ↑greedy↓
30–31	world always ⟨fights on the side of⟩ ↑⟨bends⟩↓ ↑bends men to↓ virtue

Page 243

1–2	pleasing ⟨in mode⟩ the conclusions
2–3	that ↑in↓ the ⟨m⟩ course of nature, the moral sense is ⟨always⟩ ↑steadily↓
7	But this was the ⟨dark⟩ ↑rugged↓ soil
8	English wit & ⟨poetry⟩ ↑humanity↓
9	forth sweetness. ⟨The Saxons ⟨as the Britons⟩ and the Northmen as well as the Britons had their bards, & the moment any thing like quiet possession of England was secured these showed themselves by a natural revolution the humanizers & civilizers of their countrymen. They branded the odious insanity of the Berserkers: and then, ⟨which was a great tho' natural advance⟩ the profession of ⟨the⟩ piracy.⟩
12–13	their position ↑out of↓ the pirate ⟨became⟩ ↑created↓
15	⟨The⟩ ⟨c⟩Commercial & agricultural
16–17	love of freedom ⟨& equality became⟩ ↑was↓ never
19–20	↑forgot their sanguinary . . . & slaughter↓
22	They ⟨branded⟩ succeeded
24	Saxon ↑historical↓ poem
26	93⟨8⟩4
31–32	every foe ⟨Por⟩ Should keep

Page 244

1	Glided over the ⟨earth⟩ ground
5	Nor was there ⟨ever⟩ a greater
22	⟨The followin⟩ I read a few lines

Page 245

27	the power of thy might. /

Page 246

17	Fowl God will be in heaven

481

Page 247

Lines
21   he himself inhabits. /

Page 248

17–18   romantic poetry. ⟨Caedmon⟩ The feud of Beowulf ⟨is⟩ a metri-
                     cal romance is
23   & so ⟨abundant in⟩ ↑encumbered with↓ paraphrasis,
24   new words as to be
24–27   Th⟨ese⟩is ↑is the figure . . . echo to the first. These↓ his-
                     torical poems
28   or sentence ⟨of⟩ more
30–32   Saxon so [?] . . . Alfred which . . . Chronicle a
32–33   from the Hengist & Horsa to ↑the reign of↓ Stephen.

Page 249

9   of these traits [no punctuation]
16   Humor, ⟨a sense of the ludicrous⟩ in a grave
18   Home & an adherence
22   all their arts. which
24–31   ↑Add to this a passion . . . take any unfair advantage.↓
25–26   The English⟨man⟩ from . . . lowest ↑among↓ citizen
29–30   & will ⟨take⟩ no more
33n   [The inserted passages differ from the original versions as
                     indicated below (page and line references are to the original
                     versions):]

Page 263

4–9   ↑Their literature is not less strongly marked than their manners.↓
                     The peculiar genius of the English mind may be recognised in the
                     earliest poems which have come down to us. The traits of that
                     genius are a homeliness a love . . . and a strong
14–15   636 years old.
29–31   The poems of Shakspear Jonson Herrick Herbert Raleigh, and much
                     more the ballads and natural songs betray a ⟨continual instinctive
                     endeavor⟩ ↑habit↓ in the poet to recover himself
31–32   and earthly things.
33   the farmyard, ⟨It seeks⟩ the highway, the market

Page 264

6–7   or to explain my meaning by a few examples   The favorite national
                     ballad of Chevy Chase is written in this coarse style
                              For Witherington I needs must moan
                                As one in doleful dumps
                              For when his legs were shotten off
                                He fought upon his stumps

482

Lines

The winter song
31   verse is so homely in the diction

Page 265

8–11   In Milton this earthy vein is less conspicuous so deeply was he in-
fected with the classic literature, yet it is apparent in him. The
whole L'Allegro is of this kind. And this is distinctively English
poetry. It is unborrowed and native. It is neither
13–14 their fancy are filled
16–17 who demand their constitutional

Page 276

5–8   Among the traits which steadily reappear as a permanent elements
of the Saxon character is that anciently called Gentillesse or the
doctrine of Gentle Behaviour. It adheres
14–15 This is a topic of so much permanent interest that it may be worth
while to dwell on the historic
15–16 narrow limitations to its present just and liberal acceptation.
20–22 reappear in the son not only has a foundation in experience but also
is the cause
23   son of a good man
31   jealousy it never² can¹ fail

Page 277

5   by kings nor ⟨by⟩ laws
11   liberal education."
Hist. of Eng. Vol I p 249
24   institutions that were esteemed its essential
29–30 most obvious ⟨mark⟩ of these
33   mark of a gentleman, another critic a voice of a certain tone to be
the best ⟨sign⟩ ↑criterion↓. To go still lower, "Three things

Page 278

2–3   an American measure.
3   a letter which does
5   condition ⟨of⟩ ↑in↓ the world
14–15 Suffered or done.
Let me add to this the noble remark of Addison which is itself a
theory of the gentlemanly character. "He that governs his thoughts
with the everlasting rules of reason and sense must have something
so inexpressibly graceful in his words and actions that every circumstance must become him." [*Spectator* No. 75, May 26, 1711. Signed
by Steele.] An element
22   at home. I may add what I have heard from a critic of manners
that a gentleman makes no noise.
23–24 this doctrine of Gentle Behaviour, that is, as it flows from its legitimate fountains of honor and love. In the Wife
27   But for ye speken [etc. Minor spelling variants in the quoted pas-
sage]

483

Page 279

Lines

29–35   For villain's sinful deeds make him a churl
             ⟨For gentillesse . . . thing to thy person⟩
             Thy Gentillesse cometh from God alone
             ⟨Then cometh . . . with our place⟩

Page 250

3   all we read ⟨has any⟩ recurs
5   Assyrian ⟨Empire⟩ Monarchy
9   These ⟨trifling⟩ incidents
10–11   by the moral ⟨element⟩ quality
13   forgotten. ⟨The history⟩ So it seems
14–16   than by many ⟨boo⟩ elaborate compositions /
               W
             When Alfred
             Edwin son of Ella
17   Anglia Ethelfrith
26   hall ⟨polluted⟩ ↑filled↓ with
29   cried out where
30–31   not like ⟨the⟩ vapors
33   illimitable time.

Page 251

5–6   ↑the queens words upon↓
8   missionaries. [marginal note:] A.D. 626
15–16   departs ⟨at an⟩ ↑thro the↓ other. ⟨door⟩ Whil⟨e⟩st
29   to his son. "Without

Page 252

6   poems seems ⟨an th⟩ related
8   spoken that ⟨bel⟩ adheres
11   Alfred a prince
14   embodied ↑.↓ ⟨i⟩In the middle of the 9th century⟨.⟩, ⟨H⟩he
             g⟨ives⟩ave in his
24–25   indicate with ⟨surprising⟩ ↑curious↓ fidelity the future ["future"
             circled] character

3. THE AGE OF FABLE

Page 253

5–6   forming & formed. and
6   infirm ⟨tongue⟩ ↑utterance↓
8   shall ⟨utter⟩ ↑embody↓

484

Lines

11 did not ⟨change⟩ ↑subvert↓

12 the Court was

13–14 French for ⟨near⟩ more than ⟨250 years⟩ ↑two centuries & a half↓. ⟨until the reign of Edward III.⟩ ⟨In⟩ During this ⟨period⟩ ↑coexistence↓ of two languages the ⟨vernacular⟩ common

Page 254

6 ↑The nobility . . . middle classes↓

7 the 14 century,

9 Norman words ⟨Many books perf[?]⟩ Edward III

10–11 proceedings And ⟨many books⟩ even

16–17 compositions ⟨the⟩ ↑some↓ distinctive

19 metrical romances the oral

22–27 Phrygius a great . . . Colonna ↑A.D. 1260↓. A profusion . . . Round Table on Lancelot du Lac who . . . Christ   On . . . Peers and

29 literary ⟨amusement⟩ property of Europe.

30–33 possessed the sa s [sic] common materials . . . taste or . . . intellect. In the use they made of them in the progress of ⟨their⟩ letters ⟨among them⟩ ↑in the several states↓, very strong ⟨distinctions⟩ ↑national peculiarities↓

34–35 ⟨The history of every modern literature begins with a⟩ ↑The cause of this . . . political↓ profusion of fable. If you look ⟨at the⟩ in the

36 world ⟨in the⟩ ↑from the 4th to the 9th↓ Centur⟨y⟩ies,

Page 255

2 But ⟨we may. There is⟩ ↑it is easy to indicate↓ a period ⟨in⟩ ↑during↓ which

3 dissolved. ⟨& vanished.⟩ [circled]

4 the 10 Century,

5–6 works. ⟨After that⟩, ↑Come down a few centuries &↓

7–9 glass, ↑of linen, the Compass,↓ discovery of the Solar System; of America; ⟨compass⟩ ↑manufacture of↓ watches

9–10 Tea; ⟨linen⟩ & silk

11 these ⟨War⟩terms occurs

12 War ⟨destroys⟩ ↑ruins↓

13–14 may be to ⟨strength of character⟩ ↑hardihood & strength of will↓

16 camp: ⟨everything⟩ all

17–18 justice & ⟨virtue⟩ ↑humanity↓ are

21 ⟨The⟩ Nothing is so barren ⟨of⟩ as a soldiers brain. ⟨It⟩ ↑War↓ is one

22 horses ⟨degr⟩ empties

24–25 Middle Age. ⟨centuries⟩ the people were insignificant. society being an army the ⟨pr⟩ organization

Lines

26–27 ↑To↓ Thought & freedom in individuals is the whole system ↑is↓ hostile. ⟨to.⟩

28 When these ⟨convulsions at last⟩ ↑fires↓ ⟨fires⟩ ↑of war at last↓ . . . fuel. When

30–31 the ⟨sad⟩ ↑dismal↓ effects of the disorder ⟨began⟩ shewed themselves. the

32 state of Childishness.

32–34 incapable. ↑Their eyes . . . could not see↓ Of course the Religion . . . the Government

35–36 ↑The games . . . ignorance & folly.↓

Page 256

1 ages in ⟨every country of⟩ ↑all the↓ south

2–3 The Poets ⟨began⟩ ↑sang↓ as we do ⟨with⟩ ↑to↓ children ⟨with wonder⟩ ↑of war↓ & witchcraft   The

6 nations. ⟨In those times⟩ the nobility

8 challenging ⟨to⟩ unknown

9 never saw. ⟨There are several main subjects by which the great mass of romances with which English French Spanish & Italian literature begin may be rudely classified as the Romances on Arthur & the pursuit of the Sangreal or the blood of our Saviour   2 the Romances of Charlemagne. 3 of Brut   4 of Troy⟩

10 The⟨y⟩ ↑romances↓ begin

10–11 & ⟨weave⟩ ↑spin↓ ⟨on⟩to

11 or ⟨gloo⟩ terrible

13–14 nursery the giant . . . the fairy Then

15 emperor ⟨Decius⟩ Theodosius ⟨& found⟩ after

16–17 from ↑time of↓ the persecution of Decius; ↑the tale of the wandering Jew.↓

17 of the ⟨mighty⟩ giant Ritho

19–21 slain of ⟨the giant from whose beard giant killer⟩ ↑monsters & monster killers↓ . . . giants beard the

23–26 Coasts of Africa. Of . . . his eyes.
          The . . . light   Of

27–29 issue ⟨his⟩ ↑the word of↓ command . . . 60 miles. of

32 powder ↑to hide the hero↓

Page 257

1 show his ⟨mistress⟩ friend of

3 walk ↑of themselves↓;

6 only in ⟨exhibiting⟩ ↑being joined with↓ European manners

7–8 religion, ⟨have been found⟩ ↑exist↓ in Manuscript ↑in the English public libraries of a date↓

8–9 Printing. ↑& now make . . . English tongue↓

12 printed ↑by Ellis, Warton, Ritson Southey↓

Lines

18	ear containing
21	Nobody can ↑recall↓ read these
22	between ↑the Gothic↓ these fables
24	truth ⟨is yet⟩ & believed
25	allegory ⟨containing⟩ conveying
26	Creations of the
27–28	They ⟨are⟩ beside ⟨their⟩ ↑superficial↓ beauty
32	unchosen & ⟨un⟩ miscellaneous

Page 258

3	service of men Prometheus
28–29	finding all ⟨sorts⟩ ↑kinds↓ of miseries
34	vulture ⟨or eagle⟩ stood

Page 259

1	those ↑elegant↓ pleasing fables
1–2	Greeks, ⟨& yet⟩ which
7–8	Orpheus explained of Natural & moral philosophy of
10	meaning of ⟨these⟩ ↑the ancient↓ apologues
12	convey it Whereas
14–15	from the ⟨chronicler's⟩ minstrel's intention than the discovery of a ⟨design⟩ ↑hidden sense↓
16	Yet ⟨our⟩ the obligations
16	these ⟨doughty⟩ ↑excellent↓ knights,
20–21	↑But beside . . . for the fancy↓ But ⟨as⟩ I believe
28–29	him ↑Poets, said Plato, . . . themselves understand.↓
30	⟨Thus⟩ ↑When↓ Lucian ↑quite in ye spirit of romance↓ relates

Page 260

2–3	by reading ⟨Fulton⟩ for "Pancrates" . . . *steam* For
5	skilful servants.
	⟨Moreover in the Romance the poet or novelist is always yielding to the natural wishes of man, he is making his hero successful thro' all obstacles & by preternatural means It is as easy to make his hero agreeable as odious, & so he clothes him with virtues and carries him on conquering by all splendid helps bending the refractory laws of nature⟩ /
6–30	So with the similar fictions . . . its latest form the modern Novel. [on an inserted leaf]
9–10	powers of Science.
13	hero the gift
15–16	the mind In
17	virtuous And
20	& a rose ⟨which⟩ bloom
25	that an ⟨and⟩ ingenious

Lines
25–27   as; that . . . named: that . . . trusted: ⟨and⟩ that who
30–31   modern Novel. /
              ⟨to the wishes of the mind. As far as the tale is good the soul delights in it inasmuch as it sees in a great character its own pinched features expanded to true dimensions, the shows of things to the desires of the mind.⟩ I have before me ⟨the⟩ ↑Scotts↓ fine novel The Bride of Lammermoor It

Page 261

1   industry. ⟨that⟩ We may all ↑like the hero↓ shoot
4–6   liable to great / great suffering in this world.
              Something like this
8–9   nature. ⟨What⟩ For example
9   select one ⟨an⟩ example
10   equally well) ⟨the⟩ what
11–16   Tamlane . . . lofty hall. is more
17   verses which . . . connexions from
23   child of ⟨nature⟩ ↑genius↓
28–29   inquiry the examination
30   Whilst ⟨thus⟩ the predominance of the ⟨Romantic⟩ Romance
33   had indirect⟨ly⟩ good

Page 262

1–2   restored the Poet to the people. The Latin Literature ⟨which⟩ had become . . . imitative   Nothing
7   Virgil   For
10   instead of ⟨men⟩ life
17   all that ⟨c⟩familiar
21   Meantime ⟨as⟩ War was
25   action grew wise⟨r⟩. Then ⟨followed⟩ ↑ensued↓ the
31–33   ↑And when it . . . to create it↓ But
35   mainly of ⟨common⟩ abundant
37   versifiers that

Page 263

4–5   ⟨It was the consequence then of⟩ the popular origin of English ⟨poetry⟩ ↑letters produced↓ or . . . favored the
8   homeliness ↑love of plain truth↓
12   objects it is
14–15   635 years old. /
              ⟨One peculiarity is visible in English poetry from its earliest ⟨perf⟩ compositions & that is its ⟨strong⟩ homeliness & strong tendency to describe things as they are & without ⟨poetic⟩ ↑rhetorical↓ decoration. It imports into songs & ballads the smell of the earth & breath of the cattle & th[?] seeks the

beauty that is found in low & common objects ↑It is the reverse of the Classic taste↓ Here is a ⟨love song⟩ ditty which
if Warton's reckoning be accepted is 635 years old⟩

22 Loweth after calf ⟨cow⟩ cu
23 Bullock stert⟨h⟩eth
28 Sing cuccu /
    ⟨Robert of Gloucester has left a long poem which is a
history of En⟩ [smudged out] / [next sheet inserted]
32–35 common things ⟨The⟨ir⟩ muse hath leaden eye that loves the
ground⟩ ↑The English muse loves the field & the farmyard
It holds fast by ye ⟨farmyard⟩ ↑highway↓ ye market and ye
hearthstone. The English muse mt say↓ As ↑adopt the expression of↓ Mme. de Stael ⟨said⟩ ↑about↓ of the people

Page 264

31 Raleighs ⟨is so⟩ verse⟨s⟩ are . . . their diction
32 defiance. as in

Page 265

10–15 The whole . . . useful art. [no punctuation]
12–13 ↑It is neither . . . Oriental↓
15 nature & ⟨familiar⟩ ↑useful↓ art.
16–17 not pap to . . . truth and
20–21 Chaucer, ⟨I⟩ whilst . . . metre I
22 500 years ago. [end of inserted sheet]
25 1280 I quote

Page 266

3–4 Kinde that is
7 suggested ⟨the⟩ a well known
8 It is the describes
25 Death came dry↑v↓ing
26 Kings & ⟨Kaisors⟩ knights
33 1307
    I quote
33 show ⟨the⟩ how early the

Page 268

1–2 most ⟨pleasing &⟩ musical metres
2 among the ⟨most ancient⟩ ↑oldest↓
3 The ⟨Poets⟩ writers
8–9 more ⟨in⟩ consonant with our own. ⟨habits of thought⟩

TEXTUAL NOTES AND VARIANT PASSAGES

4. CHAUCER

Page 269

Lines	
1	1328 He ⟨was a student⟩ studied
2–3	University. ⟨From⟩ At the
5–6	Edward III John of Gaunt ⟨the⟩ Duke of Lancaster the patron of Wicliffe was

Page 270

3	court 1384 respecting
8–9	liberty & ⟨offices⟩ ↑employments↓ without some dis⟨graceful recantation⟩ ↑creditable↓ confession
9–10	associates. ⟨His last years were easy⟩
12	mission to to Genoa
36–37	is the ⟨first⟩ ↑earliest↓ classical

Page 271

2	this day. ⟨In this view he⟩ He ⟨also⟩ introduced ⟨or used with success⟩ several
4	either ⟨introduced or used with success many⟩ is the
6–7	↑& more or . . . speech of men↓
7	little ⟨there⟩ ↑in his page↓
12–13	countrymen ↑now for near↓
15–16	did not ⟨separate from him⟩ ↑think of inferior merit↓.
17–18	English ↑poetical↓ triumvirate.
19	has now ⟨passed on⟩ ↑sentenced↓ Gower also ↑to silence↓ & ⟨only⟩ the name
22	average ↑physical↓ strength
25	afterward. ↑⟨The⟩ Not less stable are intellectual measures.↓
29	posterity ⟨to⟩ ↑over↓ the bard
30	What ⟨Shakspear⟩ says of Coriolanus,
35	hardly ⟨say what special gifts recommend him the⟩ show the immediate

Page 272

1	decided ↑claim of↓ preference
6	object of ⟨distinguished⟩ attention
13	love of nature. ⟨They are the writings of a man who has an earnest meaning to express & great abundance of words & images to clothe it in⟩
18	his age ⟨with⟩ before ⟨the following generations⟩ ↑posterity↓.
19	those too ⟨that are⟩ whose
23	perceives ⟨the⟩ under the
27	He possesses ⟨as none but Shakspear doth⟩ the most

490

Lines	
27–28	that of ⟨entire⟩ sympathy
29–30	that it ⟨is⟩ does not argue
30	or ↑on↓ topics
31–33	Capital ⟨defect of⟩ ↑deduction from↓ Lord Byron⟨s⟩ ↑that his↓ poems ⟨that they⟩ have but one subject; himself. ⟨But the true Poet casts himself into whatever he contemplates, & enjoys the faculty of giving making it speak that it would say⟩ It is the burden
35	persons ⟨without⟩ ↑clean of↓
37	Poet ⟨casts⟩ ↑quits↓

Page 273

1	enjoys the ⟨faculty of⟩ making
7	"sentence" that is sense to
11	And ⟨that⟩ ↑tho'↓ I do
13	dignity of of the laurel
15–16	⟨There is something quite observable in⟩ ↑No modern reader can fail to be struck with↓ . . . Poets.
18	adduced ↑with great emphasis↓
19–20	argument, ⟨for⟩ ↑because↓ thus they said ↑these writers↓
20–21	supposition that ⟨the Poet spoke⟩ there
22	that ⟨they were⟩ ↑he was↓ the teacher⟨s⟩
23	spoke not ⟨their⟩ ↑his↓
24	God ↑This exceeding respect↓ ⟨It⟩ stands
28–29	literature ↑in the Middle Age↓ as a ⟨good⟩ ↑happy↓ event;
31–32	↑With ⟨this⟩ it however . . . for the Poet.↓
34	multitude & ⟨earn⟩ win
36	²{They were forced to amuse the people} ¹{to get any audience at all}

Page 274

4	mind draws ⟨delight &⟩ excitement
7	new ⟨& noble⟩ literature
8	knowledge ⟨reclaimed⟩ ↑resumed↓ their
10	began ⟨again⟩ by instinct
11	& to ⟨feel⟩ ↑acquire↓
13	old English Poets.
15	sort is ⟨very observable⟩ ↑conspicuous↓
17–19	It is a ⟨very agreeable⟩ ↑pleasing↓ trait . . . his species Even
21	is the ⟨highest good⟩ ↑equal treasure↓ of all men And
25–26	English ⟨land⟩ ↑ground↓, when ↑Dryden↓ Pope
26	Gay ↑Darwin↓ & many
27–28	popular writers ⟨down went again⟩ with . . . thought down
29	divine man & ↑Scott,↓ Byron
32–34	↑He never writes . . . law. & has a right to be heard↓ He
35	vices of the ⟨Romish⟩ clergy.

Page 275

Lines	
2–3	pretenders ↑in science, the professions,↓ ↑He wrote a poem of stern counsel to King Richard↓ & his prophetic wisdom is ⟨always⟩ found
4	⟨After this⟩ ↑I do not feel that I have closed the↓
5	Chaucer ⟨it may yet be⟩ ↑until it is↓ added
6–7	that his ⟨talents⟩ ↑virtues↓ & genius ↑are singularly↓ is ⟨native &⟩ agreeable
8	they find ⟨in him⟩ their prominent tastes & ⟨virtues⟩ prejudices He
10–11	the ↑domestic↓ manners
12	National poets
14	habits ⟨& see⟩ sentiments
16–17	deeply tinged which

Page 276

5–6	In Chaucer are ⟨very⟩ conspicuous some of those ideas which, ⟨as I have already noticed,⟩ reappear
7–8	behaviour ↑founded upon Honor↓,
12–13	than ↑it existed in the minds of↓ Spenser, Sidney, Milton ⟨Ben Jonson, Shakspear⟩ ↑Clarendon↓ &
14–16	↑It may be worth while . . . ⟨the⟩ ↑its present↓ liberal ↑& just↓ acceptation↓
17	Anglo Saxons that ⟨pa⟩ that
19–20	And ⟨this⟩ ↑the↓ natural ⟨instinct⟩ faith
25–26	natural aristocracy. The principle of / "The principle

Page 277

13–14	afterwards ⟨upon⟩ extended
16–17	to the ⟨le⟩ this species of rank. The disuse ⟨of badges⟩ of ⟨a⟩ wearing
19	Neither ↑birth, nor↓ law,
21	gentle behaviour It
22	moral distinctions
	[upside down at the bottom of the sheet:] ⟨than that they were men who used their eyes.⟩ / ⟨The most obvious of these it has been said is a certain generosity in trifles.⟩ ↑⟨Mr Landor has finely said All titulars⟩↓
	It is not the less
23–24	& of ⟨what⟩ institutions
24–27	guards. ↑Mr Landor has . . . selfexistent."↓ ⟨It wears⟩ ↑It wears↓
28–29	they shall ⟨certa⟩ give
31	trifles. ⟨A⟩The deeper characteristic ⟨is entire truth.⟩ stand

Lines
32–33   vulgar ↑attributes↓ distinctions. ↑Lord Byron . . . a fine voice↓

Page 278

1   says ⟨the cockney⟩ ↑a lawgiver of Almacks↓ constitute
2–3   ↑I am happy . . . American witness.↓ ⟨Mr Randolph⟩
7   offers to ⟨deceive⟩ speak
12   Intent ⟨the way⟩ ↑each↓
15   ⟨It seems to me   It is a⟩An element of ⟨this idea⟩ ↑of the gentlemanly character↓ a
16   sweetness which I think, — is oftener
22   ⟨I may add what I have heard from a critic of manners that a gentleman makes no noise.⟩
25   advice ⟨that is⟩ ↑which embodies↓ the ⟨veriest⟩ ↑most↓

Page 279

5   high par⟨t⟩age
9   in such degree

         ⟨Wel can the wise poet of Florence
         That highte Dant speken of this sentence
     ⟨Full⟩ Lo in such maner rime is Dantes tale
         Full seldè riseth by his branches small
     Prowesse of man for God of his goodness
     Wol that we claim of him our gentillesse
     For of our elders may we nothing claim
     But temporal thing that man may hurt & maim
     Eke every wight wot this as well as I
     If gentiless were planted naturally
     Unto a certain linage down the line
     Prive & apert then wol they never fine
     To don of gentillesse the faire office
     They mighten do no villanie or vice⟩
12   And let ⟨them⟩ ↑men↓

Page 280

4   Coleridge. ⟨that⟩ "Religion
8   his ⟨more⟩ sustained
9–10   ↑& carries it . . . to extravagance↓ as
12–15   innocent words ⟨to sacrifice her good name⟩ ⟨honor⟩ ↑having declared ↑yt↓ she would ⟨not⟩ receive the unlawful love of Aurelius when ⟨until⟩ all . . . renews his suit↓
16   to ²{Arviragus ¹{her husband, he
17–18   keep & ⟨counsels her to yield herself to⟩ ↑bids her tell↓ Aurelius ↑she will↓ ⟨&⟩ keep her word, ⟨at all hazards,⟩
21   represented as ⟨another⟩ a historical

Lines

27–32   on ⟨the most⟩ ↑a purely↓ virtuous footing. ↑It is the consequence . . . evil or of good."↓

32–33   generous ⟨g⟩ attribute

Page 281

1   female Character.

2   sorry for it. ⟨But he also knew well what it is that is attractive
noble & ⟨even divine⟩ ↑angelic↓ in woman⟩.

5   faith ⟨as⟩ in woman,

6   woman ↑unearthly &↓ divine

Page 282

4–5   favor or fortune
⟨he g⟩ & the cry

9   She was fair ⟨for Nature had formed her with sovereign
diligence in⟩

Page 283

5   gives to ⟨Chaucer himself⟩ ↑the Clerk of Oxenford↓

22–25   The ⟨beauty⟩ ↑pious tenderness↓ . . . Cambuscan bold. [no
punctuation]

26–29   ↑The influence of Chaucer . . . is easily traced↓ From

29–30   borrowed ⟨that⟩ the English

33–(284)1   Chaucer ↑however↓ did not

Page 284

2–3   Colonna ↑a native of Messina in Sicily↓ published

4   Trojano   This

9   Caxton the (⟨first English⟩)

9–10   sources are ↑Petrarch↓ Boccacio ↑Lollius↓

13   Italian   The

15   obligations to his ↑foreign↓

18   all ⟨the⟩ works of literature

19   past. ↑Shakspear↓ Pope

20–23   shine ⟨as⟩ by ↑this↓ borrowed light. Chaucer ⟨to⟩ ↑reflects↓
Boccacio & Colonna ↑& the Troubadours↓. Boccacio & Colonna
to elder Greek & Roman ⟨originals⟩ ↑authors↓, & these in their
turn ⟨to⟩ others

26   equal degrees   He is

28   man universal ⟨reception⟩ ↑receiving↓

29   theory of ⟨Copernicus⟩ the Solar

30   Copernicus in ⟨15⟩ ↑16 cent↓

Page 285

4   proverb. Jefferson

9   never ⟨concerns⟩ troubles

Lines	
15–16	present it . . . minds eye to ⟨become aware of⟩ ↑read↓
16–17	difficult to ⟨quote⟩ appropriate
17	invent. ⟨Fine quotations are not usually found in dull books. Only an inventor can use the inventions of others⟩
18–19	great man as . . . Aristotle necessarily
19–20	current in his time It is only an inventor [blank] /
21–22	Dumont the nephew
23	Mirabeau ⟨& wh⟩ upon
25–27	Hercules And . . . food They
31	strikes us of
36	around him I

Page 286

3–5	cannot if . . . genius come . . . with which is it is hung
6	What should I be ⟨w⟩ — what
8	What have I done? ⟨What have I collected⟩
10–11	Every one of my ⟨works⟩ writings
13	& the foolish, ⟨have co[?]⟩ infancy
15–17	experience Often . . . reaped My work . . . nature. it
20	intellectual light which
21–22	sources ↑than by the composition of new works.↓ as
24	Bible. ⟨The⟩ morality
24–26	with the ⟨manner⟩ ↑spirit↓ . . . done if . . . plagiarist. if
30	obligations he frankly
31–32	says so; & ⟨so⟩ ↑thus↓ is to us in the ⟨14 century⟩ ↑remote past↓ a ↑luminous↓ solitary mind
33	to us the ⟨spirit⟩ religion

5. SHAKSPEAR [FIRST LECTURE]

Page 288

2	read ↑to ye Society↓
9	The ⟨mind⟩ ↑life↓ of Shakspear
11	mind ⟨make him singular⟩ ↑place him alone↓
12–13	reared a stone cut out ↑from the mountain↓
14–15	durable ⟨city⟩ ↑of edifices↓ add to the interest of the event. & stimulate ⟨and make⟩ ↑our inquiry into the ⟨cause.⟩ sources of his power↓
16	cause this
16	It ⟨arises⟩ ↑proceeds↓ from a

Page 289

1–2	such ⟨a mind⟩ ↑an individual↓ is to
2	the very ⟨feeble⟩ humble

Lines

4 pardon ⟨& the attention⟩ of my audience if I tax their ⟨atten-
tion with so⟩ patience

6 essential gift of / of

20 full of life Whole

22 these facts the

23–24 illustration of ⟨of⟩ a fact

28–29 seed "It . . . body It

31 light & heat But

32–33 seasons. and

33–34 grandeur ⟨&⟩ ↑or↓ pathos from that analogy. The

36 monitor a little

Page 290

1 heart then

2 sleeps become sublime. [A stray sheet, found in a much later
lecture, apparently represents part of an early draft of this
passage. It is numbered "13" in Emerson's hand, and in
another is noted: "transferred to next lecture." It was once
sewn in with Lecture I, but where is not clear, since that ms.
now has a p. 13:]

⟨The ⟨ef⟩ motion⟨s⟩ of the earth round its axis & round
the sun make the day & the year. They are brute light & heat.
But is there no intent of an analogy between man's life & the
seasons? & do the seasons gain no grandeur or pathos from
that analogy? The instincts of the ant are very unimportant
considered as the ant's; but the moment a ray of relation is
seen to extend from it to man, & the little mite is seen to be a
monitor, a little body with a mighty heart — then all the facts
that are collected of its habits even to that ⟨alleged⟩ ↑recently
asserted↓ that *it never sleeps,* become sublime.⟩ [W, I, 28]

3–4 world is itself opens

5 its borders But

6–15 The axioms of ⟨geo[?]⟩ physics . . . moral truth. [no punc-
tuation]

11 ↑Observe too↓ These propositions

15 Thus "A rolling

16–20 no moss. A bird in . . . and the like. [no punctuation]

21 analogical import [upside down at the bottom of the sheet:]

⟨In order to consider truly the function of the Imagination,
it needs to consider the relation between man & nature.

Our lowest acquaintance with the outward world is that
of commodity. It subserves perfectly the animal wants But
life soon teaches us that nature serves us in higher uses than
nourishment, clothing, & ground to stand on. It serves us as a
language, or vehicle of thought. There exists a strict relation
between the parts of nature, & the thoughts of man which
fits these to be emblems of those. All nature is a symbol of the

Lines

human spirit and every part of nature of some part of human thought.⟩

23 seen that that there

30 intellectual process⟨es⟩

Page 291

8 total mind ⟨when it uses matter as symbols⟩.

14 mind is this that

15–17 The one ⟨esteems⟩ views all nature as ⟨root⟩ fluid . . . thereon the

22–23 finds ⟨strong &⟩ picturesque

24–25 does the same He . . . the large He

30 meaning Thus

32–33 O heavens . . . sweet sway [all on one line]

Page 292

9–10 Open ⟨his⟩ any page

20 tempts me not, but it tis I

29 power to ⟨dignify or degrade an object⟩ ↑make any object great or little↓

31–32 Tempest Prospero says

   Pr The strong

Page 293

10–11 as where ⟨the⟩ Hamlet

17 sonnets a little

29 exalted to that pitch / [The entire previous three sheets to this point, or all from "The power of the Poet" (p. 289) on, appear to constitute a later insertion. The next sheet, for a page and a half, presents part of an earlier short draft which Emerson neglected to cancel when he inserted the new sheets:]

  ↑This faculty ⟨was⟩ never existed in a healthy mind with more fulness than ⟨by⟩in Shakspear↓ The ⟨predominance of this faculty a⟩ extraordinary exercise of the Imaginative power though it ⟨exist in⟩ ↑pervade↓ all his dramas was never so purely manifested as in his sonnets, a little volume of poems whose wonderful merit has been thrown into the shade by the splendor of his plays. Yet I know not where in English or in foreign poetry ⟨a⟩ more remarkable examples can be found of the tyranny of imagination or the perfect control assumed of all nature by the poet & the mastery with which he tosses the creation ↑like a bauble↓ from hand to hand to illustrate the ⟨merest toy or⟩ ↑any↓ capricious shade of thought that chances to be uppermost in his mind. These poems are

Lines

written at the same time with such closeness of thought & such ⟨sweetness⟩ even ⟨to⟩ drowsy sweetness of rhythm that they are not to be discussed in a hasty ⟨or manner⟩ ↑sketch↓ but deserve to be studied in the critical manner in which the Italians explain the sonnets of Petrarch & M. Angelo. ↑The feeling of a lover of poetry who falls in with this book is as if one should amuse himself with playing upon the ignorance of a bystander↓ One opens them as a little volume of love songs as indeed many of them are & finds them the production of a mind exalted to that pitch

30   world, ↑works of art↓

32–33   subordinated to ⟨his present⟩ the ⟨o⟩ subject that ↑for the moment↓ now

Page 294

1   them ⟨as examples⟩ to show

2   with what ⟨gravity⟩ solemn

10   discontent

           ⟨Whereto t'inviting time on fashion calls⟩

Page 295

1–2   ↑He uses time . . . which his ⟨lo⟩ beloved is ⟨locked up⟩ in-closed↓

9   they ⟨seldom⟩ ↑thinly↓ placed

12   which the ⟨time⟩ ↑robe↓ doth

17   ⟨It is the singular topic of⟩ many of ym ⟨is⟩ are

32   out of memory &c

           ⟨I am limited in my selection of ⟨ex⟩ passages by the difficulty of choice by the unfitness of the subject & chiefly by the difficulty of making poetry so ⟨c⟩dense with thought that every line & almost every word is ↑an↓ epigram, intelligible in reading.⟩

34   poems as ⟨containing⟩ ↑informed↓

35   imagination ⟨which⟩ or the

Page 296

1   nature ⟨&⟩ compelling

2–3   of this ↑⟨action or⟩↓ ⟨habit of mind⟩ ↑intellectual function↓ . . . of Literature

8   or of ⟨moulding nature into⟩ subjecting nature to the thought of ⟨the mind⟩ ↑man↓

10–11   Each ↑passing↓ thought ↑or emotion↓ filling

11   poets mind and ⟨makin⟩ bringing

23   things ⟨unseen⟩ unknown

25–26   habitation and a name.

SHAKSPEAR [FIRST LECTURE]

⟨↑This cannot be denied. Such an imagination, alone, would be a disease. Even Luther was not able always to distinguish thots from events, the symbol from the thing. The antidote provided in nature against the influence of any part is in the influence of the whole.↓

The measure is kept by the continual recovery & self recollection of the mind⟩

This cannot be denied. Such [etc. to "region above the intellect" inserted on separate leaf, with variants as noted]

28   coarseness of ⟨nature⟩ was

30   thing   The antidote

34   Reason. ⟨The healthful mind⟩

34–(297)3   minds Eye. ⟨The means it makes use of to preserve its health⟩ ↑It is ye Reason . . . thereby↓ raises us to a ⟨loftier⟩ region ⟨than⟩ ↑above ye↓ intellect⟨ual nature.⟩

The ordinary means wh. ye minds uses to keep its health [end of inserted leaf (see note above)] The healthful mind keeps itself

Page 297

7   limitations. ↑⟨It is the Reason wh. affirms⟩↓ Moreover the ⟨natural⟩ ↑special↓ check

8   is the ⟨instinctive curiosity⟩ ↑appetite↓ which

10–11   own faculties   This is philosophy. When applied to man criticism . . . works.

11   faculties ↑esteemed↓ the most

12   art, ↑because↓ ⟨to which⟩ it seems

13   poet should beleive his own

15–21   ↑Shakspeare added to this . . . fountain of our being.↓

16   force. ⟨The⟩ ⟨It is⟩ Universality

17–18   him. ⟨He⟩ It is exceedingly . . . his works so

18–19   of all ⟨personality⟩ favorite moods

19   works. And He

20   thrilling ⟨& eternal⟩ strains the ⟨awful⟩ ⟨great⟩ spiritual

21   ⟨Yet Shakspear added to this towering Imagination⟩ ↑Moreover he joined to it↓ a habit

23–24   faculties. ⟨& of⟩ ⟨He is a philosopher & a critic.⟩ ↑His reflective powers are very active↓

26   man & nature. ↑⟨THe solid globe melts away & leaves not a rack behind⟩↓

29–30   Space & Time? ↑The solid globe melts &c He doubts . . . if he doubt↓

31   himself ⟨to⟩ "Thine

33–36   ↑Ys[?] brave oerhanging firmament ys . . . congregation of vapors.↓

Page 298

Lines
8–10   ↑We are such . . . with a sleep↓
12   shake our frames. [upside down at the bottom of this sheet:]
               ⟨Now this is the poetic power. As the Cr God imparts his
               own life to brute matter in the Creation So does the mind
               impart its own life to brute matter hence is the imaginative
               man a Poet, that is a Maker.
                   This faculty has never been possessed in a higher degree
               than by the English Shakspear
15   mere beasts.
                   Hamlet
19   makes of fumes.
                   Cymbeline
24   Signifying nothing.
                   Macbeth
27   greatness What

Page 299

2   day but ⟨now⟩ ever & anon
7   upon ⟨this⟩ ↑the↓ secret
23–26   Thus singularly . . . Pyrrho Plato [written over the follow-
               ing faint list in pencil:]
                   Thad. Blood
                   David Lane [?]
                       Hosmer   Bedford
                   Amos Baker   Lincoln
                   Aaron Jones
                       Oliver
                   Tilly Buttrick
                   John Hosmer
                   Abel Davis [survivors of 1776]
23   Thus ⟨he possessed⟩ ↑singularly did he unite↓
23–24   Philosopher. ⟨in rare unison⟩.
25   still been ⟨classed⟩ ↑⟨associated⟩↓ ↑thrust↓
25–26   world ⟨with⟩ ↑into↓ the class
26   visionaries ⟨wh⟩ with
31   of thoughts ⟨There is⟩ and slight
32–(300)9   ↑Porphyry relates . . . love of comfort & use.↓

Page 299

32   ⟨Plotinus⟩ Porphyry
33   shame ⟨that⟩ ↑because↓ he had

Page 300

1   indecen⟨t⟩cies
2   impelled ⟨with⟩ ↑by↓

Lines	
3	only with ⟨a⟩ thoughts
3–4	from all ⟨relati⟩ personal
5	affection But
13–14	that is, as ⟨fathers⟩ as mortals, as fathers, as ⟨merchants⟩ ↑tradesmen↓ as householders They
18	spirit. ⟨To perceive clearly⟩ ↑Some men perceive more clearly than others↓
19	the ⟨actual⟩ ↑outward↓ or apparent world ⟨is⟩ and to act
20–21	↑The name we give to this perception↓ is Common Sense And we are ⟨accustomed⟩ ↑wont↓ to ⟨regard⟩ ↑think↓
21–22	Condition ↑of its being↓ ⟨as⟩ so
27	earthly things He soars
30–31	know of ⟨him⟩ ↑his personal history↓ falls in perfectly with this ↑impression↓ view.
34	theatre, ⟨that⟩ ↑whilst↓ Beaumont
35–36	Poets. ↑Ben Jonson . . . better writer.↓ ⟨He was a⟩ ⟨Tis said⟩ Even

Page 301

2–3	that he ↑married early↓ was
3–4	fellows, ⟨having wit combats with⟩ ↑making epigrams & biting jokes upon↓ Jonson
14–16	learning solid . . . tides tack
19–20	⟨Much Ado About Nothing⟩ [Aubrey has *Midsummer Night's Dream*]
31–32	Nature this fitness for and pleasure in the ⟨nat⟩ common

Page 302

1–2	attractive poems ↑I cannot . . . they have lain.↓
7–9	The lover . . . eyebrow [written as prose]
10–11	sort the heroic the ⟨sad⟩ ↑wretched↓ the humorous yielded
13–14	very ⟨spirit⟩ ↑impersonation↓ of ⟨F⟩ ↑fun &↓ animal ⟨delight⟩ ↑comfort↓ taking
15–19	↑must be painting himself↓ ⟨must be painting himself⟩ ↑In ye unfeigned . . . shepherds & lasses↓ In the ⟨affection⟩ ↑delicate & beseeching affection↓ of the
21	Lear ↑in the pride of Coriolanus↓
23–24	behold the ↑overflowing↓ love of life the
25	blood with
27–28	that he whilst ⟨in eminent⟩ ⟨one man⟩ ↑the author . . . Bunyan↓
30–31	Poet; ⟨like the author of the book of Job or the poems of Ossian⟩ and ⟨other men⟩ ↑whilst↓ Aristotle, or ↑David↓ Hume, or ↑Im.↓ Kant have possessed
32–34	and ↑very↓ many ⟨men⟩ ↑persons↓ have possessed the ⟨just view⟩ ↑accurate perception↓ of things as they ⟨are⟩ ↑stand↓
34–36	have been ⟨sensible & useful⟩ ↑practical↓ men: Shakspear

⟨poss.⟩ united . . . joined them he was a poet, a philosopher & a Man.
[overleaf, upside down:]
SHAKSpear
⟨The humor of the constable in A Midsummer N.D. he happened to take at Grendon in Bucks (I think it was mid-summer night yt he happened to be there) which is the road from London to Stratford & there was living that constable about 1642 when I came first to Oxon. Ben Jonson & he did gather humors wherever they came⟩
⟨Aubrey⟩

Page 303

1	draw ↑the best↓ examples
2–3	faculties of man the
8	I have ⟨rem⟩ distinguished
9	each of ⟨the⟨se⟩m⟩ them.
12–13	warmed with life. ⟨Hence he is among men a sort of Catholic or Universal Mind attracting by necessity the assent & love of all Nations⟩ /

/D/ ⟨Not like other poets known by a peculiar manner not writing on certain subjects & rapidly exhausting a certain vein, Shakspear has a genius coextensive with nature   He has no favorite subjects, & no weak side. ↑He is at home in kings palaces, & in shepherds' cabins; in the loftiest abstraction, & the lowest farce.↓ Whatever he approaches, by one word he lifts from the ground, detaches it from all the common & customary, & draws music & wisdom out of it. His Wisdom

/E/ It needs then in order to any just understanding of this shining genius that we dismiss ↑from the mind↓ at once all the tavern stories we have formerly heard about him as if he were an untutored boy who without books or ⟨cultivation⟩ ↑discipline↓ or reflection, wrote he knew not what, and ⟨regard him⟩ ↑see in↓ him what he was a Catholic or Universal Mind of very great cultivation & ⟨very good reading⟩ ↑by books, by discourse, & by thot↓, who formed his own opinions & ⟨wrote he very well knew what⟩ who wrote with intention, who knew that his record was true, & in every line he penned has left his silent appeal to the most cultivated mind.⟩

13n	[The inserted passage differed from the original version as indicated below (page and line references are to the original version):]

Page 313

33	D It is those passages in which all his rare faculties blend themselves that are the most remarkable commentaries on human life ⟨that were

ever written) ↑which all the events of our daily history are interpreting and verifying.↓
    There is a tide

34   leads on to fortune.
    Hamlet. Our indiscretion

Page 314

14   how we will.
    Enobarbus. I see men's judgments
20   all alike.
    But when we in our
26–27   To our ⟨undoing⟩ confusion ["Hamlet . . . confusion" on blank
verso of previous leaf, with no place of insertion indicated]
What profounder satire than the memorable piece of petulance in
Twelfth Night.
    Dost thou think because thou art virtuous shall be no more
cakes and ale
or the praise of Parolles in All's well that ends well
    Yet these fixed . . . ye cold wind / [E]
          our pleasant vices
    Are made the whips to plague us. [*cf.* p. 315]
    In a different
28   religion upon
29   faith to surpass
34   such thots yet."
    These wise sentences . . . the English tongue. [as on p. 313,
lines 28–30] His wisdom draws men to him. /

Page 303

15   tickled with ⟨a⟩ the tune
19   truth ↑clear wholesome & practical↓ He
23   things & not words.
        ⟨Insert E⟩
    ⟨This fact that he was a ⟨perceiver⟩ Seer & not a rhapsodist
explains to us his powers for the wonder always has been the
extent of the man the fact that he was able to depict not a
few but manifold classes of men but the fact that he aimed not
to write from fancy but to write after truth or what he saw
makes his resources inexhaustible.⟩
26   exhausted. I hasten
27–31   Lecture   Why is it that this great man. / ⟨It is⟩ Why is it
that this great man ⟨commends⟩ is his own . . . to all men.
Why is it that ⟨his wit is become the measure of congruity⟩
²{& his mind a measure of the human mind} ¹{& our power
. . . degree of culture.}
34   empyrean ⟨depth⟩ ↑centre↓

Page 304

1   nature in ⟨all⟩ selectest words of
3–4   circumference representing the ⟨vast⟩ ↑terrific↓

Lines

5	grace. that
6	enlarged mind ⟨finds⟩ ↑learns↓
11–13	circulate as if . . . not what & see in him what he was an ⟨universal m⟩ a Catholic
14–15	by thought who formed his own opinions who
16	left his ⟨appeal⟩ silent
17	most cultivated mind.

[upside down on the back of the next (blank) leaf, part of the same sheet:]

It is the Reason which affirms the laws of moral nature & thereby raises us to a loftier region than intellectual truth.

6. SHAKSPEAR [SECOND LECTURE]

Page 305

4	power the
5	incident to ⟨this faculty⟩ the mind
6–7	from him ↑both↓ by the
7	Reason or the state of the mind ⟨in equipoise⟩ when
9	freedom ⟨but that⟩ ↑and↓ also
10–11	made him ⟨a⟩ the ⟨fir⟩ extremest
12	shown that ⟨his⟩ to this double faculty of ⟨P⟩ Imagination
13–14	energy that of Common Sense a
14–15	in the ⟨whole⟩ ongoings
16	gifts ⟨mad⟩ the imaginative
17	faculties at once
18–19	necessarily ⟨of rather a⟩ ↑somewhat↓ miscellaneous, ⟨character⟩
23	read a scene even
25	superiority ⟨Yet⟩ He

Page 306

1–5	name is ⟨mentioned⟩ ↑noticed↓. & ↑B. Jonson . . . to be pardoned↓ Sir Philip Sidney ⟨the⟩ who . . . madness writes
6	Drama & d⟨id⟩oes
8–9	which, ⟨have⟩ ↑it has↓ been conjectured, ⟨to⟩ ↑might↓
11–15	Lord Bacon the English Plato who . . . works has not once ⟨named⟩ ↑alluded to the existence of↓
16–17	had not ⟨Spenser⟩ some of the ⟨bards & sages⟩ ↑lights↓
22	commendation. viz Jasper Mayne the
24–25	Falkland; ↑Selden;↓ Milton; Dryden, Addison, ⟨and then⟩ ↑since whose time↓
27–30	↑The commendation . . . eulogy: But it may be pleaded↓ There is reason
32	needs ⟨the⟩ ↑a long↓ perspective to show it ⟨well⟩ ↑truly↓

Lines

33–(307)1   assigned ⟨him⟩ a contemporary ⟨so⟩ the ⟨transcendant⟩ super-
            lative praise ⟨as⟩

Page 307

1–2	We ⟨do it⟩ ↑indulge our admiration↓ at first
3–4	220 years ⟨cannot⟩ is no longer [marginal note:]

               1835
               1616
              ‾‾‾‾
              1219 [sic]

4–5	adequate to the ⟨witchcraft⟩ which
5–6	& ↑That influence reaches↓
7	omitted to ⟨heighten⟩ carry
9	distress or ⟨expectation⟩ ↑adventure↓
9	queens his
10	delighted by the ⟨wit⟩ truth
11	of the drama; ↑⟨so that it has been said with much reason yt English know more of Eng.⟩ hist by SH. than by Hume↓ ⟨then⟩ by the wit
12	dialogue; ⟨then⟩ by the splendor
12–13	by the ⟨weig⟩ delicacy of the expression; ⟨then⟩ ↑& lastly↓ by
18–19	↑"Chewing the food . . . aught in malice"↓
20	⟨He shares with⟩ ↑Next to↓ the English Bible ⟨the⟩
21	books to the ⟨establishment⟩ ↑authority↓
23	The As it is said
23–24	lost" that ⟨what is there told of the Trinity is⟩ ↑the theological dogmas there taught are↓
24	confounded with ⟨w⟩the
28	⟨It has⟩ ↑Add↓ also
30	analysed ⟨with the supposition⟩ ↑on the belief↓
31	truly ⟨crazy⟩ insane,
32	↑& the fate of Ophelia↓
36	obeying ⟨minutely⟩ ↑with fidelity↓ the law of thought

Page 308

1	verse. ⟨It⟩ ↑There↓ is
2–4	Stael ⟨&⟩ ↑which↓ . . . foreign language She
6	all ⟨such⟩ ↑exalted↓ thoughts
7	as we we well know
9	five or six ⟨indi⟩ writers
11	In the newspapers & albums are filled with ⟨verses⟩ essays
12	metrical prose. ⟨Shakspear has no rival but Milton in the sweetness of his numbers.⟩ We feel
15	Shakspear ⟨the⟩ we are
16–17	that the ⟨though⟩ sentence was
20	numbers. ⟨This such⟩ His verse
21	tune. and this makes ⟨it⟩ ↑him↓ of all

Lines
22   mannerist ↑and so the hardest to imitate↓.
24   truly ⟨sal[?]⟩ bring out

Page 309

4–23   ↑The sweetness of this verse &c turn to A↓ [inserted page:]
       ↑A↓ The sweetness . . . stanza of Shakspear
7   muse. ⟨It⟩ This distinction
9   to him Henry VIII which
11–12   tune ⟨&⟩ ↑whilst↓ a ⟨great⟩ large proportion of the ⟨verse⟩
       lines have ↑also↓ a double
23   stanza of Shakspear Turn to B
       ↑B↓ The fair
24–25   in thy orisons
       ⟨In thy orisons⟩ be all
31   Indeed ⟨the⟩ Shakspear is

Page 310

2–3   mended the ↑harmony of↓ the phrase.
3–4   this fact Jonson
4–5   lines" & ⟨Greene⟩ ↑Meres↓ thinks
11   in that ⟨very⟩ sort.
12   necessary to ⟨speak⟩ ↑say↓ a few
14   ⟨Whilst the words are chosen⟩ One page of Shakspear
15–16   His ↑rich↓ vocabulary ⟨is rich &⟩ searches all the ⟨resources⟩
       ↑provinces↓ of language ↑the court,↓ the camp, the ⟨country⟩
       ↑farms,↓
18   his ⟨la⟩ maiden
20   introduced, ⟨f⟩ like Caliban, for whom he has ⟨found out⟩
       devised
22–23   Whilst the words ⟨are chosen as if for their beauty alone,⟩
       ↑minister↓ so much delight ⟨do they minister⟩ to the ear, ↑that
       they seem . . . beauty only↓
27–28   elevated passages.
       ⟨The perfection of the writing is such too as centuries
      of collation & revision could not amend so that one is almost
      tempted to believe in his case in a Philonic inspiration which
      guided the pen of the poet & restrained the hand of players
      scriveners & editors that none should tamper with the precious
      text. How else should⟩ /
      ⟨Of his language i⟩It must be remarked that ⟨his is preemi-
      nently⟩ it may be
30–(311)1   in 1600.
       ⟨And yet I call you servile ministers⟩
       I tax not you, ⟨ye⟩ ↑you↓ elements, with unkindness
       I never gave you kingdoms called you ⟨daughters⟩ ↑chil-
       dren↓

Lines

You owe me no subscription why then let fall
⟨And yet I call you servile ministers
That have with two pernicious daughters⟩ joined
Your horrible pleasure;

Page 311

5	battles ⟨a⟩gainst
10–11	but ⟨if I quench thee⟩ ↑once put out↓ thine Thou ⟨fairest⟩ ↑cunningest↓ pattern
14	writing ↑is↓ such ⟨too⟩
21	editing ⟨the first edition of⟩ his plays
21–22	published ↑1624↓ . . . death of Shakspear
25	& yet all ↑are↓
29–31	↑in whom all manly . . . pleasure.↓ Cleopatra ⟨whom he would⟩ ↑a female Sardanapalus, the poet↓
32–33	passion but ⟨that in no sordid manner but in a way⟩ ↑distinguished ⟨from⟩ abundantly . . . abandonment↓
34	even to ⟨the⟩ ↑her↓ devotion to her lover is

Page 312

1	even ⟨voluptuousness⟩ ↑luxury↓ sublime.
1–16	↑How noble the sentiments . . . beggars nurse & Caesars↓
10	A better life tis
18	gives him that
21–24	pleasing parts, ↑such as Duncan's . . . of the air ⟨& the⟩ indicated . . . delicate↓ ⟨the progress is so natural & the end ↑⟨event⟩↓ so just⟩ the
25	banquet ↑are↓ so just
27	& the ⟨end⟩ ↑event↓ so just
30–31	barons. ↑Gloster . . . Salisbury↓ these
34	times ⟨such as are represented⟩ these pretensions are presently tried therefore
35–(313)1	trumpets ↑It is the blazon of an approved↓ They affect us as realities They are ⟨not⟩ ⟨images but⟩ the stuff

Page 313

6	enough. W We
9–10	Prince Hal.
	⟨We are accustomed to admire the finely discriminated⟩
	⟨The women⟩
	In Dryden's time
13–16	little read. or they wd have found the ⟨sweetness &⟩ truth of Imogen, ↑purity↓ Isabel, Juliet, Catos daughter ↑heroism↓ Portia, Desdemona, ↑piety↓ Cordelia, ↑luxury↓ Cleopatra ↑ambition↓ Lady Macbeth, ↑satire↓ Beatrice

Lines

17–18   the imagination which is the highest praise Ariel

20   leave the s[?] ⟨subject⟩ ↑details↓ without

21   separated from ⟨his⟩ their

22   crown & ↑choicely↓ kept ⟨& valued⟩ for

24–25   profound ⟨observations⟩ ↑reflexions↓

30   English tongue ⟨ar⟩ being

31   that they ⟨need⟩ who

Page 314

7   the saying of [blank] in Lear?

27   satire ↑was ever uttered↓ upon ⟨the⟩ false

29   faith ⟨was ever uttered⟩ to surpass

Page 315

13   ↑⟨The Criticism of 200 years has striven to make a catalogue of Shakspeares library.⟩↓
    With all the deductions that ⟨we⟩ can be

14   enough ⟨to⟩ remains to astonish us. ⟨Still⟩ It is

15–16   separate ⟨between⟩ what is admirable ⟨&⟩ ↑from↓ what is ⟨simply⟩ ↑merely↓ fortunate ↑in the history of this genius↓,

19–22   ↑Yet the immense . . . Shakspeare has ⟨not⟩ bro't . . . much moment↓
    · ⟨Let it be con⟩ It is to be considered

24–25   action in the time ⟨of⟩ ↑when↓ ⟨Sir Walter Rale⟩ Sir Francis Drake had, ↑for the first time,↓ sailed

27   Sidney ⟨d⟩ stimulated

28   than by ↑the↓ ⟨spirit⟩ courtesy

29–30   when ↑the ambition of↓ Essex

30–31   defended ⟨the⟩ England when ⟨Bacon wa⟩ the Court was served ⟨by⟩ not only

32   transcendant ⟨genius⟩ abilities

34   Herbert, ↑Herrick↓ ⟨three⟩ poets

Page 316

4–6   commends ↑it in↓ Elizabeth that ↑Some ages . . . princess lived↓ ⟨she was preeminent⟩ in a

9   which keeps ↑the powers of↓ men ⟨of ability in⟩ tense

12–15   ↑It was impossible . . . their ⟨genius⟩ ↑accomplishments↓ & learning↓ It

16   manners & society should

17–18   conspicuous scene. ⟨It was not⟩ ↑We must not think Shakspear↓ less ⟨amenable[?]⟩ indebted to it, ⟨Shakspear⟩ that his contemporar⟨ies⟩y

20–21   it is true ⟨that he did not invent his fables⟩ ↑his fables were furnished to his hands.↓

Lines
22–23   works of ↑Homer↓
24–25   found that ⟨he very readil⟩ a great number of ⟨Phila⟩ the French
27   old plays on the ↑same↓ subjects ⟨of⟩ ↑as↓ his ⟨plays⟩ ↑own↓
29   himself. ⟨In Coriolanus⟩ Many plays
33   materials ↑Nor will it be denied↓ He
34   to us, ⟨no doubt⟩ because

Page 317

3   in his age.
4–5   Century or Nation.
[upside down at the bottom of this page:]
⟨SHAKSPear
    Rhythm
        Homekeeping youth have ever homely wits
        He leaves his friends to dignify them more
        Makes mouths at the invisible event
        Whereon the numbers cannot try the cause.⟩
The happy conception . . . than of poets   [on recto of separate leaf, facing verso of previous leaf. An insert mark occurs on that leaf between "Holinshed" and "Undoubtedly," but the sentence seems to fit this context better]
9   which ⟨had its own⟩ came solitary
10   full expansion This
12   Composition ⟨or⟩ i.e. Putting
13   It is the ⟨capital law⟩ ↑⟨charm⟩↓ ↑most powerful secret↓
13–14   ↑In Nature↓ A most
15–18   union of ⟨simple⟩ ↑common↓ elements. ⟨What⟩ ↑Fontenelle . . . Is this all! What↓ grandeur
19   many ⟨very familiar⟩ ↑similar↓ & in
20   ↑In like manner↓ In all
32   their ⟨relations⟩ ↑natural affinities↓. N ⟨Synthesis or Composition is the great instrument by which the Mind works in all great effects.⟩
35–(318)13   instruments becomes . . . attributed to him. [inserted sheet]

Page 318

2–4   with the mind." ↑Composition or ⟨putting together⟩ methodical union is this Instrument↓   The orator ↑who astonishes the senate↓ is nowise
6   whereby he ⟨charms⟩ now fires
7–8   found separate one . . . first school some
9–10   some ⟨by⟩ in his own sick bed; some through his ⟨own⟩ crimes ⟨Burke or Canning or even Patrick Henry⟩ probably admires his ↑own↓
11–12   equal unarmed that is, without . . . Synthesis to

Lines
14 ⟨instruments becomes able to perform much more & of much greater difficulty: & the case is exactly the same with the mind."⟩ This makes the difference

15 the ↑chant of the↓ improvisatore

16 be any ⟨improvisatore⟩ strictly

18 Hamlet or Lear but

23 short date   The

25 remainder   Just

26–27 instructed them to ⟨construct⟩ build the rest. ⟨No hands could make a watch   The hands brot dry sticks together & struck the flint with iron or rubbed sticks for fire & melted the ore & with stones made crowbar & hammer these again helped to make chisel & file rasp rasp [sic] & saw piston & boiler & so the watch & the steamengine are made which the hands could never have produced & these again are new tools to make still more recondite & prolific instruments⟩ So do the

27 collated [?]

31 in its ⟨own⟩ turn

31–32 was day & ⟨being⟩ ↑happiness↓ to him.

Page 319

4–5 Nature ↑least of all in her costliest productions↓.

5 never eluded ↑⟨least of all in their costliest effects.⟩↓

6 ounce and ⟨the⟩ deep

8 ↑by a profligate & buffoon. ⟨They indispensably demand↓ ⟨without⟩ habits of wisdom, ⟨without⟩ the hoarding of observation, ⟨without⟩ a the healthful action of a gentle & magnanimous mind.⟩

10 & goodness ⟨the hoarding of observa⟩tions a mind

11 with ⟨a most⟩ ↑the utmost↓ tenacity

13–14 Spirit. ↑& the more . . . study⟨h⟩ . . . most wonder↓

[The following comments, not in either journals or lectures, appear in the working notes:]

SHAKSPEAR a philosopher, a transcendentalist.

So far from Shaksp. sacrificing his own taste to the corrupt taste of the times, as is always said, he seems never to consult any taste but his own. He writes for the intelligent alone. Most of his plays seem rather poems than plays for the stage. Every speech is too fine, too wise for declamation, & demands great dramatic talent to present it at all to an audience. The wise oracles the robed primeval bards Orpheus, Hesiod, Empedocles, Hermes. that were as Gods to men cd. not speak graver than this Comedian.

"Say, if thou dar'st, proud Lord of Warwickshire,
That I am guilty of Duke Humphrey's death."

I am mightily taken with these vaunts, & the high style of the nobles; not less than a boy of fourteen, is. At the Name of "Lord of Warwickshire" my ear ⟨is⟩ immediately tingles, my imagination is stimulated, & the vision of the mountains & woods & rivers of a county rises in connection with the haughty lord who owns & represents them. I am also very sensible of the dignity of the warlike associations all along awakened in Henry VI. I am affected as boys & barbarians are, by the appearance of a few ⟨wilf⟩ rich & wilful gentlemen who ⟨defy the world &⟩ take their honor into their own keeping, & defy the world so confident are they of their courage & strength, & whose appearance is the arrival of so much life & virtue. In dangerous times, they are presently tried, & therefore their name is a flourish of trumpets. They, at least, affect us as a reality. They are not pretences, but the substance of which that age & world is made. They are true heroes for their time. They make what is, in their minds, the greatest sacrifice. They will, for an injurious word, peril all their state & wealth & go to the field. ⟨But⟩ Take away that principle, & they become pirates & Bonthrons.

But another age comes. A truer religion & ethics open and a man ⟨sets⟩ puts himself under the dominion of Principles   I see him to be the servant of truth & love & fortitude & unmoveable in the waves of the crowd. I regard no longer those tingling names that so tickled my ear. This is a baron of a better nobility & a stouter stomach. The man who without any notice of his action abroad, expecting none, takes in solitude the right step uniformly, on his private choice, does not yield, in my imagination, to any man. He is willing to be hanged at his own gate rather than consent to an ⟨surrender⟩ ↑abridgement↓ of his freedom or the suppression of his conviction. The Cause of Peace is not now the Cause of Cowardice. They uphold it who are willing to stand upon it. Those barons awed me because the brawls of the time put their vaunts to the proof & they ⟨faile⟩ made good their word. But we are fallen on times when an equal violence is breaking out & threatens presently to try the texture of every man's principles. A man had better quit the Associations of the day, & go home much, & call his thoughts to council, & lay out the map of his own road, & stablish himself in those causes he approves. ↑Coarse slander,↓ Fire, tar & feathers, & the gibbet he may freely bring home to his mind, & with what sweetness of temper he can and study himself to know how high he can fix his views of duty, braving such penalties, whenever it may please the next newspaper & a sufficient number of his neighbors to declare his opinions fanatical. I beseech him to fix them at the greatest height of his reason, & this, above all, — that having there fixed them, & made an irrevocable covenant with himself therein to die, let him hold fast the merriest heart, the cheerfullest countenance, knowing that with all his love for good men, the terrors of a Mob are unworthy to occupy the thoughts of a ↑Christian↓ gentleman.

The Merchant of Venice . . . The abundance of allusion joined with closeness to the matter in hand is the true mark of genius   A continual ⟨reference to⟩ proof of habits of meditation & proof at the same time of living at this moment

I can scarce believe my eyes, when they show me the whole speech I admire so much in Coriolanus — (all prose in Plutarch,) or the portrait of Wolsey, in Holinshed. Then first I see the secret of his inexhaustible fertility. It is that all things serve him equally well. He converts ⟨the⟩ dust & stones to gold. It is that he lifts things from their feet & thereby transforms the whole visible scene into picture instantly. He seems to reveal to us at once the immensity of our own wealth, and to deify all men.

[*Hamlet*]   Where words are best, there are they least, as in the soliloquy, for they become mere signs to denote in a general way the direction & movement of the great undercurrent of thought whose whole course is all, & the particular wave or drop, naught. . . .

The Readiness is all

I think in this play one can get more of Shakspear's private thoughts & confessions than in any other   The skill of managing presentiments & superstitions is very great & the obscure half intimations of events best not precisely known, as Ophelia's fate

7. LORD BACON

Page 320

Lines
1   class ⟨serve⟩ do us

Page 321

1	↑and degraded by crimes,↓
2–3	↑the↓ bright & ⟨eternal⟩ ↑durable↓ objects ↑of ye intellect↓
4–5	It is ↑a↓ fatal ↑blow↓ to the mind ⟨when⟩ ↑to remove from it↓
5–6	veneration. ⟨are removed.⟩ These ⟨supply such⟩ ↑restore them↓. We make ↑before these divinities↓
8–9	↑By remaining long in ye neighborhood↓ We are
9–10	orb of ⟨Shakspear⟩ ↑Milton[3]↓ or Dante[2] or Plato[1]
11	always ⟨right⟩ ↑wise↓ lose
14	& ⟨it⟩ affords
19–20	⟨Here⟩ ↑Bacon↓ is a ⟨second mind of equally universal⟩ another universal mind, one who ⟨with⟩ ↑to↓ quite different ⟨objects possessed⟩ ↑ends exercised↓
22	& adorn ⟨not⟩ the objects
23	agency of ⟨another faculty⟩ the Understanding /
23n	[inserted in pencil on next page (otherwise blank):]

We have considered Luther a scholar who by the predominance of a religious enthusiasm over a will of prodigious force introduced a great ↑religious↓ Revolution in modern times. Bacon is another Reformer of almost equal efficiency in far different sphere, who in his genius was ⟨at⟩ ↑in↓ all points a contrast to Luther and acting very remotely on the multitude has established for himself a lasting influence in all studious minds and as far as every human being has an interest in the discovery of Truth.

24 ⟨Lord Bacon who was born 1561⟩
⟨The writings of Lord Bacon make so material a portion of English literature that ⟨it is almost impossible to speak of them without a slight notice of⟩ ↑some notice is due to↓ the remarkable man who wrote them.⟩ Bacon was born in 1561

26 Cambridge ⟨at 12⟩ in his 12th year⟨s⟩,

31–32 James [new line] In 1607

32–33 Lord ⟨Chancellor⟩ ↑Keeper↓ and In 1619 ⟨he was made⟩ Lord

34–(322)3 ⟨In 1621 he fell⟩ ↑In 1621 on the . . . was ⟨tried⟩ impeached . . . pleasure   The . . . forgave him ye fine↓

Page 322

5–7 accomplished man ↑Of his rare eloquence & of his singular weight of personal character↓

7 deci⟨ded⟩sive

7–8 contemporaries ⟨of his ↑rare↓ eloquence & weight of personal character⟩.

9 Venerable Bacon.
{V. Ben Jonson ⟨next⟩ second page}

14 verse⟨ct[?]⟩d in. ↑⟨His most casual talk deserveth to be written⟩↓ ⟨So as⟩

16–17 Chirurgeon. ↑His most casual . . . written↓

19 trouble⟨d⟩

22–23 carriage ⟨he was known to own⟩ strook

24–25 from him. ⟨for fear of appearing ignorant or fancy⟩.

28 heard ↑he↓ did

29 citizen. ⟨Yet without any great if any interruption of his other studies⟩

32 ⟨Ben Jonson⟩   The testimony

Page 323

2 gravity in ↑his↓ speaking

10 ⟨My conceit of his person . . . help to make it manifest⟩ [as on p. 325]
⟨Aubrey says "All the great & good loved & honoured him."⟩
Sir Walter Raleigh said

18 courtier ↑a low intriguer↓ he

20 not ⟨the gravest⟩ ↑ a very grave↓

24–27 ↑His ⟨fall⟩ ↑ruin↓ was permitted by K James to save Buckingham ↑on↓ whom . . . himself promising to annul ye sentence↓

Lines

28   letters ⟨yield⟩ ↑are↓ too ⟨deep⟩ ↑many↓ proofs,
30   ⟨Do speak⟩ Your kind
32   suppleness ⟨to the unworthy Buckingham⟩ of such
33   without ⟨disgust⟩ pain?

Page 324

5–6   Essex one . . . men loved
10   remain ⟨ask⟩ ↑plead↓
12   which ⟨Bacon⟩ was worth
33   deformities in th⟨is⟩e
34   endowed ⟨man⟩ ↑person↓;

Page 325

2–4   exalted We . . . thoughts ↑We follow . . . masculine understanding↓ that we come . . . Archangel ⟨we follow⟩
8   We are ⟨irresistibly⟩ reminded
9   individual ⟨has⟩ ↑is afflicted with↓ intervals of insanity ⟨in⟩ ↑during↓
12   prostration fawns
15   in the ⟨s⟩ depraved
15   in the ⟨infamous⟩ hard
21   thus of him ⟨M⟩
24   proper to ⟨his person⟩ himself,
27   strength for

Page 326

1   knowledge ⟨& so our confidence⟩ in
2   Bacon, is, ⟨its Universality⟩ the extent
9   the whole ⟨frame⟩ ↑system↓,
12   No↑ne↓ ⟨man⟩ ↑ever↓ hoped more highly of ⟨the⟩
13–14   ↑It is inferior . . . greatly of it↓ ⟨The⟩ In our age
22–23   perception of ⟨Spiritual⟩ ↑sensible↓ Presence
25   cultivated, ⟨"⟩
29–30   was ⟨in his view⟩ ↑to use his expression↓ "the ⟨priest⟩ interpreter
31   to ⟨enumerat⟩ make an inventory of ⟨his⟩ ↑man's↓
33   ⟨It seems to me that Lord Bacon's mind has the best claim to the praise of universality ↑He had a right to pass the censure upon others↓ A thought which he is fond of quoting from Heraclitus that men rather explore their own little worlds than the great world which God made, for he is free from that fault himself⟩. ⟨H⟩ ⟨Less than others⟩ He has not like others

Page 327

2   lie. ⟨He⟩ & for what
5   fact & ⟨he knew⟩ ↑for he was wise enough to know↓

21–23 ↑Thence he is omnivorous . . . fancies & of falsehoods↓ ⟨Therefore he did not hastily arrange but increasingly collected facts   His own Intellect did not act much on what he collected. Very much stands as he found it mere ⟨heaps⟩ lists of facts material or spiritual. All his⟩ /

25 Literary Man ⟨He conceived it possible⟩ Believing

27–28 mind ⟨another Nature⟩ ↑a second Nature, a second Universe↓.

33 Nothing was ⟨too⟩ ↑so↓ great, nothing too ↑so↓ small, no thing ⟨too⟩ ↑so↓

34 literary man ⟨should be the master of business of courts of trades of arts of luxuries⟩ should know the whole

Page 328

1 this in no ↑general & vague way but↓ with

4 of ⟨we⟩ armies

4–5 of luxur⟨ies⟩y

5 of ⟨hypocrisy⟩ dissimulation, ↑of fraud↓

7–9 for business ↑sharpened no doubt . . . in ye ear of ye Queen↓

10 an ⟨accomplished mind⟩ ↑Education↓ to make ⟨him⟩ ↑the Scholar↓

11 useful ⟨marshalling superior⟩ oversight

16 in substance in

17 an ⟨o⟩ opinion

22–23 contemplation & doctrine." Advancement of L.
    ⟨This is not an occasional [rest of leaf torn off] ex . . . but is the settled fai . . . habitual e . . . is ↑almost↓ no⟨th⟩ . . . none o . . . has . . . expe . . . who . . . the f . . . lea . . . h . . .⟩ /
    ⟨His law tracts come to us with high commendation from English lawyers. His Advancement of Learning is professedly a survey of the whole body of Literature or the recorded thinking of Man with a view to pronounce upon its fulness & its defects
    His State of Europe written at 19 is a minute account of ye govt of each principality in Europe from ye greatest . . . ally are a proof of this . . . ects indifferently . . . Courage . . . self in . . . civil . . . Empire . . . in- . . . rtune . . . s . . .⟩ /
    ⟨masks in which he shows ye skill of an upholsterer as well as the eye of a man of taste⟩

27–28 creed. ⟨There is It determined⟩ This happy

Page 329

2 knowledge especially . . . action whereto

6 His ⟨dense pages⟩ massive

Lines

10–11	works, to ⟨show the bearing⟩ intimate
12	labor ⟨is⟩ considered
15	language. one on which the ⟨fame⟩ credit
16	depends. ⟨Its style is an imperial mantle stiff . . . vivid image. ↑No man . . . particular passages.↓⟩ [For the omitted portions, see the whole passage as Emerson transcribed it a few sentences below.] ⟨The⟩ ↑The↓ treatise
17	the world ↑the Recorded Thinking of Man↓ to
18	defects but
19–21	prescient. ↑As if the great chart of ye Intel. world lay open before him↓ He ⟨surveys⟩ ↑explores↓ every ⟨part⟩ ↑region↓ of human wit ↑ye waste & ye cultivated tracts↓
22–23	It ⟨contains⟩ ↑is made up of↓ passages ↑each↓ of
23–24	fame of a inferior writers. ⟨It is equally excellent for splendor & for sense⟩.
24	mantle stiff
30	book is ⟨a⟩ ↑one↓
30–31	so that ⟨w⟩ a passage

Page 330

19	was tho't ↑so↓ noble
26	designed to ⟨[?]⟩ invigorate
32	⟨Truth⟩ Knowledge he said, ⟨such as the doctors had⟩ was
37	observations that

Page 331

4	Idols intimating
8	Tribe or thos the
11	Den those
15	forum those
17	Theatre those
24	mankind not
27	History. And
33	Inferior men. Especially

Page 332

1	⟨The⟩ His curiosity . . . nature those
3	the ⟨twilight⟩ confines
6–7	in envy; ⟨the whole class of facts of auguries prophecies coincidences, omens.⟩ the supposed virtues of amulets,
27	physiological pointing
28–29	aid on the ⟨far⟩ superior
29	what we do It is
31	sentiments & ⟨the⟩ a most dangerous superstition to ⟨prefer⟩ raise

Page 333

Lines	
1	speculations ⟨& ex⟩ proposed
2	have ⟨of⟩ no ↑scientific↓
3	show ⟨his boundless curiosity⟩ & his
6	commentary ⟨upon⟩ ↑& exposition of↓
12	Yet ↑almost↓ all
16–17	whenever he ⟨speaks⟩ surrenders himself to his genius as when
17–31	in the ↑first↓ Essay [marginal note:] on Truth) {Insert X} ↑X How profound . . . unpleasing to ymselves." On Truth-↓
22	mummeries ⟨of⟩ & triumphs
31	⟨or⟩ and let us believe
32	for ⟨his⟩ submitting
33	Power to do good [marginal note:] ⟨on Great Place⟩

Page 334

1	in act. and that
4	being ↑more↓ a spur
24	what ⟨nicety of⟩ criticism
25	taste in ⟨yt⟩ ↑those↓ on Gardens

Page 335

3–4	↑This mt. be expected in his Nat. Hist. . . . Essays it is the same.↓
5	ground a vast
9	somewhat fragmentary / ⟨work is therefore somewhat fragmentary⟩
11	proverbs, ⟨& the⟩ ↑all wise but↓
12	mechanical ⟨& not by⟩ things ⟨being⟩ on one
13	together; ⟨&⟩ the
18	⟨It⟩ ↑So loose a Method↓ had
18–19	perpetual ⟨emendation⟩ amendment
21–22	Novum Organon that
22	⟨And now his m⟩ Many fragments
26	ended. ⟨To make Bacons works complete he must live to the end of the world.⟩ Each of Shakspears
31	1. ⟨One of⟩ a new courage
32–33	by one ⟨one⟩ scholar. This he he has

Page 336

5	2. The other ⟨refl⟩ moral of his ⟨life⟩ ↑history↓,
8–9	stand out ↑like a loathsome excrescence↓
9	nor ⟨genius⟩ ↑wit↓
10	⟨nor⟩ ↑or↓ dignify meanness.

Lines
11   front ⟨as [?]⟩ nor seems
12   obscured," ⟨&⟩ dividing

8. BEN JONSON, HERRICK, HERBERT, WOTTON

Page 338

1–2	↑I proceed . . . Charles↓ [pencil on blank verso of title leaf]
6–8	in ⟨his times⟩ ↑ye beginning of XVII Century↓. ↑Of humble birth . . . industry & resolution↓ His
10	no ↑literary↓ man
10–11	many ↑honorable↓ notices
12	the ⟨Centre⟩ ↑President↓ of that brilliant society ↑of men of letters↓
13–14	reign. consisting of ↑Spenser↓ Shakspear, Marlow ↑Camden↓
17	↑The Latin historian Camden was his teacher.↓
20	have written ⟨in his praise⟩ panegyrics
23–24	several ↑regular↓ dramas ↑both trag. & Com. He↓
24–25	a ↑sort of↓ master of ⟨the⟩ revels

Page 339

1–3	genius the . . . power & not the ↑dramatic↓ merit of ⟨single plays⟩ ↑his pieces↓
4–7	↑He who takes up . . . heavy disappointment.↓
8	indulgence. ⟨They are very heavy & worthless⟩. ⟨He⟩ They are very dull yet ⟨it⟩ with
10–11	writers ↑In his Comedies;↓ the characters ⟨of the play⟩ are usually ⟨the⟩ ↑made to↓
13–14	life as ↑ye↓ Euphuism ↑which Scott has represented in Sir P. Shafton in Monastery↓ but
16	at the ⟨pretensions of⟩ aukwardness of a ⟨new⟩
17	incident is ⟨pedantic⟩ ↑⟨pompous⟩ prosaic↓
18–20	by ⟨the⟩ one sally of wit or sparkle of ⟨vivacity⟩ ↑mirth↓ ⟨They seem so sadly unmirthful⟩ The names the ⟨desig⟩ plot the costume are ⟨all of⟩ those of comedy yet all ⟨goes⟩ ↑creeps↓ so ⟨sadly⟩ ↑heavily↓
20–21	some⟨thing else⟩ ↑popular piece↓,
22	this ↑supposition↓
23	appears ⟨excessively⟩ ↑very↓
24–25	had been ⟨damned⟩ ↑rejected↓. ⟨There never was such⟩ ↑Dulness so↓ rich & pedantic ⟨dulness And we⟩ ↑as Jonson's makes us↓
28–29	Latin reading ⟨and seem⟩ ↑but he never . . . stroke ⟨and⟩ of pity or terror; and they seem↓ to have
31–(340)1	⟨What is it then that makes the merit of Ben Jonson.⟩ ↑What

is it then . . . audience suppose . . . All savors of the kingdom of wit↓

Page 340

1	times ⟨his la⟩ he made
2–4	↑We shd. never allow . . . it is the abuse.↓
6–7	(But his especial merit is that) his moral sense
8	bard (which in the earliest times they fulfilled), namely,
9–10	Jonson ⟨worthily⟩ discharged
11	Preface to ⟨Volpone⟩ the Fox
15–16	first being ⟨ye⟩ a
19	recover them them
22	Mankind This
23	rhetoric upon." ⟨But it⟩
35–(*341*)2	spirits of ⟨ye⟩ ↑our↓ World." (Works. Vol 2 p. 112) ↑"I have laboured . . . Reason of living."↓

Page 341

5–6	virtue. ⟨In th⟩ He delights
7–24	↑Ben Jonson & Donne . . . sermon in a bear garden.↓
7	⟨There is in him⟩ ↑Ben Jonson↓ & ⟨in⟩ Donne
7–8	Marlow ↑in their better writings↓
9	thoughts, ⟨or⟩ th⟨e⟩ose moral
11–12	behind them ⟨a regard to the Pleasing⟩ ↑the study to please↓
15–16	↑They paint for eternity↓
22–23	↑Voltaire said wittily That . . . those who had none.↓
25	New Inn ↑otherwise↓ a tedious . . . piece is
26	young ⟨Platonist⟩ ↑philosopher↓
27	the ⟨doctrine or philosophy⟩ ↑doctrine↓
29–30	walks ⟨Crites &⟩ Arete ↑the goddess of Virtue & Crites her votary↓
30	sense of ⟨Epi⟩ Seneca
30–31	↑If this shows the virtue of the Poet↓
32	drama ⟨but it shows the goodness of the Poet⟩ (It is a realizing of the project of an ⟨[?]⟩ asylum for the sane.) Tis

Page 342

5	vanities of ⟨the stews⟩ braggarts
8	& ⟨is at⟩ rises at once
37	similitude ⟨of a right he⟩

Page 343

35–36	dramatic ⟨merit⟩ effect

Lines
1   intellect The same merit of clear ⟨perception⟩ ↑insight↓
5   reputation ⟨I ever read⟩ ↑in English↓.
8   equal ⟨merits⟩ interest
12   with a ⟨power of⟩ melody

Page 345

4   sport⟨s⟩ & sum it
20   pieces, an Ode
32   seats & ↑bowers↓ fires

Page 346

7–8   & upon ⟨authors⟩ books.
9–10   Herrick ↑⟨born 1591⟩↓
10–11   Numbers. a ⟨p⟩ genuine English Poet   His
11–13   lyric composed short . . . gay dainty & coarse upon
14   ⟨I c⟩ enumerate
16   birds & ⟨fl[?]⟩ bowers
30   All these ⟨subjects⟩ objects
30–31   not ⟨enumerated⟩ ↑here specified↓
34   exalted by the ⟨contemplation⟩ sight of ↑a volcano↓
37   victory of ⟨the⟩ genius over custom ⟨to s⟩ He
37–(347)1   muse ⟨has no⟩ ↑is not nice or↓ squeamish, ⟨ear eye⟩ but can
            ⟨[?]⟩ tread with ↑firm &↓ elastic step ⟨among⟩

Page 347

2–3   the sun-↑beam↓ which
3–5   Herrick ⟨if any may have⟩ ↑by the choice . . . themes, has↓
            pushed this privelege ⟨a thought⟩ too far, ↑rather I think↓
6   power, ⟨or⟩, ↑than↓
9–10   so that ↑this verse is all music, &,↓ what he writes ⟨w with⟩ ↑in
            the indulgence of↓ the most
12   this ↑felicity↓ need be ⟨adduce⟩ cited

Page 348

9   mothers breast
              Tel
19   works of ⟨kindness⟩ ↑mercy↓
27   There is ⟨something of⟩ an air
31   that ⟨it is as hard⟩ there ⟨is as much⟩ ↑may be as↓
32   as in a ⟨book⟩ ↑treatise↓. or

Page 349

5   affirmed   It
7   merit is the ⟨simplicity⟩ ↑elegance↓ and manliness ↑& 1↓ of his
8–9   sentences   He has . . . English a perfect

Lines	
25	So the ⟨spirit⟩ fancy cools,
29–30	book ⟨th I know⟩ which is apt
30	acquaintance. ⟨as many good books will.⟩
31	quaint ↑epigrammatic↓ style
32	in ⟨use⟩ ↑vogue↓ in England {& especially used by Donne & Cowley} a
34	properties of ⟨the lake the rose the star or mountain to which he makes allusion⟩ ↑natural objects↓
36	This {is not natural & may easily be overdone &}
36–37	pushed to ⟨{the last degree of}⟩ affectation. By ⟨h⟩Herbert

Page 350

2	come to be loved. /
	⟨His poems are the breathing of a devout soul reading the riddle of the world with a poets eye but with a saint's affections. The sentiments are so exalted the thought so wise the piety so fragrant that we cannot read this book without joy that our nature is capable of being so addressed & criticism is ⟨lost⟩ ↑silent↓ in ⟨higher⟩ the exercise of higher faculties.⟩
4	always ⟨perfectly⟩ simple
5–6	power of ↑exalted↓ thought
6	expression. ⟨In general according to the elevation of the soul, will the power over language always be.⟩
7	organ ⟨of⟩ on which ⟨every man⟩ ↑men↓ play⟨s⟩ with ⟨different⟩ ↑unequal↓
9	afraid or ↑when he is↓
10	when ⟨his passions are moved⟩ ↑he is angry↓, and eloquent when his ⟨mind⟩ ↑intellect↓
13	Prose is ⟨difficult enough⟩ ↑laborious↓,
14	any ⟨involved⟩ ↑difficult↓ metre
21–22	will ↑be↓ the power over language ⟨always be.⟩

Page 351

1	little piece ⟨of his⟩ called
23–24	mutilated ⟨version⟩ ↑copy↓
25–(352)8	Teach me my God . . . Makes that & the action fine / [a light pencil line is run through these five stanzas, the sixth being overleaf]

Page 352

3	Which ⟨for⟩ with this
34	Let me not . . . love thee not [written over the same in pencil]

Page 353

Lines	
3	⟨We⟩ Here poetry
8	book ⟨so⟩ that seemed
11	before 1670. within
16	Wotton ↑{born 1568}↓
21–22	Gentilis then Professor of Civil law ↑and of his fellow student Dr Donne↓
23–24	with ↑Arminius, at Leyden,↓ Theodore Beza & ↑at Geneva he lodged with↓
24	↑At Venice↓ He lived
27	Organon. & Vieta at Venice & ↑Robert↓ Bellarmine
28–30	Essex Bacon's . . . friend made Wotton his secretary. ↑& W. accompanied him in a Voyage to Spanish main↓
31	Hales, ↑⟨& Dr Donne⟩ & Cowley↓ of Sir Walter Raleigh; & Sir
36	advice ⟨touching⟩ ↑on setting forth on↓

Page 354

2–4	circle of ⟨acquaintance⟩ ↑friends each of any . . . common man↓ his
6–7	to us ⟨a⟩ though a man of ↑uncommon↓ merit ⟨himself⟩ yet ↑in↓
7–8	with the offi⟨ce⟩ ↑⟨part⟩↓ ↑relation he↓ ⟨he⟩ ⟨discharged⟩ ↑⟨played⟩↓ ↑sustained↓ to so many
11	the "happy life."
15–16	tombstone ⟨that he was⟩ ↑not his name but yt here lay↓
16–17	disputation ⟨is⟩ ↑will prove↓ . . . Church" A
18	upon Critic⟨s,⟩ism,
19	Album ⟨at⟩ ⟨when abroad⟩ ↑at Augusta in Germany↓
21–23	↑Another maxim . . . was this that . . . wiser by resting.↓
23–24	received an ⟨emp⟩ diplomatic
24	advice to whom
27–28	truth. for says Sir H.W. You shall never be believed. & by
31	& undertakings" ⟨Another of his sayings was Souls grow wiser by resting.⟩
32–33	His ⟨well⟩ advice . . . well-known il . . . stretti "Thoughts

Page 355

3–4	Angler, Isaak Walton
5	anecdotes ⟨of⟩ and
8–12	notice. Hooker ⟨the⟩ usually called "the judicious" author . . . Polity. Roger Ascham a tedious writer Donne . . . Crashaw; Raleigh ↑Hist of ye World↓ & Sir . . . Poesy. [upside down at the bottom of the sheet:] ⟨The drama of that age Ben Jonson, Ford, Beaumont Fletcher Massinger, if they

exhibit with any fidelity the ⟨existing⟩ state of ⟨s⟩ manners & the tone of fa⟨v⟩shionable society we may certainly con-gratulate ourselves upon a prodigious refinement of manners & advancement in morals.
The⟩

14 ↑I close the lecture with one general remark.↓ ⟨It will be ob-served that in the notices that we have taken of individual writers we have been compelled to select a few as representa-tives of their age.⟩ By far

17–18 remain ↑several↓ false reputations ↑on↓ which justice is yet to be done ↑of which the chief are↓ Massinger ⟨Beaumont & Fletcher⟩.

25 & if ↑these scenes of profanity & indecency↓ they really
26–28 safely ⟨congratulat⟩ thank God ⟨for⟩ ↑that he has . . . hemi-spheres to make↓

9. ETHICAL WRITERS

Page 356

1 ⟨Our⟩ {A course
2 has no ⟨great p⟩ intrinsic
5 ⟨It⟩ Wit is not
8 more mean, ⟨&⟩ prosaic

Page 357

1 indicates ⟨a better d⟩ an improved
3–4 constellations, ⟨but⟩ ↑and↓ ye laws
5 link ⟨them⟩ the writers
8 of a Class.}
8n [For some later delivery of this lecture Emerson bracketed for omission his original introduction and substituted at this point, from Lecture I, the passage "I know that the word Literature . . . in common circulation among us" on pp. 229–230. At the same time, probably, he added two other paragraphs (see pp. 359n and 360n) and possibly the last paragraph also. Textual variants follow:]

Page 229

3 The subject of the present Lecture is the Ethical writers in our English literature. I venture to name so unpopular a ⟨title⟩ ↑subject↓ because of its ↑universal↓ ⟨interest⟩ ↑importance↓ ⟨to us all⟩. {The Ethical or Moral genius is one of the most conspicuous traits of the people now inhabiting Great Britain & the United States. And the books of this character are machines of greater efficiency than all others.} I know that the word

Lines
4	sound ⟨It does not sound practical.⟩
5–6	fanciful persons ⟨& not at all . . . . of the multitude⟩
7–9	wisdom. ⟨These objections . . . anything worth. But⟩ Every
12–16	pure enjoyments. {⟨Every object in nature . . . of the perfection⟩ / of the whole . . . beauty say so.}
17–18	mind of man. ⟨{Shall not they . . . abroad the waters.}⟩
19	precious drops. It
35	tight. Once brought

Page 230

3	time. ⟨Then what⟩ a vast
4–5	Discourse of cultivated persons & come to the
9	Chaucer ↑Shakspear↓ Bacon
11–12	Circulation among us.
	Then as to the class of writings I have named.

Page 357

9	⟨A literary work has a double aim to ⟨pro⟩ give pleasure or to exhibit truth⟩ There is a very great difference in the ↑order↓ class of thots
12	scholars readers . . . learning & have
13	received ⟨great praise⟩ ↑fame↓
14–15	Pocock, ⟨&⟩ Parr, Walton, Bryant. a merit
16–17	& ⟨of⟩ very subordinate ↑when unaccompanied by other accomplishments↓.
17–18	It is a ⟨species of⟩ merit
21	will highly ⟨value⟩ ↑prize↓.
23	not of a ⟨cultivated mind⟩ ↑wise man↓.
24	date ⟨recovered⟩ in the Assyrian
24–25	↑or the fixing . . . particle↓
26	rank ⟨with a⟩ in consequence
26–27	with a ↑Byzantine↓ coin
28–29	↑enlarge ye limits of valuable knowledge↓ cheer
30	⟨So with⟩ ↑The↓ poets
32	before ↑Suckling, Prior, Gay Waller, Garth, Warton,↓ or ⟨with⟩
34	laureate poets Chaucer
34–35	Southey ⟨when⟩ ⟨these writings⟩ have no

Page 358

2	improves. as the
6–7	brief a date as those opinions as most of the partisans ["as most . . . agitated the Church" apparently inserted]
11	have no ⟨antidote against oblivion⟩ inherent vitality
13–14	thought who address ⟨a class of⟩ ↑certain↓ feelings
15	no ⟨change⟩ ↑progress↓ of arts & no ⟨differe⟩ variety . . . alter those

18   general nature of man.

⟨↑The various faculties of man have been happily represented as bearing to each other the relation of several concave spheres one within another.↓ In proportion to the inwardness of ⟨any⟩ ↑the↓ thot or feeling a writer addresses in that proportion are his compositions durable. The gossip of your street or neighborhood is impertinent in the next street or next town. A piece ↑of↓ scientific[2] or political[1] information will interest men farther off. But an utterance ⟨of a deep⟩ ↑out of the heart's↓ conviction of a social right or of a ⟨religious⟩ ↑moral↓ sentiment will be equally pertinent in the ears of all men & to the remotest times. It seems as if many of our habits of thot & action were quite superficial & temporary & scarcely call into exercise the entire man. It seems as if all evil & error were superficial. The noble aphorism "Man is good but men are bad" seems to indicate that under the vicious peculiarities of each individual is a common nature which is pure & divine.⟩

19   ⟨What I would say, is,⟩ there is a class of

19   help us (& who keep the office of literature in repute)

20   wants, ⟨those⟩ who, treat of

21–25   nature of man ⟨& whose writings keep sweet through all ages⟩ who⟨se aim is to⟩ treat of duties & aim ⟨to make⟩ ↑with Socrates to make fair &↓ perfect souls ↑& whose writings keep sweet thro all ages.↓ ⟨The perma-⟩ ↑These yield . . . feed & grow.↓ ↑The perma-↓nence of writings

27   pulpit, ⟨&⟩ the bench

28–29   sitting room which make the mottoes of ⟨coats of arms of⟩ ↑newspapers &↓ seals, ↑& signposts.↓

Page 359

2   It is the ⟨simple aphorisms⟩ Golden Sayings of Pythagoras ⟨the simple aphorisms of Diogenes of Zeno⟩

3   Plutarch, all ⟨describing⟩ ↑reciting↓

5   common society the simple

6   Socrates, & ⟨the ethical passages⟩ the books

9n   [Emerson later inserted here a revision of the paragraph "Goethe has remarked . . . kingdoms are forgotten" from Lecture II (see p. 250), with variants as follows:]

Page 250

1   I may also say that of history this is the part that abides with us. Goethe has remarked

2   few anecdotes. And most readers will have regretted on closing a voluminous history like that of Rome or of England how much is already forgotten & how much more threatens soon to be. ⟨The⟩ To those who read with care & wisdom a very small part of all recurs

Lines

with any vivacity to the memory in involuntary thinking. What does that show? It shows that the memorable events

7–9   Solon the anecdotes of ⟨Phocion⟩, Aristides, & Alexander the Great, in Plutarch, ⟨the sayings of Diogenes,⟩ the story of Alfred and the herdmans wife; of Canute on the seashore; of Columbus and his egg; of Franklin and his whistle. These incidents

Page 359

12   contrary ⟨a word⟩ a⟨n epithet⟩ ↑remark↓ dropt by any writer ⟨tending to⟩ expressing

13–16   & our ⟨courage⟩ love & courage in human beings. ⟨Such⟩ ↑It is related of Heraclitus that one day sitting ⟨in⟩ alone . . . gods are here also"↓ {It is related of Diogenes that seeing a person ⟨making⟩ ↑dressing↓ himself ⟨wi⟩ very gaily to go to an entertainment, he asked him, "whether every day were not a festival to a good man?}"

24–25   exercise the ⟨greater⟩ ↑central↓ faculties. ⟨It seems as if⟩ ↑There is a state of mind↓ all evil & error

26   men are bad" ⟨seems to⟩ indicates

Page 360

2   Muse who ⟨is⟩ alone

4–5   speaks who ⟨uttered⟩ ↑expressed↓

6–7   but ↑who↓ plain & harsh, uttering

8   perfumed, ⟨continues⟩ ↑reaches with↓ her voice ↑to↓

11   insures their ⟨prodigious⟩ ↑equal↓ efficacy

13–16   ↑In the English . . . Scandinavian race.↓ [on inserted sheet]

13–14   truth the ⟨strong⟩ decided taste for it is

16n   [The inserted sheet continues with the passage from Lecture II, "Ina laid down . . . become his friend" (pp. 250–51), with variants as follows:]

Page 250

21   Let me illustrate this contemplative genius by one or two anecdotes which come to us from a period in the history of our ancestors nearly a thousand years ago.
           Ina laid down

27   his own couch. So had

Page 251

1   relics we may ⟨perceive⟩ ↑descry↓ what

7   speech of ↑Witan↓ the noble

8   missionaries, A.D. 626.

9   beyond, ⟨of⟩ of which

15   departs ⟨at⟩ ↑thro'↓

18   dreary ⟨scene⟩ ↑waste↓ from

Lines

22–23   certainty on this dark estate it merits our belief."
When Alfred knew . . . his friend."
Thus early we mark that contemplative . . . later ages by the English and American race   From the same ethical genius flows the excellence of English laws, the precision & energy / [end of inserted sheet]

Page 360

17–19   ⟨In the English mind this capacity for Ethical truth is very conspicuous compared with other nations as the French the Italian or the Scandinavian race⟩ ↑Hence the ⟨precision⟩ excellence of English laws, the precision & energy with which ↑at every period↓ the Courts have drawn & defined the theory of rights↓ Hence the zeal

21–22   ↑Hence the fact yt↓ The island

23–24   ⟨Then⟩ ↑Hence ye early versions of ye SS↓ ⟨The bible was translated.⟩ The liturgy was ⟨In Elizabeth's⟩ ↑written in Henry & Elizabeths time↓ and pervaded

27   men may ⟨see⟩ ↑discern↓ of

30   into the ⟨verses⟩ ↑lines↓ of

32   slow ↑interrupted↓ work

33   the ⟨deep⟩ ↑fragrant↓ piety

Page 361

1   character of ⟨piety that belongs⟩ ↑religion without superstition that↓

2–3   Hebrew race.
⟨Hence the Law⟩
The effect

4–6   ↑And as the English . . . truth so has↓ ⟨Of this class of writers⟩ England ⟨has⟩ produced a large number ↑of writers who could gratify this taste↓

8–14   company John . . . More who . . . writers, Jeremy Taylor the . . . Harrington ↑& Algernon Sidney↓ the political philosophers ⟨Algernon Si⟩ Milton ↑Donne↓ ⟨Cowley & Dryden⟩ Sir Thomas . . . Bunyan who . . . historian All

18   books ⟨w⟩ ⟨by⟩ from which

22–23   of all ↑others↓ they were

25   the cause partly

26–27   the ⟨great⟩ moral revolution which commencing ⟨some reigns earlier⟩ in the reign of Henry VIII if . . . older by

27–28   the ⟨great⟩ questions of the Reformation

30   growing ⟨gathered strength⟩ ↑proceeded in private↓ ⟨in⟩ ↑during↓

31–32   civil war & ⟨expelled the⟩ changed

34   history. ↑Witness↓ The

35   the ⟨books⟩ ↑massive volumes↓

Page 362

Lines	
1	logic all
2	subject" "Jeremy
11	⟨It was a period⟩ In that memorable
15–16	physiology "which . . . age." A
17	{About the same period
19–20	French when . . . tongue as ⟨the wo Essays of Montaigne &⟩ the philosophy
22	by Cotton /
23	we have ⟨commended⟩ had occasion
27	itself is ⟨raised⟩ ↑consoled↓ & exalted
30	proportion ⟨With his⟩ We cannot
31	virtue some
32	all the ⟨elegances⟩ ↑riches↓ of learning
33–34	republican who ⟨was⟩ out

Page 363

1	argument to ⟨strengt⟩ fortify
9–14	↑The Second Book . . . Govt &c is . . . to scholars↓ [this sentence and the rest of the paragraph to "numbers" is written out again on the facing page with textual variants as follows:] Reason of Ch. Govt urged against Prelaty . . . ambition ⟨more excellent⟩ than ⟨Chivalry ever devised⟩ ↑such as was never addressed to scholars↓ and the piece . . . charming numbers.
27–28	↑He thot ⟨him only fit to write⟩ he who would . . . heroic poem.↓
29	every virtue & ↑has↓ enlarged
31–32	teacher ↑who is less known↓ is Lord Clarendon ⟨in his⟩ ↑author of the↓ History

Page 364

1–3	↑I call him an ethical writer. His book is indeed a civil history↓ But ⟨I call him an ethical writer⟩ if a book
4	reader, ⟨it is⟩ no writer
4	name of an ⟨ethical writer⟩ ↑⟨moralist⟩ philosopher↓
5	characters ⟨are a⟩ stimulate
13	Hambden
14	enemy, ↑& therefore praises sparingly.↓
24	entire yet

Page 365

20	believed the only
29–30	philosophers ↑More Smith Cudworth Norris↓

Lines

29n   Cudworth was excited . . . steel & silver & gold [written on a blank leaf opposite the mention of Cudworth in the paragraph on Locke; possibly intended for insertion before that paragraph. Textual notes:]

System a vast storehouse of ye wisdom of ⟨ancient phil.⟩ wisdom.

but & reminds us of of

31–(366)1   & ⟨after him arose⟩ ↑& his reputation & example gave leave to↓

Page 366

2   the ⟨divine⟩ unfathomable
4   clay to the
6   His ⟨great⟩ merit ↑, if it be one,↓
10   thousand ⟨S⟩ copies
11   week ⟨upon ever⟩ in & about London; & ⟨the most⟩ elegant
12–13   cast ↑into every coffee house &↓
14   place & ⟨he is⟩ his influence
23–24   encumbered ⟨possessed a⟩ ↑he↓ was
25   power ↑which always attends it↓
26–27   ⟨There is a homely majesty⟩ He is always ⟨attended⟩ ↑accompanied↓
28–29   nor ↑do↓ his observations ↑indicate↓ very profound ↑philosophy↓
30–31   so ⟨thoroughly⟩ ↑deeply↓ does ⟨he imp⟩ stamp
31–32   own ⟨beautiful⟩ mode of thot

Page 367

1   which he ⟨continually⟩ depreciates
3–4   Milton⟨:⟩. ⟨t⟩Though he hated a whig, ⟨yet⟩ he loved ⟨a Man⟩ ↑& embraced a great Man↓;
5   Milton ⟨inspires⟩ ↑fills↓ him
6   in ⟨eulogies to such⟩ heartfelt
8   displayed in ⟨Miltons⟩ Paradise Lost
9–10   confesses ⟨Milton was born for all that was great & arduous⟩ "⟨His⟩ ↑Miltons↓ great works
17   Chesterfield ↑in many of his Essays↓ but
21   assistance ⟨from⟩ ↑of↓ ye learned
30   delusive if
34   & give ⟨ye⟩ ↑their↓ second . . . form I

Page 368

7   contains ⟨thes⟩ many of those
8–9   conclusion of its ethical essays — ⟨I⟩ "that it would be found ↑exactly↓

Lines
12 no blame ⟨&⟩ or no
17 sentence from on the ⟨powe⟩ capacity
32–33 to be borne." I think it may be questioned / [Emerson is re-
minding himself that the "sublime sentence" he first quoted
follows the above passage in Johnson's text.]

Page 369

3–19 "All the performances . . . by obstinate attacks" Dr J. [writ-
ten on a separate sheet inserted before the preceding para-
graph]
17 purposes acquire
18 cannot conquer (?) &
23–24 speeches ↑beside their surpassing rhetorical merits↓
26–28 The whole body . . . Tillotson Barrow [written in pencil
on previous blank leaf opposite conclusion of preceding paragraph, presumably for insertion here]
26 ↑A↓ The whole
29–30 made of immortal ↑moral↓ sentences
31 from ↑Sir T. Browne,↓
32–33 should ↑vie with that which any language has to offer↓
quicken
33–34 inspire ⟨us⟩ men
34–35 truths ↑concerned↓ are ↑immutable↓ eternal, ⟨they are certificates of the immortality of the being who understands
them⟩ ↑⟨so the⟩↓ so our apprehension

Page 370

1–9 The law which Ethics . . . illustration; is . . . life of every
man. [added in a seemingly later hand on previous leaf
(under "The whole body" etc.); possibly contemporary with
the added introduction, etc., previously noted (see textual
notes to p. 357). Apparently for insertion here. Except as
noted here, no punctuation]

10. MODERN ASPECTS OF LETTERS

Page 372

5–6 removed ⟨out of⟩ ↑beyond↓ the circles of ⟨change⟩
7 some ⟨great names⟩ ↑masters↓ to speak
7–8 birth has ⟨made⟩ ↑placed↓ nearer
10 ⟨A⟩ Lord Byron's genius ⟨has⟩ attracted so much attention
⟨in⟩a few years
12 that ⟨people⟩ ↑men↓ begin to feel

Lines	
13–14	dubious. ⟨What faculties does he excite? What feelings does he awaken? What impression does he leave?
	The malevolent feelings certainly have their interest & awaken sympathy but only for a short time. volumes upon volumes of morbid ⟨feelings⟩ emotion disgust.⟩
	He owed . . . something Certainly
15–16	very little; ↑this taste was just↓ his
16–17	gift of ⟨mastering⟩ making
17–18	emotion ⟨is mor⟩ without ever ⟨offending⟩ ↑marring↓
18–20	remarkable in hi⟨s⟩m ⟨case⟩ as in ⟨that of⟩ any English writer since ⟨Milton⟩ ↑Dryden↓. No ⟨stanza is difficult⟩ ↑structure of verse seemed laborious↓ to him.
20–21	flow ⟨of this verse⟩ in the difficult
28	Of hasty growth
34–35	faculty & ⟨argues⟩ ↑involving as it does↓
35	association ⟨which⟩ is one of the ⟨hi⟩ rarest
36	Byron ⟨it was not⟩ as if merely from ⟨the⟩ moral

Page 373

4–5	until ⟨there is⟩ ↑our interest dies of↓
10	with & ↑under the↓ counteraction
13	↑Yet ⟨much⟩ ↑several↓ of his poetry is little else.↓
14	example of ⟨the⟩ failure ⟨of great genius⟩ from
16–17	nonsense not from
22	never more ⟨my heart⟩ ↑on me↓
35–(374)2	↑The fourth Canto . . . Venice Florence & Rome.↓ [no punctuation]
35–36	productions & ↑He↓ had made ⟨so much⟩ ↑some↓

Page 374

1	guide book ⟨in⟩ to
3	the ⟨i⟩Island
6	gang of ⟨convicts⟩ of pirates
10	philosopher ↑I believe↓ he has
13	⟨The chief value of⟩ his works ⟨consists in⟩ ↑delight us by↓
15	by ⟨the g⟩ his acquaintance
16–17	↑Every page . . . to his reading.↓
18	of all ↑choice works of↓
19	⟨Most⟩ As his book
20	most ⟨young⟩ scholars
22–23	mind, ⟨and⟩ what visions
23–24	& how ⟨sadly⟩ ↑heavily↓
26	collection of ⟨mi⟩domes
27	expectations but
29	nothing but ⟨mean or plain⟩ & narrow ↑streets & plain↓ tenements. As we ⟨go forward⟩ ↑enter↓

Lines	
32	are ⟨very⟩ interesting
33	literature on ⟨that⟩ ↑those↓ subjects

Page 375

1	on ⟨Eth⟩ the Progress of Eth. &
4–6	Scott, ⟨the number of hours he has⟩ entertainment he has given ↑to solitude↓, the relief ↑to↓ ⟨from⟩ ↑⟨he has furnished to⟩↓ headache & heartache ↑wh. he has furnished↓,
7–8	↑Though a very . . . & unaffected↓
9	↑his good nature is infinite↓
10	high & ⟨strong⟩ ↑strict↓ sense
12	Hamlet ↑& Richard↓
13	Merrilies ↑Norna↓ ⟨rather⟩ ↑only↓
14	costume. ⟨Scott has hardly made a tear flow⟩ Jeanie
16	say. ⟨His⟩ That in which
17	situations of ⟨unrivalled⟩ ↑painful↓
19	The dialogue though
20	tone of ↑vulgar↓ romances is
21	He ⟨very⟩ rarely
25–27	⟨The ⟨only⟩ main censure which must lie against Scott is that he⟩ ⟨It is not a charge against Scott but it is a criticism upon his great reputation⟩ ↑If Scott is advanced . . . standard English ⟨writer⟩ authors, ⟨it will⟩ I apprehend, it will be found↓ that ⟨it⟩ he has
28–32	↑Let it not be said . . . Sublimest verities."↓
30	writer let . . . may who
35	criticism. ⟨That which⟩ "↑What↓ comes

Page 376

1	heart: ⟨that⟩ what
2–3	↑The vice of his ⟨work⟩ literary . . . artificial.↓
5	never ⟨dreamed⟩ ↑pondered↓
5–6	minds ↑Milton . . . Rousseau↓ ↑ye enterprise↓
14–15	& true. ⟨He will always be the best of virtuos⟨os⟩↑i↓⟩ & daily loses its interest as ⟨new⟩ swarms
16	⟨One of the most⟩ A writer of elevated
17	Mackintosh ⟨with⟩ ↑who had↓
18	He ⟨is⟩ ↑has been long↓
24	His ⟨most⟩ ↑first↓ important original work ⟨is⟩ ↑was↓
25	Philosophy ⟨published⟩ of which
26	Boston. ⟨a book which is what it professes to be, a history of the progress of the science⟩ ↑a book↓ in which
30–31	a History of ye science;
31	luminous ⟨pencil⟩ ↑finger↓
33	much ⟨value⟩ ↑worth↓ as
33–34	of the ⟨Moral⟩ ↑Will↓ Emotive ↑part of nature↓ &
34–35	sentiments; ↑⟨Will.⟩↓ It ⟨contains⟩ ↑touches or opens↓

Page 377

Lines	
1	suggestion⟨s⟩ & written ⟨in⟩ ↑with↓
3–4	occupied with ⟨two Histories⟩ the History of England three
5	Cyclopaedia & the
7–9	than a ⟨perfect chronicle⟩ ↑complete narrative↓. But it is ⟨the more⟩ ↑chiefly↓ valuable ⟨for that⟩ as it ↑shows how history ought to be written↓ allowed
10	topics ⟨that arise⟩ & instead
12	all ye ↑topics↓ questions
13	nation. ↑Arts↓
14–15	history. ⟨Moreover⟩ ↑Furthermore↓ over
17	is not ⟨of⟩ a writer
18	thought ↑to justify a belief↓
22	Coleridge a man
22–23	philanthropist as ⟨it⟩ ↑he↓ show⟨s⟩ed genius
24–25	scholar ↑we↓ might think not ↑genial &↓ native
27–29	charge ⟨of superficialness⟩ we make upon the times ↑of superficialness or deficiency of interest in ⟨great⟩ ↑profound↓ inquiries↓ though
30–31	made him ↑a profound scholar↓
31	character, ⟨a profound scholar⟩ though his learning
34	lake ⟨in some places u⟩ that had some flats,
34–35	places & not ⟨a lake that was⟩ ↑one whose waters were↓
35–36	↑His interest in all sciences was equal↓ He was ⟨a Pl⟩ of that class

Page 378

5	every man as the the ⟨Temple⟩ most
6	Temple of Deity. // [E] An aristocrat
7–8	interest in ⟨the⟩ lowly
11–12	his ⟨English⟩ private soldier of the Parliament, ↑from whom he drew the sublime ⟨quotation⟩ passage in ye Friend↓ of so
14	His true ⟨province⟩ merit
17	He possessed ⟨the greatest⟩ ↑extreme↓ subtlety
18–19	dictionary surpassing all ↑men↓
20–21	with the ⟨need⟩ a needles point. ⟨How man⟩ And that
23	tongue. that he has ⟨gone o⟩ taken
26–28	position & bearings He has defined ⟨How⟩ ↑he has made↓ admirable ⟨are his⟩ definitions, ⟨how⟩ ↑& drawn↓ indelible ⟨his⟩ ⟨the⟩ lines ⟨he has drawn⟩ of distinction
30–32	↑& said that he had never . . . practical error.↓
33	explanation ⟨of Genius & Talents⟩ of the object
34	Understanding ⟨between Genius & Talent⟩;

Page 379

2	↑of the↓ of the Idea of a State

Lines
4   How ⟨different from⟩ ↑unlike↓ the defining
8–10   ↑Take the single example . . . Reason & Understanding↓
11–12   own day those . . . country without
12–14   study of ⟨Coleridge⟩ ↑this one subject↓ would have saved
         them, ⟨even if he had⟩ ↑and that with his theory of Reason
         he cd. not↓ fail⟨ed⟩ to impart
16–17   Literaria or . . . opinions is
20   adorns the whole ⟨way⟩ ↑road↓
23   a book ↑on criticism↓
25   interest, the Aids to Reflection, ↑tho' a useful book↓ Valuable
         In
27   Friend ⟨be⟩ from
28   to the end ⟨were his best works   In this wer [?] with⟩ ↑with↓
         a few of his poems were
31   all ↑good judges↓ would concur.

Page 380

4–5   which ⟨served as⟩ his critics were glad to ⟨seize as⟩ lay hold
         ⟨of⟩ ↑on↓
6   He ⟨had a petulance⟩ indulges ⟨sometimes in a petulance at
         the⟩ much in
7–8   England; ⟨&⟩ at the [cancellation dubious]
11–12   that ↑he shd. have allowed↓
12–13   Reviews ⟨should⟩ ⟨to⟩ ⟨have⟩ ⟨affect his serenity.⟩ or the very
16   rivals he who writes ⟨for eternit⟩ for the wise
23–25   unnecessary pages. ↑disinterestedness . . . lucre and pleas-
         ure↓ But the heartiness
34   loved Heraclitus,
35   St Augustine
                    ⟨Olympian bards who sung
                     Divine Ideas below
                 Which always find us young
                 And always keep us so.⟩
36   notices of ⟨the⟩ English

Page 381

6   proportion: ⟨tha⟩ It
8–9   the passion ⟨& to superfic⟩ to the love
15   has ↑been↓ unbound
16–17   has been ↑there↓ added
17–19   ⟨What⟩ ↑Where are the↓ bards have sung? ⟨what⟩ ↑Where
         are the↓ scholars ↑who have↓ collected? ↑Where are the↓
         ⟨what⟩ philosophers digested
25   among us {& in England, no less⟩ [sic]
28–29   put the ⟨true⟩ forms
31   should be ⟨urged & repeated⟩ ↑studied & published↓

Page 382

Lines	
1	have gained. / and when
7	to one ↑or both↓ of which
8	composed; Truth
11	it ⟨does not⟩ may not yet ⟨contain⟩ ↑carry↓
12	Every man ⟨has a law of his being⟩ besides
13	truth ↑has a law of *his* being.↓
15	he must ⟨write⟩ accept
17	write to him self
19	to ⟨give me⟩ ↑communicate↓ one new truth? ⟨Ar⟩ Does
20	necessity that th⟨at⟩ey
23–24	wit, ↑lyrics↓ tragedy, romance, ↑devotional writings↓
26	eternal ⟨re⟩ principle
30	⟨Yet⟩ These I take it
30–31	criticism yet ⟨are⟩ these tests
31	to the ⟨tons⟩ ↑bales↓ of books
32–35	produces ↑but a book full of words . . . imitation of imitations↓ ⟨At this moment⟩ ⟨Certainly ⟨there is⟩ a degree of humiliation must be felt by ⟨all⟩ the American Scholar, when he reviews ⟨to⟩ the constellation of great geniuses from Chaucer down, who in England have been tried by these measures Is there Truth? Is there Beauty? & it was found they had enlarged the spheres of both; & then comes to this land where ⟨the⟩ Humanity has been unbound & has enjoyed the Culture of Wisdom in the freedom of the Wilderness & ⟨sees⟩ ↑reckons↓ how little has been added to the stock of truth for mankind What bards have sung what scholars collected / What ⟨sages⟩ philosophers digested maxims ⟨for⟩ ⟨that⟩ ↑that not only issue forth into all corners of America but↓ go current in Germany in Italy & Spain. This country I know has been doing something else & instead of writing Poems has felled the woods & builded towns.⟩
	⟨Nor shall a⟩ ↑A↓ suspension
36	America ↑shall not↓ convince

Page 383

3	take in it ⟨is⟩ teach
4–5	↑sphere out of which we cannot go↓ whose
6	poorer by ⟨a⟩ so much
7	the wit & ⟨te[?]⟩ science
8–9	mind. ⟨And yet said⟩ ↑It was↓ the sublime
20	thence. but more truly seen ⟨the author of a hundred volumes is but a monad after the fashion of his little race bestirring himself immensely to hide from you what an atom he is, spinning his most seeming surface directly before the eye to conceal the Universe of his ignorance.⟩ ⟨A⟩ ↑the wise↓ man ever finds

Lines

22–23	perfect ⟨to every moment &⟩ to every mind
27–(384)16	⟨I think it of primary importance that the interest of every man should be kept as wakeful as it can be upon literature.⟩ Every man — by the gift of intellectual powers is . . . vulgarity & becomes an object of delight. [on loose leaf found inserted between "scholars collected" and "What ⟨sages⟩ philosophers" in long cancelled passage above]
34	love, ⟨the⟩ education,
35	thot the ⟨Compensation⟩ system of
36	nature & a ⟨thousand⟩ ↑hundred↓ other

Page 384

1–2	discussion nor
2–3	nor ↑Luther nor↓ Swedenborg
5	evidence ⟨to⟩ of his immortality ⟨as⟩ ↑to↓ that
7	truth a study
8–9	↑or has had half the consciousness of being↓
13	pleasing what
14	And ⟨it is⟩ the same
14–15	when ⟨the whole⟩ ↑a common↓ landscape
16	loses ⟨all⟩ its vulgarity
17	⟨I am very far from believing that the age of original poetry or philosophy is past or that the cruse of truth will run no more oil.⟩ The present moment against all time. ⟨W W[?]⟩ Wherever
19–21	been. ²{"He that has been been born has been a First Man."} ¹{I believe . . . Plato or Paul.}
23	that ⟨gave light to⟩ ↑shone on the faces of↓
24	Shakspear ⟨to⟩ ↑of↓ Dryden
27	himself of it he
28	abdicate his ⟨sovereignty⟩ ↑kingdom↓
29	constitution He
34–35	come ↑teach↓ & look at them, ↑⟨each⟩↓ once
35–(385)1	When ⟨Melchthal⟩ ↑Arnold Winkelreid↓ in the high ⟨al[?]⟩

Page 385

3	the line ↑for his comrades;↓
4–5	⟨And when & where⟩ When the bark
5–8	↑before it↓ the ⟨shore⟩ ↑beach↓ lined . . . cane the . . . around can
11–12	⟨The⟩ In the most obscure . . . to ⟨appre⟩ draw to itself [no punctuation]
15	does she ⟨order⟩ ↑bend↓ her lines
21–22	lodgers not ⟨inhabitants⟩ ↑citizens↓ of the world. The ⟨source⟩ fruitful source of all crime the ⟨source of⟩ chief source
22–23	is ⟨the⟩ inconsideration,
23	reflexion; Men

Index

Editorial references, whether in footnotes or elsewhere, are marked with an "n," to distinguish them from Emerson's references in footnotes and text. A few selected items only are included from Textual Notes.